D0363859

THE ATHEIST VIEWPOINT

THE ATHEIST VIEWPOINT

Advisory Editor:
Madalyn Murray O'Hair

AN ANALYSIS

OF

RELIGIOUS BELIEF.

BY

Viscount [John Russell] Amberley

ARNO PRESS & THE NEW YORK TIMES
New York / 1972

Reprint Edition 1972 by Arno Press Inc.

LC# 76-161318
ISBN 0-405-03621-3

The Atheist Viewpoint
ISBN for complete set: 0-405-03620-5
See last pages of this volume for titles.

Manufactured in the United States of America

AN ANALYSIS

OF

RELIGIOUS BELIEF.

BY

VISCOUNT AMBERLEY.

" Ye shall know the Truth, and the Truth shall make you Free."

From the late London Edition. Complete.

D. M. BENNETT:
LIBERAL AND SCIENTIFIC PUBLISHING HOUSE,
141 EIGHTH STREET, NEW YORK,
1877.

AMERICAN PUBLISHER'S PREFACE.

THE appearance, a few months ago, of THE ANALYSIS OF RELIG-
IOUS BELIEF caused not a little excitement in England, and its
introduction into our country had much the same effect here.
While many were more or less shocked by the Viscount's
boldness of language in examining the sources of the religious
creeds of the world, and at the freedom with which he removed
the sacred mask from many antique myths and superstitions,
the thoughtful and the enquiring were furnished with a fund
of material for new thought, and largely-increased facilities for
investigating and comparing the creeds and dogmas which have
made up the ruling religious faiths of mankind.

When the Viscount's high birth is remembered; that he was
the son of Lord John Russell, one of the first and oldest Peers
of England; that he was thus closely connected with the aris-
tocracy of that country; that he had been carefully nurtured
within the fold of the Christian Church; that he had received
the instruction of a pious Christian mother, from the days of
his early childhood, that the influence of his parents and his
early companions was to draw him him under the control of
the popular system of religion which rules in his country, it is
not a little remarkable that he had the independence and moral
bravery to come out in opposition to all his near friends, and to
avow his unbelief in a code of ethics and opinions unlike those
taught him in his childhood and youth, an unusual interest
attaches to the work which he produced.

When it is borne in mind that his amiable and sympathetic
wife toiled with him and rendered him essential service in collecting and arranging the matter for his two volumes; that she
was taken from him by the hand of death before his work was
completed; that he also sank under the hand of disease and

passed away while his work was still in the hands of the printer, it is indeed invested with peculiar interest.

When it is remembered that after his death urgent efforts were made — and from high sources too — to suppress his work; that the powerful Duke of Bedford, backed by Lord John Russell himself, tried to buy up the entire edition issued; it is enough to make every sympathetic and enquiring person anxious to read the results of his labor of years.

If some of the advanced thinkers of the day find that Viscount Amberly—as evinced in some of the later chapters of this volume — had not in all respects evolved in the line of Freethought so far as they have done they should remember that he had at least made rapid progress for the time he had devoted to the pursuit of truth. He was still a young man at the time of his death, and had it been his lot to have scored a greater number of years, with the advantage of the experience which they give, it is very possible his views might have undergone other modifications.

The London edition was issued in two volumes, 8vo and was necessarily sold at a large price. This American edition contains the entire work in one volume and is presented to the public at about one-fifth the price at which the English edition was sold. It is hoped this feature will be duly appreciated by the American public.

D. M. B.

NEW YORK, March 20th, 1877.

ADDRESS TO THE READER.

Ere the pages now given to the public had left the press, the hand that had written them was cold, the heart — of which few could know the loving depth — had ceased to beat, the far-ranging mind was forever still, the fervent spirit was at rest.

Let this be remembered by those who read, and add solemnity to the solemn purpose of the book.

May those who find in it their most cherished beliefs questioned or contemned, their surest consolations set at naught, remember that he had not shrunk from pain and anguish to himself, as one by one he parted with portions of that faith which in boyhood and early youth had been the mainspring of his life.

Let them remember that, however many the years granted to him on earth might have been, his search after truth would have ended only with his existence; that he would have been the first to call for unsparing examination of his own opinions, arguments, and conclusions; the first to welcome any new lights thrown by other workers in the same field on the mysteries of our being and of the universe.

Let them remember that while he assails much which they reckon unassailable, he does so in what to him is the cause of goodness, nobleness, love, truth, and of the mental progress of mankind.

Let them remember that the utterance of that which, after earnest and laborious thought he deemed to be the truth, was to him a sacred duty; and may they feel, as he would have felt, the justness of these words of a good man and unswerving Christian lately passed away: "A man's charity to those who differ from him upon great and difficult questions will be in the ratio of his own knowledge of them: the more knowledge, the more charity."

F. R.

INSCRIBED,

With all reverence and all affection, to the memory of the ever-lamented wife whose hearty interest in this book was, during many years of preparatory toil, my best support; whose judgment as to its merits or its faults would have been my most trusted guide; whose sympathy my truest encouragement; whose joyous welcome of the completed work I had long looked forward to as my one great reward: whose nature, combining in rare union scientific clearness with spiritual depth, may in some slight degree have left its impress on the page, though far too faintly to convey an adequate conception of one whose religious zeal in the cause of truth was rivaled only by the ardor of her humanity and the abundance of her love.

RAVENSCROFT,
November 1875.

TABLE OF CONTENTS.

EXPLANATION OF SHORT TITLES.

In order to avoid encumbering the pages with notes containing the names of books, many of which would require to be frequently repeated, I have adopted, in referring to the undermentioned works, the following abbreviations:—

A. B......The Aitareya Brahmanam of the Rig-Veda. Edited, translated, and explained by MARTIN HAUG, Ph.D. Vol. i. Sanscrit text. Vol. ii. Translation, with notes. Bombay, 1863.

A. I. C...An Account of the Island of Ceylon, by ROBERT PERCIVAL, Esq., of His Majesty's 19th Regiment of Foot. London, 1803.

A. M......Antiquities of Mexico (LORD KINGSBOROUGH'S), comprising fac similes of Ancient Mexican paintings and hieroglyphics. Together with the Monuments of New Spain, by MONS. DUPAIX ; with their respective scales of measurement and accompanying descriptions. The whole illustrated by many valuable inedited manuscripts, by AUGUSTINE AGLIO. In 9 vols. London, 1831-48.

A. N. L..Ante Nicene Christian Library ; translations of the Writings of the Fathers down to A.D. 325. Edinburgh : T. & T. CLARK, 1870, &c.

A. R......Algic Researches, comprising inquiries respecting the mental characteristics of the North American Indians. First Series, Indian Tales and Legends. In 2 vols. By HENRY ROWE SCHOOLCRAFT. New York, 1839.

Asha .....Ashantee and the Gold Coast, by JOHN BEECHAM. London, 1841.

A. S. L...History of Ancient Sanskrit Literature, by MAX MÜLLER. London, 1859.

As. Re....Researches of the Asiatic Society in Bengal. Calcutta, 1788-1839.

Av........Avesta, die Heiligen Schriften der Parsen. Aus dem Grundtexte übersetzt, mit steter Rücksicht auf die Tradition. Von Dr. FRIED. SPIEGEL. Erster Band. Der Vendidad

Leipzig, 1852. Zweiter Band. Vispered und Yacna. Leip-
zig, 1859. Dritter Band. Khorda-Avesta. Leipzig, 1863.
B. A. U ..Bibliotheca Indica. Vol. ii. part iii. The Brihad Aran-
yaka Upanishad, with the Commentary of Sánkara
A'cha'rya. Translated from the Original Sanskrit by Dr.
E. ROER. Calcutta, 1856.
Bergeron...Voyages faits principalement en Asie, dans les XIIe, XIIIe,
XIVe, et XVe siècles, par Benjamin de Tudèle, Jean du
Plan-Carpin, N. Ascelin, Guil. de Rubruquis, Marc-Paul,
Haiton, Jean de Mandeville et Ambroise Contarini ; accom-
pagnés de l'Histoire des Sarrazins et des Tartares, par P.
Bergeron. A la Haye, 1735.
Bernard...Recueil des Voyages au Nord. Amsterdam, chez JEAN
FRÉDÉRIC BERNARD, 1727.
Bh. G.....The Bhagavat-Gítá ; or a Discourse between Krishna and
Arjuna on Divine Matters. A Sanskrit Philosophical
Poem ; translated, with copious notes, an Introduction
on Sanskrit Philosophy, and other matters, by J. COCKBURN
THOMSON. Hertford, 1855.
Bib.......APOLLODORI Bibliotheca.
B. T......Buddhism in Tibet, by EMIL SCHLAGINTWEIT, LL.D. Leip-
zig and London, 1863.
C. B. A...A Catena of Buddhist Scriptures from the Chinese, by SAM'L
BEAL. London, 1871.
C. C. .....The Chinese Classics, with a translation, critical and exeget-
ical notes, prolegomena, and copious indexes, by JAMES
LEGGE, D.D. In 7 vols. Vol. i. Confucian Analects, the
Great Learning, and the Doctrine of the Mean. Vol. ii.
Works of Mencius. Vol. iii. 2 parts, The Shoo King.
Vol. iv. 2 parts, The She King. Vol. v. the Ch'un Ts'ew.
London, 1861, &c. (In course of publication.)
Ceylon....Ceylon, an Account of the Island, physical, historical, and
topographical, with notices of its natural history, antiqui-
ties, and productions, by Sir JAMES EMERSON TENNENT.
K.C.S., LL.D., &c. London, 1859.
C. G......A new and accurate Description of the Coast of Guinea,
divided into the Gold, the Slave, and the Ivory Coasts.
Written originally in Dutch, by WILLIAM BOSMAN. The
2d edition. London, 1721.
Chan. Up..Bibliotheca Indica, Nos. 78 and 181. The Chándogya
Upanishad of the Sǎma Veda, with extracts from the
Commentary of Sákara A'cha'rya. Translated from the
original Sanskrit by RÁJENDRÁLA MITRA. Calcutta. 1862.
Chinese ...The Chinese: a general Description of China and its In-
habitants, by JOHN FRANCIS DAVIS, Esq., F.R.S. A new
edition. London, 1844.

Chips.....Chips from a German Workshop, by MAX MÜLLER, M.A. 4 vols. London, 1867–75.

C. N. E...Historia General de las Cosas de Nueva España, que en doce libros y dos volumes escribió el R. P. FR, BERNARDINO DE SAHAGUN, de la Observancia de San Francisco, y uno de los primeros predicadores del Santo Evangelio en aquellas regiones. Dala a luz con notas y supplementos, CARLOS MARIA DE BUSTAMANTE. Mexico, 1829.

C. O......China Opened, by the Rev. CHARLES GÜTZLAFF, revised by the Rev. ANDREW REID, D.D. In 2 vols. London, 1838.

C. R......Primera Parte de los " Commentarios Reales, que tratan del Origen de los Yncas," Reyes que fueron del Peru, de su idolatria, leyes, y govierno en paz y en guerra ; de sus vidas y conquistas, y de toto lo que fue aquel Imperio y su Republica, antes que los Españoles passan a el. Escrito por el Ynca GARCILASSO DE LA VEGA, natural del Cozco, y Capitan de su Magestad. Lisbon, 1609.

Dervishes..The Dervishes; or Oriental Spiritualism, by JOHN P. BROWN. London, 1868.

E. M......Eastern Monachism, by ROBERT SPENCE HARDY. London,, 1850.

E. Y......Eleven Years in Ceylon, by Major FORBES, 78th Highlanders. London, 1840.

F. G......Die fünf Gâthâ's, oder Sammlungen von Liedern und Sprüchen ZARATHUSTRA'S, seiner Jünger und Nachfolger. Herausgegeben, übersetzt und erklärt von Dr. MARTIN HAUG. Erste Abtheilung. Die erste Sammlung (Gâthâ ahunavaiti) enthaltend. Leipzig, 1858. Zweite Abtheilung. Die vier übrigen Sammlungen enthaltend. Nebst einer Schlussabhandlung. Leipzig, 1860.

Gaudama..The Life, or Legend of Gaudama, the Buddha of the Burmese, with annotations. The ways to Neibban, and notice on the Phongyies, or Burmese Monks, by the Rt. Rev. P. BIGANDET. Rangoon, 1866.

G. d. M...C. G. A. OLDENDORP'S Geschichte der Mission der evangelis chen Brüder auf den Caraibischen Inseln St. Thomas, St. Croix, und St. Jean. Barby, 1777.

H. B. I....Introduction a l'Histoire du Buddhisme Indien, par E. BURNOUF. Tome premier. Paris, 1844.

H. G......DAVID CRANZ. Histoire von Grönland. Nürnberg und Leipzig, 1782.

H. I......Historia natural y moral de las Indias, en que se tratan las cosas notables del ciclo, y elementos, metales, plantas, y animales dellas; y los ritos, y ceremonias, leyes, y govierno, y guerras de los Indios. Compuesta por el Pardre JOSEPH

DE ACOSTA, Religioso de la Compañia de Jesus. Madrid, 1608.

H. N. S...Histoire naturelle et politique du Royaume de Siam, par NICHOLAS GERVAISE. Paris, 1688.

H. R. C...An Historical Relation of the Island of Ceylon in the East Indies, together with an account of the detaining in captivity the Author and divers other Englishmen now living there, and of the Author's miraculous escape, by ROBERT KNOX, a captive there nearly twenty years. London, 1681.

Ic. Ch.....Iconographie Chrétienne. Histoire de Diau, par M. DIDRON. Paris, 1843.

K.........The Koran, translated from the Arabic, the Suras arranged in chronological order; with notes and index, by the Rev. J. M. RODWELL, M.A. London and Edinburgh, 1871.

Kamtschatka..GEORGE WILHELM STELLER's Beschreibung von dem Lande Kamtschatka, dessen Einwohnern, deren Sitten, Namen, Lebensart und verchiedenen Gewohnheiten. Frankfurt und Leipzig, 1774.

K. N.....The Kafirs of Natal, by J. SHOOTER. London and Guildford, 1857.

L. L. M...Das Leben und die Lehre des Mohammad, nach bisher grösstentheils unbenutzten Quellen. Bearbeitet von A SPRENGER. 3 vols. Berlin, 1869.

Lotos.....Le Lotos de la Bonne Loi, traduit du Sanskrit, accompagné d'un commentaire, et de vingt-et-un mémoires relatifs au Buddhisme, par M. E. BURNOUF. Paris, 1852.

L. T......LAO-TSE Táo-tě-king. Der Weg zur Tugend. Aus dem Chinesischen übersetzt und erklärt von REINHOLD VON PLÄNCKNER. Leipzig, 1870.

Manu.....Institutes of Hindu Law, or the Ordinances of MENU, according to the Gloss of CULLÚCA. Comprising the Indian system of duties, religious and civil. Verbally translated from the original, with a preface, by Sir WILLIAM JONES. A new edition, collated with the Sanskrit text, by GRAVES CHAMNEY HAUGHTON., M.A., F.R.S., &c. London, 1825.

M. B......Manual of Buddhism, by R. SPENCE HARDY. London, 1860.

M. d'O....Les Moines d'Occident depuis Saint Benoit jusqu'a Saint Bernard. Parle le Comte de MONTALEMBERT. In 5 vols. Paris et Lyon, 1868.

Misc. Essays..Miscellaneous Essays, by H. T. COLEBROOKE. 2 vols. London, 1837. (The only complete edition, however, is the one published in 3 vols., London, 1873.)

M. N. W..The Myths of the New World; a Treatise on the Symbolism and Mythology of the red race of America, by DANIEL G. BRINTON, A.M., M.D. New York, 1868.

N. A......An Account of the Native Africans in the neighborhood of

Sierra Leone, by THOMAS WINTERBOTTOM. 2 vols. London, 1803.

N. F......Histoire et Description générale de la Nouvelle France, avec le journal historique d'un voyage fait par ordre du Roi dans l'Amérique Septentrionale. Par le P. DE CHARLEVOIX, de la Compagnie de Jésus 3 Vols. Paris, 1744.

N. M. E...A Narrative of Missionary Enterprises in the South Sea Islands, with remarks upon the natural history of the Islands, origin, languages, traditions, and usages of the inhabitants, by the Rev. JOHN WILLIAMS. London. 1837.

N. S. W..An account of the English Colony in New South Wales, from its first settlement in January, 1788, to August, 1801, by Lieutenant-Colonel COLLINS, of the. Royal Marines. London, 1804.

N. Y......Nineteen years in Polynesia: Missionary Life, Travels, and Researches in the Islands of the Pacific, by the Rev. GEORGE TURNER. London, 1861.

N. Z.......New Zealand and its Aborigines, by WILLIAM BROWN. London, 1845.

O-kee-pa..O-kee-pa: A Religious Ceremony; and other customs of the Mandans, by GEORGE CATLIN. London, 1867.

O. P......The Speculations on Metaphysics, Polity, and Morality of "the Old Philosopher," LAU-TSZE, translated from the Chinese, with an Introduction, by JOHN CHALMERS, A. M. London, 1868.

O. S. T...Original Sanskrit Texts on the origin and history of the people of India, their Religion and Institutions. Collected, translated, and illustrated by J. MUIR, D.C.L., LL.D. Volume First. Mythical and Legendary Accounts of the Origin of Caste, with an inquiry into its existence in the Vedic age. 2d edition. London, 1868. Volume Second. Inquiry whether the Hindus are of Trans-Himalayan Origin, and akin to the Western branches of the Indo-European Race. 2d edition. London, 1871. Volume Third. The Vedas: opinions of their authors and of later Indian writers on their origin, inspiration, and authority. 2d edition. London, 1868. Volume Fourth. Comparison of the Vedic with the later representations of the principal Indian deities. 2d edition. London, 1873. Volume Fifth. Contributions to a Cosmogony, Mythology,, Religious Ideas, Life and Manners of the Indians in the Vedic age. London, 1870.

P. A...... An Examination of the Pali Buddhistical Annals, by the Honorable GEORGE TURNOUR, of the Ceylon Civil Service. [From the Journal of the Asiatic Society for July 1837.]

P. A. B...Die Propheten des Alten Bundes, erklärt von HEINRICH

EWALD. Zweite Ausgabe in drei Bänden. Erster Band. Jesaja mit den übrigen älteren Propheten. Göttingen, 1867. Zweiter Band. Jermja und Hezequiel mit ihren Zeitgenossen. Göttingen, 1868. Dritter Band. Die jüngsten Propheten des Alten Bundes mit den Büchern Barukh und Daniel. Göttingen, 1868.

Parsees... Essays on the Sacred Language, Writings, and Religion of the Parsees, by MARTIN HAUG, Ph.D. Bombay, 1862.

Picard....The Ceremonies and Religious Customs of the various Nations of the known World, by Mr. BERNARD PICARD. Faithfully translated into English by a gentleman. London, 1733.

Popol Vuh.Popol Vuh.—Le Livre Sacré et les Mythes de l'Antiquité Américaine, avec les livres héroiques et historiques des Quichés. Texte Quiché et traduction Française en regard &c., &c. Composé sur des documents originaux et inédits, par l'Abbé BRASSEUR DE BOURBOURG. Paris, 1861.

R. B......Die Religion des Buddha und ihre Entstehung, von KARL FRIEDRICH KÖPPON. Erster Band. Die Religion des Buddha und ihre Entstehung. Berlin, 1857. Zweiter Band. Die Lamaische Hierarchie und Kirche. Berlin, 1859.

Rel. of Jews.The Book of the Religion, Ceremonies, and Prayers of the Jews, as practiced in their synagogues and Families on all Occasions; on their Sabbath and other Holidays throughout the year. Translated immediately from the Hebrew, by GAMALIEL BEN PEDAZUR, Gent. London, 1738.

R. I......Die Religiösen, Politischen, und Socialen Ideen der Asiatschen Culturvölker und der Aegypter, in ihrer historischen Entwickelung, dargestellt von CARL TWESTEN. Herausgegeben von Prof. Dr. M. LAZARUS. 2 vols. Berlin, 1872.

Roer......Bibliotheca Indica, Nos. 1 to 4. The first two Lectures of the Rig-Veda-Sanhita. Edited by Dr. E. ROER. Calcutta, 1848.

R. S. A...The Religious System of the Amazulu, by the Rev. Canon CALLAWAY, M.D. Part i. Unkulunkulu; or the Tradition of Creation as existing among the Amazulu and other tribes of South Africa, in their own words, with a translation into English, and notes. Part ii. Amatongo, or Ancestor-Worship. Part iii. Izinyanga Zokubula, or Divination. Natal, &c., 1868-70.

R. T. R. P..Rgya Tchér Rol Pa, ou Développement des Jeux, contenant l'histoire du Bouddha Cakya-Mouni, traduit sur la version Tibétaine du Bkah Hgyour, et revu sur l'original Sanscrit (Lalitavistara) par PH. ED. FOUCAUX. Première Partie.

Texte Tibétain. Paris, 1847. Deuxième Partie. Traduction Française. Paris, 1848.

R. V. S...Rig-Veda-Sanhita. The Sacred Hymns of the Brahmans, translated and explained by F. MAX MÜLLER, M. A., LL.D. Vol. i. Hymns to the Maruts or the Storm-Gods. London, 1869.

S. A......Savage Africa; the Narrative of a Tour in Equatorial, South-Western, and North-Western Africa, by W. WINWOOD READE. London, 1863.

Sale...... The Koran, commonly called the Alcoran of MOHAMMED; translated into English immediately from the original Arabic. With explanatory notes, taken from the most approved Commentators. To which is prefixed a preliminary discourse, by GEORGE SALE, Gent. A new edition, with a memoir of the translator, and with various readings and illustrative notes from Savary's version of the Koran. London, 1867.

S. L......A Voyage to the River Sierra Leone, on the Coast of Africa, by JOHN MATTHEWS, Lieutenant in the Royal Navy; during his residence in that country in the years 1785, 1786, and 1787. London, 1791.

S. L. A..Savage Life and Scenes in Australia and New Zealand, by GEORGE FRENCH ANGAS. London, 1847.

Ssabismus.Die Ssabier und der Ssabismus, von Dr D. CHWOLSOHN. Band I. Die Entwickelung der Begriffe Ssabier und Ssabismus und die Geschichte der harrânischen Ssabier, oder der Syro-hellenistischen Heiden im nördlichen Mesopotamien und in Bagdâd, zur Zeit des Chalifats. Band II. Orientalische Quellen zur Geschichte der Ssabier und des Ssabismus. St. Petersburg, 1856.

S. V......Die Hymnen des Sâma-Veda, herausgegeben, übersetzt und mit Glossar versehen, von THEODORE BENFEY. Leipzig, 1848.

T. R. A. S.Transactions of the Royal Asiatic Society of Great Britain and Ireland. London, 1827-35.

T. T. K..Lao-tse's Taò Tĕ King. Aus dem Chinesischen ins Deutsche übersetzt, eingeleitet und commentirt, von VICTOR VON STRAUSS. Leipzig, 1870.

V. G......Voyage du Chevalier DES MARCHAIS en Guinée, Isles voisines, et à Cayenne, fait en 1725.

Viti...... Viti: An Acount of a Government Mission to the Vitian or Fijian Islands in the years 1860-61, by BERTHOLD SEE-MANN, Ph.D., F.L.S., F.R.G.S. Cambridge, 1862.

Wassiljew.Der Buddhismus, seine Dogmen, Geschichte und Litteratur, von W. WASSILJEW. Erster Theil. Allgemeine Uebersicht. Aus dem Russischen übersetzt. St. Petersburg 1860.

W. E. .... The World Encompassed, by Sir FRANCIS DRAKE, 1577–80. Written by FRANCIS FLETCHER; collated with an unpublished MS. Edited with Appendices and Introduction by W. S. W. VAUX. 8vo, map. London, Hakluyt Society, 1855.

Wheel. ... The Wheel of the Law. Buddhism illustrated from Siamese sources by the Modern Buddhist, a Life of Buddha, and an account of the Phrabat, by HENRY ALABASTER, Esq. London, 1871.

Wilson. ... Rig-Veda-Sanhitá. Translated from the original Sanskrit, by H. H. WILSON, M.A., F.R.S. Vol. i. The first Ashtaka, or Book, of the Rig-Veda. 2d edition. London, 1866. Vol. ii. The second Ashtaka. London, 1854. Vol, iii. The third and fourth Ashtakas. London, 1857. Vol. iv. The fifth Ashtaka. Edited by E. B. COWELL, M.A. London, 1866.

W. u. T. . Der Weise und der Thor. Aus dem Tibetischen übersetzt und mit dem Originaltexte herausgegeben von I. J. SCHMIDT. St. Petersburg, 1843.

W. W. .... Works by the Late HORACE HAYMAN WILSON, 12 vols. London, 1862–71.

Y. .... Commentaire sur le Yaçna, l'un des Livres Religieux des Parses; ouvrage contenant le texte Zend expliqué pour la première fois; les variantes des quatre manuscrits de la Bibliothèque Royale; et la version Sanscrite inédite de Nériosengh, par EUGENE BURNOUF. Tome i. Paris, 1833. Tome ii. Paris, 1835.

Z. A. ...... Zend Avesta, Ouvrage de Zoroastre, traduit en François sur l'original Zend, avec des remarques; et accompagné de plusieurs traités propres a éclaircir les matières qui en sont l'objet, par M. ANQUETIL DU PERRON. 3 vols. Paris, 1771.

AN ANALYSIS OF RELIGIOUS BELIEF.

GENERAL INTRODUCTION.

HUMAN nature, among all the phenomena it offers to the curious inquiries of the student, presents none of more transcendent interest than the phenomenon of Religion. Pervading the whole history of mankind from the very earliest ages of which we have any authentic knowledge up to the present day; exercising on the wild and wandering tribes, which seem to have divided the earth among them in those primitive times, an influence scarcely less profound than it has ever exercised on the most polite and cultivated nations of the modern world; leading now to peace and now to war; now to the firmest of alliances, now to the bitterest enmities; uniting some in the bonds of a love so enduring as to outlast and put to shame the fleeting unions of earthly passion; separating others, even when every motive of interest and natural affection conspired to unite them, so completely as to impel them to deliver each other up to the ghastliest tortures; Religion deserves a foremost place — if not the foremost place of all — among the emotions which have in their several ways affected, modified, and controlled the current of human events.

Forming, as it does, so large an element in the constitution of our complex nature, and playing so vast a part in guiding our actions, Religion must well deserve to be made the subject of philosophical inquiry. If we can by any scientific means discover its origin, lay bare its true character to the gaze of students, and estimate the value of its pretensions to be in posses-

sion of truths of equal, if not superior, authority to those of
either natural or moral science, we shall have performed a task
which may not be wholly useless or altogether uninstructive.

Our first business, in such an inquiry as this, should be to
determine the method on which it ought to be conducted. In
analyzing the religious systems of the world, the question of
method is all-important. Indeed, it will be abundantly evident
in the course of the ensuing investigations that the conclusions
reached by those who have cultivated this field of knowledge
have often been unsound, simply because they have failed to
pursue the only proper method. Nothing can be easier, for
instance, than to construct elaborate systems of religious philosophy, the several parts of which hang so well together that
we find it difficult to urge any solid objection against them,
while yet the whole edifice rests upon so insecure a foundation
that at the least touch of its lowest stones it will fall in ruins
to the ground. This too common mistake arises from the fact
that the first principles of the system are assumed without adequate warrant, and will not bear examination. Half, if not
many more than half, the common errors of believers in the
various current creeds are due to a similar cause. These persons start from some principle which they conceive to be indisputable, and proceed to draw inferences from it with the most
complete confidence. An extreme instance of this is mentioned
by Dr. Sprenger, who was asked by a Musselman how he could
disbelieve the religion of Islam, seeing that Mahomet's name
was written on the gates of paradise. In a less palpable form,
the same mode of reasoning is constantly adopted among ourselves. Either we do not take the trouble to submit the evidence of the facts upon which we erect our arguments to a
sufficiently rigorous scrutiny, or we fail to perceive that the
axioms we take for granted are in reality neither self-evident,
as our system requires, nor capable of any satisfactory demonstration.

Another and perhaps scarcely a less common kind of error
arising from defective method is a failure to distinguish between
adequate and inadequate evidence of religious truth. A sound
and exhaustive method would not fail to disclose, if not what
kind of evidence is sufficient, at least what kind of evidence is

insufficient, to prove our doctrines.   It is plain that if we should find arguments of the same character used by the adherents of different creeds to prove contradictory propositions, we should be forced to dismiss such arguments as of comparatively little value. Supposing, for example, that a Hebrew, desirous of proving the preëminence of the Jews over the Gentiles, should rely for his justification on the miraculous deliverance of the ancient Israelites from the Egyptians, and on their subsequent special protection by the Deity, his argument, however apparently conclusive, would be considerably weakened if it were found that the annals of other nations contained similar tales evincing a similar exclusive care for their welfare on the part of their local divinities. Or if we should claim for our own school the advantage of being supported by the authority of a long succession of able, wise, and virtuous men, fully competent to judge of its truth, yet if our adversaries can produce an equally imposing list of authorities against us, we shall have gained but little by our mode of reasoning. These one-sided ways of proving the exclusive claims of a particular creed are as if a person should maintain the vast superiority of his countrymen over foreigners by a reference to the battles they had won, the territory they had conquered, and the bravery they had displayed; forgetful to inquire whether there were not other nations which had gained victories equally transcendent, made conquests equally extensive, and evinced a heroism equally admirable.

These blunders, it may be objected, do not arise exclusively from a faulty method. It is true that they have a deeper source, yet, if a correct method were pursued they would be avoided.   Hence the paramount importance of fixing upon one which shall not be likely to lead us astray.

Now, the method which in the natural sciences, and in the science of language, has led to such vast results, may be, and ought to be pursued here. This method is that of comparison.

When the philologist is desirous of discovering what elements, if any, a group of languages possesses in common, and what therefore may be considered as its fundamental stock, or essence, he compares them with one another. When the naturalist wishes to arrive at an accurate knowledge of the conformation, habits, or character of any class of animals, he can only do so by a comparison of different members of that class. How misleading our conclusions frequently are in matters like these when they are not based upon a sufficiently wide comparison, will be familiar to all. And though the analogy between these sciences and religion is far from precise, yet no good reason can be assigned why a method, which has been so successful in one case, should be totally neglected in the latter. Nor is it enough to say that this method is capable of application to the subject in hand. Religion, owing to certain characteristics which will now be explained, lends itself with peculiar facility to an inquiry thus conducted.

A merely superficial and passing glance at the phenomena presented to us by the history and actual condition of the world brings clearly to light two facts:

1. The absolute, or all but absolute universality of some kind of religious perception or religious feeling.

2. The countless variety of forms under which that feeling has made its appearance.

History and the works of travelers, amply prove that no considerable nation has ever been without religion, and that if it has ever been wanting, it has only been among the rudest savages, whose mental and moral condition was too low to be capable of any but the most obvious impressions of sense. Equally indubitable is the second proposition. We are acquainted with no period in which each country did not possess its own special variety of religious doctrine; we are acquainted with none in which there were not many and wide divergences within the bosom of each country among individuals, among sects, and among churches.

In this universality of a certain sentiment, accompanied by this variety of modes, we have at least a possible distinction between the Substance and the Form, between the universal emotion known as Religion, and the local or temporary coloring it may happen to assume.

It will be convenient if we call the substance by the name of FAITH, and the form by that of BELIEF. The use of these terms in these senses is no doubt slightly arbitrary, yet the shade of difference in their ordinary meaning is sufficient to justify it.

Faith is a term of large and general signification, referring rather to the feelings than the reason; whereas Belief generally implies the intellectual adoption of some definite proposition, capable of distinct statement in words.

The importance of the comparative method in the process of sifting, classifying, and ordering the elements of these respective spheres will now be apparent. For it is only by a comparison of the varieties of Belief that we can hope to arrive at an acquaintance with Faith. Setting one system beside another, carefully observing wherein they differ and wherein they agree, we may at length hope to discover what elements, if any, are to be set down to the account of Faith, and what other elements to that of Belief. Even after a full comparison there will still be considerable danger that we may mistake tenets which are widely held, but not universal, for primordial conceptions of the human mind. Without such a comparison, we should most undoubtedly do so, for we are ever unwilling to recognize how wide are the limits of variation of which the opinions and sentiments of men are capable.

Should we, however, succeed in eliminating by our analysis all that is local, and all that is temporary, we shall possess, in what remains to us after this process, a universal truth of human nature. Observe that I speak here of a truth of human nature as distinguished from a truth of external nature. The one does not of necessity imply the other, for it is conceivable that men might universally entertain certain hopes, fears, aspirations, or convictions which were wholly groundless; the supposed objects of which had no existence whatever beyond the mind that entertained them. In the present case, then, all that the most exhaustive comparison could do would be to lead us up to the scientific fact, that there is in human beings an irresistible tendency towards certain sentiments of a spiritual kind. Whether those sentiments can be the foundation of any rational conviction it is unable to tell us.

This question, however, is fully as important as the other, and I do not propose to pass it over in silence. It will be one object of our investigation to discover how far we are entitled to treat truths of human nature as identical with objective truths. If we are obliged to confess that no inference can be drawn from the one to the other, then it will be plain that Faith, however profoundly implanted in our hearts, does not convey to us any assurance of a single religious truth; for the impressions which we call our Faith may be as purely illusory as the fancies of delirium, or the images of our dreams. If, on the other hand, an internal sentiment may be accepted, not so much as a basis for truth, but as itself true; as leading, and not misleading us; then we must further examine what are the truths which are in a manner contained in Faith, and of which Faith is the warrant.

The first Book, therefore, will deal mainly with Belief. Its object will be, by a comparison of some of the various creeds that are, or have been, accepted by men, to discover the general characteristics of Belief, and to separate these from the more special and distinctive elements peculiar to given times, districts, and races. These general characteristics will, however, belong exclusively to the region of Belief, and not to that of Faith. In other words, they will have no title to a place in a Universal Religion.

In the second Book we shall proceed to investigate the nature of Faith. We shall endeavor to lay bare the foundation of the vast superstructure of Theology and Ritual erected by the piety of the human race. We shall seek to discover, if that be possible, the element of unity amid so much variety, of permanence amid so much change. And should we be successful in the search, we shall be in a position, if not absolutely to solve, at least to attempt the solution of the great problem which ever has interested, and ever must interest mankind: Is there any such thing as positive truth in the sphere of Religion? And if so, what is it? Or are the human faculties strictly limited to that species of knowledge which is acquired through the medium of the senses, and doomed, in all spiritual things, to be the victims of endless longings for which there is no satisfaction, and of perpetual questionings to which there is no response?

INTRODUCTION.

RELIGIOUS Feeling, like all other human emotions, makes itself objectively known to us by its manifestations. With its subjective character we are now concerned, our business in the present book being to treat it merely as an objective phenomenon. Thus regarded, its manifestations appear extremely various, but on closer examination they will be found to spring from a common principle. This principle is the desire felt by the human race in general to establish a relationship between itself and those superhuman or supernatural powers upon whose will it supposes the course of nature and the well-being of men to be dependent. Were it not for this desire, the Religious Idea — if I may venture by this term to denominate the original sentiment which is the beginning of positive religion — might remain locked up for ever in the breast of each individual who felt it. But there is innate in human beings — arriving like wanderers in the midst of a world they cannot understand — an overpowering wish to enter into some sort of communication with the mysterious agencies of whose extraordinary force they are continually conscious, but which appear to be hidden from their observation in impenetrable darkness.

Any man who seems able to give information as to the nature of these agencies; who can declare their wishes with regard to the conduct of men; who can assert, with apparent authority, their determination to reward certain kinds of actions, and to punish others, is listened to with avidity; and if he is believed to speak truly his counsels are followed. Any tradition which is held to make known the proper manner of approaching these great powers is devoutly conserved, and becomes the foundation of the conduct of many generations. Any writing which is consecrated by popular belief as either emanating directly from

these powers, or as having been composed under their authority and at their dictation, is regarded with profound reverence;
and no one is allowed to question either its statements of fact
or its injunctions. What are the particular characteristics which
enable either men, traditions, or writings to acquire so extraordinary an authority, it is difficult, if not impossible, to say.
Some approach to a reply may be made in the course of the
inquiry, but much will still remain unaccounted for: one of
those ultimate secrets of our nature which admit of no complete discovery. Certain it is, however, that this passionate
longing to enter into some kind of relation with the unknown
receives its satisfaction in the earliest stages of human society.

Man, isolated, fearful, struck with wonder at his own existence, craves to become acquainted with the Divine will, to hear
the accents of the Divine voice, to offer up his petitions to those
higher beings who are able to grant them, and to offer them up
in such a manner that they may be willing as well as able. Impelled by this craving, the Religious Idea passes out of its condition of vague emotion into that of positive opinion. It becomes manifest, or, if I may use an appropriate image, incarnate.

The means by which the wished-for intercourse between man
and the higher powers is effected are obviously twofold: such
as convey information from the worshipers to their deities, and
such as convey it from the deities back to their worshipers. In
other words they might be described as serving for communication upwards, or communication downwards; from mankind to
God, or from God to mankind. In the former case human beings are the agents; in the latter the patients. In the former,
they consciously and intentionally place themselves, or endeavor
to place themselves, in correspondence with the unseen powers;
in the latter, they simply receive the injunctions, reproofs, or
other intimations with which those powers may think fit to
favor them.

The methods by which this correspondence is sought to be
effected are very various. Let us take first those which carry
the thoughts of men's hearts upwards.

1. The earliest, simplest, and most universal method is the
performance of certain solemnities of a regularly recurrent

kind, which, as expressive of their object, I will term *consecrated actions.* Such actions are prayer, praise, sacrifice, ceremonies and rites, offerings, and, in short, all the numerous external acts comprehended under the term Worship.

2. The second is the consecration of distinct places for the purpose of carrying on such worship, or otherwise approaching the Deity more closely and solemnly than can be done on common and unsanctified ground. These I term *consecrated places.*

3. Thirdly, we have a large class of objects dedicated expressly to religious purposes. Such are votive offerings of all kinds; pictures, statues, vestments, gifts bestowed on the priesthood for employment in Divine worship, or whatever else the piety of the devotees of any deity may induce them to withdraw from their own consumption, and set apart for his service. These are *consecrated objects.*

4. Devoutly disposed persons seek to enter into a more than commonly direct relation with their god by dedication of their own persons to him, such dedication being signified by some special characteristics in their mode of life. Such are ascetics of all descriptions, whether they be known as Essenes, Nazarites, Bonzes, monks, or any other term. I describe them henceforward as *consecrated persons.*

5. Lastly, we have a class of men who are also consecrated, but who differ from the preceding in that the object of their consecration is not personal but social. They are devoted to the service of the deity not in order that they individually may enter into more intimate relations with him, but that they may carry on the needful intercourse between the community at large and its gods. To emphasize this distinction, I call them *consecrated mediators.*

The second great division of our subject is that which treats of the several modes by which divine ideas are carried downwards. And here we will follow a classification corresponding as nearly as possible to that adopted in the preceding section.

1. First, then, the Deity conveys his will or his intention through events; such as omens, auguries, miracles, dreams, and many other phenomena. All these may be termed *holy events.*

2. Secondly, there are certain spots which are either favorable to the reception of supernatural communications, or have

on some occasion been the scene of such a communication, which we will call *holy places*.

3. Thirdly, certain objects are held to possess mysterious powers, as that of healing disease. Relics, articles that have been used by holy men, and such like remains, come within this category. They may be described as *holy objects*.

4. All communities above the very lowest employ professional persons for the express object of conveying to them the will of their Deity, or discovering his intentions as to the future. The most usual name for such functionaries is that of Priest, and for the sake of embracing all ecclesiastical or quasi-ecclesiastical classes under one designation I shall call them *holy orders*.

5. The possession of a professional character distinguishes them from the next class, who serve as the fifth channel between God and man, but who differ from the fourth in the circumstance of being self-appointed. Prophets (for it is of these I am speaking) receive no regular consecration; nevertheless the part they have played in the religious history of mankind has been of such transcendent importance that they deserve to be placed in a class apart under the title of *holy persons*.

6. Sixthly, there remains a mode of communication from God to man to which there is nothing corresponding on our side; it is that of written documents. Man has never (so far as I am aware) imagined himself capable of sending a letter or written composition of any kind to God; but God is supposed, through the medium of human instruments, to have embodied his thoughts in writing for the benefit of the human race. The result is the very important category of *holy books*.

EXTERNAL MANIFESTATIONS OF RELIGIOUS SENTIMENT.

FIRST PART.

MEANS OF COMMUNICATION UPWARDS.

CHAPTER I.

CONSECRATED ACTIONS.

ADORATION, or worship, is a direct result of one of the most universal of human instincts. After the instincts which impel us to provide for the necessities of the body, and to satisfy the passion of love, there is perhaps none more potent or more general. Men are driven to pray by an irresistible impulse. Differing widely as to the object of worship; differing not less widely as to its mode; differing in a minor degree as to the blessings it secures; they are agreed as to the fundamental ideas which it involves. In the first place it presupposes a power superior to, or at any rate different from, the power of man; in the second place it assumes a belief that this super-human or non-human power can be approached by his worshippers; can be induced to listen to their desires, and to grant their petitions.

Of the first of the two elements thus implied in prayer, this is not the appropriate place to speak at length. In a very early and primitive stage of man's existence, he begins to feel his dependence upon powers invisible to his mortal eyes, whose mode of action he can but imperfectly comprehend. His way of conceiving these beings will depend upon his mental eleva-tion, upon historical influences, upon local conditions, and other

31

causes. Among very rude nations, the commonest and apparently most unimpressive objects will serve as fetishes, or incarnations of the mysterious force. Pieces of wood, stones, ornaments worn on the person, or almost anything, may under some circumstances do duty in this capacity. It is a further stage of progress when the more conspicuous objects of nature, lofty mountains, rivers, trees, fountains, and so forth, are deified, to the exclusion of more insignificant things. Still higher is the adoration of bodies which do not belong to this earth at all, and whose nature is, therefore, more mysterious—the sun, the moon, the planets or the stars, the clouds and tempests, the winds, and similar imposing phenomena. And this stage passes naturally into one where the gods, at first merely forces of nature personified, lose their character of forces, and become exclusively persons. They are then conceived as beings in human form, but endowed with much more than human faculties. Actual persons, especially the ancestors of the living generation, are also the frequent recipients of religious adoration. By other races, or by the same races at a later period, the numerous gods of polytheism are merged in one supreme god, to whom the others are subordinated as agents of his will, or before whose grandeur they disappear altogether; while this worship of powers conceived as beneficent is very frequently accompanied, more or less avowedly, by a parallel worship of powers conceived as malevolent, and whom, by reason of that very malevolence, it is occasionally deemed the more needful to conciliate.

The second element—the conviction that these deities are accessible to human requests—is shown both by the fact of worship being offered and by the mode in which it is conducted. In the first place, it is plain that prayer would not be offered at all but for the belief that it exercises some influence on the beings prayed to. But the theory does not require that they should be equally amenable to it at all times, from all persons, or in whatever way it is uttered. On the contrary, accessibility to prayer implies in these who receive it an inclination to listen with attention to the language in which they are addressed, and to be more or less moved by it according to its nature.

Reasoning from the authorities of earth whom he knows, to

those of heaven whom he does not know, the primitive man concludes that the best way of obtaining the satisfaction of his wishes from the latter will be to address them in a tone of humble supplication, intermingled with such laudatory epithets as he deems most suitable to the deity invoked, or most likely to be agreeable to his ear. Hence we have the two devotional acts of prayer and praise, which in all religions constantly accompany one another, and constitute the simplest, most natural, and most ancient expression on the part of human beings of their consciousness of an overruling power, and of their desire to enter into relations with that dreaded and venerated agency.

Prayer in its original form is simply a request for some personal advantage addressed by the worshipers to their god. Whatever loftier associations it may afterwards acquire, its intention at the outset is unquestionably this, as may be proved by reference to innumerable instances, quoted by travelers or scholars, of savage prayer, where the benefit expected from the deity is demanded in the most barefaced manner. But even after men have long ceased to be savages, the primary object of prayer may easily be discerned; sometimes plainly avowed by the persons praying, sometimes cloaked under complimentary phrases or devotional utterances. However disguised, the fact remains, that prayer was originally designed, and to a large extent is designed still, to obtain certain advantages for ourselves, either as individuals, or as a community. Private prayer, partaking to some extent of the character of a meditation, may, and no doubt often does, form an exception to this rule; but even this very frequently falls under it, and of the prayer offered by tribes or nations it always holds good.

Two excellent specimens of primitive prayer are given by Brinton in his "Myths of the New World." According to that writer, the Nootka Indian, on preparing for war, thus expresses his wishes:—"Great Quahootzee, let me live, not be sick, find the enemy, not fear him, find him asleep, and kill a great many of him."

The next instance, quoted by him from Father Breboeuf, is equally apposite. It is the prayer of a Huron:—"Oki, thou who livest in this spot, I offer thee tobacco. Help us, save us from shipwreck, defend us from our enemies, give us a good trade, and bring us back safe and sound to our villages" (M. N. W., p. 297).

The Kafirs, according to Shooter, address the "spirits" whom they worship in the following style: "Take care of me, take care of my children, take care of my wives, take care of all my people. Remove the sickness, and let my child recover. Give me plenty of children — many boys and a few girls. Give me abundance of food and cattle. Make right all my people" (K. N., p. 163).

Of the negroes on the Caribbean Islands, Oldendorp says, "Their concerns which they lay before God in their prayers, even on their knees, have reference only to the body, to health, fine weather, a good harvest, victory over their enemies, and so forth" (G. d. M., p. 325).

The Samoans, on taking their evening "cup of ava," would thus express their petitions to the gods: "Here is ava for you, O gods! Look kindly towards this family: let it prosper and increase; and let us all be kept in health. Let our plantations be productive, let fruit grow, and may there be abundance of food for us, your creatures. Here is ava for you, our war-gods! Let there be a strong and numerous people for you in this land. Here is ava for you, O sailing gods! Do not come on shore at this place; but be pleased to depart along the ocean to some other land" (N. Y., p. 200).

Mr. Turner, to whom I am indebted for the above prayer, remarks that in Tanna, another of the Polynesian islands, the chief of a village repeats a short prayer at the evening meal, "asking health, long life, good crops, and success in battle" (Ibid., p. 85).

The authors of the Vedic hymns, though standing on a far higher level of civilization, do not differ essentially from these rude people in the character of the objects for which they pray. The several deities are continually invoked to grant health, wealth, prosperity, posterity, and other temporal blessings. Thus (to quote one instance among many) in Mandala 1, Sukta 64, translated by Max Müller, the Maruts are requested to grant "strength, glorious, invincible in battle, brilliant, wealth-conferring, praiseworthy, known to all men;" and again, "wealth, durable, rich in men, defying all onslaughts; wealth a hundred and a thousandfold, always increasing " (R. V. S., i. 64, 14, 15, —Vol. i. p. 93). The liturgies of the Zend-Avesta, while sometimes assuming a loftier strain, frequently move upon the same level. The same tone is to be observed in the Hebrew Scriptures. Solomon's prayer, for instance, at the dedication of the temple, may be taken as an enumeration of the objects commonly praved for among the ancient Hebrews. It specifies among the objects to be obtained at the hands of Jehovah, the prevention of famine, of pestilence, blasting, mildew, locust or caterpillar, plague or sickness (1 Kings viii. 37). Christian liturgies contain the same universal elements, though intermingled with many others, and not in general put forward with the same crudity of language.

Besides these general objects, there are others of an ephemeral and special kind which are generally drawn within the sphere of prayer. Rain is a common object of prayer, and other changes of weather are equally prayed for if they are held to be important. Callaway, for example, was informed by a "very old man" in South Africa that "if it does not rain, the heads of villages and petty chiefs assemble and go to a black chief; they converse and pray for rain" (R. S. A., vol. i. p. 59). Another native described the mode of supplication more particularly. A certain chieftain named Utshaka "came and made his prayers greater than those who preceded him." When he desired rain, he sang the following song, which "consists of musical sounds merely, without any meaning:"—

" *One Part* — I ya wu; a wu; o ye i ye."
" *Second Part or Response* — I ya wo."

And this prayer, so touching in its simplicity, was as successful as the most elaborate composition of Jewish prophet or Christian bishop; for the narrator states that Utshaka "Sang a song and prayed to the Lord of heaven; and asked his forefathers to pray for rain to the Lord of heaven. *And it rained*" (R. S. A., vol. i. p. 92). The efficacy of prayer is plainly independent of the creed of him who offers it.

The Mexicans held an important annual festival in the month of May, of which the main purpose was to entreat for water from the sky, this being the season at which there was the greatest need of rain (H. I., b. v. ch. 28). They used to address an elaborate prayer to a god named Tlaloc, the king of the terrestral paradise, to obtain deliverance from drought. They entreated him not to visit the offenses they had committed with such severity as to continue the privation under which they were laboring.* The Tannese, when put to much inconvenience by the dust falling from a certain volcano, " were in the habit of praying to their gods for a change of wind" (N. Y., p. 75). Certain other South Sea Islanders used to pray to their gods to avert the supposed calamity of a lunar eclipse. "As the eclipse passes off, they think it is all owing to their prayers," a mode of reasoning which presents an exact parallel to that employed by many Christians.

Sir John Davis gives a very interesting specimen of a prayer for rain employed by Taou-Kuâng, the Emperor of China, in 1832, on the occasion of a long drought in that country (Chinese, vol. ii. p. 75). As may be expected from so civilized a people, this prayer rises far above the outspoken begging of savage petitions, yet it has in substance precisely the same end. The emperor describes himself as "scorched with grief," and pathetically inquires whether he has been remiss in sacrifice, has been proud or prodigal, irreverent, unjust, or wanting in discretion in the exercise of patronage. Here we see the intrusion of the theological idea that calamities are sent as punishments for sin, which plays no small part in Christian theology; but this only serves to veil, without effacing, the essential character of the prayer. The very same notion, that sin is visited by unfavorable weather, is found in the prayer of Solomon, whose mind upon this question seems to have been in the same stage of thought as that attained by the Chinese emperor. "When heaven is shut up, and there is no rain, because they have sinned against thee" (1 Kings viii. 35), is the language of Solomon: "My sins are so numerous that it is hopeless to escape their consequences," so runs the penitent confession of Taou-Kuâng. But whatever may be the cause to which the drought is attributed, the prayer, whether uttered by Chinaman, Jew, or

---

* This prayer, which is too long to quote, may be found in Aglio, A. M., v. 372, and in Sahagun, C. N. E., book vi. chap. 8. According to Sahagun, it contains " muy delicada materia."

Christian, is still simply the petition to the Amazulu, the South Sea Islander, or the native American — a request that God will so influence the phenomena of the skies as to suit our convenience. The notion that this object may sometimes be attained by our prayers is not extinct even among ourselves.

Other special occasions are sometimes held to call for prayer. Such are national calamities; as a pestilence among men or cattle, the illness of some eminent person, and other similar misfortunes. A good harvest is very generally prayed for; so is victory in time of war. The ancient Aryans, who composed the Vedic hymns one thousand years or more before Christ, continually prayed for this last blessing; and we ourselves, when engaged in warfare, piously continue the same custom.

Very frequently the notion of a bargain between the god and his worshiper appears in prayer. The worshiper claims to have rendered some service for which the god ought in equity to reward him; or he holds out the discontinuance of his former devotion as a motive to induce the concession of his desires. The constant conjunction of praise with prayer is explicable on this principle of a reciprocity of benefits. If the worshiper gains much from the god, yet the god gains something from him, being addressed in a strain of unbounded eulogy. His power, his greatness, his goodness, his excellences of all kinds are vaunted in glowing terms, no doubt sincerely used by the worshiper, but repeated and accumulated to satiety from an impression that they are pleasing to their object, and may dispose him to beneficence. Titles thus bestowed upon their deities are aptly described by the Amazulus as "laud-giving names" (R. S. A.. vol. i. p. 72, and vol. ii. p. 149). In the Vedic hymns and in the Psalms, the deities spoken of are constantly addressed by such complimentary epithets. One of the hymns to the Maruts begins by announcing the poet's intention to praise "their ancient greatness." And at the conclusion, after he has done so, he says, "May this praise, O Maruts, . . . approach you (asking) for offspring to our body, together with food. May we find food, and a camp with running water (R. V. S., vol. i. pp. 197, 201). The Psalmists were never weary of exalting the extraordinary might and majesty of Jehovah, mingling petitions with panegyric; and a large portion of the worship of Christians consists in expressions of pious admiration at the extraordinary goodness of their God, especially for his redemption of the world which he had himself condemned. All these extravagant eulogies betray a latent impression that the Deity is, after all, a very arbitrary personage, and may be moved to more merciful conduct than he would otherwise pursue by large doses of flattery.

Still more clearly does the idea of a commercial relationship with the gods make its appearance in a poet who stands on a higher intellectual and moral level than the writers of the Hebrew Psalms, namely Aischylos. In the Seven against Thebes, Eteokles implores Zeus, the Earth, and the tutelar deities of the city to protect Thebes; and subjoins as a motive for compliance, "And I trust that what I say is our common interest; for a prosperous city honors the gods " (Aisch. Sept. c. Th. 76, 77 — Dindorf). And there is a similar appeal to the divine selfishness further on in the same play, where the chorus inquires of the gods what better plain they can expect to obtain in exchange for this one, if they shall suffer it to pass into the enemy's hands (Aisch., Sept. c. Th. 304).

In the Choephoræ, Zeus is distinctly asked in the prayer of Agamemnon's children whence he can expect to obtain the sacrifice and honors which have been paid him by Orestes and Electra if he should suffer them to perish (Aisch., Choeph., 255). While in the Electra of Sophocles the converse motive of gratitude is appealed to: the god Apollon being desired to remember not what he may get, but what he already has got, from the piety of his supplicant (Soph. El., 1376 — Schneidewin). And Jacob, who was a good hand at a bargain, makes his terms with Jehovah in a thoroughly business-like spirit. "*If* God will be with me, and will keep me in this way that I go, and will give me bread to eat and raiment to put on, so that I come again to my father's house in peace; *then* shall the Lord be my God: and this stone, which I have set up for a pillar, shall be God's house: and of all that thou shalt give me I will surely give the tenth unto thee." The adoption of Jehovah as Jacob's God being thus entirely dependent on the performance by that Deity of his share in the contract " (Gen. xxviii. 20–22).

Sometimes it is quaintly suggested that were the worshiper

in the place of the god, *he* would not neglect the interests of his devotee. Thus, the author of a hymn in the Rig-Veda-Sanhita, addressing the Gods of Tempest, exclaims: "If you, sons of Prisni, were mortals, and your worshiper an immortal, then never should your praiser be unwelcome, like a deer in pasture grass, nor should he go on the path of Yama" (R. V. S., vol. i. p. 65). Another unsophisticated poet gives the following hint to the god Indra, the Hindu Jupiter: "Were I, Indra, like thee, the sole lord of wealth, the singer of my praises should be rich in cattle" (S. V., i. 2. i. 3. p. 218). And the same god is asked elsewhere in the Veda: "When wilt thou make us happy? for it is just this that is desired" (S. V., i. 5. i. 3. p 233). With equal plainness is the expectation of a *quid pro quo* enunciated in one of the most ancient hymns, contained in the sacred books of the Parsees:—"Every adoration, O True One consists in actions whereby one may obtain good possessions, full of security, and happiness round about" (F. G. vol. ii. p. 54.—Yama 51. i).

More emphatically still is this conception of a reciprocity of benefits expressed in another consecrated action, that of Sacrifice. Sacrifice holds a most important place in all religions. It originates in a stage of the human mind which, if not quite as primitive as that which gives rise to prayer, is nevertheless so early as to be practicably inseparable from it. Wherever we find prayer, we find sacrifice; but as the latter is generally found organized under definite forms, and confined to certain specified objects, we may conclude that in the state in which we recognize it, it implies a certain degree of regulation and forethought on the part of religious authorities which we do not meet with in the simplest types of prayer. Prayer is often the mere natural outpouring of our wants before a power which is considered capable of fulfilling them: sacrifice, though doubtless in the first instance an equally artless offering of gifts to beings who are regarded with veneration and gratitude, is soon converted into a formal presentation of acknowledged dues, performed under ecclesiastical supervision. No doubt prayer also tends to assume this formal character; but we have hitherto considered it in its uncorrupted aspect; its treatment in its later developments belongs to another portion of this chapter.

The idea which presides over sacrifice is obvious. The sacrificer argues that if he can make acceptable presents to the gods, they will smile upon him and be disposed to promote his ends; whereas if he keeps the whole of his possessions for worldly purposes, they will regard him with indignation, and refuse him their assistance when he may happen to stand in need of it. There is also involved in sacrifice a sense of gratitude: the gods having given us the fruits of the earth, it be hooves us to make some acknowledgment of their bounty.

Such notions, once propounded, were certain to be fertile Every motive of piety and of interest would combine to support them. The piety of the worshipers, coupled with their hopes of advantage, would be stimulated by the self-interest of the priests, who generally share in the sacrifices offered. If any piece of good fortune occurred to one who was devout and liberal in sacrificing, it would be attributed to the satisfaction felt by the gods at his exemplary conduct. If ill fortune befell those who had neglected to sacrifice, this would be an equally manifest indication of their high displeasure. As soon, therefore, as the step was taken — and it was one of the earliest in the religious history of man — of instituting sacrifices to idols or to deities, the worshipers vied with one another in the liberality of their offerings. Adopted as a mode of propitiating the celestial beings by spontaneous gifts, it became, among all nations whose religious belief had arrived at a state of flexity and consolidation, a positive duty; much as monarchs have frequently exacted large and burdensome contributions under the guise of voluntary presents.

Illustrations of this conception, that sacrifice is a sort of payment for services rendered or to be rendered, might be found abundantly in many quarters. Perhaps it is seldom more quaintly expressed than by the Amazulus, who, when going to battle, sacrifice to the Amatongo, or manes of their ancestors, in order that these, in their own language, "may have no cause of complaint, because they have made amends to them, and made them bright." On reaching the enemy, they say, "Can it be, since we have made amends to the Amadhlozi, that they will say we have wronged them by anything?" And when it comes to fighting, they are filled with valor, observing that "the Amatongo will turn their backs on us without cause" (R. S. A., vol. ii. p. 133).

The objects of sacrifice are very various, but it is noticeable that they are almost invariably things held in esteem among men, and either possessing a considerable value as commodities, or capable by their properties of ministering to their pleasure. All sacrifices of meat and corn or other edibles belong to the former class; those of flowers to the latter, for these, though of little value in the market yet give great pleasure, and are much esteemed. An exception is indeed presented by the wild hordes in Kamtschatka, who, according te Steller, offer nothing to their gods but what is valueless to themselves (Kamtschatka, p. 265). . If this statement does not originate in a misunderstanding of the traveler, the fact must be due to the singularly low religiosity of those people, who seem to have little reverence for the very objects of their worship.

The most valuable sacrifice that can possibly be made — that of human beings — has always been common among savage or uncivilized nations. Thus, in some of the South Sea Islands, human sacrifices were "fearfully common" (N. M. E., p. 547). They prevailed among some of the negro tribes known to the missionary Oldendorp (G. d. M., p. 329).

In Mexico, where the natives had arrived at a far higher condition, human sacrifices still prevailed, though the original brutality of the rite was modified by the fact of the victims being enemies. Indeed, Montezuma, when at the height of his power, expressly refused to conquer a certain province which he might easily have added to his dominions; assigning as his first reason, that he desired to keep the Mexican youth in practice; as his second and principal one, that he might reserve a province for the supply of victims to sacrifice to the gods (H. I., b. v. ch. 20).

At the great Mexican festival of the Jubilee, however, it was not an enemy, but a slave, who was offered. This slave had represented the idol during the period of a year, and had received the greatest honor during his term of office, at the end of which his head was severed from his body by the priest, who then held it as high as he could, and showed it to the Sun and to the idol (H. I., b. v. ch. 28).

Next in value to the human race are cattle, and these too are frequently immolated in honor of the gods. Thus among the Kafirs, "the animals offered are exclusively cattle and goats. The largest ox in a herd is specially reserved for sacrifices on important occasions; it is called the Ox of the Spirits, and is never sold except in cases of extreme necessity" (Kafirs. p. 165). Here we find it expressly stated that it is the best ox, in other words, the most valuable portion of the sacrificer's property, which is devoted to the gods. And the principle which leads in Natal to this reservation of the best will be found predominating over sacrifice throughout the world. The Soosoos, a people inhabiting the west coast of Africa, are so careful to propitiate their deity, that they "never undertake any affair of importance until they have sacrificed to him a bullock" (N. A., vol. i. p. 230).

Other domestic and edible animals, being of great importance to mankind, are held worthy of the honor of sacrifice. The same writer to whom I owe the last quotation tells us of the Western Africans, that "before they begin to sow their plantations, they sacrifice a sheep, goat, fowl, or fish to the ay-min, to beg that their crop may abound; for were this neglected, they are persuaded that nothing would grow there" (Ibid., vol. i. p. 223). Oldendorp, who was particularly familiar with the Caribbean Islands, describes the sacrifices of the negroes as consisting of "oxen, cows, sheep, goats, hens, palm-oil, brandy, yams, &c" (G. d. M., p. 329).

Besides porcelain collars, tobacco, maize, and skins, the American Indians used to offer "entire animals, especially dogs, on the borders of difficult or dangerous roads or rocks, or by the side of rapids." These offerings were made to the spirits who presided in these places. The great value attached by the natives of America to the dog is well known, and it is deserving of remark that the dog was the commonest victim, and that at the war-festival, which was a sort of sacrifice, it was always dogs that were offered.

In China, the animals slain are "bullocks, heifers, sheep, and pigs," which are duly purified for a certain period beforehand (C. O., vol. ii. p. 192). Among the Jews, pigs, whose flesh was regarded as impure, were not offered; bullocks, goats, and sheep were the chief sacrificial animals; and extreme care was taken in their law that they should be entirely without blemish; that is, that, like the ox of the Kafirs, they should be the best obtainable (Lev. xxii. 17–25). This is a remarkable illustration of the tendency to offer only articles of value in human estimation to God; for here that which would be good enough for men is treated as unfit for Jehovah. Animals of lesser magnitude are sometimes offered; as, for instance, the quails which the Mexicans used to sacrifice (H. I., b. v. ch. 18). Birds are not unfrequently chosen as fitting objects to present to the gods. Among the Ibos, a negro tribe, it is the custom for women, six weeks after child-birth, to present a pair of hens as an offering, which, however, are not killed, but liberated after certain ceremonies. In like manner the Hebrew woman after her delivery was enjoined to bring a lamb and a pigeon or turtle-dove; or, if she were unable to bring the lamb, two young pigeons or two turtle-doves (Lev. xii. 6–8). In addition to animals, a considerable variety of objects is sacrificed, generally the fruits of the earth or flowers. There is, however, no limit to the number of things which may be held suitable for presentation to the gods. Thus, in Samoa (in Polynesia), the offerings were principally cooked food " (N. Y. p. 241). In other Islands "the first fruits are presented to the gods " (Ibid., p. 327), a practice which corresponds, as the missionary who records it justly remarks, to that of the ancient Israelites. The Red Indians used to offer to their spirits "petun, tobacco, or birds." In honor of the Sun, and even of subordinate spirits, they would throw into the fire everything they were in the habit of using, and which they acknowledged as received from them (N. F., vol. iii. pp. 347, 348). Acosta divides the sacrifices of the Mexicans and Peruvians into three classes: the first, of inanimate objects; the second, of animals; the third, of men. In the first class are included cocoa, maize, colored feathers, seashells, gold and silver, and fine linen (H. I., b. v. ch. 18). Among the sacrifices offered by the Incas to the sun, the most esteemed, according to Garcilasso de la Vega, were lambs, then sheep, then barren ewes. Besides these, they sacrificed tame rabbits, all *edible* birds (remark the limitation), and fat of beasts, as well as all the grains and vegetables up to cocoa, and

the finest linen (observe again the care that it should be fine
(C. R., b. ii. ch. 8). At a certain Hindu festival described by
Wilson, a goddess named Varadá Chaturthi "is worshipped
with offerings of flowers, of incense, or of lights, with platters
of sugar and ginger, or milk or salt, with scarlet or saffron-
tinted strings and golden bracelets" (W. W., vol. ii. pp. 184, 185).
Among the Parsees the sacrifices consist of little loaves of
bread, and of Haoma, the sacred plant. The Indian Parsees
send from time to time to Kirman to obtain Haoma-branches
from this holy territory (Z. A., vol. ii. p. 535). The Parsees also
offer flowers, fruits, rice, odoriferous grains, perfumes, milk,
roots of certain trees, and meat. The Jews, like them, offered
the productions of the soil in sacrifice.

Beauty, and even utility, when not accompanied by considerable value in exchange, do not suffice to constitute fitness for
religious sacrifice. Common plants and shrubs, branches of
trees, wild birds or insects, are some of them among the most
beautiful productions of nature; yet they are not sacrificed.
Stones and wood are both useful, but they are obtained, as a
rule, at little cost; and they are not sacrificed. Flowers, which
certainly have no high value, were sometimes offered to idols
in the form of wreaths and garlands: they scarcely constitute
an exception to the rule, for they are prized as ornaments by
men, and the process of plucking and weaving them into appropriate shapes imposes trouble—the equivalent of cost—on the
devotee. It is plainly not owing to any accidental circumstance
that highly valuable objects have been selected by all the
nations of the earth as alone appropriate for religious sacrifice.
Two reasons may be assigned for this selection. In the first
place, the general assimilation of deities to mankind goes far
to account for it. Everywhere, and at all times—as we shall
have occasion frequently to observe in this work—men have
reasoned as to the divine nature from their knowledge of their
own. A noteworthy instance of this is to be seen in Malachi,
who does not scruple to tell the Jews that their God feels the
same kind of offense at the poverty of their offerings as a
human governor would do. "And if," says that prophet, "ye
offer the blind for sacrifice, is it not evil? and if ye offer the
lame and sick, is it not evil? *offer it now unto thy governor;*

will he be pleased with thee, or accept thy person? saith the Lord of hosts." A few verses later he recurs to the sorrow felt by Jehovah at such insults. "And ye bring that which is robbed, and the lame, and the sick; thus ye bring an offering: should I accept this of your hand? saith the Lord. But cursed be the deceiver, which hath in his flock a male, and voweth and sacrificeth unto the Lord a bad female." It would be difficult to find the theory of God's resemblance to man expressed in a cruder form. Even as a governor will show the greatest favor to those who approach him with the costliest gifts, so the mouthpiece of the Hebrew deity declares in his name that he must have the pick of his servant's flocks—the males, not the females, the sound and the perfect, not the sickly or the maimed. In a precisely similar spirit, it is enjoined in one of the sacred books of the Buddhists that no spoilt victuals or drinks may be used in sacrifice (Wassiljew, p. 211).

Men's notion of their god was often derived, like Malachi's, not only from human nature, but from those who were by no means the best specimens of human nature,—the rulers. The religious emotion, imbued with this conception of its deities, shrank through a sense of piety from the irreverent, and, as it seemed, sacrilegious act of presenting them with anything but the best. But there was another reason which, doubtless, had its weight. Not only must the offering be of a kind acceptable to the god to whom it was given; it must also impose some cost upon the worshiper. Religious sentiment imperatively required that there should be an actual sacrifice of something which the owner valued, and the surrender of which imposed a burden upon him. This seemed to be involved in the very notion of sacrifice. Its sense and purpose was, that the devotee, coming to his god, and desiring to obtain some favor from him, should show the high importance he attached to it by parting with some portion of his possessions. And plainly this portion must be such as to indicate by its character the esteem and reverence felt by the worshiper for the being whom he worshiped. To indicate this, it must be something which he would unwillingly resign but for his religious feelings. Hence a special part of the fruits of the soil would be an appropriate offering. It would involve a real diminution in the wealth of the worshiper, a real surrender of something useful and valuable to mankind. To these two reasons may be added a third, which, no doubt, must have had its weight. In many cases, a portion of the sacrifices was the property of the priests. As will be more fully shown hereafter; the priesthood frequently contrived to transfer to themselves the piety which was felt towards the gods. Hence the sacrifices, originally given to the divine beings, were in part appropriated by their ministers; and it was obviously of importance to them that the thing sacrificed should be such as they could profit by and enjoy.

It sometimes happens that the sacrifice, or a portion of it, is consumed either by the worshipers in general, or by their priests. A case of the former kind is mentioned by Oldendorp. When the young men among the Tembus (negroes) are going to battle, the old men offer sheep and hens to their god Zioo for their success; the blood and bowels they bestow upon Zioo, and the flesh they eat themselves (G. d. M., p. 330). Sometimes the thing sacrificed is itself regarded as an idol or god, and is eaten religiously, under a belief that it is a food of peculiar efficacy. Such is the case with the Christian sacrament; and such was the case, too, with the remarkable custom observed among the Mexicans at the feast of Vitziliputzli, where an idol composed of corn and honey used to be solemnly consecrated, and afterwards distributed to be eaten by the people, who received it with extreme reverence, awe, and tears, as the flesh and bones of the god himself (H. I., b. v. ch. 24). It is an exception, however, when the laity partake in the consumption of the sacrifices; they are generally reserved for the priests. Among the Jews, it was the privilege of the priests to eat certain portions of the animals brought for sacrifice; and in like manner the Parsee priest, or Zaota, eats the bread and drinks the Haoma (Av., vol. ii. p. lxxii). And it deserves especial mention, that the Haoma, a plant of which the juice is thus drunk in certain rites both in the Indian and the Parsee religions, is in both considered a god as well as a plant; just as the wine of the Christian sacrament is both the juice of the grape and the blood of the Redeemer (Av., vol. i. p. 8).

In the above cases, food consecrated to the gods is eaten by men. The converse practice, that of bestowing a portion of the ordinary food of men upon the gods, is also common. The habit of the ancients of making libations is well known. But the same practice has prevailed, or prevails still, in many distinct parts of the world. A traveler who visited Tartary in the thirteenth century states that it was the custom of the Tartar chiefs of one thousand or one hundred men, before they ate or drank anything, to offer some of it to an idol which they always kept in the middle of their dwelling place (Bergeron, Voyage de Carpin, art. iii., p. 30). In Samoa, when a family feast was held in honor of the household gods, "a cup of their intoxi-:ating ava draught was poured out as a drink-offering" (N. Y., p. 239). Among the Soosoos, on the west coast of Africa, a custom prevails "which resembles the ancient practice of pouring out a libation: they seldom or never drink spirits, wine, etc., without spilling a little of it upon the ground, and wetting the gree-gree or fetish hung round the neck: at the same time they mutter a kind of short prayer" (N. A., p. 123). Again, in Sierra Leone, "when they want to render their devil propitious to any undertaking, they generally provide liquor: a very small libation is made to him, and the rest they drink before his altar" (S. L., p. 66). While in Thibet, "the execution by a Lama is not required for the usual libations to the personal genii, nor to those of the house, the country, etc., in whose honor it is the custom to pour out upon the ground some drink or food, and to fill one of the offering vessels ranged before their images before eating or drinking one's self" (B. T., p. 247).

Great importance is in all religions attached to sacrifice. It is universally supposed to conciliate, to soften, or to appease the deity in whose honor it is offered. Sometimes it is even conceived to have an actual material power of its own, the spirits deriving a positive benefit from the food presented to them. Spiegel states that the subordinate genii in the Parsee hierarchy of angels derive from the sacrifices strength and vigor to fulfil their duties (Av., vol. ii. p. lxiii). Generally, however, the conception of the influence of sacrifice is less materialistic. The Amazulus naively express the general sentiment by saying, that, in prospect of a battle, they sacrifice to their ancestors in order that they "may have no cause of complaint." Much more mystical were the views entertained on this point by the ancient

Hindus, among whom the theory of sacrifice was probably more highly elaborated than in any other nation. Of a certain sacrificial ceremony it is stated, that the gods, after having performed it, "gained the celestial world. Likewise a sacrificer, after having done the same, gains the celestial world" (A. B., vol. ii. p. 22). And it is added, that the sacrificer who performs this rite "succeeds in both worlds, and obtains a firm footing in both worlds" (A. B., vol. ii. p. 25). While to another rite the following promise is attached: "He who, knowing this, sacrifices according to this rite, is born (anew) from the womb of Agni and the offerings, and participates in the nature of the Rik, Yajus, and Sâman, the Veda (sacred knowledge), the Brahma (sacred element), and immortality, and is absorbed in the deity" (A. B., vol. ii. p. 51). Often it is the forgiveness of some offense that is sought to be obtained by pacifying the indignant deity with a gift. In the Jewish law a large portion of the sacrifices enjoined have this object. They are termed sin-offerings or trespass-offerings.

The general idea which leads to sacrifice is in all religions the same. Respect is intended to be shown to the deity in whose honor the sacrifice is made by depriving ourselves of some valuable possession, and bestowing it on him. The pleasure supposed to be felt by God on receiving such presents is somewhat coarsely but emphatically expressed in the Hebrew Bible by the statement that when Aaron had made a sacrifice in the wilderness there came a fire from the Lord and consumed the meat which had been laid upon the altar (Lev. ix. 24).

Christianity offers only an apparent exception to the rule of the universal predominance of this idea. We do not, indeed, find among Christians the periodical and stated offerings, either of animals or of the products of the soil, which exist elsewhere. Nevertheless, the idea of sacrifice subsists among them in all its force. Indeed, it is the fundamental conception of the Christian religion itself, in which the sacrifice of the founder upon the cross embodies all those notions which are held to legitimate the custom of sacrificing among heathen nations. We have first the notion of an angry and exacting deity, who can only be rendered placable towards mankind by the surrender to him of some valuable thing; we have, consequently, the sacrifice of the most valuable thing that can possibly be offered, namely, the life of a human being; we have, lastly, the belief that this sacrifice was accepted, and that promises of mercy were in consequence held out to the human race. By a peculiar exaltation of the idea, the life thus given up is declared to be that of his own son — a conception by which the value of the sacrifice, and consequently the advantages it is capable of procuring, are indefinitely heightened.

Thus the idea of sacrifice is carried to its extreme limits in the religion of Christendom. Had it not been for the absolute necessity of some sacrifice being offered to God, there would — according to the theory of the Christian faith — have been absolutely no reason for the execution of Christ. He might have taught every doctrine associated with his name, performed every miracle related in the Gospels, have drawn to himself every disciple named in them, and yet have died, like the Buddha, in the calm of a venerated and untroubled old age. He was obliged to undergo this painful and melancholy death, if we accept the general belief of Christendom, solely because God required a sacrifice, and because without that sacrifice he could not forgive the offenses of mankind.

Simple prayer and sacrifice are, then, the most primitive and most general methods by which man approaches those whom his nature impels him to worship. But as these acts are repeated from time to time, and as their frequent repetition is suppose to be highly agreeable to their objects, it naturally happens that some particular mode of performing them comes to be preferred to others. By and by, the mode of worship usually adopted will become habitual; and a habit once formed will be strengthened by every repetition of the acts in question. Not only will certain forms of prayer, certain ways of sacrificing, certain postures, certain gestures, and a certain order of proceeding become established as usual and regular, but they will be regarded as the only appropriate and respectful forms, every attempt to depart from them being treated as a sacrilegious innovation. The form will be deemed no less essential than the substance.

Hence Ritual, which we do not find in the most primitive religions, but which is discovered in all of those that have advanced to a higher type. Even in the earliest Vedic hymns

—those of the Rig-Veda-Sanhita—we perceive clear traces of
an established ritual from the manner in which the sacrifices
are spoken of as having been duly offered. In the Zend-Avesta,
elaborate ritualistic directions are given for certain specified
purposes, especially for that of purification after any defilement.
The oldest books of the Jewish Bible are in like manner full of
instructions for the due observance of ritual. Both the Buddhists, who broke off from Brahminism, and the Christians, who
made a schism from Judaism, established a ritual of their own;
and this ritual was soon regarded as no less sacred than that
which they had abandoned. Everywhere, when religion has
passed out of its first unsettled condition, we find a fixed ritual,
and its fixity is one of its most striking features. Dogmas, in
spite of the efforts of sacerdotal orders, inevitably change. If
the words in which they are expressed remain unaltered, yet
the meaning attached to them continually varies. But ritual
does not change, or changes only when some great convulsion
uproots the settled institutions of the country. From age to
age the same forms and the same prayers remain, sometimes
long after their original meaning has been forgotten.

Thus prayer, ceasing to be spontaneous and irregular, becomes formal, ceremonial, and regular. And as there are many
occasions besides sacrifice on which men desire to pray, so there
will be many besides this on which the craving for order, and
the readiness to believe that God is better pleased with one
form of devotion than another, will lead to the establishment
of ritual.

Rites may be performed daily, weekly, or at any other interval. Sometimes, indeed, they are still more frequent, haunting
the every-day life of the devotee, and intruding upon his commonest actions. Thus the Parsees are required to repeat certain
prayers on rising, before and after eating, on going to bed, on
cutting their nails or their hair, and on several other natural
occasions, besides praying to the sun three times a day (Z. A.,
vol. ii. p. 564–567). The Jews are encompassed with obligations
which, if less minute, are of a like burdensome character. A
devout Jew has to repeat a certain prayer on rising; he has to
wear garments of a particular kind, and to wash and dress in a
particular order (Rel. of Jews, p. 1–8). Mussulmans are com-

manded to pray five times a day, turning their faces towards
Mecca (Sale, prel. discourse, pp. 76, 77).

Ritual, however, is not always of this purely personal nature,
but is generally performed by a congregation to whose needs
it refers, or by priests on their behalf. And in this case, again,
a longer or shorter interval may elapse between the recurrence
of the rites. In the Mexican temples, for instance, the ministering priests were in the habit of performing a service before
their idols four times a day (H. I., b. v. ch. p. 14). "The perpetual exercise of the priests," says Acosta, speaking of these
temples, "is to offer incense to the idols." The ritual of the
Catholic Church, like that of the ancient Mexicans, is repeated
every day. The morning and evening services of the Church of
England were framed with the same intention; and the Ritualistic clergy, rightly conceiving the teaching of their Church,
have introduced the practice of so employing them. Weekly or
bi-monthly observances prevail among Hindus, Singhalese,
Jews, and Christians. With the Hindus, the seventh lunar day,
both during the fortnight of the moon's waxing and during that
of her waning, is a festival, the first seventh day in the month
being peculiarly holy, and observed with very special rites.
More than this, the weekly period is known to them; for,
according to Wilson, "a sort of sanctity is, or was, attached
even to Sunday, and fasting on it was considered obligatory or
meritorious" (W. W., vol. ii. p. 199). In Ceylon the people
attend divine service twice a week, on Wednesdays and Satur-
days; besides which, there are in each month four days devoted
to religious acts—the 8th, 15th, 23d, and 30th (A. I. C., pp. 222,
223; H. R. C., p. 76). The Jewish ritual differs on the Sabbath-
day from that used on week-days; and such is the solemnity
attached to this festival, that a quasi-personality is attributed
to the day itself, which is exalted in the service for Friday
evening as the bride of God, and which the congregation is invited to go in quest of, and to meet (Rel. of Jews, p. 128). A
similar sanctity is considered by many Christians to pertain to
the Sunday, while all of them observe it as an important festival,
and mark it by peculiar rites. Friday, too, is regarded by the
majority of Christians as a day to be observed with distinctive
rites, of which fasting is the principal.

When the interval observed between the performance of certain rites exceeds some very short period—as a day or week—it is generally a year. In this case, the time, whether it be a month, a week, a few days, or any other period, set apart for their performance assumes the character of a Festival. Under the general term Festival I include any annually recurrent season, whether it be one of mourning or rejoicing, of fasting or feasting, which is consecrated by the observance of special ceremonies of a religious order. In all religions above the lowest stage such festivals occur. The time of their occurrence is generally marked out by the seasons of the year. Mid-winter, or the season of sowing; spring, or the time when the seed is in the ground or beginning to spring up; and autumn, when the harvest has been gathered in,—are the most natural seasons for festivals; and it is at these that they usually take place. For instance, Oldendorp states that nearly all the Guinea nations have an annual harvest-festival, at which solemn thank-offerings are presented to the Gods (G. d. M., p. 332). In China, this reference to the seasons is obvious. "At every new moon, and the change of the season, there are festivals." Of these, "the most imposing" is "the emperor's plowing the sacred field. This takes place when the sun enters the fifteenth degree of Aquarius." But the precise day is determined by astrologers. This is the winter festival, or that of sowing. The "Leih-chun, at the commencement of the spring, continues for ten days." And in autumn the feast of harvest is celebrated with great merriment (C. O., vol. ii. p. 195–199). The Parsees have numerous festivals, which it would be tedious to enumerate in detail (Z. A., vol. ii. p. 574–581.) After the Gahanbars, which refer to creation, the two principal ones are the No rouz and the Meherdjan, and of these Anquetil du Perron expressly states that the first originally corresponded to spring, and the second to Autumn (Ibid., vol. ii. p. 603). Of the Hindu festivals described by Wilson, by far the greatest are the Pongol, at the beginning of the year, and the Holi, in the middle of March (W. W., vol. ii. p. 151). Compared with these, the rest are insignificant; and these plainly refer to the processes of nature. That the great festivals of the Jews had the same reference, needs no proof; for the passover took place in spring, and the feast of Pentecost, as well as the feast of tabernacles, after harvest. Our Christmas and Easter correspond to the Pongol and Holi of the Hindus in point of time; and even the observances usual at Christmas have, as Wilson has pointed out, much resemblance to those of the Pongol.

There are in Ceylon five annual festivals, of which one, occurring at the commencement of the year (in April), is marked by the singular circumstance that "before New Year's day every individual procures from an astrologer a writing, fixing the fortunate hours of the approaching year on which to commence duties or ceremonies." Of the five festivals the most important was the Paraherra, which lasted from the new moon to the full moon in July, and consisted mainly in a series of religious processions, concluding with one in which the casket containing the Dalada, or tooth of Buddha, was borne upon an elephant. The fifth festival, called that of "New Rice," was held at the commencement of the great harvest, and was the occasion of offerings made with a view to good crops (E. Y., vol. i. p. 314–318).

The consecrated actions by which men seek to recommend themselves to their gods at these special seasons are very various. It would be useless to attempt to enumerate them at length. Of the manner in which New Year's day is observed among the Chinese, (C. O., vol. ii. pp. 194, 195) the commencement of the year among Hindus (W. W., vol. ii. p. 158 ff.), and Christmas among ourselves, it will be unnecessary to speak at all, for there is little of a religious character in these festivals. Indeed, New Year's day in China seems to be a merely secular festival; while the Christmas season in European countries, though varnished over with a religious gloss, is in reality palpably one of popular rejoicing, handed down from our pagan ancestors, and placed in a legendary relation to the birth of Christ. The religious rites which may accompany this festival have therefore a secondary importance. Those observed at other times bear reference either to the frame of mind induced by the season, or to the particular legend commemorated; or they may be purely arbitrary and enjoined by ecclesiastical authority. An example of the first kind is the Jewish feast of tabernacles, when the harvest had been gathered in, and the

Jews were enjoined to carry boughs of trees and rejoice seven days (Lev. xxiii. 40). Examples of the second class are common. Legends are frequently related in order to account for festivals, while sometimes festivals may be instituted in consequence of a legend. Thus, the extraordinary story of the manifestation of Siva as an interminable Linga, is told by the Hindus to account for their worship of that organ on the twenty-seventh of February (W. W., vol. ii. p. 211). In this case, the rites have reference to the legend; the setting up a Linga in their houses, consecrating, and offering to it, are ceremonies which refer to the event present in the minds of the worshipers; but it is more natural to suppose that the existence of the rites led to the invention of the legend, than that the legend induced the establishment of the rites. "The three essential observances," says Wilson, "are fasting during the whole Tithi, or lunar day, and holding a vigil and worshiping the Linga during the night; but the ritual is loaded with a vast number of directions, not only for the presentation of offerings of various kinds to the Linga, but for gesticulations to be employed, and prayers to be addressed to various subordinate divinities connected with Siva, and to Siva himself in a variety of forms" (ibid., vol. ii. p. 212). At another of the Hindu festivals, the effigy of Kama is burnt, to commemorate the fact of that god having been reduced to ashes by flames from Siva, and having been subsequently restored to life at the intercession of Siva's bride (W. W., vol. ii. p. 231). In like manner the jesting of the Greek woman at the Thesmophoria was explained by reference to the laughter of Demeter (Bib., i. 5. 1.). The Jewish passover was eaten with rites which were symbolical of the state of the nation just before its escape from Egypt, the time to which their tradition assigned the original passover; and the ritual in use among Christians at Easter bears reference to the story of Christ's resurrection, which in this case no doubt preceeeded the institution of the festival. The third class of rites — those which are purely arbitrary or have a merely theological significance — are the most usual of all. These, as will be obvious at once, may vary indefinitely. Fasting is one of the most usual of such observances. It is practiced by the Hindus at many of their festivals, by Mussulmans during the month of Ramadan, and by Christians in Lent. Bathing is also a common religious practice of the Hindus at their festivals. The use of holy water by Catholics on entering their churches is a ceremony of a similar kind, and no doubt having the same intention, that of purification. The Jews were to sacrifice at all their festivals, and on one of them to afflict their souls (Lev. xxiii. 27). Christians, among whom there are very numerous festivals, vary their ritual according to the character of the day.

One or two specimens of the rites observed on festival days will suffice as an illustration. The Peruvians, in their pagan days, used to have festivals every month: the greatest of these was that of the Trinity, celebrated in December. "In this feast," says Acosta, "they sacrificed a great number of sheep and lambs, and they burnt them with worked and odoriferous wood; and some sheep carried gold and silver, and they placed on them the three statues of the Sun, and the three of Thunder; father, brother, and son, whom they said that the Sun and Thunder had. In this feast they dedicated the Inca children, and placed the Guacas, or ensigns on them, and the old men whipped them with slings, and anointed their faces with blood, all in token that they should be loyal knights of the Inca. No stranger might remain during this month and feast at Cuzco, and at the end all those from without entered; and they gave them those pieces of maize with the blood of the sacrifice, which they eat, in token of confederation with the Inca" (H. I., b. 5. ch. 27). Equally curious are the rites prescribed by the Catholic Church for Holy Saturday. They are much too long to be described in full, but the following extract will convey a notion of their character: "At a proper hour the altars are covered over, and the hours are said, the candles being extinguished on the altar until the beginning of mass. In the meanwhile, fire is struck from a stone at the church-door, and coals kindled with it. The none being said, the priest, putting on his amice, alb, girdle, stole, and violet pluvial, or without his capsula, the attendants standing by him with the cross, with the blessed water and incense, before the gate of the church, if convenient, or in the porch of the church, he blesses the new fire, saying, The Lord be with you; and the attendants reply, And with thy spirit." Prayers follow. "Then he blesses five grains of incense to be placed on the wax, saying his prayer." After the prayer, incense is put in the censer, and sprinkled with water. "Meanwhile, all the lights of the church are extinguished, that they may be afterwards kindled from the blessed fire." The candles are lighted with many ceremonies. The incense having been previously blessed, "the deacon fixes five grains of the blessed incense on the wax in the form of a cross." This wax is then lighted. When "the blessing of the wax taper" is finished, the prophets are read,. and the catechumens during the reading are prepared for baptism.* These proceedings, in which the notion of the sanctity of fire—a notion shared by Roman Catholics with Parsees and others—is apparent, are particularly interesting, as showing the community of sentiment and of rites between the Church of Rome and her pagan predecessors.

In the instances hitherto given, the consecrated actions have been performed by the whole body of believers for the benefit of all. They are means by which their religious union among each other is strengthened, as well as their relation to the deity they worship solemnly expressed. But there is another class of consecrated actions which benefit, not the congregation or sect at large, but a particular individual for whose advantage they are performed. There are certain moments in the life of the individual at which he seems peculiarly to need the protection of God. Were these moments suffered to pass unobserved in a single case, it would appear as if he whose life had been thus untouched by religion stood outside the pale of the common faith, unhallowed and unblessed. And a total neglect of all these periods, even among savages, is, if not altogether unknown, at least so rare as to demand no special notice in a general analysis of religious systems. With extraordinary unanimity, those systems have pitched upon four epochs as demanding consecration by the observance of special rites. Two of them are thus consecrated wherever a definite religion exists at all. The other two are generally consecrated, though

---

* Lewis, The Bible, &c., p. 496. For a full account of the ceremonies on Holy Saturday at Rome, see A. M. Baggs, D. D., The Ceremonies of Holy Week, p. 96.

in their case exceptions more frequently occur. The four moments, or periods of life to which I refer, are

1. Birth.
2. Puberty.
3. Matrimony.
4. Death.

Of these, the first and fourth are never suffered to pass without religious observances, or at least, observances which, by their solemnity and indispensable obligation, approach to a religious character The second is usually marked by some kind of rite in the case of males; in that of females it is often suffered to pass unobserved. The third is always placed under a religious sanction, except among savages of a very low order.

Let us proceed to illustrate these propositions in the case of birth. The ceremonies attendant upon this event need not take place immediately after it; they may be deferred some days, weeks, or months; they will still fall under the same category, as designed to mark the child's entry into the world. Their form will naturally vary according to the state of civilization of the nation observing them; but notwithstanding this there is a strange similarity among them. In Samoa, for instance, "if the little stranger was a boy, the umbilicus was cut on a club, that he might grow up to be brave in war. If of the other sex, it was done on the board on which they beat out the bark of which they make their native cloth. Cloth-making is the work of women; and their wish was, that the little girl should grow up and prove useful to the family in her proper occupation " (N. Y , p. 175). I have added Mr. Turner's observation to render the nature of this ceremony plainer. It appears hardly religious; yet when we consider the symbolical means by which the end is sought to be attained, and that among savages so rude as those of Polynesia religion would have no higher practical aims than to make the boys good warriors, and the women industrious cloth-makers, we may admit that even this elementary rite has in it something of a religious consecration. When secular objects are attained by mystical ceremonials, which have no direct tendency to produce the desired result, we may generally conclude that religious belief is at the bottom of them. In the present instance this conclusion is still further strengthend by the description given by the same author of a similar ceremony in another island of the Polynesian.group. There, when a boy is born, "a priest cuts the umbilicus on a particular stone from Lifu, that the youth may be *stone*-hearted in battle. The priest, too, at the moment of the operation, must have a vessel of water before him, dyed black as ink, that the boy when he grows up, may be courageous to go anywhere to battle on a pitch-dark night, and thus, from his very birth, the little fellow is consecrated to war" (N. Y., pp. 423, 424). Here the religious nature of the operation is explicitly proved by the presence of the priest, the inevitable agent in such communications between God and man. Another missionary to the same race — the Polynesian islanders — informs us that among these people mothers dedicated their offspring to various deities, but principally to Hiro, the god of thieves, and Oro, the god of war. "Most parents, however, were anxious that their children should become brave and renowned warriors," and with this end they dedicated them, by means of ceremonies beginning before parturition, and ending after it, to the god Oro. The principal ceremony after birth consisted in the priest catching the spirit of the god, by a peculiar process, and imparting it to the child. Here again the presence of the priest, and the formal dedication to a god — even though he be a god of questionable morality — render the religious element in the natal ceremonies of these very primitive savages abundantly plain (N. M. E., p. 543).

Baptism, or washing at birth, is a common process, and is found in countries the most widely separated on the face of the earth, and the most unconnected in religious genealogy. Asia, America, and Europe alike present us with examples of this rite. It seems to be a rude form of it which prevails in Fantee in Africa, where the father, on the eighth day after birth, after thanking the gods for the birth of his child, squirts some ardent spirits upon him from his mouth, and then pronounces his name, at the same time praying for his future welfare, and "that he may live to be old, and become a stay and support to his family," and if his namesake be living, that he may prove worthy of the name he has received (Asha, p. 226). A rite of baptism at birth, says Brinton, "was of immemorial antiquity among the Cherokees, Aztecs, Mayas, and Peruvians," and this rite was "connected with the imposing of a name, done avowedly for the purpose of freeing from inherent sin, believed to produce a spiritual regeneration, nay, in more than one instance, called by an indigenous word signifying 'to be born again'" (M. N. W., p. 128). Mexico possessed elaborate rites to consecrate nativity. When the Mexican infant was four days old it was carried naked by the midwife into the court of the mother's house. Here it was bathed in a vessel prepared for the purpose, and three boys, who were engaged in eating a special food, were desired by the midwife to pronounce its name aloud, this name being prescribed to them by her. The infant, if a boy, carried with it the symbol of its father's profession; if a girl, a spinning-wheel and distaff, with a small basket and a handful of brooms, to indicate its future occupation. The umbilical cord was then offered with the symbols; and in case of a male infant, these objects were buried in the place where war was likely to occur; in case of a female infant, beneath the stone where meal was ground.* The above statements rest on the authority of Mendoza's collection. A still more complete narrative of these baptismal ceremonies is given by Bernardino de Sahagun, who records the terms of the prayers habitually employed by the officiating midwife. Their extreme interest to the study of comparative religion will justify me in extracting some of them, the more so as they have never (so far as I am aware) been published in English.†

Suppose that the infant to be baptized was a boy. After the symbolical military apparatus had been prepared, and all the relatives assembled in the court of the parents' house, the midwife placed it with the head to the East, and prayed for a blessing from the god Quetzalcoatl and the goddess of the water, Chalchivitlycue. She then gave it water to taste by moistening the fingers, and spoke as follows: "Take, receive; thou seest here that with which thou hast to live on earth, that thou mayest grow and flourish: this it is to which we owe the necessaries of life, that we may live on earth: receive it." Here-

* A. M., vol. v. p. 90 (Spanish), and vol. vi. p. 45 (English).

† Brinton has given a very imperfect version of two of them in his M. N. W., pp. 127, 128.

upon, having touched its breast with the fingers dipped in water, she continued: "Omictomx! O my child! receive the water of the Lord of the world, which is our life, and by which our body grows and flourishes: it is to wash and to purify; may this sky-blue and light-blue water enter thy body and there live. May it destroy and separate from thee all the evil that was beginning in thee before the beginning of the world, since all of us men are subject to its power, for our mother is Chal-chivitlycue." After this she washed the child's whole body with water, and proceeded to request all things that might injure him to depart from him, "that now he may live again, and be born again: now a second time he is purified and cleansed, and a second time our mother Chalchivitlycue forms and begets him." Then lifting the child in both hands towards the sky, she said: "O Lord, thou seest here thy child whom thou hast sent to this world of pain, affliction, and penitence: give him, O Lord, thy gifts and thy inspiration, for thou art the great God, and great is the goddess also." After this she deposited the infant on the ground, and then raising it a second time towards the sky, implored the "mother of heaven" to endow it with her virtue. Next, having again laid it down, and a third time lifted it up, she offered this prayer: "O Lords, the gods of heaven! here is this child; be pleased to inspire him with your grace and your spirit, that he may live on earth." After a final de-positing she raised him a fourth time towards the sky, and in a prayer, addressed to the sun, solemnly placed him under the protection of that deity. Taking the weapons she proceeded further to implore the sun on his behalf for military virtues: "Grant him the gift that thou art wont to give thy soldiers, that he may go full of joy to thy house, where valiant soldiers who die in war rest and are happy." While all this was going on, a large torch of candlewood was kept burning; and on con-clusion of the prayers the midwife gave the infant some ances-tral name. Let it be Yautl (which means *valiant man*): then she addressed him thus: "Yautl! take thou the shield! take the dart! for those are thy recreation, and the joys of the sun." The completion of the religious office was signalized by the youths of the village coming in a body to the house and seiz-ing the food prepared for them, which they called "the child's umbilicus." As they went along with this food they shouted out a sort of military exhortation to the new-born boy, and called upon the soldiers to come and eat the (so-called) umbilicus. All being over, the infant was carried back to the house, preceded by the blazing torch. Much the same was the process of baptizing a girl, except that the clothes and implements were suited to her sex. In her case, certain formularies were muttered by the midwife during the washing, in a low, inaudible tone, to the several parts of her body: thus she charged the hands not to steal, the secret parts not to be carnal, and so forth with each member as she washed it. Moreover, a prayer to the cradle, which seems in a manner to personify the universal mother earth, was introduced in the baptism of females (C. N. E. b. 6, chs. 37, 38).

If from heathen America we turn to Asia, we find that in the vast domain of the Buddhist faith the birth of children is regularly the occasion of a ceremony at which the priest is present (R. B. vol. i. p. 584,) and that in Mongolia and Thibet this ceremony assumes the special form of baptism. Candles burn, and incense is offered on the domestic altar; the priest reads the prescribed prayers, dips the child three times, and imposes on it a name (R. B. vol. ii. p. 320). A species of baptism prevails also among the Parsees, and was even enjoined by the Parsee Leviticus, the Vendidad. This very ancient code required that the child's hands should be washed first, and then its whole body (Av. vol. ii. p. xix—Vendidad, xvi. 18-20). The modern practice goes further. Before putting it to the breast, the Parsee mother sends to a Mobed (or priest), to obtain some Haoma juice; she steeps some cotton in it, and presses this into the child's mouth. After this, it must be washed three times in cow's urine, and once in water, the reason assigned being that it is impure. If the washing be omitted, it is the parents, not the child, who bear the sin (Z. A., vol. ii. p. 551).

Slightly different in form, but altogether similar in essence, is the rite administered by the Christian Church to its new-born members. Like those which have been just described, it consists in baptism; but it offers a more remarkable instance than any of them of the tenacity with which the human mind, under the influence of religious belief, insists upon the performance

of some kind of ceremony immediately after, or, at the most,
at no great interval after birth. Christian baptism was not originally intended to be administered to unconscious infants, but
to persons in full possession of their faculties, and responsible
for their actions. Moreover, it was performed, as is well known,
not by merely sprinkling the forehead, but by causing the candidate to descend naked into the water, the priest joining him
there, and pouring the water over his head. The catechumen
could not receive baptism until after he understood something
of the nature of the faith he was embracing, and was prepared
to assume its obligations. A rite more totally unfitted for administration to infants could hardly have been found. Yet such
was the need that was felt for a solemn recognition by religion
of the entrance of the child into the world, that this rite, in
course of time, completely lost its original nature. Infancy took
the place of maturity; sprinkling of immersion. But while the
age and manner of baptism were altered, the ritual remained
under the influence of the primitive idea with which it had been
instituted. The obligations could no longer be undertaken by
the persons baptized; hence they must be undertaken for them.
Thus was the Christian Church landed in the absurdity — unparalleled, I believe, in any other natal ceremony — of requiring
the most solemn promises to be made, not by those who were
thereafter to fulfil them but by others in their name; these
others having no power to enforce their fulfillment, and neither
those actually assuming the engagement, nor those on whose
behalf it was assumed, being morally responsible in case it
should be broken. Yet this strange incongruity was forced upon
the Church by an imperious want of human nature itself; and
the insignificant sects who have adopted the baptism of adults
have failed, in their zeal for historical consistency, to recognize
a sentiment whose roots lie far deeper than the chronological
foundation of Christian rites, and stretch far wider than the
geographical boundaries of the Christian faith.

The intention of all these forms of baptism — that of Ashan-
tee perhaps excepted — is identical. Water, as the natural means
of physical cleansing, is the universal symbol of spiritual purification. Hence immersion, or washing, or sprinkling, implies
the deliverance of the infant from the stain of original sin.

The Mexican and Christian rituals are perfectly clear on this head. In both, the avowed intention is to wash away the sinful nature common to humanity; in both the infant is declared to be born again by the agency of water.

Another ceremony very frequently practised at the birth of children is circumcision. The wide-spread existence of this rite is one of the most remarkable facts in comparative religious history. We know from Herodotus, that it was practised by the Colchians, Egyptians, Ethiopians, and Phœnicians (Herod., ii. 104). It has been found in modern times, not only in many parts of Africa—to which it may have come from Egypt—but in the South Sea Islands and on the American continent. Thus, according to Beecham, there are "some people," among the Gold Coast Africans, who circumcise their children (Asha, p. 225), though what proportion these circumcisers bear to the rest of the population, he does not inform us. Another traveler describes the mode of circumcising infants in the Negro kingdom of Fida or Juda, a country to which he believes that Islamism has not penetrated (V. G. vol. ii p. 159). The operation is very simple, and appears to be done without any religious ceremony; but the natives, when pressed as to the reason of the custom, can only reply that their ancestors observed it—an answer which would properly apply to a rite of religious origin whose meaning has been forgotten. Acosta, in his account of Mexican baptism, adds that a ceremony which in some sort imitated the circumcision of the Jews, was occasionally performed by the Mexicans in their baptism, principally on the children of kings and noblemen. It consisted in cutting the ears and private members of male infants (H. I., b. 5, ch. 26 No. 2). That the Jews circumcise their male children on the eighth day I need not state. The rite is performed with much solemnity, and is connected, as is common in these ceremonies, with the bestowal of a name on the child, the name being given by the father after the operation is over. Although circumcision is a ceremony which usually applies only to boys, and although it sometimes happens that the birth of girls is not marked like that of boys by any religious rite, yet the Jews do not omit to consecrate their female children as well as those of the stronger sex, though with less solemnity. "The first Saturday after the end of the month" of the mother's lying-in, she goes to the synagogue with her friends, where " the father of the girl is called up to the law on the altar, and there after a chapter hath been read to him as usual on the Sabbath morning he orders the reader to say a Mee-Shabeyrach," or a prayer for a blessing (Rel. of Jews, p. 27 1st part).

It is unnecessary, after these instances, to describe the various modes of consecrating the commencement of life which are in use in other countries. Enough has been said to show how general, if not how universal, such consecrating usages are; how religion, supported by the sentiment of mankind, siezes upon the life of the individual from the first moments of his existence; and demands, as one of the very earliest actions to be performed on his behalf, a solemn recognition of the fact that he stands under the influence, and needs the protection, of an invisible and superhuman power.

After birth, the next marked epoch in life is the arrival at manhood or at womanhood. The transition from infancy to maturity, from dependence on others to self-dependence, from an unsexual to a sexual physical and mental condition, has, like the actual entrance upon life and departure from it, been appropriated by religion with a view to its consecration by fitting rites. Since there is no precise time at which the boy can be said to become a youth, or the girl a maiden, the age at which the ceremonies attending puberty are performed varies very considerably in different countries. The range of variation is from eight to sixteen, though there are exceptional cases both of earlier and later initiation into the new stage of existence. Generally speaking, however, these ages are the limits within which the religious solemnities of puberty are confined.

More clearly, perhaps, than any of those occurring at the other crises of our lives, these solemnities are pervaded by common characteristics. Primitive man in Australia, in America, and in Africa, marks the advent of puberty in a manner which is essentially the same. When we rise to the higher class of religions, we find ceremonies of a different kind from which the ruder symbolism of the savage creeds is absent. But from the uniformity of the types of initiation into manhood among uncivilized people, it is highly probable that the progenitors of the Aryan and Semitic races also, at some period of their history, employed similar methods of rendering this epoch in life impressive and remarkable. Two distinguishing features characterize the rites of puberty — cruelty and mystery. There is always some painful ordeal to be undergone by the young men or boys who have attained the requisite age; and this ordeal is to be passed through in extreme secrecy as regards the opposite sex, and with a ceremonial of an unknown character, which is hidden from all but the initiated performers. Sometimes the puberty of women is also sanctified by religious ceremonies, and these follow the same rules, except that the female sex are not required to undergo such severe suffering as is often inflicted upon men. While, however, the cruelty is less, the mystery is the same. Men are not admitted to witness the performances gone through, and these are conducted in secluded places to which no access is allowed.

The meaning of these two features of the rites of puberty is not difficult to divine. Young men enter at that age on a period of their lives in which they are expected to display courage in danger and firmness under pain. Hence the infliction of some kind of suffering is an appropriate symbolical preparation for their future careers. Moreover, the manner in which they endure their agony serves as a test of their fortitude, and may influence the position to be assigned to them in the warlike expeditions of the tribe. But the primary motive, no doubt, is the apparent fitness of the infliction of pain at an age when the necessary pains of manhood are about to begin.

The explanation of the secrecy observed is equally simple. A mysterious change takes place in the physical condition at puberty, the generative functions, which are to play so large a part in the life of the individual, making their appearance then. It is this natural process to which the religious process bears reference. Without doubt the rites performed stand in symbolical relation to the new class of actions of which their subject is, or will be, capable. It is this allusion to the sexual instinct — a subject always tending to be shrouded in mystery — which is the origin of the jealous exclusion of women from the rites undergone by men, and of men from those undergone by women. The members of each sex are, so to speak, prepared alone for the pleasures they are afterwards to enjoy together. Religion, ever ready to seize on the more solemn moments of our existence, seeks to consecrate the time at which the two sexes are ready to enter towards one another on a new and deeply important relationship.

Bearing these characteristics in mind, we may proceed to notice a few of the ceremonies performed at puberty. Let us begin with the most barbarous of all, those witnessed by Mr. Catlin among the Mandans, a tribe of North American Indians now happily extinct. The usual secrecy was observed about the "O-kee-pa," as this great Mandan ceremony is termed, and it was only by a favor, never before accorded to a stranger, that Mr. Catlin was enabled to be present in the "Medicine Lodge," where the operations were conducted. In the first place a mysterious personage, supposed to represent a white man, appeared from the west and opened the lodge. At his approach all women and children were ordered to retire within their wigwams. Next day the young men who had arrived at maturity during the last year were summoned to come forth, the rest of the villagers remaining shut up. After committing the conduct of the ceremonies to a "medicine man," this personage returned to the west with the same mystery with which he had come. The young men were now kept without food, drink, or sleep, for four days and four nights. In the middle of the fourth day two men began to operate upon them, the one making incisions with a knife in their flesh, and the other passing splints through the wounds, from which the blood trickled over their naked, but painted bodies. The parts through which the knife was passed were on each arm, above and below the elbow; on each leg, above and below the knee; on each breast, and each shoulder. The young men not only did not wince, but smiled at their civilized observer during this process. "When these incisions were all made, and the splints passed through, a cord of raw hide was lowered down through the top of the wigwam, and fastened to the splints on the breasts or shoulders, by which the young man was to be raised up and suspended, by men placed on the top of the lodge for the purpose. These cords having been attached to the splints on the breast or the shoulders, each one had his shield hung to some one of the splints: his *medicine bag* was held in his left hand, and a dried buffalo skull was attached to the splint of each lower leg and each lower arm, that its weight might prevent him from struggling." At a signal, the men were drawn up three or four feet above the ground, and turned round with gradually increasing velocity, by a man with a pole, until they fainted. Although they had never groaned before, they uttered a heart-rending cry, a sort of prayer to the Great Spirit, during the turning. Having ceased to cry, they were let down apparently dead. Left entirely to themselves, they in time were able "*partly* to rise," and no sooner could they do thus much than they moved to another part of the lodge, where the little finger of the left hand was cut off with a hatchet. But their tortures were not over. The rest of them took place in public, and were perhaps more frightful than any. The victims were taken out of the lodge, and, being each placed between two athletic men, were dragged along, the men holding them with thongs and running with them as fast as they could, until all the buffalo skulls and weights hanging to the splints were left behind. These weights must be dragged out through the flesh, the candidates having the option of running in the race described, or of wandering about the prairies without food until suppuration took place, and the weights came off by decay of the flesh. These horrors concluded, the young men were left alone to recover as best they might. Mr. Catlin could only hear of one who had died "in the extreme part of this ceremony," and his fate was considered rather a happy one: "the Great Spirit had so willed it for some especial purpose, and no doubt for the young man's benefit" (O-kee-pa, p. 9-32).

Nor were the Mandans alone on the American continent in marking the entrance upon manhood by distinctive observances. On the contrary, a writer of the highest authority on Red Indian subjects, states that no young man among the native tribes was considered fit to begin the career of life until he had accomplished his great fast. Seven days were considered the maximum time during which a young man could fast, and the success of the devotee was inferred from the length of his abstinence. These fasts, says Mr. Schoolcraft, "are awaited

with interest, prepared for with solemnity, and endured with a
self-devotion bordering on the heroic. . . . It is at this
period that the young men and young women 'see visions and
dream dreams,' and fortune or misfortune is predicted from the
guardian spirit chosen during this, to them, religious ordeal.
The hallucinations of the mind are taken for divine inspiration.
The effect is deeply felt and strongly impressed on the mind;
too deeply, indeed, ever to be obliterated in after life." It
appears that they always in after life trust to, and meditate on,
the guardian spirit whom they have chosen at this critical
moment; but that "the *name* is never uttered, and every circumstance connected with its selection, and the devotion paid
to it, are most studiously and professedly concealed, even from
their nearest fr.ends" (A. R., vol. i. pp. 149, 150). Mystery is
certainly pushed to its highest point, when the name of the
spirit chosen at puberty, and the very circumstances of the
choice, are preserved as an inviolable secret within the breast
of the devotee.

New South Wales is distinguished by a ceremony which,
though far less severe than that of the Mandans, is nevertheless sufficiently painful. "Between the ages of eight and sixteen the males and females undergo the operation which they
term Gnanoong; viz., that of having the septum of the nose
bored to receive a bone or reed. . . . Between the same
years, also, the males receive the qualifications which are given
to them by losing one front tooth." The loss of a tooth is not
in itself a very serious matter, but the intention of the extraction being religious, the natives contrive to get rid of it in the
most barbarous mode. The final event is led up to by a series
of performances of a more or less emblematic nature. One of
them, for instance, is supposed to give power over the dog;
another refers to the hunting of the kangaroo. There is the
usual mystery about some part of the proceedings. When the
boys were being arranged for the removal of the tooth "the
author [Collins] was not permitted to witness this part of the
business, about which they appeared to observe a greater degree
of mystery and preparation than he had noticed in either of
the preceding ceremonies." After this, some of the performers
in the rite went through a number of extraordinary motions,

and made strange noises. "A particular name, *boo-roo-moo-roong*, was given to this scene; but of its import very little could be learned. To the inquiries made respecting it no answer could be obtained, but that it was very good; that the boys would now become brave men; that they would see well and fight well." When the tooth was to be taken out, the gum was first prepared by a sharply-pointed bone; and a throwing-stick, cut for the purpose with "much ceremony," was then applied to the tooth, and knocked against it by means of a stone in the hand of the operator. The tooth was thus struck out of the gum, the operation taking ten minutes in the case of the first boy on whom the author witnessed this process being performed. After the tooth was gone, "the gum was closed by his friends, who now equipped him in the style that he was to appear in for some days. A girdle was tied round his waist, in which was stuck a wooden sword; a ligature was bound round his head, in which were stuck slips of the grass-gum tree." The boy "was on no account to speak, and for that day he was not to eat." The sufferers in this ceremonial did not long remain quiescent. In the evening they had fresh duties to discharge. "Suddenly, on a signal being given, they all started up, and rushed into the town, driving before them men, women, and children, who were glad to get out of their way. They were now received into the class of men; were privileged to wield the sword and the club, and to oppose their persons in combat; and might now seize such females as they chose for wives." The sexual import of the ceremony is clearly brought into view by the last words of the writer. He adds that, having expressed a wish to possess some of the teeth, they were given him by two men with extreme secrecy, and injunctions not to betray them (N. S. W., p. 364–374).

Another observer has described the same rite as performed in a somewhat different manner, "by the tribes of the Macquarrie district" farther north. When these tribes assemble "to celebrate the mysteries of Kebarrah," as it is termed, all hostility which may exist at the time is laid aside for the nonce. "When the cooi or cowack sounds the note of preparation, the women and children in haste make their way towards the ravines and gulleys, and there remain concealed." The den-

tistry of these tribes is less scientific than that of New South
Wales. The tooth is knocked out " by boring a hole in a tree,
and inserting into it a small hard twig; the tooth is then
brought into contact with the end, and one individual holds the
candidate's head in a firm position against it, whilst another,
exerting all his strength, pushes the boy's head forwards; the
concussion causes the tooth, with frequently a portion of the
gum adhering to it, to fall out." But this is not all the poor
boy has to endure, for while "some men stand over him, brand-
ishing their waddies, menacing him with instant death if he
utters any complaint," others cut his back in stripes, and make
incisions on his shoulders with flints. It is an interesting part
of these ceremonies, that the least groan or indication of pain
is summarily punished by the utterance, on the part of the
operators, of three yells to proclaim the fact, and by the transfer of the boy to the care of the women, who are summoned to
receive him. If he does not shrink, " he is admitted to the
rank of a huntsman and a warrior " (S. L. A., vol. ii. p. 216–224).

In other parts of Australia, different ceremonies prevail.
Thus, in one of the districts visited by Mr. Angas, when boys
arrive at the age of fourteen or sixteen, they are "selected and
caught by stealth," and the hairs of their body are plucked
out, and green gum-bushes are placed "under the arm-pits and
over the os pubis." Among the privileges conferred on those
who have undergone this treatment, is that of wearing "two
kangaroo teeth, and a bunch of emu feathers in their hair."
More significant still is the permission to "possess themselves
of wives," which the young men now obtain. The "scrub-
natives" vary the initiation again. Among them the boy,
brought by an old man, is laid upon his back in the midst of
five fires which are lighted around him. An instrument, called
a wittoo wittoo, is whirled round over the fires, with the intention of keeping off evil spirits. Lastly, "with a sharp flint, the
old man cuts off the foreskin, and places it on the third finger
of the boy's left hand, who then gets up, and with another
native, selected for the purpose, goes away into the hills to
avoid the sight of women for some time. No women are allowed to be present at this rite " (S. L. A., vol. i. pp. 98, 99).

Elsewhere on the same continent, there are three stages to

be passed on the road from boyhood to manhood. "At the age of twelve or fifteen the boys are removed to a place apart from the women, whom they are not permitted to see, and then blind-folded. Among some other ceremonies their faces are blackened, and they are told to whisper, an injunction peculiarly charac-teristic of the mysteriousness which is so constant a feature of the rites of puberty. For several months this whispering con-tinues, and it is noteworthy, as a sign of the sexual nature of these proceedings, that the place where the whispers have been "is carefully avoided by the women and children." In the second ceremony, which occurs two or three years later, "the *glans penis* is slit open underneath, from the extremity to the scrotum, and circumcision is also performed." After this second stage, the *Partnapas*, as the youths are now styled, "are per-mitted to take a wife." In the third ceremony each man has a sponsor, by whom he is tatooed with a sharp quartz. These sponsors, moreover, bestow on each lad a new name, which he retains during the remainder of his life. Certain other perform-ances are gone through, such as putting an instrument termed a *witarna* round the lads' necks, and then "the ceremony con-cludes by the men all clustering round the initiated ones, enjoining them again to whisper for some months, and bestow-ing upon them their advice as regards hunting, fighting, and contempt of pain. All these ceremonies are carefully kept from the sight of the women and the children; who, when they hear the sound of the *witarna*, hide their heads and exhibit every outward sign of terror" (S. L. A.. vol. i. p. 113–116).

Leaving Australia, let us pass to Africa, and call Mr. Reade as a witness to some of the rites of puberty existing among the savages of that continent. The following extract is doubly in-teresting, as furnishing some account of the application to girls of the general principles involved in these rites, and also as supplying, in the author's opinion, that they are of a Phallic nature, a confirmation of the conclusions we had reached from a survey of the evidence as a whole:

"Before they are permitted to wear clothes, marry, and rank in society as men and women, the young have to be initiated into certain mysteries. I received some information upon this head from Mongilomba, after he had made me promise that I

would not put it into a book: a promise which I am compelled
to break by the stern duties of my vocation. He told me that
he was taken into a fetich-house, stripped, severely flogged, and
plastered with goat-dung; this ceremony, like those of Masonry,
being conducted to the sound of music. Afterwards there came
from behind a kind of screen or shrine uncouth and terrible
sounds such as he had never heard before. These, he was told,
emanated from a spirit called *Ukuk*. He afterwards brought to
me the instrument with which the fetich-man makes this noise.
It is a kind of whistle made of hollowed mangrove wood, about
two inches in length, and covered at one end with a scrap of
bat's wing. For a period of five days after initiation the novice
wears an apron of dry palm leaves, which I have frequently seen.

"The initiation of the girls is performed by elderly females
who call themselves *Ngembi*. They go into the forest, clear a
place, sweep the ground carefully, come back to the town, and
build a sacred hut which no male may enter. They return to
the clearing in the forest, taking with them the *Igonji*, or
novice. It is necessary that she should have never been to that
place before, and that she fast during the whole of the ceremony, which lasts three days. All this time a fire is kept burning in the wood. From morning to night, and from night to
morning, a *Ngembi* sits beside it and feeds it, singing, with a
cracked voice, *The fire will never die out!* The third night is
passed in the sacred hut; the *Igonji* is rubbed with black, red,
and white paints, and as the men beat drums outside, she cries,
Okanda, yo! yo! yo! which reminds one of the *Evohe!* of the
ancient Bacchantes. The ceremonies which are performed in
the hut and in the wood are kept secret from the men, and I
can say but little of them. Mongilomba had evidently been
playing the spy, but was very reserved upon the subject. Should
it be known, he said, that he had told me what he had, the
women would drag him into a fetich-house, and would flog him,
perhaps till he was dead.

"It is pretty certain, however, that these rites, like those of
the Bona Dea, are essentially of a Phallic nature; for Mongilomba once confessed, that having peeped through the chinks of
the hut, he saw a ceremony like that which is described in
Petronius Arbiter. . . .

"During the novitiate which succeeds initiation, the girls are taught religious dances—the men are instructed in science of fetich" (S. A., p. 245-247).

The Suzees and the Mandingoes, tribes of Western Africa, are distinguished by a rite which, so far as I know, is peculiar —the circumcision of women. Both sexes, indeed, are circumcised on reaching puberty, and in the case of the girls it is done "by cutting off the exterior part of the clitoris." With a view to this ceremony, "the girls of each town who are judged marriageable are collected together, and in the night preceeding the day on which the ceremony takes place, are conducted by the women of the village into the inmost recesses of a wood." Surrounded by charms to guard every approach to the "consecrated spot," they are kept here in entire seclusion for a month and a day, visited only by the old woman who performs the operation. During this close confinement they are instructed in the religion of their country, which hitherto they have not been thought fit to learn. A most singular scene is enacted at its close. They return to their homes by night, "where they are received by all the women of the village, young and old, quite naked." In this condition they go about till morning, with music playing; and should any man be indiscreet enough to imitate Peeping Tom, he is punished by death or the forfeiture of a slave. After another month of parading and marching in procession (no longer nude) the women are given to their destined husbands;—another plain indication of the nature of these rites. In such veneration is this ceremony held among the women of the country, that those who have come from other parts, and are already in years, frequently submit to it to avoid the reproaches to which uncircumcision exposes them. Indeed, "the most vilifying term they can possibly use" is applied by the circumcised female population to those who do not enjoy their religious privileges" (S. L., p. 70-83).

Puberty is recognized in much the same way among the South Sea Islanders. Thus, in Tanna "circumcision is regularly practised about the seventh year" (N. Y., p. 87). In Samoa "a modified form of circumcision prevailed," which boys of their own accord, would get performed upon themselves about the eighth or tenth year (Ib., p. 177). It may be a faint beginning of the religious ceremonies of this period of life that, in the same island, when girls are entering into womanhood, their parents invite all the unmarried women of the settlement to a feast, at which presents are distributed among them. At least it is worthy of remark that "none but females are present" on these occasions (Ib., p. 184).

When we rise higher in the scale of culture, we no longer find the painful rites by which savage nations mark the appearance of the sexual instinct. The sacred ceremony of investiture with the thread, which distinguished the twice-born classes among the Hindus, was performed at this age. The code of Manu is explicit on the subject. "In the eighth year from the conception of a Brahman, in the eleventh from that of Kshatriya, and in the twelfth from that of a Vaisya, let the father invest the child with the mark of his class." In the case of children who desire to advance more rapidly than usual in their vocation, "the investiture may be made in the fifth, sixth, or eighth years respectively. The ceremony of investiture hallowed by the gayatri must not be delayed, in the case of a priest, beyond the sixteenth year; nor in that of a soldier beyond the twenty-second; nor in that of a merchant beyond the twenty-fourth." Further postponement would render those who were guilty of it outcasts, impure, and unfit to associate with Brahmans (Manu, ii. 36–40).

Members of the kindred Parsee religion become responsible human beings after they have been girt with the kosti, or sacred girdle. The age at which this took place was formerly fifteen; and after they had once put them on, the Parsees might not remove their girdles, except in bed, without incurring serious guilt. This regulation applied equally to both sexes. Modern usage has advanced the investiture with the kosti to a much earlier period. It takes place in India at seven, and in Kirman at nine. In India, the child is held responsible in the eighth or tenth year for one half of its sins, the parents bearing the burden of the other half (Av., vol. i. p. 9; vol. ii. pp. 21., 22).

The young Jew "is looked upon as a man" at the age of thirteen, and is then bound "to observe all the commandments of the law." At this age he becomes "Bar-mizva," or a son of the law; that is, he enters on his spiritual majority (Picard, vol. i. ch. x. p. 82). Christian nations signalize the advent of the corresponding epoch by admitting those who attain it to the Sacrament of the Lord's supper, and to confirmation. At puberty they are considered, like the young Parsees, responsible for the sins which at their birth their sponsors took upon themselves, and at puberty they are admitted, like the Jews, to the full privileges of their faith, by being allowed to partake in the mystic benefits conferred by the celebration of the death of Christ in the Holy Communion.

After puberty the two sexes enter on a new relation towards one another; and though the instinct by which this relation is established is extremely apt to break loose from the control of religion, yet the latter always attempts more or less energetically to bring it within its grasp. This it does by confining the irregular indulgences to which the sexual passion is prone within the legalized forms of matrimony. To matrimony, and matrimony alone, it gives its sanction; and accordingly it confers a peculiar sacredness upon this form of cohabitation, by the performance of ceremonies at its outset. Such ceremonies are not indeed equally universal with those of birth and puberty. Among savage and slightly civilized communities we do not find them. But in all the great religions of the world they are firmly established.

Little of a distinctively religious character is perceptible in Major Forbes's account of marriage rites in the island of Ceylon. Yet it is plain that Singhalese marriages do stand under a religious sanction, for in the first place an astrologer must examine the horoscopes of the two parties, to discover whether they correspond, and then the same functionary is called upon to name an auspicious time for the wedding. On the day of its occurrence a feast is given at the bride's house, and "on the astrologer notifying that the appointed moment is approaching, a half-ripe cocoa-nut, previously placed near the board with some mystical ceremonies, is cloven in two at one blow" (E. Y., vol. i. p. 326–332).

Turning from southern to northern Buddhism, we find Köppen asserting that in Thibet and the surrounding countries, marriage consists solely in the private contract, yet adding that

none the less the lamaist clergy find business to do in regard
to engagements and weddings. The priests alone know whether
the nativity of the bride stands in a favorable relation to that
of the bridegroom, and if not, by what ceremonies and sacrifices misfortune may be averted; they alone know the day that
is most suitable and propitious for the wedding; they give the
bond its consecration and its blessing by burning incense and
by prayer (R. B., vol. ii. p. 321).

The Code of Manu is not very clear as to the sort of marriages sanctioned by religion; some irregular connections appar
ently receiving a formal recognition, though regarded with
moral disapprobation. The system of caste, moreover, introduces a confusing element, since the nuptial rites are permitted,
by some authorities, to become less and less solemn as the
grade of the contracting parties becomes lower. This opinion
having been mentioned, however, the legislator adds, that "in
this Code, three of the five last [forms of marriage] are held
legal, and two illegal: the ceremonies of Pisachas and Asuras
must never be performed." Of the two prohibited forms, the
first is merely an embrace when the damsel is asleep, drunk, or
of disordered intellect; the second is when the bride's family,
and the bride herself, have been enriched by large gifts on the
part of the bridegroom. Strangely enough, this regulation does
not exclude the marriage called Gandharva, which is "the reciprocal connection of a youth and a damsel, with mutual desire,"
and is "contracted for the purpose of amorous embraces, and
proceeding from sexual inclination." Nor does it forbid forcible
capture. But a little further on, the code encourages the more
regular modes of marrying by promising intelligent, beautiful,
and virtuous sons to those who observe them; and threatening
those who do not with bad and cruel sons. It is then stated
that "the ceremony of joining hands is appointed for those who
marry women of their own class, but with women of a different
class" certain ceremonies, enumerated in the Code, are to be
performed (Manu, iii. i. 44). It is probable that this Code was
never actually the law of any part of India; but it is none the
less interesting to see the legislator striving to bring the lawless passions with which he is dealing under the supervision of
religion.

An elaborate blessing and exhortation, beginning with the words "In the name of God," is appointed in the Zend-Avesta for the nuptial ceremonial. While marriages among Jews and Christians are, as is well known, inaugurated by solemn religious rites, and all unions not thus consecrated are, at least by the formal judgment of their respective creeds, pronounced unholy, sinful, and impure.

Death, like marriage, is held among all religions but the lowest to call for the performance of befitting rites. In these it is usually noticeable that much regard is paid to the manner in which the deceased is placed in the grave, this circumstance indicating as a general rule some form of the belief in his continued existence. Thus, Lieut.-Colonel Collins, describing the burial of a boy in New South Wales, observes that "on laying the body in the grave, great care was taken so to place it that the sun might look at it as it passed, the natives cutting down for that purpose every shrub that could obstruct the view. He was placed on his right side, with his head to the N. W. (N. S. W., p. 387 390).

If there is little trace among the rude population of this colony of a religious ceremony at the interment, we find the position of religion distinctly recognized by the natives of some parts of Africa. Oldendorp tells us of the tribes with which he was acquainted, that the funeral rites are performed by the priests, who are richly rewarded for the service. Not only are animals sacrificed at the graves, but in the case of men of rank their wives and servants are (as is well known) slaughtered to attend them (G. d. M., p. 313–317). In Sierra Leone, where "every town or village, which has been long inhabited, has a common burial-place," there is the usual attention to position in the grave. "The head of the corpse, if a man, lies either east or west; if a woman, it is turned either to the north or south. An occasional prayer is pronounced over the grave, importing a wish that God may receive the deceased, and that no harm may happen to him." Moreover, there is a ceremony which appears to be a sort of sacrifice to the manes. "A fowl is fastened by the leg upon the grave, and a little rice placed near it; if it refuse to eat the rice, it is not killed; but if it eat, the head is cut off, and the blood sprinkled upon the grave;

after which it is cooked, and a part placed on the grave, the remainder being eaten by the attendants." A tribe called the Soosoos "bury their dead with their faces to the west (S. L., vol. i. pp. 238, 239).

Sometimes we meet with the opinion that the entire removal of the deceased from his accustomed place of abode on earth depends upon due attention to the rites of interment. A primitive form of this wide-spread belief—which lingers as a survival even in Christendom—is observable in Polynesia. In Samoa, "in order to secure the admission of a departed spirit to future joys, the corpse was dressed in the best attire the relatives could provide, the head was wreathed with flowers, and other decorations were added. A pig was then baked whole, and placed upon the body of the deceased, surrounded by a pile of vegetable food." The corpse is then addressed by a near relation, who desires it with the property thus bestowed to make its way into "the palace of Tiki," and not to return to alarm the survivors. If nothing happened within a few days, the deceased was supposed to have got in; but a cricket being heard on the premises was taken as an ill omen, and led to the repetition of the offering.

Elsewhere in the same group of islands "more costly sacrifices" were presented to the gods of the celestial regions. At least at the interment of a chief it was customary for his wives to sit down severally near his body, to be strangled, and then buried along with him. "The reasons assigned for this are, that the spirit of the chief may not be lonely in its passage to the invisible world, and that by such an offering its happiness may be at once secured" (N. M. E. pp. 145, 146).

Funeral ceremonies in Mexico were performed by priests and monks, and varied in splendor according to the rank of the deceased. Offices were chanted at the graves, and at the burial of persons of quality slaves were killed to serve them in the next world. Moreover, so sensible were the Mexicans to the importance of religion in all states of being, that even the domestic chaplain was not omitted; a priest being slaughtered to accompany his lord in that capacity (H. I., b. v. ch. viii).

In Ceylon, a dying relative is taken to a detached apartment, where he is placed with his head towards the East. After death the body is turned with the head towards the West, and in the grave this position is preserved. Bodies of priests, and persons of the highest rank, are burned, and during the process of cremation the officiating priest "repeats certain forms of prayer." The same functionary returns to deliver "some moral admonitions" after seven days, when the friends revisit the pyre to collect the ashes (E. Y., pp. 334, 335).

Notwithstanding the fact that in countries professing the lamaistic form of Buddhism dead bodies are unceremoniously exposed to the open air, and left as a prey to birds or dogs, the mortality of the laity "forms, with their sicknesses, the richest source of income for the priests." A great deal, says the author from whom we draw this information, depends on the separation of soul and body taking place according to rule; and it is important that the spirit should not injure those who are left, and should meet with a happy re-birth. The Lama therefore attends the death bed, takes care to place the deceased in the correct position, and observes the hour of departure. An operation is then performed on the skin of the head, which is supposed to liberate the soul. What rites are now to be performed, how the body is to be disposed of, towards what quarter it is to be turned, and various other details, depend on astrological combinations known only to the clergy. But their most important and profitable business is the repetition of masses, for the dead, which are designed to pacify the avenging deities, and to help the soul towards as favorable a career as is possible for it. The length of time during which these masses are said varies with the wealth of the survivors; poor people obtaining them for a few days only; the richer classes for seven weeks; and princes being able to assist the spirits of their relations for a whole year (R. B., vol. ii. p. 323–325).

Among the Parsees the cemeteries consist of desolate, open places, on which the corpses are deposited and left exposed to the air. These places are called Dakhmas, and are carefully consecrated by the priests with an elaborate ceremonial. The position of the dead in the Dakhmas is fixed by the religious law. Their dying moments and those that succeed upon death are watched over by the Parsee faith, which has determined the prayers to be repeated during the last hour of life; before

the body is placed upon the bier; when it is carried out; on
the way to the Dakhma, and at the Dakhma itself. The ceremonies required on these occasions must be performed by the
Maubads, or priests. But the due disposal of the body by no
means concludes the duties of relations towards the dead. The
welfare of the soul also demands numerous prayers. Being
supposed to linger for three days in the immediate neighborhood of the corpse, it is the object during that time of especial
attention, and the rites then performed may be of use to it in
the judgment which takes place on the fourth day. Prayers
are to be recited, and offerings made on the 30th and 31st day
after death, and even then the ceremonies attending the close
of mortal existence are not concluded, for it is necessary after
the lapse of a year again to celebrate the memory of the departed. Moreover, the 26th chapter of the Yasna, a hymn of
praise and blessing, is to be said every day during the year
before eating (Av. vol. ii. p. xxxii.-xlii).

Masses for the dead are no less common in Christian countries (save where the Protestant faith is professed), than among
Buddhists and Parsees. Their object also is precisely the same;
namely, the welfare of the soul which has quitted its earthly
home to enter on a new form of being. And although no such
prayers are repeated in Protestant communities, yet there can
be no doubt that interment in due form, and with due solemnity, is held by the people, even in England, to benefit the
soul in some undefined way. Nor is any portion of the ritual
of the English Church more impressive than that passage in the
Burial Service where the officiating priest consigns " earth
to earth, ashes to ashes, dust to dust, in sure and certain hope
of the resurrection to eternal life, through our Lord Jesus
Christ."

But it is not only the due performance of these last rites
which popular opinion associates with the prospect of salvation
in the world to come. As in other religions, so in that of our
own country, the position of the body in the tomb is deemed
to be of vast importance. The head must be westward and the
feet eastward, the nominal reason being that the dead person
should rise from his temporary abode with his face to the east,
whence Christ will come; the real reason being in all probabil-

ity the survival of a much older custom, in which that venerable divinity, the Sun, stood in the place of the Savior of mankind.

CHAPTER II.

CONSECRATED actions of various kinds being the primary method of approaching the beings in whose honor they are performed, there remain various secondary methods; sometimes tending to heighten the effect of the primary method, sometimes supplementing it. These secondary means of giving effect to the religious sentiment may be divided into three classes:— the consecration of places, of things, and of persons; while the last of these falls into two subdivisions: the self-dedication of certain individuals to their deity, and the dedication of a certain class to the more special performance of religious services on behalf of the community.

Consecration of places evidently confers on the actions performed within them a higher sanctity. Prayer offered in a place which has been devoted to the service of God is more likely to be successful. Praise from within its walls will be more acceptable. Wedlock contracted under its influence will be more solemn, and will possess a more binding character. Children may most fitly enter upon life by a profession of faith made in their behalf in a consecrated temple. And the bodies of the dead will rest more peacefully in consecrated earth.

It is scarcely needful to offer evidence of the fact that in various lands, and by many kinds of belief, the performance of certain ceremonies is held to consecrate places to the purpose of communication between man and the higher powers. From the savage in Sierra Leone, where "a small shed of dry leaves" presents perhaps the rudest form of temple to be found on earth (S. L., p. 65), to the European who worships his God in St. Peter's or Westminster Abbey, the same opinion prevails. Everywhere the consecration of places is conceived to render them fitter for the celebration of religious rites, and unfit for all profaner uses.

Of the state of feeling with which such localities are endowed by the ordinary worshiper, an excellent example is offered in Solomon's speech at the dedication of the temple. He specially requests Jehovah that when prayers are made to him in this place, or toward this place, he will hear such prayers: that is, he expects that the sanctity he will confer upon the temple, by devoting it to Jehovah, will add something to the efficacy of petitions in which it is in some way concerned. The manner in which he dedicates the temple may serve, too, as a type of this kind of ceremony. "Solomon," we are told, "offered a sacrifice of peace-offerings, which he offered unto the Lord, two-and-twenty thousand oxen, and an hundred and twenty thousand sheep." With this barbaric magnificence he "dedicated the house of the Lord," and he subsequently hallowed the middle of the court by "burnt-offerings, and meat-offerings, and the fat of the peace-offerings" (1 Kings viii). How great was the respect attached to this temple by the Israelites, and how anxiously they sought to guard it against such profanation as it received at the hands of Pompey, is well known.

The lavish splendor with which Solomon adorned his temple is a common feature of consecrated places. Like the ancient Hebrews, the Mexicans and Peruvians had buildings in honor of their gods, of extreme magnificence. The temple of Pachac-amac, or the Creator, in Peru, was a very large and ancient building, richly decorated, which was found to contain an immense wealth of gold and silver vessels (H. I., b. v., chs. iii., xii). The boundless munificence with which pious Christians have sought to beautify their places of worship needs no description. Along with the more formal consecration given to such sanctuaries of the Most High by special rites, they have sought to render them more worthy of his habitation by the liberality displayed in their erection and embellishment.

CHAPTER III.

BESIDES consecration of places to religious uses, material things may be consecrated to the deity worshiped by those who thus apply them. These things may be of the most varied description, from common objects of the most trifling value, to those of the utmost possible estimation. Among consecrated objects are the furniture of temples or churches, which is reserved for divine service; the garments worn by priests in their liturgical functions; the votive tablets in which men record their gratitude for preservation in danger; pictures, statues, endowments of land for monasteries or the support of ecclesiastical offices; and anything else which the owners may part with from pious motives, and with the view of bestowing it entirely on their god or his vicegerents on earth.

Such consecrated objects were seen in abundance by Lieutenant Matthews in Sierra Leone, where the natives devoted them to the idols who reigned in the small sheds of dry leaves mentioned in the preceeding chapter. The offerings made by the natives to these superhuman beings consisted of "bits of cloth, pieces of broken cups, plates, mugs, or glass bottles, brass rings, beads, and such articles." But a still more precious object was bestowed upon these gods by the people when they wished to render them particularly complaisant. Then "they generally provide liquor," of which they make a very small libation to the object of their petitions and drink the rest. Moreover, they have also little genii, or household gods, consisting of images of wood from eight to twelve inches long, to whom they consecrate certain things. These might be of a very miscellaneous order. There might be seen, for instance, "a brass pan fastened to the stump of a tree by driving a

country axe through it — a glass bottle set up on the stump of
a tree — a broken bottle placed upon the ground with two or
three beads in it, covered with a bit of cloth, and surrounded
with stones — a rag laid upon small sticks and covered with a
broken calabash," and so forth. As in more civilized countries,
the sanctity conferred upon the objects by religion places
them under the special protection of the law. "To remove one
of them even unknowingly," continues the author, "is a great
offense, and subjects the aggressor to a *palaver*, or action in
their courts of law" (S. L., p. 65–67). The Tartar chiefs, as
described by the traveler Carpin, kept idols in their places of
abode, to whom they offered not only the first milk of their
ewes and mares, and something of all they ate, but to whom
they even consecrated horses. After this dedication to the idol
no one might mount these horses (Bergeron, Voyage de Carpin,
p. 30). Among the Singhalese a curious mode prevails of consecrating fruit to some demon, in order to prevent its being
stolen. "A band of leaves" is to be seen fastened around the
stem of a fruit-tree, and it is supposed that no thief will be so
sacrilegious as to touch the fruit that has been thus hallowed.
"Occasionally," says Sir Emerson Tennent, "these dedications
are made to the temples of Buddha, and even to the Roman
Catholic altars, as to that of St. Anne of Calpentyn. This ceremony is called Gokbandeema, 'the tying of the tender leaf,'
and its operation is to prevent the fruit from pillage, till ripe
enough to be plucked and sent as an offering to the divinity to
whom it has thus been consecrated." He adds, that a few only
of the finest are offered, the rest being kept by the owner (Ceylon, vol. i. p. 540, 3d ed). Another author, describing the same
custom, says, "To prevent fruit being stolen, the people hang
up certain grotesque figures around the orchards and dedicate
it to the devils, after which none of the native Ceylonese will
dare even to touch the fruit on any account. Even the owner
will not venture to use it, till it be first liberated from the
dedication. For this purpose, they carry some of it to   the
pagoda, where the priests, after receiving a certain proportion
for themselves, remove the incantations with which it was dedicated" (A. I. C., p. 198). Here the consecration, contrary to
the usual rule, is made with an interested motive, and is of the

nature of a direct bargain for temporal advantages. Of the common form of consecration among the same people, another visitor gives evidence; their temples are, he says, "adorned with such things as the people's ability and poverty can afford; accounting it the highest point of devotion, bountifully to dedicate such things unto their gods, which in their estimation are most precious (A. R. C., p. 73).

Sometimes consecration is held to confer special powers, not otherwise possessed, upon the objects on which it is performed. Thus, among the rude Mongolians, the consecrating rites to which sacred writings and images of Buddha are subjected are described by a word meaning to *animate,* which is held by a learned Orientalist to express their sense of the communication of living power, of which the religious ceremony is the vehicle (G. O. M., p. 330). Thus, too, among Christians, the consecration of bread and wine by a priest is regarded as the means of a still more extraordinary communication of living power to those lifeless elements. And the writer has been present at the Vatican when a vast number of rosaries, and other such trinkets, were held up by a crowd of devotees to receive the Papal blessing, which was evidently considered, by their owners, to confer upon them some kind of virtue that was otherwise lacking.

Naturally it follows from the theory of consecration — which is that of a gift from men to God — that the more valuable the objects given, the more pleasing will they be. Hence, men generally endeavor to consecrate valuable objects, though instances to the contrary may be found. The horses bestowed by the Tartars were, no doubt, among their most precious possessions. And the large endowments of land devoted in perpetuity to the Church during the middle ages, were gifts of the most permanent and most coveted form of property.

Consecration differs from sacrifice, in that the objects of sacrifice are intended for the immediate gratification of the deity, those of consecration for his continued use. Hence, things sacrificed are consumed upon the spot; things consecrated are preserved as long as their nature permits of it. So strong is the sense of permanence attaching to consecration, that there are probably even now persons among us, who would regard it as a sort of crime for the State to assume the ownership of lands once devoted to religious purposes, or to divert the proceeds to some other employment. A like sentiment, no doubt, prevails with regard to the material and the furniture of places of worship. With regard to sacrifice the case is different. Animals, fruits, or other articles intended for sacrifice, are given to the god or his representative for the single occasion, and as a requisite in the performance of some momentary rite. If a homely comparison may be permitted on so sacred a subject, it might be not inaptly said, that things sacrificed are like the meat and drink placed before a guest who is invited to dinner, while things consecrated rather resemble the present which he carries away to his own residence, and keeps for the remainder of his life.

CHAPTER IV.

CONSECRATED PERSONS.

WE have seen the religious instinct leading to the consecration of actions, to the consecration of places, and to the consecration of things. We are now to follow it in a yet more striking exhibition of its power, the consecration by human beings of their own lives and their own persons (or sometimes of the lives and persons of their children). Not only is such self-dedication to the service of religion common; it is well-nigh-universal. There is no phenomenon more constant, none more uniform, than this. Differing in minor details, the grand features of self-consecration are everywhere the same, whether we look to the saintly Rishis of ancient India; to the wearers of the yellow robe in China or Ceylon; to the Essenes among the Jews; to the devotees of Vitziliputzli in pagan Mexico; or to the monks and nuns of Christian times in Africa, in Asia, and in Europe. Throughout the various creeds of these distant lands there runs the same unconquerable impulse, producing the same remarkable effects. This is not the place to attempt a psychological explanation of asceticism as a tendency of human nature. We have now only to notice some of its most conspicuous manifestations, and thus to assign to it its proper place in a history of the mode in which man endeavors to approach and to propitiate his god.

Generally speaking, we may premise that the consecration of individuals to a life in which religion is the predominating element, means the abandonment of the ordinary pleasures of the world. This is of the very essence of self-devotion. Sanctity, and the enjoyment of all those things in which the body is largely concerned, have always been regarded as inconsistent and opposite. Hence, in the first line of things prohibited to

88

consecrated persons, we always discover the pleasures of sex. To indulge in these is usually considered the most flagrant outrage against their rules. Next to sexual delights, or equally with them, the luxuries of choice food, rich clothing, comfortable beds, well-furnished rooms, and similar ministrations to physical ease are withheld from the votaries. They are very frequently voluntary paupers or mendicants; or where this is not the case, they usually depend on some endowment derived from the liberality of others. Where their numbers are large, they are placed under rules, and bound to the strictest obedience to their superiors in the same line of life. Moreover, mere abstinence from ordinary pleasures is not enough to prove their devotion; they are called on to undergo extraordinary pains. These vary with the rule of the order, or their own fervor. Sometimes they are obliged to live in rooms which, in the coldest weather, no fire is permitted to cheer; sometimes their sleep is broken by rising at unseasonable hours to worship their deity; sometimes the garment they wear is too thick in summer, and too scanty in winter; and sometimes they tear their own flesh by scourging and flagellation. Fasting, too, is often imposed at certain times. And the zeal of individuals always outruns the compulsory hardships of their position. They will show the intensity of their devotion by fasting more rigorously than others, sleeping on harder couches, bearing greater inflictions. Self-consecration continually tends towards greater and greater self-denial; but the actual degrees of self-denial vary from the mere observance of some simple rules to the extremest possibility of self-torture. Confining ourselves, however, to the general marks which characterize this devotion of persons to religion, we may say that it involves principally two things: chastity and poverty.

When the Spaniards had established themselves in Mexico and Peru, they were astonished to find, in the religious customs and practices of the new world they had invaded, so much that resembled those of the old world they had left behind. Especially was this the case with regard to monastic institutions, in respect of which it seemed that the Christian missionaries had little to teach their heathen brothers. "Certainly it is a matter of surprise," says the Reverend Father Acosta, "that false religious opinion should have so much power with those young men and young women of Mexico, that they should do with such austerity in the service of Satan that which many of us do not do in the service of the most high God. Which is a great confusion to those who are very proud and very well satisfied with some trifling penance which they perform" (H. I., b. 5, ch. 16, sub fine). In describing more particularly the manner in which the devil had contrived to be served in Mexico, he states that around the great temple there were two monasteries, one of young women and the other of young men, whom they called monks (religiosos). Those young men who served in the temple of Vitziliputzli lived in poverty, chastity, and obedience; ministered like Levites to the priests and dignitaries of the temple, and had manual labor to do. Besides these were others who performed menial services, and carried the offerings that were made when their superiors went in quest of alms. All these had persons who took charge of them, and when they went abroad they held their heads low and their eyes on the ground, not daring to raise them to look at the women they might come across. Should they not receive enough by way of alms, they had the right of going to the sown fields, and plucking the ears of corn of which they had need. They practised penance, rising at midnight, and also cutting themselves so as to draw blood; but this exercise and penance did not last more than a year (H. I., b. 5, ch. 16).

Both in Mexico and in Peru young girls were consecrated to a religious life, but this consecration was sometimes only temporary; a certain proportion of the Peruvian nuns being drafted off into the harem of the Inca. Acosta, describing this consecration of virgins, is again impressed with the abilities of the devil. Since, he observes, the religious life is so pleasing in the eyes of God, the father of lies has contrived, not only to imitate it, but to cause his ministers to be distinguished in austerity and regularity. Thus in Peru there were many convents for girls, who were placed under the tuition of old women whom they called Mamaconas. Indoctrinated by the Mamaconas in "various things necessary for human life, and in the rites and ceremonies of their gods," they were removed, after they had attained fourteen years, either to the sanctuaries where they preserved a perpetual virginity, or to be sacrificed in some religious ceremonial, or to become wives and mistresses of the Inca and his friends. The consecration of these damsels was not, as usual in such cases, voluntary on their part, but the same idea of merit inspired the gift on the part of those who made it. For, while the surrender of female children to the monastery was compulsory when demanded by an officer named the "Appopanaca," yet "many offered their girls of their own free will, it appearing to them that they gained great merit, inasmuch as they were sacrificed for the Inca." If any of the older nuns, who presided over the children, had sinned against her honor, she was invariably buried alive or subjected to some other cruel death.

"In Mexico," continues the pious Jesuit, "the devil also found his own kind of nuns, although the profession did not last more than one year." As has been said, there were two houses, one for men and another for women. Like the monks, the nuns also wore a distinctive costume, and dressed their hair in a distinctive fashion. Like them, they had manual labor to perform; like them, they rose at midnight for matins. They had their abbesses, who occupied them in making robes for the adornment of the idols. They also had their penance, in which they cut themselves in the points of the ears. They lived with honor and circumspection, and any delinquency, even the smallest, was punished with death; for they said that the sinner had violated the honor of their god (H. I., b. 5, ch. 15).

Another author, describing the religious orders of Peru, states that fathers, anxious that their children's lives should be preserved, used to dedicate them in infancy to some form of monastic establishment, to which they were actually committed at the age of fifteen. If, for instance, they were promised to the house of Calmecac, it was that they might perform penance, and serve the gods, and live in purity and humility and chastity, and be altogether preserved from carnal vices. A Christian parent could have desired no more. "And if it were a woman, she was a servant of the temple called Civatlamacaz-qui; she had to be subject to the women who governed that order; she had to live in chastity, and abstain from every carnal act, and to live with the virgins who were called *the sisters*," who were shut up in the convent. A feast was made when the child was dedicated by its parents, and the head of the order took it in his arms in token that it was his subject till it was married; the consecration not being perpetual. Its reception was accompanied by a solemn ceremonial, in which the following prayer was offered to their god: "O Lord, most merciful, protector of all, here stand thy handmaidens, who bring thee a new handmaid, whose father and mother promise and offer her, that she may serve thee. And well thou knowest that the poor thing is thine: vouchsafe to receive her, that for a few days she may sweep and adorn thy house, which is a house of penance and weeping, where the daughters of the nobles place their hand on thy riches, praying and weeping to thee with tears and great devotion, and where they demand with prayers thy words and thy power. Vouchsafe, O Lord, to show her grace, and to receive her: place her, O Lord, in the company of the virgins who are called Tlamacazque, who do penance and serve in the temple, and wear their hair short. O Lord, most merciful, protector of all, vouchsafe to do with her whatever is thy holy will, showing her the grace which thou knowest to be suited to her." If then the girl was of age, she was marked in the ribs and breast, in evidence of her being a nun; and if she was still a child, a string of beads was put round her neck, which she wore until she could fulfil the vow of her parents (A. M., vol. v. p. 484–486).

But in addition to these temporary nuns, Peru had others, whose vows were perpetual. Vega relates in his Commentaries, that besides the women who entered into monasteries to profess perpetual virginity, there were many women of the blood-royal who lived in their own houses, subject to a vow of virginity, though not in "clausura." They went out to visit their relations on various occasions. They were held in the greatest respect for their chastity and purity, which was by no means feigned, but altogether genuine. Any failure to observe their vow was punished by burning or drowning. The writer knew one of these women when advanced in life, and occasionally saw her when she visited his mother, whose great-aunt she was. He bears witness himself to the profound veneration with which this old lady was everywhere received, the place of honor being always assigned to her, as well by his mother as by her other acquaintances (C. R., b. 4, ch. 7). Thus we find celibacy, as a mark of piety, in full force in the new world at the time of its discovery, no less than in the old; and religious chastity as much respected by the idolatrous Mexicans and Peruvians as by their Catholic invaders.

Monasticism, in countries where Buddhism reigns supreme, is a vast and powerful institution. In the early times of Buddhistic fervor, it would almost seem from the language of the legends, that to embrace the faith of Sakyamuni and to become an ascetic were one and the same thing. At least every convert who aspired to be not only a hearer, but a doer of the word, is described as instantly assuming the tonsure and the yellow robe. At the same time the distinction between Bhikshus, mendicants, and Upasakas, laymen, is no doubt an early one; and we must assume, that as soon as the religion of the gentle ascetic began to spread among the people at large, those whose circumstances did not permit them to be monks or nuns were received on easier terms. "What," asked a disciple, "must be done in the condition of a mendicant?"—"The rules of chastity must be observed during the whole of life." "That is impossible; is there no other way?"—"There is another, friend; it is to be a pious man (Upasaka)." "What is there to be done in this condition?"—"It is necessary to abstain during the whole of life from murder, theft, pleasure (the illicit pleasures of sex must be understood), lying, and the use of intoxicating liquors" (H. B. I., p. 281). To these five commandments, binding on every Buddhist, the rule imposed upon the mendicants adds five more, to say nothing of many more special obligations and regulations to which they are subject. Murder, theft, unchastity, lying, and drinking, are forbidden to them as to all others; the sixth commandment prohibits eating after mid-day; the seventh singing, dancing, and playing musical instruments; the eighth adorning the person with flowers and bands, or using perfume and ointment; the ninth sleeping on a high and large bed; the tenth accepting gold and silver. These several prohibitions aim, as is evident, at precisely the same objects which the founders of Christian orders have always had in view; that, namely, of weaning their disciples

from the world by keeping from them the enjoyment of its luxuries, and preventing the acquisition of personal property.

The obligation to observe these rules commenced with the
novitiate; a condition which, in Buddhist as in Catholic communities, precedes that of complete ordination. The novices
are termed Sramanera, a word meaning little Sramanas, while
the monks themselves are either Sramana or Bhikshu. Both
these designations serve to express the nature of their vocation;
Sramana being "an ascetic who subdues his senses," and
Bhikshu "one who lives by alms" (H. B. I., pp. 275, 276). The
sisters are called Bhikshuni, and they are said to owe their
origin to Maha Prajapati, the aunt of the great Sramana Gautama, who obtained from her nephew, through the intercession
of the beloved disciple Ananda, the permission for her sex to
follow their brothers in the way of salvation by poverty and
chastity (Ibid., p. 278).

There can be no question that, according to the original
practice of the mendicant orders, the vow was taken for life;
and this is, I believe, still the custom in most of the lands
where Buddhism is in the ascendant. But in Siam, the monastic vow can at any time be cancelled by the superior of the
monastery; and this rule, which involves a gross abuse of the
original institution, renders temporary asceticism universal in
that country (Wheel, p. 45). Another kind of degeneracy has
occurred in Nepaul, where the ministers of religion, who elsewhere must be monks, are permitted to be married (Hodgson,
T.R.A.S., vol. ii. p. 245).

The objects proposed to themselves by Buddhists, in embracing an ascetic life, are precisely the same as those proposed to
themselves by Christians. By denying themselves the pleasures
of this world, they hope to obtain a higher reward than other
mortals; whether in the shape of birth in a happier condition,
or in that of complete emancipation from all birth whatsoever,
which is the supreme goal of their religion. The means they
pursue to attain these ends are also similar. The Pratimoksha
Sutra, or Sutra of Emancipation, which forms tho universal
regula in all their monasteries, is worthy of a St. Benedict or a
St. Francis. It lays down with the minutest elaboration, not
only all the moral precepts that must be obeyed by the monk

or nun, but all the little observances in regard to dress, eating, walking, social intercourse, and so forth, to which he must attend. It contains two hundred and fifty rules, and the breach of any of these is attended with its appropriate penance, according to the magnitude of the offense.

Asceticism was deeply rooted in the native land of Buddhism long before the appearance of the reformer who gave it, by the foundation of communities, an organization and a purpose. Just as in Egypt there were many solitary saints before the time of Pachomius and Antony, so in India there were holy men who had subdued their senses before the gospel of deliverance was preached by Gautama Buddha. Some of these dispensed altogether with clothing, a custom which was frowned upon by Buddhism and put down wherever its influence was paramount. Others lived in lonely places, exposed to every sort of hardship and avoiding every form of carnal pleasure. The popular mind combined the practice of austerity with the acquisition of extraordinary powers over nature. Hence, no doubt, an additional motive for its exercise. The Ramayana abounds with descriptions of holy hermits, living on roots in the forests, and practising the utmost austerity. Visvamitra, for example, the very type of an ascetic, was a monarch, who determined to obtain from the gods the title of "Brahman saint," the highest to which he, not by birth a Brahman, could aspire. This was the manner in which he went to work:—

> " His arms upraised, without a rest,
>   With but one foot, the earth he pressed;
>   The air his food, the hermit stood
>   Still as a pillar hewn from wood
>   Around him in the summer days
>   Five mighty fires combined to blaze.
>   In floods of rain no veil was spread,
>   Save clouds, to canopy his head.
>   In the dark dews both night and day
>   Couched in the stream the hermit lay."*

Twice did the gods, alarmed at the power he was likely to

* Griffith, The Ramayan, vol. i. p. 268.

acquire, direct their efforts against his chastity. The first time the perfect nymph deputed on this errand, seen by him while bathing herself naked in the stream, caused him to forget his vow and dally with her for ten years. The second time the saint perceived the plot, but allowed himself to burst forth in words of unholy rage against the damsel who was trying to seduce him, and thus lost the merit of his former penance. After this he resolved never to speak a word, and persisted in his resolution, until the gods, in a body, addressed him in the long-desired form: "Hail, Brahman Saint" (Griffith, The Ramayan, vol. i. p. 274).

Visvamitra is of course a mythical character, and his penance imaginary; but the ascetic life he is described as leading was taken from models which the writers had before their eyes. All the marvels of the Thebaid in Christian times were, in fact, anticipated in India by at least one thousand years.

How deeply the ascetic tendency is implanted in human nature is strikingly shown in the case of the Essenes, the Nazarites, and the Therapeutæ, who sprang from a religion whose ostensible precepts are eminently opposed to all such courses, that of the Jews. Judaism powerfully encouraged all those inclinations to which monasticism is fatal: the propagation of the species, the acquisition of property, the maintenance of family ties, and the enjoyment of the good things which this world has to offer. Yet from the bosom of this sober faith sprang bodies of men who neither ate flesh, nor drank wine, nor cohabited with women. It may be that the Jewish ascetics were not very numerous; but it is clear, too, that they were not so few as to be deemed by contemporary observers altogether unimportant. And the fascination which John the Baptist, pre-eminently an ascetic, exercised over his countrymen in the first century, is a sign that this mode of living was conducive among the Jews to that spiritual supremacy which is so constantly received at the hands of Christians.

That Christianity should encourage a disposition which even Judaism could not check was no more than might be expected from the language and conduct of its founder and his earliest disciples. Christ was never married, and probably lived in complete chastity. Paul goes so far as to compare marriage unfavorably with celibacy. James upholds poverty as preferable to riches in the eyes of God. The whole of the New Testament abounds with passages in which present misery is declared to be the forerunner of future happiness, and present prosperity of future suffering. This is the very spirit of monasticism, and it is not surprising that from such a root such fruits have sprung. From a very early age devout Christians have felt that in renouncing individual property, marriage, personal freedom, and the various other joys which life in the world offers, they were fulfilling the dictates of their religion and preparing themselves for heaven. To illustrate this proposition effectually would be to write the history of the monastic orders. Beginning in the deserts of Egypt, these have extended throughout Europe, and have exercised a vast and potent influence on the extension of the Christian faith. Monks have been missionaries, preachers, martyrs, persecutors, bishops and popes. The greatest names who have ranged themselves under the banner of the Catholic Church have belonged to one or other of the several orders. And alongside of the monks, living by the same rule, helping them in their several tasks, the nuns have ever been forward in undergoing their share of austerity and undertaking their share of labor.

Very various have been the immediate motives that have led such large numbers of Christians to betake themselves to the monastery or the convent. Some have fled from riches and luxury; others from poverty and wretchedness. Some have been sick of earthly pleasures; others have sought to avoid the temptation of ever knowing them. Many have been drawn by the irresistible spell of asceticism to flee from opposing parents and unsympathizing friends in order to embrace it; others have been destined from their infancy, like the Mexican and Peruvian youth, to wear the cowl or to take the veil. But throughout the history of every order there has been the same fundamental idea sustaining its existence; the idea, namely, that in becoming an ascetic, the person was consecrated to God, and became by that consecration purer, holier, and better than those who continued to pursue the ordinary avocations of secular life.

This consecration is not given without due solemnity. It is only after a novitate, in which he has full experience of the privations to be undergone, that the candidate can be received into the order of which he desires to be a member. Should his resolution be unshaken after his year's trial as a novice, he may take the irrevocable vow of obedience, under which those of poverty and chastity are comprehended. He is now a consecrated person. He has sacrificed himself completely to his divine Master, and whatever reward he may hope to receive must be given by that Master in a future state.

It is one of the principal weaknesses of Protestantism that it has omitted to provide for the ascetic instinct. It has lost thereby the mighty hold which the Catholic Church must ever possess over those who feel themselves moved to crucify the flesh and devote themselves wholly to spiritual things. Strange to say, this remarkable instinct has nevertheless broken out afresh within the bosom of Protestantism in recent times. The Shakers are but a somewhat novel species of monks and nuns. They abstain from marriage though the two sexes live together in one community. Their chastity is said to be perfect. They give up all individual property for the common good. They wear a peculiar dress and are subject to peculiar rules. Lastly, they believe that they stand under the special guidance and protection of the Holy Spirit.

CHAPTER V.

CONSECRATED MEDIATORS.

HAVING seen the manner in which individuals devote themselves to the special service of their deities, we have now to observe the further fact that a whole class of men is devoted to this service by the demands of society. This class is the priesthood. They differ from the persons last treated of, inasmuch as the consecration of ascetics has reference exclusively to their own personal salvation, while the consecration of priests has reference exclusively to the salvation of others. A monk or a nun becomes by the act of profession a holier being; less occupied with the world; mentally nearer to God; better fitted to communicate with him than ordinary unchaste mortals. A priest becomes by the act of ordination a being endowed with special powers; better entitled to offer up the public prayers than others; more likely to be heard when he does so; more eligible as a channel of communication between men and God than unordained mortals. In other words, his functions are of a public, those of the monk of a private, kind.

We must not be confused by the fact that among Buddhists and among Catholics the two species of consecration are no longer completely distinct, the monks in both of those great religions being at the same time priests. The early writings of Buddhism sufficiently evince the fact that no kind of public ministry was at first connected with the profession of a mendicant. He had simply to observe the precepts of his order, and to aim at such perfection as should ensure the deliverance of his soul. Priestly duties are now indeed performed by monks in Buddhist countries, but this is an addition to their regular vocation, not a necessary part of it; while in Catholic countries, the ecclesiastical character which the monks at present enjoy in no way belonged to them when the monastic orders were first established. The monks, as Montalembert observes, were at first an intermediate body between laity and clergy, in whom the latter were to see an ideal which it was not possible for all to attain. Technically, however, the monks formed a part of the laity, and the steps by which they came to be considered as the "regular clergy" are, according to the same high authority, difficult to follow (M. d'O., vol. i. p. 288; vol. ii. p. 57). Self-consecration, and consecration to ecclesiastical duties were therefore two very different things, and the distinction between regular and secular clergy shows that, though somewhat obliterated in appearance, the two ideas are still kept apart.

In all religions that have risen above the rudest stage, those who desire to become priests are initiated by certain fixed ceremonies. Thus is the consecration given which fits them to convey to God the wishes of mortals, and to mortals the will of God. To take an example from a very primitive form of faith, the "Angekoks," or priests of the Greenlanders, receive their commission only after long and exhausting rites, in which a familiar spirit is supposed to appear to them, and to accompany them to heaven and hell. Should they fail ten times in obtaining the assistance of such a spirit, they are compelled to lay down their offices. The spirit, when he comes, holds a conversation with the Angekok, who is thus installed in his profession by supernatural means (H. G., p. 253-256). So also, among the American tribes in New France, we are told that the "Jongleurs" by profession never obtained this character till after they had been prepared for it by fasts, which they carried to a great extent, and during which they beat the drum, cried, shouted, sung and smoked. Their installation was subsequently accomplished in a sort of Bacchanalia, with ceremonies of a highly extravagant nature (N. F., vol. iii. p. 363). Among a certain tribe of negroes, the priests are taken from a class of men termed "living sacrifices" (G. d. M., p. 328), who live at the expense of others, taking whatever they require, and who wear their hair, like the Nazarites, unshorn. Here their consecration is marked by these peculiar characteristics, and appears to be impressed upon them by some dedication made without their own consent. In another negro nation, there is a priestess of a certain snake, who is marked in a peculiar way over the whole body, and held in great esteem. Every year some young girls are seized by force and taken to this priestess, who marks them artistically, initiates them in religious songs and dances, marries them in a manner to the snake, and consecrates them as priestesses of that divinity. With others again the priesthood is hereditary, the consecration in this case being imprinted once for all on certain families, and not imparted, as in the instances given above, by rites affecting only the individual who undergoes them. A peculiar modification of the hereditary principle is where the preference is given to him, among several sons, who dares to pull certain grains (which have been previously put in) out of the teeth of his deceased father, and place them in the mouth of the corpse. Here the consecration is partly inherited, partly personal. Elsewhere a priest or fetich-maker is made "by all sorts of silly ceremonies at a meal," and a string with consecrated objects is hung round his neck in token of his condition (G. d. M., p. 328).

Both principles, the hereditary and the personal, were known in Mexico. The priests of Vitziliputzli succeeded by right of birth; the priests of other idols by election or by an offering made in their infancy. Priests were consecrated to their holy office by an unction which, as Father Acosta justly observes, resembled that of the Catholic Church. They were annointed from head to foot, and the hair was left to hang down in tresses moist from the application of the ointment. But when they were going to perform the offices of their sacred calling on mountains, or in dark caves, they were annointed with an altogether different substance, compounded by a peculiar process from certain venomous reptiles. This was supposed to give them courage (H. I., b. 5, ch. 26).

The consecration of the Levitical priesthood, originally personal, descended from father to son, and was moreover confined to the members of this single tribe. It could not be repeated after its first performance. Hence we have in this case an interesting example, not only of an hereditary priesthood, but also of the manner in which its exclusive sanctity was supposed to have been originally established. Moses, who derived his appointment directly from Jehovah, was employed to consecrate

Aaron and his sons by means of an elaborate and imposing ritual communicated to him by that deity himself. The means thus taken (in Jehovah's own words) "to hallow them, to minister unto me in the priest's office," were effectual for all time; the descendants of Aaron after that being priests by nature. How great was the value of the consecration thus given, may be seen by the fact that Moses was ordered to threaten the penalty of death against any one who should dare to manufacture oil similar to that used in annointing Aaron and his sons (Exod. xxviii. 29; xxx. 30-33).

Priestly power among Christian nations is communicated in a solemn ceremonial, and is conferred only upon the individual recipient. It does not descend in his family, but it is capable of being imparted by bishops, who have themselves received a higher grade of priestly consecration. By some it is actually supposed that a mysterious virtue, derived directly from Christ through the apostles, is conveyed to the recipient of holy orders. But whether the apostolical succession be conveyed or not in the Ordination Service of the Church of England, it is certain that a high authority is held to be given to the priest by the laying on of the hands of the Bishop and of the other priests present at the time.

The rights which he receives are thus expressed:—

"Receive the Holy Ghost for the office and work of a priest in the Church of God, now committed unto thee by the imposition of our hands. Whose sins thou dost forgive they are forgiven; and whose sins thou dost retain, they are retained, and be thou a faithful dispenser of the Word of God, and of his holy sacraments. In the name of the Father and of the Son, and of the Holy Ghost. Amen."

After this the Bishop delivers the Bible to each of the candidates, saying:—

"Take thou authority to preach the Word of God, and to minister the holy sacraments in the congregation where thou shalt be lawfully appointed thereunto."

Here it may be observed that there are three powers conveyed by this ordination: the power of preaching, the power of administering the sacraments, and the power of forgiving and retaining sins. Since the salvation of Christians depends upon their admission to the sacraments, and upon the forgiveness of their sins, it is obvious that the priest who may debar them from the one, and refuse the other, receives in his consecration the keys of the kingdom of heaven. In their communications to the Almighty through the mediation of such priests, men are in possession of an instrument of the very highest efficacy.

The terrible reality which the belief in the ecclesiastical privilege of forgiving sins may sometimes have, is graphically exhibited in M. de Lamartine's touching poem entitled "Jocelyn." Therein a bishop, taken prisoner and condemned to death in the French Revolution, sends for a young deacon who was living in concealment in the Alps with a maiden who loved him deeply, and whom (since the irrevocable vows of a priest were not yet taken) he intended to marry. Regardless of all his pleading the Bishop, under the threat of his dying anathema, forces the unhappy youth to receive priestly orders at his hands, solely in order that he may then listen to the episcopal confession and forgive the episcopal sins. Marriage was now rendered impossible by the vow he had taken; and thus two lives were consigned to enduring misery that a bishop might die in peace. Surely the morality which could lead to such a consummation is self-condemned!

EXTERNAL MANIFESTATIONS OF RELIGIOUS SENTIMENT.

SECOND PART.

MEANS OF COMMUNICATION DOWNWARDS.

CLASSIFICATION.

WE proceed now from the several methods by which men, in all ages and in all countries, have sought to convey their wishes, aspirations, and emotions upwards, to those by which their several deities have in their opinion conveyed their commands, decisions, and intentions downwards. The classification will follow as closely as the subject permits that of the preceding part. Consecration, the quality pertaining to man's instruments of communication with God, will be replaced by holiness, the quality pertaining to God's instruments of communication with man. Thus, corresponding to the consecrated actions of prayer, sacrifice, and praise, we shall have the holy events of omens, signs, miracles, and so forth. Corresponding to the consecrated places where men pay their devotions, we shall find the holy places which some higher being has blessed with tokens of his presence. Corresponding to the consecrated objects bestowed by the creature on the Creator, we shall discover holy objects through which some peculiar grace is conveyed by the Creator to the creature. To consecrated men will correspond holy men, who speak to their fellows with an authority higher than their own; and these holy men will fall into two classes, those whose regular work it is to represent the deity on earth and those who are sent on some special occasion for some special purpose. Lastly, a separate division (having no correlative among means of commmunication upwards) must be given to holy books, for a most important place in the history of religions is occupied by treatises written by the gods for the use of men. To these then the final chapter of this portion of the work must be devoted. Pass we now to holy events.

CHAPTER I.

MANIFOLD beyond the possibility of complete computation are the signs and intimations vouchsafed to the ignorance and weakness of man by the celestial powers. They speak to him through the ordinary phenomena of nature; they instruct him through her rare and more striking exhibitions; they guide his footsteps through prodigies and marvels. Sometimes addressing him spontaneously, without any attempt on his part to elicit their intentions, they open their views or announce the future; sometimes replying to his anxious inquiries, they point out the truth and relieve his perplexity. Consider first the former class of divine manifestations, in which the human being is a merely passive recipient of the communication granted.

Dreams are an excellent example of this class of events. The belief that they are of supernatural origin is both wide-spread and ancient. Possibly there is no country in which it has not been held to a greater or less extent, even though it may not have formed an article in the established creed. Among the Africans in and about Sierra Leone, for example, a dream is received as judicial evidence of witchcraft, and the prisoner accused on this slender testimony "frequently acknowledges the charge and submits to his sentence without repining" (N. A., vol. i. p. 260). On the American continent, where dreams (says Charlevoix) "are regarded as true oracles and notices from heaven" (H. N. F., vol. iii. p. 348), it is plain that the like faith in their intimations prevails. Although explained in a variety of ways, now as the rational soul going abroad, while the sensitive soul remained behind, now as advice from the familiar spirits, now as a visit from the soul of the object dreampt of, the dream is always regarded as a sacred thing. It was thought to be the most usual way taken by the gods of making their wills known to men. Hence they took care to obey the intimations given in dreams; a savage who had dreamt that his little finger was cut off actually submitting to that operation; and another, who had found himself in his dream a prisoner among enemies, getting himself tied to a stake and burnt in various parts of the body (H. N. F., vol. iii. pp. 353, 354). The Jews have in their ritual a singular ceremony for removing the influence of bad dreams. The person who has dreamt something which seems to portend evil, is said to choose three friends, and standing before them as they sit, to repeat seven times: "A good dream have I seen." To which they reply: "A good dream thou hast seen; it is good and shall be good; the compassionate God, who is good, make it good." And the conversation between the dreamer and the interpreters continues for some time, the general effect being to convey God's blessing to the former and convert his trouble into gladness. At the end the interpreters say: "Go eat thy bread with joy, and drink thy wine with a cheerful heart, for God now accepteth thy works. And penitence and prayers and righteousnes will set aside the evil that hath been doomed, and peace be unto us and unto all Israel, Amen." To this the author of the book appends the remark that "the Jews believe that all dreams come to pass according to the interpretation that is made of them," for which reason they relate their dreams to none but friends (Rel. of Jews, p. 71-74). But that they can believe it to be in the power of their friends to *change* the meaning of the dream by an arbitrary interpretation seems scarcely possible. It may, therefore, be the meaning of this passage that an unfavorable interpretation is in itself ominous of misfortune, or that they are desirous not to hear the worst construction that can be put upon a dream.

Belief in the prophetic signification of dreams is not only not discountenanced by the Christian religion, but is explicitly taught by it. If in the present age this belief has fallen somewhat out of repute, this is not because there can be any doubt that the inspired writers of the Christian Scriptures firmly held it, but is a feature of the general relaxation of the bonds of

dogma which characterizes the modern mind. To take a few
instances: when Abraham had called Sarah his sister, and thus
permitted the king of Gerar to appropriate her, God himself
came to Abimelech by night in a dream, and told him that she
was a married woman (Gen xx. 3). Highly important information as to the future of his race was given to Jacob in a dream
(Gen. xxviii. 11–15). His son Joseph enjoyed an extraordinary
faculty, not only of dreaming true dreams himself, but also of
interpreting the dreams of others. It was his own prophetic
dreams which led to his sale into the hands of the traders by
his brothers, and it was his power of correct interpretation
which both freed him from his prison in Egypt, and led to his
promotion to the high office he afterwards held at the Egyptian
court (Gen. xxxvii, 5–11; Gen. xl., xli). Moreover, Joseph, who
must be considered an authority on the subject, expressly
informed Pharaoh, when that monarch had related his dreams
that God had showed him what he was about to do (Gen. xli.
25–28). A most important dream was granted to Solomon, to
whom " the Lord appeared in a dream by night," and told him
to ask whatever favor he might wish: on which occasion the
king preferred his celebrated request for wisdom (Kings iii, 5–15).
Another ruler, Nebuchadnezzar, was also visited by a prophetic
dream, the nature of which was revealed to the interpreter,
Daniel, "in a night vision," by God himself, who thus admitted that it was he who had sent it. A further communication
was made to Nebuchadnezzar, in the dream which he himself
has recorded in the proclamation which bears witness at the
same time to the fulfillment of its warning (Daniel ii., iv). But
of all the dreams handed down to us by the Scriptural writers,
by far the most material, as evidence of their Divine character,
is that on which the mystery of the Incarnation mainly rests.
Take away the dream in which Joseph was informed that the
Holy Ghost was the parent of Mary's first-born child (Matt. i.
20), and that mystery will depend exclusively on a story of an
angel's visit, of necessity related by Mary herself (Luke i. 35);
for obvious reasons not the most trustworthy witness on so delicate a point. But this is not all; for it was by a dream that
the Magi, after their adoration, were warned to escape the vengeance of Herod (Matt. ii. 12); and by a dream that the life of

the infant Christ was preserved in the massacre of the innocents (Matt. ii. 13). Christianity, therefore, may be said to owe
its very existence to the celestial intimations conveyed in
dreams, and Christians cannot consistently embrace any theory
which would lead to a denial of their holy and prophetic character. Since, moreover, we have numerous instances in the
Bible of such dreams being granted to heathens and idolaters
it is plain that the Christian deity does not confine his noctur-
nal visitations to orthodox believers. If the chief butler, the
chief baker, Pharaoh, and Nebuchadnezzar dreamt propheti-
cally, so may any of us at any time according to this teaching.
On the other hand, this power may be due to a special outpouring of the Holy Spirit, as implied in the prediction of Joel
that "your sons and your daughters shall prophecy, your old
men shall dream dreams, your young men shall see visions"
(Joel ii. 28). So that we may completely endorse the conclusion
of the Rev Principal Barry, who discusses this subject with
much solemnity in Smith's "Dictionary of the Bible," "that
the Scripture claims the dream, as it does every other action of
the human mind, as a medium through which God may speak
to man, either directly, that is, as we call it, 'providentially,'
or indirectly, in virtue of a general influence upon all his
thoughts; but whether there is anything to be said in support
of the further inference that "revelation by dreams" may be
expected to pass away, is not equally clear. Assuredly no passage can be produced which, even by implication, states that
this method of communication was temporary or transient; and
considering that it continued in operation from the days of
Abraham to those of Jesus, it is hard to see how the Bible can
be made to support the notion that it is to cease entirely at
any period of human history. On the contrary, the Scriptural
writers, both old and new, would practically have agreed with
Homer: "The dream also is from Zeus" (Iliad, i. 63). Indeed,
the passage in which that deity sends the personified Dream to
bear a message to Agamemnon (Ibid., ii. 8–15), differs only in
its mythological coloring from the representations in the Bible
of dreams in which God comes or appears to the sleeper, or in
which he charges an angel to convey to him his purpose or his
will. And the discrimination commanded to be exercised

between prophecies or dreams deserving attention, and prophecies or dreams contrived merely to test the fidelity of the
Israelites, and therefore not to be received as true, fully corresponds to the distinction drawn in the Odyssey between dreams
passing through the iron gate, and dreams passing through the
ivory gate. Those that came through the horn gate brought
true intimations; but those that came through the ivory gate
were sent to deceive (Od. xix. 560–568).

Another involuntary action through which God communi-
cates with man is sneezing. From the lowest savages to the
most educated nation on the face of the earth, this simple physical event is viewed as an omen. A peculiarity attending this
particular kind of manifestation is, that it is usual for those
present when it occurs to notice it by saying something of favorable augury. In Samoa, one of the Polynesian islands, it was
common to say. "Life to you!" (N. Y., p. 347.) an exclamation
which in sense corresponds almost exactly to the German
"Gesundheit!" (health) to the Italian "Salute!" and to our
own "God bless you!" on the same occasion. South African
savages have the same sentiment of the religious nature of the
omen involved in sneezing. Thus, among the Kafirs we learn
that "it used always to be said when a man sneezed, 'May
Utikxo [God] ever regard me with favor.'" Canon Callaway,
who has acutely noticed the parallelism among various nations
in respect of the feeling associated with this action, further
informs us that "among the Amazulu, if a child sneeze, it is
regarded as a good sign; and if it be ill, they believe it will
recover. On such an occasion they exclaim, 'Tutuka,' Grow.
When a grown up person sneezes, he says, 'Bakiti, ngi hambe
kade,' Spirits of our people, grant me a long life. As he believes
that at the time of sneezing the spirit of his house is in some
especial proximity to him, he believes it is a time especially
favorable to prayer, and that whatever he asks for will be given;
hence he may say, 'Bakwiti, inkomo,' Spirits of our people,
give me cattle, or 'Bakwiti, abntwana,' spirits of our people
give me children. Diviners among the natives are very apt to
sneeze, which they regard as an indication of the presence of
the spirits; the diviner adores by saying, 'Makosi,' Lords, or
Masters" (R. S. A., part i. p. 64). A similar belief prevails among

the Parsees, who consider a sneeze as a mark of victory obtained over the evil spirits who besiege the interior of the body by the fire which animates man, and who accordingly render thanks to Ahuramazda when this event happens (Z. A., vol. ii. p. 598).

Classical antiquity presents us with an example of a famous sneeze. At a critical moment in the expedition of the Ten Thousand against Artaxerxes, when they were left in a hostile country surrounded with perplexities and perils, Xenophon encouraged them by an address in which he urged that if they would take a certain course, they had with the favor of the gods, many and good hopes of safety. Just at these words, "somebody sneezes," and immediately the drooping hearts of the soldiery were comforted by this assurance of divine protection. With one impulse they worshipped the god; and Xenophon remarked that since, when they were in the very act of speaking of safety, this favorable augury of Zeus the Savior had appeared, it seemed proper to him that they should vow thank-offerings to this deity, to be presented on their first arrival in a friendly country, and also that they should make a vow to sacrifice to the other gods according to their ability (Xen. Anab. iii. 2. 9). Not only is it customary in Germany to welcome a sneeze with the above-mentioned exclamation of "Gesundheit!" but a notion is stated to prevail that should one person be thinking of something in the future, and another sneeze at the moment he is thus engaged, the thing thought of will come pass. So that the commonest character ascribed to sneezing is that of an auspicious omen.

Other phenomena may serve as omens, and such phenomena may be either natural or preternatural. In the first case their prophetic or significant character is entirely due to the interpretation put upon them by men; in the second, it is inherent in their very nature, which at once renders them conspicuous as exceptions to the usual course. Those of the first class have thus a dual function: contemplated on the other side, they are merely events belonging to the regular sequence of causes and effects; contemplated on the other, they are especially contrived as indications of the divine purposes. Hence, to one observer they may bear the appearance of ordinary phenomena; to an-

other, better informed, they may convey important intimations
of the future. Tacitus mentions, for example, the favorable
augury that was granted to the Romans on the eve of a battle
with the Germans by the flight of eight eagles who sought the
woods (Tac. Ann., ii. 17. 2). The same author informs us of a
melancholy omen which occurred to Paetus when he and his
army were crossing the Euphrates. Without apparent cause, the
horse which bore the consular insignia turned backwards (Ibid.,
xv. 7. 3). Each of these signs was of course followed by its
appropriate exents. A belief which is thus found in a civilized
nation naturally has its prototype among the uncivilized. The
Kafirs believe that the spirits send them omens. Thus a wild
animal entering a kraal is "regarded as a messenger from the
spirit to remind the people that they have done something
wrong." Another omen which is considered very terrible is the
bleating of a sheep while it is being slaughtered. A councilor,
to whom it occured to hear this sign, was told by a prophet
that it "foreboded his death." Strange to say, his chief soon
after sent soldiers to kill him, and the man only averted his
threatened fate by escaping to Natal. Among other natural
events which are omens to the Kafirs are, "a child born dead;
a woman two days in parturition; a man burnt while sitting by
the fire, unless he were asleep or drunk" (K. N. pp. 162, 163).
"An unexpected whirlwind will suggest to" the Chinese "the
contest of evil spirits; and the flying of a crow in a peculiar
direction fill them with consternation. In such a deplorable
state," gravely observes the missionary who records these facts,
"is the heathen mind" (C. O., vol. ii. p. 208). Perhaps he did
not consider that there were many in more enlightened countries who would be alarmed at the omen implied by a dinner-
party of thirteen, and who would regard it as of evil augury to
begin a journey on Friday. In such a deplorable state is the
Christian mind.

Ceylon appears to be remarkable for the faith placed by its inhabitants in omens, which are even said to regulate their whole
conduct and to intimate their destiny from birth onwards.
Children, of whose future the astrologers predict evil, are sometimes destroyed in order to avoid their pre-determined misery.
On going out in the morning, the Singhalese anxiously remark

the object they encounter first, in order to deduce from it a
favorable or unfavorable augury for the business of the day.
"I, as a European," says the author who tells us these facts,
"was always a glad sight to them;" for "a white man or a
woman with child" were good omens; but beggars and deformed
persons so unlucky, as even to stop these hapless folk from proceeding in the work they were about during the day on which
these boding signs were the first things to meet their gaze (A.
I. C., p. 194). Another phenomenon of a somewhat less ordinary kind serves as an omen to the Singhalese, though apparently only in reference to a single fact. There is visible in Ceylon "a peculiar and beautiful meteor," termed "Buddha rays,'
which "is supposed by the natives only to appear over a temple or tomb of Buddha's relics, and from thence to emanate."
The appearance of these rays is taken by believers as a sign
that the Buddhist faith will last for the destined span of five
thousand years from its founder's death (E. Y., vol. i. p. 337);
much as the rainbow is held by Jews and Christians to be the
token of a promise that God will never again punish the world
by a universal deluge.

The next class of omens need not consist of phenomena
which are absolutely beyond the range of physical law, provided they be sufficiently rare to strike the imagination of observers as marvelous occurrences. For example, an eclipse of
the sun may be an omen to savage or very uninstructed people;
a comet, being more unusual, will seem ominous to nations
standing on a much higher grade of culture. Advancing still
higher, extraordinary and inexplicable sights in the heavens or
on earth will stand for portents to all but the scientifically
minded. An example of the latter class is found in the temporary withering of the Ruminal tree, which had sheltered the
infancy of Romulus and Remus 840 years before (Tac. Ann.,
xiii. 58). At the time at which Tacitus begins his history, there
were, he says, prodigies in the sky and on earth, warnings of
lightnings and presages of future things (Tac. Hist., i. 3. 2).
Popular imagination, besides converting natural, but rare, phenomena into omens, invents others which are altogether supernatural. In the disturbed days of Otho and Vitellius, it was
rumored that a form of larger than human dimensions had

issued from the shrine of Juno; that a statue of Julius on the Tiberine island had turned round from west to east without any perceptible agency; that an ox in Etruria had spoken; that animals had brought forth strange progeny; and that other alarming exceptions to the laws of nature had been observed (Ibid., i. 86. i). The supposed contraction of a man's shadow is thought in South Africa to portend his death (R. S. A., pt. i. p. 126). The Irish Banshee is a being who does not belong to any species recognized by science, and who, moreover, is heard to scream only before a death in the family to which she is attached. The ticking sound produced by a small insect in the wooden furniture of a room is termed in Scotland the death-watch, and has the same ominous significance. To one family, a drummer heard to drum outside the castle is significant of death; in another, it may be that a particular ghost, seen by a casual visitor who knows nothing of its meaning, conveys a similar intimation. The birth of great men is often supposed to be marked by extraordinary signs. "At my nativity," says Owen Glendower,

> " The front of heaven was full of fiery shapes,
>   Of burning cressets; and at my birth,
>   The frame and huge foundation of the earth
>   Shak'd like a coward."

And again:—

> " The goats ran from the mountains, and the herds
>   Were strangely clamorous to the frighted fields.
>   These signs have marked me extraordinary;
>   And all the courses of my life do show
>   I am not in the roll of common men."*

From signs which the bounty of nature supplies without effort on the part of human beings, we proceed to those which are granted only in reply to solicitations on the part of some person or persons in quest of supernatural information. Of these, a leading place must be assigned to those which are obtained through the medium of diviners. Divination is in many parts of the world a highly-developed and lucrative art.

* Henry IV., pt. 1, act iii. scene 1.

The natives of South Africa, being in any perplexity, resort to the professional diviner to help them out of it. Should cattle be lost, should a goat be too long in giving birth to its kids, should a relation be ill, the diviner is asked to inform those who consult him, both what it is that has happened, and what they are to do. Sometimes his replies are assisted by sticks held by the people, who beat them vehemently on the ground when he divines correctly, and gently when he divines incorrectly; sometimes he himself makes use of small sticks or bones, which indicate by their movements the thing desired to be known; sometimes again mysterious voices, supposed to be those of spirits, are heard to speak. In a case related by one of Canon Callaway's informants (who was quite sceptical as to that class of diviners who required the people to strike the ground), a correct answer was given by a diviner who employed bones as his professional instruments. He had gone to inquire about a goat of his brother's, which had been yeaning some days, and had not brought forth. The diviner discovered from his bones what was the matter; he declared that the she-goat had been made ill by sorcerers, and told them that when they reached home it would have given birth to two kids. The prediction was fulfilled. On reaching home there were two kids, a white and a grey one; the very colors the diviner had seen in his inspired vision. "I was at once satisfied," observes the narrator (R. S. A., pt. iii. p. 334-336). Another mode of divining is by the aid of "familiar spirits," who address the consulting party without being themselves visible. A native relates that his adopted father went to inquire of a diviner by spirits (named Umancele) concerning his wife's illness. When the relations of the sick woman entered to salute, some heard the spirits saluting them, saying, "Good-day, So and So." The person thus addressed started, and exclaimed, "Oh, whence does the voice come? I was saluting Umancele yonder." The divination in this case was not successful, and the narrator pathetically regrets that a bullock was given to the diviner for his false information. In another case a woman, who likewise divined by means of spirits, was perfectly correct in all she said. Some members of a family in which a little boy suffered from convulsions went to consult her; and she discovered, or rather the spirits discovered for her, what was the matter with him; what was the relationship of those who had come; and what were their circumstances. She prescribed a remedy, and predicted a complete recovery. The cause of the illness was, according to her, the displeasure of ancestral spirits. A sacrifice was to be offered to them; and the village was to be removed to another place. These things done, she declared that the boy would have no more of the convulsions from which he suffered. If he did, they might take back their money. All turned out as she had said, to the very letter (R. S. A., pt. iii. p. 361-374).

The priests of the North American tribes have a peculiar method of divination. Having received a handful of tobacco as a fee, they will summon a spirit to answer the inquiries of their visitors. This they do by enclosing themselves in lodges, in which they utter incantations. As may be supposed, the spirits who obey the summons of the Indian priest are not much more useful as guides to action than those who figure at the *seance* of his civilized competitor, the medium. Their replies, "though usually clear and correct, are usually of that profoundly ambiguous purport which leaves the anxious inquirer little wiser than he was before" (M. N. W., p. 268). Brinton, however, having stated this, proceeds to speak of cases, apparently well attested, in which the diviners have foreseen coming events with unaccountable clearness. For instance, when Captain Jonathan Carver, in 1767, was among the Killistenoes, and that tribe was suffering from want of food, the chief priest consulted the divinities, and predicted with perfect accuracy the hour on the following day when a canoe would arrive. Brinton adds, on the authority of John Mason Brown, that when Mr. Brown and two companions were pursuing an "apparently hopeless quest" for a band of Indians, they were met by some warriors of that very band, who declared that the appearance of the white man had been exactly described by the medicine-man who had sent them. And what renders the story remarkable is, that "the description was repeated to Mr. Brown by the warriors before they saw his two companions." The priest was unable to explain what he had done, except by saying that "he saw them coming, and heard them talk on their journey" (M. N. W., pp. 270, 271).

Among the Ostiacks in former days, the priests, when they intended to divine, caused themselves to be bound, threw themselves on the ground, and made all sorts of grimaces and contortions till they felt themselves inspired with a reply to the question that had been put to the idol. Those who had come to consult the oracle, sighed and moaned and struck upon certain vessels so as to make a noise, till they saw a bluish vapor, which they conceived to be the spirit of prophecy, and which, while spreading over all the spectators, seized the diviner and caused him to fall into convulsions (Bernard, vol. viii. p. 412).

In ancient China, "the instruments of divination were the shell of the tortoise and the stalks of a certain grass or reed" (C. C., vol. iii. Proleg. p. 196). These are frequently spoken of in the sacred books as the "tortoise and milfoil," and there are historical examples of their employment. The following rules for divination are given by a speaker in the Shoo King:—

"Having chosen and appointed officers for divining by the tortoise and by the milfoil, they are to be charged *on occasion* to perform their duties. *In doing this*, they will find *the appearances* of rain, clearing up, cloudiness, want of connection, and crossing; and *the symbols*, solidity and repentance. In all, *the indications* are seven;—five given by the tortoise, and two by the milfoil, by which the errors of *affairs* may be traced out. These officers having been appointed, when the operations with the tortoise and milfoil are proceeded with, three men are to obtain and interpret the indications and symbols, and the consenting words of two of them are to be followed" (C. C., vol. iii. p. 335).

Further instructions are then given in case the Emperor, nobles, officers, or people, and any or all of these, should disagree with the tortoise and milfoil; the greater weight being given to the latter (Ibid., p. 327).

Of modern divination in China, Dr. Legge recounts the following story:—

"I once saw a father and son divining after one of the fashions of the present day. They tossed the bamboo roots, which came down in the unlucky positions for a dozen times in succession. At last a lucky cast was made. They looked into each other's faces, laughed heartily, and rose up, delighted, from their knees. The divination was now successful, and they dared not repeat it!" (Ibid., Proleg. p. 197).

Here it seems that heaven was merely called in to give its sanction to a foregone conclusion.

The Singhalese have a curious method of discovering, by a species of divination, what god it is who has caused the illness of a patient. "With any little stick," says Knox, "they make a bow, and on the string thereof they hang a thing they have to cut betel-nuts, somewhat like a pair of scissors; then holding the stick or bow by both ends, they repeat the names of all, both god and devils: and when they come to him who hath afflicted them, then the iron or the bowstring will swing" (H. R. C., p. 76).

Divination, as is well known, was regularly practiced by the ancients, who read the will of the gods in the entrails of animals, and who employed, as a help in forseeing the future and guiding their conduct, the class of professional diviners known as augurs.

Another method, by which it has often been supposed that God entered into communication with man, is that of the movements of the stars and planets. Hence the pseudo-science of astrology, which was so much cultivated in the middle ages before its supersession by astronomy. In India, observes Karl Twesten, the stars were very early consulted as oracles. Manu excludes astrologers from the sacrifices; and in later times astrology became very general. According to Twesten, there is an astrologer in almost every Hindu community, who is much consulted, and determines the favorable moment for every important undertaking (R. I., p. 285). Antiquity, wide extension, and great persistency may all be pleaded on behalf of the notion that terrestrial events are forshadowed by a system of celestial signals. There is a touch of astrological belief in the evangelical narrative that the birth of Christ was intimated to the Magi by a star in the east.

Sometimes, when it was desirable not to ascertain future events, but to decide between guilt and innocence, truth and falsehood, the divine Being himself was called in as umpire, and was supposed to convey his judgment by the turn of events in a pre-arranged case. This is the theory of those communi-

cations from God to man which are made by ordeals. Ordeals
were of various kinds, according to the nature of the issue to
be tried. Did one man charge another with some kind of disgraceful conduct, the accuser was summoned to put his words
to the test of a single combat, in which truth was held to lie
on the side of the victor; was an old woman suspected of witchcraft, she was thrown into the nearest pond, with thumbs and
toes tied together, where her floating was regarded as certain
evidence of her guilt. Innocence of legal crime, or in the case
of women, of adultery, has very frequently been established by
the method of ordeals. Several authors have noticed the ordeals in use among the natives on the west coast of Africa.
One of them, writing of Sierra Leone, informs us that if an
accused person can find a chief to patronize him, he is permitted to clear himself by submitting either to have a hot iron
applied to his skin, or to dip his hand in boiling oil to pull out
some object put into it, or to have his tongue stroked with a
red-hot copper ring. Since his being burnt is considered as a
proof of guilt, it would not appear that the chances of escape
were great. "Upon the Gold Coast, the ordeal consists in
chewing the bark of a tree, with a prayer that it may cause
his death if he be not innocent. In the neighborhood of Sierra
Leone," a very peculiar ordeal is practiced, that, namely, of
drinking water prepared from the bark of a certain tree, and
termed "red water." Before taking it, the drinker repeats a
prayer containing an imprecation on himself if guilty. Should
this decoction cause purging or pains in the bowels, it is a
proof of guilt; should it, on the contrary, excite vomiting, and
produce no effect on the bowels for twenty-four hours, an acquittal ensues, and the person who has thus successfully undergone the trial is held in higher esteem than he enjoyed before
(N. A., vol. i. p. 129–133). Sometimes this singular mode of trial
is employed in cases where a corpse is supposed to have accused
some person of causing the death of its former owner (S. L., p.
124–127). On the Gold Coast, "every person entering into any
obligation is obliged to drink the swearing liquor." Thus,
should one nation intend to assist another, "all the chief ones
are obliged to drink this liquor, with an imprecation that their
fetiche may punish them with death if they do not assist them

with utmost vigor to extirpate their enemy." Since, however, a dispensing power over such oaths has been exercised by the priests, some negroes observe the precaution, before taking oaths, of causing the priest to swear first, and then drink the red water, with an imprecation that the fetich may punish him if he absolves any one without the consent of all the parties interested in the contract (D. C. G., pp. 124, 125).

The sanction of Scripture is given to an ordeal of precisely this nature is the case of women charged with adultery; and it is curious to find the very same mode of testing the fidelity of wives employed both by the ancient Hebrews and modern negroes. The law of Moses was, that if a man suspected his wife of unfaithfulness, and the "spirit of jealousy" came upon him, he might take her to the priest (with an offering, of course), and leave him to deal with her in the following manner: Taking holy water in an earthen vessel, the priest was to mix in it some of the dust of the floor of the tabernacle, and set the woman with her head uncovered, and the jealousy offering in her hands, "before the Lord." He was then to "charge her with an oath," saying, that if she was pure, she was to be free from the bitter water that caused the curse, but if not, the Lord was to make her a curse and an oath among her people, causing her hips (or thighs) [to disappear and her belly to swell. The water was to go into her bowels to produce these effects. Hereupon the woman was to say, "Amen, amen." According to the effects of the bitter water upon her constitution, was her guilt or her innocence adjudged to be (Num. v. 11-31).

Now the procedure of the negroes, in similar cases, is almost an exact reproduction (it can scarcely be an imitation) of that enjoined by Jehovah. "Red water" is administered, instead of "bitter water;" but with this exception, precisely the same method is pursued, and precisely the same doctrine underlies the use of the ordeal. God is expected, both by Jews and negroes, to manifest the truth where human skill is incompetent to discover it. The negroes, according to Bosman, believe that where the red water is drunk by one who makes a false declaration, he will either "be swelled by that liquor till he bursts," or will "shortly die of a languishing sickness; the first punishment they imagine more peculiar to women, who take this draught to acquit them of any accusation of adultery :" a belief which curiously reminds us of the old Jewish superstition, that the hips will fall away and the belly swell in the case of the adulterous wife who has taken the bitter water on a false pretence. Bosman himself has correctly observed on the remarkable similarity of the two procedures (D. C. G., p. 125).

A slightly different mode of trying suspected adultresses by ordeal prevails among the Ostiacks (in Northern Asia). Should an Ostiack entertain doubts of his wife's fidelity, he cuts off a handful of hair from a bear's skin, and takes it to her. If innocent, she receives it without hesitation; but if guilty, she does not venture to touch it, and is accordingly repudiated. The conviction reigns among these people, that were a woman to lie under these circumstances, the bear to whom the hair belonged would revive in three days and come to devour her (Bernard, vol. viii. pp. 44, 45).

More important, however, and more universal than any of the above means of communication from God to man, is the method of communication by miracles. There is probably no great religion in the world, the establishment of which has been altogether dissociated from miracles. They form the most striking, most indisputable, most intelligible proof of the divine will. Not indeed that there is any close logical connection between the performance of a wonder, and the truth of the wonder-worker's doctrines; but popular imagination jumps readily to the conclusion that a man, whom rumor or tradition has invested with supernatural powers over nature, must also be in possession of correct opinions, or even of superhuman knowledge, on the mysterious questions with which religion deals. Hence ecclesiastical historians, of all ages and countries, have sought to show that those from whom they deduced the systems in which they wished their readers to believe, were either themselves gifted with thaumaturgic faculties, or were the subjects of special marvels worked upon them. Such miracles have always served as their credentials, indicating their high character, and entitling them to demand the obedience of mankind to the commands they brought.

The establishment of Buddhism, for example, was attended by the performance of extraordinary miracles. Not only did the

Buddha himself frequently perform supernatural feats; not only did his disciples, when they attained a certain grade of sanctity, receive the faculty of flying and doing other wonderful things; but he actually proved the superiority of his claims over those of others by a pitched battle in thaumaturgy. Certain Tirthyas, or heretical teachers, had the audacity to challenge him to contend with them in working miracles, and the trial of skill ended, of course, in their ignominious defeat (H. B. I., p. 162–189). Much in the same way did Moses enter into a rivalry with Pharaoh's magicians, who were overcome by his superior miracles as the Tirthyas were by those of Gautama Buddha. As Jewish prophets and Christian saints received by spiritual inheritance the power of performing miracles, so also did the Fathers of Buddhism. Of one of the greatest of these, named Nagardjuna, it is related that a Brahman who had entered into a dispute with him produced a magical pond, in the middle of which was a lotus with a thousand leaves, but that Nagardjuna produced a magical elephant which destroyed the magical pond (Wassiljew, p. 234). This again may remind us of the serpent of Moses, which swallowed up the serpents of the magicians; or of the fire brought down from heaven by Elijah in his controversy with the prophets of Baal. Another eminent Buddhist, Asvagosha, was remarkable as a preacher. The officials at the court of a certain king reproached him with holding this holy man in too high esteem. The king thereupon took seven horses, kept them six days without food, and then led them to the place where Asvagosha was preaching to be fed. The horses would not touch the food that was offered, but shed tears at the words of the preacher (Wassiljew, p. 232).

The history of the Mongols records some equally wonderful performances on the part of a Lama (or priest) named Bogda. When some messengers came to meet him, he raised his hand in a threatening way against a river, the waters of which immediately began to run upwards instead of downwards; "by which miracle," observes the historian, "an unshakeable faith was established in all minds." No wonder. The division of the Red Sea and the Jordan were child's play to this. The same man caused many others to believe by suddenly producing a spring in a dry place. In another country which he visited, he subdued all the dragons and other baneful creatures to his will (G. O. M., p. 227).

If the founder of the Mussulman religion did not claim any direct power of performing miracles, yet the communication to him of the Suras which compose the the Koran was a standing miracle. He professed to fall into an ecstatic condition, in which he received the direct instructions of his God; and his care, when entering the sick-room of a friend, to avoid treading on the angels' wings which he saw extended in all directions, indicates a pretension to more than human faculties. The present votaries of the Mohammedan faith believe in the power of their saints to work miracles, for we read of the sick being taken to their Sheik to be cured by the imposition of his feet (Dervishes, p. 347).

That the Christian religion was largely indebted to miracles for its success during its early years need hardly be remarked. Not only did Christ himself perform miracles of the most extraordinary kind, but the power was, if not wholly, yet to some extent, transmitted to his apostles, and was frequently exercised by the saints and Fathers of the early Church. Jesus himself, according to tradition, relied largely on his miracles as proofs of his divine mission; for when John the Baptist sent disciples to inquire who he was, he replied by telling them to report to their master that the blind received sight, the lame walked, the lepers were cleansed, the deaf heard, the dead were raised up, and the poor had the gospel preached to them. So that the possession of this unusual gift of healing and re-animating, was regarded by him (or, more accurately, by his biographers) as a sufficient answer to the doubt entertained by John whether he were really the Messiah, or whether another were to come.

How great was the importance attached to the possession of miraculous powers by the early Christian Church, may be gathered from a passage in which Irenæus endeavors to cover certain heretics with confusion, by asserting that they are unable to do the things that are commonly done by the adherents of the true faith. "For they can neither confer sight on the blind, nor hearing on the deaf, nor chase away all sorts of demons — [none, indeed], except those that are sent into others

by themselves, if they can even do so much as this. Nor can
they cure the weak, or the lame, or the paralytic, or those who
are distressed in any other part of the body, as has often been
done in regard to bodily infirmity. Nor can they furnish effec-
tive remedies for those external accidents which may occur.
And so far are they from being able to raise the dead, as the
Lord raised them, and the apostles did by means of prayer, and
as has been frequently done in the brotherhood on account of
some necessity—the entire Church in that particular locality
entreating [the boon] with much fasting and prayer, the spirit
of the dead man has returned, and he has been bestowed in
answer to the prayers of the saints—that they do not even
believe this can possibly be done, [and hold] that the resurrection from the dead is simply an acquaintance with that truth
which they proclaim."* Thus, the cure of infirmities and diseases by supernatural means were every-day achievements of
the early Christians; and even the dead were sometimes restored
to life, when sufficient pains were taken to obtain the favorable
attention of the Almighty. "It is not possible," observes the
same author in another place, "to name the number of the
gifts which the Church [scattered] throughout the whole world
has received from God, in the name of Jesus Christ, who was
crucified under Pontius Pilate, and which she exerts day by day
for the benefit of the Gentiles."†

Hence the Mormons, who claim to possess at the present day
the powers which have departed from Christians in general, are
perfectly in accordance with Irenæus in holding that signs like
these are invariably attendant on the kingdom of God. Revelations, visions, the powers of prophecy, of healing, of speaking
with tongues, of casting out devils, and working other miracles,
are (they contend) the prerogatives of those who belong to this
kingdom. History, in relating first the miracles of the Jewish
patriarchs and prophets, then those of the Christian Fathers,
powerfully supports this theory. Scripture in several unambiguous passages entirely confirms it. And the daily experience of
the Latter-day Saints, if we accept their statements, bears witness to its truth, by presenting abundant examples of the

* Irenæus adv. Hæreses, II. xxxi. 2.—A. N. L., vol. v. p. 241.   † Ibid., II.,
xxxii. 4.—A. N. L., vol. v. p. 246.

actual exercise of such supernatural gifts within their own society. Thus, one person is cured of blindness; another of dislocation of the thigh; another has his fractured backbone restored; in the fourth case it is a rupture that is healed; in the fifth convulsive fits that are stopped.* I have myself been present at a Mormon meeting for public worship, and have heard the saints who were gathered together narrate, with perfect solemnity and apparent good faith, the miraculous cures which they themselves experienced, or which they had personally witnessed. One after another rose to bear his testimony to some case of the kind which had fallen within his immediate knowledge. To these uncultivated and fanatical people, holy events still were what they have long ceased to be to the ordinary Christian world—living realities; and we may still study in them the mental condition of those who could accept as phenomena occurring in their own day the restoration of sight, hearing, or speech; the expulsion of devils; and the resurrection of the dead.

* For the evidence of these miracles, see a paper by the author on " The Latter-day Saints," in the *Fortnightly Review* for December, 1869.

CHAPTER II.

"DRAW not nigh hither," said the occupant of the burning bush to Moses; "put off thy shoes from off thy feet; for the place whereon thou standest is holy ground" (Exod. iii. 5). This verse embodies the universal theory of holy places. They are spots occupied in a special and peculiar manner by the deity or his representative; and where he finds it easier to communicate with mankind than it is elsewhere. Hence, those who hope or desire to receive some celestial intimation, resort to such holy places. The oracles of the ancient world, and the temple at Jerusalem, are instances of holy places where the respective gods worshiped by those who frequented them gave responses, or manifested their presence. Holy places are not always consecrated places. Sometimes — as in the case of the Delphian oracle — the consecration is the work of nature; the divinity intimates in some unmistakable way his presence in the sanctuary which he has himself selected; and human beings have nothing to do but humbly to receive such communications as he may desire to make. Frequently, however, holy places have only become holy by the act of consecration; the local god has not occupied them until they have been duly prepared for him by human labor. On the other hand, consecrated places are always holy places. Not indeed that there are always conspicuous intimations of the divine presence; but it is nevertheless vaguely supposed to haunt the buildings where worship is offered, and rites are performed, more than it does the outer world.

To begin with a few instances of holy places which have not undergone consecration. On the coast of Guinea "almost every village hath a small appropriated grove. ' Offerings are made in these groves, and they are regarded as so sacred that no one ventures to injure the trees by plucking, cutting, or breaking their branches. "Universal malediction" would be one of the consequences of such misconduct (D. C. G., p. 128). Mr. Turner states that "as of old in Canaan, sacred *groves* for heathen worship, with and without temples, were quite common in the islands of the Pacific" (N. Y., p. 329). These are instances of the sacredness so frequently attached to woods and forests by primitive nations.

> "The groves were God's first temples. Ere man learned
> To hew the shaft, and lay the architrave,
> And spread the roof above them; ere he framed
> The lofty vault, to gather and roll back
> The sound of anthems,—in the darkling wood,
> Amidst the cool and silence he knelt down,
> And offered to the Mightiest solemn thanks
> And supplication."*

Natural characteristics in the same manner determine the quality of holiness attributed to certain spots by the natives of Africa. Holy places among them are those where a god dwells either visibly or invisibly; particular buildings, huts, or hills; or trees which are remarkable for age, size and strength. They have also sacred groves into which no negro, not being a priest ventures to intrude. One of the tribes asserts that their god has his dwelling-place in the cavern of a rock that is situated in the bushes (G. d. M., p. 326).

A singular example of a holy place in a more advanced religion is the neighborhood of the Bo tree, or Bogaha tree, in Ceylon, under whose shade the people worship at the great festival. This tree derives its sanctity from the circumstance of its having sheltered Buddha at an eventful crisis of his life. Near it ninety kings are interred; huts are erected around it for the use of the devotees who repair to it; and as "every sort of uncleanness and dust must be removed from the sacred spot," the approaches are continually swept by persons appointed for the purpose. Besides the Bo tree, and the pagodas—or public

* Bryant, a Forest Hymn.

temples — many of the Singhalese have private holy places in their own houses. They "build in their yards *private* chapels, which are little houses like to closets," and in these they place an image of the Buddha which they worship (H. R. C., p. 73).

Graves of the dead whom we have loved are apt to become holy places to us all; and in some religious creeds, such as those of Islam and Christianity, this veneration is extended to the tombs of persons who have been distinguished by their sanctity. Mussulmans "pray at the tomb of those they repute saints;" and expect by offering vows at such places, to obtain "relief, through their saintly intercession, from sickness, misfortune, sterility, &c." Miracles take place at these tombs, and supernatural lights float over them (Dervishes, pp. 79, 80). It is believed, too, that "the merits of the deceased will insure a favorable reception of the prayers which they offer up in such consecrated places" (Dervishes, p. 272).

Sometimes, again, the place where some striking event in the history of religion has occurred, acquires a holiness of its own. Thus the Scala Santa at Rome enjoys a preëminent holiness possessing the merit of procuring a considerable remission of punishment for those who perform the task of ascending it on their knees.

The oracle of Clarius Apollo at Colophon, mentioned by Tacitus, is an example of a large and important class of holy places which were not consecrated places. Here it was not a woman, as at Delphi (observes Tacitus), who gave the responses; but a priest, who descended into a cavern, and drank water from a secret fountain (Tac. Ann., ii. 54). In Jewish history we meet with a remarkable instance of a place originally hallowed by the actual appearance of God, in the case of Beth-el, "the house of God," where Jacob was favored with his remarkable dream. "How dreadful is this place!" exclaimed the patriarch on waking; "this is none other but the house of God, and this is the gate of heaven" (Gen. xxviii. 17). In the spot whose holiness had thus been rendered manifest, Jacob proceeded to perform consecrating rites; but, contrary to the usual order, the holiness preceeded and induced the consecration.

More generally, consecration forms a sort of invitation to the deity to inhabit the place which has thus been rendered

suited to his abode. Of the holy places which are also consecrated, a conspicuous place is due to Solomon's temple; in the
dedication of which the theory just stated is clearly embodied.
Solomon, or his historians, perceived the difficulty of causing a
being so transcendently powerful as Jehovah to dwell within
local limits. The monarch, in his consecrating prayer, explains
that he is well aware that even the heaven of heavens cannot
contain him; much less this house that he has built. Nevertheless, he cannot give up the notion that this house may, in some
degree, be peculiarly favored by having his especial attention
directed towards it. His eyes at least may be open towards it,
and if he cannot be there himself, his name may. Moreover,
when prayers are offered in the temple, he may listen to them
more graciously than to other supplications; and when the
asseverations of contending parties are confirmed by oaths
taken before the altar it contains, he may take unusual pains
to execute justice between them. Jehovah fully approves of his
servant's proposals. He emphatically declares in reply that he
has hallowed this house which he has built, to put his name
there for ever; and that his eyes and his heart shall be there
pepetually (Kings viii. 22—ix. 3).

Very primitive peoples hold similar views of the relation of
their deities to their temples. Just as there was "an oracle"
in the Jewish temple, where "the glory of the Lord filled the
house of the Lord, as it had filled the corresponding place in
the tabernacle, so in most of the Fijian temples there is "a
shrine, where the god is supposed to descend when holding
communication with the priests; and there is also a long piece
of native cloth hung at one end of the building, and from the
very ceiling, which is also connected with the arrival and
departure of the god invoked" (Viti, p. 393). It seems to have
been a general rule in the temples of these islands to have
some object specially connected with the deity, and through
which he might manifest his presence in the place. Thus, in
one of them there was a conch shell, which "the god was supposed to blow when he wished the people to rise to war" (N. Y.,
p. 240). Nay, there was even an altar erected to Jehovah and
Jesus Christ in one of the islands, "to which persons afflicted
with all manner of diseases were brought to be healed; and so

great was the reputation which this maræ obtained, that the
power of Jehovah and Jesus Christ became great in the estimation of the people" (N. M. E., p. 28). Here an altar, erected of
course by a man not yet converted to Christianity, received a
blessing no less conspicuous than that granted in ancient times
to Solomon's temple.

The Mexicans and Peruvians entertained a precisely similar
belief to that which we have observed among the Fijians and
the Hebrews. Father Acosta describes the ruins of a very large
building in Peru which had been a place of worship, where
immense plunder had been carried off by the Christians. In
this temple there was a sure tradition that "the devil" had
spoken, and given responses in his oracle. The fact of the devil
speaking and answering in these false sanctuaries is, according to
the learned father, a very common thing in America; but the
father of lies has become silent since the sign of the cross has
been raised in those regions of his previous power (H. I., b. v.
ch. 12). Not only were the temples holy in Peru, but the whole
of the imperial city of Cozco, the residence of the Incas, enjoyed
an exceptional holiness. So much was this the case, that if two
natives of equal rank met one another on the road, the one
coming from Cozco, and the other going to it, the one coming
from it received respect and reverence from the one going to
it, which was enhanced to a higher degree if he were a native
of Cozco (C. R., b. iii. ch. 20). In approaching the great temple at Cozco, there were certain limits where all who passed were
obliged to take off their shoes: the very same sign of regard for
holy places which Moses was commanded to observe at the burning bush; which is practiced by Parsee priests when ministering
in their temples, and by Mussulmans in reference to their
mosques (Ibid., b. iii. ch. 23).

Prohibition to all but holy persons to enter holy places is
not uncommon. The holy of holies in the Jewish temple might
be entered by no one but the high priest, and the utmost horror was felt by the Jews at the violation of their sanctuary by
Pompey. A European traveler in Africa, finding a grove with
a mat hung before it, wished to enter; but was entreated not
to do so by the negroes, who informed him that a great spirit,
who might kill him if displeased, dwelt within. He, however,

went in, and found a delightful place; this being one of those to which only priests were admitted (G. d. M., p. 326). Similarly among the Parsees, the Atesch-gâh, or holy place where worship is performed, may be entered only by the priests, except under special circumstances, when laymen may enter it after due observance of preparatory rites, and with the face covered. Such a case would occur if there were no priest to keep up the sacred fire (Z. A., vol. ii. p. 569). In Mexico, where there were two important holy places—the Cu, or great temple of Vitzili-putzli, and the temple of Tezcatlipuca—the priests alone had the right of entry to this last (H. I., b. 5, ch. 13).

We thus find, among the several nations of the world, a consistent and all-pervading theory of holy places. These are not always the scenes of divine revelations, or of striking events produced by the divine agency; but they are much more likely to be so favored than other places, and if communications are distinctly sought, it must generally be by resorting to such local sanctuaries as are commonly reputed to be fitted for the purpose. Where no revelation is either given or expected, the holy place is yet the abiding home of the deity whose worship is celebrated within its enclosure. And although Christians may consider their God as present everywhere, yet they are conscious on entering a church, of coming, in a peculiar sense, into his presence; and they indicate that consciousness by removing their hats, if men, and keeping the head covered, if women. For such is the outward indication of respect which the Christian God is supposed to require of those who set their feet within his holy places.

CHAPTER III.

WHILE a highly-exalted conception of the First cause of nature would see him equally in everything, and believe the whole world to be alike natural and divine, no actual religion, believed by any considerable number of persons, has ever reached so abstract an idea. To all of them some things are more sacred than others; in the more primitive forms of faith these things are either a species of divinities themselves, or they are the abode of some divinity; in the more advanced types, they are held to be sanctified by the power of God, or to be the earthly representatives of his invisible majesty. To the class of holy objects belong all charms, amulets, fetishes, sacred animals, and other things of whatever kind, which are believed in any country to possess a different order of powers from those which scientific investigation discovers in them.

The theory underlying the use of such objects among the negroes — and it is practically the same as that of more civil- ized nations — is well explained by a German missionary. "Fe- tishes, or Shambu," according to him, "are holy things, which are supposed to have received a particular power from God, both to drive away evil spirits, as also to be useful in all ill- nesses and dangers, especially against sorcery." They cover both themselves and their gods with fetishes. These descend from father to son, and are preserved with the greatest care. Some are kept in sanctuaries of their own. There exists among these negroes (the Mavu) a class of professional fetish-makers, who are mostly old women, and who wear a peculiar dress. A man, who had fetishes at the bottom of his staircase, informed the writer that their use was to keep the devil from getting into his house. Another tribe of negroes prefer to take things which

132

have been struck by lightning for their fetishes: the lightning-stroke being, as the missionary justly concludes, an indication that a divine power has united itself to these objects (G. d. M., pp. 322, 323).

The natives of Sierra Leone are described as placing unlimited faith in "griggories," or charms. These are made of goats' skin; texts of the Koran are written upon them, and they are worn upon various parts of the person. They have distinct functions, each one being designed to preserve the wearer from a certain kind of evil or danger (S. L., p. 132).

Numerous objects were holy in Peru. Rivers, fountains, large stones, hills, the tops of mountains, are mentioned by Acosta as having been adored by the Peruvians; indeed, he says that they adored whatever natural object appeared very different from the rest, recognizing therein some peculiar deity.

A certain tree, for instance, which was cut down by the Spaniards, had long been an object of adoration to the Indians, on account of its antiquity and size (H. I., b. 5, ch. 5). In another part of the American continent, the neighborhood of Acadia, a traveler tells us of a venerable tree which was likewise holy. Many marvels were recounted of it. and it was always loaded with offerings. The sea having washed the soil from about its roots, it maintained itself a long time "almost in the air," which confirmed the savages in their notion that it was "the seat of some great spirit;" and even after it had fallen, its branches, so long as they were visible above the surface of the water, continued to receive the worship of the people (N. F., vol. iii. p. 349).

Not unfrequently the holy object is an animal, and then it may be regarded either as itself a god, or as sacred to some god, who either makes it in some sense his abode, or regards it with favor and takes it under his care. Among animals, there is none more frequently worshiped than the serpent; and it has been supposed, with some plausibility, that the Hebrew legend of the fall was directed against serpent-worship. However this may be, that worship is clearly discernible in the story of the brazen serpent which healed the sickness of the Israelites in the wilderness (Num. xxi. 8). This would seem to be a dim tradition of a time at which the adoration of the ser-

pent was still practiced by the people of Jehovah. Many other
countries afford examples of the same worship. To take a
single case; the Chevalier des Marchais, who traveled in the
last century, relates that serpents of a certain kind were worshiped in Guinea. There was one, however, which was called
the father of these gods, and was reputed to be of prodigious
size. It was kept in a place of its own, where it had "secret
apartments," and none but the chief sacrificer was permitted to
enter this holy of holies. The king himself might only see it
once, when, three months after his coronation, he went to present his offerings (V. G., vol. ii. p. 169).

Even Christianity did not entirely put an end to the worship of the serpent; for an early Christian writer, in a treatise against all heresies, makes mention of a sect of Ophites
who (he says) "magnify the serpent to such a degree, that they
prefer him even to Christ himself; for it was he, they say, who
gave us the origin of the knowledge of good and evil. His
power and majesty (they say) Moses perceiving, set up the
brazen serpent; and whoever gazed upon him obtained health.
Christ himself (they say further) imitates Moses serpent's
sacred power in saying: 'And as Moses upreared the serpent in
the desert, so it behoveth the Son of man to be upreared.'
Him they introduce to bless their eucharistic [elements]" (Adv.
omn. haereses., II.— A. N. L., vol. 18, p. 262).

Holy objects are very often connected with some eminent
man, from whose relation to them they derive their sanctity.
Such are all the innumerable relics of saints to which so much
importance is attached in Catholic countries. Such is that pre-
eminently sacred relic, the tooth of Buddha, so carefully preserved and guarded in Ceylon. When Major Forbes witnessed
the tooth festival at Kandy, fifty-three years had passed since
the last exhibition of this deeply revered member of the founder
of the faith. It was kept in its temple within six cases; of
which the three larger ones having been first removed, the
three inner ones, containing it, were placed "on the back of an
elephant richly caparisoned." It was shown to the people on a
temporary altar, surrounded with rich hangings; the festival
being attended by crowds of pious worshipers, who thought
that the privilege of seeing the tooth, so rarely exhibited to the

public, was a sufficient proof of the merits they had obtained in former lives (E. Y), vol. i. p. 290–293).

Mussulmans have their holy objects, consisting of verses of the Koran, suspended or written on their dwellings, which are supposed to insure their protection. Such verses, or short Suras, are sometimes carried on the person engraved on stones (Dervishes, p. 313).

Conspicuous among holy objects for the extraordinary virtues ascribed to them, are the bread and wine of the Lord's supper. These are believed by Christians either to be or to represent (according to their several doctrines) the actual flesh and blood of Jesus; and the mere fact of eating and drinking them, in faith, is held to exercise a mystic efficacy over the life of the communicant. A more singular instance of the holiness attributed by an act of the imagination to material things can scarcely be produced. Another curious case of the same notion is the belief in holy water; which enjoys so great a power, that some drops of it dashed upon an infant's forehead contribute to ensure its eternal happiness; while it has also the gift of conferring some kind of advantage upon the worshipers who, on entering a church, sprinkle it upon their persons.

Images of the gods or saints worshiped in a country form a large and important class of holy objects. Such were the "teraphim" or "gods" stolen by Rachel from her father, and which she concealed in the furniture of her camel (Gen. xxxi. 19, 30–35). Similar images are employed by the Tartars, who place them at the heads and feet of their beds in certain fixed positions, and who carry them about with them wherever they go (Bergeron, Voyage de Rubruquis, ch. 3, p. 9).

CHAPTER IV.

RITES, acts of worship and sacrifices, originally performed by each individual at his own discretion, or by each household in its own way, fall (as we have seen) with advancing development into the hands of professional persons consecrated for this especial purpose. Very great importance attaches to these consecrated persons. The place they occupy in all societies above the level of barbarism is one of peculiar honor; and their influence on the course of human history has in all ages with which that history is acquainted been conspicuous and profound. Once devoted to their religious duties, they become the authorized representatives of deity on earth. In treating of their consecration, we consider them as channels of communication from earth to heaven; we have now to consider them as channels of communication from heaven to earth.

Endowed by the general wish of all human society with a special right to convey their petitions to the divine beings whom they worship, they do not fail to claim for themselves the correlative right of conveying to men the commands, the intentions, the reproofs, and the desires of these divine beings. It is the priests alone who can pretend to know their minds. It is the priests alone who can correctly interpret their often enigmatic language. It is the priests alone through whom they generally deign to converse with mortals.

Such is the ecclesiastical theory throughout the world; and it is as a general rule accepted by the communities for whose guidance it is constructed. Exceptions do indeed present themselves, above all in the case of the remarkable men whose careers we shall deal with in the ensuing chapter, who have founded new religions independently of, or even in spite of, very powerful existing priesthoods. And, speaking generally, the holy class is not always coëxtensive with the consecrated class. We shall notice further on an important order among the Jews who were universally received as holy, without being consecrated. Moreover, there has often existed a species of men who, without regular consecration, have nevertheless served as a channel of communication from God or from inferior spirits to man. Such were magicians, astrologers, "et hoc genus omne," in ancient times; such are the so-called mediums in the present day. Conversely, consecration, though by its very nature implying holiness as its correlative, implies it less and less as we rise in the scale of culture. Thus, in the more advanced forms of Protestantism, such as the Presbyterian or the Unitarian, the minister is scarcely more than a mere teacher; he has little or no more power to convey commands or intimations from God than any member of his congregation. So that we should have a rough approximation to the truth were we to say that in the lower grades of religious culture we have holy orders without consecration; while in the higher grades we have consecrated orders without holiness.

Between these extremes there lies the great body of regular and qualified priests, appointed to communicate upwards, and entitled to communicate downwards. Invasions of their authority by irregular pretenders are the exceptions, not the rule. It is the usual order of things, that the decisions of priests on matters pertaining to religion should be accepted in submissive faith, by the societies to which they belong. Where, as in the case of Jesus of Nazareth, some bold individual brushes aside successfully the pretentions of ecclesiastical castes, the theory is only modified to suit the individual instance. Ecclesiastical castes, deriving their title from the innovator himself, spring up again at once; and differ only in so far as the God whose will they expound is either another God, or a new modification of the same God.

Numerous privileges are generally accorded to priests. Sometimes they enjoy exemptions from the operation of the ordinary laws; sometimes they are permitted a disproportionate share in the government of their country; sometimes, without possessing recognized legislative powers, they control the destinies of nations by the expression of their views. Often, the whole physical force of the government is at their disposal, for the propagation and support of the system they uphold; occasionally, when their authority has reached its highest point, the mere solemn declaration of their commands is enough to ensure the acquiescence of monarchs and the obedience of their subjects. Corresponding to these considerable rights, they perform a considerable variety of functions, which are regarded by the societies who employ them as not only useful, but indispensable. We find them in all primitive communities acting as the recognized doctors of the people, treating their diseases by the method of supernatural inspiration. Rising a little higher, they predict that class of events which is so interesting to each individual, namely, the prospects of his or her life. In other words, they become fortune-tellers, astrologers, or (by whatever means) readers of the future. Or they control the weather, calling down from heaven the needful rain. They are inspired by the deity in whose service they are enrolled, and they announce his will. In his name they threaten evil-doers with punishment, and promise rewards to the faithful and obedient. Benefits from on high are declared to be the lot of those who pay them honor. They proclaim the fact that their presence is essential to the performance of important rites, and that their assistance at these must be duly rewarded. Sometimes they are in possession of knowledge which is only permitted to be imparted to their own caste. They are at all times the authorized expositors of theological dogma, and the authorized guardians of public ritual.

Let us enter on a more detailed account of these several characteristics of the priestly order.

First, it has to be noted that the differentiation of this order from the rest of society is in primitive communities very incomplete. Fathers of families, or any venerable and respected men, act as priests, and perform the requirements of divine worship according to their own notions of propriety. Thus in Samoa, Mr. Turner tells us that "the father of the family was *the high-priest*, and usually offered a short prayer at the evening meal, that they might all be kept from fines, sickness, war, and death." He also directed on what occasions religious festivals should be held, and it was supposed that the god sometimes spoke through the father or another member of the family (N. Y., p. 239). So in the early period of the history of the Israelites, there was no formal and regular priesthood, and no established ritual. The Levites were not devoted to the functions they subsequently discharged, until, in the course of the Exodus, they had proved their qualification by the holy zeal with which they slaughtered their brethren. It was for the perpetration of this massacre that they were promised by Moses the blessing of God (Exod. xxxii. 25–29). With advancing culture, the necessity for separating priests from laymen is always felt. The ministrations of unskilled hands are not held to be sufficient. Ritual grows fixed; and for a fixed ritual there must be a special apprenticeship. Ceremonies multiply; and the original family prayer having grown into a more elaborate system of worship, takes more time, and demands the attention of a class who make this, and kindred matters, their exclusive occupation.

While, however, the ministers of the gods are thus differentiated from the people at large, they are not differentiated until a later stage from the ministers of the human body. Medicine and priestcraft are for a long time united arts. On this connection, Brinton very justly remarks, that "when sickness is looked upon as the effect of the anger of a god, or as the malicious infliction of a sorcerer, it is natural to seek help from those who assume to control the unseen world, and influence the fiats of the Almighty" (M. N. W., p. 264). Thus in America the native priests were called by the European colonists, "medicine men." The New Zealand priests were "expert jugglers," and when called in to the sick would ascribe some diseases to a piece of wood lodged in the stomach; this they pretended to extract, and produced it in evidence of their assertion. An acquaintance of the author from whom I borrow this fact, saw one of these doctors tear open the leg of a rheumatic patient, and (apparently) take out of it a knotted piece of wood (N. Z., p. 80). In the Fiji islands they occasionally use their medical powers malevolently, instead of benevolently. In Tanna, there was a class of men termed "disease-makers," and greatly dreaded by the people, who thought that these men could exer-

cise the power of life and death, the calamity of death being
the result of burning rubbish belonging to the sufferer. When
a Tannese was ill, he believed that the disease-maker was burning his rubbish, and would send large presents to induce him
to stop; for if it were all burned he would die (N. Y. p. 89–91).
The Samoans believed disease to be the result of divine wrath,
and sought its remedy at the hands of the high-priest of the
village. Whatever he might demand was given; in some cases,
however, he did not ask for anything, but merely commanded
the family of the patient to "confess, and throw out." Confessing, and throwing out, consisted of a statement by each
member of the family of the crimes he had committed, or of
the evil he had invoked on the patient or his connections, accompanied by the ceremony of spurting out water from the
mouth towards him (N. Y., p. 224). Like the Fijians, the natives
of Australia employ priests to cure their illnesses. Their ecclesiastical practitioners "perform incantations over the sick," and
also pretend to suck out the disease, producing a piece of bone
which they assert to be its cause (S. L. A., p. 226). The Africans have an exactly similar belief in the influence of fetish
over disease. Reade observes that epileptic attacks are (as is
natural from their mysterious character) ascribed to demoniacal
possession, and that fetish-men are called in to cure them. This
they attempt to accomplish by elaborate dances and festivities,
"at the expense of the next of kin," which sometimes end in
driving the patient into the bush in a state of complete insanity. When cured, he "builds a little fetish-house, avoids certain kinds of food, and performs certain duties" (S. A., p. 251).
The negroes on the coast of Guinea, when ill, apply to their
priest, who informs them what offerings are required to ensure
their recovery (D. C. G., p. 213). When an Amazulu is troubled
by bad dreams, he applies to a diviner, who recommends certain ceremonies by which the spirit causing the dreams is supposed to be banished. Should he be ill, his friends apply to the
diviner, who discovers the source of the illness, and probably
demands the sacrifice of a bullock. A remarkable sensitiveness
about the shoulders indicates the spiritual character of the doc-
tor. If he fail to remove disease, he is said to have no "It-
ongo," or spirit, in him (R. S. A., pt. ii. pp. 159, 160, 172). The

Fida negroes sent to consult their divine snake through a priest
when ill, and the priest (unless he announced that the disease
would be fatal) received a reward for indicating the remedies to
be used. Moreover, the priests were the physicians of the negroes. Two theories prevailed among the people as to the origin of illnesses. Some tribes held them to be due to evil spirits,
who were accordingly driven away by a prescribed system of
armed pursuit. But the priests in other places regarded them
as a consequence of discord between spirit and soul, and required
the patient in the first instance to confess his sins. This being
done, they obtain from their deity an indication of the offerings
to be made, or the vows to be fulfilled, to restore mental harmony. They then undertook the treatment of the body by
physical means (G. d. M., pp. 335, 336). In Sierra Leone, as in
other parts of Africa, "the practice of medicine, and the art of
making greegrees and fetishes, in other words, amulets . . .
is generally the province of the same person." Those who
practice medicine are looked upon as witches, and believed not
only to converse with evil spirits, but to exercise control over
them (N. A., vol. i. p. 251). In New France, in the eighteenth
century, the principal occupation of the native priests was medicine (N. F. vol. iii. p. 364). In Mexico, the people came from
all parts to the priests to be annointed with the peculiar ungent used in the special consecration mentioned above (*Supra*,
p. 116). This they termed a "divine physic," and considered as
a cure for their diseases (H. I., b. 5, ch. 26).

Such rude notions as these, implying a supernatural as opposed to a natural thory of the physical conditions of the body,
are not wholly extinct even among ourselves They exist, like
so many of the crude conceptions of the savage, in the form of
respected survivals wholly inconsistent with our practical habits.
True, we do not call in the clergyman to assist or to direct at
the sick-bed. But we do ask him to put up prayers for the
recovery of the sick; and in the case of royal princes, the clergy
throughout the land are set to work to induce the divine Being
to give their illnesses a favorable turn. Now, this proceeding,
however disguised under refined and imposing forms, is practically on a level with that of the Amazulu, who seeks to pacify
the offended spirit that has attacked him with pain by the sac-

rifice of a bullock; or with that of the Fijian who, when his
friend is ill, blows a shell for hours as a call to the disease-
maker to stop burning the sick man's rubbish, and as a sign
that presents will speedily reach his hands. Nay, the very missionary who relates this Fiji custom gives at least one proof of
his fitness to understand the native mind, in a passage showing
that in reference to beliefs like these his own was almost on a
par with it. A war, of which the missionaries disapproved, had
been going on for four months, "and the end of it was, the war
was raised against ourselves. After they had been fighting for
months among themselves, contrary to all our entreaties, God
commenced to punish them with a deadly epidemic in the form
of dysentery." Now, the conviction that diseases are punishments sent by some god, or at any rate direct results of an
intention on the part of some god to harm the sufferer, is at
the root of the priestly, as opposed to the scientific, treatment.
For if God punishes with a deadly epidemic, it is an obvious
inference that the mode of cure and of prevention is not to take
physical remedies, and observe physical precautions, but to
avoid the sin for which the punishment is given. And this is
the common conclusion of the savage and the Christian, though
the superior information of the Christian renders his conduct
self-contradictory and confused, where that of the savage is
logical and simple.

Nearly related to the supposed influence of priests over physical suffering, is their supposed power to foretell the future.
Here, however, a number of unauthorized and schismatic priesthoods often enter into competition with those sanctioned by the
state. Technically, they would not be termed priests at all; but
tested by the true mark of priesthood, the gift, alleged by themselves and admitted by others, of forming channels of communication from the celestial powers to man, they are entitled to
that name, and this although they may perhaps receive no regular consecration to their office. The Roman Senate during the
Empire came into frequent collision with these irregular priests.
It endeavored from time to time to combat the growing belief
in the unorthodox practices of astrologers and magi, by decree-
ing their expulsion from Italy, and occasionally by visiting some
of them with severer penalties; but such endeavors to stem the

tide of popular superstition are naturally useless (Tac. Ann., ii. 32; xii. 52). Magic of some description is universal. In New Zealand the priest "seems to unite in his person the offices of priest, sorcerer, juggler, and physician." He predicts the life or death of members of his tribe (N. Z., p. 80). By the Kafirs the prophet is consulted on all kinds of domestic occasions, and (while the people beat the ground in assent to what he says) he is held to see in a vision the event which has led to the consultation (K. N., p. 167 ff). The inhabitants of Sierra Leone have other methods of divining. Their diviners make dots and lines in sand spread upon a goat's skin, which dots and lines they afterwards decipher; or they place palm-nuts in heaps upon a goat's skin, and by shifting them about suppose that an answer is obtained (N. A., vol. i. p. 134). The heathen Mexican had the habit, on the birth of a child, of consulting a diviner in order to ascertain its future. The diviner, having learnt from the child's parents the hour at which it was born, turned over his books to discover the sign under which its nativity had occurred. Should that sign prove to be favorable, he would say to the parents: "Your child has been born under a good sign; it will be a senor, or senator, or rich, or brave," or will have some other distinction. In the opposite case he would say: "The child has not been born under a good sign; it has been born under a disastrous sign." In some circumstances there was hope that the evil might be remedied; but if the sign were altogether bad, they would predict that it would be vicious, carnal, and a thief; or that it would be dull and lazy; or possibly that it would be a great drunkard; or that its life would be short. A third alternative was when the sign was indifferent, and the expected fortune was therefore partly good and partly bad. The diviner, in this case and in that of a bad, but not hopelessly bad, sign, assisted the parents by pointing out an auspicious day for the baptism of the infant (A. M., vol. v. pp. 479, 480).

Prediction of coming events was practiced by the priests in North America, as it was elsewhere. They pursuaded the multitude, says Charlevoix, that they suffered from ecstatic transports. During these conditions, they said that their spirits gave them a large acquaintance with remote things, and with the future (N. F., vol. iii. p. 347). Moreover, they practiced magic, and with such effect that Charlevoix felt himself compelled to ascribe their performances to their alliance with the devil. They even pretended to be born in a supernatural manner, and found believers ready to think that only by some sort of enchantment and illusion had they formerly imagined that they had come into the world like other people. When they went into the state of ecstasy, they resembled the Pythoness on the tripod; they assumed tones of voice and performed actions which seemed beyond human capacity. On these occasions they suffered so much that it was hard to induce them, even by handsome payment, thus to yield themselves to the spirit. So often did they prophesy truly, that Charlevoix can only resort again to his hypothesis of a real intercourse between them and the "father of seduction and of lies," who manifested his connection with them by telling them the truth. Thus, a lady named Madame de Marson, by no means an "esprit faible," was anxious about her husband, who was commanding at a French outpost in Acadia, and who had stayed away beyond the time fixed for his return. A native woman, having ascertained the reason of her trouble, told her not to be distressed, for that her husband would return on a certain day at a certain hour, wearing a grey hat. Seeing that the lady did not believe in her, she returned on the day and at the hour named, and asked her if she would not come to meet her husband. After much pressing, she induced the lady to accompany her to the bank of the river. Scarcely had they arrived, when M. de Marson appeared in a canoe, wearing a grey hat upon his head. The writer was informed of this fact by Madame de Marson's son-in-law, at that time Governor-General of the French dominions in America, who had heard it from herself (N. F., vol. iii. p. 359–363). The priests of the Tartars are also their diviners. They predict eclipses, and announce lucky and unlucky days for all sorts of business (Bergeron, Voyage de Rubruquis, ch. 47).

Among the Buddhist priesthood of Thibet, there is a class of Lamas who are astrologers, distinguished by a peculiar dress, and making it their business to tell fortunes, exorcise evil spirits, and so forth. The astrologers "are considered to have intercourse with Sadag," a spirit who is supposed to be "lord

of the ground," in which bodies are interred, and who, along
with other spirits, requires to be pacified by charms and rites
known only to these priests. To prevent them from injuring
the dead, the relations offer a price in cattle or money to Sadag;
and the astrologers, when satisfied with the amount, undertake
the necessary conjuration (B. T., pp. 156, 271).

In the Old Testament, this class of unofficial priests is mentioned with the reprobation inspired by rivalry. The Hebrew
legislator is at one with the Roman Senate in his desire to expel
them from the land. "There shall not be found among you any
one that . . . useth divination, or an observer of times, or an
enchanter, or a witch, or a charmer, or a consultor with familiar
spirits, or a wizard, or a necromancer. For all that do these
things are an abomination unto the Lord: and because of these
abominations the Lord thy God doth drive them out from
before thee" (Deut. xviii. 10-12). The very prohibition evinces
the existence of the objects against whom it is aimed; and
proves that, along with the recognized worship of Jehovah,
there existed an unrecognized resort to practices which the
sterner adherents of that worship would not permit.

In addition to their claim to be in possession of special
means of ascertaining the occult causes of phenomena (as in illness), and of special contrivances for penetrating the future (as
in astrology or fortune-telling), priesthoods pretend to a more
direct inspiration from on high, qualifying them either to announce the will of their god on exceptional occasions, or to intimate his purpose in matters of more ordinary occurrence.
This inspiration was granted to the native North American
priests at the critical age of puberty, "It was revealed to its
possessor by the character of the visions he perceived at the
ordeal he passed through on arriving at puberty; and by the
northern nations was said to be the manifestation of a more
potent personal spirit than ordinary. It was not a faculty, but
an inspiration; not an inborn strength, but a spiritual gift"
(M. N. W., p. 279). So in India; among the several meanings
of the word Brahman, is that of a person "elected by special
divine favor to receive the gift of inspiration" (O. S. T., vol. i.
p. 259). The missionary Turner, who has an eye for parallels,
observes, among other just reflections, that "the way in which

the Samoan priests declared that the gods spoke by them, strikingly reminds us of the mode by which God of old made known his will to man by the Hebrew prophets " (N. Y., p. 349). Although the Levites were said to be the Lord's, and to have been hallowed by him instead of all the first-born of Israel, yet it does not appear that they were in general endowed with any high order of inspiration. The high-priest no doubt received communications from God by the Urim and Thummim. Priests were also the judges whom the Lord chose, and whose sentence in court was to be obeyed on penalty of death; but the inspiration that was fitted to guide the Israelites was supplied not so much by them as by the prophets, a kind of supplementary priesthood of which the members, sometimes priests, sometimes consecrated by other prophets, were as a rule unconsecrated, deriving their appointment directly from Jehovah. While, therefore, it was attained in a somewhat unusual way, the general need of an inspired order was supplied no less perfectly among the Israelites than elsewhere. Christian priests enjoy two kinds of inspiration. In the first place, they are inspired specially when assembled in general councils, to declare the truth in matters of doctrine, or in other words, to issue supplementary revelations; in the second place, they are inspired generally to remit or retain offenses, their sentence being — according to the common doctrine of Catholics and Episcopalian Protestants — always ratified in the Court above.

Consistently with this exalted conception of their authority, priestly orders threaten punishment to offenders, and announce the future destiny of souls. Thus the Mexican priests warned their penitents after confession not to fall again into sin, holding out the prospect of the torments of hell if they should neglect the admonition (A. M., vol. v. p. 370). The priests in some parts of Africa know the fate of each soul after death, and can say whether it has gone to God or to the evil spirit (G. d. M., p. 335).

Sometimes the priests are held to be protected against injury by the especial care of heaven. To take away a Brahman's wife is an offense involving terrible calamities, while kings who restore her to the Brahman enjoy "the abundance of the earth " (O. S. T., vol. i. p. 257). A king who should eat a Brah-

man's cow is warned in solemn language of the dreadful consequences of such conduct, both in this world and the next (Ibid.,
vol. i. p. 285). The sacred volumes declare that "whenever a
king, fancying himself mighty, seeks to devour a Brahman,
that kingdom is broken up, in which a Brahman is oppressed"
(Ibid., vol. i. p. 287). "No one who has eaten a Brahman's cow
continues to watch (*i.e.*, to rule) over a country." The Indian
gods, moreover, "do not eat the food offered by a king who
has no . . . Purohita," or domestic chaplain (A. B., p. 528).
The murder of a king who had honored and enriched the Buddhist priesthood, is said to have entailed the destruction of the
power and strength of the kingdom of Thibet, and to have
extinguished the happiness and welfare of its people (G. O. M.,
p. 362). And Jewish history affords abundant instances of the
manner in which the success or glory of the rulers was connected, by the sacerdotal class, with the respect shown towards
themselves as the ministers of Jehovah, and with the rigor
evinced in persecuting or putting down the ministers of every
other creed. That the same bias has been betrayed by the
Christian priesthood and their adherents in the interpretation
of history needs no proof.

The presence of a priest or priests at important rites is held
to be indispensable by all religions. With the negroes visited
by Oldendorp, the priest was in requisition at burials; for he
only could help the soul to get to God, and keep off the evil
spirit who would seek to obtain possession of it (G. d. M., p.
327). "For most of the ceremonies" (in Thibet) "the performance by a Lama is considered indispensable to its due effect;
and even where this is not so, the efficacy of the rite is
increased by the Lama's assistance (B. T., p. 247). Much the
same thing may be said here. For certain ceremonies, such as
confirmation, the administration of the sacrament, the conduct
of divine service on Sundays, the priest is a necessary official.
For others, such as marriage, the majority of the people prefer
to employ him, and no doubt believe that "the efficacy of the
rite is increased" by the fact that he reads the words of the
service. Nor is this surprising when we consider that, until
within very recent times, no legitimate child could be produced
in England without the assistance of a priest.

Not only is the ecclesiastical caste required to render religious rites aceptable to the deity, but they are often endowed
with the attribute of ability to modify the course of nature.
Tanna, one of the Fiji group, "there are rain-makers and
thunder-makers, and fly and musquito makers, and a host of
other ' sacred men;'" and in another island "there is a rain-
making class of priests" (N. Y., pp. 89, 428). In Christian
countries all priests are rain-makers, the reading of prayers for
fine or wet weather being a portion of their established duties.

Naturally, the members of a class whose functions are of
this high value to the community enjoy great power, are
regarded as extremely sacred, and above all, are well rewarded.
First, as to the power they enjoy. This is accorded to them
alike by savage tribes and by cultivated Europeans. According
to Brinton, all North American tribes "appear to have been
controlled" by secret societies of priests. "Withal," says the
same authority, "there was no class of persons who so widely
and deeply influenced the culture, and shaped the destiny of
the Indian tribes, as their priests" (M. N. W., p. 285). Over
the negroes of the Caribbean Islands the priests and priestesses
exercised an almost unlimited dominion, being regarded with
the greatest reverence. No negro would have ventured to
transgress the arrangements made by a priest (G. d. M., p. 327).
On the coast of Guinea there exists, or existed, an institution
by which certain women became priestesses; and such women,
even though slaves before, enjoyed, on receiving this dignity, a
high position and even exercised absolute authority precisely in
the quarter where it must have been sweetest to their minds,
namely, over their husbands (D. C. G., p. 363). Writing of the
Talapoins in Siam, Gervaise says, that they are exempted from
all public charges; they salute nobody, while everybody pros-
trates himself before them; they are maintained at the public
expense, and so forth (H, N. S., troisième partie, chs. 5, 6). Of
the enormous power wielded by the clerical order in Europe,
especially during the Middle Ages, it is unnecessary to speak.
The humiliation of Theodosius by Ambrose was one of the
most conspicuous, as it was one of the most beneficent, exercises of their extensive rights.

Secondly, the sanctity attached to their persons is usually

considerable, and may often, to ambitious minds, afford a large compensation for the loss (if such be required) of some kinds of secular enjoyment. The African priestesses just mentioned are "as much respected as the priest, or rather more," and call themselves by the appellation of "God's children." When certain Buddhist ecclesiastics were executed for rebellion in Ceylon, the utmost astonishment was expressed by the people at the temerity of the king in so treating "such holy and reverend persons. And none heretofore," adds the reporter of the fact, "have been so served; being-reputed and called *sons of Boddon*" (H. R. C., p. 75), or Buddha; a title exactly corresponding to that of God's children bestowed upon the priestesses. In Siam the "Talapoins," or priests, are of two kinds: secular, living in the world; and regular, living in the forest without intercourse with men. There is no limit to the veneration given by the Siamese to these last, whom they look upon as demigods (H. N. S., troisième partie, p. 184). "The Brahman caste," according to the sacred books of the Hindus, "is sprung from the gods" (O. S. T., vol. i. p. 21); and the exceptional honor always accorded to them is in harmony with this theory of their origin. The title "Reverend," man to be revered, given to the clergy in Europe, implies the existence, at least originally, of a similar sentiment of respect.

Lastly, the services of priests are generally well rewarded, and they themselves take every care to encourage liberality towards their order. Payment is made to them either in the shape of direct remuneration, or in that of exceptional pecuniary privileges, or in that of exemptions from burdens. Direct remuneration may be, and often is, given in the shape of a fixed portion abstracted from the property of the laity for the benefit of the clergy. Such are the tithes bestowed by law upon the latter among the Jews, the Parsees, and the Christians. Or, direct remuneration may consist in fees for services rendered, and in voluntary gifts. Such fees and gifts are always represented by the priesthood as highly advantageous to the givers. If the relatives of a deceased Parsee do not give the priest who officiates at the funeral four new robes, the dead will appear naked before the throne of God at the resurrection, and will be put to shame before the whole assembly (Av., vol.

ii. p. xli.; iii. p. xliv). Moreover, those Parsees who wish to
live happily, and have children who will do them honor, must
pay four priests, who during three days and three nights perform the Yasna for them (Z. A., vol., ii. p. 564). In Thibet
there is great merit in consecrating a domestic animal to a certain god, the animal being after a certain time "delivered to
the Lamas, who may eat it" (B. T., p. 158). Giving alms to the
monks is a duty most sedulously inculcated by Buddhism, and
the Buddhist writings abound in illustrations of the advantages
derived from the practice. Similar benefits accrue to the
clergy from the custom, prevailing in Ceylon, of making offerings in the temples for recovery from sickness; for when the
Singhalese have left their gift on the altar, "the priest presents
it with all due ceremony to the god; and after its purpose is
thus served, very prudently converts it to his own use" (A I.
C., p. 205). Of the Levites it is solemnly declared in Deuteronomy that they have "no part nor inheritance with Israel,"
and that "the Lord is their inheritance." But "the Lord" is
soon seen to be a very substantial inheritance indeed. From
those that offer an ox or a sheep the priests are to receive
"the shoulder, the two cheeks, and the maw;" while the
first-fruits of corn, wine, and oil, and the first of the sheep's
fleeces are to be given to them (Deut. xviii. 1-5). Moreover,
giving to the priest is declared to be the same thing as giving
to the Lord (Num. v. 8). A similar notion, always fostered by
ecclesiastical influence, has led to the vast endowments bestowed
by pious monarchs and wealthy individuals upon the Christian
clergy.

Occasionally, the priests enjoy exemptions from the taxes, or
other burdens levied upon ordinary people. A singular instance
of this is found in the privilege of the Parsee priests, of not
paying their doctors (J. A., vol. ii. p. 555). Large immunities
used to be enjoyed by ecclesiastics among ourselves, especially
that of exemption from the jurisdiction of the ordinary courts
of law.

While the life of a priest often entails certain privations, he
is nevertheless frequently sustained by the thought that there
is merit in the sacrifices he makes. Thus, it is held by a Buddhist authority, that the merit obtained by entering the spiritual

order is very great; and that his merit is immeasurable who either permits a son, a daughter, or a slave, to enter it, or enters it himself (W. u. T., p. 107).

Priesthoods may either be hereditary or selected. The Brahmins in India, and the Levites in Judæa, are remarkable types of hereditary, the Buddhist and the Christian clergy of selected, sacerdotal orders. Curious modifications of the hereditary principle were found among the American Indians. Thus, "among the Nez Percés of Oregon," the priestly office "was transmitted in one family from father to son and daughter, but always with the proviso that the children at the proper age reported dreams of a satisfactory character." The Shawnees "confined it to one *totem:*" but just as the Hebrew prophets need not be Levites, "the greatest of their prophets . . . was not a member of this clan." The Cherokees "had one family set apart for the priestly office," and when they "abused their birthright" and were all massacred, another family took their places. With another tribe, the Choctaws, the office of high-priest remained in one family, passing from father to son; "and the very influential piaches of the Carib tribes very generally transmitted their rank and position to their children." A more important case of hereditary priesthood is that of the Incas of Peru, who monopolized the highest offices both in Church and State. "In ancient Anahuac" there existed a double system of inheritance and selection. The priests of Huitzilopochtli, "and perhaps a few other gods," were hereditary; and the high-priest of that god, towards whom the whole order was required to observe implicit obedience, was the "hereditary pontifix maximus." But the rest were dedicated to ecclesiastical life from early childhood, and were carefully educated for the profession (M. N. W., p. 281–291).

Christianity entirely abandoned the hereditary principle prevalent among its spiritual ancestors, the Jews, and selected for its ministers of religion those who felt, or professed to feel, an internal vocation for this career. Doubtless this is the most effectual plan for securing a powerful priesthood. Those who belong to it have their heart far more thoroughly in their work than can possibly be the case when it falls to them by right of birth. Just the most priestly-minded of the community become

priests; and a far greater air of zeal and of sanctity attaches
to an order thus maintained, than to one of which many of the
members possess no qualification but that of family, tribe, or
caste.

Nothing can be more irrational than the denunciation of
priests and priestcraft which is often indulged in by Liberal
writers and politicians. If it be true that priests have shown
considerable cunning, it is also true that the people have fostered that cunning by credulity. And if the clergy have put
forth very large pretensions to inspiration, divine authority, and
hidden knowledge, it is equally the fact that the laity have demanded such qualifications at their hands. An order can
scarcely be blamed if it seeks to satisfy the claims which the
popular religion makes upon it. Enlightenment from heaven
has in all ages and countries been positively demanded. Sacrifices have always had to be made; and when it was found more
convenient to delegate the function of offering them to a class
apart, that class naturally established ritualistic rules of their
own, and as naturally asserted (and no doubt believed) that all
sacrifices not offered according to these rules were displeasing
to God. And they could not profess the inspiration which they
were expected to manifest without also requiring obedience to
divine commands. Priests are, in fact, the mere outcome of
religious belief as it commonly exists; and partly minister to
that belief by deliberate trickery, partly share it themselves,
and honestly accept the accredited view of their own lofty commission.

Divine inspiration leads by a very logical process to infallibility. A Church founded on revelation needs living teachers to
preserve the correct interpretation of that revelation. Without
such living teachers, revealed truth itself becomes (as it always
has done among Protestants) an occasion of discord and of
schism. But the interpreters of revelation in their turn must
be able to appeal to some sole and supreme authority, as the
arbiter between varying opinions, and the guide to be followed
through all the intricacies of dogma. Nowhere can such an arbiter and such a guide be found more naturally than in the
head of the Church himself. If God speaks to mankind through
his Church, it is only a logical conclusion that within that Church

there must be one through whom he speaks with absolute certainty, and whose prophetic voice must therefore be infallible. There cannot be a more consistent application of the general theory of priesthood; and there is no more fatal sign for the prospects of Christianity than the inability of many of its supporters to accept so useful a doctrine, and the thoughtless indignation of some among them against the single Church which has had the wisdom to proclaim it.

CHAPTER V.

ALTHOUGH for the ordinary and regular communications from the divine Being to man the established priesthoods might suffice, yet occasions arise when there is need of a plenipotentiary with higher authority and more extensive powers. What is required of these exceptional ambassadors is not merely to repeat the doctrines of the old religion, but to establish a new one. In other words, they are the original founders of the great religions of the world. Of such founders there is but a very limited number.

Beginning with China, and proceeding from East to West, we find six:—

1. CONFUCIUS, or KHUNG-FU-TSZE, the founder of Confucianism.
2. LAO-TSE, the founder of Taouism.
3. SAKYAMUNI, or GAUTAMA BUDDHA, the founder of Buddhism.
4. ZARATHUSTRA, or ZOROASTER, the founder of Parseeism.
5. MOHAMMED, or MAHOMET, the founder of Islamism.
6. JESUS CHRIST, the founder of Christianity.

All these men, whom for convenience sake I propose to call *prophets*, occupy an entirely exceptional position in the history of the human race. The characteristics, or marks, by which they may be distinguished from other great men, are partly external, belonging to the views of others about them; partly internal, belonging to their own view about themselves.

1. The first external mark by which they are distinguished is, that within his own religion each of these is recognized as the highest known authority. They alone are thought of as having the right to change what is established. While all other teachers appeal to them for the sanction of their doctrines

there is no appeal from them to any one beyond. What they have said is final. They are in perfect possession of the truth. Others are in possession of it only in so far as they agree with them. No doubt, the sacred books are equally infallible with the prophets; but the sacred books of religions founded by prophets derive their authority in the last resort from them, and are always held to be only a written statement of their teaching. Thus, the sacred books of China are partly of direct Confucian authorship; partly by others who recognize him as their head. The only sacred book of the Tao-tsé is by their founder himself. The sacred books of the Buddhists are supposed discourses of the Buddha. The Avesta is the reputed work of Zarathustra. The Koran is the actual work of Mahomet. And lastly, the New Testament is all of it written in express subordination to the authority of Christ, to which it constantly appeals. These books, then, are infallible, because they contain the doctrines of their founders.

The same thing is true where there is an infallible Church. The Church never claims the same absolute authority as it concedes to its prophet. Its infallibility consists in its power to interpret correctly the mind of him by whom it was established. He it is who brought the message from above which no human power could have discovered. It is the Church's function to explain that message to the world; and, where needed, to deduce such inferences therefrom as by its supernatural inspiration it perceives to be just. Beyond this, the power of the Church does not extend.

A second external mark, closely related to the first, is, that the prophet of each religion is, within the limits of that religion, the object of a more or less mythical delineation of his personality. His historical form is, to some extent, superseded by the form bestowed upon him by a dogmatic legend. According to that legend there was something about his nature that was more than human. He was in some way extraordinary. The myths related vary from a mere exaltation of the common features of humanity, to the invention of completely supernatural attributes. But their object is the same: to represent their prophet as more highly endowed than other mortals. Even where there is little of absolute myth, the representation we

receive is one-sided; we know nothing of the prophet's faults,
except in so far as we may discover them against the will of the
biographers. To them he appears all-virtuous. These remarks
will be abundantly illustrated when we come to consider the
life of Jesus, and to compare it with that of his compeers.

2. The internal mark corresponds to the first external mark,
of which it is indeed the subjective counterpart. These prophets
conceive themselves deputed to teach a faith, and they virtually
recognize in the performance of this mission no human authority superior to their own. In words, perhaps, they do acknowledge some established authority; but in fact they set it aside.
No Church or priesthood has the smallest weight with them, as
opposed to that intense internal conviction which appears to
them an inspiration. Hence it was observed of Jesus, that he
taught with authority, and not as the scribes. Without being
able themselves to give any explanation of the fact, they feel
themselves endowed with plenary power to reform. And it is
not, like other reformers, in the name of another that they do
this; they reform in their own right, and with no other title
than their own profound consciousness of being not only permitted, but charged to do it.

Nevertheless, it must not be imagined that the prophets
sweep away everything they find in the existing religion. On
the contrary, it will be found on examination that they always
retain some important element or elements of the older faith.
Without this, they would have no hold on the popular mind of
their country, from which they would be too far removed to
make themselves understood. Thus, Allah was already recognized as God by the Arabians in the time of Mahomet, whose
reform consisted in teaching that he was the only God. Thus,
the Messiah was already expected by the Jews in the time of
Jesus, whose reform consisted in applying the expectation to
himself. Prophets take advantage of a faith already in existence, and making that the foundation of a new religion, erect
upon it the more special truths they are inspired to proclaim.

No prophet can construct a religion entirely from his own
brain. Were he to do so, he would be unable to show any reason why it should be accepted. There would be no feeling in
the minds of his hearers to which he could appeal. A religion

to be accepted by any but an insignificant fraction, must find a response not only in the intellects, but in the emotions of those for whom it is designed.

This, it appears to me, is the weak point of Positivism. Auguste Comte, having abolished all that in the general mind constitutes religion at all, attempted to compose a faith for his disciples by the merely arbitrary exercise of his own ingenuity. He perhaps did not consider that in all history there is no example of a religion being invented by an individual thinker. It is like attempting to sell a commodity for which there is no demand. Even if his philosophical principles should be accepted by the whole of Europe, there can be no reason why the special observances he recommends should be adopted, or the special saints whom he places in the calendar be adored. Those who receive his philosophy will have no need for his ceremonies. While even if ceremonies cannot be entirely dispensed with; it is not the mere fact of a solitary thinker planning it in his own mind that can ever ensure the adoption of a ritual.

Very different has been the procedure of the prophets of whom we are now to speak. Intellectually, they were no doubt far inferior to the founder of the Positive Philosophy. But emotionally, they were fitted for the part which he unsuccessfully endeavored to play. They entered into the religious feelings of their countrymen, and gave those feelings a higher expression than had yet been found for them. Instinctively fixing on some conspicuous part of the old religion, they made that the starting-point for the development of the new. They reformed, but the reformation linked itself to some conviction that was already deeply rooted in the nature of their converts. They assumed boundless authority; but it was authority to proclaim a pre-existing truth, not to spin out of their purely personal ideas of fitness a system altogether disconnected from the past evolution of religion, and to impose that system upon the remainder of mankind.

SECTION I.—CONFUCIUS.*

The life of the prophet of China is not eventful. It has

*After some hesitation, I have determined to adhere to the Latinized neither the charm of philosophic placidity and retirement from the world which belongs to that of Lao-tsè, nor the romantic interest of the more varied careers of Sakyamuni, Christ, or Mahomet. For Confucius, though a philosopher, did not object, indeed rather desired, to take some share in the government of his country, but his wishes received very little gratification. Rulers refused to acquiesce in his principles of administration, and he was compelled to rely for their propagation mainly on the oral instruction imparted to his disciples. His life, therefore, bears to some extent the aspect of a failure, though for this appearance he himself is not to blame. Another cause, which somewhat diminishes the interest we might otherwise take in him, is his excessive attention to proprieties, ceremonies, and rites. We cannot but feel that a truly great man, even in China, would have emancipated himself from the bondage of such trifles. Nevertheless, after all deductions are made, enough remains to render the career and character of Confucius deserving of attention, and in many respects of admiration.

Descended from a family which had formerly been powerful and noble, but was now in comparatively modest circumstances, he was born in B.C. 551, his father's name being Shuh-leang Heih, and his mother's Ching-Tsae. The legends related of his nativity I pass over for the present. His father, who was an old man when he was born, died when the child was in his third year; and his mother in B.C. 528. At nineteen, Confucius

form of the name of the prophet of China, as more familiar to English ears. As a general rule, I consider the movement in literature which is restoring proper names to their original spellings,—giving us Herakles for Hercules, and Oidipous for Œdipus,—as deserving of all support. But where the common form, in addition to being the more familiar, may be considered as English proper and not Latin used in English (as in such names as Homer, Aristotle, Jesus Christ), I conceive it to be more convenient to retain the accustomed designation, even though it may be regretted that it has come into general use. Hence, I think, we may retain Confucius, who would scarcely be recognized by English readers under his full name, Khung-fu-tsze, or under his more usual abridged name, Khung-tsze, or under the name elsewhere given him, Chung-ne. No similar justification appears to me to exist for the Greek form Zoroaster, as compared with Zarathustra, which last form is as easy to pronounce as the other, and not very dissimilar from it in sound.

My authorities for the life of Confucius have been Dr. Legge's Chinese Classics, vol. i. Proleg. p. 54-113, and the Lun Yu and Chung Yung, translated in the same volume.

was married; and at twenty-one he came forward as a teacher.
Disciples attached themselves to him, and during his long
career as a philosopher, we find him constantly attended by
some faithful friends, who receive all he says with unbounded
deference, and propose questions for his decision as to an
authority against whom there can be no appeal. The maxims
of Confucius did not refer solely to ethics or to religion; they
bore largely upon the art of government, and he was desirous
if possible of putting them in actual practice in the administration of public affairs. China, however, was in a state of great
confusion in his days; there were rebellions and wars in progress: and the character of the rulers from whom he might
have obtained employment was such, that he could not, consistently with the high standard of honor on which he always
acted, accept favors at their hands. One of them proposed to
grant him a town with its revenues; but Confucius said: "A
superior man will only receive reward for services which he has
done. I have given advice to the duke king, but he has not
obeyed it, and now he would endow me with this place! very
far is he from understanding me" (C. C., vol. i., Prolegomena,
p. 68). In the year 500 the means were at length put within his
reach of carrying his views into practice. He was made "chief
magistrate of a town" in the state of Loo; and this first appointment was followed by that of "assistant-superintendent of
works," and subsequently by that of "minister of crime." In
this office he is said to have put an end to crime altogether;
but Dr. Legge rightly warns us against confiding in the "indis-
criminating eulogies" of his disciples. A more substantial service attributed to him is that of procuring the dismantlement of
two fortified towns which were the refuge of dangerous and
warlike chiefs. But his reforming government was brought to
an end after a few years by the weakness of his sovereign,
duke Ting, who was captivated by a present of eighty beautiful
and accomplished girls, and one hundred and twenty horses,
from a neighboring State. Engrossed by this present, the
duke neglected public affairs, and the philosopher felt bound to
resign.

We need not follow him during the long wanderings through
various parts of China which followed upon this disappoint-

ment. After traveling from State to State for many years, he
returned in his sixty-ninth year to Loo, but not to office. In
the year 478 his sad and troubled life was closed by death.

Our information respecting the character of Confucius is
ample. From the book which Dr. Legge has entitled the "Confucian Analects," a collection of his sayings made (as he
believes) by the disciples of his disciples, we obtain the most
minute particulars both as to his personal habits and as to the
nature of his teaching. The impression derived from these
accounts is that of a gentle, virtuous, benevolent, and eminently
honorable man; a man who, like Socrates, was indifferent to
the reward received for his tuition, though not refusing payment
altogether; who would never sacrifice a single principle for the
sake of his individual advantage; yet who was anxious, if possible, to benefit the kingdom by the establishment of an administration pénetrated with those ethical maxims which he conceived to be all-important. Yet, irreproachable as his moral
character was, there is about him a deficiency of that bold originality which has characterized the greatest prophets of other
nations. Sakyamuni revolted against the restrictions of caste
which dominated all minds in India. Jesus boldly claimed for
moral conduct a rank far superior to that of every ceremonial
obligation, even those which were held the most sacred by his
countrymen. Mahomet, morally far below the Chinese sage,
evinced a far more independent genius by his attack on the
prevalent idolatry of Mecca. Confucius did nothing of this kind.
His was a mind which looked back longingly to antiquity, and
imagined that it discovered in the ancient rulers and the ancient
modes of action, the models of perfection which all later times
should strive to follow. Nor was this all. He was so profoundly
under the influence of Chinese ways of thinking, as to attach
an almost ludicrous importance to a precise conformity to certain rules of propriety, and to regard the exactitude with which
ceremonies were performed as matter of the highest concern.
In fact, he could not emancipate himself from the traditions of
his country; and his principles would have resulted rather in
making his followers perfect Chinamen than perfect men.

A far more serious charge is indeed brought against him by
Dr. Legge — that of insincerity (C. C., vol. i. — Prolegomena —

p. 101). I hesitate to impugn the opinion of so competent a scholar; yet the evidence he has produced does not seem to me sufficient to sustain the indictment. Granting that he gave an unwelcome visitor the excuse of sickness, which was untrue, still, as we are ignorant of the reasons which led him to decline seeing the person in question, we cannot estimate the force of the motives that induced him to put forward a plea in conformity with the polite customs of his country. It does not appear, moreover, that he practiced an intentional deceit. And though on one occasion he may have violated an oath extorted by rebels who had him in their power, therein acting wrongly (as I think), it is always an open question how far promises made under such circumstances are binding on the conscience. Whatever failings, however, it may be necessary to admit, there can be no question of the preëminent purity alike of his life and doctrine. His is a character which, be its imperfections what they may, we cannot help loving; and there have been few, indeed, who would not have been benefited by the attempt to reach even that standard of virtue which he held up to the admiration of his disciples.

A few quotations from the works in which his words and actions are preserved, will illustrate these remarks. In the tenth Book of the Analects (C. C., vol. i. p. 91–100), his manners, his garments, his mode of behavior under various circumstances, are elaborately described. There are not many personages in history of whom we have so minute a knowledge. We learn that "in his village" he "looked simple and sincere, and as if he were not able to speak." His reverence for his superiors seems to have been profound. "When the prince was present, his manner displayed respectful uneasiness; it was grave, but self-possessed." When going to an audience of the prince, "he ascended the dais, holding up his robe with both his hands, and his body bent; holding in his breath also, as if he dared not breathe. When he came out *from the audience* (the italics, here and elsewhere, are in Legge), as soon as he had descended one step, he began to relax his countenance, and had a satisfied look. When he had got to the bottom of the steps, he advanced rapidly to his place, *with his arms* like wings, and on occupying it, his manner *still* showed respectful uneasiness." He was rather particular about his food, rejecting meat unless "cut properly," and with "its proper sauce."

Whatever he might be eating, however, "he would offer a little of it in sacrifice." "When any of his friends died, if the deceased had no relations who could be depended on for the necessary offices, he would say, 'I will bury him.'" "In bed, he did not lie like a corpse." And it is satisfactory to learn of one who was such a respecter of formalities, that "at home he did not put on any formal deportment." Notwithstanding this, he does not appear to have been on very intimate terms with his son, to whom he is reported to have said that unless he learned "the odes" he would not be fit to converse with; and that unless he learned "the rules of propriety" his character could not be established. The disciple, who was informed by the son himself that he had never heard from his father any other special doctrine, was probably right in concluding that "the superior man maintains a distant reserve towards his son" (Lun Yu, xvi. 13).

But with his beloved disciples Confucius was on terms of affectionate intimacy which does not seem to have been marred by "the rules of propriety." For the death of one of them at least he mourned so bitterly as to draw down upon himself the expostulation of those who remained (Ibid., xi. 9). The picture of the Master, accompanied at all times by his faithful friends, who hang upon his lips, and eagerly gather up his every utterance, is on the whole a pleasant one. "Do you think, my disciples," he asks, "that I have any concealments? I conceal nothing from you. There is nothing that I do which is not shown to you, my disciples;—that is my way" (Ibid., vii. 23). And with all the homage he is constantly receiving, Confucius is never arrogant. He never speaks like a man who wishes to enforce his views in an authoritative style on others; never threatens punishment either here or hereafter to those who dissent from him.

"There were four things," his disciples tell us, "from which the Master was entirely free. He had no foregone conclusions, no arbitrary predeterminations, no obstinacy, and no egoism" (Lun Yu, ix. 4). And his conduct is entirely in harmony with this statement. It is as a learner, rather than a teacher, that he regards himself. "The Master said, 'When I walk along with two others, they may serve me as my teachers. I will select their good qualities, and follow them; their bad qualities, and avoid them'" (Ibid., vii. 21). Or again: "The sage and the man of perfect virtue, how dare I *rank myself with them?* It may simply be said of me, that I strive to become such without satiety, and teach others without weariness" Ibid., vii. 33). "In letters I am perhaps equal to other men, but *the character* of the superior man, carrying out in his conduct what he professes, is what I have not yet attained to" (Ibid., vii. 32).

Notwithstanding this modesty, there are traces — few indeed, but not obscure — of that conviction of a peculiar mission which all great prophets have entertained, and without which even Confucius would scarcely have been ranked among them. The most distinct of these is the following passage: — "The Master was put in fear in K'wang. He said, 'After the death of king Wan, was not the cause of truth lodged here *in me?* If Heaven had wished to let this cause of truth perish, then I, a future mortal, should not have got such a relation to that cause. While Heaven does not let the cause of truth perish, what can the people of K'wang do to me?'" (Lun Yu, ix. 5. These remarkable words would be conclusive, if they stood alone. But they do not stand alone. In another place we find him thus lamenting the pain of being generally misunderstood, which is apt to be so keenly felt by exalted and sensitive natures. "The Master said, 'Alas!' there is no one that knows me.' Tsc-kung said, 'What do you mean by thus saying — that no one knows you?' The Master replied, 'I do not murmur against Heaven. I do not grumble against men. My studies lie low, and my penetration rises high. But there is Heaven; — that knows me!'" (Ibid., xiv. 37). Men might reject his labors and despise his teaching, but he would complain neither against Heaven nor against them. If he was not known by men, he was known by Heaven, and that was enough. On another occasion, "the Master said, 'Heaven produced the virtue that is in me, Hwan T'uy — what can he do to me?'" *

* Ibid., vii. 22. The occasion of this utterance is said to have been an attack by the emissaries of an officer named Hwan T'uy, with a view of killing the sage.

These passages are the more remarkable, because Confucius was not in the ordinary sense a believer in God. That is, he never, throughout his instructions, says a single word implying acknowledgment of a personal Deity; a Creator of the world; a Being whom we are bound to worship as the author of our lives and the ruler of our destinies. He has even been suspected of omitting from his edition of the Shoo-king and the She-king everything that could support the comparatively theistic doctrine of his contemporary, Lao-tsè (By V. von Strauss, T. T. K., p. xxxviii). That his high respect for antiquity would have permitted such a proceedure is, to say the least, very improbable; and Dr. Legge is no doubt right in acquitting him of any willful suppression of, or addition to, the ancient articles of Chinese faith (C. C., vol. i. Prolegomena, p. 99). For our present purpose it is enough to note that he avoided all discussion on the higher problems of religion; and contented himself with speaking, and that but rarely, of a vague, and hardly personal Being which he called heaven. Thus, in a book attributed (perhaps erroneously) to his grandson, he is reported as saying, "Sincerity is the very way of Heaven" (Chung Yung, xx. 18). Of king Woo and the duke of Chow, two ancient worthies, he says: "By the ceremonies of the sacrifices to Heaven and Earth they served God" (where he seems to distinguish between Heaven and God, whom I believe he never mentions but here); "and by the ceremonies of the ancestral temple they sacrificed to their ancestors. He who understands the ceremonies of the sacrifices to Heaven and Earth, and the meaning of the several sacrifices to ancestors, would find the government of a kingdom as easy as to look into his palm" (Ibid., xix. 6). Elsewhere, he remarks that "he who is greatly virtuous will be sure to receive the appointment of heaven" (Ibid., xvii. 5). Again: "Heaven, in the production of things, is surely bountiful to them, according to their qualities" (Ibid., xvii. 3). Nothing very definite can be gathered from these passages, as to his opinions concerning the nature of the power of which he spoke thus obscurely. Yet it would be rash to find fault with him on that account. His language may have been, and in all probability was, the correct expression of his feelings. His mind was not of the dogmatic type; and if he does not teach his disciples any very intelligible principles concerning spiritual matters, it is simply because he is honestly conscious of having none to teach.

There are, indeed, indications which might be taken to imply the existence of an esoteric doctrine. "To those," he says, "whose talents are above mediocrity, the highest subjects may be announced. To those who are below mediocrity, the highest subjects may not be announced" (Lun Yu., vi. 19). We are further told that Tsze-kung said, "the Master's *personal* displays *of his principles*, and *ordinary* descriptions of them may be heard. His discourses about *man's* nature, and the way of Heaven, cannot be heard" (Ibid., v. 12). This last passage appears to mean that they were not open to the indiscriminate multitude, nor perhaps to all of the disciples. But we may reasonably suppose that the intimate friends who recorded his sayings were considered by him to be above mediocrity, and were the depositaries of all he had to tell them on religious matters.

Yet this, little as it was, may not always have been rightly understood. Once, for example, he says to a disciple, "Sin, my doctrine is that of an all-pervading unity." This is interpreted by the disciple (in the Master's absence) to mean only that his doctrine is "to be true to the principles of our nature, and the benevolent exercise of them to others" (Ibid., iv. 15). I can hardly believe that Confucius would have taught so simple a lesson under so obscure a figure; and it is possible that the reserve that he habitually practiced with regard to his religious faith may have prevented a fuller explanation. "The subjects on which the Master did not talk were — extraordinary things, feats of strength, disorder, and spiritual beings" (Lun Yu, vii. 20). And although, in the Doctrine of the Mean (a work which is perhaps less authentic than the Analects) we find him discoursing freely on spiritual beings, which, he says, "abundantly display the powers that belong to them" (Chung Yung, 16). There are portions of the Analects which confirm the impression that he did not readily venture into these extra-mundane regions. Heaven itself, he once pointed out to an over-curious disciple. preserves an unbroken silence (Lun Yu, xvii. 19). Interrogated "about serving the spirits of the dead," he gave this striking answer: "While you are not able to serve men, how can you serve their spirits?" And when "Ke Loo added, 'I venture to ask about death?' he was answered, 'While you do not know life, how can you know about death?'" (Ibid., xi. 11). Another instance of a similar reticence is presented by his conduct during an illness. "The Master being very sick, Tsze-Loo asked leave to pray for him. "He said, 'May such a thing be done?' Tsze-Loo replied, 'It may. In the prayers it is said, Prayer has been made to the spirits of the upper and lower worlds.' The Master said, 'My praying has been for a long time'" (Ibid., vii. 34). I am unable to see "the satisfaction of Confucius with himself," which Dr. Legge discovers in this reply. To me it appears simply to indicate the devout attitude of his mind, which is evinced by many other passages in his conversation. In short, though we may complain of the indefinite character of the faith he taught, and wish that he had expressed himself more fully, there can scarcely be a doubt that Confucius had a deeply religious mind; and that he looked with awe and reverence upon that power which he called by the name of "Heaven," which controlled the progress of events, and would not suffer the cause of truth to perish altogether.

It is true, however, that he confined himself chiefly, and indeed almost entirely, to moral teaching. His main object undoubtedly was to inculcate upon his friends, and if possible to introduce among the people at large, those great principles of ethics which he thought would restore the virtue and well-being of ancient times. Those principles are aptly summarized in the following verse: "The duties of universal obligation are five, and the virtues wherewith they are practiced are three. The duties are those between sovereign and minister, between father and son, between husband and wife, between elder brother and younger, and those belonging to the intercourse of friends. Those five are the duties of universal obligation. Knowledge, magnanimity, and energy, these three are the virtues universally binding; and the means by which they carry the duties into practice is singleness" (Chung Yung, xx. 7). In the Analects, "Gravity, generosity of soul, sincerity, earnestness, and kindness," are said to constitute perfect virtue (Lun Yu, xvii. 6).

It is as an earnest and devoted teacher, both by example and by precept, of these and other virtues, that Confucius must be judged. And in order to assist the formation of such a judgment, let us take his doctrine of Reciprocity, to which I shall return in another place. "Tsze-kung asked, saying, 'Is there one word which may serve as a rule of practice for all one's life?' The Master said, 'Is not RECIPROCITY such a word? What you do not want done to yourself, do not do to others'" (Lun Yu, xv. 23). On a kindred topic he thus delivered his opinion: "Some one said, 'What do you say concerning the principle that injury should be recompensed with kindness?' The Master said, 'With what, then, will you recompense kindness? Recompense injury with justice, and recompense kindness with kindness'" (Ibid., xiv. 26).

If in the above sentence he may be thought to fall short of the highest elevation, there are some among his apophthegms, the point and excellence of which have, perhaps, never been surpassed. Take for instance these:—"The superior man is catholic and no partizan. The mean man is a partizan and not catholic." "Learning without thought is labor lost; thought without learning is perilous" (Ibid., ii. 14, 15). Or these:—"I will not be afflicted at men's not knowing me; I will be afflicted that I do not know men" (Ibid., i. 16). "A scholar, whose mind is set on truth, and who is ashamed of bad clothes and bad food, is not fit to be discoursed with" (Ibid., iv. 9). "The superior man is affable, but not adulatory; the mean is adulatory, but not affable" (Ibid., xiii. 23). "Where the solid qualities are in excess of accomplishments, we have rusticity; where the accomplishments are in excess of the solid qualities, we have the manners of a clerk. When the accomplishments and solid qualities are equally blended, we then have the man of complete virtue" (Lun Yu, vi. 16). Lastly, I will quote one which, with a slight change of terms, might have emanated from the pen of Thomas Carlyle: "There are three things of which the superior man stands in awe:—He stands in awe of the ordinances of heaven; he stands in awe of great men; he stands in awe of the words of sages. The mean man does not know the ordinances of heaven, and *consequently* does not stand in awe of them. He is disrespectful to great men. He makes sport of the words of sages" (Ibid., xvi. 8).

These, and various other recorded sayings, go far to explain,

if not to justify, the unbounded admiration of his faithful follower, Tsze-kung: "Our Master cannot be attained to, just in
the same way as the heavens cannot be gone up to by the steps
of a stair. Were our Master in the position of the prince of a
State, or the chief of a family, we should find verified the description *which has been given of a sage's rule:* — he would plant
the people, and forthwith they would be established; he would
lead them on, and forthwith they would follow him: he would
make them happy, and forthwith *multitudes* would resort to *his
dominions;* he would stimulate them, and forthwith they would
be harmonious. While he lived, he would be glorious. When
he died, he would be bitterly lamented. How is it possible for
him to be attained to?" (Ibid., xix. 25.)

SECTION II. — LAÒ-TSÈ.*

Concerning the life of Lao-tsè, the founder of the smallest
of the three sects of China (Confucians, Buddhists, and Taouists),
we have only the most meagre information. Scarcely anything
is known either of his personal character or of his doctrine,
except through his book. His birth-year is unknown to us, and
can only be approximately determined by means of the date
assigned to his famous interview with his great contemporary,
Confucius. This occurred in B. c. 517, when Lao-tsè was very
old. He may, therefore, have been born about the year B. c.
600.† All we can say of his career is, that he held an office in
the State of Tseheu, that of "writer (or historian) of the ar-
chives." When visited by Confucius, who was the master of a
rival school, he is said to have addressed him in these terms:—
"Those whom you talk about are dead, and their bones are
mouldered to dust; only their words remain. When the superior man gets his time, he mounts aloft; but when the time is
against him, he moves as if his feet were entangled. I have
heard that a good merchant, though he has rich treasures
deeply stored, appears as if he were poor; and that the superior man, whose virtue is complete, is yet to outward seeming
stupid. Put away your proud air and many desires; your insin-

---

* For authorities on Lao-tse, see vol. ii. chap. vi. section ii.

† Julien assigns B. c. 604 as the date, but confesses that he has no
authority but historical tradition. L. V. V. xix

uating habit and wild will. These are of no advantage to you.
This is all which I have to tell you." After this interview,
Confucius thus expressed his opinion of the older philosopher
to his disciples:—"I know how birds can fly, how fishes can
swim, and how animals can run. But the runner may be
snared, the swimmer may be hooked, and the flyer may be shot
by the arrow. But there is the dragon. I cannot tell how he
mounts on the wind through the clouds and rises to heaven.
To-day I have seen Lao-tsè, and can only compare him to the
dragon" (C. C., vol. i. Proleg. p. 65.—T. T. K., p. liii.—L. T..
p. iv).

Troubles in the State in which he held office induced him to
retire, and to seek the frontier. Here the officer in command
requested him to write a book, the result of which request was
the Tao-te-king. "No one knows," says the Chinese historian,
"where he died. Lao-tsè was a hidden sage" (T. T. K., p. lvi).

To this very scanty historical information we may add such
indications as Lao-tsè himself has given us of his personality.
One of these is contained in the twentieth chapter of his work,
in which he tells us that while other men are radiant with
pleasure, he is calm, like a child that does not yet smile. He
wavers to and fro, as one who knows not where to turn. Other
men have abundance; he is as it were deprived of all. He is
like a stupid fellow, so confused does he feel. Ordinary men
are enlightened; he is obscure and troubled in mind. Like the
sea he is forgotten, and driven about like one who has no certain resting-place. All other men are of use; he alone is clown-
ish like a peasant. He alone is unlike other men, but he honors
the nursing mother (T. T. K., ch. xx.

It is obvious that an estimate so depreciatory is not to be
taken literally. To understand its full significance, it should
be compared to the magnificent description in Plato's Theæletus
of the outward appearance presented by the philosopher, who,
in presence of practical men, is the jest alike of "Thracian
handmaids," and of the "general herd;" who is "unacquainted
with his next-door neighbor;" who is "ignorant of what is
before him, and always at a loss;" and who is so awkward and
useless when called on to perform some menial office, such as
"packing up a bag, or flavoring a sauce, or fawning speech."

Yet this philosopher, like Lao-tsè, "honors his nursing Mother;" he moves in a sphere of thought where men of the world cannot follow him, and where they in their turn are lost (Theætetus, 174–176). Just such a character as that drawn by Plato, Lao-tsè seems to have been. Living in retirement, and devoted to philosophy, he appeared to his contemporaries an eccentric and incompetent person. Yet he says that they called him great (Ch. lxvii), which seems to imply that his reputation was already founded in his life-time.

One other reference to himself must not be omitted, for it evinces the sense he had of the nature of his work in the world. "My words," so he writes in his paradoxical manner, "are very easy to understand, very easy to follow,—no one in the world is able to understand them, no one is able to follow them. The words have an author, the works have one who enjoins them; but he is not understood, therefore I am not understood" (Ch. lxx). On this Stanislas Julien observes, "There is not a word of Lao-tsè's that has not a solid foundation. In fact, they have for their origin and basis Tao and Virtue " (L. V. V. p. 269, n. 2). These expressions, then, suffice to show that Lao-tsè was not destitute of that sense of inspiration of which other great prophets have been so profoundly conscious.

SECTION III.— GAUTAMA BUDDHA.*

SUBDIVISION 1. *The Historical Buddha.*

Were we to write the history of the Buddha according to the fashion of Buddhist historians, we should have to begin our story several ages before his birth. For the theory of his disciples is, that during many millions of years, through an almost innumerable series of different lives, he had been preparing himself for the great office of the savior of humanity which he at length assumed. Only by the practice of incredible

---

* The following works may be advantageously consulted with reference to the Buddha Sakyamuni:—Notices on the Life of Shakya, by C-oma Korosi; Asiatic Researches, vol. xx, part ii. p. 285: the Rgya Tch'er Rol Pa, par Ph, Ed. Foucaux; Hardy's Manual of Buddhism; Bigandet's Life or Legend of Gautama, the Buddha of the Burmese; Alabaster's Wheel of the Law; and Koeppen's Religion des Buddha, vol. i. p. 71, ff. Some information will also be found in my article on " Recent Publications on Buddhism, in the *Theological Review* for July, 1872.

self-denial, and unbounded virtue, during all the long line of human births he was destined to undergo, could he become fitted for that consummate duty, the performance of which at last released him forever from the bonds of existence. For the total extinction of conscious life, not its continuation in a better sphere, is, or at any rate was, the goal of the pious Buddhist. And it was the crowning merit of the Buddha, that he not only sought this reward for himself, but qualified himself by ages of endurance to enlighten others as to the way in which it might be earned.

But we will not encumber ourselves with the pre-historic Buddha, the tales of whose deeds are palpable fictions, but will endeavor to unravel the thread of genuine fact which probably runs through the accepted life of Sakyamuni in his final appearance upon earth. And here we are met with a preliminary difficulty. That life is not guaranteed by any trustworthy authority. It cannot be traced back to any known disciple of Buddha. It cannot be shown to have been written within a century after his death, and it may have been written later. Ancient, however, it undoubtedly is. For the separation of northern from southern Buddhism occurred at an early period in the history of the Church, probably about two hundred years after the death of its founder; and this life is the common property of all sections of Buddhists. It was consequently current before that separation. But its antiquity does not make it trustworthy. On the contrary, it is constructed in accordance with an evident design. Every incident has a definite dogmatic value, and stands in well-marked dogmatic relations to the rest. There is nothing natural or spontaneous about them. Everything has its proper place, and its distinct purpose. And it is useless to attempt to deal with such a life on the rationalistic plan of sifting the historical from the fabulous; the natural and possible from the miraculous and impossible elements. The close intermixture of the two renders any such process hopeless. We are, in fact, with regard to the life of Gautama Buddha, much in the position that we should be in with regard to the life of Jesus Christ, had we no records to consult but the apocryphal gospels

Nevertheless, while holding that his biography can never now

be written, it is by no means my intention to imply that it is
impossible to know anything about him. On the contrary, a
picture not wholly imaginary may unquestionably be drawn of
the character and doctrines of the great teacher of the Asiatic
continent. Let us venture on the attempt.

An imposing array of scholars agrees in fixing the date of
his death in B.C. 543, and as he is said to have lived eighty
years, he would thus have been born in B.C. 623. Without entering now into the grounds of their inference, I venture to
believe that they have thrown him back to a too distant date.
I am more inclined to agree with Köppen, who would place his
death from B.C. 480 to 460, or about two centuries before the
accession of the great Buddhist king Asoka. Westergaard, it is
true, would fix this event much later, namely about B.C. 370. Supposing the former writer to be correct in his conclusions, the
active portion of the Buddha's life would fall to the earlier
years of the fifth century B.C., and possibly to the conclusion of
the sixth. His birth, about B.C. 560–540, occurred in a small
kingdom of the north of India, entitled Kapilavastu. Of what
rank his parents may have been, the accounts before us do not
enable us to say. The tradition according to which they were
the king and queen of the country, I regard with Wassiljew as
in all probability an invention intended to shed additional
glory upon him. The boy is said to have been named Siddhartha, though possibly this also was one of the many titles
bestowed on him by subsequent piety. At an early age he felt
—as so many young men of lofty character have always done—
the hollowness of worldly pleasures, and withdrew himself from
men to lead a solitary and ascetic life. After he had satisfied
the craving for self-torture, and subdued the lusts of the flesh,
he came forth, full of zeal for the redemption of mankind, to
proclaim a new and startling gospel. India was at that time,
as always, dominated by the system of caste. The Buddha,
boldly breaking through the deepest prejudices of his countrymen, surrounded himself with a society in which caste was
nothing. Let but a man or even a woman (for it is stated that
at his sister's request he admitted women) become his disciple,
agree to renounce the world, and lead the life of an ascetic,
and he or she at once lost either the privileges of a high caste,

or the degradations of a low one. Rank depended henceforth
exclusively upon capacity for the reception of spiritual truth;
and the humblest individual might, by attending to and practicing the teacher's lessons, rise to the highest places in the
hierarchy. "Since the doctrine which I teach," he is represented as saying in one of the Canonical Books, "is completely
pure, it makes no distinction between noble and commoner,
between rich and poor. It is, for example, like water, which
washes both noblemen and common people, both rich and poor,
both good and bad, and purifies all without distinction. It
may, to take another illustration, be compared to fire, which
consumes mountains, rocks, and all great and small objects
between heaven and earth without distinction. Again, my doctrine is like heaven, inasmuch as there is room within it, without exception, for whomsoever it may be; for men and women,
for boys and girls, for rich and poor" (W. u. T., p. 282). This
was the practical side of Sakyamuni's great reform. Its theo-
retical side was this. Life was regarded by Indian devotees,
not as a blessing, but as an unspeakable misery. Deliverance
from existence altogether, not merely transposition to a happier
mode of existence, was the object of their ardent longing. The
Buddha did not seek to oppose this craving for annihilation,
but to satisfy it. He addressed himself to the problem, How is
pain produced, and how can it be extinguished? And his meditations led him to what are termed "the four truths"—the cardinal dogma of Buddhism in all its forms. The four truths are
stated as follows:—

1. The existence of pain.
2. The production of pain.
3. The annihilation of pain.
4. The way to the annihilation of pain.

The meaning of the truths is this:—Pain exists; that is, all
living beings are subject to it; its production is the result of
the existence of such beings; its annihilation is possible; and
lastly, the way to attain that annihilation is to enter on the
paths opened to mankind by Gautama Buddha. In other
words, the way to avoid that awful series of succeeding births
to which the Indian believed himself subject, was to adopt the
monastic life; to practice all virtues, more especially charity;

to acquire a profound knowledge of spiritual truths; and, in fine, to follow the teaching of the Buddha. Renounce the world, and you will—sooner or later, according to your degree of merit—be freed from the curse of existence; this seems to sum up, in brief, the gospel proclaimed with all the fervor of a great discovery by the new teacher. After about forty-five years of public life devoted to mankind, he died at the age of eighty, at Kusinagara, deeply mourned by a few faithful disciples who had clustered around him, and no doubt regretted by many who had found repose and comfort in his doctrines, and had been strengthened by his example. The names of his principal disciples become almost as familiar to a reader of Buddhist books as those of Peter, James, and John, to a Christian. Maudgalyayana and Sariputtra, the eminent evangelists, and Ananda, the beloved disciple, the close friend and servant of the Buddha, are among the most prominent of this little group. With them rested propagation of the faith, and the vast results, which in two centuries followed their exertions, prove that they were not remiss. The stories of the thousands who embraced the proffered salvation in the life-time of the Buddha are pious fancies. It was the apostles and Fathers of the Church who, while developing his doctrines and largely adding to their complexity and number, almost succeeded in rendering his religion the dominant creed of India.

Such is, in my opinion, the sum total of our positive knowledge with regard to the life lived, and the truths taught, by this great figure in human history. The two points to which I have adverted—namely, the formation of a society apart from the world in which caste was nothing, and the hope held out of annihilation by the practice of virtues and asceticism—are too fundamental and too ancient to be derived from any but the founder. After all, ecclesiastical biographers, while they adorn their heroes with fictitious trappings, do not invent them altogether. A man from whose tuition great results have flowed, cannot be a small man; something of those results must needs be due to the impulse he has given. And if the Buddha must have taught something, must have inaugurated some reform, what is he more likely to have taught, than the way to the annihilation of pain? what reform more likely to have inaugurated than the creation of a society held together by purely spiritual ties ? Both are absolutely essential to Buddhism as we know it. Both are closely connected. For Buddhism would have had nothing to offer without the hope of extinction; and this hope, while leading to the practice of an austere and religious life, can itself be fulfilled only by that life; implying as it does a detachment from the bonds of carnality which hold us to this scene of suffering. Thus, these corner-stones of Buddhism—flowing as they must have done from a mastermind—may, with the highest probability, be assigned to its author.

On one other point there is no reason to call in question the testimony of the legend. We need not doubt he really was the pure, gentle, benevolent, and blameless man which that legend depicts him to have been. Even his enemies have not attempted (I believe) to malign his character. He stands before us as one of the few great leaders of humanity who seem endowed with every virtue, and free from every fault.

SUBDIVISION 2. *The Mythical Buddha.*

Buddhistic authorities divide the life of their founder into twelve great periods, under which it will be convenient to treat of it:—

1. His descent from heaven.
2. His incarnation.
3. His birth.
4. His display of various accomplishments.
5. His marriage, and enjoyment of domestic life.
6. His departure from home, and assumption of the monastic character.
7. His penances.
8. His triumph over the devil.
9. His attainment of the Buddhaship.
10. His turning the Wheel of the Law.
11. His death.
12. His cremation, and the division of his relics.

1. Following, then, the guidance of the accepted legend, we must begin with his resolution to be born on earth for the salvation of the world. After thousands of preparatory births, he

was residing in a certain heaven called Tushita, that being one of the numerous stages in the ascending series of the abodes of the blessed. At length, the end of his sojourn in this heaven arrived. He determined to quit the gods who were his companions there, and to be born on earth. Careful consideration convinced him that the monarch Suddhodana, and his queen, Maya Devi, alone possessed these preëminent qualifications which entitled them to become the parents of a Buddha. Suddhodana lived in the town of Kapila, and belonged to the royal family of the Sakyas, the only family which the Bodhisattva (or destined Buddha) had discovered by his examination to be free from faults by which it would have been disqualified to receive him as one of its members. His wife, in addition to the most consummate beauty, was distinguished for every conjugal and feminine virtue. Here, then, was a couple worthy of the honor about to be conferred upon their house.

2. At this critical moment Maya had demanded, and obtained, the permission of the king to devote herself for a season to the practice of fasting and penance, While engaged in these austerities, she dreamt that a beautiful white elephant approached her, penetrated her side, and entered her womb. At this very time, Bodhisattva actually descended in the shape of a white elephant, and took up his abode within her body. On waking, she related the dream to her husband, who called upon the official Brahmins to interpret it. They declared it to be of good augury. The queen, they said, carried in her womb a being who would either be a "Wheel King," or Sovereign of the whole world; or if he took to a monastic career, would become a Buddha. All things went well during Maya's pregnancy. According to all accounts she underwent none of the discomforts incidental to that state. One writer states that "her soul enjoyed a perfect calm, the sweetest happiness; fatigue and weariness never affected her unimpaired health." Another remarks that she enjoyed "the most perfect health, and was free from fainting fits." An additional gratification lay in the fact, that she was able to see the infant Bodhisattva sitting calmly in his place within her person.

3. Ten months having passed (a Buddha always takes ten), the queen expressed a desire to walk in a beautiful garden

called Lumbini; and, with the king's ready permission, proceeded thither with her attendants. In this garden the hour
of her delivery came on. Standing under a tree (the *ficus relig-
iosa*), which courteously lowered its branches that she might
hold on by them during labor, she gave birth to the child who
was afterwards to be the first of human-kind. Gods from heaven
received him when born, and he himself at once took several
steps forward, and exclaimed: "This is my last birth—there
shall be to me no other state of existence: I am the greatest
of all beings." Ananda, his cousin, and afterwards his disciple,
was born at the same moment. Maya, notwithstanding her
excellent health, died seven days after her child's birth. This
was not from any physical infirmity, but because it is the invariable rule that the mother of a Buddha should die at that
exact time. The reason of this, according to the Lalitavistara,
is, that when the Buddha became a wandering monk her heart
would break. Other respectable authorities assert, that the
womb in which a Bodhisattva has lain is like a sanctuary where
a relic is enshrined. "No human being can again occupy it,
or use it" (P. A., No. III. p. 27). Maya was born again in one
of the celestial regions, and the infant was confided to her sister, his aunt Prajapati, or Gautami, who was assisted in the
care of her charge by thirty-two nurses. He was christened
Sarvarthasiddha, usually shortened into Siddhartha. He is also
known as Gautama Buddha, by which name he is distinguished
from other Buddhas: as Sakyamuni, the hermit of the Sakya
race; as the Tathagata, he who walks in the footsteps of his
predecessors; as Bhagavat, Lord; and by other honorific titles.

Soon after the birth of the Bodhisattva, he was visited and
adored by a very eminent Rishi, or hermit, known as Asita (or
Kapiladevila), who predicted his future greatness, but wept at
the thought that he himself was too old to see the day when
the law of salvation would be taught by the infant whom he
had come to contemplate.

4. When the appropriate age for the marriage of the young
prince arrived, a wife, possessing all the perfections requisite
for so excellent a husband, was sought. She was found in a
maiden named Gopa (or Yasodhara), the daughter of Dandapani, one of the Sakya race. An unexpected obstacle, however,

arose. The father of the lovely Gopa complained that Siddhartha's education had been grossly neglected, and that he was
wanting alike in literary accomplishments and in muscular pro-
ficiency — things which were invariably demanded of the husbands of Sakya princesses. It does, indeed, appear that Suddhodana had taken little pains to cultivate his son's abilities,
and that he had mainly confined himself to the care of his personal safety by surrounding him with attendants. Accordingly,
he asked the prince whether he thought he could exhibit his
skill in those branches of knowledge, the mastery of which
Dandapani had declared to be a necessary condition of his consent. Siddhartha assured his father that he could; and in a
regular competitive examination, which was thereupon held, he
completely defeated the other princes, not only in writing,
arithmetic, and such matters, but in wrestling and archery. In
the last art, especially, he gained a signal victory, by easily
wielding a bow which none of the others could manage.

5. Gopa was now won, and conducted by her husband to a
magnificent palace, where, surrounded by a vast harem of beautiful women, he spent some years of his life in the enjoyment
of excessive luxury. But worldly pleasure was not to retain him
long in its embrace.

6. A crisis in his life was now approaching. Suddhodana had
been warned that Siddhartha would assume the ascetic character if four objects were to meet his sight; an old man, a sick
man, a corpse, and a recluse. Suddhodana, who would have
much preferred his son being a universal monarch to his becoming a Buddha, anxiously endeavored to guard him from
coming across these things. But all was in vain. One day,
when driving in the town, he perceived a wrinkled, decrepit,
and miserable old man. Having inquired of the coachman what
this strange creature was, and having learnt from him that he
was only suffering the general fate of humanity, the Bodhisattva
was much affected; and, full of sad thoughts, ordered his chariot to be turned homewards. Meeting on two other occasions,
likewise when driving, with a man emaciated by sickness, and
with a corpse, he was led to still further reflections on the
wretchedness of the conditions under which we live. Prepared
by these meditations, he yielded completely to the tendencies

aroused within him when, on a fourth excursion, he came across a monk. The aspect of this man—his calmness, his dignity, his downcast eyes, his decent deportment—filled him with desire to abandon the world like him.

The die was cast. Nothing could now retain the Bodhisattva, at this time a young man of nine-and-twenty, from the course that approved itself to his conscience. In vain did his father cause his palace to be surrounded with guards. In vain did the ladies of the harem (acting under instructions) deploy their most ravishing arts to captivate and to amuse him. His resolution was finally fixed by a singular circumstance. The beautiful damsels who ministered to him had sought to engage his attention by an exhibition of the most graceful dancing, accompanied by music, displaying their forms before his eyes as they executed their varied movements. But the Boddhisattva, deep in his meditations, was wholly unaffected. He fell asleep; and the women, baffled in their attempts and wearied out, soon followed his example. But in the course of the night the prince awoke. And then the sight of these girls, slumbering in all sorts of ungainly and ungraceful postures, utterly disgusted him. Summoning a courtier, named Chandaka, he ordered him at once to prepare his favorite horse Kantaka, that he might quit the city of his fathers, and lead the life of a humble recluse. But before thus abandoning his home, there was one painful parting to be gone through. One tie still held him to the world. His wife had just become a mother. Anxious to see his infant son, Rahula, before his departure, he gently opened the door of his wife's apartment. He found her sleeping with one hand over the head of the child. He would fain have taken a last look at his little boy, but fearing that if he withdrew the mother's hand she would awake and hinder his departure, he retired without approaching the bed. In the dead of night, mounted on Kantaka, and with the one attendant whom he had taken into the secret, he managed to leave Kapilavastu unperceived, never to return to it again till he had attained the full dignity of a Buddha.

7. Having sent back Chandaka with the horse, the Boddhisattva commenced, alone and unaided, a course of austerities fitted to prepare him for his great duty. He tried Brahminical

teachers, but was soon dissatisfied with their doctrine. Five of the disciples of one of these teachers followed him for six years in the homeless and wandering life he now began. He adopted the most rigid asceticism, reducing his body to the last degree of feebleness and emaciation. But this too discovered itself to his mind as an error. He took to eating again, and regained his strength, whereupon the five disciples left him, viewing him as a man who had weakly abandoned his principles.

8. After this period of gradual approach to the required perfection the Boddhisattva went to Boddhimanda, the place appointed for his reception of the Buddhaship. Here he had to withstand a furious attack by the demon Mara, who first endeavored to annihilate him by his armies, and then to seduce him by the fascination of his three daughters. But Gautama withstood his male and female adversaries with equal calmness and success. Of the latter he had possibly had enough in his princely palace.

9. All these trials having been surmounted, he placed himself under the Bodhi (or Intelligence) tree, and there, engaging in the most intense meditations, gradually reached the intellectual and moral height towards which he had long been climbing. He was now in possession of Bodhi, or that complete and perfect knowledge which constitutes a Buddha. He was thus fit to teach the law of salvation, but the Lalitavistra represents him as still doubting for a moment whether he should engage in a task which he feared would be thankless and unavailing. Men, he thought, would be incapable of receiving so sublime a doctrine, and he would incur fatigue and make exertions in vain. Silence and solitude recommended themselves at this moment to his spirit. But from a resolution so disastrous he was turned aside by the intercession of the god Brahma.

10. He proceeded accordingly to "turn the Wheel of the Law," or to preach to others, during the forty-five remaining years of his long life, the truths he had arrived at himself. The current lives speak, in their exaggerated manner, of his magnificent receptions by the kings whose countries he visited, and of the thousands of converts whom he made by his preaching, or who, in technical language, obtained Nirvana through him. His father and other members of his family were among

his followers. But among the first-fruits of his teaching were the five Brahmins who had abandoned him when he had relaxed in his ascetic habits. These, on first perceiving him, spoke of him with contempt as a glutton and a luxurious fellow spoilt by softness. But his personal presence filled them with admiration, and they at once acknowledged his perfect wisdom. During this time the two orders of monks and nuns, with their strict regulations enforcing continence and temperance, were founded. Gautama's aunt and nurse, Prajapati, was the first abbess; the Buddha, who had intended to exclude women from his order, having consented to admit them at her request. Rahula, his son, received the tonsure.

11. After he had firmly established his law in the hearts of many devoted disciples, the Buddha "entered Nirvana" at the age of eighty, at Kusinagara. That his death was deeply mourned by the friends who had hung upon his lips, and drawn their knowledge of religious truth from him, need not be related.

12. A pompous account is given of his funeral rites, of which it will be sufficient to mention here that his body was laid upon a pyre, and burnt after the manner of burning in use for Chakravartins, or Universal Monarchs. The princes of Kusinagara wished to keep his relics to themselves; but seven kings, each of whom demanded a share, made threatening demonstrations against them, and after some quarrelling it was agreed to distribute the relics among the whole number. They were therefore divided into eight portions, the royal family of each country taking one. A dagoba, or monument, was erected over them in each of the capitals governed by these royal Buddhists.

Of the numerous stories that are told with regard to the effects of the Buddha's preaching, of the amazing miracles he is said to have performed, and of the wonders reported to have happened at his death and his cremation, there will be an opportunity of speaking in another place. For the present, it is enough to relate the legend of his life in its main features, according to the version piously believed by the millions of human beings who—in China, Tartary, Mongolia, Siam, Burmah, Thibet, and Ceylon—look to him as their law-giver and their savior.

SECTION IV. — ZARATHUSTRA.[*]

Slaves, condemned to make bricks without straw, would
hardly have a more hopeless task than he who attempts to
construct, from the materials now before him, a life of Zarathustra. Eminent as we know this great prophet to have been,
the details of his biography have been lost forever. His name
and his doctrines, with a few scattered hints in the Gâthâs, are
all that remain on record concerning the personality of a man
who was the teacher of one great branch of the Aryan race,
and whose religion, proclaimed many centuries, possibly even a
thousand years, before Christ taught in Galilee, was a great and
powerful faith in the days when Marathon was fought, and is
not even now extinct. We will gather from these fragmentary
sources what knowledge we can of the Iranian prophet, but we
will refuse to fill up the void created by the absence of historical documents with ingenious hypotheses or subtle speculations.

Something approaching to a bit of biography is to be found
in the opening verses of the fifth Gâthâ, which are to this
effect:—

"It is reported that Zarathustra Spitama possessed the best
good; for Ahura Mazda granted him all that may be obtained
by means of a sincere worship, forever, all that promotes the
good life, and he gives the same to all those who keep the
words and perform the actions enjoined by the good religion.

"Thus may Kava Vistaspa, Zarathustra's companion, and the
most holy Frashaostra, who prepare the right paths for the
faith which He who Liveth gave unto the priests of fire, faithfully honor and adore Mazda according to his (Zarathustra's)
mind, with his words and his works!

"Pourutschista, the Hetchataspadin, the most holy one, the
most distinguished of the daughters of Zarathustra, formed the
doctrine, as a reflection of the good mind, the true and wise
one."[†]

---

[*] For an account of all that is to be made out concerning this prophet, see
Haug's Parsees, p. 258-264.

[†] Yasna liii. 1-3. The translations contained in this section are taken
either from Dr. Haug's F. G., or his Parsees. Here and there I have ventured
to amend his English without altering the sense.

Here we find an allusion to the interesting fact that the Zarathustra had a daughter who contributed to the formation of the Parsee creed. The phrase, most distinguished of the daughters, probably does not mean that the prophet was the father of several daughters, but merely that this one was celebrated as his coadjutor. Spiegel has in vain endeavored to discover the name of this lady's husband, but it seems to be doubtful whether anything is known of her matrimonial relations. The fact which it concerns us to notice is, that already in these primitive ages we have a female saint appearing on the scene. In addition to St. Pourutschista, mention is made of two disciples, who were evidently leaders in the apostolic band. The evangelic ardor of Frashaostra is touched upon in the preceding Gâthâ, where it is stated that "he wished to visit my Highlands (i. e., Bactria) to propagate there the good religion," and Ahura Mazda is implored to bless his undertaking. Rava Vistaspa is celebrated in the same place as having obtained knowledge which the living Wise One himself had discovered (Yasna li. 16, 17. Parsees, p. 161). The names of both are well known, being frequently mentioned in the Gâthâs. They appear to have been intimate associates of the prophet. Thus a supposed inquiry is addressed to Zarathustra, "Who is thy true friend in the great work? who will publicly proclaim it?" and the answer is, "Kava Vistaspa is the man who will do this" (Yasna, xlvi. 14). And Frashaostra is spoken of as having received from God, in company with the speaker (probably the prophet himself), "the distinguished creation of truth" (Ibid., xlix. 8). It is added, "for all time we will be thy messengers," or in other words, Evangelists.

Not only do we obtain from the Gâthâs a glympse of Zarathustra attended by zealous disciples, eager to proclaim the good tidings he brought: we learn something also of the opposition he encountered from the adherents of the older faith. And since he actually names himself in the course of one of these compositions, which bears every appearance of genuineness and antiquity, we need not doubt the authenticity of the picture therein given of his relations to these opponents. They were the adherents of the old Devas, the gods whom Zarathustra dethroned;—polytheists, averse to this unheard-of introduction of monotheism into their midst. And they formed, at least during a part of the prophet's life-time possibly during the whole of it, by far the stronger party, for he refers to them in these terms:—

"To what country shall I go? where shall I take refuge? what country gives shelter to the master (Zarathustra) and his companion? None of the servants pay reverence to me, nor do the wicked rulers of the country. How shall I worship thee further, living Wise One?

"I know that I am helpless. Look at me being amongst few men, for I have few men (I have lost my followers or they have left me); I implore thee weeping, thou living God who grantest happiness as a friend gives *a present* to his friend. The good of the good mind is in thy own possession, thou True One! . . .

"The sway is given into the hands of the priests and prophets of idols, who, by their *atrocious* actions, endeavor to destroy the life of man. . . .

"To him who makes this very life increase by means of truth to the utmost for me, who am Zarathustra myself, to such an one the first (earthly) and the other (spiritual) life will be granted as a reward together with all good things to be had on the imperishable earth. Thou, living Wise One, art the very owner of all these things to the greatest extent; thou, who art my friend, O Wise One!" (Yasna. xlv. 1, 2, 11, 19.)

And elsewhere we come across this exclamation: "What help did Zarathustra receive, when he proclaimed the truths? What did he obtain through the good mind?" (Ibid., xlix. 12.)

And the piteous question is put to Ahura Mazda: "Why has the truthful one so few adherents, while all the mighty, who are unbelievers, follow the Liar in great numbers?" (Ibid., xlvii. 4.)

These simple and natural verses point to a prophet who was —for a time at least—without honor in his own country. Whereas the later representations of his career depict him as the triumphant revealer of a new faith, before whose words of power the "Devas," or god of polytheism, flee in terror and dismay, we meet with him here in the character of a persecuted and lonely man, unsupported by the authorities of his nation, opposed by a powerful majority, and imploring, in the distress and desolation of his mind, the all-powerful assistance of his God. Such is the reality; how widely it differs from the fiction we have already seen. But as is always the case with great prophets, who are rejected in their own days and honored after their death, the reality is forgotten; the fiction is universally accepted.

Little need be said of the doctrines taught by Zarathustra. His main principle is belief in the one great God, Ahura Mazda, whom he substitutes for the many gods of the ancient Aryans. He was in fact the author of a monotheistic reformation. The worshipers of these deities are often referred to in opprobrious terms, more especially as "liars," or "adherents of lies," while the devotees of Ahura are spoken of as the good, or as those who are in possession of the truth. It is only through the spirit of lying that the godless seek to do harm; through the true and wise God they cannot do it (Yasna, xlvii. 4). This God, the friend of the prophet, is honored in language of deep and simple adoration; not with the mere vapid epithets of praise which become common in the later sections of the Zend-Avesta. Zarathustra feels himself entirely under his protection, and describes himself ready to preach whatever truths this great Spirit may instruct him to declare.

Beyond this great central dogma — which he announces with all the fervor of a discoverer — there is nothing of a very distinctive kind in his theology. The doctrine of a separate evil spirit opposed to Ahura Mazda does not hold in the Gâthâs that place which it afterwards obtained in the sacred literature of the Parsee. Dr. Haug considers that Zarathustra held merely a philosophical dualism, the two principles of existence — bad and good — being united in the supreme nature of the ultimate Deity. From this great and all-wise Being every good thing emanates. He is the inspirer of his prophet; the teacher of his people; the counselor in the many perplexing questions that harass the minds of his worshipers. To him the pious souls resorts in trouble; by him both earthly possessions and spiritual life are granted to those who rightly seek him. Ahura Mazda is the true God; and there is no other God but Ahura Mazda.

Section V. — Mahomet.*

The last man who has obtained the rank of a prophet is Mohammed, or Mahomet, the son of Abdallah and Amina. Since his time none has succeeded in founding a great, and at the same time an independent religion. Many have wrought changes in preëxisting materials; but no one has built from the foundation upwards. The religion of Mahomet, though compounded of heathen, Judaic, and Christian elements, is not a mere reformation of any of the faiths in which these constituents were found. It depends for its original sanction upon none of these, but derives its *raison d'etre* exclusively from the direct inspiration of its author.

This prophet was born at Mecca in 571, and was the posthumous child of Abdallah, by his wife Amina. His mother died when he was six years old, and he was then taken charge of by his grandfather Abd-al-Mottalib, who, dying in two years, left the child to the care of his son Abu Talib. Mahomet was poor, and had to work for his living in a very humble occupation. In process of time, however, he obtained a comfortable employment in the service of a rich widow, named Khadija, who was engaged in business, and whom he served in the capacity of a commercial traveler; or at first perhaps in a lower situation. His mercenary relation to her was soon superseded by a tenderer bond. He married her in 595, she being then thirty-eight or thirty-nine years of age, and fifteen years older than himself. She was evidently a woman of strong character, and retained an unbroken hold upon the affection of Mahomet until her death in 619. He subsequently married many wives, of whom Ayisha was the most intimate with him; but none of them appears to have exercised so much influence upon his character as Khadija.

She it was who was the first to believe in the divine inspiration which her husband began to disclose in the year 612, at the mature age of forty; and she it was who encouraged and

* The source from which this notice is mainly drawn is Sprenger, "Das Leben und die Lehre des Mohammed," 3 vols. In addition to this I have consulted Muir's "Life of Mahomet;" Caussin de Perceval, "Les Arabes;" Gustav Weil, "Mohammed der Prophet," and other works. The facts here stated will generally be found in Sprenger. The translations of Koranic passages are taken from Rodwell's Koran.

comforted the rising prophet during his early years of trouble and persecution. His first revelation was received by him in 612. It purported to be dictated by the angel Gabriel, who was Mahomet's authority for the whole of the Koran.

"Recite thou," thus spoke his heavenly instructor, "in the name of thy Lord who created;—created man from clots of blood:—Recite thou! For thy Lord is the most beneficent, who hath taught the use of the pen;—hath taught man that which he knoweth not" (K., p. 1.—Sura xcvi).

After this first reception of the word of God, Mahomet passed through that period of extreme depression and gloom which appears to be the universal lot of thoughtful characters, and which Mr. Carlyle has designated "the Everlasting No." For many months he recived no more revelations, and in his despondency he entertained a wish to throw himself down from high mountains, but was prevented by the appearance of the angel Gabriel. In time another communication came to strengthen him in his work; and revelations now began to pour down abundantly. His earliest disciples, besides his wife and his daughters, were his cousin Ali, and the slave Zayd, whom he had adopted as a son. By and by he obtained other important converts, among whom were Abu Bakr, Zobayr, and Othman, afterwards the Chalif.

His earliest revelations were inoffensive to the Meccans; and it was only when he began to preach distinctly the unity of God, the resurrection, and responsibility to the Deity, that opposition was aroused. Persecution followed upon disapproval. Some of Mahomet's followers were compelled to take refuge in Abyssinia, and he himself told the Meccans instructive legends of nations whom God had destroyed for their wickedness in rejecting the prophets who had been sent to them. In 616, however, Mahomet was guilty of a relapse, for he published a revelation recognizing three Meccan idols, Lat, Ozza, and Manah, as intercessors with Allah. In consequence of this concession to their faith, the Koraysch!tes—his own tribe—fell down on their faces in adoration of Allah, and the exiles in Abyssinia returned to their native land. But the prophet was soon ashamed of the weakness by which he had purchased public support. The verse was struck out of the Koran, and the passing recognition of idolatry attributed to the suggestion of the devil. Tradition assigns to this occasion the following verses:

"We have not sent any apostle or prophet before thee, among whose desires Satan injected not some wrong desire; but God shall bring to nought that which Satan had suggested. Thus shall God affirm his revelations, for God is Knowing-Wise! That he may make that which Satan hath injected, a trial to those in whose hearts is a disease, and whose hearts are hardened " (K. p. 593— Sura xxii. 51, 52).

After his renewed profession of Monotheism, Mohomet and his followers were naturally subjected to renewed persecutions. Conversions, however, did not cease; and that of Omar, in 617, was of great importance to the nascent community. Yet matters were at last pushed to extremities by the unbelievers. Mahomet's family, the Haschimites, were excluded from all commercial and social intercourse by the other Korayschites, and compelled to withdraw into their own quarter. This state of quarantine probably lasted from the autumn of 617 to that of 619. At its conclusion Mahomet lost his wife Khadija, and his uncle Abu Talib, who had given him protection.

He was now exposed to many insults and much annoyance. The insecurity in which he lived at Mecca forced him to seek supporters elsewhere. Now the Caaba or holy stone at Mecca was the scene of an annual pilgrimage from the surrounding country. Mahomet made use of the advent of the pilgrims in 621 to enlist in his cause six inhabitants of Medina, who are reported to have bound themselves to him by the following vow:—Not to consider any one equal to Allah; not to steal; not to be unchaste; not to kill their children; not willfully to culumniate; to obey the prophet's orders in equitable matters. Paradise was to be the guerdon of the strict observance of this vow, which from the place where it was taken was called the first Akaba. In the following year, 622, Mahomet met seventy-two men of Medina by night at the same ravine, and the oath now taken was the second Akaba. The believers swore to receive the prophet and to expend their property and their blood in his defense. Twelve of the seventy-two disciples were selected as elders, the prophet following therein the example of Christ.

A place of refuge from the hostility of their countrymen was now open to the rising sect. All the Moslems who were able and willing gradually found their way to Medina. At length none of the intending emigrants remained at Mecca but the prophet himself and his two friends Abu Bakr, and Ali. The designs of the Korayschites against Mahomet's life failed, and he effected his escape to a cave at some little distance from Mecca, and in the opposite direction from Medina. Here he remained in concealment with Abu Bakr for three days, the daughter of the latter bringing food for both. After this time a guide brought three camels with which they proceeded in safety to Medina. The prophet reached Koba, a village just outside it, on the 14th of September 622. He remained here three days, and received the visits of his adherents in Medina every day. This was the celebrated Hegira, or flight, from which the Mussulman era is dated.

In the course of a year, the majority of the inhabitants of Medina had adopted Islam, and a little later those who remained heathens were either compelled or persuaded to embrace, or at least to submit to, the new creed and its apostle. The Jews alone retained their ancient religion. But while Mahomet was thus successful with Medina, he was still exposed to the bitter hostility of Mecca. War between the two cities was the result of the hospitality accorded to him by the former. Mahomet, who now united in his person the temporal and spiritual supremacy in his adopted home, did not shrink from the contest, but carried it on with vigor and success. In the year 624, having gone in pursuit of a Meccan caravan, he met the army of the Korayschites at Badr, and defeated them; although he had not much more than three hundred men, while they commanded from nine hundred to one thousand. In the following year indeed the Moslems were defeated in the battle of Ohod; but in 627 the seige of Medina, undertaken by Abu Sofyân at the head of ten thousand men, was raised after three weeks without serious loss on either side.

Notwithstanding the enmity of its inhabitants, Mecca still retained in the eyes of Mahomet and his disciples its ancient prerogative of sanctity. The Kibla, or point towards which the Moslem was to turn in prayer, had for a time been Jerusalem;

but Mahomet had restored this privilege to his native town two years affer the Hegira. There too was the sacred stone, no less venerated by the pious worshiper of Allah than by the adherents of Lat, Ozza and Manah; and thither it was that the religious pilgrimage had to be performed, for Mahomet had no intention of giving up this part of his ancestral faith. He was desirous in the spring of 628 of performing the pilgrimage to Mecca. The Koreish, however, came out to meet him with an army, determined to preclude his entrance to the city. The design was therefore abandoned; but an important treaty was concluded between Mahomet and Sohayl, who acted as envoy from Mecca. By this compact both parties agreed to abstain from all hostilities for ten years; Mahomet was to surrender fugitives from Mecca, but the Meccans were not to surrender fugitives from him; no robbery was to be practiced; it was open to any one to make an alliance with either party; Mahomet and his followers were to be permitted to enter Mecca for three days in the following year for the festival. After making this agreement Mahomet, yielding to circumstances, performed the ceremonies of the festival at Hodaybiya near Mecca and then withdrew.

The treaty caused great dissatisfaction among the Moslems, as well it might; and the humiliation was heightened when the prophet, shortly after making it, was compelled to fulfil its provisions by giving up certain proselytes who had fled to him, from Mecca. Nevertheless his power continued to grow, and a tribe residing near Mecca took advantage of the treaty to conclude an alliance with him.

Mahomet now began to place himself on a level with crowned heads. In 628 he had a seal made with the inscription upon it: "Mahomet the messenger of God." Furnished with this official seal, he despatched six messengers with letters to the Emperor Heraclius; to the King of Abyssinia; to the Shah of Persia; to Mokawkas, lord of Alexandria; to Harith the Ghassanite chief; and to Hawda in Yamama, a province of Arabia. The purport of all these missives was an exhortation to the various sovereigns and chiefs to embrace the new religion, and a promise that God would reward them if they did, with a warning that they would bear the guilt of their subjects if they did not.

In the same year Mahomet besieged the town of Chaybar, whose inhabitants were Jews. Many of them were killed; the rest were permitted to withdraw with their families. Kinana, their chief, was executed; and his wife Cafyya was added to the already numerous harem of the victor.

The following year, 629, witnessed the performance by the Moslems of the pilgrimage to Mecca for the first time since the Hegira. The prophet summoned those who had accompanied him to Hodaybiya the year before to go with him now. The Koreish, according to the stipulations of the treaty, left the city; the Moslems entered it, performed their devotions, and retired after three days. This year was also marked by a signal victory over a Ghassanite chief, who had executed a Mussulman envoy.

In January, 630, taking advantage of the invitation of an allied tribe who had quarreled with Mecca, Mahomet quitted Medina with a large army for the purpose of taking that city. The exploit was facilitated by the desertion of the general of the Koreish, Abû Sofyân, who privately escaped to the Moslem camp and made his confession of faith. Next day the forces of the prophet entered Mecca with scarcely any resistance. In the following year he laid down the terms upon which the conquered city was to be dealt with. Abu Bakr, accompanied by 300 Moslems, was sent to Mecca as leader of the pilgrims. Ali was charged to make the proclamation to the people which is found in the 9th Sura of the Koran.

"An Immunity from God and his Apostles to those with whom ye are in league, among the Polytheist Arabs! (those who join gods with God). Go ye, therefore, at large in the land four months: but know that God ye shall not weaken; and that those who believe not, God will put to shame — And a proclamation on the part of God and his Apostle to the people on the day of the greater pilgrimage, that God is free from any engagement with the votaries of other gods with God as is his Apostle! If therefore ye turn to God it will be better for you; but if ye turn back then know that ye shall not weaken God: and to those who believe not, announce thou a grievous punishment. But this concerneth not those Polytheists with whom ye are in league, and who shall have afterwards in no way have failed you, nor aided any one against you. Observe, therefore, engagement with them through the whole time of their treaty: for God loveth those who fear him. And when the sacred months are passed, kill those who join other gods with God wherever ye shall find them; and seize them, besiege them, and lay wait for them with every kind of ambush: but if they shall convert, and observe prayer, and pay the obligatory arms, then let them go their way, for God is gracious, merciful. If any one of those who join gods with God ask an asylum of thee, grant him an asylum, that he may hear the Word of God, and then let him reach his place of safety. This, for that they are people devoid of knowledge" (K., p. 611.—Sura ix. 1-6).

Without quoting the proclamation at full length, we may observe that in substance the terms granted were these. Those of the heathen with whom treaties had been made were informed that they should be free for four months. These are the "sacred months" alluded to in the text, and which had always been observed as a time of truce by the heathen Arabs, but which Mahomet deprived of their privilege. After this period was past the Moslems might kill the heathens or take them prisoners wherever they might find them. With other heathens, with whom there was no treaty in existence, Allah announced that he would have nothing further to do. Moreover, the heathen were excluded by this proclamation from approaching the holy places of Mecca in future. "O believers!"—such are the words of this last decree—"only they who join gods with God are unclean! Let them not, therefore, after this year, come near the sacred Temple" (K., p. 615.—Sura ix. 28).

The prophet was now at the climax of his power. All Arabia was his; both materially and spiritually subdued beneath his authority. The city of his birth, which had spurned him as one of her humble citizens, was now compelled to receive him as her lord. No triumph could be more complete; and it is a rare, if not a unique, example of a new religion being persecuted, imperilled, well-nigh crushed, rescued, strengthened, contending for supremacy, and supreme, within the life-time of its founder. But that life-time was now approaching its end. Mahomet in 632 celebrated the last festival he was destined to witness with the utmost pomp. He went with all his wives to

Mecca, and thousands of believers assembled around him there. He preached to them from his camel. He sacrificed one hundred camels. On the 8th of June, 632, he expired in the hut of Ayischa of a remittant fever from which he had been suffering a short time.

The character of the prophet Mahomet is an open question. Between the glowing admiration bestowed upon him by Carlyle, and the sneering depreciation of Sprenger, there lie numerous intermediate possibilities of opinion. His sincerity, his veracity, his humanity, his originality, are all topics of discussion admitting of varied treatment. The old and simple method of treating Mahomet as an impostor scarcely merits notice. Among serious students of his life it may be pronounced extinct. But between positive imposture and a degree of truthfulness equal to that which all would concede to Confucius, or to Jesus, there are many degrees, and a man may be more or less sincere in many particulars which do not involve the fundamental honesty of his conduct. It is in such particulars that the character of Mahomet is most open to suspicion. Few, I believe, would be able to read the earlier Meccan Suras, instinct as they are with a spirit of glowing devotion to a new idea, without entire conviction of the sincerity of their author. Nor can we reasonably doubt that he himself fully believed in the inspiration he professed to receive. The Koran is written precisely in that loose, rambling, and irregular style, which would indicate that its author was above the laws of human composition. If (as is said by some) there is beauty in the original Arabic, that beauty entirely evaporates in translation. The man whose work it is gave utterance to the thoughts of the moment as they were borne in upon him, in his opinion by an external power. But while he no doubt conceived himself as the instrument of the divine being, it is also exceedingly probable that in his later life he abused the weapon which he had thus got into his possession. That is to say, instead of waiting patiently for the revelation, and allowing Allah to take his own time, he in all likelihood put forth as revealed whatever happened to suit the political purpose of the day, and that at whatever moment was convenient to himself. In other words, he may have become less of a passive, and more of an active agent in the composition of the Koran. Take, for example, the two following Suras, belonging to his earliest period, as specimens of the inspired poetic style:—"Say: O ye unbelievers! I worship not that which ye worship, and ye do not worship that which I worship; I shall never worship that which ye worship, neither will ye worship that which I worship. To you be your religion; to me my religion." "Say: He is God alone: God the eternal! He begetteth not, and is not begotten; and there is none like unto him" (K., pp. 12, 13.—Suras cix., cxii).

Contrast these fervent exclamations with such a passage as this, from one of the latest Suras:—

"This day have I perfected your religion for you, and have filled up the measure of my favors upon you: and it is my pleasure that Islam be your religion; but whoso without willful leanings to wrong shall be forced by hunger to transgress, to him, verily, will God be indulgent, merciful. They will ask thee what is made lawful for them. Say: Those things which are good are legalized to you, and the prey of beasts of chase which ye have trained like dogs, teaching them as God hath taught you. Eat, therefore, of what they shall catch for you, and make mention of the name of God over it, and fear God: Verily, swift is God to reckon: This day, things healthful are legalized to you, and the meats of those who have received the Scriptures are allowed to you, as your meats are to them. And you are permitted to marry virtuous women of those who have received the Scriptures before you, when you shall have provided them their portions, living chastely with them without fornication, and without taking concubines" (K., p. 632.—Sura v. 5–7).

The doctrine of direct inspiration, applied to matters like these, is almost a mockery. Yet Mahomet may have continued to think that God assisted him in the task of laying down laws for the believers, and we cannot accuse him of positive insincerity, even though his revelations were no longer the spontaneous outpourings of an overflowing heart.

A more difficult question is raised when we inquire how much of his teaching was borrowed from others, and whether there was any one who acted as his prompter in the novel doctrines he announced. Now there is evidence enough, some of it supplied by the Koran itself, that Mahomet was preceded by a sect called Hanyfites, who rejected the idolatry of their countrymen and held monotheistic doctrines. He spoke of himself as belonging to this sect, of which the patriarch Abraham was considered the representative and founder. Abraham is referred to in the Koran with the epithet "Hanyf," and as one of those who do not join gods with God (E.g., Sura iii. 89; vi. 162; xvi. 121). A dozen or so of the contemporaries of the prophet renounced idolatry before him, and were Hanyfites. Three of these became Christians, and a fourth, by name Zayd, professed to be neither Jew nor Christian, but to follow the religion of Abraham. Zayd was acknowledged as his forerunner by Mahomet himself. But besides these sources of conversion which lay open to the prophet, it is plain from the Koran itself that he had had much intercourse with a person (or persons) of the Jewish faith. Mahomet was not a scholar, and his continual allusions to events in Jewish history plainly indicate a personal source. Moreover, the narratives are given in that somewhat perverted form which we should expect to find if they were derived from loose conversation rather than from study. His belief in the unity of God is not therefore a peculiarity which cannot be explained by reference to the circumstances in which his youth was passed. What was original with him was not the doctrine so much as the intensity with which it took possession of his mind, and the fervor which allowed him no rest until he had done his best to impart to others the profound conviction he entertained of this great truth.

Mahomet in fact began his public career as a simple preacher. The resistance he met with at home, and the necessity of relying for self-preservation on the swords of the men of Medina, converted him from a prophet to a potentate. The change was not one which he could avoid without sacrificing all chances of success; but it does appear to have exercised an unfortunate influence upon his character. As the governor of Medina he became tyrannical and even cruel. Among the worst features of his life is his conduct to the Jews after his attempts at conciliation had been shown to be fruitless. For instance, a Jewish tribe, the Banu Kaynoka, with whom a treaty of friendship had been concluded, were expelled from Medina. Another tribe of

the same religion, the Banu Nadhyr, were blockaded in their
quarter, and driven to capitulate, on condition of being allowed
to leave Medina with their movable property. On the very day
upon which the seige by Abû Sofyân in 627 came to an end,
Mahomet blockaded the Banu Koraytza, also Jews, and compelled them to surrender at discretion. All the men, six hundred in number, were put to death, and the women were sold
as slaves; a punishment which, even on the supposition that
the tribe was hostile to the prophet, was unpardonably severe.
In the ensuing year he marched against Chaybar, a town
inhabited by Jews, besieged and took it. All the Jews taken in
arms were put to death, whereupon the rest surrendered on
condition of being permitted to withdraw with their families
and their portable goods, exclusive of weapons and the precious metals. Kinana, their leader, was executed, and it is a
suspicious circumstance that Mahomet married his widow Cafyya. Nor were these the worst of the prophet's misdeeds. He
even stooped to sanction, if not to order, private assassination.
Shortly after his victory at Badr, a woman and an old man,
both of whom had rendered themselves offensive by their anti-
Mussulman verses, were murdered in the night; and in both
instances the murderers received the protection and countenance
of the prophet and his followers.

Unbridled authority had in fact corrupted him. All those
who did not adhere to his cause committed in his eyes the
crime of opposing the will of God. To a man empowered
by a special commission like his, the ordinary restraints of
morality could not apply. Hence also, if he required a larger
number of wives than was permitted to any other Moslem, a
special revelation was produced to justify the excess. This was
one of the weakest points in the prophet's character. Instead
of setting an example to the community, he was driven to justify his self-indulgence by means which were nothing short of
a perversion of religion to his own ends. There would have
been nothing reprehensible, considering his age and country,
in his indulgence in polygamy, had he observed any kind of
moderation as to its extent. Where he happened to take a
fancy to a woman, and that woman did not object to him, the
moral sense of his countrymen would not have revolted by his

taking her to wife. But it was revolted by the unrestricted freedom with which he added wife to wife, and concubine to concubine; a freedom so great as to degenerate into mere debauchery. He married women whom he had never seen, and who were sometimes already married. Mere beauty seems to have justified in his own eyes the addition of a new member to his harem, and there could be no pretence of real affection in the case of the women whom, without previous acquaintance he took to his matrimonial bed. Exclusive of Khadija, the total number of his wives was thirteen, of whom nine survived him. He had also three concubines.

That his procedure scandalized the faithful is shown by the necessity he felt of defending it by the pliant instrument of revelation. Not only did he obtain from God a special law entitling him to exceed the usual number of wives; other pecularities in his conduct were justified, either by an *ex post facto* decision applicable to all, or by an appeal to his extraordinary rights in his character of prophet. He had, for example conceived a desire to possess Zaynab, the wife of his adopted son Zaid. Zaid obligingly divorced her, and received the greatest favor from the prophet for this friendly conduct. Zaynab made it a condition of her compliance that the union with Mahomet should be sanctioned by revelation, and this sanction was of course procured. Marriage with an adopted son's wife was somewhat shocking, and the following reference in the Koran indicates the manner in which the affair was regarded:

"And, remember, when thou saidst to him unto whom God had shown favor [*i. e.*, to Zaid], and to whom thou also hadst shown favor, 'Keep thy wife to thyself, and fear God;' and thou didst hide in thy mind what God would bring to light, and didst fear man; but more right had it been to fear God. And when Zaid had settled concerning her to divorce her, we married her to thee, that it might not be a crime in the faithful to marry the wives of their adopted sons, when they have settled the affair concerning them. And the behest of God is to be performed. No blame attacheth to the prophet where God hath given him a permission " (K., p. 566. — Sura xxxiii. 38.39).

In another case he wished to induce a cousin, who was already married, though only to a heathen husband living at

Mecca, to become his wife; but she, believer as she was, refused to be untrue to her conjugal duties. He permitted himself also to accept the love of women who simply surrendered themselves to him without the sanction of their relations, conduct which placed them in a highly disadvantageous position, since in case of dismissal by her husband, a woman thus informally married was not entitled to the dowry which other married women would receive, nor could she claim the protection of her family. "Among the heathen Arabs," observes Sprenger, "a man who accepted such a favor would have been killed by the woman's family" (L. L. M,, vol. iii. p. 84). But for the case of the cousin and for the case of such obliging female devotees the Koran had its suitable provisions:—

"O Prophet! we allow thee thy wives whom thou hast dowered, and the slaves whom thy right hand possesseth out of the booty which God hath granted thee, and the daughters of thy uncle, and of thy paternal and maternal aunts who fled with thee *to Medina*, and any believing woman who hath given herself up to the prophet, if the prophet desired to wed her — a privilege for thee above the rest of the faithful. . . . Thou mayest decline for the present whom thou wilt of them, and thou mayest take to thy *bed* whom thou wilt, and whomsoever thou shalt long for of those thou shalt have before neglected; and this shall not be a crime in thee. Thus will it be easier to give them the desire of their eyes, and not to put them to grief, and to satisfy them with what thou shalt accord to each of them. God knoweth what is in your hearts, and God is knowing, gracious."

By a combination of qualities which is not uncommon, he added to an unrestricted license in his own favor an equally unrestricted jealousy concerning others. He could not bear the thought that any other man might possibly enjoy one of his wives even after his death. His followers were told that they "must not trouble the Apostle of God, nor marry his wives after him, for ever. This would be a grave offense with God." In the same paltry spirit he orders them, when they would ask a gift of any of his wives, to ask it from behind a veil. "Purer will this be for your hearts and for their hearts." Lest any stranger should trouble this uneasy husband by obtaining a sight of his wives' naked faces, he required them invariably to wear a veil in public, and never to expose themselves unveiled except to near male relations, slaves, or women (K., p. 569. — Sura xxxiii. 51, 53, 55).

Texts like these exhibit the degeneracy of the prophet's character in his later days. He wanted the stimulus of adversity to keep him pure. But he had done his work, and that work was on the whole a good one. Not indeed that there was anything very original or striking in the doctrines he announced. The Koran rings the changes on the unity of God, his power, his mercy, and his other well-known qualities; on the resurrection, with its delights for the faithful and its terrible judgments for the wicked; and on the vast importance of belief in the prophet and submission to his decrees. But this religion, though containing no elements that did not already exist in its two parents, Judaism and Christianity, was an improvement on the promiscuous idolatry which it superseded. It was less sensual and more abstract; and its moral tone was higher. Greater still than the improvement in the creed of the Arabs was the improvement in their material *status*. Unity of faith brought with it unity of action. From a number of scattered, independent, and often hostile tribes, the Arabs became a powerful and conquering nation. Other peoples were in course of time converted, and the religion of Mahomet was in the succeeding centuries carried in triumph over vast districts where the name of Christ had hitherto reigned supreme. Districts of heathen Africa have also accepted it. Were the prophet able to speak to us now, he would be entitled to say that the manifest blessing of Allah had rested upon the work he had begun in obscurity and persisted in through persecution; and that the partiality of heaven was evident from the fact that Christianity had never succeeded-and had no prospect of succeeding, in regaining the vast territory in Europe and in Africa from which Islam has expelled it.

Section VI. — Jesus Christ.

When we endeavor to write the life of Jesus Christ, the greatest of the prophets, we are beset by peculiar difficulties arising from the nature of the materials. While in the case of the Buddha we receive from authorities a life which, though largely composed of fiction, is at least uniform and consistent, in the case of Jesus we have biographies from several sources, all of them partly historical, partly legendary, and each in some respects at issue with all the rest. Hence the labor of sifting fact from fiction, as also that of reproducing and classifying the fictitious element itself, is far more difficult. In sifting fact from fiction we have to judge, among two, three, or four versions of an occurrence, which is likely to be the most faithful statement of the truth, and within this statement itself how much we may accept, how much we must reject. And in reproducing and classifying the fictitious element we have not merely to relate a simple story, but to combine into our narrative varying, and sometimes conflicting, forms of the same fundamental myth.

Hence further subdivision will be needed in the case of Jesus than was requisite in treating the lives of any of the other prophets. We may in fact discern in the gospels three distinct strata: a stratum of fact; a stratum of miracle and marvel; and a stratum (in John) of mere imagination *within* the realm of natural events. Correspondently to these divisions in the sources we will treat Jesus first as historical; secondly, as mythical; thirdly, as ideal. The historical Jesus is the actual human figure who remains after abstraction has been made of the miraculous and legendary portions of his biography. The mythical Jesus, who is found in the three first gospels, is the human subject of legendary narratives; the ideal Jesus, who is found in John, is a completely superhuman conception.

Finally, it may be needful to remark that the names affixed to the several gospels are merely traditional, and that in using them as a brief designation for these works, no theory as to their actual authorship is intended to be implied. The gospels (excepting perhaps the fourth) were the work of many authors, though ultimately compiled and edited by a single hand. Who this editor was is of little moment; and who the original authors were we never can discover. So that the gospels are to all intents and purposes anonymous; but it will be convenient, after noting this fact, to continue to describe them by their current titles.

Subdivision 1. — *The Historical Jesus.*

In attempting to sketch the outline of the actual life of Jesus — and anything more than an outline must needs be highly conjectural — there are some general principles which it is advisable to follow. Recollecting that we have to deal with biographers who have mingled in promiscuous confusion the supernatural with the natural, impossibilities with probabilities, fables with facts, it becomes our duty to endeavor to separate these heterogeneous elements according to some consistent plan. That this can ever be perfectly accomplished is not to be expected. The figure of Jesus must ever move in twilight, but we may succeed in reducing the degree of unavoidable obscurity.

The first of the maxims to be observed will be furnished by a little consideration of the kind of thing likely to be the earliest committed to writing, as also to be the most accurately handed down by tradition. This, it appears to me, would be sayings, rather than doings. Nothing in the life of Jesus is more characteristic and remarkable than his oral instruction; this would impress itself deeply upon the minds of his hearers, and nothing, we may fairly conjecture, would be so soon committed to writing either by them or by their followers. Moreover, the records of discourses and parables would be, in the main, more accurate than those of events; slight differences in the words attributed to a speaker being (except in special cases) less material than divergences in the manner of portraying his actions. Historical confirmation of this hypothesis is not wanting. There is the well-known statement of Papias that Matthew wrote down the "sayings" of Christ in Hebrew [Syro-Chaldaic]. And if we look for internal evidence, we find it in the far greater agreement among the synoptical gospels as to the doctrines taught by Jesus than as to the incidents of his career. The incidents bear traces of embellishment undergone in passing from mouth to mouth from which the doctrines are free. In some cases, moreover, there is concurrence as to the doctrines taught along with divergence as to the place where, and the circumstances under which, they were delivered. Added to which considerations there is the all-important fact that the events in the life of Christ are often of a supernatural order,

while his discourses (excepting those in John) present nothing
irreconcilable with his position in regard either to his epoch,
his presumable education, or his nationality.

Giving this preference to sayings in general, over doings in
general, we may next establish an order of preference among
doings themselves. Of these, some are natural and probable;
others unnatural and improbable; others again supernatural
and impossible. The first kind will, of course, be accepted
rather than the second; while the third kind must be rejected
altogether. And as a corollary from this general principle, it
follows that where one narrative gives a simpler version than
another of the same event or series of events, the simpler version is to be preferred.

A third rule of the utmost importance is that when any
statement is opposed, either directly or by its implications, to
subsequent tradition, that statement may be confidently received. For when the whole course of opinion in the Christian
Church has run in a given direction, the preservation in one of
our Gospels of an alleged or implied fact conflicting with the
established view, is an unmistakable indication that the truth
has been rescued from destruction in a case where succeeding
generations would gladly have suppressed it.

A fourth maxim, which is likely to be useful, is that wherever
we can perceive traces of faults or blemishes in the character
of Christ, we may presume them to have actually existed. For
his biographers were deeply interested in making him appear
perfect, and they would have been anxious wherever possible to
conceal his weaknesses. Where, therefore, they suffer such
human frailties to be perceived, their unconscious testimony is
entitled to great weight. For although they themselves either
do not see or do not acknowledge that what they record is really
evidence of faultiness at all, yet it is plain that circumstances
conveying such an impression to impartial minds are not likely
to have been invented. The conduct ascribed to Jesus might be
capable of justification from his peculiar mission or his peculiar
conception of his duties, but admiring disciples would not wan-
tonly burden him with a load not rightly his. Yet this principle, though unquestionable in the main, must be tempered with
the qualification that there are cases where his followers may

have misunderstood and misrepresented him. It must be added that a similar presumption of truth attaches to the record of faults or blunders in the ·conduct of the disciples, whose characters their disciples were likewise anxious to exalt.

In the fifth place, it is a reasonable supposition that the less complete the outline of the life of Jesus contained in any Gospel, the more authentic is that Gospel. Gaps in the story told by one writer which, in another writer, have been filled up, are strong indications of actual gaps in the life as known to the first Christians. While it is true that the compiler of one Gospel might, from ignorance or from design, omit some historical fact which the compiler of another would insert, yet it is unlikely that whole years would be passed over in silence, or remarkable events left out, where any genuine knowledge of those years or those events was possessed by the biographer. But nothing is more natural than that a space, subsequently felt to be a serious and almost intolerable void, should in process of time be removed by the exercise of the imagination craving to fill the empty canvas with living figures. Nor even where there is no positive blank, is it surprising that many actions conformable to the notion formed of Christ should be fitted into his career, and made to take their places alongside of others of a more unquestionable nature. We shall therefore prefer the scantiest account of the life of Jesus to the fullest.

A careful comparison of the first three Gospels — which alone can pretend to an historical character — will establish the fact that the second, ascribed to Mark, is the most trustworthy, or to speak accurately, the least untrustworthy, according to these canons. For in the first place, it absolutely omits many of the most noteworthy events comprehended by the other Gospels in the life of Jesus. Secondly, it sometimes gives a natural version of a circumstance which appears in the others as supernatural; or a comparatively simple version of a circumstance which the others have converted into something mystical. It surpasses the others in statements, and still more in omissions, implying divergence from well-established subsequent tradition; and in general the far greater scantiness of detail, the failure to fill up blanks as the other Evangelists have done, the almost fragmentary character of this Gospel, are points telling largely in its favor. That, however, we have the earliest, or anything approaching the earliest form of the life of Jesus in Mark it would be a great error to assume. As much as Mark differs from Matthew and Luke, so much at least did the primitive story differ from his, and in the same direction. Nay, it must have differed far more, for by the time the second Gospel was committed to its present form, a cloud of marvels had already surrounded the person of Jesus, and obscured his genuine figure. Through the mist of this cloud we must endeavor to discern such of his lineaments as have not been totally and forever hidden from our scrutinizing gaze.

Very little is known of the parents of Jesus, and even that little has rather to be inferred from casual references than gathered from direct statements. Joseph, his father, was a carpenter or builder, but his status is nowhere clearly defined. He and his family appear, however, to have been well known in their native country, and he was probably, therefore, not a mere workman, but a tradesman in comfortable circumstances.* At any rate, he was the father of a considerable family, consisting of five sons and of more than one daughter (Mt. xiii. 55, and xii. 46; Mk. vi. 3, and iii. 31; Lu. viii. 19). The names of the brothers of Jesus,—James, Joses, Simon, and Judas,—have been preserved, while those of his sisters are unknown.

Whether there is not some confusion here, may indeed be doubted, for we hear also of another Mary, the mother of James and Joses (Mk. xv. 40; Mt. xxvii. 56), and it is possible (as M. Renan supposes), that the names of her children have been substituted for those of the genuine brothers of Christ which had been forgotten. Paul certainly mentions James, the Lord's brother (Gal. i. 19), and it would be natural to interpret this literally. But the question does not admit of any positive decision. Of the actual existence, however, of both brothers and sisters there can be no reasonable doubt; for they are spoken of as personages who were familiar to their neighbors, while the very fact that they play no part in the subsequent history is a

---

* The author of "The Messiah" (London, 1872) contends that he was not only a master builder, but the principal builder of Nazareth. His remarks on this subject (pp. 91 ff.) deserve consideration, though they are not conclusive.

guarantee that they have not been invented for a purpose. Little is known of his mother Mary, her genuine form having been transfigured at a very early period by the Christian legend. The first and third Gospels have made her the subject of a story which would force us — if we accept it at all — to consider Jesus as her illegitimate child, born of some other father than Joseph. But there is no adequate ground to ascribe to her such laxity of conduct. For aught we can discern to the contrary, she seems to have borne a fair reputation among her countrymen, who undoubtedly, according to the incidental and therefore unbiased testimony of all four Evangelists, believed Jesus to have been the son of Joseph, begotten, like the rest of his family, in wed-lock (Mt. xiii. 55; Mk. vi. 3; Lu. iv. 22; Jo. vi. 42,)

Beyond the fact that Joseph and Mary occupied a respecta-ble position in Nazareth, we can say little of them. The lineage of both was plainly unknown to the compilers of the Gospels, since Joseph has been endowed with two different fathers, while the parentage of Mary has not even been alluded to. All that we can venture to assert is, that neither of them were reputed to be of the family of David, for Jesus took pains to prove that the Messiah need not, as was commonly believed, be descended from that monarch (Mt. xxii. 41–46; Mk. xii. 35–37; Lu. xx. 41–44). There would have been no occasion for his ingenious suggestion that David, by calling the Messiah Lord, disproved the theory that this Lord must be his son, unless he had felt that his belonging to a family which could not claim such a pedigree might be used as an argument against his Messianic character. We may confidently conclude then that his lineage was obscure.

That his birth took place at Nazareth is abundantly obvious from the very contrivances resorted to in Matthew and Luke to take his parents to Bethlehem for that event. According to either of these narratives one fact is plain: that the habitual dwelling-place of the family was Nazareth; while Matthew has preserved the valuable information that he was called a Naza-rene (Mt. ii. 23), a statement which is confirmed by the manner in which he is alluded to in John, as "Jesus of Nazareth, the son of Joseph" (Jo. i. 45). Jesus therefore passed in his life-time for a native of Nazareth, and as it does not appear that he ever contradicted the current assumption, as moreover the only two authorities which are at issue with this assumption are also at issue with one another on all but the bare fact of the birth at Bethlehem, we need not hesitate to draw the inference that he was born at Nazareth.

In his youth the son of Joseph was apprenticed to his father's trade, and he may have practiced it for many years before he took to his more special vocation of a public teacher. He was at any rate known to his neighbors as "the carpenter," and his abandonment of that calling for one in which he seemed to pretend to a position of authority over others, caused both astonishment and indignation among his old acquaintances.

His public career was closely preceded by that of an illustrious prophet, by whom he must have been profoundly influenced — John the Baptist. Very little of the doctrine of John has been preserved to us, his fame having been eclipsed by that of his successor. But that little is sufficient to evince the great similarity between his teaching and that of Jesus. He was in the habit of baptizing those who resorted to him in the Jordan, and of inculcating repentance, because the kingdom of heaven was at hand (Mt. iii. 2). Now precisely the same tone was adopted by Jesus after the captivity of John. Repentance was inculcated on account of the approaching advent of the kingdom of heaven, and a mode of instruction similar to that of John was practiced. Both these prophets, affected no doubt by the troubled condition of Judea, enjoined the simple amendment of the lives of individuals as the means towards a happier state of things. Both attracted crowds around them by the force and novelty of their preaching. Jesus, according to a probable interpretation of the narrative, was so much impressed by the lessons of his predecessor, and by the baptism received from him, that he for a time retired to a solitary place, living an ascetic life, and pondering the stirring questions that must have burnt within him. During this retirement Jesus could mature his designs for the future, and on emerging from it he was able at once to take up the thread of John the Baptist's discourses. Possibly John himself had perceived the high capacity of the young Nazarene, and had appointed him to the prophetic office. But the story of his baptism by John has been unfortunately so surrounded with mythical circumstances, that the true relations between these teachers can no longer be discerned.

Meditating in the wilderness on the words of John the Baptist, and on the state of his country, the notion may have entered the mind of Jesus that he himself was the destined Messiah. While the power he felt within him may have given birth to the idea, the idea once born would react upon his nature and increase the power within him. But whether the conception of his own Messiahship arose now or at some other period, it is plain that he was animated by it during his public career, and that it gave to all his teaching its peculiar tone of independent authority. How far he was completely convinced of his own claim to the Messianic title will be considered in another place; it is sufficient to say here that he was plainly anxious that this claim should be acknowledged, and the rights it conferred upon him recognized.

On emerging from his retreat, he began the public promulgation of his doctrines; at first, however, with caution and reserve, and keeping within the lines marked out by John the Baptist. Attracted by the young enthusiast, a select band of followers gathered around him, and while he inspired them with implicit trust, they no doubt inspired him in their turn with higher confidence. The reticence which modesty or hesitation had produced gradually melted away, and he began boldly to put forth pretensions which, while they repelled and scandalized many, drew others into a closer companionship and a more implicit submission. Simon and Andrew, James and John, were the first, or among the first, of his disciples. Eight others joined him at about the same period of his life, their names being Philip, Bartholomew, Matthew, Thomas, James the son of Alpheus, Thaddeus, Simon the Canaanite, and Judas (Mk. iii. 14-19; Mt. x. 1-4). While these formed the inner circle, we must suppose that he had many other admirers and followers, who were either less intimate with him, or less constant in their attendance. And there may even have been others of equal intimacy with the twelve apostles, whose names have not been handed down to us. For all the apostles did not enjoy an equally close and unreserved friendship with their master.

Three of their number—Simon, James, and John—stood towards him in an altogether special and peculiar relationship. They are far more prominent than any of the other nine. They were selected to accompany Jesus when others were left behind. They formed an inmost circle within the circle of his more constant companions. Them alone he is said to have distinguished by names of his own invention. On Simon he conferred the name of Peter. To James and John, the sons of Zebedee, he applied the familiar nickname of Boanerges, or sons of thunder, which seems to indicate that they were distinguished by the fervor of their zeal (Mk. iii. 16, 17).

The admirers of Jesus were scarcely, if at all, less numerous among the female than among the male sex. Indeed, he seems to have exercised a very marked fascination over women. When he went to Jerusalem, he was followed by many women from Galilee, who had been accustomed to contribute to his wants, and to give him that personal attention which kindly women know so well how to confer. Mary Magdalene whom he had healed of some mental ailment, Mary the mother of James, Salome the mother of the sons of thunder, were among the most devoted of these, while two sisters, Mary and Martha, Joanna the wife of Chuza, Herod's steward, and Susanna, are also mentioned (Mk. xv. 40, 41; Lu. viii. 2, 3, x. 38, 39). If we may believe one of the Evangelists, who stands alone in this respect, the homage of women was particularly agreeable to Jesus, who received it with words of the highest praise (Lu. vii. 36-50 x. 38-42). That some among these many female followers were drawn to him by the sentiment of love is, at least, highly probable. Whether Jesus entertained any such feeling towards one of them it is impossible to guess, for the human side of his nature has been carefully suppressed in the extant legend.

Supported then by adherents of both sexes, Jesus entered upon his career of a public teacher. His own house was at Capernaum (Mt. iv. 13), but he wandered from place to place in the exercise of his vocation, staying, no doubt, with friends and disciples. It is not necessary to follow him in these peregrinations, of which only the vaguest accounts have been preserved by the Evangelists. But two remarkable circumstances deserve to be noted; namely, that his own family rejected his pretensions, and that he met with no success in his own district. Of the former, in addition to the negative evidence furnished by the fact that neither Mary nor the brothers of Jesus are mentioned among the believers, we have the positive evidence of John that his brothers did not believe (Jo. vii. 5), confirmed by the statement in the other Gospels that his family attempted to see him during the earlier part of his career, and that Jesus positively refused to have anything to do with them (Mk. iii. 31–35; Mt. xii. 46–50; Lu. viii. 19–21). This desire on the part of the family to confer with him, and the manner in which Jesus, disavowing all special ties, adopts all who " do the will of God " as mother, brother and sister, admits of but one construction. Mary and her other children were anxious to draw him away from the rash and foolish mode of life — as they deemed it — on which he had entered, and Jesus, understanding their design, avoided an unpleasant interview by simply declining to be troubled with them. And if, as is highly probable, it was they who thought him mad (Mk. iii. 21), we have further proof that neither his mother nor any of the other members of his family can be counted among his converts, at any rate during his life-time. The second circumstance, his complete failure in his own neighborhood, is attested by a saying of his own, recorded by all four Evangelists. A prophet, he is reported to have said, is without honor in his own country, among his own kin, and in his own house (Mk. vi. 4). To which it was added that he was unable to perform any work of power there, beyond curing a few sick people. And these cures evidently did not impress the skeptical Nazarenes, for we are told that " he marveled because of their unbelief " (Mk. vi. 5, 6).

Leaving, therefore, these hard-hearted neighbors, he proceeded to address the people of Galilee and Judea in discourses which excited great attention; sometimes inculcating moral truths in plain but eloquent language, sometimes preferring to illustrate them by little stories, the application of which he either made himself or left to his hearers to discover. Had these stood alone, they would have sufficed to give him a high reputation. But he did not depend on words alone for his success among the people. The peculiar condition of Palestine at this epoch gave him a favorable opportunity of supplementing words by deeds. The trials and sufferings they had undergone, both from the Herodian family and the Romans; the constant outrage to their deepest feelings afforded by the presence of an alien soldiery; the insults, humiliations, and cruelties they endured at the hands of their conquerors, had wrought the people up to a state of almost unbearable tension and extreme excitement. That under the pressure of such a state of things nervous disorders should be widely prevalent, is not to be wondered at. And these affections, as is well known, are peculiarly infectious, easily spreading through a whole village and raging in a whole country (See, for example, Hæcker's Epidemics, *passim*). Hysteria, moreover, takes many forms. Now it may show itself as species of madness; now as the imagination of some positive disease. Here it may be violent and outrageous; there morbid and gloomy. Another peculiarity is its tendency to increase the more, the greater the attention paid to it by friends and onlookers. To be an object of interest to those around is enough to inflame the symptoms of the hysterical patient. And when this interest took shape in a belief that he was inhabited by some bad spirit—which was equally the theory of the Jews in the time of Christ, and of Christians up to the middle ages—it was natural that the evil should be magnified to the highest degree. There are, however, some individuals who exercise a peculiar power over sufferers of this description. Their looks, their touch, their words, are all soothing. By addressing the victims of hysteria in tones of authority, by taking their hands, or otherwise endeavoring to calm their excited nerves, these physicians of nature may put a stop to the pain, or expel the illusion. In modern days they would be called mesmerists, and though the pecularities of temperament to which they owe their mesmeric faculty are not yet understood, their influence is well known to those who have examined into the subject.

Among the Jews, the subjects of these current maladies were said to be possessed by devils. And it was a common profession to cast out these so-called devils,* for we are told that it was

---

* Lu. xi. 19. I use this verse, not as evidence that Jesus actually spoke the words ascribed to him, but that the practice of casting out devils was common to Jesus and the disciples of the Pharisees.

practiced by the adherents of the Pharisees. What means they employed we do not know. Probably they were not of the mesmeric order, but consisted in charms and exorcisms which, being believed by the patients to have the power of curing them, actually had it. At any rate, the fact remains that Jesus and the Pharisees are reputed to have possessed a similar influence over the demons, and if we accept the statement as true in the one case we cannot consistently reject it in the other. It remains to be considered, however, whether the evidence is such as to induce us to believe it in either. Now it is quite true that a great many absurd and impossible miracles are ascribed to Jesus in the Gospels. But considering the important place occupied in his life — as it has come down to us — by his cures of sick people; considering the possibility above suggested that many of these might have taken place by known methods; considering too the extremely easy field which Palestine presented for their application, it would appear more likely that there might be a basis of truth in the numerous accounts of sudden recoveries effected by him, than that they were all mere inventions. We may then assume, without here entering into details, that a number of unfortunate people, thought to be possessed by devils, either met him on his way, or were brought to him by relations, and were restored to health by the authoritative command addressed to the evil spirit to depart; mingled with the sympathetic tone and manner towards the tormented subject of possession. Individual examples of these apparently miraculous cures may be open to doubt from the very inaccurate character of the records, and for this reason it will be better for the present to admit the general fact without binding ourselves to this or that special instance of its occurrence.

Possessing this power himself, and ignorant of its source, Jesus attempted to communicate it to his disciples. It is expressly stated that he gave them power to heal sicknesses and cast out devils (Mk. iii. 15), though it is doubtful whether they met with much success in this vocation. On one occasion, at least, a signal failure is reported, and as the fact stated redounds neither to the glory of Christ, who had appointed his disciples to the work, nor of the disciples who had received the appoint-

ment, we may believe it to be true (Mk. ix. 14–29). A parent
had brought his little son to the apostles to be delivered from
some kind of fits from which he suffered. The apostles could
do nothing with him. When Jesus arrived he ordered the spirit
to depart, and the boy, after a violent attack, was left tranquil.
We are not told indeed how long his calmness lasted, nor
whether the fits were permanently arrested. For the moment,
however, a remedy was effected, and the disciples naturally inquired why they had not been equally successful. The extreme
vagueness of the reply of Jesus renders it probable that his
remedial influence was due to some personal characteristic
which he could not impart to others. This conclusion is confirmed by the noteworthy fact that an unknown person exercised
the art of casting out devils in the name of Jesus, though not
one of his company (Mk. ix. 38–40). Here the name would be
valuable only because of its celebrity, the expulsion of the devils
being due, as in the case of Jesus himself, to the personal endowments of the exorcist. At any rate, we have the broad facts
that the Pharisees, Jesus himself, and the unknown employer
of his name, were all proficient in the art of delivering patients
from the supposed possession of evil spirits. Possibly too the
apostles did the same, and it was certainly the intention of Jesus
that they should.

Such exhibitions of power, though they might tend to
strengthen the influence of Jesus among the multitude, were
not the principal means on which he depended for acceptance.
His sermons and his parables were both more remarkable and
more original. In addition to the fact that he taught, in the
main, pure and beautiful moral doctrines, he well knew how to
exemplify his meaning by telling illustrations. The parables
by which he enforced his views have become familiar to us all,
and deserve to remain among our most precious literary possessions. What more especially distinguished his mode of teaching
from that of other masters was the air of spiritual supremacy
he assumed, and his total independence of all predecessors but
the writers of Scripture. Not indeed that he ventured upon
any departure from the accepted tradition with regard to the
history of his nation, or the authority of the Old Testament.
On the contrary, he was entirely free from any approach to a

critical or inquiring attitude. But in so far he did not teach
like the scribes, that he boldly put forth his own interpretations
of Scripture and his own views of ethics, without the smallest
regard for the established opinions of the schools, and without
seeking support from any authority but his own. In this course
he was evidently strengthened by an inward conviction that he
was the destined Messiah of the Jewish people. Deputed, as
he conceived, directly from God, he could afford to slight the
restrictions which others might place upon their conduct. He
was not bound by the rules which applied to ordinary men.

This assumption, with its corresponding behavior, could not
fail to give great offense to those by whom his title was not
conceded. And we accordingly find that he comes into constant
collision with the recognized legal and religious guides of the
Jews. Among the first of the shocks he inflicted on their sense
of propriety was his claim to be authorized to forgive sins (Mk.
ii, 7). To the Jewish mind this pretension was highly blasphemous; no one, they thought, could forgive sins but God, and
they did not understand the credentials in virtue of which this
young man acted as his ambassador. Further scandal was
caused by his contempt for the common customs observed on
the Sabbath day (Mk. ii. 24, and iii. 6), which appeared to him
inconsistent with the original purpose of that institution. The
language he was accustomed to use to his disciples, and to his
hearers generally, was not of a nature to soothe their growing
animosity. Designating himself by the Messianic term of " the
Son of man," he announced the approach, even during the generation then extant, of a kingdom of heaven wherein he himself
was to return clothed with glory, and his followers were to be
gathered round him to enjoy his triumph. Along with these
promises to his friends, there flowed forth indignant denunciation of the Pharisees and Scribes, who were held up to the
scorn of the populace.

Having thus provoked them to the utmost, he imprudently
accepted the honor of a sort of triumphal entry into Jerusalem,
the pomp of which, however, has probably been somewhat exaggerated (Mk. xi. 1-11). Nor was this all. He proceeded to an
act of violence which it was impossible for the authorities to
overlook. The current Roman money not being accepted at the

temple, the outer court of this building was used by money-changers, who performed the useful and necessary service of receiving from those who came to make their offerings the ordinary coinage, and giving Jewish money instead of it. Doves being also required by the law to be offered on certain occasions, there were persons outside the temple who sold these birds. Indignant at what seemed to him a violation of the sanctity of the spot, Jesus upset the tables of these traffickers, and described them all as thieves. It is added in one account that he interfered to prevent vessels being carried through the temple (Mk. xi. 15-17). That, after this, the spiritual rulers should ask him to produce his authority for such conduct, was not unnatural. Nor is it surprising that, after his unsatisfactory reply to their inquiry, they should take steps to prevent the repetition of similar scenes.

The efforts of the chief priests to bring about his destruction are described in two of our Gospels as the direct result of his proceedings about the temple, the impression he had made on the multitude being a further inducement (Mk. xi. 18; Lu. xix. 48). Aware of the indignation he had excited, Jesus soon after these events retired into some private place, known only to his more intimate friends. So at least I understand the story of his betrayal. Either Judas never betrayed him at all, or he was lurking in concealment somewhere in the neighborhood of Jerusalem. That the conduct attributed to Judas should be a pure invention appears to me so improbable, more especially when the history of the election of a new apostle is taken into account, that I am forced to choose the latter alternative. The representation of the Gospels, that Jesus went on teaching in public to the very end of his career, and yet that Judas received a bribe for his betrayal, is self-contradictory. The facts appear to be that Jesus ate the passover at Jerusalem with his disciples, and that immediately after it, conscious of his growing danger, he retired to some hidden spot where he had lived before, and where friends alone were admitted to his company. Judas informed the authorities of the temple where this spot was. They thereupon apprehended Jesus, and brought him before the Sanhedrim for trial.

So confused and imperfect is the account of this trial given by the Evangelists, that we are unable to make out what was the nature of the charge preferred against him, or of the evidence by which it was supported. It is clear, however, that the gravamen of the accusation was that he had put forth blasphemous pretensions to be the Messiah, "the Son of the Blessed One." And this was supported by a curious bit of evidence. Two witnesses deposed, either that they had heard him say he *would* destroy this temple made with hands and build another made without hands within three days, or that he *was able* to destroy the temple, and to rebuild it in three days (Mt. xxvi. 61; Mk. xiv. 58). The witnesses are called false witnesses, both in Mark and in Matthew. But if we turn to John (Jo. ii. 19), we find the probable source of the charge brought against him by these two witnesses, and we find reason also to think that they were not perjurers. There we are told that after he had driven the money-changers and traders from the temple, the Jews asked him for a sign that might evince his right to do such things. In reply to their demand, Jesus is reported to have said, "Destroy this temple, and in three days I will raise it up." Connecting this statement in the one Gospel with the evidence given on the trial according to others, we may form a tolerably clear notion of the actual fact. Pressed by his opponents for some justification of his extraordinary conduct, Jesus had taken refuge in an assertion of his supernatural power. If they destroyed the temple he would be able, with the favor bestowed on him by God, to rebuild it in three days. These words might possibly be misconstrued by some of his hearers into a threat that he himself would destroy the temple, an outrage which would in their view have been less difficult to imagine after his violence to those engaged in business in its outer court. But whether so understood or not, there could be no question about the pretension to something like divinity in the promise to rebuild it in three days. There is not a shadow of probability in favor of the interpretation put upon the words in the fourth Gospel, that he spoke of the temple of his body. And even had that been his secret meaning, the witnesses who appeared against him could have no conception that he was thinking of anything but the material temple, to which the whole dialogue had immediate reference. They were therefore simply repeating, to the best of their ability, words which had actually fallen from the prisoner. The evidence for the prosecution being concluded, the high priest appealed to Jesus to know whether he had nothing to reply. Jesus being silent, the high priest proceeded to ask him directly whether he was "Christ, the Son of the Blessed One." Jesus answered that he was, and that they would hereafter see him "sitting on the right hand of power, and coming in the clouds of heaven." Such an answer was an explicit confession of the very worst that had been alleged against him. After it, there was no option but to convict him, and we read accordingly that they all condemned him as worthy of death. But capital punishment could not be inflicted except by Roman authority. He was accordingly taken before the procurator, Pontius Pilate, charged with the civil crime of claiming to be king of the Jews. Pontius appears to have regarded him as a harmless fanatic, and to have been anxious to discharge him, in accordance with a custom by which one prisoner was released at the festival which fell at this time. But the Jews clamored for the release of a man named Barabbas, who was in prison on account of his participation in an insurrectionary movement in which blood had been shed. Barabbas accordingly was set at liberty, and Jesus, though with some reluctance on the part of the procurator, was sentenced to crucifixion. The sentence was carried into effect immediately. Unable, probably from exhaustion through his recent sufferings, to carry his own cross, Jesus was relieved of the burden by one Simon, on whom the soldiery imposed the duty of bearing it. He was crucified along with two thieves, and an inscription in which he was entitled "King of the Jews" was placed upon his cross, apparently in mockery of the Jewish nation much more than of him. His ordinary disciples had fled in terror from his melancholy end, but he was followed to the cross by some affectionate women, who had previously attended him in Galilee. And after he was dead, his body was honorably interred by a well-to-do adherent, named Joseph of Arimathæa.

Subdivision 2.—*The Mythical Jesus.*

The life of the mythical Jesus is found in the synoptical Gospels, but more especially in the first and third. It is by no means pure fiction, but an indistinguishable compound of fact and fiction, in which the fictitious elements bear so large a proportion that it is impossible to disentangle from them the elements of genuine history. Part of this life moreover is wholly mythical, and of this wholly mythical portion there are certain sections that are constructed on a common plan, the biographers in these sections having only fitted the typical incidents in the lives of great men to the special case of Jesus, the son of Joseph, Not that this need have been done consciously; the probability is that the circumstances and mode of thought which led to the invention of such typical incidents in the lives of others, led to it equally in that of Jesus. However this may be, we shall find in the mythical life of Jesus the following three classes of myths: 1. Myths of the typical order, common to a certain kind of great men in certain ages, and therefore purely unhistorical; 2. Myths peculiar to Jesus, in which the miraculous element so predominates, that it is impossible to recognize any, or more than the very slightest, admixture of history; 3. Myths, peculiar to Jesus, in which there is a more or less considerable admixture of history; And 4. Statements not of necessity mythical, which may or may not be historical, but of which the evidence is inadequate.

At the outset of our task we are met by the assumed genealogy of Jesus, which has caused some trouble to theologians, and which is mainly important as an indication of the degree of credit due to writers who could insert such a document. For these awkward pedigrees afford an absolute proof of the facility with which the Christians of the earliest age supplemented the actual life of Jesus by free invention. We are happily in possession of two conflicting lists of ancestors, and happily also they are both of them lists of the ancestors of Joseph, who, according to the very writers by whom they are supplied, stood in no relation whatever to Christ, the final term of the genealogies. Double discredit thus falls upon the witnesses. In the first place, both lists cannot be true, though both may be false; one of them therefore must be, and each may be, a deliberate fiction. In the second place, both the Gospels bear unconscious testimony to the fact that Joseph was originally supposed to be, by the natural course of things, the father of

Jesus, for otherwise why should the early Christians have been
at the trouble to furnish the worthy carpenter with a distinguished ancestry? They thus discredit their own story that
Jesus was the son of Mary alone. Either then Jesus was the
son of Joseph, or neither of the two genealogies is his genealogy at all. The solution of these inconsistencies is to be found
in the fact that two independent traditions have been blended
together by the Evangelists. The one, no doubt the more
ancient of the two, considered Jesus as the child of Joseph and
Mary, and the ingenuity of his biographers has not succeeded
in obliterating the traces of this tradition (Mt. xiii. 55). Another
and much later one, treated him as the offspring of Mary without the aid of a human father. Those who believed in the first
and more authentic story had busied themselves with the discovery of a royal descent for their hero, in order that he might
fulfill what they considered the conditions of the Messiahship.
They had naturally traced his ancestry upwards from his
father, not from his mother, according to the usual procedure.
But the Gospels of Matthew and Luke were written entirely on
the hypothesis that he had no father but God; all necessity for
showing that Joseph was of the house of David was therefore
gone. Nevertheless the writers or the editors of these Gospels
did not like to neglect entirely what seemed to them to
strengthen their case, and, forgetful of the ridiculous jumble
they were making, inserted an elaborate pedigree of Joseph
along with the statement that Jesus was not his son.

Let us now examine the genealogies in detail, placing them
in columns parallel to one another. Luke begins a stage
earlier than Matthew, making God his starting-point instead of
Abraham. From Abraham to David the two authorities proceed
together. Matthew, who has cut his genealogical tree into
three sections of fourteen generations each, makes this his first
division. After this the divergence begins:—

MATTHEW.	LUKE.
1. Solomon.	1. Nathan.
2. Rehoboam.	2. Mattatha.
3. Abia.	3. Menan.
4. Asa.	4. Melea.
5. Jehoshaphat.	5. Eliakim.

Matthew (*continued*)—
6. Joram.
  [*Ahaziah.*
  Joash.
  Amaziah.*]
7. Ozias (or Uzziah).
8. Jotham.
9. Ahaz.
10. Hezekiah.
11. Manasseh.
12. Amon.
13. Josiah.
  [*Jehoiakim.*]
14. Jeconiah (or Jehoiachin).

Here the captivity closes the second period. After the captivity we have—

1. Jeconiah.
2. Salathiel (or Shealtiel)
3. Zerubbabel.
4. Abiud.
5. Eliakim.
6. Azor.
7. Sadoc.
8. Achim.
9. Eliud.
10. Eleazar.
11. Matthan.
12. Jacob.
13. Joseph.
14. JESUS.

Luke (*continued*)—
6. Jonan.

7. Joseph.
8. Juda.
9. Simeon.
10. Levi.
11. Matthat.
12. Jorim.
13. Eliezer.

14. Jose.

15. Er.
16. Elmodam.
17. Cosam.
18. Addi.
19. Melchi.
20. Neri.
21. Salathiel.
22. Zorobabel.
23. Rhesa.
24. Joanna.
25. Juda.
26. Joseph
27. Semei.
28. Mattathias.
29. Maath.
30. Nagga.
31. Esli.
32. Naum.
33. Amos.
34. Mattathias.
35. Joseph.
36. Janna.
37. Melchi.
38. Levi.
39. Matthat.
40. Heli.
41. Joseph.
42. JESUS.†

* Kings omitted in the Gospel are inserted in brackets and italicized.

† Mt. i. 1–17; Lu. iii. 23–38.

Various observations offer themselves on these discrepant
genealogies. In the first place it will be observed that Matthew, in his anxiety to show that the whole period comprised is
divisible into three equal parts of fourteen generations each,
has actually omitted no less than four generations contained in
the authorities he followed. For since he traced the descent of
Joseph through the royal line of Judah, we are enabled to check
his statements by reference to the Book of Chronicles (1 Chron.
iii.), and thus to convict him of positive bad faith. In the first
instance he omits three kings, representing Uzziah as the son
of Joram, who was his great great grandfather; in the second
he passes over Jehoiachim, making Jehoiachin the son instead
of the grandson of Josiah. In the third period we have no
authority by which to verify his statements beyond Zerubbabel,
but his determination to carry out his numerical system at all
hazards is shown by the double reckoning of Jehoiachin, at the
close of the second and the beginning of the third division.
The latter has in fact but thirteen generations, and it was only
by this trick — a little concealed by the break effected through
his allusion to the captivity — that the appearance of uniformity
was maintained. Luke has adopted a different method. Leaving the line of kings, he connects Joseph with David through
Nathan instead of Solomon. Now beyond the fact that Nathan
was the offspring of David and Bathsheba, nothing whatever is
known about him. Indeed it may have been his very obscurity,
and the consequent facility of creating descendants for him,
that led to his selection in preference to Solomon, though
unless it were that his name stood next above Solomon's (2
Sam. v. 14) — there is no obvious reason for his being preferred
to several other children of David. However, he answered the
purpose as well as any, and after him it was not a difficult
operation to invent a plausible list of names to fill up the gap
between him and Joseph. The compiler of the list in Matthew
had the advantage in so far that he did not require to draw on
his imagination except for nine names between Zerubbabel and
Joseph, while the compiler of the list in Luke had to supply
the whole period from Nathan downwards with forefathers.
But the second compiler had the advantage over the first inasmuch as his fraud did not admit of the same easy exposure by

reference to its sources, and it was, on the whole, a safer course to desert history altogether than to falsify it in favor of an arithmetical fancy.

Another discrepancy between the two writers remains to be noted; it is the enormous disproportion in the number of generations between David and Joseph. Matthew has twenty-five generations, and Luke forty, excluding Joseph himself. A difference of this magnitude —involving something like 400–450 years — is not to be surmounted by any process of harmonizing. To which it may be added that the two Evangelists, by assigning to Joseph different fathers, clearly inform us that his true father was unknown.

We have here, in short, an excellent instance of the first order of myth, or myth typical. It has been a common practice in all ages, more especially among ignorant and uncultivated nations, to endow those who had risen from obscurity to greatness with illustrious ancestors. Royal connections have always been regarded with especial favor for such purposes. Thus, the Buddha is represented as the descendant of the great Sakya monarchs. Thus, the ancestors of Zarathustra, in the genealogy provided for him in Parsee authorities, were the ancient kings of Persia. Thus, Moslem biographers declare that Mahomet sprang from the noblest family of the noblest nation, and many historians give him even a princely lineage (L. L. M., vol. i. p. 140). Thus, according to Sir John Davis, "the pedigree of Confucius is traced back in a summary manner to the mythological monarch *Hoang-ty*, who is said to have lived more than two thousand years before Christ" (Chinese, vol. ii. p. 45). Thus, the founder of Rome was placed by popular legend in a family relationship to Æneas.

Leaving these genealogies — which are important only from the light they shed on the literary character of their authors and transmitters — we pass to the first legend directly concerning Jesus himself, that of his birth. Here again the second and fourth Evangelists are silent, leaving us to suppose that Jesus was the natural son of Joseph and Mary, and certainly never hinting that they entertained any other belief themselves. But the first and third each relate a little fable on this subject, though unhappily for them the fables do not agree.

Both had to observe two conditions. The first was that Jesus should be born of a virgin mother; the second that he should be born at Bethlehem. Matthew accomplishes this end by informing us that Mary, when espoused to Joseph, was found to be with child. Joseph, who thereupon contemplated the rupture of his engagement, was informed by an angel in a dream that his bride was with child by no one but the Holy Ghost; that she was to bear a son, and that he was to call him Jesus. Being satisfied by this assurance, he married Mary, but respected her virginity until she had brought forth her first-born son, whom in obedience to his dream he named Jesus. The child was born in Bethlehem where it would appear from this account that Mary lived, and it is only after a journey to Egypt that this Gospel brings the parents of Christ to Nazareth where a tradition too firm to be shaken placed their residence (Mt. i. 18–25; ii. 23).

Widely different is the treatment of this subject in Luke. According to him there was a priest named Zacharias whose wife Elizabeth was barren. The couple were no longer young, but they were not old enough to have lost all hope of progeny, for we are told that when Zacharias was engaged in his duties in the temple, an angel appeared to him and informed him that his prayer was heard, and that his wife was to have a son whom he was to call John. Zacharias had therefore been praying for offspring, though when the angel — who announced himself as Gabriel — appeared, he was troubled with some impious doubts, in punishment of which he was struck dumb. After this Elizabeth conceived, and went into retirement. From five to six months after the above scene Gabriel was again despatched from heaven, this time to a virgin named Mary, living at Nazareth. Arrived at her house, he addressed her thus: "Hail, thou that art highly favored; the Lord is with thee; blessed art thou among women." Seeing Mary's confusion he reassured her; and informed her that she should have a son called Jesus, who was to possess the throne of David, and reign over the house of Jacob forever. Like Zacharias, Mary was disposed to raise troublesome questions, and she accordingly inquired of Gabriel how she could bear a child, "seeing I know not a man." But Gabriel was ready with his answer. The Holy Ghost would come upon her; moreover, her cousin Elizabeth had conceived (which, however, was not a parallel case), and nothing was impossible with God. Soon after this visit, Mary went to see Elizabeth, who interpreted an ordinary incident of pregnancy as a sign that the fruit of Mary's womb was blessed, and that Mary was to be the mother of her Lord. The virgin replied in a very elaborate little speech, which if uttered must have been carefully prepared for the occasion. In due time the child of Zacharias and Elizabeth was born, and named John by his parents' desire. What Joseph thought of his bride's condition we are not told, nor do we know whether she made known to him her interview with the angel Gabriel. At any rate he did not repudiate her, for we find him taking her with him, about five months later, to Bethlehem, for the purpose of the census which took place when Quirinus was governor of Syria, his descent from David requiring him to attend at that town. During this census it was that Jesus was born, and because of the crowded condition of the inn at this busy time, he was placed in a manger (Lu. i. 1; ii. 7). There let us leave him for the present, while we compare these narratives with others of a like description.

Birth in some miraculous or unusual manner is a common circumstance in the lives of great persons. We have here therefore another instance of the typical species of myth. Thus, in classical antiquity, Here is said to have produced Hephaistos "without the marriage bed" (Bib., i. 3–5). Turning to a remote part of the globe, there was in the present century a person living in New Zealand who, according to native tradition, was "begotten by the attua," a species of deity, "his mother being then unmarried. The infant was produced at her left arm-pit, but there was no visible mark left. . . . He is held as a great prophet; when he says there will be no rain there will be none " (N. Z., p. 82). An example of 'the same kind of legend occurs in the ancient history of China. The hero is one Howtseih, who was the founder of the royal house of Chow. His mother, it appears, was barren, like Elizabeth, for she "had presented a pure offering and sacrificed, that her childlessness might be taken away." Her devotion received a fitting reward, for :—

"She then trod on a toe-print made by God, and was moved,
In the large place where she rested.
She became pregnant, she dwelt retired;
She gave birth to, and nourished [a son],
Who was How-tseih."

His mode of coming into the world was peculiar too:—

"When she had fulfilled her months
Her first-born son [came forth] like a lamb.
There was no bursting, nor rending;
No injury, no hurt:—
Showing how wonderful he would be.
Did not God give her the comfort ?
Had he not accepted her pure offering and sacrifice,
So that thus easily she brought forth her son ?"*

The gestation of the Buddha was in many ways miraculous.
He entered the womb of his mother by a voluntary act, resigning
his abode in heaven for the purpose. At the time of his descent
upon earth Mâyâ Dêvi dreamt that a white elephant of singular
beauty had entered into her, a dream which portended the
future greatness of the child (R. T. R. P., vol. ii. p. 61). During
the time of his remaining in the womb, his body, which was
visible both to his mother and to others, had a resplendent and
glorious appearance.* "Mâyâ the queen, during the time that
Boddhisattva remained in the womb of his mother, did not feel
her body heavy, but on the contrary light, at ease and in comfort, and felt no pain in her entrails. She was nowise tormented
by the desires of passion, nor by disgust, nor by trouble, and
had no irresolution against desire, no irresolution against the

---

* C. C. vol. iv. p. 465.—She King, Part iii. Bk. 2, i, 1. 2.

* Ibid,, vol. ii. p. 73. It is very remarkable that the same notion is
expressed in Christian paintings of the middle ages. On a painted glass
of the sixteenth century, found in the church of Jouy, a little village in
France, the virgin is represented standing, her hands clasped in prayer,
and the naked body of the child in the same attitude appears upon her
stomach, apparently supposed to be seen through the garments and body
of the mother. M. Didron saw at Lyons a Salutation painted on shutters,
in which the two infants, likewise depicted on their mothers' stomachs,
were also saluting each other. This precisely corresponds to Buddhist
accounts of the Boddhisattva's ante-natal proceedings.—Ic. Chr. p. 263.

thought of evil or of vice. She suffered the sensation neither
of cold, nor of heat, nor of hunger, nor of thirst, nor of trouble,
nor of passion, nor of fatigue: she saw nothing of which the
form, the sound, the smell, the taste and the touch did not
seem to her agreeable. She had no bad dreams. The tricks of
women, their inconstancy, their jealousy, the defects of women
and their weaknesses, she did not share " (Ibid., vol. ii. p. 77)
And although it is never expressly stated that the Buddha's
nominal father had no part in his production, it is remarkable
that at the time of her conceiving, Mâyâ was living in a place
apart from him, having craved permission to retire for a season, to practice fasting and penance. During this time she had
told the king that she would be "completely delivered from
thoughts of stealing, desire and pride," and that she would not
"yield to one illicit desire" (R. T. R. P., vol. ii. pp. 54, 55).
Some sects of Buddhists are more explicit, and maintain that
Boddhisattvas do not pass through the earlier stages of fœtal
development; namely, those of *Kalalam*, mixing up, the period
of the first week, when the future body is like milk: *arbudam*,
the period of the second week, where a form rises like something
inflated; *peci*, thickening: and *ghana*, hardening, the periods of
the third and fourth weeks (Wassiljew, p. 260). But all this does
not exclude the coöperation of a human father. Passing to
another great religion, we find that even the sober philosopher
Confucius did not enter the world, if we may believe Chinese
traditions, without premonitory symptoms of his greatness. It
is said that one day as his mother was ascending a hill, "the
leaves of the trees and plants all erected themselves and bent
downwards on her return. That night she dreamt the Black *Te*
appeared, and said to her, 'You shall have a son, a sage, and
you must bring him forth in a hollow mulberry tree.'" In
another dream she received a prophecy of the importance of
her coming progeny (C. C., vol. i. p. 59 — Proleg). Another account states that "various prodigies, as in other instances, were
the forerunners of the birth of this extraordinary person. On
the eve of his appearance on earth, two dragons encircled the
house, and celestial music sounded in the ears of his mother.
When he was born, this inscription appeared on his breast—
' The maker of a rule for settling the world'" (Chinese, vol. ii.

p. 44). The mother of Mahomet is said to have related of her pregnancy, that she felt none of the usual inconveniences of that state; and that she had seen a vision in which she had been told that she bore in her womb the Lord and Prophet of her people. A little before her delivery the same figure appeared again, and commanded her to say, "I commend the fruit of my body to the One, the Eternal, for protection against the envious" (L. L. M., vol. i. p. 142).

Miraculously born, it was necessary that Jesus should also be miraculously recognized as a child of no common order. The story would have been incomplete without some one to acknowledge his superhuman character even in his cradle. Matthew and Luke again accomplish the common end by widely different means. Luke's is the simpler narrative, and it will be more convenient to begin with. He tells us that there were in the same country, that is, near Bethlehem, shepherds watching their flocks. An angel appeared to them and said that a Savior, Christ the Lord, was born in the city of David. They were to know him by his being in a manger wrapped in swaddling clothes. In this humility of his external circumstances immediately after birth, as in the supernatural recognition which he received, he again resembles the Chinese hero. How-tseih

> "was placed in a narrow lane,
> But the sheep and oxen protected him with loving care.
> He was placed in a wide forest,
> Where he was met by the woodcutters.
> He was placed on the cold ice,
> And a bird screened and supported him with its wings." *

"And suddenly," the narrative in Luke proceeds, "there was with the angel a multitude of the heavenly host, praising God and saying, 'Glory to God in the highest, and on earth the peace of good-will among men'" (Lu. ii. 8–14). Similar demonstrations of celestial delight were not wanting at the birth of the Buddha Sakyamuni. He was received by the greatest of the gods, Indra and Brahma. All beings everywhere were full of joy. Musical instruments belonging to men and gods played of

* C. C., vol. iv. p. 468.—She King, Pt. iii. Bk. 2, i. 3.

themselves. Trees became covered with flowers and fruit. There fell from the skies a gentle shower of flowers, garments, odoriferous powders, and ornaments. Caressing breezes blew. A marvelous light was produced. Evil passions were put a stop to, and illnesses were cured; miseries of all kinds were at an end (R. T. R. P., vol. ii. pp. 90, 91). So also we read in Moslem authorities that at the birth of Ali, Mahomet's great disciple, and the chief of one of the two principal sects into which Islam is divided, "a light was distinctly visible, resembling a bright column, extending from the earth to the firmament" (Dervishes, p. 372). But let us complete the narrative in Luke.

Urged by the angelic order, the shepherds went to Bethlehem and found the infant Christ, whose nature, as revealed by the angels, they made known to the people with whom they met. Returning, they praised and glorified God for all they had heard and seen (Lu. ii. 15-20).

Quite dissimilar is the form in which the same incident appears in Matthew. Here, instead of shepherds, we have magi coming from the East to discover the King of the Jews. A star in the East had revealed to them the birth of this King of the Jews *de jure*, and in the search for him they run straight into the very jaws of Herod, the king *de facto*. The author is obliged to make them take this absurdly improbable course for the sake of introducing Herod, whom he required for a purpose shortly to be explained. How utterly superfluous the visit to Herod was is evinced by the fact that, after that monarch has found out from the chief priests the birthplace of the Messiah, the magi are guided onwards by the star, which had been omitted from the story since its first appearance in order to allow of their journey to Jerusalem, a mistake for which the star could not be made responsible. However, after leaving Herod, they were led by that luminary to the very spot where Christ lay. On seeing the infant they worshiped him, and offered him magnificent presents, after which a dream informed them — what their waking senses might surely have discovered — that it was not safe to return to Herod after having thus acknowledged a rival claimant to the throne. They accordingly went home another way.

Interwoven with this visit of the magi we have a myth which

belongs to a common form, and which in the present instance is merely adapted to the special circumstances of the age and place. I term it the myth of THE DANGEROUS CHILD. Its general outline is this: A child is born concerning whose future greatness some prophetic indications have been given. But the life of this child is fraught with danger to some powerful individual, generally a monarch. In alarm at his threatened fate, this person endeavors to take the child's life; but it is preserved by the divine care. Escaping the measures directed against it, and generally remaining long unknown, it at length fulfills the prophecies concerning its career, while the fate which he has vainly sought to shun falls upon him who had desired to slay it. There is a departure here from the ordinary type, inasmuch as Herod does not actually die or suffer any calamity through the agency of Jesus. But this failure is due to the fact that Jesus did not fulfill the conditions of the Messiahship, according to the Jewish conception which Matthew has here in mind. Had he — as was expected of the Messiah — become the actual sovereign of the Jews, he must have dethroned the reigning dynasty, whether represented by Herod or his successors. But as his subsequent career belied these expectations, the Evangelist was obliged to postpone to a future time his accession to that throne of temporal dominion which the incredulity of his countrymen had withheld from him during his earthly life (Mt. xxiv. 30, 31; xxv. 31 ff.; xxvi. 64).

In other respects the legend before us conforms to its prototypes. The magi, coming to Herod, inquire after the whereabouts of the king of the Jews, whose star they have seen in the East. Herod summons the chief priests and scribes to council, and ascertains of them that Christ was to be born at Bethlehem. This done, he is careful to learn from the magi the exact date at which the star had appeared to them. He further desires them to search diligently for the young child, that he also may worship it. They, as previously related, returned home without revisiting Herod, whereupon that monarch, in anger at the deception practiced upon him, causes all the children under two years of age, in and about Bethlehem, to be slaughtered. All is in vain. Joseph, warned by a dream, had taken his wife and step-son to Egypt, where they remained until after the death of Herod, when another dream commanded them to return. When afraid to enter the dominions of Archelaus, another of these useful dreams guided them to Galilee, where they took up their quarters at Nazareth (Mt. ii).

How wide-spread and of what frequent recurrence is this myth of the Dangerous Child, a few examples may suffice to show. In Grecian mythology the king of the gods himself had been a dangerous child. The story of Kronos swallowing his children in order to defeat the prophecy that he would be dethroned by his own son; the manner in which Rhea deceived him by giving him a stone, and Zeus, armed with thunder and lightning, deposed him from the government of the world, are familiar to all (Bib. 1. 1. 5-7, and 1. 2. 1). If we descend from gods to heroes, we find a similar legend related of Perseus, whose grandfather, Akrisios, vainly tried to avert his predicted fate, first by scheming to prevent his grandson's birth, and then by seeking to destroy him when born (Ibid., 2. 4. 1. 4); and of Oidipous, who in spite of the attempt to cut short his life in infancy, inevitably and unconsciously fulfilled the oracle by slaying his father and marrying his mother. Within historical times, Kyros, the son of Kambyses is the hero of a similar tale. His grandfather, Astyages, had dreamt certain dreams which were interpreted by the magi to mean that the offspring of his daughter Mandane would expel him from his kingdom. Alarmed at the prophecy, he handed the child to his kinsman Harpagos to be killed; but this man having entrusted it to a shepherd to be exposed, the latter contrived to save it by exhibiting to the emissaries of Harpagos the body of a stillborn child of which his own wife had just been delivered. Grown to man's estate, Kyros of course ·justified the prediction of the magi by his successful revolt against Astyages and assumption of the monarchy (Herodotos, i. 107-130). Jewish tradition, like that of the Greeks and the Persians, has its dangerous child in the person of the national hero Moses, whose death Pharaoh had endeavored to effect by a massacre of innocents, but who had lived to bring upon that ruler his inevitable fate. From these well-known examples it is interesting to turn to the chronicles of the East-Mongols, and find precisely the same tale repeated there. We read that a certain king of a people called

Patsala, had a son whose peculiar appearance led the Brahmins
at court to prophesy that he would bring evil upon his father,
and to advise his destruction, Various modes of execution having failed, the boy was laid in a copper chest and thrown into
the Ganges. Rescued by an old peasant who brought him up
as his son, he in due time learnt the story of his escape, and
returned to seize upon the kingdom destined for him from his
birth. This was in B. C. 313 (G. O. M., pp. 21, 23). This universal
myth—of the natural origin of which it would lead me too
far to speak—was now adapted to the special case of Christ,
who runs the usual risk and escapes it with the usual good
fortune of dangerous children.

Having thus preserved the infant Christ from the dangers
that threatened him, Matthew tells us absolutely nothing about
him until he has arrived at manhood, and is ready to enter on
his public life. Luke is much less reticent. True, he knows
nothing whatever of the star that appeared in the East; nothing of Herod's inquiries as to the birthplace of Christ; nothing of the massacre of the innocents, nor of the flight into
Egypt and the return from that country to Nazareth. On the
contrary, his narrative by implication excludes all this, for he
makes Joseph and Mary go up to Bethlehem for the census
only, and return to Nazareth soon after it; so that Herod could
have had no occasion to kill the infants up to the age of two
years, for Christ could not have been above a few weeks old at
most (Lu. ii. 39). Moreover, we learn definitely from one verse
that his parents went up *from Nazareth* to Jerusalem every
year at the passover (Ibid., ii. 41). But the absence of any
statements like those just taken from the first Gospel is amply
compensated in the third by several pleasing details relating to
his infancy and boyhood. In the first place we learn that after
eight days he was circumcised, and named Jesus according to
the angel's desire (Ibid., ii. 21). Next, we are told that after
his mother's purification—which would last thirty-three days
after the circumcision—she and his step-father took him to the
temple to be presented, and to make the customary offering.
There was in the temple a man named Simeon who had been
promised by the Holy Ghost that he should not die till he had
seen Christ. This man, who came by the Spirit into the temple,

took the baby in his arms and gave vent to his emotion in the beautiful little hymn known as the *Nunc Dimittis:*— "Now, O Lord, thou dost release thy servant according to thy word in peace, because mine eyes have seen thy salvation, which thou hast prepared before the face of all nations; a light for the revelation of the Gentiles and the glory of thy people Israel" (Lu. ii. 29–32).

Less exquisite in its simplicity, but not altogether dissimilar in tone. is the prophecy of the Rishi Asita on the infant Buddha. This old and eminent ascetic had come to see the child whose marvelous gifts had been known to him by supernatural signs. Having embraced its feet, and predicted its future preëminence, he had surprised the king by bursting into tears and heaving long sighs. Questioned about the meaning of this he replied: "Great king, it is not on account of this child that I weep; truly there is not in him the smallest vice. Great king, I am old and broken; and this young prince (Literally, Sarvarthasiddha) will certainly clothe himself with the perfect and complete intelligence of Buddha, and will cause the wheel of the law that has no superior to turn. . . . After becoming Buddha he will cause hundreds of thousands of millions of beings to pass to the other border of the ocean of wandering life, and will lead them forever to immortality. And I—I shall not see this pearl of Buddhas ! Cured of illness, I shall not be freed by him from passion ! Great king, that is why I weep, and why in my sadness I heave long sighs" (R. T. R. P., vol. ii. pp. 106, 107).

So Abd-al-mottalib, Mahomet's grandfather, on seeing his grandchild immediately after his birth, is reported to have exclaimed: "Praise be to Allah, who has given me this glorious youth, who even in the cradle rules over other boys. I commend him to the protection of Allah, the Lord of the four elements, that he may show him to us when he is well grown up. To his protection I commend him from the evil of the wicked spirit" (L. L. M., vol. i. p. 143).

Prognostications of greatness in infancy are, indeed, among the stock incidents in the mythical or semi-mythical lives of eminent persons. Not content with Simeon's recognition, Luke introduces an old prophetess called Anna, living in the temple,

and represents her as giving thanks, and speaking of the child
to all who looked for redemption in Jerusalem (Lu. ii.). -3893

Twelve years are now suffered to elapse without further
account of the young Jesus than that he grew and strengthened,
filled with wisdom, and that the grace of God was upon him
(Ibid., ii. 40). At twelve years old, the blank is filled by a single event. His parents had gone to Jerusalem to keep the passover, taking Jesus with them. On their way back they missed
him, and having failed to find him among their traveling companions, returned to look for him at Jerusalem. There they
found him in the temple sitting among the doctors of the law,
listening to them and putting questions. Those who heard him
are said to have been astonished at his intelligence. Questioned
by his mother as to this extraordinary conduct, he replied,
"How is it that ye sought me? wist ye not that I must be
about my Father's business?" (Lu. ii. 41-50.) Were this incident
confirmed by other authorities, and did it stand in some kind
of connection with the events that precede and follow it, we
might accept it as a genuine reminiscence of the boyhood of
Jesus. That a precocious boy, eager for information, should
take the opportunity of a visit to the head-quarters of Hebraic
learning to seek from the authorities then most respected a
solution of questions that troubled his mind, would not in
itself be so very surprising. And those who are familiar with
the kind of inquiries made by clever children, especially on
theological topics, will not think it strange that his youthful
wits should occasionally be too much for those of professed
theologians. But the isolation in which this single event stands
in the first thirty years of Christ's life, and the total absence of
confirmation from any other source, compel us to regard it as
an invention designed to show an early consciousness in Jesus
of his later mission, and also to prove the inability of the doctors to cope with him, We must, therefore, reject it along with
the other myths of the infancy, of which some are typical
myths, others (like this) myths peculiar to Jesus, but none in
the smallest degree historical.

Before entering on the later life of Jesus, let us note certain
differences between Matthew and Luke in their treatment of
the infancy, which will confirm the above conclusion. In the

first place, it is to be observed that they effect the desired end by totally unlike methods. Given the problem of getting the infant Christ born without the assistance of a father, there were various ways in which readers could be assured of the truth of such a miracle. One was to inform Joseph in a dream of the coming event; another was to announce it to Mary by means of an angel. In choosing between these expedients each Evangelist is guided by his own idiosyncracy. Matthew selects the dream; Luke the angel; and it is noteworthy that on other occasions they exhibit similar preferences. Matthew gets out of every difficulty by a dream. In the course of his two first chapters he uses this favorite contrivance no less than five times; four times for Joseph, and once for the magi (Mt. i. 20, and ii. 12, 13, 22). Twice, it is true, he mentions an angel of the Lord as appearing in the dream, but the angel in his narrative plays a very subordinate part, and is, indeed, practically superfluous. With Luke, on the contrary, the principal agent in the events of the infancy is the angel, who supplies the place of the dream in Matthew. An angel informs Zacharias that his wife is to have a son; an angel declares to Mary that she is destined to give birth to the Son of God; an angel announces that event to the shepherds after its occurrence; and angels appear in crowds above them as soon as the announcement has been made (Lu. i. 11, 26, and ii. 9, 13). Another striking difference is the extreme fondness of Matthew for ancient prophecies, and of Luke for little anthems and for songs of praise. The diverse natures of the two writers are well exemplified by this distinction; the former being the more penetrated with the history and literature of the Jewish race; the latter the more flexible and the more imbued with the spirit of his ago. Hence, Matthew almost avowedly constructs his narrative in such a manner as to ensure the fulfillment of the prophecies. After describing Mary's miraculous conception, he says that all this was done to fulfill Isaiah's words: "Behold, a virgin shall conceive" (more accurately; the maiden has conceived), "and shall bear a son, and shall call his name Immanuel" (Mt. i. 23; Isa. vii. 14). And this he quotes, regardless of the fact that Christ never was called Immanuel, and that if the one clause of the prophecy is to be understood literally, so must the other.

Thus also he reveals his reason for assigning to Bethlehem the honor of being Christ's birthplace, when he places in the mouths of the priests at the court of Herod a verse from Micah, in which it is asserted that from Bethlehem Ephratah shall come a man who is to be ruler in Israel (Mt. ii. 6; Mic. v. 2). Further, he massacres the innocents in order to corroborate a saying of Jeremiah (Mt. ii. 18; Jer. xxxi. 15), and he takes Joseph and Mary to Egypt to confirm an expression of Hosea (Mt. ii. 15; Hos. xi. 1). In each case, he perverts the natural sense of the prophets; for in Jeremiah, the children are to return to their own land, which the innocents could not do; and in Hosea, the son who is called out of Egypt is the people of Israel. Lastly, in his exceeding love of quoting the Old Testament, he commits the most singular blunder of all in applying to Christ the words spoken of Samson by the angel who announced his birth. If, indeed, the allusion be to this passage (and it can scarcely be to any other), the Evangelist is barely honest; for he converts the angelic words, "he shall *be a Nazarite,*" into the words "he shall *be called a Nazarene*" (Mt. ii. 23; Judg. xiii. 5). So Judaic a writer could hardly be ignorant that a Nazarite was not the same thing as an inhabitant of Nazareth. But from whatever source the quotation may come, its object plainly is to lead to the belief that notwithstanding his birth at Bethlehem, Jesus was called by his contemporaries a Nazarene.

Luke does not trouble himself with the search for ancient oracles, but indulges a far freer and more inventive genius. His personages give utterance to their feelings in highly finished songs, which are sometimes very beautiful, but most certainly could never have been uttered by the simple people to whom he attributes them. Among these are the salutation of Elizabeth to Mary, and the still more elaborate answer of Mary. Zacharias, the very instant he recovers his speech, recites a complete hymn of no inconsiderable length (Lu. i. 68–79). Again, Simeon expresses his joy at the birth of the Savior in a similar manner (Ibid., ii. 29–32); but in his case it may be said that he had so long expected to see the Christ that his hymn of thanksgiving might well be ready.

Passing now to the manhood of Jesus, we find the four

Evangelists all agreed in recording the baptism by John as the earliest known event in his adult career, and it is unquestionably with this consecration by a great man that his authentic life begins. Mark and John indeed were unaware of anything previous to this period, and the former introduces it by the words, "The beginning of the gospel of Jesus Christ the Son of God" (Mk. i. 1), showing that for him at least the history of his Master began at this point. As usual, the myth appears in its simplest form in his pages. After applying to John the Baptist a prophecy by Isaiah, he states that this prophet was engaged in baptizing in the wilderness, and that all Judea and all the Jerusalemites went out to him and were baptized, confessing their sins. He declared that a mightier than he was coming after him, the latchet of whose shoes he was unworthy to unloose. Jesus, like the rest of the world, went to be baptized, and as he came out of the water he saw the heavens opened, and the Spirit descending on him like a dove. There was a voice from the heavens, "Thou art my beloved Son, in thee I am well pleased." Matthew and Luke describe the baptism of John in a similar manner, Matthew adding a conversation between Jesus and John. They also mention the baptism of Jesus, the descent of the dove, and the voice, but with slight variations. For whereas Mark merely says that *Jesus saw* the heavens opened and the Spirit like a dove descending, and Matthew, in substantial accordance with him, relates that the heavens were opened [to him], and that *he saw* the Spirit descend as a dove, Luke going further, pretends that the heavens *were* opened, and that the spirit did ascend in a bodily form like a dove upon him (Mk. i, 1–12; Mt. iii.; Lu. iii. 1–22). Thus is the subjective fact in the consciousness of Jesus gradually changed into an objective fact, a transition deserving to be noted as illustrative of the trivial changes of language by which a myth may grow. Several other examples of a like process will meet us in the course of this inquiry. The scene at the baptism is described differently again in the fourth Gospel. There the testimony of John the Baptist to Christ is rendered far more emphatic; he receives him with the words, "Behold the Lamb of God, who taketh away the sins of the world;" and he explains his knowledge of him by the fact that he has received a special revelation concerning him. On whomsoever he saw the Spirit descend and remain, that was he who was to baptize with the Holy Ghost. Now he had seen the Spirit descend like a dove on Jesus, and therefore had borne witness that he was the son of God (John i. 6-37). Of the opening of the heavens and of the voice nothing is said, and the meaning of the whole story evidently is that this descent of the Spirit was a private sign arranged between God and John the Baptist, but of which the bystanders either perceived nothing, or understood nothing. For had they known that the Holy Ghost itself was thus bearing witness to Jesus, what need was there of the witness of John? It is evident, however, that even if they saw the dove flying down and alighting upon Jesus, they were not informed that it represented the Holy Spirit. Thus the whole fact is reduced to a peculiar interpretation given by John to a natural occurrence. We have then three versions of the baptismal myth: — in the first certain circumstances are perceived by Jesus; in the second they are perceived by John; in the third they actually occur.

Strangely inconsistent with this distinct acknowledgment of Christ as the son of God, is the inquiry addressed to him at a subsequent period by John the Baptist through his disciples. It appears that on hearing of the extraordinary fame of Jesus and of the course he was pursuing, John sent two disciples from the prison where he was confined to put this question to him, "Art thou he that should come, or do we expect another?" in other words, Are you the Messiah? Thus interrogated, Jesus replied, not by appealing to the testimony of the dove at his baptism, or the voice from heaven, but by citing the miraculous cures he was then performing. Nor did he in the least resent the doubt implied in John the Baptist's query. On the contrary, he immediately entered upon a glowing panegyric of his precursor, describing him as the messenger sent before his face to prepare his way, and as the prophet Elias who was expected to come — (Mt. xi. 1-15; Lu. vii. 18-30) — a title which in another Gospel the Baptist had expressly repudiated (Jo. i. 21). This remarkable transaction between the two teachers could not easily have occurred, if the elder had previously discovered "him that should come" in the person of Jesus. For then we must suppose that since the baptism he had seen reason to hesitate as to the correctness of his opinion. And in that case, could he have referred the question to Jesus himself for his decision? And could Jesus have employed the terms of praise here given, in speaking of one who had lapsed from his former faith into a state of doubt? Plainly not. The Evangelists have overshot the mark in their narrative of the baptism. Eager to make John bear witness to Jesus, they have forgotten that it was only at a later period that he was convinced — if he was convinced at all — of the Messianic claims of the young man who had passed under his influence, and derived from him some of his earliest inspirations. His doubts are historical; his conviction is mythical.

Temporary retirement into solitude naturally followed upon the consecration administered by John in the baptismal rite. Jesus spent some time wandering in a lonely place, the period of forty days assigned to this purpose being naturally suggested by the forty years of Israel's troubles in the wilderness. If there mingled among his meditations any lingering feelings of reluctance to follow the course pointed out by the Baptist, he would have afterwards described such feelings as temptations of the devil. Hence, it may be, the story of his conversations with Satan. These are not alluded to at all in Mark, who simply mentions the fact that he was tempted by Satan. Neither is there any reference in Mark to fasting for the whole of the forty days or any part of them. Greatly improving upon this bald version, the other two Synoptics tell us that he ate nothing during all this time, and describe the very words of his dialogues with the tempter. Satan had besought him to make bread out of stones; to cast himself down from a high place, and to accept at his hands all the kingdoms of earth in return for a single act of worship (Mk. i. 12, 13; Mt. iv. 1-11; Lu. iv. 1-13). Jesus, like the Buddha at the corresponding period of his life, emerged triumphant from the trial. It was by no means equal in severity to that which Sakyamuni underwent. He also was obliged to overcome the devil before he could attain perfection. "Mârâ the sinner," the Indian Satan, assailed him not only by force of arms, despatching an immense army against him; but finding this onslaught a failure, he tried the subtler mode of attempting to corrupt his virtue by the seductions of women. His beautiful daughters were despatched with orders to display all their charms, and employ all their fascinations before the young monk. They faithfuly executed the commission, but all was in vain. Calm and unmoved, the Boddhisattva regarded them with complete indifference, and emerged from this severest of trials a perfect Buddha (R. T. R. P., vol. ii. p. 286-327). In like manner Zarathustra was tempted by the Parsee devil, Angra-mainyus, who held out a promise of happiness if he would but curse the good law. Like Jesus, Zarathustra repelled the suggestion with indignation: "I will not curse the good Mazdayasna law, not even if limbs, soul, and life were to part from one another " Av., vol. i. p. 244. — Fargard xix. 23-26.

Not long after his return from the desert, Jesus took up his abode at the village of Kapharnaoum, or Capernaum, in Galilee, Nazareth being in several ways uncongenial to him (Mk. ii. 1; Mt. iv. 12-16). In the first place it was the abode of his family, who did not believe in the pretensions he now began to advance. Moreover, he was well known to the Nazarenes as the carpenter, or the carpenter's son, and it seemed an unwarrantable presumption in their young townsman, undistinguished by advantages either of birth or education, to claim to become their teacher (Mk. vi. 3). His relations also not only discredited him by their unbelief, but occasionally took active measures to stop his proceedings (Mk. iii. 21, 31). From these and perhaps other causes, he entirely failed to accomplish any important miracle at Nazareth, and he had to excuse his failure by the remark that a prophet is not without honor except in his own country, among his own relations, and in his own house (Ibid., vi. 4). The more natural version — that of Mark — adds that he marvelled because of their unbelief. With less simplicity Matthew relates, not that he was unable to do, but that he did not do many mighty works there because of their unbelief (Mt. xiii. 54-58). Further confirmation of the incredulity of the Nazarenes is afforded by their reception of a remarkable sermon said to have been delivered by Jesus in their synagogue, It seems that after he had preached in various parts of Galilee, and had been well received, he came to Nazareth and, having read a Messianic prophecy from Isaiah, proceeded to apply it to himself. Having noticed the demand which he expected would be addressed to him, that he should repeat there such works as he was reported to have performed at Capernaum, he proceeded to convey by some pointed illustrations from the Old Testament the unflattering intimation that Nazareth was to be less favored by God than his adopted home. Hereupon a storm arose in the synagogue, and an effort was made by the enraged audience to cast him from the brow of a hill. But he escaped in safety to his own residence at Capernaum (Lu. iv. 14-30).

Whether or not any such sermon was preached or any such attempt upon his life was made, the narrative bears further witness to the fact of ill success in the town where he had been brought up, and to his possession of a house or lodging at Capernaum. Whether he himself was the owner of the abode, or whether it belonged to a disciple who received him (of which latter there is no evidence), makes little difference; the representation afterwards made that foxes had holes, and birds had nests, but the son of man had not where to lay his head (Mt. viii. 19, 20; Lu. ix. 57, 58), is equally negatived by either supposition. Mark and John know nothing of this condition of the son of man. In John's Gospel, indeed, it is distinctly contradicted by the statement that two of the Baptist's disciples asked him to show them where he lived; that he did so, and that they staid with him that day (Jo. i. 39). Indirect evidence of the same kind is afforded by the notice of an entertainment given by Jesus at his own house, to which he invited a very promiscuous company. Luke, indeed, represents this feast as having been given by Levi, but this is evidently for the sake of an artistic connection with the summons to Levi, which in all three narratives immediately precedes it. For the same reason he departs from both other Evangelists in making the scribes at this very feast put the question why Jesus and his disciples did not fast, which, according to the more trustworthy version, is put by the disciples of the Baptist (Mk. ii. 18-22; Mt. ix. 14-17; Lu. v. 33-39). Thus Luke contrives to convert three unconnected stories into a single connected one. That Jesus received the more degraded classes of his countrymen on equal terms, and that his habits were not ascetic, are the important facts which we have to gather from these several statements.

The inference from the evidence on the whole is that Jesus was in comfortable, though not opulent circumstances; and even had he been in want, he had friends enough whose devotion would never have allowed him to remain without a good lodging and sufficient food.

These friends he seems to have begun collecting round him as soon as he entered upon his career of preaching in Galilee. Among the earliest were four fishermed, Simon and his brother Andrew, James and his brother John. The first pair of brothers Jesus called away from their occupation, saying, "Follow me, and I will make you fishers of men" (Mk. i. 16-20; Mt. iv. 18-22). So say two Gospels, but a very different account appears in John. There we are told that two of the disciples of John the Baptist having heard Jesus, left their master to follow him. One of these two was Andrew, Simon's brother, and it was Andrew who went and informed Simon that he had discovered the Messiah. On seeing Simon, Jesus addresses him, "Thou art Simon the son of John; thou shalt be called Kephas" (Jo. i. 38-43). Not a word is said here of the calling of fishermen pursued by these brothers, nor of the remarkable promise to make them fishers of men. Moreover it is they who present themselves to Jesus; not he who summons them. The two accounts are mutually exclusive.

Luke has a third version, not absolutely irreconcilable with that of Mark and Matthew, though inconsistent in all its details. According to him, Jesus had once been speaking to the people from Simon's boat, which was lying on the lake of Gennesaret. The address concluded, he desired Simon to launch into the lake and let down the nets. Simon replied that they had toiled all night and caught nothing; yet he would obey. On casting out the net it was found to inclose so great a multitude of fishes that it broke. Simon called to his partners, James and John, to come to his assistance, and both vessels were not only filled with fish, but began to sink with the weight. Peter, ascribing this large haul to the presence of Jesus, begged him to depart from him, for he was a sinful man. Jesus told him, as in the other Gospels he tells him and his brother Andrew (who does not appear here), that he shall henceforth catch men. Hereupon all the three forsook all, and followed him; from which it must clearly be understood that they had not followed him before. Thus, that which the simpler version represents as a mere summons, obeyed at once, is here converted into a summons enforced upon the fishermen by a professional success so great as to appear to them miraculous, and to lead in their minds to the inference that since Jesus had commanded them to let down the nets, and their obedience had been thus rewarded, he was in some obscure manner the cause of the good fortune which had attended their efforts (Lu. v. 1–11).

Leaving aside for the present all that is peculiar to John, who alone mentions the calling of Philip, there is but one other disciple concerning whom we have any information as to the mode in which he was led to join Jesus. This is Levi, or Matthew, the publican. Jesus found him sitting at the receipt of custom, and commanded him to follow him, which he instantly did (Mk. ii. 14; Mt. ix. 9; Lu. v. 27, 28). But we are not compelled to suppose that from this time forward Levi did nothing but accompany Jesus or go through the country preaching the new faith. He may have done so, or he may only have left his business from time to time to listen to the prophet who had so deeply impressed him. For while three Evangelists mention this circumstance, only one of them, and that the least trustworthy, adds that in following Jesus he left all things.

The names of the other seven disciples are given with but a single variation in all of the synoptical Gospels (Mk. iii. 14–19; Mt. x. 1–4; Lu. vi. 12–16). To these twelve their master gave power to heal diseases and to cast out devils, and sent them forth into the world to preach the coming of the kingdom of heaven, giving them instructions as to the manner in which they should fulfill their mission (Mk. iii. 14, 15; Mt. x. 5–15; Lu. ix. 1–6). When not thus engaged, they were to remain about his person, and form an inner circle of intimate friends, to receive his more hidden thoughts, and help him in the work he had undertaken.

The four who were the first to join him seem to have stood towards him in a closer relationship than anyone else, and to have been in fact his only thorough disciples during the earliest period of his life. For we read that after the cure of a demoniac effected in the synagogue at Capernaum(Mk. i. 21–28; Lu. iv.

31–37), he retired into the house of Simon and Andrew, with James and John, and there healed Simon's mother-in-law of a fever by the touch of his hands, a species of remedy which requires no miracle to render it effectual (Mk. i. 29–31; Mt. viii. 14, 15; Lu. iv. 38, 39). His reputation as a thaumaturgist had now begun to spread, and crowds of people besieged his door, whom he relieved of various diseases, and from whom he expelled many devils (Mk. i. 32–34; Mt. viii. 16, 17; Lu. iv. 40, 41). The anxiety of the devils to bear witness to his Messiahship he repressed, on this as on other occasions. Mentioning these circumstances, Matthew, ever prone to strengthen his case by the authority of a Hebrew prophet, cites Isaiah, "He himself took our infirmities, and bore our sicknesses." Certainly not a very happy application of prophecy; since it nowhere appears that Jesus bore the diseases he cured, or was possessed by the devils he expelled.

Anxious to escape from the pressure of the people, who clamored for miracles, he retired to a desert place to pray. But here Simon and others followed him and told him that all men were seeking him. He replied that he must carry his message to other villages also, and proceeded on a tour through Galilee, preaching and casting out devils (Mk. i. 35–39; Lu. iv. 42–44). It was on some occasion during this Galilean journey, when crowds, eager to hear his doctrine and see his wonders, had pressed around him from every quarter that he delivered the celebrated sermon the scene of which is laid by Matthew on a mountain, and by Luke in a plain (Mt. chs. v.—vii., inclusive; Lu. vi. 20–49). A part only of this discourse has been preserved to us, for Matthew has evidently collected into one a great number of his best sayings, which were no doubt actually uttered on many different occasions and in many different places. Luke, with more sense of fitness, has scattered them about his Gospel, assigning to some an earlier, to others a later date. Notably is this unlike arrangement remarkable in the case of the Lord's prayer, and in nothing is the untrustworthiness of these Gospels, as to all exterior circumstances, more conspicuous than in their assigning to the communication of this most important prayer totally different times, different antecedents, and different surroundings. For whereas Matthew brings it within his all-comprehensive sermon on the mount, Luke causes it to be taught in "a certain place" where Jesus was praying. The former makes Jesus deliver it spontaneously; the latter in answer to the request of a disciple; the former to a vast audience; the latter to the disciples alone (Mt. vi. 9-13; Lu. xi. 1-4).

Discrepancies like these evince the hopelessness of attempting to follow with accuracy the footsteps of Christ. We can obtain nothing beyond the most general conception of his movements, if even that; and of the order of the several events in his life we can have scarcely any notion. Discourses, parables, conversations, miracles, follow one another now in rapid succession. Leaving the consideration of the doctrines taught for another place, we will notice here, without aiming at a chronological arrangement, the principal scenes of his life; and, beginning with his miracles, we will take before any others those in which devils are expelled; or as we should say, maniacs are restored to sanity.

A strange miracle of this kind is related of a man in the country of the Gadarenes or Gergasenes. Matthew indeed, according to a common habit of his, has made him into two men, but the other two Evangelists agree that there was but one. This man was a raving lunatic, who had defeated every effort to confine him hitherto made, and who lived among tombs, crying and cutting himself with stones. Seeing Jesus, he addressed him as the Son of the Most High God, and adjured him not to torment him. On being asked his name, he said it was Legion, for they were many. Having been ordered out by Jesus, he begged for leave to enter into a herd of swine which was feeding near at hand; this was granted, and the herd ran violently down a steep place into the sea and were all drowned, their number being about two thousand (Mk. v. 1-20; Mt. viii. 28-34; Lu. viii. 26-39). After this wanton destruction of property, it is not surprising that the people "began to pray him to depart out of their coasts." Jesus on this occasion certainly displayed a singular tenderness towards the devils, and very little consideration for the unfortunate owners of the pigs. Nor did the Legion gain much by the bargain; for they lost their new habitation the moment they had taken possession of it.

The disciples, as we have seen, had received power over devils, but it appears from a remarkable story that they were not always able to master them. For on returning to them after the transfiguration, Jesus found a crowd about them engaged in some disputation. Having demanded an explanation, a man told him that he had brought his son, who was subject to violent fits, probably epileptic (Mark alone makes him deaf and dumb), and begged the disciples to cure him, which they had been unable to do. Hereupon, Jesus, bursting into an angry exclamation against the "faithless and perverse generation" with whom he lived, took the boy and healed him. Luke omits the private conversation with the disciples which followed on this scene. They asked him, it is said, why they had been thus unsuccessful. The answer is different in Matthew and in Mark. In the former Gospel, he assigns a plain reason: "because of your unbelief;" adding afterwards, "this kind does not come out except by fasting and prayer." In Mark, the latter statement constitutes the whole reply, no allusion being made to the disciples' unbelief. It is noticeable, however, that in Mark alone the father is required to believe before the boy is healed; a singular condition to exact, since belief may generally be expected to follow on a miracle rather than to precede it (Mk. ix. 14-29; Mt. xvii. 14-21; Lu. ix. 37-43).

In the case of the Syro-phœnician woman, however, there was no need to impose it, for her faith, founded on the reputation of Jesus was perfect. This woman came to him when he had gone upon an excursion to the neighborhood of Tyre and Sidon, and begged him to cast out a devil from her daughter, who was not present. He at first refused on the ground of her being a Gentile, but after a remarkable dialogue, confessed himself convinced by her arguments, and told her that on her return she would find the daughter cured, which actually happened (Mk. vii. 24-30; Mt. xv. 21-28). Here we have an instance of a remedy effected at a distance, which can scarcely be credited at all unless on the supposition that the daughter knew of her mother's expedition, and had equal faith in Jesus. The probability is, however, that her recovery is an invention, though the argument with the woman may possibly be historical.

Belief in the production of diseases by demoniacal possession, and in the power of exorcism over diseases so produced, is the common condition of mind in barbarous or semi-civilized nations. The phenomena which occurred in the first century in Judea are reproduced at the present day in more than one quarter of the globe. Take, to begin with, the theory of possession in Abyssinia, which I find quoted by Canon Callaway from Stern's "Wanderings among the Falashes." Canon Callaway observes that "in Abyssinia we meet with the word *Bouda*, applied to a character more resembling the Abatakadi or wizards of these parts [South Africa]. . . . The *Bouda*, or an evil spirit called by the same name and acting with him, takes possession of others, giving rise to an attack known as 'Bouda symptoms,' which present the characteristics of intense hysteria, bordering on insanity. Together with the *Boudas* there is, of course, the exorcist, who has unusual powers, and, like the *inyanga yokubula*, or diviner among the Amazulu, points out those who are *Boudas*, that is, Abatakati" (R. S. A., part iii. pp. 280, 281). Describing the diseases of the Polynesian islanders, the missionary Turner says: "Insanity is occasionally met with. It was invariably traced in former times to the immediate presence of an evil spirit" (N. Y., p. 221). Rising somewhat higher in the scale of culture, the Singhalese, as depicted by Knox, present the spectacle of patients whose symptoms are an almost exact reproduction of those which afflicted the objects of the mercy of Jesus. "I have many times," he relates, "seen men and women of this country strangely possest, insomuch that I could judge it nothing else but the effect of the devil's power upon them, and they themselves do acknowledge as much. In the like condition to which I never saw any that did profess to be a worshiper of the holy name of Jesus. They that are thus possest, some of them will run mad into the woods, screeching and roaring, but do mischief to none; some will be taken so as to be speechless, shaking and quaking, and dancing, and will tread upon the fire and not be hurt; they will also talk idle, like distracted folk." The author proceeds to say that the friends of these demoniac patients appeal to the devil for their cure, believing their attacks to proceed from him (H. R. C., p. 77).

The striking successes of Jesus with maladies of this order naturally brought him the reputation of ability to deal no less powerfully with other diseases. Accordingly, a leper presented himself one day, and kneeling to him said that if he wished he could make him clean. He did so, and the leper, though enjoined to keep silence, went about proclaiming the power of Jesus, who was consequently besieged by still further throngs of applicants and of curious spectators (Mk. i. 40–45; Mt. viii. 1–4; Lu. v. 12–16).

Illustrating the manner in which he was pursued, we find a curious story. Jesus was in his own house at Capernaum, when a paralytic, borne upon a couch, was brought to him to be healed. Unable from the concourse about him to penetrate to Jesus, his bearers let him down through an opening in the roof. After forgiving the man's sins, which he claimed a right to do, he told him to take up his bed and walk. This the paralytic at once did, to the amazement of the bystanders (Mk. ii. 1–12; Mt. ix. 1–8: Lu. v. 18–26). Matthew, telling the same story, omits the crowd and the circumstance of letting down the patient through the roof; and these adjuncts may be fictitious in the special case, but in so far as they bear witness to the thaumaturgic repute of Jesus, have in them an element of genuine history.

Of various other miracles of healing with which Jesus is credited, one of the most interesting is the alleged resuscitation of Jairus' daughter. Jairus was a ruler of the synagogue; a personage therefore of some note in his district; and his daughter, a little girl of twelve years old, was dangerously ill, and supposed by her friends to be at the point of death. At this critical moment Jairus repaired to Jesus, and requested him to come and lay his hands on the little maid, that she might live. Jesus consented, but before he could reach the house messengers arrived who informed Jairus that his child was already dead; he need not trouble the master. None the less did Jesus proceed to the house, taking with him only the most intimate disciples, Peter, James, and John. Here a strange scene awaited him. About, and probably in the sick-room had gathered a crowd of people, relations, friends, and dependants of Jairus, who were engaged in raising a wild clamor of grief around the child.   Flute-players were performing on their instruments, while their lugubrious music was accompanied by the tumultuous wailing and howling of the mourners.   Jesus, having entered the place, declared that the maiden was not dead, but sleeping; or as we should say, in a state of insensibility.   The people laughed in derision at the assertion, but Jesus at once took the very proper and sensible measure of turning them all out of the room (which was either the sick-room itself or one close to it), and taking the damsel's hand, commanded her to rise.   She did so, and Jesus (again exhibiting excellent sense) ordered that she should have something to eat (Mk. v. 21-24, and 35-43; Mt. ix. 18, 19, and 23-26; Lu. viii. 40 42, and 49 56).   In this case we have a peculiarly valuable instance of the manner in which miracles may be manufactured.   Analyzed into its elements of fact and its elements of inference, we find in it nothing which cannot be easily understood without supposing either any exercise of supernatural power or any deliberate fraud in the narrators. Observe first, that in two out of the three versions the girl is reported by Jairus not to be dead, but dying.   True, before Jesus can get to her it is announced that she is actually dead. But Jesus, having reached the house, and having evidently seen the patient (though this fact is only suffered to appear in Luke's version), expressly contradicts this opinion, declaring that she is not dead, but unconscious.   On what particular symptom he founded this statement we do not know, but we cannot, without accusing Jesus of deliberate untruthfulness, believe that he made it without reason.   At any rate, the measures taken by him implied a decided conviction of the accuracy of his observation.   If she were, as he asserted, not dead, though dangerously ill, the hubbub in the house, if suffered to continue, would very likely have rendered her recovery impossible.   Quiet was essential; and that having been obtained, it was perfectly possible that under the soothing touch and the care of Jesus she might awake from her trance far better than before, and to all appearance suddenly restored to health.   The crisis of her case was over, and it may have been by preventing her foolish friends from treating that crisis as death, that Jesus in reality saved her life.   And when she awoke, the order to give her food implied a state of debility in which she could be assisted, not by supernatural, but by very commonplace measurès. Observe, however, the manner in which in this case the myth has grown. In two of the Gospels, Mark and Luke, Jairus comes to Jesus, not when his daughter is dead, but only when she is supposed to be at the last gasp. There is no reason from their accounts to believe that she died at all, her friends' opinion on that point being contradicted by Jesus. But in Matthew the miracle is enhanced by the statement of the father to Jesus that she was just dead (Mt. ix. 18). Consistently with this account the message afterwards sent to him from his house is omitted. Again, while it seems from the manner in which Matthew and Mark relate what happened, that the words of Jesus, "The maiden is not dead, but sleepeth," preceeded his entry into her room, it is clear from Luke that they succeeded it. And this is consistent with the requirements of the case. Some of the mourners and attendants must obviously have been by the bedside, and he could not turn them out till he was himself beside it. Then clearing the sick-chamber of useless idlers, he could proceed in peace to treat the patient; while if we suppose that these people were all outside the door, there is far less reason for their prompt expulsion. That this is the true explanation of the miracle I do not venture to assert; I have only been anxious to show, by a single instance, how easily the tale of an astounding prodigy might arise out of a few perfectly simple circumstances.

A curious incident took place on the way to the house of Jairus. A woman who had had an issue of blood for twelve years, came behind Jesus and touched his clothes, whereupon she was instantly healed. Jesus, turning round, told her that her faith had saved her (Mk. v. 25–34; Mt. ix. 20–22; Lu. viii. 43–48). Such is the fact as related by the first Evangelist; but the other two, magnifying the marvel, place Jesus in the midst of a throng of people pressing upon him, and make him supernaturally conscious that some one has touched him in such a manner as to extract remedial power out of him. Discovered by this instinct, the woman tremblingly confesses her deed.

Neither contact, however, nor even the presence of Jesus on the spot, were essential to a miracle of healing. A centurion, having a paralytic servant, either went or sent others to Jesus, requesting that he would heal him. Before Jesus could reach the house, he declared that he was unworthy of receiving him within it, but entreated that the word might be spoken, adding that his servant would then be healed. This was done; and Jesus took occasion to point the moral by contrasting the faith of this heathen with that of the Jews, dwelling on the superior strength of the former (Mt. viii. 5–13; Lu. vii. 1–10). This myth which appears only in two Gospels, and in them with considerable variations, seems to have been designed to glorify Jesus by making a Roman officer acknowledge his powers. This intention is more evident in Luke than in Matthew; for in Matthew the centurion comes himself; but in Luke he sends "the elders of the Jews" to prefer his request, their appearance evincing his importance, and therefore increasing the honor done to Jesus by the suppliant attitude in which he stands. When Jesus is near his house the officer still does not approach in person, but sends friends, distinctly stating that he thought himself unworthy to come himself, and intimating his belief that a mere word will be enough to heal his servant. It is impossible to see why this message might not have been sent in the first instance by the elders, and the cure effected at once, but the two embassies to Jesus make a better story. Thus, in this version the centurion, who in the other version gives an interesting account of his official status, and receives the highest praise for his faith, never actually sees Jesus at all; and the eulogy is spoken not *to* him, but *of* him. Here, then, is another example of the way in which tales of this kind grow in passing from mouth to mouth.

Sometimes much more materialistic means of healing were adopted. One day, by the sea of Galilee, a deaf and dumb man was brought to Jesus. In this case he took the man aside, put his fingers into his ears, spat, touched his tongue, looked up to heaven, sighed, and said, Ephphatha, or, Be opened (Mk. vii. 31-37). When a word was sufficient, it was singular to go through all these performances, and the whole proceeding has somewhat the air of a piece of jugglery. At Bethsaida he dealt in like manner with a blind man, leading him out of the town, spitting upon his eyes, and then putting his hands upon him. Asked whether he saw, the man replied that he saw men as trees walking, whereupon a further application of the hand to his eyes caused him to see clearly (Mk. viii. 22-26). Here the remark presents itself that if anything of the sort ever occurred, the man could not have been born blind, since he would then have been unable to distinguish either men or trees by sight. It must have been a blindness due to accident or disease of the eyes, and might not have been total. But the whole story is probably mythical.

Two more miracles of healing rest on the authority of the third Gospel alone. By one of them ten lepers, who had asked for mercy, were suddenly cleansed after they had gone away. One only of the ten, a Samaritan, turned round to glorify God and to utter his gratitude. Jesus then observes: "'Were not the ten cleansed? Where are the nine? Were there none found that returned to give glory to God, except this stranger?' And he said to him, 'Arise, go; thy faith hath saved thee'" (Lu. xvii. 11–19). Here the intention of exalting the Samaritan above the Jews is very evident.

Another prodigy was worked at the town of Nain, where the only son of a widow was just dead, and his body was being carried out to the burial-place. Jesus touched the bier, and the widow's son rose to life, to the terror of the spectators, who declared that a great prophet had been raised up, and that God had looked upon his people (Lu. vii. 11–17).

Though the miracles of Jesus were principally of a remedial character, there were others which were rather designed to evince his power. Conspicuous among this class is that of feeding a multitude of five thousand people who had followed him into a desert place, and whose hunger he satisfied by the supernatural multiplication of five loaves and two fishes (Mk. vi. 30-45, and viii. 1-9; Mt. xiv. 14-21, and xv. 29-38; Lu. ix. 10-17; Jo. vi. 1-15). Of this wonder a double version, slightly different in details, has been embodied in the first two Gospels. It is plainly the same story coming from different sources. John, whose miracles are seldom identical with those of the synoptics, relates this one nearly in the same way; except that according to him it was a lad and not (as in the other Gospels) the disciples, who had the food on which the marvel was operated. The number of persons is stated in all four Gospels to be five thousand (and on the second occasion in the two first Gospels four thousand); but Matthew alone has striven to enhance the miracle still further by adding to these numbers the words, "besides women and children."

Immediately after this miracle the disciples entered a boat to cross the lake of Galilee, leaving their master on land. A storm overtook them at night, and as they were laboring through it, they saw Jesus walking towards them on the water. Alarmed at such an apparition they cried out in fear; but Jesus reassured them, and was received into their boat, whereupon the wind fell (Mk. vi. 45-52; Mt. xiv. 22-33; Jo. vi. 16-21). To this Matthew, unlike Mark and John, adds that Peter also attempted the feat of walking on the lake; but being timid, began to sink, and had to be rescued by Jesus. John alone adds to the first miracle a further one: namely, that immediately upon his entrance into the ship, they were at the land whither they went.

A somewhat similar performance is that of stilling a violent storm on the lake of Galilee, which seems to have astonished even the disciples in the boat, accustomed as they must have been to prodigies. At least their exclamation, "What sort of man then is this, that even the wind and the sea obey him?" looks as if all his influence over devils and diseases had failed to convince them of his true character (Mk. iv. 35-41; Mt. viii. 23-27; Lu. viii. 22-25).

All doubt upon this score must have been removed in the minds of three at least of the disciples by a scene which occurred in their presence. Peter, James and John accompanied him one day to a high mountain, where he was transfigured before them; his raiment becoming white and shining. Elijah and Moses were seen with him, and Peter, evidently bewildered, proposed to make three tabernacles. A voice came from heaven: "This is my beloved son: hear him." Suddenly the apparition vanished; Jesus alone remained with the disciples, and on the way down charged them to tell no one of what they had seen till after the resurrection (Mk. ix. 2-13: Mt. xvii. 1-13; Lu. ix. 28-36). This is a suspicious circumstance, which means, if it mean anything, that the transfiguration was never thought of till after the death of Jesus, and that this order of his was invented to account for the otherwise unaccountable silence of the three disciples. For is it to be imagined that Peter, James, and John could keep the secret of this marvelous event, which was so well fitted to confirm the faith of believers, and to convince the Jews in general of the Messianic nature of the prophet? And if they did keep the secret, what weight is to be attached to their evidence, given long after the event, and when exalted views of the divinity of the Christ who had risen from death were already current?

Such are some of the "mighty works" for which Jesus claimed, and his disciples yielded, the title of "son of man," or "son of God," and assumed the authority of the "Messiah" whom the Jewish nation expected. But this claim was recognized neither by the spiritual heads of the Jews, nor by the great bulk of the people. Indeed he had given great offense to their religious sentiment both by putting forward such pretensions, and by the opinions he had expressed on various topics. The language which had caused their hostility, as belonging to his historical and not to his mythical personality, will be considered elsewhere. But the accounts — semi-mythical, semi-historical — which have reached us of the closing scenes of his life, must be passed under review now.

Long before his actual arrest, the Gospels tell us that he had predicted to his disciples the sufferings that were to befall him. Peter, according to one of the versions, had remonstrated with him on these forebodings, and had received from him in consequence one of the sharpest reprimands he had ever given, with the opprobrious epithet of "Satan." It is further stated that he prophesied his resurrection, and his return to earth in glory with the angels of his Father. To this was added another prediction which proved false, that there were some standing there who should not taste of death till the son of man came in his kingdom. Gloomy expressions as to the necessity of his followers taking up their crosses and being ready to lose their lives also escaped him (Mk. viii. 31-ix. 1; Mt. xvi. 21-28; Lu. ix. 22-27). A little later, he is said to have distinctly given vent to similar expectations as to his approaching end, though without being able to make himself understood by his disciples (Mk. ix. 30-32; Mt. xvii. 22, 23; Lu. ix. 44, 45). Again, on the way to Jerusalem where he intended to celebrate the passover, he took all his twelve disciples aside, and distinctly foretold his execution there, and his resurrection on the third day (Mk. x. 32-34; Mt. xx. 17-19; Lu. xviii. 31-34).

Those portions of his prophecies which related to his death at the hands of the Jewish rulers, though not those which related to his return in glory, were destined to be soon fulfilled. Determined to insist publicly upon his title to the Messianic throne, Jesus resolved upon a triumphal entry into Jerusalem. Having sent two disciples from the Mount of Olives to fetch a colt, hitherto unridden, which he informed them the owners would surrender on hearing that the Lord had need of it, he mounted this animal and rode into the city amid the shouts and acclamations of his supporters. Many are said to have spread their garments in his path; others to have cut down branches from trees, and strewed them before him. Those that went before and behind him kept cheering as he rode, exclaiming: "Hosanna, blessed is he who cometh in the name of the Lord; blessed is the coming kingdom of our father David; hosanna in the highest" (Mk. xi. 1-11; Mt. xxi. 1-11: Lu. xix. 29-39; Jo. xii. 12-16).

This remarkable scene is described in all the Gospels; but while the three first represent Jesus as sending to fetch the colt, or the ass and colt, which he in some mysterious manner knows that the man will give up, the fourth makes him take the ass and mount it; not as in the other versions before the triumphal reception, but after it had begun. So that as to these important circumstances the two accounts are entirely at issue; that of John being the more natural. That Jesus actually entered Jerusalem in this fashion is highly probable, for we find in the Gospels themselves a motive assigned which might well have led him to select it for his approach to the capital. There was a prophecy in Zechariah with which he was no doubt familiar: "Rejoice greatly, O daughter of Zion: shout, O daughter of Jerusalem: behold, thy King cometh unto thee, just and victorious is he; lowly, and riding upon an ass, and upon a foal, the young of asses" (Zech. ix. 9). With the views he held as to his Messiahship, Jesus may well have been anxious to show that this prophecy was fulfilled in his person.

On the day after his entry on the ass, on coming from Bethany he was hungry, and finding a fig-tree without fruit, he cursed it. Mark says that the disciples found it withered the next day; Matthew increasing the marvelous element, that they saw it wither "immediately." Mark also adds that it was not the season for figs, which, if correct, would have made it absurdly irrational in Jesus to expect them (Mk. xi. 12–14, and 20–26; Mt. xxi. 18–22). If we accept the more natural supposition that it was the season, but that this individual tree was barren, then we may easily understand that the absence of fruit and the withered condition of the tree were both parts of the same set of phenomena, and that the disciples may have observed them about the same time.

Human beings were the next victims of the wrath of Jesus. The money-changers and dove-sellers were turned out of the temple by him; the fourth Gospel alone mentioning a scourge of small cords as the weapon employed (Mk. xi. 12–14, Mt. xxxi. 12, 13; Lu. xix, 45, 46; Jo. ii. 15–18). A question put by the authorities as to his right to act thus was met by a counter-question, and finally left unanswered (Mk. xi. 27–33; Mt. xxi. 23–27; Lu. xx. 1-8.) The chief priests now consulted together as to the measures to be taken with a view of bringing him to trial, but hesitated to do anything on the feast-day for fear of popular disturbances. Matthew tells us, what the other two do not know, that they assembled at the palace of the high priest Caiaphas, and also puts in the mouth of Jesus a distinct prophecy that after two days he will be betrayed to be crucified (Mk. xiv. 1, 2; Mt. xxvi. 1-5; Luke xxii. 1, 2.)

A similar foreboding is expressed, according to Matthew, Mark, and John, in reference to an incident which is variously described by these three Evangelists. Matthew and Mark agree in saying, that on this occasion he was taking a repast at the house of Simon the leper, when a woman came up to him with a box of very precious ointment and poured it on his head. Here, according to Mark, "some," according to Matthew, "the disciples," were indignant at the waste of the ointment, which might, they said, have been sold "for much," or "for three hundred pence," and the proceeds given to the poor. But Jesus warmly took up the woman's cause, for, he remarked, "she has wrought a good work on me. For you always have the poor with you, but me ye have not always. For in pouring this ointment on my body she has done it for my burial." Mark now how strangely this simple story has been perverted in the fourth Gospel to suit the purposes of the writer. The date he assigns to it — six days before the passover — is nearly the same as that given in the second Gospel, where it is placed two days before that festival. The place, Bethany, is also identical. But the other circumstances are widely different. In this Gospel alone is anything known of an intimate friend of Jesus, Lazarus by name. In it alone is there any mention of one of his most astounding miracles, the restoration of Lazarus to life. Consistently with his peculiar notion of the relations of Jesus with this man's family he says nothing of Simon the leper, but without telling us in whose house Jesus was, mentions that Lazarus was among the guests, and that his sister Martha was serving. Further, he asserts that the woman who brought the ointment was Mary, the other sister. Instead of pouring it on his head, she is made to anoint his feet, and wipe them with her hair. Instead of the disciples, or some unknown people, being angry at the waste, it is Judas Iscariot in whose mouth the obnoxious comment is placed. The sum he names, three hundred pence, is the same as that assigned in Mark as the value of the ointment. But in order to cover Judas with still further obloquy, the Evangelist charges him with a desire to obtain this sum, not for the poor, but for himself; he being the bearer of the common purse, and being in the habit of dishonestly appropriating some portion of its contents (Mk. xiv. 3-9; Mt. xxvi. 6-13; Jo. xii. 3-8). Of such an accusation not a trace is to be found in the other Gospels, whose writers were assuredly not likely to spare the reputation of Judas if it were open to attack. Nor does the author of this insinuation offer one particle of evidence in its support.

The steps by which a story grows from an indefinite to a definite, from a historical to a mythical form, are admirably illustrated in this instance. A tradition is preserved in which, while the main event is clear, many of the surrounding circumstances have been suffered to escape from memory. Writer after writer takes it up, and finding it thus imperfect, adds to it detail after detail until its whole complexion is altered.

Even the main event may not always be exempted from the transfiguring process; as here, where the feet of Jesus are substituted for the head, and the interesting picture introduced of Mary wiping them with her hair, and consequently placing herself in a situation of the deepest humility. And if the central incident is thus unsafe, still more so are its adjuncts. First, the woman is unknown, as are those who murmur against her. Then, in the second stage, the woman is still unknown, but the murmurers are known generally as the disciples. But no bad motive is as yet assigned for their censure. Lastly, in the third stage, the woman is known, the murmurer is known specifically as *one* disciple, and a bad motive is assigned for his censure. Such is the way in which myths grow up.

The circumstance we have next to deal with is obscure, not because too much has been added, but because something has been omitted. Jesus had now drawn upon him the mortal hatred of the priests of the temple. He was well aware of his danger, as many of his expressions show. He endeavored to avoid it by living in concealment in or near Jerusalem. Not that we are told of this in so many words, but that the course of the story renders it a necessary assumption. For all the Gospels inform us that one of his disciples, Judas named Iscariot, went to the chief priests and betrayed him, receiving a pecuniary reward for the service thus rendered (Mk. xiv. 10, 11; Mt. xxvi. 14-16; Lu. xxii. 3-6; Jo. xiii. 2, 27). As to this fact there is complete unanimity, and it is borne out by the manner of his arrest as subsequently depicted. We cannot then treat it as a fiction; but it is plain that had Jesus been leading the open and public life described in the Gospels, there would have been no secret to betray, and no reward to be earned. A period, more or less long, of retirement to some spot known only to friends, must therefore be taken for granted. John alludes to something of the sort, though not distinctly, when he relates that there was a garden across the brook Cedron, to which he often resorted with his disciples, and which was known to Judas. But the Christian tradition did not like to acknowledge that Christ, whom it represents as braving death, ever lurked in hidden places like a criminal, and at the same time it wished to brand the memory of Judas with infamy. Hence the sup-

pression of a fact without which the story cannot be understood. The expressions, "he sought how he might conveniently
betray him" (Mk. xiv. 11); or "he sought opportunity to betray
him (Mt. xxvi. 26), plainly point to the same inference.

There are some differences in the manner in which the proceedings of Judas are related. All the Gospels agree that he
received money, but Matthew alone knows how much. This
Evangelist had in his mind a passage in Zechariah, which he
erroneously attributes to Jeremiah, and which moreover he mis-
quotes (Mt. xxvii. 9). In the original it runs thus: "And I said
unto them [the poor of the flock], If it is good in your eyes,
give me my hire; and if not, forbear. And they weighed for
my hire thirty pieces of silver."* Matthew and Mark merely
state that Judas betrayed his master, giving no reason for his
conduct. Luke, however, represents it as a consequence of
Satan having entered into him (Lu. xxii. 3); while John in like
manner states that the devil put it into his heart, and even
knows the very moment when Satan entered into him (Jo. xiii.
2, 27). This Evangelist alone places the first steps taken by
Judas after the last supper, instead of before it, and strangely
enough so arranges the course of events, that he only acts upon
the resolution to betray him after a distinct declaration by Jesus
that he was about to do so.

Slightly anticipating the course of the narrative, we may
mention here the singular myth of the unhappy end of the
traitor Judas; a myth which is of peculiar interest inasmuch as
its origin is distinctly traceable to a mistranslation of a verse
in Zechariah. The passage quoted above continues thus: "And
Jehovah spoke to me: Throw it to the treasure, the costly
mantle with which I am honored by them; and I took the
thirty pieces of silver and threw them into the temple of
Jehovah to the treasure." But the word here used for the treasure commonly signifies potter, and was hence interpreted "Throw
it to the potter." Out of this mistake arose the story that
Judas, ashamed of his bargain, returned the money to the chief
priests, who, deeming it unlawful to put it in the treasury,
bought therewith the "potter's field to bury strangers in."

* Zech. xi. 12, 13. According to Ewald, this portion of Zechariah is by an
anonymous prophet contemporaneous with Isaiah.

Thus, observes Matthew, "was fulfilled that which was spoken by Jeremy the prophet." Judas, having parted with his ill-gotten gain, committed suicide by hanging (Mt. xxvii. 3-10). So at least says Matthew; but Luke, making confusion worse confounded, represents Judas himself as purchasing the field "with the reward of iniquity;" after which he fell headlong, and bursting in the middle, his bowels gushed out (Acts i. 18, 19). Of this notorious fact, "known," according to the Acts of the Apostles, "to all the dwellers at Jerusalem," Matthew at least was wholly ignorant. But both versions equally originate in the defective Hebrew of the translators of Zechariah.

In all the synoptical Gospels, the celebration of the passover by Jesus and his disciples succeeds the secret arrangement of Judas with the high priests. He kept it in Jerusalem, in the house of a man whose name is not mentioned, but who must have been one of his adherents. The encounter with this man is represented in two of the three versions as something miraculous. On the first day of unleavened bread Jesus told two of his disciples (according to Mark), James and John (according to Luke), to go into Jerusalem, where they would meet a man bearing a pitcher of water. Him they were to follow, and wherever he went in, they were to say to the master of the house, "Where is the guest-chamber, where I may eat the passover with my disciples?" He would then show them a large furnished upper room, where they were to prepare it. Nothing but a perfectly natural version of all this appears in Matthew. There Jesus tells his disciples to go into the city to So-and-so (the name therefore having been given), and tell him that he wished to keep the passover at his house (Mk. xiv. 12-16; Mt. xxvi. 17-19; Lu. xxii. 7-13). Here again we see how easily a wondrous tale may originate in a very simple fact.

Supper was accordingly prepared in the man's house, and Jesus ate the passover there with his disciples. At this supper, according to all the Gospels, he mentioned the fact that one of them would betray him. Whether in so doing he actually named the traitor is uncertain. Mark's account is that when he had predicted that one would betray him, the disciples in sorrow inquired one by one, "Is it I?" and that Jesus told them it was the one who dipped with him in the dish. Luke leaves it still more indefinite. There Jesus merely says, "the hand of him that betrays me is with me on the table," and no further inquiry is made by any one. Matthew, like Mark, represents each disciple as asking whether he was the one, and Jesus as giving the same indication about the dish. But he adds that Judas himself asked, "Is it I?" and that Jesus answered, "Thou hast said." Quite different is the account in John. There, instead of all the disciples inquiring whether it was he, a single disciple, leaning on the breast of Jesus, asks, on a sign from Peter, who it was to be. Jesus does not reply that it was he who dipped in the dish, but he to whom he should give a sop. He then gives the sop to Judas, and tells him to do quickly that which he is about to do; words understood by no one present.* The improbability of any of these stories is obvious. In the three first, Judas is pointed out to all the eleven as a man who is about to give up their master to punishment, and probable death, yet no step was taken or even suggested by any of them either to impede the false disciple in his movements, or to save Jesus by flight and concealment. The announcement is taken as quietly as if it were an every-day occurrence that was referred to. John's narrative avoids this diffiulty by supposing the intimation that Judas was the man to be conveyed by a private signal understood only by Peter and the disciple next to Jesus. These two may have felt it necessary to keep the secret, but why then could they not understand the words of Jesus to Judas, or why not at least inquire whether they had reference to his treachery, which had just before been so plainly intimated? That Jesus, with his keen vision, may have divined the proceedings of Judas, is quite possible; that he could have spoken of them at the table in this open way without exciting more attention, is hardly credible.

It was at this same passover that Christ, conscious of his approaching end, blessed the bread and the cup of wine, and giving them to his disciples, told them that the one was his body, and the other his blood in the new testament, or the new testament of his blood (Mk. xiv. 22-25; Mt. xxvi. 26-29; Lu. xxii. 14-21; I Cor. xi. 23-25). John who was confused about dates in

* Mk. xiv. 17-21; Mt. xxvi. 20-25; Lu. xxii. 21, 22; Jo. xiii. 21-28.

his biography, supposes that this supper took place before the feast of the passover, instead of at it, and, consistently with this view, he says nothing of the institution of the Eucharist, which had a peculiar reference to the Jewish feast-day. Instead thereof, he introduces another ceremony, of which neither the other Evangelists nor Paul say a word; that of washing the disciples' feet by Jesus. This was done to make them "clean every whit" (though it had no such effect on Judas), and also to set them an example of mutual kindness (Jo. xiii. 4-17).

The passover eaten, Jesus retired with his disciples to the Mount of Olives. Being in a prophetic mood, he foretold that all his disciples would forsake him in the hour of danger now approaching, and that Peter would deny him. This Peter resented, though it was destined to be soon fulfilled. After this Jesus went to Gethsemane, and taking his three principal disciples apart from the rest, told them that his soul was sorrowful unto death, and begged them to remain and watch while he prayed. Going a little forward, he prayed earnestly that the coming trial might pass from him, yet with submission to God's will. Returning, he found his three friends asleep, and this happened twice again, these devoted men sleeping calmly on until the very moment when the officers of the Sanhedrim came to arrest their Lord. Luke adorns this scene — which he places at the Mount of Olives without mentioning the garden of Gethsemane — with ampler details. Mark and Matthew know nothing of the exact distance of Jesus from his disciples; Luke knows that it was about a stone's throw. Moreover, all the number are present, not only Peter, James, and John. Sweat like drops of blood falls from Christ. An angel appears to strengthen him. All this is new; as is the representation that the disciples were sleeping from sorrow,—a motive which the Evangelist no doubt felt it needful to assign in order to vindicate their honor. The other two biographers, who content themselves with saying that "Their eyes were heavy," certainly keep more within the limits of probability (Mk. xiv. 32-42; Mt. xxvi. 36-46; Lu. xxii. 39-46).

No sooner was the prayer concluded than Judas, accompanied by a large *posse comitatus* armed with swords and staves, came from the Jewish authorities. Resistance to the arrest must have been expected, and not wholly without reason; for as soon as the officers, in obedience to the preconcerted signal of a kiss from Judas, had seized Jesus, one of his party drew a sword and cut off the ear of the high priest's servant. This incident is related in various ways in all the Gospels. In Mark, Jesus addresses no rebuke to the disciple who commits this action. In Matthew, he tells him to put up his sword, for all who take the sword shall perish by the sword. In Luke, the progress to greater definiteness which has been noted as characterizing these semi-historical myths has begun. In the first place, before going to the Mount of Olives, the disciples provide themselves with two swords; and Jesus, on their mentioning the fact, says, "It is enough." Then the writer knows that it was the right ear which was cut off. More than this, he gives artistic finish to the whole by making Jesus touch the place and heal the wound: though whether a new ear grew, or the old one was put on again, he does not tell us. More definite still is the version in John. This Evangelist, as we saw in another case, is fond of supplying names. Thus, he pretends to know here that it was Peter who cut off the ear, and that its owner was called Malchus. Peter is called to order in his version, but Malchus is not healed. Plainly it was the sense of justice of the third Evangelist that made him shrink from leaving an innocent dependent in this mutilated condition, when he knew that Christ might so easily have restored the missing member.

While in the synoptical Gospels it is Judas who by a kiss points out Jesus, in John it is Jesus himself who comes forward to declare himself. Hereupon the party deputed by the priests go backwards and fall to the ground. They soon recover themselves enough to arrest him. In all the versions he suffers himself to be quietly taken, while in all but John he resents, with much dignity, the sending of such a force against him, as though he had been a thief; while in fact he had often taught openly in the temple and had not been stopped. Their master once taken, the courage of the disciples was at an end. They all fled. Jesus was brought before the Sanhedrim, and evidence, of the tenor of which we are not informed, was produced against him. Lastly, two witnesses deposed that they had heard him say, "I am able to destroy this temple, and in three days to rebuild it;" or, "I will destroy this temple made with hands, and will build another not made with hands in three days." Mark endeavors to depreciate these witnesses by saying that their evidence did not agree; and he himself is liable to the remark that his report of their evidence does not agree with that of Matthew, while in neither Gospel does the utterance attributed by these men to Jesus tally exactly with that assigned to him in John, "Destroy this temple, and in three days I will raise it up" (Jo. ii. 19). The agreement, however, is close enough to render it probable that some such expression was used, and some such evidence given. Neither Luke nor John know anything of witnesses against Jesus. But Luke, in common with the other synoptical Gospels, asserts that he not only admitted, but emphatically confirmed the charge—distinctly put to him by the high priest—of being the Son of God. On this confession he was unanimously found guilty of blasphemy.

Wholly different is the conduct of the trial in John, whose account, moreover, is confused and ill-written in the extreme. With his usual proneness to give names, he says that Jesus was taken first before Annas, the father-in-law of Caiaphas the high priest. Annas sent him bound to Caiaphas. The high priest (the council is not alluded to) carried on an informal conversation with Jesus, inquiring about his doctrine and disciples; questions which the latter, on the plea of the publicity of his teaching, refused to answer. There is no mention of blasphemy; no conviction on any charge; no expression of opinion on the part of Caiaphas; though from the fact that he committed the prisoner for trial before the Roman court, it may be inferred that he considered him guilty.*

During the trial by the Sanhedrim, a singular scene was passing in the ante-room. There Peter, who alone of the disciples had followed his master (for the mention of another is peculiar to John), was warming himself among the attendants. Questioned by maids and officers of the court whether he had not been among the disciples of the accused, he vehemently, three several times, repudiated the supposition, though his

* Mk. xiv. 43-65; Mt. xxvi. 47-68; Lu. xxii. 47-53, and 63-71; Jo. xviii. 3-14 and 19-24.

Galilean accent told heavily against him. According to John, the question was put on the third occasion by a relative of Malchus, who had seen him in the garden. The other Evangelists are less specific. Now Jesus had foretold that Peter would thus deny him, and that his falsehoods would be followed by the crowing of a cock. Immediately after the last denial, this signal occurred; and Peter, according to all the Gospels but the fourth, went out and wept over his meanness.

Convicted by the Sanhedrim, the prisoner was now placed at the bar of the civil tribunal. The procurator of Judea at this time was a man named Pontius Pilatus. His character does not stand high. Neander terms him "an image of the corruption which then prevailed among distinguished Romans" (Leben Jesu, p. 687). Appointed in the year 23, he was recalled in 37 on account of the slaughter of some Samaritans in a battle. He had insulted the prejudices of the people he governed by setting up the standards of the Roman army within the walls of Jerusalem, and had threatened an armed attack upon the peaceable Jews who went to Cæsarea to remonstrate against this novel measure. On another occasion he had taken some of the revenues of the temple to construct an aqueduct, and when the work was interrupted by the people, had set disguised soldiers upon them, who killed them without mercy.

Such a man was not likely to be excessively troubled by scruples about the execution of an innocent victim. On the other hand it is perfectly possible that he might, comparing the prisoner with the prosecutors, prefer the former. Having no love for the Jewish people, an object of their antipathy might become to a certain extent an object of his sympathy. But beyond this, it would be absurd to suppose that a man of the character of Jesus would inspire him with any sort of regard, or that he would hesitate to take his life if it suited his purpose. The simplest account of the trial bears out this expectation. Questioned by Pilate as to the charge preferred against him, of claiming to be the king of the Jews, the prisoner answered by an admission of its truth: "Thou sayest it." To other accusations urged against him by the priests he made

* Mk. xiv. 26-30, and 66-72; Mt. xxvi. 30-35, and 69-75; Lu. xxii. 33, 34, and 55-62; Jo. xiii. 37, 38, and xviii. 15-18, and 25-27.

no reply. Pilate wondered at his silence, and endeavored, but without success, to extract an answer. While the conduct of the accused man must have appeared to him not a little strange, Pilate may also have thought that the pretensions to kingship of a peaceable fanatic, with but few and obscure followers, were nowise dangerous to the Roman government. It was his custom at this festival to release a prisoner, leaving the people, or the Jewish authorities, to decide whom. He now proposed to release Jesus, but the suggestion was not accepted, and the liberation of a well-known political prisoner, who had been engaged in an insurrectionary enterprise, was demanded instead. Pilate naturally enough preferred the would-be Messiah to the actual rebel. The Jews as naturally preferred the rebel. They clamored for the crucifixion of Jesus, and Pilate—afraid perhaps that by too much anxiety to save him he would expose himself to misrepresentation before Tiberius—gave way to their demand.

So far Mark; and as to the charge against Jesus, and the procurator's treatment of it, the other Evangelists are all at one with him. But each has adorned the trial with additional incidents after his own fashion. Matthew has a ridiculous story of an interference with the course of justice by Pilate's wife, who on the strength of a dream entreated him to have nothing to do with "that just man." Matthew, as we have seen before, was a great believer in dreams. Then he is so desirous of clearing the character of the Roman, that he describes him as washing his hands in token of his innocence before the multitude, who cry out that the blood of Jesus is to be on them and their children. In Luke, there is a new variation. Learning that Jesus was a Galilean, Pilate sent him to Herod, who had long been anxious to see him, but who could not now induce him to answer any of his questions. Herod, like Pilate, found no fault in him, and sent him back after treating him with ridicule. Pilate's reluctance to convict Jesus is much magnified in this Gospel. He insists on Herod's inability, as well as his own, to discover any capital offense committed by him, and three several times proposes to the prosecution to chastise him and then dismiss him. In John, the conversation of Pilate with Jesus is wholly different. In the first place, it takes place alone, or at

any rate in the absence of the accusers, for these had refused
to be defiled by entering the court; and Pilate is represented
as going out to them to inquire into the charge. This is to
suit the blunder about dates committed in this Gospel, according to which the last supper was before, and the trial at the
very time of, the passover. The Jews, therefore, stand without,
and the prisoner is within. The prisoner does not refuse, as in
all the other versions, to answer Pilate's questions, but enters
at some length into his doctrine, explaining the unworldly
nature of his kingdom. Pilate places the purple robe and the
crown of thorns upon him before his condemnation, instead of
after it, and then tells the Jews that he finds no fault in him.
Yet after this he desires them to crucify him, although he was
guiltless. Hereupon the Jews tell him that he had made himself the Son of God. At this, Pilate is frightened, and enters
into further conversation with Jesus. After hearing him expound another theory, he is still very anxious to release him,
but is forced to yield by an intimation that no friend of Cæsar's
would protect a rival to the throne (Mk. xv. 1-14; Mt. xxvii. 1,
2, and 11 25; Lu. xxiii. 1-23; Jo. xviii. 28-40). Anything more
utterly improbable than this scene it is difficult to imagine.
The picture of the Roman governor of Judea going backwards
and forwards between accusers and accused; listening to the
theological fancies of the accused; helpless against the pressure
of the accusers; alarmed at the pretensions to divinity of a
young Galilean artisan; are sufficient in themselves to stamp
this Gospel with the mark of unveracity.

Sentenced to death, Jesus was now scourged; a purple robe
was put upon him, and a crown of thorns about his head (not
upon it as was afterwards said): he was saluted in mockery as
king of the Jews, and smitten with a reed upon the head. After
this cruel ceremony he was led out to Golgotha to be crucified.
a man named Simon being compelled to bear his cross (Mk. xv.
15-21; Mt. xxvii. 26-32; Lu. xxiii. 24-26; Jo. xix. 1-16). Luke is
singular in the introduction of a large company of women who
follow Jesus to the crucifixion and draw from him a prophecy
of terrible evils to come upon them and their children; for
themselves, and not for him, they were to weep (Lu. xxiii.
27-31). The other versions say nothing of any friends or follow-

ers, male or female, as being present at this period, though
they do mention many women as looking on from a distance
during the crucifixion.   These, however, were not daughters of
Jerusalem (like the women in Luke), but Galilean admirers who
had followed him to the capital.   His mother was certainly not
among them, or she could not fail to have been mentioned in
the synoptical Gospels; whereas the only names we meet with
are those of Mary Magdalene; Mary, mother of James and
Joses; and Salome, apparently the same person as the mother
of Zebedee's children (Mk. xv. 40, 41; Mt. xxvii. 55, 56).

These were among the spectators of the melancholy end of
him who had been their teacher and their friend.   He was crucified between two criminals, with an inscription on his cross
which is differently reported in every Gospel, but of which the
substance was that he was the king of the Jews.   A stupifying
drink which Matthew (in accordance with a supposed prophecy)
(Ps. lxix. 21) calls vinegar and gall, was offered him by the
executioners; not as Luke supposes, in mockery, but with the
humane intention of allaying the pain.   His clothes were divided
among the party of soldiers; a circumstance in which the Evangelists as usual endeavor to see the fulfillment of prophecy.
In Psalm xxii. 18, we read: "They part my garments among
them, and cast lots upon my vesture."   The Synoptics content
themselves here with stating that the soldiers drew lots for his
clothing, but John anxious to fulfill this prophecy in the
most literal manner possible, pretends that they divided
the articles of his apparel into four parts, but finding the coat
without seam, agreed not to tear it, but to apportion it by lot.
Luke is the sole reporter of a saying of Jesus uttered in his
last moments: "Father, forgive them, for they know not what
they do" (Mk. xv. 23-28; Mt. xxvii. 34-38; Lu. xxiii. 32-34, 36;
Jo. xix. 17-24).

The pangs of death must have been greatly embittered to
Jesus if it be true that not only the priests and passers by, but
the very criminals who were crucified with him, ridiculed his
claim to be king of Israel, and suggested that he should prove
it to demonstration by saving himself from the cross.   All the
synoptical Gospels agree in this account, with the single exception that Luke includes only one of the malefactors among the

scorners. According to this Gospel, the other rebuked his fel-
low-convict for his misbehavior, and addressed to him a few
moral remarks; which, however, were perhaps not quite disin-
terested, for at its close he requested Jesus to remember him
in his kingdom, and received an ample reward in the shape of
a promise from the latter that he should be with him that day
in Paradise. But where was the impenitent criminal to be?
About his fate there is an ominous obscurity, and it evidently
did not occur to the writer that the forgiveness which Jesus
had just been praying his Father to grant his enemies, he
might himself have extended to this miserable man (Mk. xv.
29–32; Mt. xxvii. 39–44; Lu. xxiii. 35–43).

Another incident of the closing hours of Jesus is known to
the fourth Exangelist alone. According to the others, the
women who watched him expire were standing far off. But
according to John, his mother Mary, her sister, and Magdalene
wore all at the foot of the cross. There also was the disciple
whom Jesus loved, and who in the three other Gospels had run
away. Before he died, Jesus committed his mother to the care
of this disciple as to a son, and he afterwars took her home.
The dogmatic purpose of this story is evident. Mary had not
been converted by her son during his life-time, and it was
important to bring her to the foot of the cross at his death, and
to place her in this close connection with one of his principal
disciples (Jo. xix. 25 27).

As to the last words of Jesus, there is an amount of divergence which shows that no account can be regarded as trustworthy. Mark and Matthew both relate that he called out,
"Eloi, Eloi, lama sabachthani?" an exclamation which he may
really have uttered, or which, as coming from a prophetic
Psalm, may have seemed to them appropriate. Hereupon a
sponge of vinegar was offered him under the impression that
he was calling Elias, and with a loud cry he gave up the ghost.
In Luke he cries loudly, and then says, "Father, into thy
hands I commend my spirit." With these words (also from one
of the Psalms) upon his lips, he dies. In John he says, "I am
thirsty:" and after receiving some vinegar, adds, "It is fin.
ished;" and bowing his head, gives up the ghost (Mk. xv. 34–
37; Mt. xxvii. 46–50; Lu. xxiii. 46; Jo. xix. 28–30),

With the death of Christ, and indeed immediately before it, we pass from the region of mixed history and mythology into that of pure mythology. With the exception of his burial, all that follows has been deliberately invented. The wonders attendant upon his closing hours belong in part to the typical order of myths, and in part to an order peculiar to himself. The darkness from the sixth to the ninth hour, the rending of the temple veil, the earthquake, the rending of the rocks, are altogether like the prodigies attending the decease of other great men. The centurion's exclamation, "Truly this man was just," or "Truly this man was the son of God" (it is differently reported), is a myth belonging peculiarly to Christ, and designed to exhibit the enforced confession of his greatness by an incredulous Roman. In Matthew, where the more modest narratives of Mark and Luke are greatly improved upon by additional details, it is further added that many bodies of saints arose, and after the resurrection appeared to many in Jerusalem (Mk. xv. 33-39; Mt. xxvii. 45, and 51-54; Lu. xxiii. 44-47))

John, who knows nothing whatever of the darkness, the accident to the temple veil, the revival of the saints, or the centurion's exclamation, has a myth of his own constructed for the especial purpose of fulfilling certain prophecies. The next day being a festival, the Jews, he says, were anxious that the bodies should not remain on the crosses. They therefore requested Pilate to break their legs and remove them. He ordered this to be done, and the legs of the two criminals were broken, but not those of Jesus, who was already dead; one of the soldiers, however, pierced his side, from which blood and water gushed out. The writer adds a strong asseveration of his veracity, but immediately betrays himself by letting out that in relating the omission to break the legs of Jesus he was comparing him to the Paschal lamb, of whom not a bone was to be broken; while in telling of the soldier who pierced his side, he was thinking of a phrase in Zechariah: "They shall look upon me whom they have pierced" (Zech. xii. 10; Jo. xix. 31-37).

The burial of the body took place quietly. Joseph of Arimathæa, a secret admirer of Jesus, placed it in a new sepulchre of his own. With him John associates a character who exists only in his Gospel, Nicodemus, and whom he introduces here as taking some part in the interment. To the circumstance of the burial in the rock sepulchre, Matthew adds an audacious fiction of his own; namely, that the chief priests, remembering Christ's prediction that he should rise on the third day, obtained leave to seal the stone of the tomb and keep it watched, lest the disciples should take the body by night and pretend that he was risen (Mk. xv. 42–47; Mt. xxvii. 57–66; Lu. xxiii. 50–56; Jo. xix. 38–42).

Certainly if the Evangelist had meant to convey the impression that no human means could prevent the resurrection of Christ, he would have been perfectly right. An actual body was not necessary for the purpose. For the legends appertaining to the resurrection belong to a region in which imagination, unhampered by the controlling influence of historical fact, has been permitted the freest play. Of the appearances of Jesus after his death we have accounts by no less than seven different hands, each story being distinct from, though not always inconsistent with, the other six. Let us begin with what is probably the oldest of all, containing but a germ of the rest; the first eight verses of the last chapter of Mark. There we are told that on the day after the Sabbath, Mary Magdalene, Mary James's mother, and Salome went to the sepulchre at sunrise. They found it empty, the stone having been rolled away. A young man in white clothes was sitting in it. He told them that Jesus was risen, and desired them to tell the disciples that he was going to Galilee, where they would see him. All that follows in this Gospel is added by a later hand, and the very first verse of the addition is plainly written in total disregard of what has just preceded it. Observe then that *the simplest form of the story of the resurrection contains no mention of any actual appearance of Jesus whatever*, but merely an assertion that the body was not in the tomb, and that a man, sitting inside it, made certain statements to three women. To this the forger has added that Jesus appeared first to Magdalene, whose account, given to the disciples, was disbelieved by them; secondly, to two disciples while walking, whose evidence was also disbelieved; thirdly, to the eleven at dinner, to whom he addressed a discourse (Mk. xvi).

The writer of thee first Gospel is much more elaborate. He

was a little embarrassed by the guards whom he had set to watch the tomb, whom it was essential to find some convenient method of getting out of the way. Like Mark, he takes the two Marys (not Salome) to the sepulchre early on the first day of the week; unlike Mark, he does not make them examine the tomb and find it deserted. On the contrary, there is an earthquake (the author is rather fond of these natural convulsions), and an angel with a face like lightning, clothed in the purest white, descends. He rolls back the stone and sits upon it. His appearance so terrifies the keepers that they become like corpses. The angel tells the women that Jesus is risen, and that they are to let the disciples know that he would go before them to Galilee, where they would see him. As they are engaged on this errand, Jesus himself appears and gives them a similar injunction. The second appearance occurred before the eleven disciples, who saw him at an appointed place in Galilee, "but some doubted." Here Jesus addressed to them a parting discourse, and this Gospel does not state how or when he quitted them. The awkward circumstance of the presence of the guards, who had certainly not testified to the angel's descent, had still to be surmounted. This is accomplished by a ridiculous story that they had been heavily bribed by the priests and elders to say that the disciples had stolen the body while they were asleep (Mt. xxviii).

Unlike either of the preceding writers, Luke conceives the first appearance of the risen Christ to have been, not to the women, but to two disciples. He does indeed relate that on the morning of the first day of the week Magdalene, Mary, Joanna, and other women went to the tomb, and found the stone rolled away and the body gone. While they were wondering at this, two men in shining garments stood by them, and told them that he whom they sought was risen. They returned to report to the apostles, to whom their words seemed as idle tales. Peter, however, ran to the sepulchre to verify their statement, and found only the clothes in it. Two of the disciples were going that same day to Emmaus. While walking and talking, a stranger joined them and entered into a conversation, in which he expounded the prophecies relating to the Messiah. They requested this man to remain with them for the night at the house where they were lodging. During supper he took bread, blessed it, broke it, and gave it to them; whereupon they recognized him as Jesus, and he vanished from their eyes. On returning to Jerusalem, they found the eleven and the rest asserting that Christ was risen and had appeared to Peter. The two wanderers related their experiences in their turn. While the disciples were talking, Jesus himself appeared in their midst, and said, "Peace unto you." Some skeptical doubts, however, troubled them even now, for Jesus thought it necessary to prove his actual carnality by showing his hands and feet, as well as by eating some broiled fish and a piece of honeycomb. After this he "opened their understanding," by an expository discourse in reference to some of his own sayings and to the Scriptures; concluding with an exhortation to remain at Jerusalem till they were endowed with power from on high (Lu. xxii. 1-49). This last passage is explained by the same author in the Acts of the Apostles to refer to the descent of the Holy Ghost upon the apostles, which in that work is much more definitely promised by Jesus (Acts i. 5, 8). We also find in it an important addition to the details furnished by the Gospel about the resurrection; namely, that Jesus was seen by his disciples for forty days after his physical death, during which time he kept speaking to them about matters pertaining to the kingdom of God (Acts i. 3).

Directly contradicting Mark and Matthew, John states that Magdalene (no one else is mentioned) went to the sepulchre while it was still dark (not at dawn or sunrise), and found the stone taken away. Making no further inspection, she ran to Peter and to the beloved disciple, saying that the body had been abstracted. The two ran together to the place, and going in, found the clothes lying in the tomb, whereupon the beloved disciple "saw and believed," though what he believed is not stated. Magdalene was standing outside; but after the two men had concluded their examination she entered, and saw what they had not seen—two angels, sitting one at each end of the place where the body had been. These angels asked her why she was weeping; she answered, because her Lord's body had been taken. Turning round, she saw a man whom she at first took for the gardener, but whom she soon recognized as Jesus. She returned and informed the disciples that she had seen him. The same day, in the evening, Jesus appeared to the disciples, said, " Peace unto you," and showed them his hands and feet. He then breathed the Holy Ghost into them, and gave them authority to remit or retain sins. Thomas, who was not present on this occasion, roundly refused to believe these facts unless he himself could touch the marks of the nails, and put his hand into the side. A week later Jesus again appeared, and Thomas was now enabled to dispel his doubts by actual examination of his person. To these three appearances, with which the genuine Gospel closed, a later hand has added a fourth. According to this new writer, a number of disciples were about to fish on the lake of Tiberias, when Christ was observed standing on the shore. The miraculous draught of fishes is introduced here in a form slightly different from that which it has in Luke. By acting on a direction from Jesus, the disciples caught a vast number. He then bade them come and dine with him, which they did. After dinner, he instructed Peter to feed his flock, and hinted that the beloved disciple might possibly live till his return in glory (Jo. xx. xxi).

Completely different from any of these narratives is the account of the resurrection contributed by Paul. It is somewhat confused and difficult to understand. Christ, he says, rose on the third day according to the Scriptures, and was seèn by Cephas; then by the twelve; after that by more than five hundred brethren; after that by James; next by all the apostles; and lastly by himself (1 Cor. xv. 3–8). It is to be noted that since Paul does not say that Christ appeared *first* to Cephas, we may if we please combine with this account one of those which make him appear first to Magdalene, or to her and other women. But even then the difficulties do not disappear. For how could so notorious an event as the manifestation of Christ to five hundred people be passed over *sub silentio* in all the Gospels and in the Acts? And granting that Paul may by an oversight have put "the twelve" for "the eleven," are we not compelled to suppose that "all the apostles" are distinct from "the twelve," and if so, who are they? What, again, are we to think of the appearance to James, of which nothing is said elsewhere? Above all, what are we to think of the fact that the purely spiritual vision granted to Paul, which was not even seen by his traveling companions, is placed by him exactly on a level with all the other reappearances of Christ, the physical reality of which so much trouble has been taken to prove?

Comparing now the several narratives of the resurrection with one another, we find this general result. In Mark, Jesus is said to have appeared three times: —

1. To Mary Magdalene.
2. To two disciples.
3. To the disciples at meat.

Two such appearances only are recorded in Matthew:—

1. To the women.
2. To the eleven in Galilee.

In Luke he appears:—

1. To Cleopas and his companion.
2. To Peter.
3. To the eleven and others.

In the two last chapters of John the appearances amount to four:—

1. To Mary Magdalene.
2. To the disciples without Thomas.
3. To the disciples with Thomas.
4. To several disciples on the Tiberias lake.

Paul extends them to six:—

1. To Peter.
2. To the twelve.
3. To more than 500.
4. To James.
5. To all the apostles.
6. To Paul.

Upon this most momentous question, then, every one of the Christian writers is at variance with every other. Nor is this all, for two of the number bring the earthly career of Jesus to its final close in a manner so extraordinary that we cannot even imagine the occurrence of such an event, of necessity so notorious and so impressive, to have been believed by the other

biographers, and yet to have been passed over by them without
a word of notice or allusion. Can it be for a moment supposed
that two out of the four Evangelists had heard of the ascension
of Christ — that the most wonderful termination of a wonderful
life — and either forgot to mention, or deliberately omitted it?
And may it not be assumed that Paul, when detailing the
several occasions on which Christ had been seen after his crucifixion, must needs, had he known of it, have included this, perhaps the most striking of all, in his list? In fact the ascension
rests entirely on the evidence of two witnesses, both of them
comparatively late ones, the forger of the last verses of Mark,
and the third Evangelist. Neither of them stand as near the
events described as the true author of Mark, as Matthew, or as
Paul, from no one of whom do we hear a word of the ascension.
Nor do even these two witnesses relate their story in the same
terms. The finisher of Mark merely tells us that after his parting charge to the eleven, he was received into heaven and sat
at God's right hand; a statement couched in such general
terms as even to leave it doubtful whether there was any distinct and visible ascension, or whether Jesus was merely taken
to heaven like any other virtuous man, though enjoying when
there a higher precedence (Mk. xvi. 19). Especially is this
doubt fostered by the fact that this Gospel, when speaking of
the witnesses to Christ's resurrection, never alludes to any of
the physical proofs of his actual existence so much dwelt upon
in Luke and the last chapter of John. Very much more definite
is the statement at the close of the third Gospel. There it is
related that Jesus led his disciples out to Bethany, where he
blessed them and that, in the very act of blessing, he was
parted from them and carried up into heaven (Lu. xxiv. 50, 51).
The same author subsequently composed the Acts of the Apostles, and in the interim he had greatly improved upon his previous conception of the ascension. When he came to write the
Acts, he was able to supply, what he had omitted before, the
last conversation of the master with the disciples he was about
to leave; he knows too that after the final words — no blessing
is mentioned here — he was taken up and received by a cloud;
that while the disciples were gazing up, two men in white —
no doubt the very couple who had been seen at the sepulchre —

were perceived standing by them, and that these celestial visitors told them that Jesus would return from heaven in the same way in which he had gone to it (Acts i. 9-11). Unhappy Galileans! little could they have dreamt for how many centuries after that day their successors would watch and wait, watching and waiting in vain, for the fulfillment of that consoling prophecy.

Casting a retrospective glance at the stories of the Resurrection and the Ascension, we may perhaps discern at least a psychological explanation of their origin and of the currency they obtained. Whatever other qualities Jesus may have possessed or lacked, there can be no question that he had one — that of inspiring in others a strong attachment to himself. He had in his brief career surrounded himself with devoted disciples; and he was taken from their midst in the full bloom of his powers by a violent and early death. Now there are some who have been taught by the bitter experience of their lives how difficult, nay, how impossible it is to realize in imagination the fact that a beloved companion is in truth gone from them forever. More especially will this mental difficulty be felt when he whom death has parted from our sides is young, vigorous, full of promise; when the infinite stillness of eternal rest has succeeded almost without a break upon the joyous activity of a well-spent life; when the being who is now no more was but a moment ago the moving spirit of a household, or the honored teacher of a band of friends who were linked together by his presence.

Where the association has been close and constant; where we have been accustomed to share our thoughts and to impart our feelings: where, therefore, we have habitually entwined not only our present lives, but our hopes and wishes for the future around the personality of the dead, this refusal of the mind to comprehend its loss is strongest of all. Emotion enters then upon a strange conflict with Reason. Reason may tell us but too distinctly that all hope of the return of the beloved one to life is vain and foolish. But Emotion speaks to us in another language. Well nigh does it prevent us from believing even the ghastly realities which our unhappy eyes have been compelled to witness. Deep within us there arises the craving for the presence of our friend, and with it the irrepressible thought that he may even yet come back to those who can scarcely bear to live without him. Were these inevitable longings not to be checked by a clear perception that they originate in our own broken hearts, we should fancy that we saw the figure of the departed and heard his voice. In that case a resurrection would have taken place for us, and for those who believed our tale. So far from the reappearance of the well-known form seeming to be strange, it is its failure to reappear that is strange to us in these times of sorrow. We fondly conceive that in some way the dead must still exist; and if so, can one, who was so tender before, listen to our cry of pain and refuse to come? can one, who soothed us in the lesser troubles of our lives, look on while we are suffering the greatest agony of all and fail to comfort? It cannot be. Imagination declines to picture the long future of solitude that lies before us. We cannot understand that we shall never again listen to the tones of the familiar voice; never feel the touch of the gentle hand; never be encouraged by the warm embrace that tells us we are loved, or find a refuge from miserable thoughts and the vexations of the world in the affectionate and ever-open heart. All this is too hard for us. We long for a resurrection; we should believe in it if we could; we do believe in it in sleep, when our feelings are free to roam at pleasure, unrestrained by the chilling presence of the material world. In dreams the old life is repeated again and again. Sometimes the lost one is beside us as of old, and we are quite untroubled by the thought of parting. Sometimes there is a strange and confusing consciousness that the great calamity has happened, or has been thought to happen, but that now we are again together, and that a new life has succeeded upon death. Or the dream takes a less definite form. We are united now; but along with our happiness in the union there is an oppressive sense of some mysterious terror clouding our enjoyment. We are afraid that it is an unsubstantial, shadowy being that is with us; the least touch may dissipate its uncertain existence; the slightest illness may extinguish its feeble breath. Granting only a strong emotion and a lively phantasy, we may comprehend at once how, in many lands, to many mourners, the images of their dreams may also become the visions of their waking hours. They see him again; they know that he is not gone; he is beside them still.

But for us, who live in a calmer age, and see with scientific eyes, there is no such comfort. Not to us can the bodily forms of those who have gone before us to the grave appear again in all the loveliness of life. In the first shock of our bereavement we may indeed indulge in some such visionary hope; but as day after day passes by and leaves us in a solitude that does but deepen with the lapse of time, we learn to understand only too well that we are bereft forever. Hope gradually dwindling to a fainter and fainter remnant, is crushed at last by the miserable certainty of profound despair. Yet even then, the mind of man refuses to accept its fate. The scene of the reunion, which we cannot but so ardently desire, is postponed to another season and to a better world. Many are they to whom this final hope is ah enduring consolation, But if even that should fail us in the hour of darkness, as the more primitive and simpler hope failed before it; if here again emotion is reluctantly compelled to yield to reason; then there is still one refuge in despondency, and a refuge of which we can never be deprived. It is the thought that death, so cruel now, will one day visit us with a kinder touch; and that the tomb, which already holds the nearest and the dearest within its grasp, will open to receive us also in our turn to its everlasting peace.

SUBDIVISION 3.—*The Ideal Jesus.*

The Gospel attributed by the current legend to St. John differs from the other three Gospels in almost every respect in which difference is possible. The events recorded are different. The order of events is different. The conversations of Jesus are different. His sermons are different. His opinions are different. The theories of the writer about him are different. Were it not for the name and a few leading incidents, we should be compelled to say that the subject of the biography himself is different. A more conspicuous unlikeness than that of the synoptical to the Johannine Jesus it is not easy to conceive in two narratives which depict the same hero. In the synoptical Gospels Jesus is plain, direct, easy of comprehension, and fond

of illustrating his meaning by short and simple parables. In
John he is obscure, mystical, symbolic, and of his favorite
method of teaching by parables there is not a trace. Both descriptions cannot be true. It would be monstrous to suppose
either that the synoptical Gospels omitted some of his most extraordinary miracles and some of his most remarkable discourses, or that the Gospel of John passed over in silence the
whole of that side of his character which is portrayed in the
ethical maxims, the parables, and the exhortations of its predecessors. Were it so, none of the four could be accepted as
other than an extremely one-sided and imperfect biography, and
each of them is plainly regarded by its author as complete
within itself. None of them refers to extraneous sources to
supplement its own deficiencies. The concluding verse of the
fourth Gospel does indeed allude to many unrecorded actions of
Jesus, which, if they were all written, would fill more books
than the world could contain. But, not to rely on the fact that
the last chapter is spurious, these words contain no intimation
that a mode of teaching completely different from that here
recorded was ever employed by Jesus. And this is the point in
which John's narrative is peculiar. Again, to turn to the Synoptics, there is no shadow of an intimation in them that, between
the last supper and arrest, Jesus addressed to his disciples a
long and remarkable discourse, full of the most interesting revelations. Can we suppose that they could have forgotten it, delivered as it was at such a moment as this, the very last before
their master's condemnation at which he was able to speak to
them? Such a supposition is utterly untenable. The two traditions embodied in these versions of his life do not therefore, as
some learned men — Ewald, for example — have supposed, supplement, but exclude one another.

Let us enter into detail into some of the peculiar characteristics of the Jesus of John. In the first place, we may note
that his miracles are altogether new. One of them at least is
so astounding that no biographer who had heard of it could
have passed it by. The raising of Lazarus is the greatest feat
that Jesus ever performed. In other cases he brought persons
who were supposed to be just dead to life, but skeptical Jews
might have suspected that they had never in reality died at all.

Ample precautions against such cavils were taken in the case of Lazarus. This man lived at Bethany, and his sisters, Mary and Martha, were devoted admirers of Jesus. These women sent word to Jesus, who had retired "beyond Jordan," to say that their brother was ill. He replied that this illness was for the glory of God. Afer he had heard of it he remained two days in the same place. Then, disregarding the dissuasions of the disciples, who reminded him that the Jews had recently sought to stone him, he proceeded towards Judea. He informed them in that obscure manner which he almost invariably affects in this Gospel, that Lazarus was asleep; but on their misunderstanding him, consented to speak plainly and say that he was dead. He added that for their sakes he was glad he had not been there, in order that they might believe — even the disciples' faith being apparently still in need of confirmation. On reaching Bethany, he found that Lazarus had been buried four days. Martha, who came to meet him, observed that had he been there, her brother would not have died, and that even now whatever he asked of God would be given. Jesus told her that her brother would rise again; a saying which she interpreted as referring to the general resurrection; but he replied that whoever believed in him would never die, and required of her an explicit declaration of her faith in this dogma. Martha evaded the inquiry by a profession of her conviction that he was the Christ and went to summon Mary. She too remarked that if he had been there Lazarus would not have died. Distressed by her distress, Jesus himself wept. Going to the grave, he ordered the stone which covered it to be removed, in spite of Martha's objection that putrefaction had set in. A curious scene followed. "Jesus lifted up his eyes and said, 'Father, I thank thee that thou hast heard me. And I know that thou hearest me always, but because of the people which stand by I said it, that they may believe that thou hast sent me.'" We must suppose these last words to have been spoken *sotto voce*, for "the people which stood by" would have been little likely to believe in him had they known that the thanksgiving to God was a mere pious pretence, offered up for the purpose of impressing their imaginations by the event that was to follow. Knowing that his father always heard him, he certainly had no

occasion to thank him on this one occasion; if indeed he could
properly be thanked at all for taking the necessary measures
to ensure the credit of his own son, in whom he desired mankind to believe, and who is over and over again described as
one with himself. This is perhaps the only instance in any of
the Gospels in which something like hypocrisy is ascribed to
Jesus; in which he is represented as consciously acting a part
for the benefit of the bystanders, and speaking simply with a
view to effect. Happily for his reputation we are not obliged
to believe in the accuracy of his biographer. After this he called
loudly, "Lazarus, come forth." The dead man accordingly
arose, and came forth from the tomb clad in his grave-clothes
(Jo. xi. 1-46). His restoration to life was permanent, for we find
him afterwards among the guests at a supper to which Jesus
was invited (Jo. xii. 2).

Another singular miracle to which there is no allusion in any
other Gospel is that which is here declared to be the first; the
conversion of water into wine. Jesus was at a wedding in Cana
of Galilee, and when the wine provided for the entertainment
had all been consumed, his mother informed him of the state
of things. He gave her a repelling answer; but she told the
servants to do what he bade them. He then ordered six water-
pots to be filled with water, and the contents to be drawn. It
was found that they contained wine of a superior quality to
that at first provided (Jo. ii. 1-11).

The second miracle according to John is not unlike some of
those recorded elsewhere. It consisted in the cure by a mere
word, without visiting the place, of a nobleman's son who was
on the point of death. This time also Jesus was at Cana,
though the patient lay at Capernaum (Jo. iii. 46-54). Another
cure was wrought at the pool of Bethesda, the healing virtues
of which are known only to this Gospel. A man who had long
been lying on its steps, too infirm to descend at the proper
moment, was enjoined to rise and walk, which he did (Jo. v.
1-9). It is singular that although "a great multitude of impotent folk" were waiting at the pool, many of whom must
needs have been kept long, since only one could be cured each
time the water was troubled, this man alone was selected for the
object of a miracle. Why were not all of them healed at once?

Not only are the most wonderful proofs of Christ's divinity contained in this Gospel unknown to the rest, but its *dramatis personæ* are in several respects altogether novel. Nathanael, whose difficulties about thinking that any good thing can come from Nazareth are overcome in a conversation with Jesus (Jo. i. 45-51); Nicodemus, the secret adherent who came by night and received instruction in the doctrine of regeneration (Jo. iii. 1-21), who at a later period supported him against the attacks of the Pharisees (Jo. vii. 51), and lastly brought spices to his interment (Jo. xix. 39); Lazarus, brother of Mary and Martha, who owed him his life (Jo. xi. 44; xii. 2); the woman of Samaria, to whom an important prophecy was made, and whose past life he knew by intuition (Jo. iv. 1-30); are all new personages, and they hold no mean place in the story. The immediate attendants on his person are no doubt the same; but the representation that there was one disciple "whom Jesus loved" above the rest, and to whom a greater intimacy was permitted (Jo. xiii. 23), is uncountenanced by anything in the other Gospels; and indicates a fixed purpose of exalting the apostle John above his compeers.

While the scene, the persons, and the plot are thus diverse, the style of the principal actor is in striking contrast to that which he employs elsewhere. Its most conspicuous characteristic is the continual recurrence to symbols. It is true that in the other Gospels Jesus frequently exchanges the direct explanation of his views for the indirect method of illustration. But an illustration serves to clear up the meaning of a speaker, a symbol to disguise it. Illustrations cast light upon the principal thesis; symbols merely darken it. And this is the difference between the synoptical and the Johannine Jesus. The one is anxious to be understood; the other, in appearance at least, is seeking to perplex. Hence the exchange of the parable for the symbol. The number of such symbols in John is considerable. Jesus is continually inventing new ones. Near the beginning of the Gospel, he explains to Nicodemus that it is needful to be born again; a statement by which Nicodemus is considerably perplexed (Jo. iii. 3, 4). But his symbols are more generally applied to himself or his relations to the Father. He is the bread of life or the bread of God (Jo. vi.

33–48); again, he is the living water (Jo.), or he gives a water which prevents all future thirst (Jo. iv. 14); he is the true vine, his Father the husbandman, and his disciples the branches (Jo. xv. 1–5); elsewhere he is both the good shepherd and the door by which the sheep enter the fold (Jo. x. 7–16); he is the way, the truth, and the life (Jo. xiv. 6); he is the light that came into the world (Jo. xii. 46; iii. 19)); or he is the Resurrection and the Life (Jo. xi. 25). John the Baptist, also, unlike the John of the other Gospels, adopts the same manner. Christ is spoken of by him as the Lamb of God, which takes away the sins of the world (Jo. i. 29); or as the Bridegroom whose voice he rejoiced to hear, while he himself was but the Bridegroom's friend (Jo. iii. 29). Sometimes "the Jews," as they are termed in this Gospel, are puzzled by the enigmatical style of Jesus, the sense of which they cannot unriddle. Thus, when he tells them that if they destroy the temple he will rebuild it in three days, they are naturally unable to perceive that he is speaking of the temple of his body (Jo. ii. 19–21). They murmured because he spoke of himself as the Bread that came down from heaven, nor was any explanation offered them beyond a reiteration of the same statement (Jo. vi. 41–51). Not only the Jews, but also many of his own partisans. were hopelessly perplexed by the statement that no one could have life in him who did not eat his flesh and drink his blood (Jo. vi. 53, 60), a statement which differs materially from that made at the passover (in the other Gospels), where the bread and wine were actually offered as signs of his flesh and blood, and the apostles alone (who were present) were required to receive them. At other times he confused them by mysterious intimations that he was going somewhere whither they could not come, and that they should seek him and be unable to find him (Jo. vii. 33–36; viii. 21, 22). On one occasion, his auditors were unable to comprehend his assertion that he must be lifted up, and requested him to explain it. The only reply was another enigma, namely, that the light was with them but a little while, and that they should believe in it while they had it (Jo. xii. 32–36). To such language they might well have retorted, that what they had from him was not light, but a twilight in which no object could be distinctly seen, and which never advanced towards clear daylight.

Closely connected with this tendency to speak in obscure images was his predilection for argument with the Jews on abstruse theological topics. In the other Gospels he teaches the people who surround him, and the subject of his teaching is generally the rules of moral conduct; comparatively seldom theology. In John he does not so much teach as dispute, and the subject of the dispute is not morals — a field he scarcely ever enters — but his personal pretensions. Upon these he carries on a continual wrangle, supporting his claims by his peculiar views of the divine nature and of his relation to it (Jo. v. 16–47; vi. 41–59; vii. 14–36; viii. 12–29; ix. 39–41; x. 19–37). In the same spirit the blind man whom he cures enters into a discussion with the Pharisees on the character of him who had restored his sight (Jo. ix. 24–34). The Jews are depicted as continually occupied about this question. Even their own officers receive from them a reproof for making a laudatory remark about him (Jo. vii. 47, 48), while Nicodemus, who interposes in arrest of judgment, is sharply asked whether he also is of Galilee (Jo. vii. 51–52).

The very best instruction of Jesus is not given, as in the other Gospels, to a multitude, but is reserved for a select circle of his own followers. It is in the 14th, 15th, and 16th chapters that he rises to the sublimest heights of his doctrine, and the whole of this remarkable discourse is delivered to the disciples after Judas has left the supper-table in order to betray him. The substance of his teaching is no less peculiar than its occasions. The writer conceives of him as holding an altogether singular relation to the Father, and that relation he represents his Christ as continually expounding and insisting upon as of vital moment. The Evangelist himself begins his work by a concise statement of his doctrine on this point. The Logos, he says, was with God in the beginning; the Logos was God. All things were made by it, and nothing was made without it. In it was life, and the life was the light of men. This Light came into the world, but the world did not know him. Even his own, whoever these may have been, did not receive him. To those who did receive him, he gave power to become the sons of God; and these were born, not of blood, nor of the will of the flesh, nor of the will of man, but of God. The Logos was made flesh, and dwelt among us, and we beheld his glory, as of the only-begotten of the Father (Jo. i. 1–14).

The language of Christ is duly adjusted to this very speculative theory. Thus, he scandalizes the Jews by the bold assertion that he and his Father are one; and adds to their horror by further maintaining that he is in the Father, and the Father in him (Jo. x. 30, 38). Elsewhere, Philip is required to believe in the same truth. In reply to his ignorant request that he may be shown the Father, he is told that seeing Jesus is equivalent to seeing the Father. Moreover, the Father who dwells in Christ performs the works which are apparently done by Christ alone (Jo. xiv. 9–11). The disciples, too, are included in this mystic unity, for they are in Jesus in the same sense in which he is in God (Jo. xiv. 20; xvii. 21, 23). His Father, nevertheless, is greater than himself (Jo. xiv. 28). Jesus has been glorified with the Father before the world existed, and looks forward to a return to that glory. He wishes that those who have been given him on earth may be with him to behold the glory which God, who loved him before the foundation of the world, has given him. That glory he has given them, and they are to be one, even as he and his Father are one; he in them, and God in him (Jo. xvii. 5, 22–24).

After these preliminary observations, we need not dwell long on the historical incidents of the Gospel, of which there are but few. The meeting of Jesus with Andrew and Simon, and his reception of Nathanael, related in the first chapter, have already been noticed. It only remains to be said, that Nathanael was deceived by a prophecy which was not fulfilled; for at the end of the interview, Jesus, referring to his amazement that he had been discovered under the fig-tree, which had quite put him off his balance, tells him that he shall see greater things than these, and especially mentions among them the opening of the heavens and the descent of angels upon the Son of man. Nathanael never saw anything of the kind (Jo. i. 35–51).

The conversion of water into wine follows next. A peculiari.y in the notions of this writer is evinced by the assertion that his mother and brothers went with him to Capernaum, for his family do not accompany him, according to any other statement, while here his mother not only is with him, but is aware that he is able to work a miracle (Jo. ii. 1-12). Jesus, after visiting Capernaum, proceeded for the passover to Jerusalem, where it is said that many believed in him because of his miracles. His expulsion of the money-changers, however, brought him into collision with the authorities of his nation, who asked him for a sign; a question to which he replied by the undertaking to rebuild the temple, if destroyed, in three days (Jo. ii. 13-25). But one of the Jewish rulers, named Nicodemus, was disposed to believe in his pretensions. This man came to him by night, and heard from him a long theological disquisition (Jo. iii. 1-21). Jesus then went into Judea, and remained there with his disciples baptizing his converts. John the Baptist is made to bear an emphatic testimony to his superiority (Jo. iii. 22-36). A visit to Samaria is the occasion for an interesting dialogue with a Samaritan woman who had come to draw water at a well; and her report leads the inhabitants to come out and see the prophet by whom she had been so much impressed.

This incident is reproduced with curious fidelity in Buddhist story. Ananda, one of Sakyamuni's disciples, met with a Matangi woman, one of a degraded caste, who was drawing water, and asked her to give him some of it to drink. Just as the Samaritan wondered that Jesus, a Jew, should ask drink of her, one of a nation with whom the Jews had no dealings, so this young Matangi girl warned Ananda of her caste, which rendered it unlawful for her to approach a monk. And as Jesus nevertheless continued to converse with the woman, so Ananda did not shrink from this outcast damsel. "I do not ask thee, my sister," he replied, "either thy caste or thy family; I only ask thee for water, if thou canst give me some." The Buddha himself, to whom the Matangi girl afterwards presented herself, treated her with equal kindness. He contrived to divert the profane love she had conceived for Ananda into a holy love of religion; much as Jesus led the Samaritan from the thought of her five husbands, and of him who was not her husband, to the conception of the universal Father who was to be worshiped "in spirit and in truth." And as the disciples "marveled" that Jesus should have conversed with this member of a despised race, so the respectable Brahmins and householders who adhered to Buddhism were scandalized to learn that the young

Matangi had been admitted to the order of mendicants (Jo. iv.
1-42; H. B. I., pp. 205, 206).

After two days spent at Samaria Jesus went on to Galilee,
where he healed the nobleman's sons (Jo. iv. 43-54). Having
returned to Jerusalem for another feast, he cured the impotent
man on the Sabbath, which endangered his life at the hands of
the indignant Jews, and led him to deliver a long vindication
(Jo. v). The feeding of the five thousand was followed by an
attempt to make him king, from which he prudently escaped.
The disciples took ship to go to Capernaum, and Jesus joined
them by walking on the water. On the ensuing day he preached
to the people who followed him, and shocked even some of the
disciples by the loftiness of the claims he advanced. Many of
them are said to have left him at this time (Jo. vi).

A singular proceeding is now mentioned. Urged by his
brothers, who were still incredulous, to go to Jerusalem for the
feast of tabernacles, he declined on the ground that his time
was not yet come. When they were gone he himself went also,
though secretly (Jo. vii. 1-10). There is no reason assigned for
this little stratagem, and he soon emerged from his incognito
and taught openly in the temple. The public mind was much
divided about his character, some maintaining him to be Christ,
others contending that Christ could only come from the seed of
David and the town of Bethlehem. An attempt to arrest him
failed, owing to the impression he made upon the police (Jo.
vii. 11-53). A discussion with the Jews was terminated by their
taking up stones to throw at him, a peril from which he escaped
apparently by miracle (Jo. viii. 12-59; verses 1-11 are spurious).
Further offense was given by the restoration of a blind man's
sight on the Sabbath (Jo. ix). A discourse on his title to authority provoked divisions, and at the feast of the dedication he
was plainly asked whether he was the Christ. His answer
again led to an attempt to stone him, from which he escaped
to the place beyond Jordan where John had formerly baptized
(Jo. x). The raising of Lazarus and the anointing by Mary are
the next events recorded (Jo. xi. 1-xii. 9). The passover followed
six days after the latter incident, and his preaching at this festival was interrupted in a singular manner. Jesus had used the
words, "Father, glorify thy name!" whereupon a voice was

heard from heaven, saying, "I both have glorified it, and will glorify it again." Thereupon Jesus observed that this voice came not for his sake, but for that of the bystanders. It seems, however, to have produced but little effect upon them, for a few verses later we find a complaint that, in spite of his many miracles, they did not believe on him (Jo. xii. 12–50). The last supper with the disciples was immediately succeeded by a parting discourse of much beauty, conceived in an elevated tone; and his last moments of freedom were occupied in a prayer of which the pathos has been rarely equaled (Jo. xiii.-xvii).

The remainder of his career—his trial, execution, and alleged resurrection—have been fully treated in another place.

SUBDIVISION 4. — *What did the Jews think of him?*

Victorious over Jesus Christ at the moment, the Jewish nation have, from an early period in Christian history, been subject in their turn to his disciples. Their polity—crushed under the iron heel of Vespasian, scattered to the winds by Hadrian—vanished from existence not long after it had successfully put down the founder of the new faith. Their religion, tolerated by the heathen Romans only under humiliating and galling conditions, persecuted almost to death by the Christians, suffered until modern times an oppression so terrible and so cruel, that but for the deep and unshakeable attachment of its adherents, it could never have survived its perils. Hence the course of events has been such that this unhappy nation has never until quite recently enjoyed the freedom necessary to present their case in the matter of Jesus the son of Joseph; while the gradual decay of the rancor formerly felt against them, at the same time that it gives them liberty, renders it less important for them to come forward in what would still be an unpopular cause. Thus it happens that one side only in the controversy, that of the Christians, has been adequately heard. They certainly have not shrunk from the presentation of their views. Every epithet that scorn, hatred, or indignation could suggest has been heaped upon the generation of Jews who were the immediate instigators of the execution of Jesus, while all the subsequent miseries of their race have been regarded—by the party which delighted to inflict them — as exhibitions of the divine vengeance against that one criminal act. Nor have even freethinkers shrunk from condemning the Jews as guilty of gross and unpardonable persecution, and that towards one who, if they do not think him a God, nevertheless appears to them singularly free from blame. On the one side, according to the prevailing conception, stands the innocent victim; on the other the bloodthirsty Jewish people. All good is with the one; all evil with the other. It is supposed that only their hard-heartedness, their aversion to the pure doctrine of the Redeemer, their determination to shut their eyes to the light and their ears to the words of truth, could have led them to the commission of so great a crime.

Whether or not this theory be true, it at least suffers from the vice of having been adopted without due examination. An opinion can rest on no solid basis unless its opposite has been duly supported by competent defenders. Now in the present instance this has not happened. Owing to the causes mentioned above, the Christian view has been practically uncontested, and writer after writer has taken it up and repeated it in the unreflecting way in which we all of us repeat assertions about which there is no dispute. Yet a very little consideration will show that so simple an explanation of the transaction has at least no *a priori* probability in its favor. That a whole nation should be completely in the wrong, and a few individuals only in the right, is a supposition which can be accepted only on the most convincing evidence. And in order even to justify our entertaining it for a moment, we must be in possession of a report of the circumstances of the case from the advocates of the nation, as well as from the advocates of the individuals who suffered by its action. A one-sided statement from the partizans of a convicted person can never be sufficient to enable us to pronounce a conclusive verdict against his judges. The most ordinary rules of fairness prohibit this. Yet this is what is commonly done. No account whatever of the trial of Jesus has reached us from the side of the prosecution. Josephus, who might have enlightened us, is silent. On the other hand, the side of the defense has furnished us with its own version of what passed, and from the imperfect materials thus supplied

we must endeavor to discriminate
can. To do this justly, we must bear
the charges produced against Jesus sho
the indignation of his accusers, it is at lea
indignation was altogether without reasonab
ful as it may be to be compelled to think that
wrong, it would surely—had not long habit perv
ural sentiments—be quite as painful to believe t
multitude of men, impelled by mere malignity agains
ous citizen, had conspired to put him to death on charges
were absolutely groundless. The honor of an heror, and i
all, of a deeply religious people, is here at stake. It is no l
matter to deal in wholesale accusations of judicial mord
against them. It would surely be a happier solution if it could
be shown that the individual condemned was not absolutely
guiltless. But possibly we may be able to elude either alternative. Just as, according to the able reasoning of Grote, the upright character of Socrates may be compatible with a sense of
justice on the part of the Athenians who condemned him to
death, so it is conceivable that the innocence of Jesus may consist with the fact that the Jews who caused him to be crucified
were not altogether without excuse.

An examination of this question must be conducted with a
careful regard to the hereditary feelings of orthodox Hebrews
in matters of religion; with an attention to the conceptions
they had formed of holiness, and consequently of blasphemy,
its negation; with a desire to do justice if possible to the very
prejudices that clouded their vision, and to realize the intensity
of the sentiment that ruled their national life and bound them
to uphold their law in all its severe integrity. We must
remember that the Jews were above all things monotheists.
Ever since, after the captivity, they had put away every remnant of idolatry, they had clung to the unity and majesty of
Jehovah with a stern tenacity which no alluring temptations,
no extremity of suffering, had been able to break. If they were
now ready to persecute for this faith, they had at least shown
themselves able—they soon showed themselves able again—to
bear persecution for its sake. Their law, with its monotheistic
dogmas and its practical injunctions, was to them supremely holy.

to infringe its precepts, or to question its authority, than that which it recognized, to teach any other
of that which rested on this foundation, was blasphemy
... yes.   The happiness, nay, the very existence, of the
... as bound up with its strict observance. This may have
... delusion, but it was one for which the existing genera-
... as not responsible. It had been handed down from their
... tors, and had reached them with all the sanctity of ven-
... le age. If it were a delusion, it was one which the compil-
... of the Pentateuch; which Josiah, with his reforming meas-
... es; which Ezra, with his purifying zeal; which the prophets
... and priests of olden times who had fought and labored for the
religion of Jevovah, had mainly fostered. They had succeeded
but too well in impressing upon the mind of the nation the
profound conviction that, in order to ensure the favor of God,
they must maintain every iota of the revealed truth they had
received, and that his anger would surely follow if they suffered
it to be in the smallest degree corrupted or treated with neglect.

Nevertheless the utmost efforts of the people to guard the
purity of the faith had been rewarded hitherto with little but
misery. Their exemption from troubles did not last long after
the rebuilding of the temple. A prey now to the Seleucidæ,
now to the Ptolemies, their native land the scene of incessant
warfare, they enjoyed under the Asmonean kings but a brief
period of independence and good government. Their polity
received a rude shock from the capture of Jerusalem by Pompey; maintained but a shadow of freedom under the tyranny of
Herod; and fell at last—some time before the public appearance of Christ—under the direct administration of the unsym-
pathetic Romans. A more intolerable fate could hardly be
imagined. The Romans had no tenderness for their feelings, no
commiseration for their scruples, no comprehension of their
peculiar practices. Hence constant collision between the governors and the governed. It is needless to enter in detail upon
the miserable struggles between those who were strong in the
material force and those who were strong in the force of conscience. Suffice it to say, that provocation on provocation was inflicted on the Jews, until at length the inevitable rebellion came,

to be terminated by the not less inevitable su,
attendant cruelties. But in the time of Jesus the
yet come. All things were in a state of the utmost
was of the highest importance to the people, and their ι
were well aware of it, that there should be nothing do.
could excite the anger of their rulers. The Romans kne
course, that no loyalty was felt towards them in Palesti..
And the least indication of resistance was enough to provoke
them to the severest measures. All that remained of independence to the Jews — the freedom to worship in their own way;
their national unity; their possession of the temple; their very
lives — depended on their success in conciliating the favor of
the procurator who happened to be set over them, The assertion by any one of rights that might appear to clash with those
of Rome, even the foolish desire of the populace to honor some
one who did not pretend to them, were fraught with the utmost
danger. It was necessary for the rulers to prove that they did
not countenance the least indication of a wish to set up a rival
power.

Their task was more difficult because the people were continually looking for some great national hero who should re-
deem them from their subjection. The conception of the "Messiah," the Anointed One, the King or High Priest who should
restore, and much more than restore, the ancient glory of their
nation, who should lead them to victory over their enemies and
then reign over them in peace, was ineradicably imbedded in
their minds. Consequently they were only too ready — especially
in those days of overstrung nerves and feverish agitation under
a hateful rule — to welcome any one who held out the chance
of deliverance. The risk was not imaginary. Prophets and
Messiahs, if they were not successful, could do nothing but
harm. Theudas, a leader who did not even claim Messiahship,
had involved his followers in destruction. Bar-cochab, who at a
later time was received by many as the Messiah, brought upon
his countrymen not only enormous slaughter, but even the crowning misfortune of expulsion from Jerusalem. Now, although the
high priests and elders no doubt shared the popular expectation
of a Messiah, they were bound as prudent men to test the pretensions of those who put themselves forward in that character,

and if they were imperi'ing the public peace, to put a stop to their careers. It was not for them, the appointed guides of the people, to be carried away by every breath of popular enthusiasm. They would have been wholly unworthy of their position had they permitted floating reports of miracles and marvels, or the applauding clamor of admirers, to impose upon their judgment. Calmly, and after examination of the facts, it was their duty to decide.

Jesus had professed to be the Messiah. So much is undisputed. Could his title be admitted? Now, in the first place, it was the central conception of the Messianic office that its holder should exercise temporal power. He was not expected to be a teacher of religious doctrines, for this was not what was required. The code of theological truth was, so far as the Jews were aware, completed. The Revelation they possessed never hinted, from beginning to end, that it was imperfect in any of its parts, or that it needed a supplementary Revelation to fill up the void which it contained. Whatever Christians, instructed by the gospel, may have thought in subsequent ages, the believers in the Hebrew Bible neither had ascertained, nor possibly could ascertain, that Jehovah intended to send his Son on earth to enlighten them on questions appertaining to their religious belief. This they thought had long been settled, and he who tried either to take anything from it or add anything to it was in their eyes an impious criminal. Such persons, they knew, had been sternly dealt with in the palmy days of the Hebrew state, and the example of their most honored prophets and their most pious kings would justify the severest measures that could be taken against them. A spiritual reformer, then, was not what they needed: a temporal leader was. And this they had a perfect right to expect that the Messiah would be. The very word itself — the Anointed One, a word commonly applied to the king — indicates the possession of the powers of government. Their prophecies all pointed to this conception of the Messiah. Their popular traditions all confirmed it. Their political necessities all encouraged it. The very disciples themselves held it like the rest of their nation, for when they met Jesus after his resurrection we find them inquiring, "Lord, wilt thou at this time restore the kingdom of Israel? (Acts i. 6.) The conversation may be imaginary, but the state of mind which such a question indicates was doubtless real. The author represented them as speaking as he knew that they had felt. Now, if ever they, who had enjoyed the intimate friendship of Jesus, could still look to him as one who would restore to Israel something of her bygone grandeur, was it to be expected that the less privileged Jews, who had inherited from their forefathers a fixed belief in this temporal restoration, should suddenly surrender it at the bidding of Jesus of Nazareth? For he at least did not realize the prevailing notions of what the Messiah ought to be. For temporal sovereignty he was clearly unfit, nor does he seem to have ever demanded it. There was a danger no doubt that his enthusiastic followers might thrust it upon him, and that, thus urged, he might be tempted to accept it. But his general character precludes the supposition that he could ever be fit to stand at the head of a national movement. The absence, moreover, of all political enthusiasm from his teaching proved him not to be the Savior for whom they were looking. His assertions that he was the Son of God, though they might provoke sedition and endanger the security of his countrymen, could bring them no corresponding good.

Christians have maintained that the Jews were entirely wrong in their conception of the Messiah's character, and that Jesus by his admirable life brought a higher and more excellent ideal than theirs into the world. They admire him for not laying claim to temporal dominion, and laud his humility, his meekness, his submissiveness, the patience with which he bore his sufferings, and the whole catalogue of similar virtues. It was, according to them, the mere blindness of the Jews that prevented them from recognizing in him a far greater Messiah than they had erroneously expected. Moreover, they tell us that another of the mistakes made by this gross nation was the expectation of an earthly kingdom in which Christ was to reign, whereas it was only a spiritual kingdom which he came to institute. But who were to be judges of the character of the Messiah if not the Jews to whom he was to come? The very thought of a Messiah was peculiarly their own. It had grown up in the course of their national history, and was embodied in their national prophecies. They alone were its authorized interpreters; they alone could say whether it was fulfilled in the case of a given individual. It is surely a piece of the most amazing presumption on the part of nations of heathen origin to pretend that they are more competent than the Jews themselves to understand the meaning of a Jewish term; a term, moreover, which neither had nor could have before the time of Jesus any sense at all except that which the Jews themselves attached to it. Christians, who derive not only their idea of the Messiah's character, but their very knowledge of the word, from the case of Jesus alone, undertake to set right the Jews, among whom it was a current notion for centuries before he had been conceived in his mother's womb!

Granting, however, that this difficulty might have been surmounted, supposing that it was a spiritual kingdom which the ancient prophets under uncouth images referred to, the question still remains whether Jesus in other respects fulfilled the conditions demanded by Scripture. For this purpose it will be the fairest method to confine ourselves to the discussion of those prophecies alone which are quoted by the Evangelists, and are therefore relied upon by them as proving their case. Where, however, they have quoted only a portion of a prophecy, and the remainder gives a somewhat different complexion to the passage extracted, justice to their opponents requires that we should consider the whole.

Take first the circumstances of Christ's birth. It was expected that the Messiah was to be of the family of David, and born at Bethlehem Ephrathah. Now, according to two of our authorities, he fulfilled both of these conditions. But, without at all discussing the point whether their statement is true, it is abundantly sufficient for the vindication of the Jews to observe, that they neither knew, nor could know, anything at all, either of his royal lineage or of his birth at Bethlehem. For he himself never stated either of the two capital facts of which Luke and Matthew make so much, nor does it appear that any of his disciples alluded to them during his life-time. He was habitually spoken about as Jesus of Nazareth. Matthew, in endeavoring to account for the name by misquoting a prophecy, bears witness to the fact that it expressed the general belief. Luke makes him speak of Nazareth as his own country. Nowhere does it appear that he repudiated the implication conveyed by his ordinary title. Still less did he ever maintain—what his over-busy biographers maintained for him—that he was of the seed of David. Quite the reverse. He contends against the Pharisees that the Messiah was not to be a descendant of David at all. The dialogue as given by Matthew runs thus: "'What is your opinion about the Christ? whose son is he?' They say to him, 'David's.' He says to them, 'How then does David in the spirit call him Lord, saying, The Lord said to my lord, Sit on my right hand until I place thine enemies under thy feet? If then David calls him lord, how is he his son?'" (Mt. xxii. 42–46). No answer was given by the Pharisees, nor was any explanation of the paradox ever granted them by Jesus. In the absence, then, of any further elucidation we can only put one interpretation upon his argument. It was clearly intended to show not only that the Messiah *need* not, but that he *could* not be of the house of David. David in that case would not have called him Lord. The Pharisees may have been but little impressed by the force of the argument, but of one thing they could scarcely entertain a doubt. Jesus wished it to be thought that he was the Messiah. He also wished it to be thought that the Messiah was not a son of David. He himself therefore was certainly not a son of David. But if anything more were needed to excuse the ignorance—supposing it such—of the Jewish rulers about the birthplace and family of Jesus, we find it even super-abundantly in the work of one of his own adherents—the fourth Evangelist. Not that this writer is to be taken as an authority on the facts, but he is an authority on the views that were current, at least in a portion of his own sect, and on that which he himself—writing long after the death of Christ—had received by tradition. Now, in the beginning of his Gospel he describes Philip the disciple as going to Nathanael, and saying, "We have found him of whom Moses in the law and of whom the prophets wrote, Jesus *the son of Joseph from Nazareth*." At this Nathanael skeptically asks, "Can anything good come from Nazareth?" and Philip replies, "Come and see" (Jo. i. 45, 46). According to this account, then, the very disciples of Jesus believed in his Nazarene nativity, as also (by the way) in his generation by a human father. Nor is this all the evidence. In another chapter an active discussion is represented as going on among the Jews as to whether Jesus was the Christ or not. Opinions differed. Foremost among the arguments for the negative, however, was the appeal to the Scriptural declaration that the Christ must be of David's seed, and emanate from the village of Bethlehem (Jo. vii. 42). No answer to this was forthcoming from the partizans of Jesus, nor is any suggested by the Evangelist. There is but one rational inference to be drawn from his silence. He either had not heard, or he purposely ignored, the story of Christ's birth at Bethlehem, and the genealogies which connected him with David. His mind (if he had ever been a Jew) was to no small extent emancipated from Jewish limitations, and with his highly refined views of the Logos, he did not believe in the necessity of these material conditions. It was nothing to him that they were not fulfilled. More orthodox believers in the prophecies of the Old Testament may be pardoned if they could not so lightly put them aside. But what shall be said of the conduct of Jesus? If he really were a descendant of David, born at Bethlehem, and wrongly taken for a Nazarene, can we acquit him of an inexcusable fraud upon the Jews in not bringing these facts under their notice? Assuredly not. If, knowing as he did the weight they would have in the public mind, he kept them back; knowing that they would overcome some of the gravest objections that were taken against his claim, he did not urge them in reply; knowing at the close of his life that he was charged with an undue assumption of authority, he did not produce them as at least a portion of his credentials,— he played a part which it would be difficult to stigmatize as severely as it deserves. He believed that his reception by his nation would be an immense benefit to themselves, yet he did not speak the word which might have helped them to receive him. He thought he had a mission from God, yet he failed to use one potent argument in favor of the truth of that idea. He saw finally that he was condemned to death for supposed impiety, yet he suffered the Sanhedrim to incur the guilt of his condemnation without employing one of his strongest weapons in his defense. Happily we are not obliged to suspect him of this iniquity. The contradictory stories by which his royal descent and his birth at

Bethlehem are sought to be established sufficiently betray their origin to permit us to believe in the honor and honesty of Jesus.

Another Messianic prophecy which he is supposed to have fulfilled is that of birth from a virgin, the necessity of which was deduced from an expression of Isaiah's. That the writer of the fourth Gospel was ignorant of this virgin-birth we have already shown, and that the Jewish people in general took him to be the son of Joseph is obvious enough from their allusions to his father (Mk. vi. 3; Mt. xiii. 55, 56; Lu. iv. 22; Jo. vi. 42). Here again he never contradicted the prevalent assumption. But even had they known of the miraculous conception, the Jews might have denied that the passage from Isaiah bore any such construction as that put upon it by Matthew. He renders it: "Behold, the virgin shall be with child, and bear a son" (Mt. i. 23). But a more proper translation would be: "The maiden shall conceive, and bear a son," for the word translated *virgin* by Matthew does not exclude young women who have lost their virginity. Nay, it curiously enough happens to be used elsewhere of maidens engaged in the very conduct by which they would certainly be deprived of it.

Moreover, the two prophecies quoted by Matthew, which were, no doubt, familiar to the Jews, could by no possibility be applied by them to a person of the character of Jesus. Even the small fragments torn away from their context by the Evangelist convict him of a misapplication. In the first fragment, the Virgin's son is called Immanuel, a name which Jesus never bore (Mt. i. 23). In the second, he is described as "a ruler, who shall govern my people Israel," which Jesus never was (Mt. ii. 6). But the unlikeness of the predicted person to Jesus is still further shown by comparing the circumstances as conceived by the prophet with the actual circumstances of the time. Immanuel's birth is to be followed, while he is still too young to choose between good and evil, by a terrible desolation of the land. Hosts, described as flies and bees, are to come from Egypt and Assyria, and camp in the valleys, the clefts of the rocks, the hedges and meadows. Cultivable land will produce only thorns and thistles. Cultivated hills will be surrendered to cattle from fear of thorns and thistles (Isa. vii. 14-25). Nothing of all this happened in the time of Jesus. But the prophecy of Micah is still more inappropriate. The "ruler" who is to be born in Bethlehem is to lead Israel to victory over all her enemies. He is to deliver his people from the Assyrian. The remnant of Jacob is to be among the heathen, like a lion among the beasts of the forest, like a young lion among flocks of sheep. Its hand is to be lifted up against its adversaries, and all its enemies are to be destroyed (Micah v).

These references to prophecy were certainly not happy. An allusion by Matthew to the words, "The people who walk in darkness see a great light," is not much more to the purpose, for Isaiah in the passage in question proceeds to describe the child who is to bring them this happiness as one who shall have the government upon his shoulder, who is to be on the throne of David, to establish and maintain it by right and justice for ever (Mt. iv. 15, 16; Is. ix. 1-7). Another extract from Isaiah, beginning, "Behold my servant whom I have chosen," and depicting a gentler character, is more appropriate, but is too vague to be easily confined to any one individual.

Jesus himself is reported by one of his biographers to have relied on certain words from the pseudo-Isaiah as a confirmation of his mission. If the account be true, the circumstance is of great importance as showing the view he himself took of his office, and the means he employed to convince the Jews of his right to hold it. Entering the synagogue at Nazareth, he received the roll of the prophet Isaiah, and proceeded to read from the sixty-first chapter as follows: "The Spirit of the Lord Jehovah is upon me, because Jehovah has anointed me to announce glad tidings to the poor; he has sent me to bind up the broken-hearted; to cry to the captives, Freedom, and to those in fetters, Deliverance; to cry out a year of good-will from Jehovah." Here Jesus broke off the reading in the middle of a verse, and declared that this day this scripture was fulfilled (Lu. iv. 16-21). But let us continue our study of the prophetic vision a little further. "To cry out a year of good-will from Jehovah, and *a day of vengeance from our God:* to comfort all that mourn; to appoint for the mourners of Zion,—to give them ornaments for ashes, the oil of joy for mourning, a garment of praise for a desponding spirit; that they may be called oaks of righteousness, a plantation of Jehovah to glorify himself. And they will build up the ruins of old times, they will restore the desolations of former days; and they will renew desolate cities, the ruins of generation upon generation. And strangers shall stand and feed your flocks, and the sons of foreigners shall be your husbandmen and your vine-dressers. And you shall be called 'Priests of Jehovah;' 'Servants of our God,' shall be said to you; the riches of the Gentiles you shall eat, and into their splendor you shall enter " (Is. lxi. 1-6). Had Jesus concluded the passage he had begun, he could scarcely have said, "This day is the scripture fulfilled in your ears." The contrast between the prediction and the fact would have been rather too glaring.

Perhaps the most striking apparent similarity to Jesus is found in the man described in such beautiful language by an unknown prophet in the fifty-third chapter of Isaiah. But these words could hardly be applied to him by the Jews; in the first place, because they would not be construed to refer to him until after his crucifixion, seeing that they describe oppression, prison, judgment, and execution; in the second place, because there was no reason to believe that he bore their diseases, and took their sorrows upon him. And although the familiar words —doubly familiar from the glorious music of Handel,—"He was a man of sorrows, and acquainted with grief," may seem to us, who know his end, to describe him perfectly, they could hardly describe him to the Jews, who saw him in his daily life. In that, at least, there was nothing peculiarly unhappy.

Failing the prophecies, which were plainly two-edged swords, Jesus could appeal to his remarkable miracles. He and his disciples evidently thought them demonstrations of a divine commission. But, in the first place, it is clear that the evidence of the most wonderful of these consisted only of the rumors circulating among ignorant peasants, which the more instructed portion of the nation very properly disregarded. Their demand for a sign (Mt. xii. 38) proves that they were not satisfied by these popular reports, if they had ever heard them. And in the second place, those miracles which were better attested were not convincing from the fact that others could perform them. Jesus, charged with casting out devils by Baäl-zebub, the prince of devils, adroitly retorted on the Pharisees by asking, if that were so, by whom their sons cast them out? (Mk. iii. 22; Mt. xii. 24–30; Lu. xi. 14–24). But thus he admitted that he was not singular in his profession. Miracles, in short, were not regarded by the Jews as any proof of Messiahship. Their own prophets had performed them. Their own disciples now performed them. Others might possibly perform them by diabolic agency. The Egyptian magicians had been very clever in their contest with Moses, though Moses had beaten them, and had performed far more amazing wonders than those of Jesus, in so far as these latter were known to the Pharisees.

Miracles being too common to confer any peculiar title to reverence on the thaumaturgist, there remained the doctrine and personal character of Jesus by which to judge him. It must be borne in mind that the impression which these might make upon his antagonist would depend mainly upon his bearing in his relations with them. He might preach pure morals in Galilee, or present a model of excellence to his own followers in Judea; but this would not entitle him to reception as the Messiah, nor would it remove an unfavorable bias created by his conduct towards those who had not embraced his principles. Let us see, then, what was likely to be the effect on the Pharisees, scribes, and others, of those elements in his opinions and his behavior by which they were more immediately affected.

There existed among the Jews, as there still exists among ourselves, an institution which was greatly honored among them, as it is still honored, though in a minor degree, among ourselves. The institution was that of a day of rest sacred to God once in every seven days. This custom they believed to have been founded by the very highest authority, and embodied by Moses in the ten commandments which he received on Sinai. Nothing in the eyes of an orthodox Jew could be holier than such an observance, enjoined by his God, founded by the greatest legislator of his race, consecrated by long tradition. Now the ordinary rules with regard to what was lawful and what unlawful on this day were totally disregarded by Jesus. Not only did his disciples make a path through a cornfield on the Sabbath, but Jesus openly cured diseases, that is, pursued his common occupation, on this most sacred festival (Mk. ii. 23—

iii. 7; Mt. xii. 1–14; Lu. vi. 1–11, xiii. 10–17, xiv. 1–6). When these violations of propriety (as they seemed to them) first came under the notice of the Pharisees, they merely remonstrated with Jesus, and endeavored to induce him to restrain the impiety of his disciples. Not only did he decline to do so, but he expressly justified their course by the example of David, and by that of the priests, who, according to his mode of reasoning, profane the Sabbath in the temple by doing that to which by their office they were legally bound. Such an argument could scarcely convince the Pharisees, but they must have been shocked beyond measure when he proclaimed himself greater than the temple, and asserted his lordship even over the Sabbath-day. They then inquired of him — a perfectly legitimate question — whether it was lawful to heal on the Sabbath, to which he replied that if one of their own sheep had fallen into the pit they would pick it out. Confirming his theory by his practice, he at once healed a man with a withered hand. It is noteworthy that the desire of the Pharisees to inflict punishment upon Jesus is dated by all three Evangelists from this incident; so that the hostility towards him may be certainly considered as largely due to his unsabbatarian principles.

Now in this question it is almost needless for me to say that my sympathies are entirely with Jesus. Although I do not perceive in his conduct any extensive design against the Sabbath altogether, yet it is much that he should have attempted to mitigate its rigor. For that the world owes him its thanks. But surely it cannot be difficult, in this highly sabbatarian country, to understand the horror of the Pharisees at his apparent levity. Seeing that it is not so very long since the supposed desecration of the Sunday in these islands subjected the offender to be treated as a common criminal; seeing that even now a total abstinence from labor on that day is in many occupations enforced by law; seeing that a custom almost as strong as law forbids indulgence in a vast number of ordinary amusements during its course, — we can scarcely be much surprised that the sabbatarians of Judea were zealous to preserve the sanctity of their weekly rest. The fact that highly conscientious and honorable persons entertain similar sentiments about the Sunday is familiar to all. We know that any one who neglected the usual customs; who, for example, played a game at cricket, or danced, or even pursued his commercial avocations on Sunday, would be visited by them with perfectly genuine reproaches. Yet this was exactly the sort of way in which Christ and his disciples shocked the Jews. To make a path through a cornfield and pluck the ears was just one of those little things which the current morality of the Sabbath condemned, much as ours condemns the opening of museums or theatrical entertainments. Their piety was scandalized at such a glaring contempt of the divine ordinances. Nor was the reasoning of Jesus likely to conciliate them. To ask whether it was lawful to do good or evil, to save life or to kill on the Sabbath-day was nothing to the purpose. The question was what *was* good or evil on that particular day, when things otherwise good were by all admitted to be evil. Nor were the cures effected by Jesus necessary to save life. All his patients might well have waited till evening, when the Sabbath was over. One of them, for instance, a woman who had suffered from a "spirit of weakness" eighteen years, being unable to hold herself erect, was surely not in such urgent need of attendance that a few hours more of her disease would have done her serious harm. Jesus, with his principles, was of course perfectly right to relieve her at once, but it is not to be wondered at that the ruler of the synagogue was indignant, and told the people that there were six working days; in them therefore they should come and be healed, and not on the Sabbath. The epithet of "hypocrite," applied to him by Jesus, was, to say the least, hardly justified (Lu. xiii. 10–17).

Another habit of Jesus, in itself commendable, excited the displeasure of the stricter sects. It was that of eating with publicans and sinners. This practice, and the fact of his neglecting the fasts observed by the Pharisees, gave an impression of general laxity about his conduct, which, however, unjust, was perfectly natural (Mk. ii. 15–22; Mt. ix. 10–17; Lu. v. 29–39). Here again I see no reason to attribute bad motives to his opponents who merely felt as "church-going" people among ourselves would feel about one who stayed away from divine service, and as highly decorous people would feel about one who kept what they thought low company.

Eating with unwashed hands was another of the several evidences of his contempt for the prevalent proprieties of life which gave offense. The resentment felt by the Pharisees at this practice was the more excusable that Jesus justified it on the distinct ground that he had no respect for "the tradition of the elders," for which they entertained the utmost reverence. This tradition he unsparingly attacked, accusing them of frustrating the commandment of God in order to keep it (Mk. vii. 1–13; Mt. xv. 1–9). Language like this was not likely to pass without leaving a deep-seated wound, especially if it be true (as stated by Luke) that one of the occasions on which he employed it was when invited to dinner by a Pharisee. Indifferent as the washing of hands might be in itself, courtesy towards his host required him to abstain from needless outrage to his feelings. And when, in addition to the first offense, he proceeded to denounce his host and host's friends as people who made the outside of the cup and the platter clean, but were inwardly full of ravening and wickedness, there is an apparent rudeness which even the truth of his statements could not have excused (Lu. xi. 37–39).

Neither was the manner in which he answered the questions addressed to him, as to a teacher claiming to instruct the people, likely to remove the prejudice thus created. The Evangelists who report these questions generally relate that they were put with an evil intent: "tempting him," or some such expression being used. But whatever may have been the secret motives of the questioners, nothing could be more legitimate than to interrogate a man who put forward the enormous pretensions of Jesus, so long as the process was conducted fairly. And this, on the side of the Jews, it apparently was. There is nowhere perceptible in their inquiries a scheme to entrap him, or a desire to entangle him in difficulties by skillful examination. On the contrary, the subjects on which he is questioned are precisely those on which, as the would-be master of the nation, he might most properly be expected to give clear answers. And the judgment formed of him by the public would naturally depend to a large extent on the mode in which he acquitted himself in this impromptu trial. Let us see, then, what was the impression he probably produced.

On one occasion the Pharisees came to him, "tempting him," to ascertain his opinion on divorce. Might a man put away his wife? Jesus replied that he might not, and explained the permission of Moses to give a wife a bill of divorce as a mere concession to the hardness of their hearts. A divorced man or woman who married again was guilty of adultery. Even the disciples were staggered at this. If an unhappy man could never be released from his wife, it would be better, they thought not to marry at all (Mk. x. 1–12; Mt. xix. 1–12). Much more must the Pharisees have dissented from this novel doctrine. Rightly or wrongly, they reverenced the law of Moses, and they could not but profoundly disapprove this assumption of authority to set it aside and substitute for its precepts an unheard of innovation.

Another question of considerable importance was that relating to the tribute. Some of the Pharisees, it seems, after praising him for his independence, begged him to give them his opinion on a disputed point: Was it lawful or not to pay tribute to the Emperor? All three biographers are indignant at the question. They attribute it as usual to a desire to "catch him in his words," or, as another Evangelist puts it, to "entangle him in his talk." Jesus (they remark) perceived what one calls their "wickedness," a second their "hypocrisy," and the third their "craftiness." "Why do you tempt me?" he began. "Bring me a denarium that I may see it." The coin being brought, he asked them, "Whose image and superscription is this? "Cæsar's." "Then render to Cæsar the things that are Cæsar's, and to God the things that are God's" (Mk. xii. 13–17; Mt. xxii. 15–22; Lu. xx. 20–26). One of the Evangelists, reporting this reply, rejoices at the discomfiture of the Pharisees, who "could not take hold of his words before the people." Doubtless his decision had the merit that it could not be taken hold of, but this was only because it decided nothing. Taking the words in their simplest sense, they merely assert what nobody would deny. No Pharisee would ever have maintained that the things of Cæsar should be given to God; and no partizan of Rome would ever have demanded that the things of God should be given to Cæsar. But practically it is evident that Jesus meant to do more than employ an unmeaning form of words. He meant to assert that the tribute was one of the things of Cæsar, and that because the coin in which it was paid was stamped with his image. More fallacious reasoning could hardly be imagined, and it is not surprising that the Pharisees "marveled at him." Nobody doubted that the Emperor possessed the material power, and no more than this was proved by the fact that coins bearing his effigy were current in the country. The question was not whether he actually ruled Judea, but whether it was lawful to acknowledge that rule by paying tribute. And what light could it throw on this question to show that the money used to pay it was issued from his mint ? It must almost be supposed that Jesus fell into the confusion of supposing that the denarium with Cæsar's image and superscription upon it was in some peculiar sense Cæsar's property, whereas it belonged as completely to the man who produced it at the moment as did the clothes he wore. Had the Roman domination come to an end at any moment, the coin of the Empire would have retained its intrinsic value, but the Romans could by no possibility have founded a right of exacting tribute upon the circumstance of its circulation. Either, therefore, this celebrated declaration was a mere verbal juggle, or it rested on a transparent fallacy.

After the Pharisees had been thus disposed of, their inquiries were followed up by a puzzle devised by the Sadducees in order to throw ridicule on the doctrine of a future state. These sectaries put an imaginary case. Moses had enjoined that if a man died leaving a childless widow, his brother should marry her for the purpose of keeping up the family. Suppose, said they, that the first of seven brothers marries, and dies without issue. The second brother then marries her with the like result; then the third, and so on through all the seven. In the resurrection whose wife will this woman be, for the seven have had her as their wife? To this Jesus replies: first, that his questioners greatly err, neither knowing the Scriptures nor the power of God; secondly, that when people rise from death they do not marry, but are like angels; thirdly, that' the resurrection is proved by the fact that God had spoken of himself as the God of Abraham, Isaac, and Jacob, and that he is not the God of the dead, but of the living (Mk. xii. 18–27; Mt. xxii. 23–33; Lu.

xx. 27-40). Whether the Sadducees were or were not satisfied by
this answer we are not told, but it is quite certain that their
modern representatives could not accept it. For the inquirers
had hit upon one of the real difficulties attending the doctrine
of a future life. We are always assured that one of the great
consolations of this doctrine is the hope it holds out of meeting
again those whom we have loved on earth, and living with them
in a kind of communion not wholly unlike that which we have
enjoyed here. Earthly relationships, it is assumed, will be prolonged into that happier world. There the parent will find
again the child whom he has lost, and the child will rejoin his
parent; there the bereaved husband will be restored to his wife,
and the widow will be comforted by the sight of the companion
of her wedded years. All this is simple enough. Complications
inevitably arise, however, when we endeavor to pick up again
in another life the tangled skein of our relations in this. Not
only may the feelings with which we look forward to meeting
former friends be widely different after many years' separation
from what they were at their death; but even in marriage there
may be a preferance for a first or a second husband or wife,
which may render the thought of meeting the other positively
unpleasant. And if the sentiments of the other should nevertheless be those of undiminished love, the question may well
arise, whose husband is he, or whose wife is she of the two?
Are all three to live together? But then, along with the comfort of meeting one whom we love, we have the less agreeable
prospect of meeting another whom we have ceased to love. Or
will one of the two wives or two husbands be preferred and the
other slighted? If so, the last will suffer and not gain by the
reunion. Take the present case. Assume that the wife loved
only her first husband, but that all the seven were attached to
her. Then we may well ask, whose wife will she be of them?
Will her affections be divided among the seven, or will they all
be given to the first? In the former case, she will be compelled
to live in a society for which she has no desire; in the latter,
six of her seven husbands will be unable to enjoy the full benefit of her presence. The question is merely evaded by saying
that in the resurrection there is neither marriage nor giving in
marriage, but that men are like angels. Either there is no con-

solation in living again, or there must be some kind of repetition of former ties. Still less logical is the argument by which Jesus attempts to prove the reality of a future state against the Sadducees. In syllogistic form it may be thus stated:—

God is not the God of the dead, but of the living. God told Moses in the bush that he was the God of Abraham, Isaac, and Jacob. Therefore they are not dead, but living (Mk. xii. 18–27; Mt. xxii. 23–33; Lu. xx. 27–40).

What is the evidence of the major premiss? The moment it is questioned it is seen to be invalid. Nothing could be more natural than that Moses, or any other Hebrew, should speak of his God as the God of Abraham, Isaac, and Jacob, meaning that those great forefathers of his race had adored and been protected by the same Jehovah in their day, but not therefore that they were still living. The Sadducees must have been weak indeed if such an argument could weigh with them for a moment.

After this a scribe or lawyer drew from Jesus the important declaration that in his opinion the two greatest commandments were that we should love God with the whole heart, soul, mind, and strength; and our neighbors as ourselves (Mk. xii. 28–34; Mt. xxii. 34–40; Lu. x. 25–37). How gratuitous the imputations of ill-will thrown out against those who interrogate Jesus may be, is admirably shown in the present instance. One Gospel (the most trustworthy) asserts that the question about the first commandment was put by a scribe, who thought that Jesus had answered well, and who, moreover, expressed emphatic approval of the reply given to himself. Such (according to this account) was his sympathy with Jesus, that the latter declared that he was not far from the kingdom of God. Mark now the extraordinary color given to this simple transaction in another Gospel. The Pharisees, we are told, saw that the Sadducees had been silenced, and therefore drew together. Apparently as a result of their consultation (though this is not stated), one of *them* who was a lawyer asked a question, *tempting him*, namely, Which is the great commandment in the law? Diverse, again, from both versions is the narrative of a third. In the first place, all connection with the preceding questions is broken off, and without any preliminaries, a lawyer stands up, and, *tempting him*, inquires, "Master, by what conduct shall I inherit eternal life?" To which Jesus replies by a counter-question, "What is written in the law?" and then, strange to say, these two great commandments are enunciated, not by him, but by the unknown lawyer, whose answer receives the commendation of Jesus.

The bias thus evinced by the Evangelists, even in reporting the fairest questions, seems to show that Christ did not like his opinions to be elicited from him by this method, feeling perhaps that it was likely to expose his intellectual weaknesses. In this way, and possibly in others, a sentiment of hostility grew up between himself and the dominant sects, which, until the closing scenes of his career, was far more marked on his side than on theirs. Beautiful maxims about loving one's enemies and returning good for evil did not keep him from reproaching the Pharisees on many occasions. Unfortunately, a man's particular enemies are just those who scarcely ever appear to him worthy of love, and this was evidently the case with Jesus and the men upon whom he poured forth his denunciations. Judging by his mode of speaking, we should suppose that all religious people who did not agree with him were simply hypocrites. This is one of the mildest terms by which he can bring himself to mention the Pharisees or the scribes. Of the latter, he declares that they devour widows' houses, and for a pretence make long prayers; therefore they would receive the greater damnation (Mk. xii. 40; Mt. xxiii. 14). The scribes and the Pharisees, it is said, bind heavy burdens on others, and refuse to touch them themselves (surely an improbable charge). They do all their works to be seen of men (their outward behavior then was virtuous). One of their grievous sins is that they make their phylacteries broad, and enlarge the borders of their garments. Worse still: they like the best places at dinner-parties and in the synagogues (to which perhaps their position entitled them). They have a pleasure in hearing themselves called "Rabbi," a crime of which Christ's disciples are especially to beware. They shut up the kingdom of heaven, neither entering themselves, nor allowing others to enter. They compass sea and land to make one proselyte, but all this seeming zeal for religion is worthless: when they have the proselyte, they make him still more a child of hell than themselves. They pay tithes regularly, but omit the weightier virtues; unhappily too common a failing with the votaries of all religions. They make the outside of the cup and platter clean, but within they are full of extortion and excess. Like whited sepulchres, they look well enough outside, but this aspect of righteousness is a mere cloak for hypocrisy and wickedness. They honor God with their lips, but their heart is far from him.*

He uses towards them such designations as these: "Scribes and Pharisees, hypocrites;" "you blind guides;" "you fools and blind;" "thou blind Pharisee;" "you serpents, you generation of vipers." If we may believe that he was the author of a parable contained only in Luke, he used a Pharisee as his typical hypocrite, and held up a publican — one of a degraded class — as far superior in genuine virtue to this self-righteous representative of the hated order (Lu. xviii. 9-14).

Had the Pharisees been actually guilty of the exceeding wickedness which Jesus thought proper to ascribe to them, his career would surely have been cut short at a much earlier stage. As it was, they seem to have borne with considerable patience the extreme license which he permitted himself in his language against them. Nay, I venture to say that had he confined himself to language, however strong, he might have escaped the fate which actually befell him. And the evidence of this proposition is to be found in the extreme mildness with which his apostles were afterwards treated by the Sanhedrim, even when they acted in direct disobedience to its orders (Acts iv. 15-21, and v. 27-42). Only Stephen, who courted martyrdom by his language, was put to death, and that for the legal offense of blasphemy. Ordinary prudence would have saved Jesus. For his arrest was closely connected with his expulsion of the money-changers from the temple court. Not indeed that he was condemned to death on that account, but that this ill-considered deed was the immediate incentive of the legal proceedings,

---

* Mt. xxiii. 1-33; Mk. vii. 6. I omit the concluding verses in Mt. xxiii., as the allusion in verse 35 renders it impossible that Christ could have uttered them. Indeed, the whole chapter is suspicious; but as portions of it are confirmed by Mark, I conclude that the sentiments at least, if not the precise words, are genuine.

which subsequently ended, contrary perhaps to the expectation
of his prosecutors, in his conviction by the Sanhedrim on a capital charge. Let us consider the evidence of this. For the convenience of persons going to pay tribute to the temple, some
money-changers — probably neither better nor worse than others
of their trade — sat outside for the purpose of receiving the current Roman coinage and giving the national money, which
alone the authorities of the temple received in exchange. Certain occasions in life requiring an offering of doves, these too
were sold in the precincts of the temple, obviously to the advantage of the public. Had Jesus disapproved of this practice,
he might have denounced it in public, and have endeavored to
persuade the people to give it up. Instead of this, he entered
the temple, expelled the buyers and sellers (by what means we
do not know), upset the money-changers' tables and the dove-
sellers' seats, and permitted no one to carry a vessel through
the temple. "Is it not written," he exclaimed, "'My house
shall be called a house of prayer for all nations?' but you
have made it a den of thieves" (Mk. xi. 15–18; Mt. xxi. 12, 13;
Lu. xix. 45–48). The action and the words were alike unjustifi-
able. The extreme care of the Jews to preserve the sanctity of
their temple is well known from secular history. Nothing that
they had done or were likely to do could prevent it from remaining a house of prayer. And even if they had suffered it to be
desecrated by commerce, was it, they would ask, for Jesus to
fall suddenly upon men who were but pursuing a calling which
custom had sanctioned, and which they had no reason to think
illegal or irreligious? Was it for him to stigmatize them all
indiscriminately as "thieves"? Plainly not. He had, in their
opinion, exceeded all bounds of decorum, to say nothing of law,
in this deed of violence and of passion. Thus, there was nothing for it now but to restrain the further excesses he might
be tempted to commit.

No immediate steps were, however, taken to punish this
outrage. It is alleged that Jesus escaped because of the reputation he enjoyed among the people. At any rate, the course
of the authorities was the mildest they could possibly adopt.
They contented themselves with asking Jesus by what authority
he did these things, a question which assuredly they had every

right to put. He answered by another question, promising if they answered it, he would answer theirs. Was John's baptism from heaven or from men? Hereupon the Evangelists depict the perplexity which they imagine arose among the priests. If they said, from heaven, Jesus would proceed to ask why they had not received him; if from men, they would encounter the popular impression that he was a prophet. All this, however, may be mere speculation; we return within the region of the actual knowledge of the Evangelists when we come to their answer. "And they say in answer to Jesus, ' *We do not know.*' And Jesus says to them, '*Neither do I tell you* by what authority I do these things.'" (Mk. xi. 27–33; Mt. xxi. 23–27; Lu. xx. 1–8). Observe in this reply the conduct of Jesus. He had promised the priests that if they answered his question he would also answer theirs. They *did* answer his question as best they could, and he refused to answer theirs! Even in the English version, where the contrast between him and them is disguised by the employment of the same word "tell" as the translation of two very different verbs in the original, the distinction between "We *cannot* tell" and "I *do not*," that is "will not tell" is palpable enough. But it is far more so in the original. The priests did not by any means decline to answer the question; they simply said, what may very likely have been true, that they did not know whence the baptism of John was. In the divided state of public opinion about John, nothing could be more natural. They could not reply decidedly if their feelings were undecided. Their reply, "We do not know," was then a perfectly proper one. The corresponding reply on the part of Jesus would have been, "I do not know by what authority I do these things;" but this of course it was impossible to give. The chief priests, scribes and elders had more right to ask Jesus to produce his authority for his assault than he had to interrogate them about their religious opinions. But Jesus, though he had for the moment evaded a difficulty, must have been well aware that he was not out of danger. He found it necessary to retire to a secret spot, known only to friends. Here, however, he was discovered by his opponents, and brought before the Sanhedrim to answer to the charges now alleged against his character and doctrine.

To some extent these charges are matter of conjecture. The Gospels intimate that there was much evidence against him which they have not reported. Now it is impossible for us to do complete justice to the tribunal which heard the case unless we know the nature and number of the offences of which the prisoner was accused. One of them, the promise to destroy the temple and rebuild it in three days, may have presented itself to their minds as an announcement of a serious purpose, especially after the recent violence done to the traders. However this may be, there was now sufficient evidence before the court to require the high priest to call upon Jesus for his reply. He might therefore have made his defense if he had thought proper. He declined to do so. Again the high priest addressed him, solemnly requiring him to say whether he was the Christ, the Son of God. Jesus admitted that such was his conviction, and declared that they would afterwards see him return in the clouds of heaven. Hereupon the high priest rent his clothes, and asked what further evidence could be needed. All had heard his blasphemy; what did they think of it? All of them concurred in condemning him to death (Mk. xv. 53-64; Mt. xxvi. 57-66; Lu. xxii. 66-71).

The three Evangelists who report the trial all agree that the blasphemy thus uttered was accepted at once as full and sufficient ground for the conviction of Jesus. Now, I see no reason whatever to doubt that the priests who were thus scandalized by his declaration were perfectly sincere in the horror they professed. All who have at all realized the extremely strong feelings of the Jews on the subject of Monotheism, will easily understand that anything which in the least impugned it would be regarded by them with the utmost aversion. And a man who claimed to be the Son of God certainly detracted somewhat from the sole and exclusive adoration which they considered to be due to Jehovah. As indeed the event has proved; for the Christian Church soon departed from pure Monotheism, adopting the dogma of the Trinity; while Christ along with his Father, and even more than his Father, became an object of its worship. So that if the Jews considered it their supreme obligation to preserve the purity of their Jehovistic faith, as their Scriptures taught them to believe it was, they were right in putting down Jesus by forcible means. No doubt they were wrong in holding such an opinion. It was not, in fact, their duty to guard their faith by persecution. They would have been morally better had they understood the modern doctrine of religious liberty, unknown as it was to Christians themselves until some sixteen centuries after the death of Christ. But for their mistaken notions on this head they were only in part responsible. They had inherited their creed with its profound intolerance. Their history, their legislators, their prophets, all conspired to uphold persecution for the maintenance of religious truth. They could not believe in their sacred books, and disbelieve the propriety of persecution. Before they could leave Jesus at large to teach his subversive doctrines, they must have ceased to be Jews; and this it was impossible for them to do. We must not be too hard upon men whose only crime was that they believed in a false religion.

According to the dictates of that religion, Jesus ought to have been stoned. But the Roman supremacy precluded the Jews from giving effect to their own laws. Jesus was therefore taken before the procurator, and accused of "many things." The charge of blasphemy of course would weigh nothing in the mind of a Roman; and it is evident that another aspect of the indictment was brought prominently before Pilate: namely, the pretension of Jesus to be king of the Jews. As to the substantial truth of this second charge, we are saved the necessity of discussion, for Jesus himself, when questioned by Pilate, at once admitted it. But whether it was made in malice, and in a somewhat different sense from that in which Pilate understood it, is not so clear. Jesus at no time, so far as we know, put forward any direct claim to immediate temporal dominion. At the same time it must be remembered that the ideas of Messiahship and possession of the kingdom were so intimately connected in the minds of the Jews, that they were probably unable to dissociate them. Unfit as Jesus plainly was for the exercise of the government, they might well believe that, if received by any considerable number of the people, it would be forced upon him as the logical result of his career. Nor were these fears unreasonable. His entry into Jerusalem riding on an ass (an animal expressly selected as emblematic of his royalty),

with palm-branches strewed before him, and admirers calling
"Hosanna!" as he went, pointed to a very real and serious
danger. Another such demonstration might with the utmost
ease have passed into a disturbance of the peace, not to say a
tumult, which the Romans would have quenched in blood unsparingly and indiscriminatingly shed. Jesus was really therefore a dangerous character, not so much to the Romans, as to
the Jews. Not being prepared to accept him as their king in
fact, they were almost compelled in self-preservation to denounce
him as their would-be king to Pilate.

His execution followed. His supposed resurrection, and the
renewed propagation of his faith, followed that. It has been
widely believed that because Christianity was not put down by
the death of its founder, because, indeed, it burst out again in
renewed vigor, therefore the measures taken against him were
a complete failure, and served only to confer additional glory
and power on the religion he had taught. But this opinion
arises from a confusion of ideas. If they aimed at preserving
their own nation from what they deemed an impious heresy —
and I see no proof that they aimed at anything else — the Jewish authorities were perfectly successful. Christianity, which, if
our accounts be true, threatened to seduce large numbers of
people from their allegiance to the orthodox creed, was practically extinguished among the Jews themselves by the death of
Christ. They could not possibly believe in a crucified Messiah.
Only a very small band of disciples persisted in adhering to
Jesus, justifying their continued faith by asserting that he had
risen from the tomb. But it was no longer among the countrymen of Jesus, whom he had especially sought to attach to his
person and his doctrine, that this small remnant of his followers could find their converts. Neither then, nor at any subsequent time, has Christianity been able to wean the Jews from
their ancient faith. The number of those who, from that time
to this, have abandoned it in favor of the more recent religion
has been singularly small. If, as is probable, there was during
the earthly career of Jesus a growing danger that his teaching
might lead to the formation of a sect to which many minds
would be attracted, that danger was completely averted.

True, Christianity, when rejected by the Jews, made rapid

progress among the Gentiles. But it was no business of the authorities at Jerusalem to look after the religion of heathen nations. They might have thought, had they foreseen the future of Christianity, that a creed which originated among themselves, and had in it a large admixture of Hebrew elements, was better than the worship of the pagan deities. Be this as it may, the particular form of error which the Gentiles might embrace was evidently no concern of theirs. But they had a duty, or thought they had one, towards their own people, who looked to them for guidance, and that was to preserve the religion that had been handed down from their forefathers uncorrupted and unmixed. This they endeavored to do by stifling the new-born heresy of Jesus before it had become too powerful to be stifled. Their measures, having regard to the end they had in view, were undoubtedly politic, and even just.

For were they not perfectly right in supposing that faith in Christ was dangerous to faith in Moses? The event has proved it beyond possibility of question. Not indeed that they could perceive the extent of the peril, for neither Jesus nor any of his disciples has ventured then to throw off Judaism altogether. But they did perceive, with a perfectly correct insight, that the Christians were setting up a new authority alongside of the authorities which alone they recognized,— the Scriptures and the traditional interpretation of the Scriptures. And it was precisely the adoption of a new authority which they desired to prevent. So completely was their foresight on this point justified, that not long after the death of Christ, his assumed followers received converts without circumcision, that all-essential rite; and that, after the lapse of no long period of time, Judaism was entirely abandoned, and a new religion, with new dogmas, new ritual, and new observances, was founded in its place. Surely the action of the men who sat in judgment upon Jesus needs no further justification, from their own point of view, than this one consideration. They had no more sacred trust, in their own eyes, than to prevent the admission of any other object of worship than the Lord Jehovah. Christ speedily became among Christians an object of worship. They owned no more solemn duty than to observe in all its parts the law delivered by their God to Moses. That law was almost instantly abandoned by the Christian Church. They knew of no more unpardonable crime than apostasy from their faith. That apostasy was soon committed by the Jewish Christians.

On all these grounds, then, I venture to maintain that the spiritual rulers of Judea were not so blameworthy as has been commonly supposed in the execution of Jesus of Nazareth. Judged by the principles of universal morality, they were undoubtedly wrong. Judged by the principles of their own religion, they were no less undoubtedly right.

SUBDIVISION 5.—*What did he think of himself?*

Having endeavored, as far as our imperfect information will admit, to realize the view that would be taken of Jesus by contemporary Jews, let us seek if possible to realize the view which he took of himself. In what relation did he suppose himself to stand to God the Father? And in what relation to the Hebrew law? What was his conception of his own mission, and of the manner in which it could best be fulfilled?

Though, in replying to these questions, we suffer somewhat from the scarcity of the materials, we do not labor under the same disadvantages as those we encountered in the preceding section. For there we had to judge between two bitterly hostile parties, of which only one had presented its case. And from the highly colored statement of this one party we had to unravel, as best we could, whatever circumstances might be permitted to weigh in favor of the other. Here we have no conflicting factions to obscure the truth. The opinion formed by Jesus of himself has been handed down to us by his own disciples, who, even if they did not perfectly understand him, must at least have understood him far better than anybody else. And if the picture they give us of the conception he had formed of his own office be consistent with itself, there is also the utmost probability that it is true. Especially will this hold good if this conception should be found to differ materially from that not long afterwards framed about him by the Christian Church.

Consider first the idea he entertained concerning his Messianic character, and his consequent relation to God. His conviction that he was the Messiah, who was sent with a divine message to his nation, was evidently the mainspring of his life. It was under this conviction that he worked his cures and preached his sermons. Probably it strengthened as he continued in his career, though of this there is no possible evidence. Possibly, however, the instructions he gave on several occasions to those whom he had healed, and once to his disciples, to tell no man about him, arose from a certain diffidence about the power by which his miracles were effected (*E.g.*, Mk. i. 44; Mt. ix. 30), and a reluctance to accept the honor which the populace would have conferred upon him. However this may be, he certainly put forward his belief on this subject plainly enough, and its acceptance by his disciples no doubt confirmed it in his own mind, while its rejection by the nation at large, especially the more learned portion of it, gave a flavor of bitterness to the tone in which he insisted upon it. The title by which he habitually designates himself is the Son of man. This was, no doubt, selected as a more modest name than "Son of God." The latter was never (if we exclude the fourth Gospel) applied by Jesus to himself, but when applied to him by others, he made no objection to it, but accepted it as his due. The inference from his behavior is, that he liked to be thought the Son of God (as indeed is shown by his eulogy of Peter when that apostle had so described him) (Mt. xvi 17; vers. 18 and 19 are probably interpolations), but that he did not quite venture to claim the title for himself. That he was ever imagined, either by himself or others, to be the Son of God in the literal, materialistic sense in which the term was afterwards understood, it would be an entire mistake to suppose. No such notion had ever been formulated by the Jewish mind, and it would, no doubt, have filled his earliest disciples with horror. As Mr. Westcott truly observes, "Years must elapse before we can feel that the words of one who talked with men were indeed the words of God" (Canon of New Testament, p 64). Nor was the Hebrew Jehovah the sort of divinity who would have had a son by a young village maiden. Proceedings of that kind were left to the heathen deities. Nor did Christ, in claiming a filial relationship to God, ever intend to claim unity with the divine essence, still less to assert that he actually was God himself. This notion of identity would receive no sanction even from the fourth Gospel, which

does, quite unlike its predecessors, lend some sanction to that
of unity in nature. The best proof of this is that Jesus never,
at any period of his life, desired his followers to worship him,
either as God or as the Son of God. Had he believed of himself what his followers subsequently believed of him, that he
was one of the constituent persons in a divine trinity, he must
have enjoined his apostles both to address him in prayer themselves, and to desire their converts to address him. It is quite
plain that he did nothing of the kind, and that they never supposed him to have done so. Belief in Christ as the Messiah
was taught as the first dogma of apostolic Christianity, but adoration of Christ as God was not taught at all. But we are not
left in this matter to depend on conjectural inferences. The
words of Jesus are plain. Whenever occasion arose, he asserted
his inferiority to the Father (as Milton has proved to demonstration),* though, as no one had then dreamt of his equality,
it is natural that the occasions should not have been frequent.
He made himself inferior in knowledge when he said that of
the day and hour of the day of judgment no one knew, neither
the angels in heaven, nor the Son; no one except the Father
(Mk. xiii. 32). He made himself inferior in power when he said
that seats on his right hand and on his left in the kingdom of
heaven were not his to give (Mk. x. 40); inferior in virtue when
he desired a certain man not to address his as "Good master,"
for there was none good but God (Mk. x. 18). The words of his
prayer at Gethsemane, "all things are possible unto thee," imply that all things were not possible to him; while its conclusion, "not what I will, but what thou wilt," indicates submission to a superior, not the mere execution of a purpose of his
own (Mk. xiv. 36). Indeed, the whole prayer would have been a
mockery, useless for any purpose but the deception of his disciples, if he had himself been identical with the Being to whom
he prayed, and had merely been giving effect by his death to
their common counsels. While the cry of agony from the cross,
"My God, my God, why hast thou forsaken me?" (Mk. xv. 34,)
would have been quite unmeaning if the person forsaken and
the person forsaking had been one and the same. Either, then,
we must assume that the language of Jesus has been misre-

* Milton, Treatise on Christian Doctrine, Sumner's translation, p. 100 ff.

ported, or we must admit that he never for a moment pretended to be co-equal, co-eternal, or con-substantial with God.

Throughout his public life he spoke of himself as one who was sent by God for a certain purpose. What was that purpose? Was it, as the Gentile Christians so readily assumed, to abolish the laws and customs of the Jews, and to substitute others in their stead? Did he, for example, propose to supplant circumcision by baptism? the Sabbath by the Sunday? the synagogue by the church? the ceremonial observances of the law of Moses by observances of another kind? If so, let the evidence be produced. For unless we find among his recorded instructions some specific injunction to his disciples that they were no longer to be Jews, but Christians, we cannot assume that he intended any such revolution. Now, not only can no such injunction be produced, but the whole course of his life negatives the supposition that any was given. For while teaching much on many subjects, he never at any time alludes to the Mosaic dispensation as a temporary arrangement, destined to yield to a higher law. Yet it would surely have been strange if he had left his disciples to guess at his intentions on this all-important subject. Moreover, it came directly in his way when he censured the Pharisees. He frequently accuses them of overlaying the law with a multitude of unnecessary and trouble-some rules; but while objecting to these, he never for a moment hints that the very law itself was now to become a thing of the past. Quite the reverse. The Pharisees were very scrupulous about paying tithes and disregarded weightier matters; these, he says, they ought to have done, and not to have left the other undone. If those tithes were no longer to be paid (at least not for the same objects), why does he not say so? Again, he charges them with transgressing the commandment of God by their tradition; where it is the accretions round the law, and not the law itself, which he attacks. In one case he even directly imposes an observance of the legal requirements on a man over whom he has influence (Mk. i. 44). Moreover, he himself evidently continued to perform the obligations of his Jewish religion until the very end of his life, for one of his last acts was to eat the passover with his disciples. The only institution which he apparently desires to alter at all is the

Sabbath, and there it is plain that he aims at an amendment
in the mode of its observance, not at its entire abolition,
Indeed. he justifies his disciples by invoking the example of
David, an orthodox Hebrew; and very happily remarks, that
the Sabbath was made for man, not man for the Sabbath—one of
his best and most epigrammatic sayings. But an institution
made for man was indeed one to be rationally observed, but by
no means one to be lightly tampered with. Jesus, in fact, was
altogether a Jew, and though an ardent reformer, he desired to
reform within the limits of Judaism, not beyond them.

If further proof were needed of this than the fact that he
himself neither abandoned the religion of his birth, nor sought
to obtain disciples except among those who belonged to it, it
would be found in his treatment of the heathen women whose
daughter was troubled with a devil. To her he distinctly
declared that he was not sent except to the lost sheep of the
house of Israel. In reply to her further persistence, he told her
that it was not well to take the children's meat and throw it to
dogs. Nothing but her appropriate yet modest answer induced
him to accede to her request (Mt. xv. 21–28). Further confirmation is afforded by his instructions to his disciples, whom he
desired not to go either to the Gentiles or the Samaritans, but
to the lost sheep of the house of Israel (Mt. x. 5, 6). His own
practice was altogether in conformity with these instructions.
He markedly confined the benefits of his teaching to his fellow-
countrymen. Once only is he said to have visited the neighborhood of Tyre and Sidon, and then he was anxious to preserve
the strictest incognito (Mk. vii. 24). Even when the Jews
refused to believed in him, he sought no converts among the
Gentiles. He never even intimated that he would receive such
converts without their previous adoption of the Jewish faith,
and after his decease his most intimate disciples were doubtful
whether it was lawful to associate with uncircumcised people
(Acts x. 28; xi. 2, 3). Not only, therefore, had he himself never
done so, but he had left no instructions behind him that such a
relaxation of Jewish scruples might ever be permitted. True,
when disappointed among his own people, he now and then
contrasted them in unflattering terms with the heathen. Chorazin and Bethsaida were worse than Tyre and Sidon; Caper-

naum less open to conviction than Sodom (Mt. xi. 20–24). The faith of the heathen centurion was greater than any he had found in Israel (Mt. viii. 10). But all these expressions of embittered feeling imply that it was in Israel he had looked for faith, towards Israel that his desires were turned. To discover faith out of it might be an agreeable surprise, but as a general rule, was neither to be expected nor sought.

Having, then, determined, what the purport of his mission was not, let us try to discover what it was. The quest is not difficult. The whole of his teaching is pervaded by one ever-recurring keynote, which those who have ears to hear it cannot miss. He came to announce the approach of what he termed "the kingdom of heaven." A great revolution was to take place on earth. God was to come, accompanied by Jesus. to reward the virtuous and to punish the wicked. A totally new order of things was to be substituted in lieu of the present unjust and unequal institutions. And Jesus was sent by God to warn the children of Israel to prepare for this kingdom of heaven. There was but little time to lose, for even now the day of judgment was at hand. The mind of Jesus was laden with this one great thought, to which, with him, all others were subordinate. It runs through his maxims of conduct, his parables, his familiar converse with his disciples. Far from him was the notion of founding a new religion, to be extended throughout the world and to last for ages. It was a work of much more immediate urgency which he came to do. "Prepare for the kingdom of heaven, for it will come upon you in the present generation;" such was the burden of his message. Let us hear his own mode of delivering it to men.

The very beginning of his preaching, according to Mark, was in this strain: "The time is fulfilled, and the kingdom of God has approached; repent, and believe the Gospel" (Mk. i. 15). Precisely similar is the purport of his earliest doctrine according to Matthew (Mt. iv. 7). How thoroughly he believed that the time was fulfilled is shown by his decided declaration that there were some among his hearers who would not taste of death till they had seen the kingdom of God come with power (Mk. ix. 1), a saying which, as it would never have been invented, is undoubtedly genuine. He told his disciples that Elias, who was expected to precede the kingdom of heaven, had already come (Mk. ix. 13).

Over and over again, in a hundred different ways, this absorbing thought finds expression in his language. The one and only message the disciples are instructed to carry to the "lost sheep of the house of Israel" is that the kingdom of heaven is at hand (Mt. x. 17. When a city does not receive them, they are to wipe off the dust of it against them, and bid them be sure that the kingdom of God is near them (Lu. x. 11). In the coming judgment, Chorazin, Bethsaida, and above all his own place Capernaum, were to suffer more than Tyre and Sidon. Earthly matters assume, in consequence of this conviction of their temporary nature, a very trivial aspect. The disciples are to take no thought for the morrow; the morrow will take thought for itself. Nor are they to trouble themselves about food and clothing, but to seek first the kingdom of God (Mt. vi. 31-34). They are not to lay up treasure on earth, but in heaven, in order that their hearts may be there (Mt. vi. 19-21). Moreover, they must be always on the watch, as the Son of man will come upon them at an unexpected hour. It would not do then to be engaged as the wicked antediluvians were when overtaken by the flood, in the occupations of eating and drinking, or marrying and giving in marriage. Instead of this, they must be like the faithful servant whom his master on returning to his house found watching (Mt. xxiv. 38, 42, 43; Lu. xii. 37, 38). Preparation is to be made for the kingdom which their Father will give them by selling what they have and bestowing alms, so laying up an incorruptible treasure; by keeping their loins girded and their lights burning (Lu. xii. 32). Neglect of these precautions will be punished by exclusion from the joys of the kingdom, as shown in the parable of the ten virgins (Mt. xxv. 1-13). But the indications of the great event are not understood by the people, who are able to read the signs of the coming weather, but not those of the times (Lu. xii. 54-57); an inability which might have been due to the fact that they had had some experience of the one kind of signs and none of the other. On another occasion, he observes that the law and the prophets were till John; since then the kingdom of God has been preached, and every man presses into it (Lu.

xvi. 16). Here he specially proclaims himself as the preacher of the kingdom; the man who brought mankind this new revelation. Such was the manner in which this revelation was announced, that some at least of those who heard him thought that the kingdom was to come immediately. To counteract this view he told the parable of the nobleman who went from home to receive a kingdom, leaving his servants in charge of certain monies, and rewarded them on his return according to the amount of interest they had obtained by usury, punishing one of them who had made no use of the sum intrusted to him (Lu. xix. 11-27). He himself, of course, was the nobleman who received his kingdom and returned again to judge his servants. So urgent was the message he had to deliver, that (according to one Evangelist) a man who wished to bury his father before joining him was told to let the dead bury their dead, but to go himself and announce the kingdom of God; while another, who asked leave to bid farewell to his family, was warned that no man, having put his hand to the plough, and looking back, was fit for that kingdom Lu. ix. 58-62).

The arrival of the kingdom was to be preceded by various signs. There would be false Christs; there would be wars; earthquakes, and famines; there would be persecutions of the faithful; but the Gospel (that is, the announcement of the approach of this new state of things) must first be published in all nations.* Then the sun and moon would be darkened and the stars fall; the Son of man would come in power and glory, and gather his elect from all parts of the earth. The existing generation was not to pass till all these things were done. Not even the Son knew when this would happen; but as it might come suddenly and unexpectedly upon them, they were to be continually on the watch (Mk. xiii.; Mt. xxiv). The apostles would not even finish the cities of Israel before the Son of man had come (Mt. x. 23).

Little is said in description of the nature of the kingdom of heaven except by the method of illustration. The main result to be gathered from numerous allusions to it is that justice is to prevail. Thus, the kingdom of heaven is said to be like a man

---

* This verse is so inconsistent with other declarations of Christ, especially with Mt. x. 23, that I am disposed to regard it as an interpolation.

who sowed good seed in his field, but in whose property an enemy maliciously mingled tares. At the harvest the tares are to be burnt, and the wheat gathered into the barn. This parable Jesus himself explained. The tares are the wicked; the wheat represents "the children of the kingdom." And as tares are burnt, so "the Son of man shall send his angels, and collect from his kingdom all offenses, and those who do wickedness, and shall throw them into the furnace of fire; there shall be weeping and gnashing of teeth. Then the just shall shine out like the sun in the kingdom of their Father." The same idea is expressed in the illustration of the net cast into the sea, which gathers good fish and bad. Just as the fishermen separate these, so the angels at the end of the world will separate the wicked from the midst of the just. Other comparisons represent the influence on the heart of faith in the kingdom. Thus, the kingdom of heaven is like a grain of mustard seed, which, though the smallest of seeds, becomes the largest of herbs. Or it is like leaven leavening three measures of meal. Again, it is like treasure hid in a field, or a pearl of great price (Mt. xiii. 24-50).

The best qualification for preëminence in the kingdom was humility.

When asked who was to be greatest in the kingdom of heaven, Jesus replied that it would be he who humbled himself like a little child (Mt. xviii. 1-4). He delights in the exhibition of striking contrasts between the present and the future state of things. The first are to be the last, and the last first. Those who have made great sacrifices now are then to receive vast rewards (Mk. x. 29-31). He who has lost his life for his sake is to find it, and he who has found it is to lose it (Mt. x. 39). The stone rejected by the builder is to become the head of the corner (Mk. xii. 10). The kingdom of God is to be taken from the privileged nation and given to another more worthy of it (Mt. xxi. 43). Publicans and harlots are to take precedence of the respectable classes in entering the kingdom (Mt. xxi. 31). It is scarcely possible for rich men to enter it all, though God may perhaps admit them by an extraordinary exertion of power (Mk. x. 23-27). Many even who trust in their high character for correct religion will find themselves rejected. But they will be safe who have both heard the sayings of Jesus and done them.

They will have built their houses on rocks, from which the storms which usher in the kingdom will not dislodge them. Those, however, who hear these sayings, and neglect to perform them, will be like foolish men who have built their houses on sand, where the storms will beat them down, and great will be their fall (Mt. vii. 22–29). That the kingdom is to be on earth, not in some unknown heaven, is manifest from the numerous references of Jesus to the time when the Son of man will "come;" a time which none can know, yet for which all are to watch. He never speaks of men "going" to the kingdom of heaven; It is the kingdom of heaven which is to come to them. And the most remarkable of the many contrasts will be that between the present humiliation of the Son and his future glory. He will return to execute his Father's decrees. His judges themselves will see him "sitting on the right hand of power, and coming in the clouds of heaven" (Mt. xxvi. 64). instead of standing as a prisoner at the bar, he will then be enthroned as a judge. "When the Son of man shall come in his glory, and all the angels with him, then he shall sit on the throne of his glory; and all the nations 'shall be collected before him, and he shall separate them from one another, as the shepherd separates the sheep from the goats; and he shall put the sheep on his right hand, but the goats on his left." The goats, who have done harm, are then to go into everlasting punishment; and the sheep, who have done good, are to pass into eternal life (Mt. xxv. 31–46).

This equitable adjustment of rewards and punishments to merit and demerit is the leading conception in the revolution which the kingdom of heaven is to make. The faithful servant is to be made ruler over his master's goods; the unfaithful one to be cut off and assigned a portion with the hypocrites. The virgins whose lamps are ready burning will be admitted to the marriage festival. The servants who make the best use of the property committed to their charge will be rewarded, while those who have failed to employ it properly will be cast into outer darkness (Mt. xxiv. 42–xxv. 30). So also the wicked husbandman in the vineyard, who ill-treated their master's servants and killed his heir, are to be destroyed when he comes, and the vineyard is to be committed to other cultivators (Mk.

xii. 1–9). All those, on the other hand, who have made great
sacrifices for the sake of Christ will receive a hundred-fold compensation for all that they have now abandoned (Mt. xix. 29, 30).

Such was the sort of notion — rude, yet tolerably definite —
which Jesus had formed of the kingdom his Father was about
to found. and for the coming of which he taught his disciples
to pray. This hope of a reign of justice, of an exaltation of the
lowly and virtuous, and a depression of the proud and wicked,
animated his teaching and inspired his life. To make known
this great event, so shortly to overtake them, to mankind, was
a duty with which in his opinion he had been charged by God;
to receive this message at his hands was in his judgment the
first of virtues, to spurn it the most unpardonable of crimes.

SUBDIVISION 6.—*What did his disciples think of him?*

There is on record a remarkable conversation which affords
us a glimpse, both of the rumors that were current about Christ
among the people, and also of the view taken of him by his
nearest friends during his life-time. Jesus had gone with his
disciples into the towns of Cæsarea Philippi. On the way, being
apparently curious about the state of public opinion, he asked
them, "Whom do men say that I am?" To this they replied,
"John the Baptist; and some say Elias, and others that thou
art one of the prophets." To which Jesus rejoined, "But you,
whom say you that I am?" Peter returned the answer, "Thou
art the Messiah;" or "Thou art the Messiah, the Son of the
living God." It is remarkable that Peter alone is represented
as replying to this second question, as if the others had not yet
attained to the conviction which this apostle held of the Messiahship of Jesus. Especially would this conclusion be confirmed
if we adopted the version of Matthew, where Jesus expresses
his high approbation of Peter's answer (Mk. viii. 27–30; Mt. xvi.
13–20). If this apostle was peculiarly blessed on account of his
perception of this truth, it may be inferred that his companions
had either not yet perceived, or were not yet sure of it. That
Peter did not mean by calling him the Messiah to state that he
was a portion of the deity himself, is evident from what follows; for Jesus having predicted his future sufferings, "Peter

began to rebuke him," anxious to avert the omen. Had he believed that it was God himself with whom he was conversing, he could hardly have ventured to question his perfect knowledge of the future.

The doctrine of the divinity of Christ is not, in fact, to be found in the New Testament. Even the writer of the fourth Gospel, who holds the highest and most mystical view of his nature, does not teach that. Often indeed in that Gospel does Jesus speak of himself as one with the Father. But the dogmatic force of all these expressions is measured by the fact that precisely in the same sense he speaks of the disciples as one with himself. As the Father and he are in one another, so he prays that the disciples may be one in them (Jo. xvii. 21). Moreover, when the Jews charged him with making himself God, he met them by inquiring whether it was not written in their law, " I said, Ye are gods." If, then, those to whom the word of God came were called gods, was it blasphemy in him, whom the Father had sanctified and sent, to say, "I am the Son of God?" (Jo. x. 33-37). Here, then, the term which Jesus appropriates is "Son of God," and this he considers admissible because the Hebrew people generally had been called gods. Evidently, then, he does not admit the charge of making himself God.

The authority of the fourth Gospel is, of course of no value in enabling us to determine what Jesus said or did, but it is of great value as evidence of the view taken about him by those of his disciples who, at this early period, had advanced the furthest in the direction of placing him on a level with God himself. It is either the latest, or one of the latest, compositions in the New Testament, and it proves that, at the period when its author lived, even the boldest spirits had not ventured on the dogma which afterwards became the corner stone of the Christian creed.

Throughout the rest of the canonical books, Jesus is simply the Messiah, the Son of God; in whom, in that sense, it is a duty to believe. Whoever believes this much is, according to the first epistle of John, born of God (1 John v. 1).

Clearer still is the evidence that, in the opinion of those most competent to judge, Jesus had no intention of abolishing

the observance of the law of Moses. So far were his disciples
from imagining that he contemplated any such change, that
they were at first in doubt whether it was allowable for them
even to relax the rules which forbade social intercourse with
heathens. The writer of the Acts of the Apostles, however, informs us that, when an important convert was to be won over
from the pagan ranks, Peter had the privilege of a vision which
enjoined him not to call anything which God had cleansed
common or unclean. Interpreting this to mean that he might
associate with the Gentiles, he received the heathen convert,
Cornelius, with all cordiality, and even preached the gospel of
Jesus to the uncircumcised company by whom he was surrounded. That this was a novel measure is plainly evinced by
the fact that the Jewish Christians who were present were
astonished that the gift of the Holy Ghost should be poured
out upon the Gentiles. They therefore had conceived that
Christianity was to be confined to themselves (Acts x).

But there is more direct evidence of the same fact. When
Peter returned to Jerusalem, the circumcised believers there
found fault with him because he had gone in to uncircumcised
men, and had eaten with them. Peter, of course, related his
vision in self-defense, and since there was no reply to be made
to such an argument as this, they accepted the new and unexpected fact which he announced: "Well, then, God has given
repentance to life to the Gentiles also" (Acts xi. 1–18). Paul,
who was too strong-minded to need a revelation to teach him
the best way of promoting Christian interests, also received
heathen converts without requiring them to come under Jewish
obligations. But the conduct of these apostles was far from
meeting with unmixed approbation in the community. Some
men from Judea came to Antioch, where Paul and Barnabas
were, and informed the brethren there that unless they were
circumcised they could not be saved. So important was this
question deemed, that Paul and Barnabas, after much disputing
with these Judaic Christians, agreed to go with them to Jerusalem to refer the matter to a council of the apostles and elders. Obviously, then, it was a new case which had arisen. No
authoritative *dictum* of Jesus could be produced. The possibility of having to receive heathens among his disciples was one

he had never contemplated. Called to deal with this supremely important question, on which the whole future of the Church turned, the apostles displayed moderation and good sense. Acting on the concurrent advice of Peter, Paul, James, and Barnabas, they wrote to the brethren in Antioch, Syria, and Cilicia, that they had determined to lay no greater burden upon them than these necessary things:—1. Abstinence from meat offered to idols; 2. from blood; 3. from things strangled; 4. from fornication. Hence it will be seen that they absolved the heathen believers from all Jewish observances except two, those that forbade blood and things strangled. These, from long habit and the fixed prejudices of their race, no doubt appeared to them to have some deeper foundation than a mere arbitrary command. These therefore they enjoined even upon pagans (Acts xv. 1-31).

Be it observed, however, that this dispensation applied only to those who were not of Hebrew blood. The apostles and elders assembled at Jerusalem had no thought of dispensing *themselves* from the binding force of the law of Moses. To observe it was alike their privilege and their duty. They did not conceive that, in becoming Christians, they had ceased to be Jews, any more than a Catholic who becomes a Protestant conceives that he has ceased to be a Christian. The question whether those who had been born Jews should abandon their ancient religion was not even raised at this time among them. The only question was whether those who had not been born Jews should adopt it.

Innovation, however, is not to be arrested at any given point. Liberty having been conceded to the Gentiles, it was not unnatural that some of the apostles, when living among the Gentiles, should take advantage of it for themselves. No overt rule was adopted on this subject. It seems to have been tacitly understood that all Jews should continue to be bound by the rigor of their native customs, except in so far as they had been modified by common consent: and the attempt of some to escape from this burden was an occasion of no small scandal to the more orthodox members of the sect (Acts xxi. 20; Gal. ii. 12). Both Peter and Paul indeed, at separate times, were compelled to make some concessions to the extremely strong feeling in favor of the law which existed at headquarters. The conduct of these two eminent apostles merits examination.

Peter, it appears, never gave up Judaism in his own person; but when staying at Antioch he mixed freely with Gentiles, making no attempt to impose the law upon them, and approving of the proceedings of Paul. It so happened, however, that there came to Antioch some brethren from James at Jerusalem. These men were strict Jews, and Peter was so much afraid of them, that he "withdrew and separated himself" from his former companions. The other Jewish Christians, and even Barnabas, the former friend of Paul, were induced to act in the same way. Paul, who was not likely to lose the opporunity of a little triumph over Peter, ruthlessly exposed his misconduct. According to his account, he publicly addressed him in these terms: "If thou, being a Jew, livest like a Gentile and not like a Jew, why dost thou compel the Gentiles to be like Jews?" (Gal. ii. 11–14.) What answer Peter returned, or whether he returned any, Paul does not inform us. His charge against Peter I understand to be, not that the apostle had positively adopted heathen customs, and then taken up Jewish ones again, but that he had relaxed in his own favor the rules which forbade Jews from eating with Gentiles. On the appearance of the stricter Christians from Jerusalem he put on the appearance of a strictness equal to their own. Such conduct was consistent with the character of the disciple who had denied his master.

Paul himself, on the other hand, was a complete freethinker. Once converted, the system of which he had formerly been the zealous upholder no longer had any power over his emancipated mind. His robust and logical intellect soon delivered him from the fetters in which he had been bound. Far, however, from following his example, the Christians at Jerusalem were shocked at the laxity of his morals. The steps he took to conciliate them are graphically described in the Acts of the Apostles. On visiting the capital, Paul and his companions went to see James, with whom were assembled all the elders; and Paul described the success he had met with among the Gentiles. Hereupon the assembled company, or more probably James as their spokesman, informed Paul what very disadvantageous reports were current concerning him. "Thou seest, brother," they

began, "how many thousands of believers there are among the
Jews, and all are zealots for the law; and they have been informed of thee that thou teachest the Jews among the Gentiles
apostasy from Moses, saying that they should not circumcise
their children, nor walk in the customs. What is it, then? It
is quite necessary that the multitude should meet, for they will
hear that thou art come. Do then this that we tell thee. We
have four men who have a vow upon them; take these and be
purified with them, and bear the expense with them of having
their heads shaven; and all will know that there is nothing in
what they have heard about thee, but that thou also walkest
in the observation of the law" (Acts xxi. 20-24). This sensible
advice was adopted by Paul; and the "zealots for the law,"
who composed the Christian community at Jerusalem, had the
satisfaction of seeing him purify himself and enter the temple
with the men under the vow. On a later occasion, too, when
charged with crime before Felix, Paul mentioned the fact that
twelve days ago he had gone up to worship at Jerusalem, as if
he had been an orthodox Jew (Acts xxiv. 11).

But although he might think it expedient to satisfy James
and his friends at Jerusalem by a concession to public opinion,
the rumor which had reached the brethren there, if unfounded
in the letter, was in fact an accurate representation of the inevitable outcome of Paul's teaching. Possibly he did not wish
to press his own views upon others of his nation, and therefore
did not interfere with such of them as, though living among
heathens, yet adhered religiously to their national customs.
But unquestionably his own feelings were strongly enlisted in
favor of the abolition of the law, and if the Jewish Christians
read and accepted his writings, they could hardly fail to adopt
his practice. The law in his opinion was no longer necessary
for those who believed in Christ. He is not the true Jew who
is one outwardly, nor is that the true circumcision which is
outward. He is a Jew who is so internally, and circumcision is
of the heart in the spirit, not in the letter. If it be asked what
advantage the Jew has, Paul replies that he has much: the
first of all, that to his nation were confided the oracles of God
(Rom. ii. 28, 29, iii. 1, 2). He knows, he says, and is persuaded
in the Lord Jesus, that there is nothing unclean in itself, though

to him who thinks it so it may be unclean. It is well to abstain from eating flesh or drinking wine, or anything else that
may give offense to others, but these things are all unimportant
in themselves. One man esteems one day above another; another man esteems them all alike; let each be fully persuaded
in his own mind. Only let us not judge one another, nor put
stumbling-blocks in one another's way (Rom. xiv).

From these considerations it appears that the suspicions
entertained of Paul at Jerusalem were substantially true. Possibly he did not absolutely teach the Jews to abandon the law;
possibly he did not even completely abandon it himself. But in
his writings he constantly treats it as a thing indifferent in
itself; Christians might or might not believe in its obligations,
and provided they acted conscientiously, all was well. Along
with these very skeptical opinions, however, Paul strongly held
to the necessity of worldly prudence. He is very indignant with
the "false brethren privily introduced, who slipped in to spy
out the liberty we have in Jesus Christ, that they might enslave
us; to whom," he adds, "we did not yield by subjection even
for an hour" (Gal. ii. 4, 5). But whether the brethren at Jerusalem required him to clear himself from the report that he
was not an observer of the law, there came in another principle
of action, which he has himself explained with praiseworthy
frankness. "To the Jews," he tells the Corinthians, "I became as a Jew, that I might gain the Jews; to those under
the law as under the law, not being myself under the law,
that I might gain those under the law; to those without law,
as without law (not being without law to God, but law-abid-
ing to Christ), that I might gain those without law; to the
weak I became weak, that I might gain the weak; I became all
things to all men, that by all means I might save some" (1
Cor. ix. 20–22). Acting on this elastic rule, Paul might easily
comply with all the demands of James and his zealots. To the
Jews he became a Jew for the nonce. It was perhaps in the
same spirit of worldly wisdom that he took the precaution of
circumcising a young convert who was Jewish only on the
mother's side, his father having been a Greek (Acts xvi. 1–3).

While such was the conduct of this strong-minded reformer,
it is plain that his attitude towards the law was not shared by

the personal friends of Jesus. James at Jerusalem adhered strictly to Judaism. The other apostles, so far as we know, did the same. The rest of the brethren there did the same. Paul was tolerated, and even cordially received, as the apostle of the Gentiles, but it does not appear that he had any following among the Jews. Had any of the original apostles followed him in his bold innovations, he would surely have mentioned the fact, as he has mentioned the partial adhesion of Peter. On the contrary, he seems in his epistles, when attacking the Judaic type of Christianity, to be arguing as much against them as against the unchristian Jews or the heathen.

Stronger evidence than mere inference is, however, obtainable on this point. The Jewish Christians, who had received their doctrines direct from the companions of Jesus, soon came to form a sect apart, and were known by the name of Ebionites. Of these men, Irenæus tells us that "they use the Gospel according to Matthew only, and repudiate the apostle Paul, maintaining that he was an apostate from the law." Moreover, "they practice circumcision, persevere in the observance of those customs which are enjoined by the law, and are so Judaic in their style of life, that they even adore Jerusalem as if it were the house of God" (Adv. Hær. i. 26). It was a strange fate that befell these unfortunate people, when, overwhelmed by the flood of heathenism that had swept into the Church, they were condemned as heretics. Yet there is no evidence that they had ever swerved from the doctrines of Jesus, or of the disciples who knew him in his life-time. Jesus himself had been circumcised, and he certainly never condemned the rite, or spoke of it as useless for the future. He was so Judaic in his style of life that he reverenced the temple at Jerusalem as "a house of prayer for all nations," and deemed it his special duty to purify it from what he regarded as pollution. But the torrent of progress swept past the Ebionites, and left them stranded on the shore.

Should the position here maintained with reference to the Judaic character of the early Christians be thought to require further confirmation, I should find it in the weighty words of a theologian who, while entirely Christian in his views, is also one of the highest authorities on the history of the Church. Nean-

der, speaking of this question, observes that the disciples did
not at once arrive at the consciousness of that vocation which
Christ (in his opinion) had indicated to them, namely, that they
should form a distinct community from that of the Jews. On the
contrary, they attached themselves to this community in every re-
respect, and all the forms of the national theocracy were holy to
them. " They lived in the conviction that these forms would continue as they were till the return of Christ, by which a new and
higher order of things was to be founded ; and this change they
expected as one that was near a hand. Far from them, therefore,
lay the thought of the foundation of a new cultus, even if from
the light of belief in the Redeemer new ideas had dawned upon
them about that which belonged to the essence of the true
adoration of God. They took part as zealously in the service of
the temple as any pious Jews. Only they believed that a sifting would take place among the theocratic people, and that the
better part of it would be incorporated in *their* community by
the recognition of Jesus as the Messiah" (Neander, Pflanzung
der Christlichen Kirche, vol. i. p. 38). Neander proceeds to
point out — and here too his remarks are valuable — that the
outward forms of Judaism gave facilities for the formation of
such smaller bodies within the general body, by means of the
division into synagogues. The Christians, therefore, constituted
merely a special synagogue, embraced within the mass of
believers who all accepted the law of Moses, all worshiped at
the temple of Jerusalem. It will be seen, however, that I differ
from Neander in so far as he supposes that the members of
the Christian synagogue, in adhering to Judaism, were neglecting any indications given by their founder. On the contrary, it
appears to me a more reasonable explanation of their conduct
that the founder himself had never contemplated that entire
emancipation from Judaic forms which was soon to follow.

On these two points, then — the humanity of Jesus and his
Judaism — the early history of the Church affords our position
all possible support. How is it about the third — his announcement of a kingdom of heaven soon to come? Paul must
have derived his doctrine on this point, whatever it was,
from those who were disciples of Christ before him, for it
does not appear that he had any special revelation on the sub-

ject. Let us hear what was the impression made upon his mind by their report of the teaching of Jesus. "We do not wish you to be ignorant, brethren "—so he writes to the Thessalonians — "that you may not grieve like the rest who have no hope. For if we believe that Jesus died and rose again, thus also will God bring those who sleep through Jesus. For this we say to you *by the word of the Lord* " (Paul therefore is speaking with all the authority of his apostolic commission), "*that we who are alive and are left for the coming of the Lord* shall not take precedence of those who are asleep. For the Lord himself shall descend from heaven with the word of command, with the voice of the archangel, and with the trumpet of God, and the dead in Christ will rise first. Then we who are alive and are left shall be snatched with them in the clouds to meet the Lord in the air, and thus we shall always be with the Lord" (1 Thess. iv. 13 17). Clearer than this it is difficult to be. There can be no question whatever, unless we put an arbitrary significance on these words, that Paul looked for the second coming of Christ and the final judgment long before the existing generation had passed away. Some will fall asleep before that day, but he fully expects that he himself and many of those whom he is addressing will be alive to witness it. So confident is he of this, that he even describes the order in which the faithful will proceed to join their Lord, the dead taking a higher rank than the living. He differs from Jesus, and probably from the other apostles, in placing the kingdom of heaven somewhere in the clouds, and not on earth. But he entirely agrees with them as to the date of the revolution. Quite consistent with the above passage is another (of which, however, the correct reading is doubtful): "We shall not all sleep, but we shall all be changed."

Filled with the like hope, he prays that the spirit, mind, and *body* of the Thessalonians may be preserved blameless to the coming of Christ (1 Thess. v. 23). And he comforts them in a subsequent letter by the promise that they who are troubled shall have "rest with us in the revelation of the Lord Jesus from heaven with the angels of his power (2 Thess. i. 7). While, in writing to the Corinthians, he speaks of the existing generation as those "upon whom the ends of the ages have come."

Not less clear is the language of the other apostles. Peter on that memorable day of Pentecost when the apostles exhibit the gift of tongues, and some irreverent spectators are led to charge them with inebriety, explains to the assembly that the scene which had just been witnessed was characteristic of the "last days," as foretold by the prophet Joel. In those days their sons and their daughters were to prophesy, their young men to see visions, and their old men to dream dreams; the Spirit was to be poured out on God's servants and handmaidens; there were to be signs and wonders; blood, fire, and smoke; the sun was to be turned into darkness, and the moon into blood; and whoever called on the name of the Lord was to be saved. Thus Peter, than whom there could be no higher authority as to the mind of Christ, applied to his own time the prophetic description of the "day of the Lord" given by Joel (Acts ii. 14-2). James exhorts his disciples not to be in too great a hurry for the arrival of Christ. They are to imitate the husbandman waiting for the ripening of his crops. "Be you also patient: confirm your hearts; for the coming of the Lord draws near" (James v. 7, 8). The author of the first epistle of Peter distinctly informs the Christian community that "the end of all things is at hand." And he warns them not to think it strange concerning the fiery trial which is to try them, "but rejoice, inasmuch as you share in the sufferings of Christ; that in the revelation of his glory you may also rejoice with exceeding joy" (1 Pet. iv. 7, 12, 13). Further on he promises that when the chief Shepherd appears, they shall receive "the unfading crown of glory" (1 Pet. v. 4). In the first epistle of John the disciples are thus exhorted: "And now, little children, remain in him, that when he comes we may have boldness, and may not be ashamed before him at his coming" (1 Jo. ii. 28).

In the next chapter he tells them that "when he appears we shall be like him, for we shall see him as he is" (1 Jo. iii. 2). Of the Apocalypse it cannot be necessary to speak in detail. The one great thought that inspires it from beginning to end is that of the speedy return of Jesus, accompanied as it will be by the judgment of the wicked, the reward of the faithful, and the establishment of a new heaven and a new earth far more glorious and more beautiful than those that are to pass away,

The end of the book is conclusive as to its meaning: "I, Jesus, have sent my angel to testify these things to you in the churches." "He that testifies these things says, 'Surely I come quickly. So be it; come, Lord Jesus'" (Rev. xxii. 16, 20).

There is another passage bearing on this subject, which, as it appears to have been written at a later date than any of those hitherto quoted, may best be considered last. It is found in the second epistle attributed to Peter. The epistle was probably written after the first generation of Christians had passed away, but the forger endeavors to assume the style of the apostle whose name he borrows. From the language he employs it is evident that there was some impatience among believers in his day on account of what seemed to them the long delay in the second coming of Christ. Scoffers had arisen, who were putting the awkward question, "Where is the promise of his coming? for since the fathers fell asleep, all things continue as they were from the beginning of creation." Such scoffers, he tells them, are to come "in the last days," and he warns them how to resist the influence of their specious arguments. For this purpose he reminds them of the former destruction of the earth by water, and assures them that the present heavens and the present earth are to be destroyed by fire. They are not to let the consideration escape them that with the Lord one day is a thousand years, and a thousand years as one day. Hence God is not really slow about fulfilling his promise, as some people believe; he is only waiting out of kindness, not being willing that any should perish, but desiring that all should come to repentance. But the day of the Lord will come unexpectedly, like a thief in the night; wherefore the Christians who are looking for new heavens and a new earth, according to his promise, must take care to be ready that they may be found by him spotless and blameless (2 Pet. iii). Here, then, we have a further proof of the hopes entertained by the early Christians; for this writer, who evidently felt that the promises held out by the original apostles were in danger of being discredited by the long delay in the expected catastrophe, concerns himself to show that the postponement of its arrival is not after all so great as it may seem, and seeks to dispel the doubts that had grown up concerning it. He thus bears important testimony to the nature of the expectations entertained by those who had gone before him.

But even if we had not this epistle, we should find some evidence of the same fact in the writings of the earliest fathers. Thus, in the first epistle of Clement, the Christians are warned in the following language:—

"Far from us be that which is written, 'Wretched are they who are of a double mind and of a doubting heart;' who say, 'These things we have heard even in the time of our fathers; but behold, we have grown old and none of them has happened unto us!' Ye foolish ones! compare yourselves to a tree; take [for instance] the vine. First of all it sheds its leaves, then it buds, next it puts forth leaves, and then it flowers; after that comes the sour grape, and then follows the ripened fruit. Ye perceive how in a little time the fruit of a tree comes to maturity. Of a truth, soon and suddenly shall his will be accomplished, as the Scripture also bears witness, saying, 'Speedily will he come, and not tarry;' and, 'The Lord shall suddenly come to his temple, even the Holy One, for whom ye look'" (First Ep. of Clement, ch xxiii.—A. N. L., vol. i. p. 24).

Further on, the same writer expressly states that what the apostles of Christ preached was the speedy advent of the new order of things. "Having therefore received their orders, and being fully assured by the ressurrection of our Lord Jesus Christ, and established in the word of God, with full assurance of the Holy Ghost, they went forth proclaiming that the kingdom of God was at hand" (Ibid., ch. xli.—A. N. L., vol. i. p. 37). Here, then, we have authority of this very early writer for the statement that such was the view taken of the mission of Jesus by his original disciples.

Again, in the second epistle of Clement, this expression occurs:—"Let us expect, therefore, hour by hour, the kingdom of God in love and righteousness, since we know not the day of the appearing of God" (Second Ep. of Clement, ch. xii.—A. N. L., vol. i. p. 62). Thus it appears that the apostles received from Jesus, and the early Christians from the apostles, the doctrine that the return of the Messiah in his glory would take place soon,

SUBDIVISION 7.—*What are we to think of him?*

We come now to the most important question of all, namely, what opinion the evidence we possess should lead us to form of the moral character of Jesus, and of the value of his teaching. In considering this subject, we are met at the threshold of the inquiry by the extreme difficulty of discarding the traditional view which has gained currency among us. Not only believers in the Christian religion, but freethinkers who look upon Christ as no more than an extraordinary man, have united to utter his praises in no measured terms. His conduct has been supposed to present an ideal of perfection to the human race, and his aphorisms to embody the supreme degree of excellence and of wisdom. Some critics, not being Christians, have even gone so far as to assume that whatever items in his reported language or behavior seemed to reflect some discredit upon him could not be genuine, but must be due to the imaginations of his disciples.

All this unbounded panegyric naturally raises in the minds of critics who have freed themselves from the accepted tradition a slight prejudice against him, and this may lead them to regard his errors with too unsparing a severity, and to mete out scant justice to the merits he may really possess. No task can be less easy than that of approaching this question with a mind entirely devoid of bias on the one side or on the other. For my own part, I shall endeavor, if I cannot attain perfect impartiality, at least neither to praise nor to blame without adequate reason.

Before proceeding, however, it may be well to state that I shall not attempt to discriminate between the authentic and the unauthentic utterances of Jesus, but shall take for granted that his reporters—excluding the fourth Evangelist—have in the main reported him correctly. No doubt this position is not strictly true. There must be errors, and there may be grave errors in the record, since those who transmitted the language of their master trusted only to memory. But it is on the whole much more likely that the parables, sermons, and short sayings ascribed to Jesus represent with some approach to fidelity what he really said, than that they, or any considerable portion of them, were invented by any of his disciples afterwards. They have, moreover, a characteristic flavor which it would have been difficult for a forger to give to the fictitious utterances he might have added to the genuine remains. It is, however, a question of minor import whether the synoptical writers are or are not faithful reporters. Jesus is presented to our admiration by them as the Son of God, and as a pattern of virtue and of wisdom. Therefore, even if we are not criticising a portrait from life, we are at least criticising the ideal portrait which they have held up as an object of worship, and which Christendom has accepted as such.

Omitting (as already considered) those very considerable portions of his doctrine which refer to himself and to his kingdom, we may proceed to the more strictly ethical elements which are to be found scattered about in his instructions to his hearers, sometimes contained in those striking parables which, following the habit of his nation, he was fond of relating; sometimes in the short, clear, and incisive sentences of which he was a master. In considering the value and originality of his views, it will be of advantage to compare them, where we can, with those of other great teachers of mankind.

Perhaps one of the most conspicuous peculiarities is his fondness for impressive contrasts. He has a peculiar pleasure in contemplating the reversal of existing arrangements. The first are to be last; the humble exalted; the poor preferred to the rich; the meanest to become the greatest, and so forth. Strangely similar to this favorite idea, so continually making its appearance in his moral forecasts, is the language frequently used by his Chinese predecessor Laò-tsé, who in more than one respect greatly resembles him. Thus Jesus tells his disciples that he who is greatest among them shall be their servant, and that he who exalts himself shall be abased, while he who humbles himself shall be exalted (Mt. xxiii. 10, 11). Elsewhere he declares that if any man desire to be first, he shall be last, and servant of all (Mk. ix. 35). Presenting a child, to render his lesson the more impressive, he tells them that he who humbles himself like this little child is greatest in the kingdom of heaven (Mt. xviii. 4). Exactly in the same tone Laò-tsè observes that "the holy man places himself behind, and comes to the front;

neglects himself and is preserved " (T. t. k., ch. vii). Heaven, according to the same sage, does precisely as Jesus expects his Father to do in the kingdom of heaven. "It lowers the high, it raises the low. The way of heaven is to diminish what is superfluous, to complete what is deficient. The way of man is not this; he diminishes what is deficient to add it to what is superfluous " (T. t. k., ch. lxxvii).

On the same subject of humility, an opinion of the philosopher Mang, or Mencius, may be compared with one of Christ's. There was a strife among the disciples of the latter which should be accounted the greatest. Christ said: "The kings of the earth have dominion over them, and they who have authority over them are called benefactors. But be not you so: but let the greater among you be as the younger, and he that leads as he that serves " (Lu. xxii. 26, 26). Now Mang in like manner warns his disciples against the craving for authority. "Mencius said: 'The superior man has three things in which he delights, and to be ruler over the empire is not one of them. That his father and mother are both alive, and that the condition of his brothers affords no cause for anxiety; — this is one delight. That, when looking up, he has no occasion for shame before heaven; and below, he has no occasion to blush before men; — this is a second delight. That he can get from the whole empire the most talented individuals, and teach and nourish them; — this is the third delight. The superior man has three things in which he delights, and to be ruler over the empire is not one of them '" (Mang, vii. 1, 20 — C. C., vol. ii. p. 334). This definition of the pleasures of the high-minded man is quite equal of its kind to anything that has been said on the same subject by Jesus. It is true that Mang ranges over a somewhat wider field, and that therefore the sentences just quoted do not admit of exact comparison with anything coming from Jesus. But while both agree in reprobating the desire to exercise power, Mang goes beyond Jesus in proposing to substitute other interests for that of political ambition. And these interests are of the best kind. His "superior man" rejoices in the prosperity of his family, in the consciousness of his innocence of any disgraceful conduct, and in his opportunities of teaching those who are most worthy of his instructions and most likely to carry on his work. The latter is a pleasure which is rarely mentioned, and it shows much thoughtfulness on the part of the philosopher to have upheld it as an object in life.

Curiously enough, another Chinese sage has anticipated another of the best points in the doctrine of Jesus. Jesus enjoined his hearers not to practice charity in a public and ostentatious manner, like the hypocrites, "but when thou doest alms, let not thy left hand know what thy right hand doeth" (Mt. vi, 3). In this admirable maxim he would have had the support of all true Confucians, for one of their canonical writers had also told them that "it is the way of the superior man to prefer the concealment of his virtue, while it daily becomes more illustrious, and it is the way of the mean man to seek notoriety, while he daily goes more and more to ruin" (C. C., i. 295. — Chung Yung, ch. xxxiii. 1).

On another question, that of the admonition of an erring friend, Jesus gave an opinion which is in perfect accord with an opinion given by Confucius. If a man's brother trespass against him, he is first, according to Jesus, to take him to task in private; should that fail, to call in two or three witnesses to hear the charge; and should the offender still be obdurate, to inform the Church.* If his impenitence continue even after this, he is to become to him "as a heathen and a publican" (Mt. xviii. 15–17). Turning to the conversations of Confucius, we find the following: — "Tsze-kung asked about friendship. The Master said, ' Faithfully admonish your friend, and kindly try to lead him. If you find him impracticable, stop. Do not disgrace yourself '" (Lun Yu, b. xii. ch. 33. — C. C., i. 125). The steps inculcated by the two teachers are, making allowance for difference of country, almost identical.

The thoughts as well as the language of Jesus are often reproduced with singular fidelity in the sacred works of Buddhists. As the Buddha is, on the whole, the prophet whose character approaches most closely to that of Jesus, so we are almost certain to find in the literature of Buddhism nearly all the most exalted features of his ethical teaching. Thus Jesus praises the poor widow who contributes her mite to the temple

---

* The use of this word casts suspicion on the authenticity of the verse where it occurs.

treasury, because she has given all that she had. In one of
the numerous legends supposed to have been related by Sakyamuni an exactly similar incident occurs. A former Buddha was
traveling through various countries, accompanied by his attendant monks. The rich householders presented them with all
kinds of food as offerings. A poor man, who had no property
whatever, and lived by collecting wood in the mountains and
selling it, had gained two coins by the pursuit of his industry.
Perceiving the Buddha coming from a visit to the royal palace,
he devoutly gave him these two coins; his sole possession in
the world. The Buddha received them, and mercifully remembered the donor, who (as Sakyamuni now explained) was richly
rewarded during ninety-one subsequent ages (W. u. Th., p. 53).
The widow's mite is no less closely reflected in the following
anecdote from the same collection. In the time of a former
Buddha, a certain monk belonging to his train had gone out
to collect the offerings of the pious. He arrived at the hut
of a miserable couple, who had nothing between them but
an old piece of cotton-wool. When the husband went out to
beg, the wife sat at home naked in the hay; and when the
wife went out, the husband remained in the same condition.
To these people then the monk approached, crying out as
usual, "Go and prostrate yourself before Buddha! present
him with gifts!" It happened that the wife was wearing the
cotton-wool on this occasion. She therefore requested the holy
man to wait a little, promising to return. Hereupon she entered the house and requested the permission of her husband
to offer the cotton-wool to Buddha. He, however, pointed out
that as they had not the smallest property beyond this, extreme
inconvenience would result from the loss of it, for both of them
must then remain at home. To this she replied that they must
needs die in any case, and that their hopes for the future would
be much improved if they died after presentation of an offering. She then returned to the monk, and requested him to turn
away his eyes a moment. But he told her to give her alms
openly in her hands, and that he would then recite a benediction over them. The full delicacy of her situation had now to
be explained. "Except this cotton-wool stuff on my body I
have nothing, and no other clothing; since, then, it would be

improper for thee to behold the foul-smelling impurity of the female body, I will reach thee out the stuff from within. So saying she retired into the house and handed out her garment. When the monk delivered it to Buddha, it caused great offense to the king's courtiers, who surrounded him, on account of its being old and dirty. But Buddha, who knew their thoughts, said, "I find, that of all the gifts of this assembly, no single one surpasses this in cleanliness and purity" (W. u. Th., p. 150).

Not only in the case of the widow at the treasury did Jesus dwell upon the value of even trifling gifts made for the sake of religion. Another time he declared to those about him that whoever gave them a cup of cold water in his name, because they belonged to Christ, would not lose his reward. In Buddhist story the very same ideas are to be found; almost the same words. An eminent member of the Buddha's circle says that "whoever with a purely-believing heart offers nothing but a handful of water, or presents so much to the spiritual assembly or to his parents, or gives drink therewith to the poor and needy, or to a beast of the field;—this meritorious action will not be exhausted in many ages" (W. u. Th., p. 37).

The simile of fishing for men, employed by Jesus in his summons to Simon and Andrew, is likewise to be discovered in the works of the great Asiatic religion. The images of the Boddhisattvas, or Buddhas yet to come, frequently hold in their hands a snare, which is thus explained in the *Nippon Pantheon:*—"He disseminates upon the ocean of birth and decay the Lotus-flower of the excellent law as bait; with the loop of devotion, never cast out in vain, he brings living beings up like fishes, and carries them to the other side of the river, where there is true understanding" (B. T., p. 213). And in the book from which some illustrations have already been taken, it is said of a believer that "he had been seized by the hook of the doctrine, just as a fish, who has taken the line, is securely pulled out" (W. u. Th., p. 114).

Hitherto we have noticed a few of the minor points in the doctrine of Jesus, and while there has been little in these to object to, there has also been little to excite excessive admiration. The extreme exaltation of humility, and the evident anxiety to see, not equality of conditions, but a reversal of the actual inequalities, are not among the best features of his ideal system. We cannot but suspect something of a personal bias. Thus, in the parable of the Pharisee and the publican, aimed at a hostile and detested order, the publican is justified by nothing but his humility; while in that of Lazarus and Dives, Lazarus is eternally rewarded for nothing but his poverty. It is no doubt well to be humble, and we should be glad to see poverty removed; but it is not to be assumed that the Pharisee, conscious of leading an honorable life, is therefore a bad man; nor that the rich proprietor should be tormented in hell merely because he does not give alms to all the beggars who throng about his gates. When Jesus desires that virtuous actions should be done as quietly and even as secretly as possible, he inculcates an important principle of morals, and it is devoutly to be wished that we had among us more of this unconspicuous kindness, and less ostentatious charity. Where, however, he preaches on the virtue of bestowing alms on his disciples, he does but echo a sentiment which is natural to religious teachers in all ages, and to which, as we have seen, the emissaries of another and earlier faith, were equally alive. Passing from these comparatively trifling questions, let us consider some of his decisions on the greater moral problems with which he felt called upon to deal.

On a vast social subject — that of divorce — he pronounced an opinion which gives us a little insight into his mode of regarding that most important of all topics, the relations of the sexes. The Pharisees, it appears, came to him and asked him whether it was permissible for a man to put away his wife, Moses having allowed it. Jesus explained that this precept had been given for the hardness of their hearts. His own view was, that man and wife are one flesh, and that if either should leave the other, except on account of unfaithfulness, and marry again, that one would be guilty of adultery. This severe doctrine he supported by one of his short sayings: "What God hath joined together, let not man put asunder" (Mk. x. 1-12; Mt. xix. 1-12; and v. 31, 32). But surely this judgment assumes the very point at issue. The joining together in wedlock is ascribed to God; the putting asunder to man. But granting the sacredness of the marriage tie, it would still be no less possible to invoke the

divine sanction for its dissolution than for its original formation. And in many instances the maxim might be exactly
reversed. So unfortunate is the result of many marriages,
that it would be easy for a religious reformer to say of them,
with perfect sincerity, "What man hath joined together, let
God put asunder." There is, in fact, almost as much to be said
on moral grounds for the divorce of unhappy couples as for the
marriage of happy ones. Nor does Jesus by any means face the
real difficulties of the question by allowing divorce where either
of the parties has been guilty of adultery. This, no doubt, is
the exteme case, and if divorce is not to be given here, it can
be given nowhere. But why is adultery to be the sole ground
of separation? Why is an institution which may bring so much
happiness to mankind to be converted into one of the most fertile sources of human misery? Why, when both parties to the
contract desire separation, is an external authority, whether
that of opinion or of law, to enforce union? None of these
questions appear to have presented themselves to the mind of
Jesus. Supposing even that his decision were right, he assigns
no reasons for it, but simply lays down the law in a trenchant
manner, without giving us the least clue to the process by
which he arrived at so strange a conclusion. Nor is it in the
least likely that the many perplexities encompassing this, and
all other questions affecting the morals of sex, had ever troubled
him. His mind was not sufficiently subtle to enter into them;
and thus it is that, throughout the whole course of his career,
he lays down no single doctrine (if we except this one on
divorce) which can be of the smallest service to his disciples in
the many practical troubles that must beset their lives from
the existence of a natural passion of which he takes no account.

Another weak point in the system of Jesus is his aversion to
wealth and wealthy men, apart from the consideration of the
good or bad use they may make of their property. Thus, the
only advice he gives to the rich man who had kept all the
commandments was to sell everything he had and give the proceeds to the poor; a measure of very questionable advantage to
those for whose benefit it is intended. When the man naturally
declined to take this course — practically a mere throwing off of
the responsibilities of life — Jesus remarked that it was hard

for those who had riches to enter the kingdom of God. Seeing the amazement of his disciples, he emphasized his doctrine by adding that it was easier for a camel to pass through the eye of a needle than for a rich man to enter that kingdom. Hereupon his disciples, "excessively astonished," asked who then could be saved, and Jesus left a loophole for the salvation of the rich by the declaration that, impossible as it might be for men to pass a camel through a needle's eye, all things are possible with God (Mk. x. 17-27). A like *animus* against the wealthier classes is evinced in the story of the king who invited a number of guests to a wedding festivity. Those who had received invitations made light of them, one going to his farm, another to his merchandise, and so forth; or, according to another version, alleging their worldly affairs as excuses. Seeing that they would not come, the king bade his servants go out into the highways, and bring in whomsoever they might find; or, as Luke puts it, the poor, the maimed, the halt, and the blind (Mt. xxii. 1-10; Lu. xiv. 16-24).

More indiscriminately still is this averson to the rich expressed in the parable of Lazarus and Dives. Here we are not told that the great proprietor had been a bad man, or had acted with any unusual selfishness. The utmost we may infer from the language used about him is that he had not been sufficiently sensitive to the difference between his own condition and that of the beggar. But no positive unkindness is even hinted at. Nor had the beggar done anything to merit reward. He had only led one of those idle and worthless lives of dependence on others which are too common among Southern nations. Yet in the future life the beggar appears to be rewarded merely because in this life he had been badly off; and the rich man is punished merely because he had been well off (Lu. xvi. 19-25). A stronger instance of apparently irrational prejudice it would be difficult to find.

In connection with these notions about wealth there is a curious theory of social intercourse deserving to be considered. Jesus has expressed it thus: "When thou makest a supper or a dinner, do not invite thy friends, or thy brothers, or thy relations, or thy rich neighbors, lest they also should invite thee in return, and thou shouldst have a recompense. But when thou

makest a feast, invite the poor, the maimed, the lame, the
blind; and thou shalt be blessed because they have not the
means of making thee a recompense. For thou shalt be recompensed at the resurrection of the just " (Lu. xiv. 12–14). Nobody can object to charitable individuals asking poor people or
invalids without rank to dinner at their houses; indeed, it is to
be wished that the practice were more common than it is. But
we cannot admit that this kind action ought to be rendered obligatory, to the exclusion of other modes of conduct. Society,
properly speaking, cannot exist except by reciprocity. That
sort of friendly intercourse between equals which constitutes
society implies giving and taking; and it is eminently desirable that we should do exactly what Christ would forbid us
doing, namely, invite our neighbors and be invited by them as
circumstances may require. The fear that we may receive a
recompense for the dinner-parties we may give is surely chimer-
ical. Pleasantness and mutual advantage are alike promoted by
this reciprocity, which, moreover, avoids the discomfort produced when the obligation is wholly on one side. Jesus, in
fact, overlooks entirely the more intellectual side of society,
and dwells exclusively on the moral side. What he wishes to
establish, is not converse between men, but charity. So that a
person acting on his views would be excluded from the society
of those who might benefit him either materially or morally,
and would be confined to those whom he might benefit. Such
an arrangement would not in the end be good either for the
benefactors or the benefited.

His conceptions of justice are seemingly not more perfect than
his conceptions of social arrangements. The parable of the laborers is intended to justify the deity in assigning equal rewards
to those who have borne unequal burdens, and also to illustrate
his doctrine that the first will be last, and the last first. A
householder hires a number of laborers to work in his vineyard;
some of whom he engages in the morning, others later in the
day, others towards its close. All of them receive a denarium
in payment, though some had worked the whole day, and others
only an hour. At this result the class which had worked the
longer time grumble; but the householder defends himself by
appealing to the strict terms of his contract, by which he had

bound himself to give the same wages to all (Mt. xx. 1-16). No doubt the laborers who had borne the burden and heat of the day had no *legal* standing-point for their complaint; but the sentiment that prompted it was none the less a just one. Granting the validity of the master's plea that he had honorably fulfilled his bargain, it may still be urged that the bargain itself was not of an equitable character. Plainly, a sum which is adequate pay for an hour, is inadequate for ten or twelve; and that which is sufficient for a day is excessive for an evening. And the same argument applies to a future state. If, as is so often urged, it is to be a compensation for the sufferings of this state, then it ought to bear some proportion to those sufferings. But how can this be effected? Jesus saw the difficulty, and endeavored, but not successfully, to meet it by this parable.

But the imperfection of his sense of justice is nowhere more conspicuously shown than in the conduct he ascribes to God. To recur again to the case of Lazarus and Dives. Not only is the rich man punished with frightful torture, but his humble and kindly request that Lazarus might be allowed to warn his five brothers of their possible fate is met with a peremptory refusal. The only reason alleged for this cruelty is that they have Moses and the prophets, who certainly did not inform them that the mere possession of wealth or enjoyment of luxury was punished by everlasting misery (Lu. xvi. 27-31), In other places, too, the horrible doctrine of unending punishment is asserted by Jesus, and all the efforts of his modern disciples will not explain away this fact. The tares are to be bound up in bundles to be burnt. The wicked are to be cast into a furnace of fire, where there will be wailing and gnashing of teeth (Mt. xiii. 30, 42, 50). It is better to enter into life mutilated than to be thrown unmutilated into the fire (Mt. xviii. 8, 9) of hell which is never quenched (Mk. ix. 43-46). The servant who had made no money by usury is cast into outer darkness (Mt. xxv. 30). The righteous go into eternal life; the wicked to eternal punishment (Mt. xxv. 46). Blasphemy against the Holy Ghost cannot be forgiven, but involves eternal damnation (Mk. iii. 29). It is almost needless to observe that no wickedness could ever justify punishment without an end; that is, punishment for punishment's sake; and that the creation of human beings whose existence *terminated* in torture would be itself a far more terrible crime than any which the basest of mankind can ever commit.

There is one more point as to which his teaching will not bear investigation. It is the doctrine of the power of prayer. He tells his hearers, in the most absolute manner, that they will receive whatever they may ask in prayer, provided they believe (Mk. xi. 24; Mt. xxi. 22). Faith is the grand and sole condition of the accomplishment of all desires. This is the explanation of the withered fig-tree. It was faith that had wrought the change. By faith the disciples might effect not only such matters as the destruction of fig-trees, but far more stupendous miracles (Mt. xxi. 19–21). This is the explanation of the disciples' failure with the lunatic child. It was owing to their want of faith. Had they but faith as a grain of mustard seed — so Jesus told them — they would be able to say to a mountain, "Remove hence thither," and it would be removed. Nothing would be impossible to them (Mt. xvii. 20). And if they had faith themselves, if they really believed in their master's words, and ever attempted the experiment of working such transformations in nature, they must have experienced the bitter disappointment so graphically described by the authoress of "Joshua Davidson" in the case of that sincere Christian. But short of this extreme trial of the power of faith over matter, many generations of pious believers will bear sad witness to the fact that they have asked many things in prayer which they have *not* received; not least among the number being moral excellence, which they have but imperfectly attained. Yet this, it would seem, might be the most easily granted without interference with the physical universe. And if it be pleaded that no Christian has ever really succeeded in acquiring the degree of faith required to move mountains, what becomes of the promise of Jesus? Is it not a mere form of words, depending for its truth on a condition which human nature never can fulfill?

The opinions of Jesus on the question of the lawfulness of the tribute, and his reply to the Sadducean difficulty about due adjustment of matrimonial relations in a future state, have been already noticed. Neither of these decisions, it has been shown, can be regarded as evincing wisdom or depth of thought. On the other hand, his answer to the scribe who asked him which was the first commandment fully deserves the approbation which his questioner bestowed. After this, remarks the Evangelist triumphantly, no man dared to interrogate him. Passing from these isolated judgments, let us consider now the fullest exposition to be found anywhere of the moral system of Jesus,— the so-called Sermon on the Mount (Mt. v.-vii. inclusive). As reported by Matthew, this is a vast collection of precepts on many different subjects, delivered no doubt on many different occasions. Taken together, they contain the concentrated essence of his teaching, and offer therefore the fairest field for discussion and criticism. He opens his discourse with a series of blessings, in which his extreme fondness for contrasting the present with the future order is markedly exhibited. Those whom he selects as the objects of benediction are the poor in spirit; mourners; the meek; those who hunger and thirst after righteousness; the merciful; the pure in heart; the peacemakers; those who are persecuted for righteousness' sake; the disciples when reviled, persecuted, and unjustly accused. Of the nine classes of those who are thus blessed, five are composed of those whose present condition makes them objects of pity, and who are consoled with the assurance that they shall be rewarded in the kingdom of heaven. After this, the followers of Jesus are admonished that they are the salt of the earth, and that they must cause their light to shine before men. This is followed by that remarkable declaration (already noticed) as to the permanence of the law, and by a warning that, if they wished to enter the kingdom of heaven, their righteousness must exceed that of those odious people, the scribes and Pharisees.

Hereupon Jesus takes up three great commandments—not to kill, not to commit adultery, not to commit perjury—and proceeds to expand their meaning beyond the literal signification of the words. Thus, it had been said, "Thou shalt not kill." But he says, that whoever is angry with his brother shall be liable to the judgment; that whoever says "Raka" to his brother shall be liable to the Sanhedrim; but that whoever says "Fool," shall be liable to hell, or literally, to "the gehenna of fire." The punishment is of undue severity in proportion to the offense; but when, in the following verses, Jesus insists on the importance of doing justice to men before performing religious obligations, he speaks in the truest spirit of humanity, Proceeding to the commandment not to commit adultery, he enjoins an excess of self-discipline. It is *not* desirable to pluck out the right eye and cut off the right hand because they offend us, though it is well to train them to obey the higher faculties. The argument of Jesus rests only on the assumption that the sinful members, if not destroyed by such violent measures as this, may land the whole body in hell. Dealing next with the question of oaths, he enlarges the prohibition of perjury into a prohibition of all swearing whatsoever, assigning the strangest reasons for avoiding the employment, when taking oaths, of the names of various objects. They are not to swear by heaven, because it is God's throne; nor by the earth, because it is his footstool; nor by Jerusalem, because it is the city of the great king; nor by the head, because we cannot make a single hair black or white. Granting even that the advice is good, what is to be said of these reasons? What would be thought of a Member of Parliament using an exactly parallel argument: namely, that it is wrong to swear by the New Testament, because the person taking the oath cannot make a single type larger or smaller?

The theory embodied in the following verses occupies so cardinal a place in the philosophy of Jesus, that in order to do him justice they must be quoted at length. "You have heard that it has been said, An eye for an eye, and a tooth for a tooth. But I tell you not to resist evil; but whoever shall smite thee on the right cheek, turn to him the other also. And as for him who wishes to sue thee, and take thy coat, give him thy cloak also. And whoever shall compel thee to go one mile, go two with him. Give to him that asketh thee; and turn not away from him that wishes to borrow of thee. You have heard that it has been said, Thou shalt love thy neighbor and hate thine enemy. But I say unto you, Love your enemies, and pray for them who persecute you, that you may be sons of your father in heaven; for he causes his sun to rise on bad and good, and sends rain on just and unjust" (Mt. v. 38–45).

Perhaps there is no single point in the moral teaching of

Jesus which has been more celebrated than this. It is thought to represent the very acme of perfection, and Christianity takes credit to itself for the embodiment of so magnificent a doctrine in its moral system. And certainly the words of Jesus are so sublime as almost to extort admiration and disarm criticism. Nor would it at all detract from his merits if the principle here laid down should turn out to be no new discovery of his own, but one already reached by great teachers in other lands; for it was through him that it was made known to the Jews of his own age, and thus to the whole of Christendom. Moreover, we cannot suppose that he had ever heard of those who had anticipated the sentiments, and almost the words, of these beautiful sentences in the Sermon on the Mount. Nevertheless, these anticipations exist; and whatever glory this rule may confer on the religion of Christ must belong equally, and even by prior right, to the religion of Lao-tsze and the religion of Buddha. Thus Lao-tsze says, "Return enmity by doing good" (T. t. k., 63). Or again, "I treat the good man well; the man who is not good I also treat well" (Ibid., 49). The very perfection of patience under injustice, extending to the length of blessing those who curse, and turning the other cheek to those who smite the one — is exhibited in the old Buddhistic legend of Purna. Purna is a convert who spontaneously betakes himself as a missionary to a savage nation. The Buddha asks him what he will do if they address him in coarse and insolent language. He replies that he will consider them good and gentle people not to strike him with their fists or stone him. Should they strike him with their fists or stone him, he will still think them good and gentle neither to strike him with sticks or swords; should they strike him with sticks or swords, he will equally praise them for not killing him; should they even kill him, he will still say, "They are certainly good people, they are certainly gentle people, they who deliver me with so little pain from this body full of impurity" (H. B. I., p. 253). This is certainly a most consistent application of the principle of non-resistance to evil, and of loving one's enemies. No Christian saint or martyr could have followed his master's precepts more faithfully than this Buddhist apostle. But whether those precepts admit of general adoption into the scheme of human morals is a much more difficult question than whether in occasional instances here and there they have led to admirable conduct. Let us call in another Chinese philosopher to our assistance on this point.

The doctrine of returning good for evil, proclaimed, as we have seen, by Lao-tsze, was thus dealt with by his great rival, Confucius. "Some one said, 'What do you say concerning the principle that injury should be recompensed with kindness?' The Master said, 'With what, then, will you recompense kindness? Recompense injury with justice, and recompense kindness with kindness.'" How shall we decide between these authorities? None can question the nobility of the conduct enjoined by Jesus in certain instances. There are cases where the return of good for evil, of blessing for cursing, of benevolence for persecution, is not only the highest practicable virtue, but also the best punishment of the evil-doers. Nevertheless, there is great force in the observations of Confucius. If we are to reward injury by kindness, how are we to reward kindness? Is there to be no difference made between those who do us good and those who do us harm? To so pertinent a question we are compelled to answer that the practical results of such conduct on our part would be simply disastrous. Unkindness would not receive its natural and appropriate penalty, nor kindness its natural and appropriate reward. Not only should we ourselves be losers by our failure to resist injustice, but the worst classes of mankind would receive by that non-resistance a powerful stimulus to evil. Imagine, for example, that, instead of opposing an extortionate claim, we give up our cloak also to the man who wishes to take our coat. Plainly such conduct can have but one result. We shall become the victims of extortionate claims, and our property will be squandered among the undeserving instead of being kept for better uses. Or suppose that persecution for the sake of our opinions, instead of being met with armed resistance, wherever that resistance is likely to be successful, is received only with blessings showered on the heads of the oppressors; without doubt, the hands of the persecuting party will be strengthened, and liberty, which is everywhere the result of resisting evil, will never be established. The freedom we ourselves enjoy, both as a nation in respect of other nations, and as individuals in respect of our domestic government, is the consequence of acting on a principle the direct reverse of that laid down by Jesus. Our ancestors, who were good Christains but much better patriots, would have been amazed indeed at any attempt to persuade them to turn the left cheek to him who smote them on the right. A doctrine more convenient for the purposes of tyrants and malefactors of every description it would be difficult to invent.

At the same time it must be conceded that there is in it some truth, provided we discriminate between fitting and unfitting occasions for its application. It is not the violent man who assaults us, the unscrupulous man who sues us, or the persecutor who tramples on our freedom, who should be met by a benevolent return. But there are offenses of so personal a nature, affecting our individual interest so largely, and the public interest so slightly, that the best way of dealing with them may often be not to resent them, but to receive them with unruffled gentleness. Each person must judge for himself what are the cases to which this possibility applies. But the guiding rule in thus acting must be that we expect by thus returning good for evil to soften the heart of him who has done us wrong, and in the language of Paul to "heap coals of fire on his head." Should the effect be simply to relieve him from the penalty of our resentment without inducing him to change his course, we shall have done him a moral injury and society a material injury, and the probability or improbability of such result should be measured in deciding upon the conduct to be pursued. Properly guarded, and borne in mind as the occasional exception, by no means as the rule, the return of injustice or ill-will by benevolence and kindly feeling may be of the utmost value, both in cultivating the best emotions in those who practice it, and in calling forth the repentance of those towards whom it is practiced; but as a universal and absolute principle it must be utterly rejected. Lao-tsze and Jesus when they affirmed it undoubtedly struck one of the highest notes in human nature. Yet it must be granted that Khung-tsze took a wider view, and that his injunction to recompense injury with justice, and kindness with kindness, is more consistent with a philosophic regard for the interests of mankind, and with a practicable scheme of social ethics.

Jesus proceeds to enjoin his disciples neither to give alms, nor to pray, nor to fast in an ostentatious manner; and in connection with this excellent advice he teaches them the short prayer which has become so famous under his name. The clauses of this prayer may be worth some consideration. It begins with a formula of adoration addressed to "Our father in heaven." Then follows a petition full of meaning to Jesus and those to whom he imparted it, but of little or no signification in the mouths of the millions of modern Christians who daily repeat it: "Thy kingdom come." Jesus hoped, and his disciples caught the hope, that God's kingdom would come very soon; and this prayer was a request for the early realization of the glories of that kingdom. Those who then employed it believed that at any moment it might be granted, and that at no distant period it certainly would be granted. "Thy will be done, as in heaven so also on earth;" a clause embodying the popular conception of another region in which God's will is perfectly obeyed, while here it is met by some counteracting influence. "Give us this day our daily bread," for beyond the daily provision they were not to look; a doctrine which we shall notice shortly. "And forgive us our debts" (or, in Luke, our sins) "as we forgive our debtors; and lead us not into temptation, but deliver us from evil." Passing over the singular conception of God as leading men into temptation, let us rather notice the preceding petition, on which Jesus himself has supplied a commentary, that we may be forgiven, as we forgive others. In reference to this he tells his hearers, that if they forgive men their trespasses, their heavenly father will forgive theirs; and that if they do not thus behave, neither will he. A kindred doctrine is laid down in the beginning of the next chapter, where he tells them not to judge, that they may not be judged; that with what measure they mete, it shall be measured to them again. And this illustrated in another place by the parable of the servant who, having been excused from the immediate payment of a large debt by his master, refused to excuse a fellow-servant from the payment of a small one; whereupon his master flew into a passion, and "delivered him to the tormentors" (Mt. xviii. 23-35). There is an apparent justice and real emotional satisfaction in the harsh treatment of those who are harsh themselves. But we must not be misled by the immediate gratification we experience at the punishment of the unforgiving servant, supposing that it is right to mete out to each man the measure he metes out to others. Assuredly it does not follow that because a man is unjust or cruel, he should be treated with injustice or cruelty himself. Either it is right to forgive a man's sins, or it is not. If right, then his own harshness in refusing forgiveness to another is one of the sins which should be forgiven. If not right, then neither that nor any other offense should be forgiven by the supreme dispenser of justice. For what reason should the one crime of not forgiving those who trespass against us be selected for a punishment of such extraordinary severity, while it is implied that the penalty of other and graver crimes may by God's mercy be remitted? The fact is, that Jesus is misled by a false analogy between the conduct of one man towards another, in a case where he is personally concerned, and the conduct of a judge towards criminals. Offenses against morality are treated as personal offenses against God, who has therefore the same right to forgive them as a creditor has to excuse his debtor from payment. But in a perfect system of justice, human or divine, there could be no question of forgiveness at all. Every violation of the law would bring its appropriate penalty, *and no more*. The penalty being thus proportioned to the offense, there could be no question of that sort of "forgiveness" which implies a suspicion that it is, or may be, too severe. No doubt, the temper of the offender, and the probability of his repeating the crime, would be elements to be considered in awarding the sentence. But it must always be borne in mind that either the hope of complete pardon, or the threat of a punishment far heavier than is needed to deter, equally tend to neutralize the effects of our system of justice. And thus it has been in Christendom. The threat of everlasting torture, accompanied with the expectation of complete forgiveness, has been less efficacious than would have been the most moderate of earthly penalties, provided they had been certain. But Jesus was encumbered with a system in which there were no gradations. Thus he represents the deity now as extending complete forgiveness to sins which should have received their fitting retribution; now as visiting with immoderate severity offenses for which more lenient measures would have amply sufficed.

Proceeding to another subject, the speaker dwells upon the comparative unimportance of terrestrial affairs. He advises men not to lay up treasure on earth, but in heaven, for where their treasure is, there will their heart be also; and he goes on to say, "Take no thought for your life what you shall eat or what you shall drink, nor for your body what you shall put on. Is not the life more than nourishment, and the body than raiment? Look at the birds of the sky, for they sow not, neither do they reap nor gather into barns, and your heavenly father feeds them. Are you not much better than they? And which of you by taking thought can add a single cubit to his stature? And why do you take thought for raiment? Consider the lilies of the field, they toil not, neither do they spin: and I say to you that not even Solomon in all his glory was clothed like one of these. And if God so clothe the grass of the field which exists to-day and to-morrow is cast into the oven, will he not much more clothe you, O you of little faith?" Therefore his disciples are to take no thought about eating, drinking, or clothing (as the Gentiles do), for their heavenly father knows that they have need of these things. They are to seek the kingdom of God and his righteousness, and these will be added. They are to take no thought for the morrow, but let the morrow take thought for itself (Mt. vi. 25-34). Upon which extraordinary argument it would have been interesting to ask a few questions. In the first place, how did Jesus suppose that it had happened that men had in fact come to trouble themselves about food, drink, and clothing? Did he imagine that an inherent pleasure in labor had driven them to do so? Would he not rather have been compelled to admit that, not by any choice of their own, but just because their heavenly father had *not* provided these things in the requisite abundance, they had been forced to "take thought" for the morrow; all their primitive inclinations notwithstanding? Every tendency of human nature would have prompted men to take no thought either for food or raiment, had not hunger and cold brought vividly before them the necessity of doing so. But for this they would only have been too glad to live like the birds of the air or the lilies of the field. But let us examine a little more closely the reasoning of Jesus. Birds neither sow nor reap; God feeds them; therefore he will feed us without sowing or reaping. A more unfortunate illustration of the care of Providence for his creatures it would be difficult to find. Was Jesus ignorant of the fact that he feeds some birds upon others whom they seize on as their prey; and these again upon an inferior class of animals? So that, if he is careful of the hawk, it is at the expense of the dove; and if he is careful of the sparrow, it is at the expense of the worm. Cannibalism, or at least a recourse to wild animals as the only obtainable diet, must have been the logical results of the doctrine of Jesus. Not less singular would be the effects of his teaching as to clothes. The lily which remains in a state of nature is more beautifully arrayed than was Solomon. Granted; but does it therefore follow that we are to imitate the lily? We might agree with Jesus that nudity, alike in flowers and in human beings, is more beautiful than the most superb dressing: yet there are conveniences in clothes which may even justify taking a little thought in order to obtain them, and those who really omit to do this are generally the lowest types of the human race. That God would not give us clothing if we ourselves made no effort to obtain it, is not only admitted, but almost asserted, in the argument of Jesus; for he refers us to the grass of the field, which remains in its natural condition, as an example of the kind of raiment which our heavenly father provides. So absurd are these precepts, that no body of Christians has ever attempted to act upon them. Some there have been, indeed, who took no thought for the morrow, and who never exerted themselves to procure the necessaries of life. But then they lived in the midst of societies where these things were provided by the labor of others, and where they well knew that their pious indolence would not leave them a prey to hunger, but would rather stimulate the charitable zeal of their more secular brethren.

After laying down the rule against judging others, which has been already referred to, Jesus gives the excellent advice to those who would pull the mote out of their brother's eye to attend first to the beam in their own. This is followed by the proverbial warning not to cast pearls before swine. A singular passage succeeds, in which the doctrine is broadly stated that whatever men desire of God they are to ask it, "for every one who asks receives, and he who seeks finds." And it is added, that as they give their children good gifts, so their heavenly father gives good things to those who ask him. But what of those who do not ask him? Does he, like an unwise human parent, give most to those who are the loudest in their petitions, neglecting the humble or retiring children who make no noise? These verses allow us no option but to suppose that Jesus thought he did, and this inference receives strong confirmation from the parable of the unjust judge, who yielded to clamor what he would not give from a sense of justice (Lu. xviii. 1–5), as also from the illustration of the man who was wearied by the importunity of his friend into doing what he would not have done for the sake of friendship (Lu. xi. 5–9). In the former case, the parable is related for the express purpose of showing "that men ought always to pray and not to faint;" in the latter, the illustration is given in connection with the very verses which we are now criticising. There is, then, no escape from the conclusion that the conceptions Jesus had of the deity were of a nature to lead to the belief that God might be worried by continual prayer into concessions and favors which would not otherwise have been granted.

Excepting a single verse, the remainder of the sermon is occupied with a warning that the way to life is narrow, that to destruction broad; with a caution against false prophets, and a very fine description of the future rejection from heaven of many who have made loud professions of religion, and contrariwise, of the reception of those who have done their father's will, and whom he likens to one who has built his house upon the solid rock as distinguished from one who has built it on the sand. One verse, however, remains, and that not only the most important in the whole of this discourse, but ethically the most important in the whole of its author's system. That verse is the well-known commandment: "All things whatsoever you may wish men to do to you, thus also do you to them. For this is the law and the prophets" (Mt. vii. 12; Lu. vi. 31).

Whether Jesus perceived that in this brief sentence he was enunciating the cardinal principle of all morality is of necessity uncertain. But from the addition of the phrase "this is the law and the prophets," it is probable that he regarded it as a summary of the moral teachings of the religion he professed. If so, he has rightly laid the foundation of scientific ethics. Utilitarians, who believe that the object of morality is human happiness, may claim him (as one of them has already done) as the father of their system. While Kant, who gives the fundamental law, so to act that the rule of your conduct may be such as you yourself would wish to see adopted as a general principle, will be equally in agreement with him. Nor does it detract from the merits of Jesus that this very doctrine should have been announced in China about five centuries before he proclaimed it in Judea. He remains not less original; but we, while giving him his due, must be careful to award an equal tribute to his great predecessor, Confucius. Twice over did that eminent man assert the principle taught in the Sermon on the Mount. In the first instance, "Chung-kung asked about perfect virtue. The Master said, 'It is, when you go abroad, to behave to every one as if you were receiving a great guest; to employ the people as if you were assisting at a great sacrifice; *not to do to others as you would not wish done to yourself;* to have no murmuring against you in the country, and none in the family'" (C. C., vol. i. p. 115.—Lun Yu, xii. 2). Much more strikingly is this law enunciated in the second case. "Tsze-kung asked, saying, 'Is there one word which may serve as a rule of practice for all one's life?' The Master said, 'Is not RECIPROCITY such a word? What you do not want done to yourself, do not do to others'" (C. C., vol. i. p. 165.—Lun Yu, xv. 23). And we have another statement of the rule in the work ascribed to the grandson of Confucius, where he is reported to have said, "What you do not like when done to yourself, do not do to others" (Chung Yung, xiii. 3.—C. C., vol. i. p. 258). It is true, as remarked by the translater, that the doctrine is here stated negatively, and not positively; but practically this can make little difference in its application. Not to do to others what we wish them not to do to us would amount to nearly the same thing as doing what we wish them to do. Obviously it

prohibits all actual injury which we should resent if inflicted on
ourselves. But it also enjoins active benevolence; for as we do
not like the lack of kindness towards ourselves when in distress
or want, so we must not be guilty of showing such lack of kindness to others. Take the parable of the good Samaritan, told
in illustration of the kindred maxim to love our neighbors as
ourselves. Plainly we should not like the conduct of the priest
and the Levite were we in the situation of the plundered man.
And if so, the behavior of the good Samaritan is that which
the Chinese as well as the Jewish prophet would require us to
pursue.

Much more might be said of the doctrines of Jesus, but it is
time to bring this over-long section to a close. What answer
shall we now return to the query which stands at the head of
this final division. What are we to think of him? Is our judgment to be mainly favorable or mainly unfavorable? or must
it be a mixture of opposing sentiments? The reply may be
given under three separate heads, relating the one to his work
as a prophet, the next to his intellectual, and the last to his
moral character. Considered as a prophet, he forms one of a
mighty triad who divide among them the honor of having
given their religions to the larger portion of Asia and to the
whole of Europe. Confucius, to whom Eastern Asia owes its
most prevalent faith; Buddha Sakyamuni, whose faith is
accepted in the south and centre of that continent; and Christ,
to whom Europe bows the knee, are the members of this great
trinity not in unity. All three are alike in their possession of
prophetic ardor and prophetic inspiration. Two of them, the
Chinaman and the Jew, speak as the conscious agents of a
higher Power. The other, of whom his creed prevents us from
saying this, is yet represented in his story as predestined to a
great mission, becoming aware of that destiny at a certain
epoch of his life, and thenceforth feeling that no temptations
and no sufferings can induce him to swerve from his allotted
task. Of these three men it would perhaps be accurate to say
that Confucius was the most thoughtful, Sakyamuni the most
eminently virtuous, and Christ the most deeply religious. Not
that a description like this can be regarded as exhaustive.
Each trespasses to some degree on the special domain of the

others. Especially is it hard to compare the moral excellence of Jesus with that of Buddha. The Hindu, as depicted in his biographies, offers a character of singular beauty, and free from some of the defects which may be discerned in that of the Jew. History, however, was too much despised by these Oriental sectaries to enable us to form a trustworthy comparison. All we can affirm is, that, assuming the pictures of both prophets to be correctly drawn, there is in Sakyamuni a purity of tone, an absence of violence or rancor, an exemption from personal feeling and from hostile bias, which place him even on a higher level than his Jewish fellow-prophet. Supposing, on the other hand, that either picture is not historical, then it must be conceded that primitive Buddhism attained a more perfect ideal of goodness than primitive Christianity. Both ideals, however, are admirable, and they closely resemble one another.

Morally not unlike, Jesus and Sakyamuni have another point of similarity in a certain mournfulness of spirit, a sorrowing regret for the errors of human kind, and a tender anxiety to summon them from those errors to a better way. Each in his own manner felt that life was very sad; each desired to relieve that sadness, though each aimed at effecting his end by different means. Sakyamuni offered to his disciples the peace of Nirvana; Jesus, the favor of God and the rewards to be given in his kingdom. There is a striking similarity in the manner in which the summons to suffering humanity is expressed in each religion. Here are the words ascribed to Buddha: "Many, driven by fear, seek an asylum in mountains and in woods, in hermitages and in the neighborhood of sacred trees. But it is not the best asylum, it is not the best refuge, and it is not in that asylum that men are delivered from every pain. He, on the contrary, who seeks a refuge in Buddha, in the Law and in the Assembly, when he perceives with wisdom the four sublime truths, ... that man knows the best asylum, the best refuge; as soon as he has reached it, he is delivered from every pain " (H. B. I., 186). Still more beautifully is the like sentiment expressed by Jesus: "Come unto me, all ye that labor and are heavy laden, and I will give you rest. Take my yoke upon you and learn of me, for I am meek and lowly of heart, and you shall find rest unto your souls.   For my yoke is easy and my burden is light " (Mt. xi. 28-30).

While in tenderness and sympathy for human sorrow Christ resembles Buddha, in the nature of his moral precepts he sometimes resembles Confucius. The plain duties of man towards his fellow-man are inculcated in the same spirit by both, while in Buddhism it is generally the most extreme and often prodigious examples of charity or self-sacrifice that are held up to admiration.   Buddhism, moreover, teaches by means of long stories; Confucius and Jesus by means of short maxims. To a certain extent, indeed, Jesus combines both methods, the first being represented in his parables; but these are much simpler, and go far more directly to the point, than the complicated narratives of the Buddhistic canon.   On the whole, we may safely say that Jesus is certainly not surpassed by either of these rival prophets, and that in some respects, if not in all, he surpasses both.

Another comparison is commonly made, and may be just touched on here. It is that between the Hebrew prophet and the Athenian sage, "who," in the words of Byron, "lived and died as none can live or die." Without fully endorsing this emphatic opinion of the poet, we may admit that Socrates is not unworthy to stand beside Jesus in the foremost rank of the heroes of our race. He shares with the prophets who have been already named the inspiring sense of a divine mission which he is bound to fulfill. At all hazards and under all conditions he will carry on the special and peculiar work which the divine voice commands him to do. And this plenary belief in his own inspiration is not accompanied, as sometimes happens, by mental poverty. Intellectually his superiority to Jesus cannot be disputed. It is apparent in the very manner of his instruction. Socrates could never have enunciated the truths he had to tell in that authoritative tone which is appropriate to the religious teacher. Whatever knowledge he thinks it possible to acquire at all must be acquired by reasoning and inquiry; and must be tested by comparison of our own mental condition with that of others. Nothing must be assumed but what is granted by the hearer. Socrates would have thought that there was little gained by the mere dogmatic assertion of moral or spiritual truths. He must carry his interlocutor along with him; must compel him to admit his errors; must stimulate his desire of improvement by bringing him face to face with his own ignorance. Much as we must value the moral teaching of Christ, it must be confessed that the peculiar gift of Socrates is one of a far rarer kind. The power of inculcating holiness, purity, charity, and other virtues, either directly by short maxims (as in the Confucian Analects, in Mencius, or in Marcus Aurelius), or indirectly by stories (as in Buddhagosha's parables), is by no means so uncommon as the Socratic gift of searching examination into men's minds and souls. If Jesus is unsurpassed in the former — "primus inter pares" — Socrates is absolutely without a rival in the latter.

Whether the shock of the *elenchus* of Socrates, or the touching beauty of the parables and the Sermon on the Mount, produced the greatest benefit to the hearers is a question that can hardly be determined. The effect of either method must depend upon the character of those to whom it is applied. Outward appearances would lead us to assign more influence to the method of Jesus; for Socrates left no Socratics, while Christ did leave Christians to hand on his doctrine. But, in the first place, it may be confidently asserted that no lasting sect could have been formed upon the basis of the few truths taught by Jesus himself; and, in the second place, the fact that he became the founder of a new religion must be attributed as much to the state of Judea at the time as to his personal influence. That the influence of Socrates was not small in his own life-time might be inferred from the bitterness of the prosecution alone, even if Plato had not remained to attest the abiding impress he left upon an intellect by the side of which those of Peter, James, and John are but as little children to a full-grown athlete. We can imagine the havoc that would have been made in the statements and arguments of Jesus had Socrates met him face to face and subjected him to his testing method. How ill would his loose popular notions have borne a close examination of their foundations; how easily would his dogmatic assertions have been exposed in all their naked presumption by a few simple questions; how quickly would his careless reasoning have been shattered by the dialectic art which would have forced him to exhibit its fallacies himself before the assembled audience! But there was no one competent to the task, and when his opponents attempted to perplex him by what they thought awkward questions, he was able to baffle them without much trouble by his superior skill.

It is not, however, as an intellectual man that we must consider Jesus. He himself laid no claim to the character, and, if we would do him justice, we must judge him by his own idea of his function and his duties. So judging, there can be no question that we must recognize in him a man of the highest moral grandeur, lofty in his aims, pure in his use of means, earnest, energetic, zealous, and unselfish. No doubt he was sometimes misled by that very ardor which inspired him with the courage required to pursue his work. No doubt he suffered himself to forget the charity that was due to those who could not accept his mission nor bow before his preaching. No doubt he returned curse for curse, and hatred for hatred, with unsparing hand. Perhaps, too, he was sometimes the first to give way to angry passion, and to express in scathing words the bitterness he felt. Yet his failings are those of an upright and honorable character, and while they ought not to be extenuated or denied, neither ought they to outweigh his great and unquestionable merits. Appointed, as he believed, to a special work, he bravely and honestly devoted his powers to the fulfillment of that work, not even shrinking from his duty when it led him to the cross.

His unhappy end has cast its shadow over his life. He has been continually spoken of as "a man of sorrows and acquainted with grief." There is no reason to suppose that in any special sense he corresponded to the prophetic picture. Undoubtedly he had his sorrows; undoubtedly he was acquainted with grief. But unless there had been in his private life some tragedy of which we are not informed, those sorrows were .not of the bitterest, nor was that grief of the deepest. There is no doubt in his language a tinge of that sadness which all great natures who are not in harmony with their age must needs experience. He believed that he had great truths to tell, and he found his countrymen unwilling to receive them. Here was one source of unhappiness; and another he had in common with all who are deeply conscious of the miseries of human existence. But in no special or transcendent sense can he be termed a man of sorrows and acquainted with grief. So far as our evidence goes, he was exempt from the most terrible calamities that befall mankind. Free from all earthly ties but those of friendship with his chosen companions, he was not exposed to many of the anxieties and trials which afflict more ordinary men. Dying young, he did not suffer (so far as we know) from any serious illness, nor from the troubles, both physical and mental, that scarcely ever fail to beset a longer life. Bereavement, the most terrible of human ills, never afflicted him. Whether in his youth he had suffered the pains of unrequited love at the hands of some Galilean maiden we cannot tell. But there is nothing in his language or his career that would lead us to see in him an embittered or disappointed man.

Judging by the representation given in the Gospels, it does not appear that his life was in any special measure sad or gloomy. On the contrary, his circumstances were in the main conducive to a fair share of happiness. Surrounded by admiring friends of his own sex, and attended by sympathizing (perhaps loving) women, he passed from place to place, drawing crowds around him, speaking his mind freely, and receiving no inconsiderable homage. Granting that he had enemies, he was able until his prosecution to meet them on equal terms, and was not prohibited (as he would have been in most Christian countries until recent times) from proclaiming aloud his unorthodox opinions. True, this liberty was not allowed to continue for ever, but it was no small matter for him that it had continued so long. True, he suffered a painful death; but far less painful than many a humble martyr has undergone for his sake; far less painful even than those torturing illnesses which so often precede the hour of rest. Nor is it possible that his death could reflect its agonies back upon his life. His life, on the whole, seems to have been one, if not of abundant happiness, yet of a fair and reasonable degree of cheerfulness and of comfort. The notion that he had not where to lay his head is of course utterly unfounded. Not only had he his own house at Nazareth, but he had friends who at all times were happy to receive him. If he himself ever drew this sad picture of his desolation (which I doubt), he must have done it for a special purpose, and without regard to the literal accuracy of his words.

While, then, I see no proof of the peculiar sorrow ascribed to him on the strength of a prophecy, I freely admit that he had the melancholy which belongs to a sympathetic heart. His words of regret over Jerusalem are unsurpassed in their beauty. At this closing period of his career we may indeed detect the sadness of disappointment. And in the bitter cry that was wrung from him at the end, "My God, my God, why hast thou forsaken me?" we look down for a moment into an abyss of misery which it is painful to contemplate; physical suffering and a shaken faith, the agonies of unaccomplished purposes, and the still more fearful agony of desertion by the loving Father in whom he had put his trust.

But Jesus, though he knew it not, had done his work. Nay, he had done more than he himself intended. After-ages saw in him — what he saw only in his God — an ideal to be worshiped and a power to be addressed in prayer. We, who are free from this exaggeration of reverence, may yet continue to pay him the high and unquestioned honor which his unflinching devotion to his duty, his gentle regard for the weak and suffering, his uncorrupted purity of mind, and his self-sacrificing love so abundantly deserve.

CHAPTER VI.

VAST, and even immeasurable, as the influence has been which has been exercised on the course of human development by the great men of whom we have spoken, it has been equaled, if not surpassed, by the influence of the peculiar class of writings which we have grouped together under the designation of Holy Books. Of this, the last manifestation of the Religious Idea, it will be necessary to speak in considerable detail; both on account of its intrinsic importance, and because it is a branch of the subject which has not hitherto received the attention it deserves.

We have been far too much accustomed in Europe to treat the Bible as a book standing altogether by itself; to be admired, reverenced and loved, or, it may be, to be criticised, objected to and rejected, not as one of a class, but as something altogether peculiar and unparalleled in the literary history of the world. And, undoubtedly, if we compare it with ordinary literature of whatever description, whatever age, and whatever nation, this opinion is just. Neither in the poetry, the history, or the philosophy of any other nation do we find any work that at all resembles it. Nevertheless it would be a very rash conclusion to arrive at, that because in the whole field of Greek or Roman, Italian or French, Teutonic or Celtic literature, there is nothing that admits of being put in the same category with the Bible, therefore the Bible cannot be placed in any category at all. It is one of a numerous class; a class marked by certain distinct characteristics; a class of which some specimen is held in honor from the furthest East of Asia, to the extreme West of America, or, in other words, throughout every portion of the surface of the earth which is inhabited by any race with the smallest pretense to civilization and to culture. Wherever there is literature at all, there are Sacred Books. If in some isolated cases it is not so, these cases are exceptions too trifling in extent to invalidate the rule. Speaking generally we may say, that every people which has risen above the conditions of savage life; every nation which possesses an organized administration, a settled domestic life, a religion with developed and complex dogmas, possesses also its Sacred Books. If this truth has been too generally forgotton; if the Bible has been too commonly treated as something exceptional and peculiar which it was the glory of Christianity to possess, this omission is probably in great part due to the fact that the attention of scholars has been too much confined to the literature, the religion, and the general culture of the Greeks and Romans. From special circumstances these nations had no Sacred writings among them. Their religion was independent of any such authorities; and our notions of pagan religion have been largely drawn from the religions of Greece and Rome. But the Greeks and Romans were only an insignificant fraction of the Aryan race; and other far more numerous branches of that race had their recognized and authoritative Scriptures, containing in some portions those most ancient traditions of the original stock which entered into the intellectual property of the Hellenic family, in the form of mythological tales and current stories of their gods. We must not therefore be led by the example of classical antiquity to ignore the existence of these writings, or to overlook their importance.*

We may classify the Sacred Books to which reference will be made in this chapter as follows, proceeding (as in the case of prophets) from East to West:—

1. The Thirteen King, or Canon of the Confucians.
2. The Tao-tè-king, or Canon of the Taò-sè.
3. The Veda, or Canon of the Hindus.
4. The Tripitaka, or Canon of the Buddhists.
5. The Zend Avesta, or Canon of the Parsees.

* See on this subject the truly admirable remarks of Karl Otfried Muller, in his Prolegomena zu einer Wissenschaftlichen Mythologie (Gottingen, 1825), pp. 282-284.

6. The KORAN, or Canon of the Moslems.

7. The OLD TESTAMENT, or Canon of the Jews.

8. The NEW TESTAMENT, or Canon of the Christians.

The works included in the above list,—which are more numerous than might at first appear, owing to the vast collections comprised under the titles "Vedas," and "Tripitaka,"— are distinguished, as has been already stated, by certain common characteristics. It would be an exaggeration to say that all of these characteristics apply to each one of the writings accepted by any portion of mankind as canonical. This cannot be so, any more than the peculiar qualities which may happen to distinguish any given race of men can ever belong in equal measure to all its members. Hence there will necessarily be some exceptions to our rules, but on the whole I believe we may say with confidence that canonical or sacred books have the following distinctive marks:—

A. There are certain external marks, the presence of which is essential to constitute them sacred at all.

1. They must be accepted by the sectaries of the religion to which they belong as being either inspired, or, if the nature of the faith precludes this idea, as containing the highest wisdom to which it is possible for man to attain, and indeed a much higher wisdom than can be reached by ordinary men. Nor do those who accept these books ever expect to attain it. They regard the authors, or supposed authors, as enlightened to a degree which is beyond the reach of their disciples, and receive their words as utterances of an unquestionable authority. But wherever a divine being is acknowledged, these books are regarded as emanating from him. Either they have fallen direct from heaven and been merely "seen" by their human editors, as was the case with the Vedic hymns; or their contents have been communicated in colloquies to holy men by the Deity himself, as happened with the Avesta; or an angel has revealed them to the prophet while in a fit or a state of ecstacy, as Mahomet was made acquainted with the Suras of the Koran; or lastly, as is held to have been the case with the Jewish and Christian Scriptures, the mind of the writer has been at least so guided and informed by the Spirit of God, that in the words traced by his pen it was impossible he should err.

Such a conviction is expressly stated in the Second Epistle to Timothy, where it is said that "all Scripture is given by inspiration of God." And a claim to even more than inspiration is put forward in the Apocalypse, whose author first calls his work "the Revelation of Jesus Christ," which he says God sent to him by an angel deputed for the purpose, and then proceeds to describe voices heard, and visions perceived; thus resting his prophetic knowledge not on supernatural information communicated to the mind, but on the direct testimony of his senses.

2. With this theory of inspiration, or of a more than human knowledge and wisdom, is closely connected an idea of *merit* to be obtained by reading such books, or hearing them read. With tedious iteration is this notion asserted in the later works of the Buddhist Canon. These indeed represent the degeneracy of the idea. One of them is so filled with the panegyrics pronounced upon itself by the Buddha or his hearers, and with the recital of the advantages to be obtained by him who reads it, that the student searches in vain under this mass of laudations for the substance of the book itself (H. B. I., p. 536). A Sutra translated by Schlagintweit from the Thibetan, and bearing the marks (according to its translator) of having been written at a period of "mystic modification of Buddhism," promises that, at a future period of intense and general distress this Sutra "will be an ablution for every kind of sin which has been committed in the meantime: all animated beings shall read it, and on account of it all sins shall be wiped away" (B. T., p. 139). In another Sutra, termed the Karanda vyuha, a great saint is introduced as exhorting his hearers to study this treatise, the efficaciousness of which he highly exalts (H. B. I., p. 222 . Another speaker recites in several stanzas the advantages which will accrue to him who either reads the Karanda vyuha or hears it read (Ibid., p. 226). Such was the force of the idea that the mere mechanical reading or copying of the sacred texts was in itself meritorious, that, by a still further separation of the outward action from its rational signification, the purely unintelligent process of turning a cylinder on which sentences of Scripture were printed came to be regarded as equally efficacious. An author who has given an interesting account of these cylinders observes that, as few men in Thibet knew how to

read, and those who did had not time to exercise their powers,
"the Lamas cast about for an expedient to enable the ignorant
and the much-occupied man also to obtain the spiritual advantages" (namely, purification from sin and exemption from metempsychosis) "attached to an observance of the practice mentioned; they taught that the mere turning of a rolled manu-
script might be considered an efficacious substitute for reading
it." So completely does the one process take the place of the
other that "each revolution of the cylinder is considered to be
equal to the reading of as many sacred sentences or treatises as
are enclosed in it, provided that the turning of the cylinder is
done slowly and from right to left;" the slowness being a sign
of a devout mind, and the direction of turning being a curious
remnant of the original practice of reading, in which, as the
letters run from left to right, the eye must move over them in
that direction (B. T., pp, 230, 231). Similar sentiments, though
not pushed to the same extravagance, prevail among the Hindus. One of the Brahmanas, or treatises appended to the metrical portion of the Vedas, lays down the principle that "of all
the modes of exertion, which are known between heaven and
earth, study of the Veda occupies the highest rank (in the case
of him) who, knowing this, studies it" (O. S. T., vol. iii. p. 22).
Manu, one of the highest of Indian authorities, observes that
"a Brahman who should destroy these three worlds, and eat
food received from any quarter whatever, would incur no guilt
if he retained in his memory the Rig Veda. Repeating thrice
with intent mind the Sanhita of the Rik, or the Yajush, or the
Saman, with the Upanishads, he is freed from all his sins.
Just as a clod thrown into a great lake is dissolved when it
touches the water, so does all sin sink in the triple Veda"
(Ibid., vol. iii. p. 25). Reading the Holy Scriptures is with the
Parsees a positive duty. And these works, read in the proper
spirit, are thought to exert upon earth an influence somewhat
similar to that of the primeval Word at the origin of created
beings (Z. A. Q., p. 595). It is needless to speak of the importance attached among Jews and Christians to the reading and
re-reading of their Bibles, or of the spiritual benefits supposed
to result therefrom. It is worth remarking, however, that this
constant perusal of Holy Writ is altogether a different operation

from that of studying it for the sake of knowing its contents. People read continually what they are already perfectly familiar with, and they neither gain, nor expect to gain, any fresh information from the performance. And this is a species of reading to which among Christian nations the Bible alone is subjected.

The genesis of this notion is not difficult to follow. Once let a given work be accepted as containing information on religious questions which man's unaided faculties could not have attained, and it is evident that there is no better way of qualifying himself for the performance of his obligations towards heaven than by studying that work. Its perusal and re-perusal will increase his knowledge of divine things, and render him more and more fit, the oftener he repeats it, to put that knowledge into practice. But if it is thus advantageous to the devout man to be familiar with the sacred writings of his faith, it is plain that the attention he gives to them must be in the highest degree agreeable to the divinity from whom they emanate. For, to put it on the lowest ground, it is a sign of respect. It renders it evident that he is not indifferent to the communication which his God has been pleased to make. It evinces a pious and reverential disposition. Hence not only is the reader benefited by such a study, but the Deity is pleased by it. Or if the books are not conceived as inspired by any deity, yet a careful attention to them shows a desire for wisdom, and a humble regard for the instructions of more highly-gifted men who in these religions stand in the place of gods. Thus the action of reading these works, and becoming thoroughly familiar with their contents, is for natural reasons regarded as meritorious. But this is not all. An act which at first is meritorious as a means, tends inevitably to become meritorious as an end. Moreover, actions frequently repeated for some definite reason come to be repeated when that reason is absent. Thus, the reading of Sacred Books, originally a profitable exercise to the mind of the reader, is soon undertaken for its own sake, whether the mind of the reader be concerned in it or not. And the action, having become habitual, is stereotyped as a religious custom, and therefore a religious obligation. The words of the holy books are read aloud to a congregation, without effort or intelligence on their part, perhaps in a tongue which they do not

comprehend. Even if the vernacular be employed, there is not
the pretence of an effort to penetrate the sense of difficult passages. Holy Writ has become a charm, to be mechanically read
and as mechanically heard, and the notion of merit — arising in
the first instance from the high importance of understanding
its meaning with a view to practicing its precepts — now attaches
to the mere repetition of the consecrated words.

3. The exact converse of this unintelligent reverence for the
sacred writings is the excessive and over-subtle exercise of intelligence upon them. It is the common fate of such works to
be made the subject of the most minute, most careful, and
most constant scrutiny to which any of the productions of the
human mind can be subjected. The pious and the learned
alike submit them to an unceasing study. No phrase, no word,
no letter, passes unobserved. The result of this devout investigation naturally is, that much which in reality belongs to the
mind of the reader is attributed to that of the writer. Approached with the fixed prepossession that they contain vast
stores of superhuman wisdom, that which is so eagerly sought
from them is certain to be found. Hence the natural and simple meaning of the words is set aside, or is relegated to a secondary place. All sorts of forced interpretations are put upon
them with a view of compelling them to harmonize with that
which it is supposed they ought to mean. Statements, doctrines, and allusions are discovered in them which not only have
no existence in their pages, but which are absolutely foreign to
the epoch at which they were written. This process of false
interpretation is greatly favored by distance of time. When an
ancient book is approached by those who know but little of the
external circumstances, or of the intellectual and spiritual atmosphere, of the age in which it was composed, much that was
simple and plain enough to the contemporaries of the writer
will be dubious and obscure to them. And when they are determined to find in the venerable classic nothing but perfect
truth, the result of such conditions is an inevitable confusion.
Their own actual notions of truth must at all hazards be discovered in the sacred pages. The assumption cannot be surrendered; all that does not agree with it must therefore be suit-
ably explained.

Are proceedings or actions which shock the improved morality of a later age spoken of with approbation in the canoni.al
books? Some evasion must be d.scovered which will reconcile
ethics with belief. Are doctrines which the religion of a later
age rejects plainly enunciated, or statements of facts, which
later investigation has shown to be impossible, unequivocally
made? The inconvenient passages must be shown to bear another construction. Are there portions whose character appears
too trivial or too mundane to be consistent with the dignity of
works given for the instruction of mankind? These portions
must be shown to possess a mystical significance; a spirit hidden beneath the letter; profound instruction veiled under ordinary phrases. Are the dogmas cherished as of supreme importance by subsequent generations unhappily not to be found
in the text of Revelation? These dogmas must be read out of
them by putting a strain upon words which apparently refer to
some other subject. Perhaps, if they are not contained in
them *totidem verbis*, they may be *totidem syllabis:* or if not
even *totidem syllabis*, at least *totidem literis*. And the absence
of a letter (like the k in shoulder-knots) can always be got
over somehow. Lastly, are there palpable contradictions? At
whatever cost they must be explained away, for Holy Writ,
being inspired, can never contradict itself.

Let us consider a few of the most striking examples of these
methods of treatment. China, usually so matter of fact, has
manifested in this field a subtlety of interpretation not altogether unworthy of the more mystical India. The Ch'un
Ts'ëw, one of the books of the Chinese Canon, is a historical
compilation attributed to Confucius himself, and is therefore of
more than ordinary authority even for a Sacred Book. Concerning one of the years of which it contains a record, the following statements are made:—

"In the ninth month, on Kang-seuk, the first day of the
moon, the sun was eclipsed.

"In winter, in the tenth month, on Kang-shin, the first day
of the moon, the sun was eclipsed" (C. C., vol. v. p. 489.—Ch'un
Ts'ëw, b. 9, ch. xxi. p. 5, 6).

Two eclipses in such close proximity were of course an impossibility. Chinese scholars were fully aware of this, and

knew, moreover, that the second eclipse mentioned did not take place. A similar mistake occurred in another chapter, so that there were two unquestionable blunders to be got over. No wonder then that "the critics," as Dr. Legge says, "have vexed themselves with the question in vain." But one of them proposes an explanation. "In this year," he remarks, "and in the twenty-fourth year, we have the record of eclipses in successive months. According to modern chronologists such a thing could not be; but *perhaps it did occur in ancient times!*" (Ibid., vol. v. p. 491). Dr. Legge has italicized the concluding words, and put an exclamation after them, as if they embodied a surprising absurdity. But his experience of Biblical criticism must have presented him with abundant instances of similar interpretations of the glaring contradictions to modern science found in Scripture. Is it more ridiculous to suppose that the two eclipses might have occurred in two months than to believe that the sun stood still, in other words, that the revolution of the earth on its axis ceased for a space of time? or that an ass could be endowed with human speech? or that a man, instead of dying, could rise from earth to heaven? And if these and similar strange occurrences be explained as miracles, then such miracles "did occur in ancient times," and do not now. Or if it be attempted, as it is by interpreters of the rationalistic school to get over the difficulty by supposing a natural event as the foundation of the story — as one writer suggests that the descent of the Holy Ghost at Pentecost was a strong blast of wind — then European critics, like those of China, "vex themselves in vain."

No country, however, has done more than India, possibly none has done so much, in the peculiar exercise of ingenuity by which all sorts of senses are deduced from sacred texts. The Veda formed in that highly religious land the common basis on which each variety of philosophy was founded, and by which each was thought to be justified. Dr. Muir has collected a number of facts in proof of the diverse interpretations that found defenders among the champions of the several schools. In these facts, according to him, " we find another illustration (1) of the tendency common to all dogmatic theologians to interpret in strict conformity to their own opinions the unsystematic and not always consistent texts of an earlier age which have been

handed down by tradition as sacred and infallible, and to represent them as containing, or as necessarily implying, fixed and
consistent systems of doctrine; as well as (2) of the diversity of
view which so generally prevails in regard to the sense of such
texts among writers of different schools, who adduce them with
equal positiveness of assertion as establishing tenets and principles which are mutually contradictory or inconsistent" (O. S.
T., vol. iii. p, xx).

Exactly the same methods were applied to the sacred books
of Buddhism. "It is in general," says Burnouf, "the same
texts that serve as a foundation for all doctrines; only the explanation of these texts marks the naturalistic, theistic, moral
or intellectual tendency" (H. B. I., p. 444). To meet the case
of contradictions occurring in the Buddhistic Sutras a theory of
a double meaning has been invented. The various schools that
had arisen in the course of time did not venture to reject the
Sutras that failed to harmonize with their own opinions, as not
having emanated from Buddha, but maintained he had not expressed them in the form of absolute truth. He had often, they
thought, adapted himself to the conceptions of his hearers, and
uttered what was directly contradictory to his veritable ideas.
Hence his words must be taken in two senses; the palpable and
the hidden sense (Wassiljew, pp. 105, 329). As it has been with
the Chinese Classics, with the Veda, and with the Tripitaka, so
it has been with the Zend Avesta. Speaking of the progress of
scholarship in deciphering the sense of that ancient work, Professor Max Müller justly observes that "greater violence is done
by successive interpreters to sacred writings than to any other
relics of ancient literature. Ideas grow and change, yet each
generation tries to find its own ideas reflected in the sacred
pages of their early prophets, and in addition to the ordinary
influences which blur and obscure the sharp features of old
words, artificial influences are here at work distorting the natural expression of words which have been invested with a sacred
authority. Passages in the Veda or Zend Avesta which do not
bear on religious or philosophical doctrines, are generally explained simply and naturally, even by the latest of native commentators. But as soon as any word or sentence can be so
turned as to support a doctrine, however modern, or a precept,

however irrational, the simplest phrases are tortured and mangled till at last they are made to yield their assent to ideas the most foreign to the minds of the authors of the Veda and Zend Avesta " (Chips, vol. i. p. 134).

It is remarkable that almost identical expressions are employed by a Roman Catholic writer in reference to the efforts that have been made by theologians to discover the doctrine of the Trinity in the pages of the Hebrew Bible. I am glad to be able to quote an authority so unexceptionable as that of M. Didron for the proposition, that the poverty of the Old Testament in texts relating to the Trinity has caused the commentators to torture the sense of the words and the signification of facts. He adds the interesting information that artists, pushed on by the commentators, have represented the signs of the Trinity in scenes which did not admit of them. Thus, commentators and artists have united to find a revelation of the three persons of the Godhead in the three angels whom Abraham met in the plain of Mamre; in the three companions of Daniel who were thrown into the fiery furnace, and in other passages of equal relevance. No wonder, when such are the texts relied upon to prove the presence of this cardinal dogma, that M. Didron should observe that the Old Testament contains very few texts that are clear and precise upon the subject, and that in this portion of the Sacred Books we do not see a sufficient number of real and unquestionable manifestations of the Holy Trinity (Ic. Ch., pp. 514–517).

Perhaps, however, the most conspicuous instance of the power of preconceptions in deciding the sense of Holy Writ is the traditional interpretation of the Song of Solomon. In this little book, which is altogether secular in its subject and its nature, the love of a young damsel to her swain is described in peculiarly plain and sensuous language. But precisely because it was so plain was it necessary to find allegorical allusions under its rather glowing phrases. Hence such expressions as "let him kiss me with a kiss of his mouth; thy caresses are softer than wine," are held to refer to "the Church's love unto Christ," and an enthusiastic encomium passed by the Shulamite upon the physical perfections of her lover is called " a description of Christ by his graces." So, when another speaker, in

this case a man, flatters a women by enumerating the beauties
of her form, the feet, the joints of her thighs, the navel, the
belly, the two breasts so passionately praised by her admirer,
are thought in some mystic way to signify the graces of the
Church. A passage referring to a young girl not yet fully developed is made out to be a foreshadowing of "the calling of the
Gentiles," and the natural and simple appeal to a lover to
make haste to come is "the Church praying for Christ's coming."

Equal, or nearly equal, absurdities are found in the Chinese
interpretations of certain Odes contained in their classics.
These Odes are, like the Song of Songs, mere expressions of human love. But the critics find in them profound historical
allusions; history being the staple of the Chinese sacred books,
as theology is of the Hebrew ones. Now it happened in China,
as it has happened in Europe, that there was a traditional
meaning attached to this portion of the sacred books; and the
traditional meaning was embodied in a Preface which was generally supposed to have descended from very ancient times,
which came to be incorporated with the Odes, and thus appeared to rest on the same authority as the text itself. But a
Chinese scholar, named Choo He, who examined the preface in
a freer spirit than was usual among the commentators, formed
a very different opinion as to its age and its authority, He
believed it to be of much more recent date that was commonly
supposed, and by no means to form an integral portion of the
Odes. The prevailing theory was that the Preface had existed
as a separate document in the time of a scholar named Maou,
"and that he broke it up, prefixing to each Ode the portion belonging to it. The natural conclusion," observes Choo He, is that
the Preface had come down from a remote period, and Hwang"
(a scholar who, in one account, is said to have written the Preface) "merely added to it and rounded it off. In accordance
with this, scholars generally hold that the first sentences in the
introductory notices formed the original Preface which Maou
distributed, and that the following portions were subsequently
added. This view may appear reasonable, but when we examine those first sentences themselves we find some of them
which do not agree with the obvious meaning of the Odes to

which they are prefixed, and give merely the rash and baseless
expositions of the writers." Choo He adds, that after the pref-
atory notices were published as a portion of the text, "they
appeared as if they were the production of the poets themselves
and the Odes seemed to be made from them as so many
themes. Scholars handed down a faith in them from one to
another, and no one ventured to express a doubt of their
authority. The text was twisted and chiseled to bring it into
accordance with them, and nobody would undertake to say
plainly that they were the work of the scholars of the Han
dynasty" (C. C., vol. iv. Proleg., p. 33).

Ample confirma ion of the justice of Choo He's opinion will
be found on turning to the Odes and comparing them with the
notices in the Preface, which bear a family likeness to the
headings of the chapters in the Song of Songs. Here, for example, is an Ode :—

> "If you, Sir, think kindly of me,
> I will hold up my lower garments, and cross the Tsin.
> If you do not think of me,
> Is there no other person [to do so ?]
> You foolish, foolish fellow !"*

The second stanza is identical, with this exception, that the
name of the river is changed. Now this young lady's coquet-
tish appeal to her lover is said in the Preface to be an expression "of the desire of the people of Ch'ing to have the condition of the State rectified" (C. C., vol. iv. Proleg., p. 51).
Another Ode runs thus :—

> 1. "The sun is in the east,
>   And that lovely girl
>   Is in my chamber.
>   She is in my chamber;
>   She treads in my footsteps, and comes to me.
>
> 2. "The moon is in the east,
>   And that lovely girl
>   Is inside my door.

* C. C., vol. iv. p. 140.—She King, pt. i. b. 7, ode 13.

> She is inside my door;
> She treads in my footsteps, and hastens away."*

This simple poem is supposed by the Preface to be "directed against the decay [of the times]." Observe the theory that anything appearing in a sacred book must have a moral purpose. "The relation of ruler and minister was neglected. Men and women sought each other in lewd fashion; and there was no ability to alter the customs by the rules of propriety" (C. C., vol. iv. Proleg., p. 52). A commentator, studious to discover the hidden moral, urges that the incongruous fact of the young woman's coming at sunrise and going at moonrise "should satisfy us that, under the figuration of these lovers, is intended a representation of Ts'e, with bright or with gloomy relations between its ruler and officers" (C. C., vol. iv. p. 153, note). In another Ode a lady laments her husband's absence, pathetically saying that while she does not see him, her heart cannot forget its grief:

> "How is it, how is it,
> That he forgets me so very mnch?"

is the burden of every stanza. This piece, according to the Preface, was directed against a duke, "who slighted the men of worth whom his father had collected around him, leaving the State without those who were its ornament and strength" (C. C., vol. iv. p. 200, and the note.—She King, pt. i. b. 11, ode 7).

With such methods as these there is no marvel which may not be accomplished. And when, by the lapse of many centuries, the very language of the sacred records has been forgotten —as the Sanscrit of the Vedas was forgotten by the Hindus, the Zend by the Parsees, and the Hebrew by the Jews—the process of perversion is still further favored. The original works are then accessible but to a few; and when these few undertake to explain them in the ordinary tongue, they will do so with a gloss suggested by their own imperfect comprehension of the thoughts and language of the past.

These, then, may be accepted as the external marks of Sacred Books: 1. The unusual veneration accorded to them by the ad-

* C. C., vol. iv. p. 153.—She King, pt. i, b. 8, ode 4.

herents of each religion, on the ground that they contain truths beyond the reach of human intelligence when not specially enlightened; or in other words, the theory of their *inspiration*. 2. The notion of *religious merit* atttached to reading them. 3. The application to them of *forced interpretation*, in order to bring them into accordance with the assumptions made regarding them.

B. Passing now to the internal marks by which writings of this class are distinguished, we shall find several which, taken together, constitute them altogether a peculiar branch of literature.

1. Their subjects are generally confined within a certain definite range, but in the limits of that range there is a considerable portion which has the peculiarity that their investigation transcends the unaided powers of the human intellect. Almost the whole of the vast field of theological dogma comes under this head. The sublimer subjects usually dealt with, and not only dealt with, but emphatically dwelt upon, in the Sacred Books are, the nature of the Deity and his mode of action towards mankind; the creation of the world and its various constituent parts, including man himself; the motives of the Deity in these exercises of his power; the dogmas to be believed in reference to the Deity himself and in reference to other superhuman powers or agencies, whether good or bad; and the condition of the soul after death with the rewards and the punishments of vicious conduct. Coming down to matters of a less purely celestial character, but still beyond the reach of the uninspired faculties of ordinary minds, they treat of the primitive condition of mankind when first placed upon the earth; of his earliest history; of the rites by which the divine being is to be worshiped; of the sacrifices which are to be offered to him; of the ceremonies by which his favor is to be won. Here we move in a region which is at least intelligible and free from mysteries, though it is plain that we could not arrive at any certain conclusions on such things as these without divine assistance and superhuman illumination.

Lastly, the Sacred Books of all nations profess to give information on a subject the nature of which is altogether mundane, and with regard to which truth is accessible to all, inspired or uninspired;—the rules of moral conduct. These are, I believe, the main subjects which will be found treated of in the various books that lay claim to the title of Sacred. These subjects may be briefly classified as, 1. Metaphysical speculations as to the nature of the Deity. 2. Doctrines as to the past or future existence of the soul. 3. Accounts of the creation. 4. Lives of prophets or collections of their sayings. 5. Theories as to the origin of evil. 6. Prescriptions as to ritual. 7. Ethics. That this does not pretend to be an exhaustive classification, I need hardly say; other topics are treated in some of them to which no allusion is made, and all of these topics themselves are not treated at all. But they are those with which the Sacred Books are principally concerned; and more than this, they are those in the treatment of which these books are especially peculiar. One important feature both of the Chinese and the Jewish Canon is passed over, namely, their historical records. If these records were not exceptional appearances in sacred works, or if, though exceptional, they presented some essential singularity marking them off from all ordinary history, they should be included in the list of subjects. But as the Chinese Shoo King are perfectly commonplace annals of matters of fact; and as the Books of Samuel, Kings, and Chronicles are not otherwise distinguished from secular history than by their theological theories—in respect of which they are included under the previous heads—I see no reason to include history among the matters generally treated in Sacred Books. It is right, however, to note in passing that in these two instances it is found in them.

2. Since, however, it will be obvious to all that these great topics are discussed in many other works which have no pretention to be thought sacred, we must seek for some further and more definite criterion by which to separate them from general literature. And we shall find it in the *manner* in which the above-named subjects are treated. The great distinction between sacred and non-sacred writings in their manner of dealing with these great questions is the tone of authority, and if the expression may be used, of finality, assumed by the former. There is no appeal beyond them to a higher authority than their own. Having God as their author and inspirer, or being the product

of the supreme elevation of reason, they take for granted that human beings will not question or cavil at their statements. While other writers, when seeking to enforce the doctrines of any positive religion, invariably rest their contentions, implicitly or explicitly, on some superior authority, referring their readers or hearers either to the Vedas, the Koran, the Bible, the Church, or some other recognized standard of belief and would think it in the last degree presumptuous to claim assent except to what can be found in or deduced from that standard; while those teachers who are not the exponents of any positive, revealed religion, endeavor to prove their conclusions from the common intuitions or the common reasoning faculties of mankind; the writers of these books do neither. They seem to speak with a full confidence that their words need no confirmation either from authority or from reason. If they tell us the story of the creation of the world, they do not think it needful to inform us from what sources the narrative is derived. If they reveal the character of God, it is without explaining the means by which their insight has been obtained. If they lay down the rules of religious or moral conduct, it is not done with the modesty of fallible teachers, but with the voice of unqualified command emanating from the plentitude of power. Of their decisions there can be no discussion; from their sentences there is no appeal.

3. It corresponds with this character that Sacred Books should very generally be anonymous; or more strictly speaking, impersonal; that is, that they should not be put forward in the name of an individual, and that no individual should take credit for their authorship. Understanding the expression in this somewhat wider sense, we may say that anonymity is a general characteristic of this class of writings. Their authors do not desire to invite attention to their own personality, or to claim assent on the ground of respect or consideration towards themselves. On the contrary, they withdraw entirely from observation; they appear to be thoroughly engrossed in the greatness of the subject; and to write not from any deliberate design or with any artistic plan, but simply from the fullness of the inspiration by which they are controlled. Hence not only are the names of the authors in most cases completely lost to

us, but they have left us not a hint or an indication by which we could discover what manner of men they were. Even where the name of a writer has been preserved to us, it is often rather by some accident altogether independent of the book, and which in no way alters its anonymous character. We happen to know, on what seems to be good authority, that Laò-tsè composed the Taò-te-king, but assuredly there is not a syllable in the work itself which indicates its author. We happen to know beyond a doubt that Mahomet composed the Koran; but the theory of the book is that it had no human author at all, and it was put forth, not as the prophet's composition, but as the literal reproduction of revelations made to him from heaven. The most noteworthy exceptions are the prophets of the Old Testament and the Pauline, Petrine and Johannine Epistles of the New. But of the prophets, though their names are indeed given, the great majority are little more than a mere name to us; while large portions of the prophecies, attributed in the Jewish Canon to some celebrated prophet, are in reality the work of unknown writers. This is notoriously the case with the whole of the latter part of our Isaiah; it is the case with parts of Jeremiah; it is the case with Malachi (whose real name is not preserved); it is the case with Daniel.

The Pauline Epistles offer indeed a marked exception to the rule; and some of them are of doubtful authenticity. The Epistles of Peter, of John, of James and Jude, even if their authorship be correctly assigned, are of too limited extent to constitute an exception of any importance. The rest of the Christian Bible follows the rule. Like the Vedic hymns, like the Sutras of Buddhism, like the records of the life and doctrines of Khung-tsé, like the Avesta, all the larger books of the Bible—except the prophets—are anonymous. The whole of the historical portion of the Old Testament, the four Gospels, the Acts of the Apostles, the Epistle to the Hebrews, are—whatever names tradition may have associated with them—strictly the production of unknown authors. This characteristic is one of very high importance, because it indicates—along with another which I am about to mention—the spirit in which these works were written. They were written as it were unconsciously and undesignedly; not of course without a knowledge on the writer's part of what he was about, but without that conscious and distinct intention of composing a literary work with which ordinary men sit down to write a book. Flowing from the depths of religious feeling, they were the reflection of the age that brought them forth. Generations past and present, nations, communities, brotherhoods of believers, spoke in them and through them. They were not only the work of him who first uttered them or wrote them; others worked with him, thought with him, spoke with him; they were not merely the voice of an individual, but the voice of an epoch and of a people. Hence the utter absence of any apparent and palpable authorship, the disappearance of the individual in the grandeur of the subject. This phenomenon is not indeed quite peculiar to Sacred Books. It belongs also to those great national epics which likewise express the feelings of whole races and communities of men; to the Mahabharata, to the Ramayana, to the Iliad and the Odyssey, to the Volsungen and Nibelungen Sagas, to the Eddas, to the legends of King Arthur and his knights. These poems, or these poetical tales, are anonymous, and they occupy in the veneration of the people a rank which is second only to that of books actually sacred. In some other respects they bear a resemblance to Sacred Books, but these books differ from them in one important particular, which of itself suffices to place them in a different category. What that particular is must now be explained.

4. If I were to describe it by a single word, I should call it their *formlessness*. The term is an awkward one, but I know of no other which so exactly describes this most peculiar feature of Sacred Books. Like the earth in its chaotic condition before creation, they are "without form." That artistic finish, that construction, combination of parts into a well-defined edifice, that arrangement of the whole work upon an apparent plan, subservient to a distinct object, which marks every other class of the productions of the human mind, is entirely wanting to them. They read not unfrequently as if they had been carelessly jotted down without the smallest regard to order, or the least attention to the effect to be produced on the mind of the reader. Sometimes they may even be said to have neither beginning, middle, nor end. We might open them anywhere and close them anywhere without material difference. Sometimes

there is a distinct progress in the narrative, but it is nevertheless wholly without methodical combination of the separate
parts into a well-ordered whole. Herein they differ also from
those poetical Epics which we have found agreeing with them
in being virtually anonymous. Nothing can exceed the grace,
the finish, the perfection of style, of those immortal poems
which are known as Homeric. The northern Epics are indeed
simpler, ruder, far more destitute of literary merit. The first
part, for instance, of the Edda Saemundar (which perhaps
ought not to be called an Epic at all) is to the last degree
uncouth and barbarous. But then the subject-matter of this
portion of the Edda is such as belongs properly to Sacred
Books, and had it ever been actually current among the Scan-
dinavians as a canonical work — of which we have no evidence —
it would be entitled to a place among them. When we come
to the second or heroic portion of this Edda, the case is different. The mode of treatment is still rude and unattractive, but
if, unrepelled by the outward form, we study the longest of the
narratives which this division contains — the Saga of the Val-
sungs — we shall discover in it a tale, which for the exquisite
pathos of its sentiments, for the deep and tragic interest which
centres round the principal characters, for the vivid delineation
by a few brief touches of the intensest suffering, is scarcely
surpassed even by the far more finished productions of Hellenic
genius. No doubt the foundation of the story is mythological,
and this throws over many of its incidents a grotesqueness
which goes far in modern eyes to mar the effect. But the mythological incidents of the Iliad and the Odyssey are grotesque
also, and it requires all the genius of the poet to render them
tolerable. Apart from this groundwork, the Volsunga-Saga
treats its personages as human, and claims from its readers a
purely human interest in their various adventures. It relates
these adventures in a connected form, it depicts the feelings of
the several actors with all the sympathy of the dramatist, and
draws no moral, teaches no lesson. In the whole range of
sacred literature I recollect nothing like this. Stories are doubtless told in it, but we are made to feel that they are subservient
to an ulterior purpose. In the Old Testament and in the New,
they serve to enforce the theological doctrines of the writers; in

the works of the Buddhists they generally impress on the hearers some useful lesson as to the reward of merit, and the punishment of demerit, in a future existence. Of the genuine and simple relation of a rather elaborate romance, terminating in itself, there is probably no instance. Such stories as are related are moral tales, and not romances; and they are generally too short to absorb, in any considerable degree, the interest of the reader.

While this is the difference between secular and Sacred Books in respect of their narrative portions, the sacred are as a whole even more decidedly below the secular in all that belongs to style and composition. The dullest historian generally contrives to render his chronicle more lucid, and therefore more readable, than the authors of canonical books. In these last there is the most absolute disregard of artistic or literary excellence. Hence they are, with scarcely an exception, very tedious reading. M. Renan observes of the Koran that its continuous perusal is almost intolerable. Burnouf hesitates to inflict upon his readers the tedium he himself has suffered from the study of certain Tantras. The inconceivable tediousness of the Buddhistic Sutras — excepting the earlier and simpler ones — is well known to those who have read or attempted to read such works, as, for instance, the Saddharma Pundarika. The Chinese Classics are less repulsive, but few readers would care to study them for long together. The Vedic hymns, though full of mythological interest, are yet difficult and unpleasant reading, both from their monotony and the looseness of the connection between each verse and sentence. The Brahmanas are barely readable. The Avesta is far from attractive. The Bible, though vastly superior in this respect to all the rest of its class, is yet not easy to read for any length of time without fatigue. Doubtless, if taken as a special study, with a view to something which we desire to ascertain from it, we may without difficulty read large portions at a time; yet we see that Christians, who read it for edification, invariably choose in their public assemblies to confine themselves to very moderate sections of it indeed, while they will listen to sermons of many times the length. There can be little doubt that a similar practice is pursued in private devotion. Single chapters, or at most a few chapters, are selected; these are perused, and perhaps made the object of meditation; but even the most fervent admirers of the Bible would probably find it difficult to read through its longer books without pausing. They do not, so to speak, "carry us on." It was essential to dwell on this tediousness of Sacred Books, because it forms one of their most marked characteristics. Nor does it arise, as is often the case, from indifference or aversion on the part of the reader. Other books repel us because we have no interest in the subjects with which they deal. In these, the keenest interest in the subjects with which they deal will not suffice to render their presentation tolerable.

Section I. — The Thirteen King.*

Sacred Books in general are in China termed *King*. But as the Chinese Buddhists have their own sacred literature, and as Taou-ists are in possession of a sacred work of their founder, Laò-tsé, I call the Books of the State religion, that is, of the followers of Confucius, *the* King *par excellence*. For Confucianism is the official creed of the Government of China, and the Confucian Canon forms the subject of the Civil Service examinations which qualify for office. According to a competent authority, "a complete knowledge of the whole of them, as well as of the standard notes and criticisms by which they are elucidated, is an indispensable condition towards the attainment of the higher grades of literary and official rank" (Chinese, vol. ii. p. 48).

* In treating of the Sacred Books of the Confucian School in China, I rely entirely upon the admirable and (so far as it has yet gone) complete work of the Rev. Dr. James Legge. Although I have consulted other publications, I have not drawn my information from them, because it was at once evident that Dr. Legge's "Chinese Classics" was immeasurably superior to all that had preceded it on the same subject. Unfortunately, the very thoroughness of the work renders it voluminous; and it thus happens that the author has not fulfilled more than a portion of the promise held out at its commencement. It must be the earnest hope of all who are interested in these studies that the learned missionary will live to complete his design; meantime, we are obliged to confine ourselves to a notice of that portion of the Classics which he has translated. For Pauthier,s French translation of the Chinese Classics (in the Pantheon Litteraire: "Les Livres Sacres de l'Orient") embraces only that portion of the King which is to be found in the hitherto-published volumes of Dr. Legge.

The writings now recognized as especially sacred in China are "the five King," and "the four Shoo." * *King* is a term of which the proper signification is "the warp, the chain of a web: thence that which progresses equally, that which constitutes a fundamental law, the normal. Applied to books, it indicates those that are regarded as canonical; as an absolute standard, either in general or with reference to some definite object" (T. T. K., p. lxviii). In the words of another Sinologue, it is "the Rule, the Law, a book of canonical authority, a classical book" (L. T., p. ix). The word seems therefore on the whole to correspond most nearly to what we mean by a "canonical book." *Shoo* means "Writings or Books." The four Shoo, of which I shall speak first, are these: — A 1. The Lun Yu, or Digested Conversations (of Confucius). A 2. The Ta Hëo, or Great Learning. A 3. The Chung Yung, or Doctrine of the Mean. A 4. The Works of Mang-tsze, or Mencius. The five King are these: — B 1. The Yih, or Book of Changes (Noticed in Pauthier, p. 137). B 2. The Shoo, or Book of History. B 3. The She, or Book of Poetry. B 4. The Le Ke, or Record of Rites. B 5. The Ch'un Ts'ew, or Spring and Autumn, a chronicle of events from B. C. 721-B. C. 480. The oldest enumeration specified only the five King, to which the Yoko, or Record of Music (now in the Le Ke), was sometimes added, making six. There was also a division into nine King; and in the compilation made by order of Tâe-Tsung (who reigned in the 7th century A. D.) there are specified thirteen King, which consist of: † — 1-7. The five King, including three editions of the Ch'un Ts'ew. 8. The Lun Yu (A 1). 9. Mang-tsze (A 4). 10. The Chow Le, or Ritual of Chow. 11. The E Le, or Ceremonial Usages. 12. The Urh Ya, a sort of ancient dictionary. 13. The Heaou King, or Classic of Filial Piety. The apparent omission of the Ta Hëo (A 2) and the Chung Yung (A 3) is accounted for by the fact that both are included in the Le Ke (B 4). The only works

* Of which an English translation by David Collie, entitled "The Chinese Classical Work, commonly called the Four Books," was published at Malacca in 1828.

† Sir J. Davis (The Chinese ii. 48) reckons only nine King, those enumerated above. I presume that the remaining four enjoy an inferior degree of veneration.

which it is at present in my power to speak of in detail are those classified as A 1 to A 4, and as B 2.

The authenticity of these works is considered to be above reasonable suspicion; for though an emperor who reigned in the third century B. C., did indeed order (B. C. 212) that they should all be destroyed, yet this emperor died not long after the issue of his edict, which was formally abrogated after twenty-two years; and subsequent dynasties took pains to preserve and recover the missing volumes. As it is of course improbable that every individual would obey the frantic order of the emperor who enjoined their destruction, there appears to be sufficient ground for Dr. Legge's conclusion, that we possess the actual works which were already extant in the time of Confucius, or (in so far as they referred to him) were compiled by his disciples or their immediate successors.

SUBDIVISION 1.—*The Lun Yu.*

1. The first of the four Books is the Lun Yu, or "Digested Conversations." From internal evidence it seems to have been compiled in its actual form, not by the immediate disciples of Confucius, but by their disciples. Its date would be "about the end of the fourth, or beginning of the fifth, century before Christ;" that is, about 400 B.C. It bears a nearer resemblance to the Christian Gospels than any other book contained in the Chinese Classics, being in fact a minute account, by admiring hands, of the behavior, character, and doctrine, of the great Master, Confucius. Since, however, it contains no notice of the events of his life in chronological order, it answers much more accurately to the description given by Papais of the "λόγι" composed by Matthew in the Hebrew dialect than to that of any of our canonical Gospels.

Biographical materials may indeed be discovered in it; but they occur only as incidental allusions, subservient to the main object of preserving a record of his sayings. In the minute and painstaking mode in which this task is performed there is even a resemblance to Boswell's "Johnson;" as in that celebrated work, we have as it were a photographic picture of the great man's conversation, taken by a reverent and humble follower.

And as there is a total absence of that fondness for the marvelous and that tendency to exaggerate the Master's powers which so generally characterize traditional accounts of religious teachers, we may fairly infer that we have here a trustworthy, and in the main, accurate representation of Confucius' personality and of his teaching. As I have largely drawn upon this work in writing the Life of that prophet, I need not now detain the reader with any further quotations.

SUBDIVISION 2.—*The Ta Heo*

Passing to the Ta Hëo, or Great Learning, we find ourselves occupied with a book which bears the same kind of relationship to the Lun Yu as the Epistle to the Hebrews does to the Gospels. This work is altogether of a doctrinal character; and as in the Epistle, the exposition of the doctrines is by no means so clear and simple as in the oral instructions of the founder of the school. The Ta Hëo is attributed by Chinese tradition to K'ung Keih, the grandson of Confucius; but its authorship is in fact, like that of the Epistle, unknown. It was added to the Le Ke, or Record of Rites, in the second century A.D.

It begins with certain paragraphs which are attributed, apparently without authority, to Confucius; and all that follows is supposed to be a commentary on this original text. The text begins thus:—

1. "What the Great Learning teaches, is—to illustrate illustrious virtue; to renovate the people; and to rest in the highest excellence. . . . .

4. "The ancients who wished to illustrate illustrious virtue throughout the Empire, first ordered well their own States. Wishing to order well their States, they first regulated their families. Wishing to regulate their families, they first cultivated their persons. Wishing to cultivate their persons, they first rectified their hearts. Wishing to rectify their hearts, they first sought to be sincere in their thoughts. Wishing to be sincere in their thoughts, they first extended to the utmost their knowledge. Such extension of knowledge lay in the investigation of things."

After a few more verses of text, we come to the "Commentary of the philosopher Tsang," which is mainly occupied with what purports to be an explanation of the process described in the foregoing verses. For instance, the sixth chapter "explains making the thoughts sincere," the seventh, "rectifying the mind and cultivating the person;" until at last we arrive at the right manner of conducting "the government of the State, and the making of the Empire peaceful and happy." The object of the treatise is therefore practical, and the subject a favorite one with the Chinese Classics, that of Government. Great stress is laid on the influence of a good example on the part of the ruler; and those model sovereigns, "Yaou and Shun," are appealed to as illustrations of its good effect in such hands as theirs. In the course of the exposition of these principles, we meet with dry maxims of political economy, worthy of modern times, such as this:—

"There is a great course also for the production of wealth. Let the producers be many and the consumers few. Let there be activity in the production, and economy in the expenditure. Then the wealth will always be sufficient" (Ta Hëo).

Subdivision 3.—*The Chung Yung.*

The composition of the Chung Yung, or "Doctrine of the Mean," is universally attributed in China to K'ung Keih, or Tsze-sze, the grandson of Confucius. The external evidence of his authorship is, in Dr. Legge's opinion, sufficient; though if that which he has produced be all that is extant, it does not seem to be at all conclusive. Some quotations from it have already been made in the notice of Confucius, many of whose utterances are contained in it.

Its principal object is, or seems to be, to inculcate the excellence of what is called "the Mean," but the explanation of what is intended by the Mean is far from clear. The course of the Mean, however, is that taken by the sage; the virtue which is according to the Mean is perfect; the superior man embodies it in his practice; ordinary men cannot keep to it; mean men act contrary to it; and Shun, a model emperor, "determined the Mean" between the bad and good elements in men, "and employed it in his government of the people." The Mean, from the attributes thus assigned to it, would appear to be a state of complete and hardly attainable moral perfection, of which they who have offered an example in their conduct have (at least in modern times) been rare indeed. In the beginning of the treatise we learn that:—

1. "What Heaven has conferred is called THE NATURE; an accordance with this nature is called THE PATH *of duty;* the regulation of this path is called INSTRUCTION."

4. "While there are no stirrings of pleasure, anger, sorrow or joy, the mind may be said to be in the state of EQUILIBRIUM. When those feelings have been stirred, and they act in their due degree, there ensues what may be called the state of HARMONY. This EQUILIBRIUM is the great root *from which grow all the human actings* in the world, and this HARMONY is the universal path *which they all should pursue* (The italics, here and in future quotations, are in Legge).

5. "Let the states of equilibrium and harmony exist in perfection, and a happy order will prevail throughout heaven and earth, and all things will be nourished and flourish" (Chung Yung).

In another part of the work, "the path" is described as not being "far from the common indications of consciousness;" and the following rule is laid down with regard to it:—

"When one cultivates to the utmost the principles of his nature, and exercises them on the principle of reciprocity, he is not far from the path. What you do not like, when done to yourself, do not do to others" (Ibid., xiii. 3).

A large and important portion of the goodness required of those who would walk in the path is sincerity. Sincerity is declared to be the "way of Heaven" (Ibid., xx. 18), and it is laid down that "it is only he who is possessed of the most complete sincerity that can exist under Heaven, who can give its full development to his nature." Having this power, he is said to be able to give development to the natures of other men, animals, and things, and even "to assist the transforming and nourishing powers of Heaven and Earth," so that "he may with Heaven and Earth form a ternion" (Chung Yung, xx. 7).

The doctrine of "Heaven" as a protecting power holds no inconsiderable place in this short treatise. Thus it is stated that "Heaven, in the production of things, is surely bountiful to them, according to their qualities" (Ibid., xvii. 3). "In order to know men" the sovereign "may not dispense with a knowledge of Heaven" (Ibid., xxii). "The way of Heaven and Earth may be completely declared in one sentence. They are without any doubleness, and so they produce things in a manner that is unfathomable.

"The way of Heaven and Earth is large and substantial, high and brilliant, far reaching and long enduring"(Chung Yung, xxvi. 7, 8).

And in a very high-flown passage on the character of the sage — said to refer to the author's grandfather — he is spoken of as "the equal of Heaven" (Ibid., xxxi. 3).

Heaven, however, is not the only superhuman power that is mentioned in the Chung Yung. In one of its chapters we are told that Confucius thus expressed himself:—

"How abundantly do spiritual beings display the powers that belong to them!

"We look for them, but do not see them; we listen to, but do not hear them; yet they enter into all things, and there is nothing without them.

"They cause all the people in the Empire to fast and purify themselves, and array themselves in their richest dresses, in order to attend at their sacrifices. Then, like overflowing water, they seem to be over the heads, and on the right and left *of their worshipers*" (Chung Yung, xvi. 1-3).

This positive expression of opinion is scarcely consistent with the habitual reserve of Kung-tse on subjects of this kind (Lun Yu, vii. 20), and were it not that it rests apparently on adequate authority, we might be tempted to reject it as apocryphal.

SUBDIVISION 4.—*The works of Mang-tsze.*

The next place in the Chinese Scriptures is occupied by the works of Mang-tsze, the philosopher Mang, or as he is frequenty called, Mencius. Mang lived nearly two hundred years later than Confucius, having been born about 371, and having died in 288 B. C. He was not an original teacher asserting independent authority, and has no claim to the title of prophet. On the contrary, he was an avowed disciple of Confucius, to whose *dicta* he paid implicit reverence, and whom he quoted with the respect due to the exalted character which the sage had already acquired in the eyes of his school.

The so-called "Works of Mang" are not original compositions of this philosopher, but collections of his sayings, resembling the Lun Yu, or Confucian Analects. Whether he compiled them, or took any part in their compilation himself, is uncertain. But, considering their character, the more probable hypothesis seems to be that they were committed to writing by his friends, or disciples, either during his own life, or immediately after his death.

The evidence of their antiquity and authenticity must be very briefly touched upon. The earliest notice of Mang is antecedent to the Ts'in dynasty (255-206 B. C.), that is, within thirty-three years after his death. We are indebted for it to Seun K'ing, who "several times makes mention of" Mang, and who in one chapter of his works, "quotes his arguments and endeavors to set them aside." In the next place, we have accounts of him, and references to his writings, in K'ung Foo, prior to the Han dynasty, that is, before 206 B. C. Thirdly, he is quoted by writers from 186-178 B. C., under the Han dynasty. About 100 B. C. occurs the earliest mention now known of Mang's works. It emanates from Sze-ma Tseen, who attributes to Mang himself the composition of "seven books." While in a category of the date A. D. 1, the works of Mang are entered as being "in eleven books;" a discrepancy which has given rise to perplexities among Chinese scholars, with which we need not concern ourselves. Suffice it to say, that Mang's works, as we now possess them, consist only of seven books, and are not known to have ever consisted of more.

This evidence would appear to be sufficient to prove the antiquity of the collection, though not its Mencian authorship. Whoever may have been its author, it was not admitted among the Sacred Books till many centuries after it had been received among scholars as a valuable, though not classical, work. Under the Sung dynasty, which began to reign about A. D. 960-970, the works of Mang were at length placed on a level with the Lun Yu, as part of the great Bible of China.

On the whole, Mang's writings are of little interest for European readers, and I shall not trouble mine with any elaborate account of them. They are mainly occupied with the question of the good government of the Empire. What constitutes a good ruler? on what principles should the administration of public affairs be carried on? how can the people be rendered happy and the whole Empire prosperous? these are the sort of inquiries that chiefly engaged the attention of Mang, and to which he sought to furnish satisfactory replies. At the courts of the monarchs who received him, he inculcated benevolent conduct towards their subjects, with a paternal regard for their welfare, and sometimes boldly reproved unjust or negligent rulers. Holding, in common with the rest of his school, the doctrine of a superintendence of human affairs by a power named Heaven, he asserted in uncompromising terms the theory that Heaven expresses its will through the instrumentality of the people at large. "Vox populi, vox Dei," is the sentiment that animates the following passage, which contains one of the most courageous assertions of popular rights to be found in the productions of any age or country:—

"Wan Chang said, 'Was it the case that Yaou gave the empire to Shun?' * Mencius said, 'No. The emperor cannot give the empire to another.'

"'Yes;—but Shun had the empire. Who gave it to him?'

"'Heaven gave it to him,' was the answer.

"'Heaven gave it to him:—did *Heaven* confer its appointment on him with specific injunctions?'

"*Mencius* replied, 'No. Heaven does not speak. It simply showed its will by his personal conduct, and his conduct of affairs.'

"'It showed its will by his personal conduct and his conduct of affairs:—how was this?' Mencius' answer was, 'The empire [? emperor] can present a man to Heaven, but he cannot make Heaven give that man the empire. A prince can present a man to the emperor, but he cannot cause the emperor to make that

* Yaou and Shun are the ideal Chinese emperors, and belong to a mythical age. Shun was not the legitimate successor of Yaou, who had raised him from poverty, and given him his two daughters in marriage. On Yaou's death, his son at first succeeded him, and Shun withdrew; but the latter was soon called to the throne by the general desire.

man a prince. A great officer can present a man to his prince, but he cannot cause the prince to make that man a great officer. Yaou presented Shun to Heaven, and the people accepted him. Therefore I say, Heaven does not speak. It simply indicated its will by his personal conduct and his conduct of affairs.'

"*Chang* said, 'I presume to ask how it was that *Yaou* presented *Shun* to Heaven, and Heaven accepted him; and that he exhibited him to the people, and the people accepted him." *Mencius* replied, 'He caused him to preside over the sacrifices, and all the spirits were well pleased with them;—thus Heaven accepted him. He caused him to preside over the conduct of affairs, and affairs were well administered. so that the people reposed under him;—thus the people accepted him. Heaven gave *the empire* to him. The people gave it to him. Therefore I said, The emperor cannot give the empire to another.

"'Shun assisted Yaou in the government for twenty and eight years;—this was more than man could have done, and was from Heaven. After the death of Yaou, when the three years' mourning was completed, Shun withdrew from the son of Yaou to the south of South river. The princes of the empire, however, repairing to court, went not to the son of Yaou, but they went to Shun. Singers sang not the son of Yaou, but they sang Shun. Therefore I said, Heaven *gave him the empire*. It was after these things that he went to the Middle kingdom, and occupied the emperor's seat. If he had, *before these things*, taken up his residence in the palace of Yaou, and had applied pressure to the son of Yaou, it would have been an act of usurpation, and not the gift of Heaven.

"'This sentiment is expressed in the words of The great Declaration, — *Heaven sees according as my people see; Heaven hears according as my people hear*'" (The Italics are mine.— Mang-tsze, b. 5, pt. i. ch. v.)

Mang's notion of what a really good government should do is fully explained at the end of the first part of the first book, in an exhortation to the king of Ts'e. His Majesty, he observed, should "institute a government whose action shall all be benevolent," for then his kingdom will be resorted to by officers of the court, farmers, merchants, and persons who are aggrieved by their own rulers. The king must take care "to regulate the

livelihood of people," in order that all may have enough for
parents, wives, and children; for "they are only men of education, who without a certain livelihood, are able to maintain a fixed heart. As to the people, if they have not a certain livelihood, it follows that they will not have a fixed
heart. And if they have not a fixed heart, there is nothing
which they will not do, in the way of self-abandonment, of
moral deflection, of depravity, and of wild license. When they
have thus been involved in crime, to follow them up and punish them, — this is to entrap the people. How can such a thing
as entrapping the people be done under the rule of a benevolent man?" With a view then to their material and moral
well-being, mulberry trees should be planted, the breeding seasons of domestic animals he carefully attended to, the labor
necessary to cultivate farms not be interfered with, and "careful attention paid to education in schools." And it has never
been known that the ruler in whose State these things were
duly performed "did not attain to the Imperial dignity" (Mang-
tsze, b. 1 pt. i. ch. vii. p. 18–24). The only virtue required for
"the attainment of Imperial sway" is "the love and protection
of the people; with this there is no power which can prevent a
ruler from attaining it" (Ibid., b. 1, pt. i. ch. vii. p. 3). In accordance with his decided opinions as to the right of the people to be consulted in the appointment of their rulers, he advised the same king to be guided entirely by popular feeling in
assuming, or not assuming, the government of a neighboring
territory which he had conquered· "If the people of Yen will
be pleased with your taking possession of it, then do so. . . .
If the people of Yen will not be pleased with your taking possession of it, then do not do so" (Mang-tsze, b. 1, pt. ii. ch. x.
p. 3).

Mang was something of a political economist as well as a
statesman. There is in his writings a just and striking defense
of the division of labor, in opposition to the primitive simplicity
recommended by a man named Heu Hing, who wished the
rulers to cultivate the soil with their own hands. Mang's
answer to Heu Hing's disciple is in the form of an *ad hominem*
argument, showing that, as Heu Hing himself does not manufacture his own clothes or make his own pots and pans, but

obtains them in exchange for grain, in order that all his time may be devoted to agriculture, it is absurd to suppose that government is the only business which can advantageously he pursued along with husbandry, as Heu Hing desired (Mang-tsze, b. 1, pt. ii. ch. x. p. 3).,

It was not enough, however, in Mang's eyes that a sovereign should conduct the government of his country in accordance with the great ethical and economical maxims he laid down; he must also pay strict attention to the rules of Chinese etiquette. On some occasions Mang insisted even haughtily on the observance towards himself of these rules by the princes who wished to see him, even though one of his own disciples plainly told him that in refusing to visit them because of their supposed failure to attend to such minutiæ he seemed to him to be "standing on a small point" (Ibid., b. 3. pt. i. ch. iv). In fact the "rules of propriety" held in his estimation no less a place than in that of his Master and predecessor. It is gratifying, however, to find him admitting that cases may arise where their operation should be suspended. Indecorous as it is for males and females to "allow their hands to touch in giving or receiving anything," yet when "a man's sister-in-law" is drowning he is permitted, and indeed bound to, "rescue her with the hand." Nay, Mang in his liberality goes further, and emphatically observes, that "he who would not so rescue a drowning woman is a wolf" (Mang-tsze, b. 4. pt. i. ch. xvii. p. 1).

The most important doctrine of a moral character dwelt upon by Mang is that of the essential goodness of human nature, on which he lays considerable stress. According to him, "the tendency of man's nature to good is like the tendency of water to flow downwards," and it is shared by all, as all water flows downwards. You may indeed force water to go upwards by striking it, but the movement is unnatural, and it is equally contrary to the nature of men to be "made to do what is not good" (Ibid., b. 0, pt. i. ch. ii. pp. 2, 3). Yaou and Shun were indeed great men, but all may be Yaous and Shuns, if only they will make the necessary effort (Ibid., b. 6, pt. ii. ch. ii. pp. 1-5). "*Men's* mouths agree in having the same relishes; their ears agree in enjoying the same sounds; their eyes agree in recognizing the same beauty;—shall their minds alone be without that which they similarly approve. What is it then of which they similarly approve? It is, I say, the principles *of our nature*, and the determinations of righteousness. The sages only apprehended before me that of which my mind approves along with other men. Therefore the principles of our nature and the determinations of righteousness are agreeable to my mind, just as the flesh of grass [?-fed] and grain-fed animals is agreeable to my mouth" (Mang-tsze, b. 6, pt. i. ch. vii. p. 8). It ought not to be said that any man's mind is without benevolence and righteousness. But men lose their goodness as "the trees are denuded by axes and bills." The mind, "hewn down day after day," cannot "retain its beauty." But "the calm air of the morning" is favorable to the natural feelings of humanity, though they are destroyed again by the influences men come under during the day. "This fettering takes place again and again," and as "the restorative influence of the night" is insufficient to preserve the native hue, "the nature becomes not much different from that of the irrational animals," and then people suppose it never had these original powers of goodness. "But does this condition," continues Mang, "represent the feelings proper to humanity?" (Ibid., b. 6, pt. i. ch. viii. p. 2 . What some of these feelings are he has plainly told us. Commiseration, shame, and dislike, modesty and complaisance, approbation and disapprobation, are according to him four principles which men have just as they have their four limbs. The important point for all men to attend to is their development, for if they are but completely developed, "they will suffice to love and protect all within the four seas" (Ibid., b. 2, pt. i. ch. vi. pp. 5–7). And in another place he insists on the importance of studying and cultivating the nature which he asserts to be thus instinctively virtuous. "He who has exhausted all his mental constitution knows his nature. Knowing his nature, he knows Heaven.

"To preserve one's mental constitution, and nourish one's nature, is the way to serve Heaven" (Ibid., b. 7, pt. i. ch. i. pp. 1, 2).

The moral tone of Mang's writings is exalted and unbending, and evinces a man whose character will bear comparison with those of the greatest philosophers or most eminent Christians of the western world.

SUBDIVISION 5.—*The Shoo King.*

In this work are contained the historical memorials of the Chinese Empire. The authentic history of China extends, as is well known, to an earlier date than that of any extant nation. It possesses records of events that occurred more than two thousand years before the Christian era, although these events are intermixed with fabulous incidents. "From the time of T'ang the Successful, however," Dr. Legge informs us, "commonly placed in the eighteenth century before Christ, we seem to be able to tread the field of history with a somewhat confident step" (C. C. vol. iii. Proleg., p. 48). The exact dates, however, cannot be fixed with certainty till the year 775 B. C. "Twenty centuries before our era the Chinese nation appears, beginning to be" (Ibid., p. 90).

Without entering into the history of the text of the Shoo King, it may be stated that its fifty-eight books may probably be accepted as "substantially the same with those which were known to Seun-tsze, Mencius, Mih-tsze, Confucius himself, and others" (C. C., vol. iii. Proleg., p. 48).

Its earliest books—which must be regarded as in great part legendary—contain accounts of three Chinese Emperors—Yaou, Shun, and Yu—whose conduct is held up as a model to future ages, and who represent the *beau ideal* of a ruler to the Chinese mind.

These admirable sovereigns were succeeded by men of very inferior virtue. T'ae-k'ang (B. C. 2187), the grandson of Yu, "pursued his pleasure and wanderings without any restraint." An insurrection against his authority took place, and his five brothers took occasion to admonish him by repeating "the cautions of the great Yu in the form of songs." The first of these songs may be quoted as a good specimen of the doctrine of the Shoo King with reference to the imperial duties:—

"It was the lesson of our great ancestor:—
  The people should be cherished;
  They should not be down-trodden:
  The people are the root of a country;

The root firm, the country is tranquil.
When I look throughout the empire,
Of the simple men and simple women,
Any one may surpass me,
If I, the one man, err repeatedly:—
Should dissatisfaction be waited for till it appears?
Before it is seen, it should be guarded against.
In my relation to the millions of the people,
I should feel as much anxiety as if I were driving six horses with
 rotten reins.
The ruler of men—
How can he be but reverent *of his duty?* *

Many successive dynasties, comprising sovereigns of various characters, succeed these original Emperors. Throughout the Shoo King we find great stress laid on the doctrine, that the rulers of the land enjoy the protection of Heaven only so long as their government is good. Should the prince become tyrannical, dissolute, or neglectful of his exalted duties, the favor of the Divine Power is withdrawn from him and conferred upon another, who is thus enabled to drive him from the throne he is no longer worthy to fill. The emphatic and reiterated assertion of this revolutionary theory is very remarkable. Thus, a king who has himself just effected the overthrow of an incompetent dynasty, is represented as addressing this discourse to the "myriad regions:"—

"Ah! ye multitudes of the myriad regions, listen clearly to the announcement of me, the one man. The great God has conferred *even* on the inferior people a moral sense, compliance with which would show their nature invariably right (the same doctrine insisted on by Mang). *But* to cause them tranquilly to pursue the course which it would indicate, is the work of the sovereign.

"The king of Hea (the monarch whom the speaker had superseded,) extinguished his virtue and played the tyrant, extending his oppression over you, the people of the myriad regions. Suffering from his cruel injuries, and unable to endure the wormwood and poison, you protested with one accord your

* Shoo King, b. 3, pt. iii. ch. i. pp. 6, 7.

innocence to the spirits of heaven and earth. The way of Heaven is to bless the good and punish the bad. It sent down calamities on *the House of* Hea, to make manifest its crimes.

"Therefore I, the little child, charged with the decree of Heaven and its bright terrors, did not dare to forgive *the criminal*. I presume to use a dark-colored victim, and making clear announcement to the spiritual Sovereign of the high heavens, requested leave to deal with the ruler of Hea as a criminal. Then I sought for the great sage, with whom I might unite my strength, to request the favor of Heaven on behalf of you, my multitudes. High Heaven truly showed its favor to the inferior people, and the criminal has been degraded .and subjected " (Shoo King, iv. 3. 2).

It is true that this speech, proceeding from an interested party naturally anxious to set his own conduct in the fairest light, is liable to suspicion, But there is abundant evidence in the pages of the Shoo King that the views expressed above were participated in by its writers, who constantly hold the fate that befalls wicked Emperors as a punishment from Heaven, and laud those who effect their own downfall as Heaven's agents. They also frequently introduce sage advisers who reprove the reigning Emperor for his faults, and admonish him to walk in the ways of virtue in a spirit of the utmost frankness. One of these monarchs candidly confesses the benefit he has derived from the instructions of such a counselor, whose lessons have led him to effect a complete reformation of his character (Ibid., iv. 5. pt. ii). Another charged his minister to be constantly presenting instructions to aid his virtue, and to act towards him as medicine which should cure his sickness (Ibid., iv. 8. pt. i. 5-8). If, however, a dynasty persisted in its evil courses, in spite of all the warnings it might receive, it was doomed to perish. Losing the attachment of the people, it fell undefended and unregretted. Such was the case with the house of Yin. The Viscount of Wei, who is stated by old authorities to have been a brother of the Emperor, thus described its career:—

"The Viscount of Wei spoke to the following effect:— 'Grand Tutor and Junior Tutor, *the House of* Yin, we may conclude, can no longer exercise rule over the four quarters of the empire. The great deeds of our founder were displayed in for-

mer ages, but by our being lost and maddened with wine, we
have destroyed *the effects of* his virtue, in these after times.
The people of Yin, small and great, are given to highway robberies, villainies, and treachery. The nobles and officers imitate one another in violating the laws; and for criminals there
is no certainty that they will be apprehended. The lesser people
consequently rise up, and make violent outrages on one another.
The dynasty of Yin is now sinking in ruin;—its condition is
like that of one crossing a large stream, who can find neither
ford nor bank. That Yin should be hurrying to ruin at the
present pace!'—

"He added, 'Grand Tutor and Junior Tutor, we are mani-
festing insanity. The venerable of our families have withdrawn
to the wilds; and now you indicate nothing, but tell me of the
impending ruin;—what is to be done?'

"The Grand Tutor made about the following reply:—'King's
son, Heaven in anger is sending down calamities, and wasting
the country of Yin.'" And after mentioning the crimes of the
Emperor, he proceeds:—"'When ruin overtakes Shang, I will
not be the servant *of another dynasty. But* I tell you, O king's
son, to go away as being the course *for you.* . . . Let us
rest quietly in our several parts, and present ourselves to the
former kings. I do not think of making my escape'" (Shoo
King, iv. 11).

In another portion of the Shoo the causes which lead to the
preservation or loss of Heaven's favor are thus described by
"The Duke of Chow:"—"The favor of Heaven is not easily preserved. Heaven is hard to be depended on. Men lose its favoring appointment because they cannot pursue and carry out
the reverence and brilliant virtue of their forefathers." Again:
—"Heaven is not to be trusted. Our course is simply to seek
the prolongation of the virtue of the Tranquilizing king, and
Heaven will not find occasion to remove its favoring decree
which King Wan received" (Shoo King, xvi. 1).

The paramount importance to the national welfare of a wise
selection of ministers and officials receives its full share of
attention in the Chinese Bible. The Duke of Ts'in, another
province of the Empire, is represented as speaking thus:—

"I have deeply thought and concluded;—Let me have but

one resolute minister, plain and sincere, without other abilities, but having a simple, complacent mind, and possessed of generosity, regarding the talents of others, as if he himself possessed them: and when he finds accomplished and sage-like men, loving them in his heart more than his mouth expresses, really showing himself able to bear them:—such a minister would be able to preserve my descendants and my people, and would indeed be a giver of benefits' (Shoo King, v. 30. See also v. 19. 2).

These extracts, without giving an adequate notion of the very miscellaneous contents of the Shoo King, a work which could not be accomplished without an undue extension of the subdivision referring to it, will serve to show that its moral tone on matters relating to the government of a nation is not inferior to that of any of the productions of classical or Hebrew antiquity.

Subdivision 6. — *The She King.*

Whatever sanctity or authority may attach to the She King in the minds of the Chinese, must belong to it solely on account of its antiquity, for there is certainly nothing in the character of its contents that should entitle it to a place in the consecrated literature of a nation. Similar phenomena, however, are not unknown among more devout races than the Chinese. Thus the Hebrews admitted into their Canon the Books of Ruth and Esther, and the Song of Solomon, which contain but little of an edifying nature, though full of human interest. The same may be said of the She King. The play of human emotions is vividly represented in it, but there is not much in which moral or religious lessons are to be found, except by doing violence to the text.

The She King is a collection of ancient poems. Tradition attributes the arrangement and selection of the Odes now contained in it to Confucius, who is supposed to have selected them in accordance with some wise design from a much larger number. The present translator, however, assigns reasons for rejecting this tradition, and for believing that the She King was current in China long before his time in a form not very different from that in which we now possess it. At the present day,

its songs have not lost their ancient popularity, for it is stated
that they are "the favorite study of the better informed at the
present remote period. Every well-educated Chinese has the
most celebrated pieces by heart, and there are constant allusions
to them in modern poetry and writings of all kinds" (Davis'
Chinese, ii. 60).

The poems, which were collected from many different prov-
inces, relate to a great variety of subjects. Some are political,
some domestic, some sacrificial, others festive. We have rulers
addressing the princes of their kingdom in laudatory terms, and
princes in their turn extolling the ruler; complaints of unem-
ployed politicians, and groans from oppressed subjects; husbands deploring their absence from their wives on military service; forlorn wives longing for the return of absent husbands;
stanzas written by lovers to their mistresses, and maidens' in-
vocations of their lovers; along with a few allusions to amatory
transactions of a more questionable character. All these miscellaneous matters are treated in short, simple, and rather monotonous poems, which, if they have any beauty in the original,
have completely lost it in the process of translation. There is
sometimes pathos in the feelings uttered; but the expressions
are of the most direct and unornamental kind, and the whole
book partakes largely of that artlessness which we have noted
as one of the ordinary marks of Sacred Books.

A few specimens will suffice. Here is the "protest of a
widow against being urged to marry again:"—

1. "It floats about, that boat of cypress wood,
　　There in the middle of the Ho.
　　With his two tufts of hair falling over his forehead;
　　He was my mate;
　　And I swear that till death I will have no other.
　　O mother, O Heaven,
　　Why will you not understand me?

2. "It floats about, that boat of cypress wood,
　　There by the side of the Ho.
　　With his two tufts of hair falling over his forehead;
　　He was my only one;

And I swear that till death I will not do the evil thing.
O mother, O Heaven,
Why will you not understand me?"*

In the following lines a young lady begs her lover to be
more cautious in his advances, and that in a tone which may
remind us of Nausikaa's request to Odysseus to walk at some
distance behind her, lest the busybodies of the town should take
occasion to gossip:—

1. "I pray you, Mr. Chung,
  Do not come leaping into my hamlet;
  Do not break my willow-trees.
  Do I care for them?
  But I fear my parents.
  You, O Chung, are to be loved,
  But the words of my parents
  Are also to be feared.

2. " I pray you; Mr. Chung,
  Do not come leaping over my wall;
  Do not break my mulberry-trees.
  Do I care for them?
  But I fear the words of my brothers.
  You, O Chung, are to be loved,
  But the words of my brothers
  Are also to be feared.

3. " I pray you, Mr. Chung,
  Do not come leaping into my garden;
  Do not break my sandal-trees.
  Do I care for them?
  But I dread the talk of people,
  You, O Chung, are to be loved,
  But the talk of people
  Is also to be feared."†

The following Ode, conceived in a different spirit, will serve
to illustrate one of the most prominent features of Chinese

* She King, i. 4. 1.   † She King, i. 7. 2.

character as depicted in these ancient books,—its filial piety.
It is supposed to be the composition of a young monarch who
has just succeeded to the government of his kingdom:—

> "Alas for me, who am [as] a little child,
> On whom has devolved the unsettled State !
> Solitary am I and full of distress.
> Oh my great Father,
> All thy life long, thou wast filial.

> "Thou didst think of my great grandfather,
> [Seeing him, as it were] ascending and descending in the court.
> I, the little child,*
> Day and night will be so reverent.
> "Oh ye great kings,
> As your successor, I will strive not to forget you."†

SUBDIVISION 7.—*The Ch'un Tsew.*

According to Chinese tradition, the Ch'un Ts'ëw, or Spring
and Autumn, was the production of Confucius himself; not
indeed his original composition, but a compilation made by him
from preëxisting sources. The title of Ch'un Ts'ëw was not of
his own making. It was the name already in use for the annals
of the several States. The annals were arranged under the four
seasons of each year, and then two of the seasons—Spring and
Autumn—were used as an abbreviated term for all the four.
And so strictly is this principle of parceling out the annals of
each year under the several seasons adhered to in the work,
that even when there is no event to be recorded we have such
entries as these: "It was summer, the fourth month." "It
was winter, the tenth month."

The classical Ch'un Ts'ëw was compiled from the Ch'un
Ts'ëw of the State of Loo. It is even doubtful whether Confucius did anything more than copy what he found in the annals
of that country. Dr. Legge evidently inclines to the belief that

---

* Not literally a child. "Little child" is the usual style of Chinese
rulers when designing to express feelings of modesty and religious reverence.
† She King, iv. 1. [iii.] 1.

he altered nothing. At any rate, the work can only be regarded as very particularly his own. More than this, it is questionable whether the text we have at present is that of the original Ch'un Ts'ëw at all. This classic is indeed said to have been recovered in the Han dynasty after the destruction of the book. But there are circumstances which may well make us hesitate before we accept the Chinese account of this recovery as a fact. Mang, who had the best opportunities of knowing what his master was believed to have written, if not what he actually had written, speaks of the Ch'un Ts'ëw in terms wholly inapplicable to the work before us. He asserts expressly that it was composed by him because right principles had dwindled away, because unseemly language and unrighteous deeds were common, and he attributes to its completion the result that "rebellious ministers and villainous sons were struck with terror." Now we may allow what limits we please for the exaggeration natural to a disciple when speaking of the labors of a revered master. But can we believe that Mang, a man whose own teaching proves him to have been a moderate and sensible thinker, would have spoken thus of a compilation which from beginning to end contains absolutely no moral principles whatever? Yet such is the case with the "Spring and Autumn" as we possess it. There is not in it the faintest glimmer of an ethical judgment on the historical events which it records. A birth, an eclipse, a fall of snow, a plague of insects, a murder, a battle, the death of a ruler, are all chronicled in the same dry, lifeless, unvarying style. Nowhere would it be possible for an unprejudiced critic to detect the opinions of the compiler, or to gather from his words that he viewed a virtuous action with more favor than an abominable crime. Such being the case, I hesitate, notwithstanding the high authority of Dr. Legge, to accept the genuineness of this work as beyond cavil.

It has in fact been questioned in China, not indeed on very valid grounds, by a scholar whose letter he has translated in his Prolegomena, and he himself candidly acknowledges the extreme difficulty of reconciling the character of our present text with the statement of Mang. But he considers the external testimony to the recovery of the book sufficiently weighty to dispose of this and other difficulties. Yet, without disputing the strength of the grounds on which this conclusion rests, we may still permit ourselves to entertain a modest doubt whether this compilation was really the handiwork of such a man as we know Confucius to have been, and that doubt will be strengthened when we recall the common tendency of the popular mind to connect the authorship of standard works with names of high repute. And the bare existence of such a doubt will compel us to suspend our judgment on the very serious charges of misrepresentation and falsehood which Dr. Legge has brought against Confucius in his capacity of historian. If the actual Ch'un Ts'ëw be shown to be identical with that edited by Confucius, and if he simply adopted, without alteration, or with very trivial alteration, the labors of his predecessors, the gravity of these charges will be very considerably diminished. For we know not but what some feeling of respect for that which he found already recorded may have stayed his hand from revision and improvement.

Passing to the work itself, we shall find little in it worthy of attention, unless by those who may be desirous of studying the history of China. Chinese commentators have indeed discovered all kinds of recondite meanings in it, as is usually the case with the commentators on Sacred Books, but these are of no more value than the similar discoveries of types and mystic foreshadowings in the Hebrew Scriptures. In itself, the text is profoundly uninteresting. Here is one of the shortest chapters as a specimen. The title of the Book from which it is taken is "Duke Chwang:"—

XXVI. 1. "In his twenty-sixth year, in spring, the duke invaded the Jung.

2. "In summer, the duke arrived from the invasion of the Jung.

3. "Ts'aou put to death one of its great officers.

4. "In autumn, the duke joined an officer of Sung and an officer of Ts'e in invading Seu.

5. "In winter, in the twelfth month, on Kwei-hae, the first day of the moon, the sun was eclipsed" (Ch'un Ts'ëw, iii. 26).

The events noted in these annals refer to various States—for it appears that the several States were in the habit of communicating remarkable occurrences to each other—but they are of a very limited class, and are invariably recorded in the brief manner of the chapter that has just been quoted. Eclipses of the sun are duly registered, and the record thus acquires a chronological value of high importance in historical researches. Among the other facts commonly mentioned are sacrifices for rain, which occur very frequently; wars, with the results of great battles; the marriages or deaths of rulers and important persons; their journeys; occasionally their murder; meetings of rulers for the purpose of common action in matters of State; diplomatic missions, invasions of locusts or other troublesome insects; and lastly, peculiarities of various kinds in the state of the weather. It is plain that annals of this kind have no religious significance beyond that which they derive from the mere fact of being reputed sacred. And in this aspect the Ch'un Ts'ëw is certainly curious. Having been assigned — rightly or wrongly — to the pen of the prophet of China, it seems to have become a point of honor with Chinese scholars to extract from it, by hook or by crook, the profoundest lessons on politics and morals.

SECTION II. — THE TAO-TE-KING.*

There are in China three recognized sects or "religiones licitæ:" — Confucianism, Buddhism, and Tao ism. We have examined the Sacred Books of the first; those of the second will come under review in another section. There remains the comparatively small and unimportant sect of the Taò-ssé, or "Doctors of Reason," who derive their origin from Laò-tsé, and who possess as their classic the single written composition which emanated from their founder. It is entitled the Taò-té-King.

Ancient as this book is (probably about B.C. 520), there is no

* By far the best European work on the Tao-te-King is that of Victor von Strauss, and I have followed his translation, though not without consulting those of others. I am fully sensible of the inconvenience of a double translation, and I should have preferred to follow Chalmers' English rendering of Lao-tse, had not the obscurity of his version been so great as to render it almost unintelligible to the general reader. Reinhold von Planckner's translation errs on the other side by excess of clearness. It is a palpable attempt to force upon the ancient Chinaman a connected system professedly unraveled from the text by the ingenuity of the modern German. It should be used only with extreme caution, or not at all.

reason to doubt its authenticity.* This is sufficiently guaranteed by quotations from it which are found in authors belonging to the fourth century B.C., and by the fact that a scholar who wrote in B.C. 163 made it the subject of a commentary, which accompanies it sentence by sentence. Nor does Chinese tradition state that it perished in the Burning of the Books (B.C. 212–209), which was a measure leveled against the Confucian school, and took place under an Emperor who was favorable to the Taò-ssé. We may safely conclude that we are in possession of the genuine composition of the ancient philosopher (T. T. K., lxxiii., lxxiv).

Of the three words which compose its title, King has already been explained (Supra p. 30). The full meaning of Taò will appear in the sequel: we may here term it the Absolute. Te means Virtue; and the title would thus imply either that this Canonical Book deals with the Absolute *and* with Virtue, or with that kind of virtue which emanates from, and is founded upon, a belief in and a spiritual union with the Absolute.†

Whatever the signification of its name, its principal subjects undoubtedly are Taò and Te: the Supreme Principle and human Virtue. Let us see what is Laò-tsè's description of Taò, the great fundamental Being on whom his whole system rests. "Taò, if it can be pronounced, is not the eternal Taò. The Name, if it can be named, is not the eternal Name. The Nameless One is the foundation of Heaven and Earth; he who has a Name is the Mother of all beings " (Ch. 1). These enigmatical sentences open the Taò philosophy. The idea that Taò is unnameable is a prominent one in the author's mind, although

* It deserves to be noted, as a peculiarity of the Chinese prophets—Confucius and Lao-tse—that they alone among their peers have left authentic written compositions. The Koran can scarcely be said to have been written by Mahomet, in the sense in which we talk of writing a book. And neither Zarathustra, Jesus, nor the Buddha, were authors. The calmer Chinese temperament permitted, in the case of these two great teachers, a mode of conveying instrucions which is repugnant, as a rule, to the fervid prophetic nature. Observe that of the Jewish (so-called) prophets, those who committed their prophecies to writing, generally belonged to a comparatively late age, in which oral prophecy was no longer in vogue, and the state of feeling that had inspired it no longer prevalent.

† The former view is that of Stan. Julien; the latter that of von Planckner.

he seems also to recognize a subordinate creative principle —
like the Gnostic Æons — which is nameable. Thus we read:
"Taò, the Eternal has no Name. . . . . . He who begins to
create, has a Name" (Ch. 32). Again: "For ever and ever it is
unnameable, and returns into non-existence." Or; "I know
not its Name; if I describe it, I call it Taò" (Ch. 25). We are
reminded of Faust's reply in Goethe:—

> "Ich habe keinen Namen
> Dafür? Gefühl ist alles;
> Name ist Schall und Rauch
> Umnebelnd Himmelsgluth."

Nor is Taò only without a Name; it is sometimes described
as if devoid of all intelligible attributes. Thus, in one chapter,
we learn that it is eternally without action, and yet without
non-action (Ch. 37). Nay, the entire absence of all activity is
not unfrequently predicated of Taò, whose great merit is stated
to be complete quiescence. Taò is moreover incomprehensible,
inconceivable, undiscoverable, obscure (Ch. 21). Its upper part
is not clear, its lower part not obscure. It returns into non-
existence. It is the form of the Formless; the image of the
Imageless (Ch. 14). Mysterious as this Being is, yet in other
places attributes are ascribed to it which go far to elucidate the
author's conception of its nature. Productive energy, for instance, is plainly attributed to Taò, for it is stated that Taò produces one, one two, and two three, while three produces all
creatures (Ch. 32). The following account is less mystical:
"Taò produces them [creatures], its Might preserves them, its
essence forms them, its power perfects them: therefore of all
beings there is none that does not adore Taò, and honor its
Might. The adoration of Taò, the honoring of its Might, is commanded by no one and is always spontaneous. For Taò produces them, preserves them, brings them up, fashions them,
perfects them, ripens them, cherishes them, protects them.
To produce and not possess, to act and not expect, to bring up
and not control, this is called sublime Virtue."* In addition
to these creative and preservative qualities, it has moral

---

* Ch., 51. I have borrowed some expressions from Chalmers, O. P.

attributes of the highest order. Thus, its Spirit is supremely
trustworthy. In it is faithfulness (Ch. 21.) All beings trust to it
in order to live. When a work is completed, it does not call it its
own. Loving and nourishing all beings, it still does not lord
it over them. It is eternally without desire. All beings turn
to it, yet it does not lord it over them (Ch., 34). It is eminently straightforward. It dwells only with those who are
not occupied with the luxuries of this world (Ch., 53). Nay, it
is altogether perfect (Ch., 25). The last assertion is found in a
chapter which, as it is probably the most important in the
book for the purpose of understanding the theology of the
author, deserves to be translated in full:—"There existed a
Being, inconceivably perfect, before Heaven and Earth arose.
So still! so supersensible! It alone remains and does not
change. It pervades all and is not endangered. It may be regarded as the Mother of the World. I know not its name; if
I describe it, I call it Taò. Concerned to give it a Name, I call
it Great; as great, I call it Immense; as immense, I call it Distant; as distant, I call it Returning. For Taò is great; Heaven
is great; the Earth is great; the King is also great. In the
world there are many kinds of greatness, and the King remains
one of them. The measure of Man is the earth; the measure
of earth, Heaven; the measure of Heaven, Taò; Taò's measure
itself."*

Such is the picture of Taò; but the Taò-te-king is much
more than a treatise on theology; it is even more conspicuously
a treatise on morals. Taò is indeed the transcendental foundation on which the ethical superstructure is raised; but the
superstructure occupies a much more considerable space than
the foundation, and seems to have been the main practical end
for which the latter was laid down. Intermingled with the
image of Taò we find the image of the good man, or, as we
may call him, in Scriptural phraseology, the righteous man; an
ideal of perfect virtue, whom the author holds up, not as an
actual person, but as an imaginary model for the guidance of
human conduct. By putting together the scattered traits of his

---

* Ch., 25. For the sake of enabling the reader to compare the interpretations of this important chapter given by various Sinologues, I subjoin
in an appendix four other translations.

character, we may arrive at a tolerable comprehension of the
author's conception of perfect goodness. In the first place, the
righteous man is in harmony in his actions with Taò; he becomes one with Taò, and Taò rejoices to receive him (Ch., 23).
He places himself in the background, and by that very means
is brought forward (Ch., 7). He does not regard himself, and
therefore shines; he is not just to himself, and is therefore distinguished; does not praise himself, and is therefore meritorious; does not exalt himself, and is therefore preëminent. As
he does not dispute, none can dispute with him (Ch., 22). If he
acts, he sets no store by his action; for he does not wish to
render his wisdom conspicuous (Ch., 77). He knows himself, but
does not regard himself; loves himself, but does not set a high
price on himself (Ch., 72). Unwilling lightly to promise great
things, he is thereby able to accomplish the more; by treating
things as difficult, he finds nothing too difficult during his
whole life (Ch. 63). Inaccessible alike to friendship and enmity,
uninfluenced by personal advantage or injury, by honor or dis-
honor, he is honored by all the world (Ch., 56). He is characterized by quiet earnestness; should he possess splendid palaces,
he inhabits them or quits them with equal calm (Ch., 26). He
clothes himself in wool (a very coarse material in China), and
hides his jewels (Ch., 70). He is ever ready to help others; for
the good man is the educator of the bad, the bad man the
treasure of the good (Ch., 27). "The righteous man does not ac-
cumulate. The more he spends on others, the more he has; the
more he gives to others, the richer he is" (Ch., 81). He who
knows others is clever; he who knows himself is enlightened"
(Ch. 33). Thus the sage, like Socrates, makes νῶθι σέαντον a
main principle of his conduct. Should he be called to the
administration of the realm, he adopts a policy of *laisser faire*,
for he has observed the evils produced by over-legislation. It
is his belief that if he be inactive, the people will improve by
themselves; if he be quiet, they will become honorable; if he
abstain from intermeddling, they will become rich; if he be
free from desires, they will become simple (Ch., 57). Compelled to engage in war, he will not make use of conquest to
triumph or exalt himself, neither will he take violent measures
(Ch. 30). Mercy is a quality that must not be despised; the

merciful will conquer in battle (Ch. 67). Endowed with these characteristics, the good man need fear nothing. Like Horace's

"Integer vitæ scelerisque purus,"

he is preserved from danger. The horn of the rhinoceros, the claws· of the tiger, the blade of the sword, cannot hurt him (Ch., 50). He is like a new-born child: serpents do not sting it, nor wild beasts seize it, nor birds of prey attack it.*

A few features, which do not directly enter into the delineation of the character of the sage, must still be added to complete that image. And first, a prominent place must be assigned to a quality which is a large ˙ingredient in Laò-tsé's conception of goodness, both human and divine. It is that of gentleness, or, as he would call it, weakness. It is a favorite principle of his, that the weak things of the earth overcome the strong, and that they overcome in virtue of that very weakness. He has an aversion to all conspicuous exercise of force. The deity of his philosophy is one who is indeed all-powerful, but who never displays his power. The method of Heaven—and it should also be that of man—is *apparent* yielding, leading to real supremacy. "It strives not, yet is able to overcome. It speaks not, yet is able to obtain an answer. It summons not, yet men come to it of their own accord; is long-suffering, yet is able to succeed in its designs" (Ch., 73). The superiority of the weak—or the seeming weak—to the strong, is further illustrated by Laò-tsé in several parallels. We enter life soft and feeble; we quit it hard and strong. Therefore softness and feebleness are the companions of life; hardness and strength of death (Ch., 76). And does not the wife overcome her husband by her quietness? (Ch., 61.) Is not water the softest and weakest of all things in the world, yet is there anything which ever attacks the hard and strong that is able to surpass it? (Ch., 78.) Thus, the most yielding of all substances overcomes the most inflexible. Hence is manifest the advantage of inactivity and of silence (Ch., 43). It is fully in accordance with these notions that Laò-tsé should distinctly deprecate warfare, and should assert that the most competent general will not be warlike.

---

* Ch. 55. Von Strauss explains this to mean that he is like the child in its unconsciousness of danger from these sources.

Calmly conscious of his power, he is not quarrelsome or eager for battle, and thus possessing the virtue of peaceable and patient strength, he becomes the peer of Heaven (Ch., 68). War is altogether to be condemned, as pregnant with calamity to the state (Ch., 30). "The most beauteous weapons are instruments of misfortune; all creatures abhor them; therefore he who has Taò does not employ them." They are not the instruments of the wise man. If he must needs resort to them, yet he still values peace and quietness as the highest aims. He conquers with reluctance. "He who has killed many men, let him weep for them with grief and compassion. He who has conquered in battle, let him stand as at a funeral pomp" (Ch., 31).

Another striking characteristic of Laò-tsé's moral system is his dislike of luxury, and his earnest injunction to all men to be contented with modest circumstances. We have seen that the sage is depicted as wearing coarse clothing, and Laò-tsé considers that the very presence of considerable riches indicates the absence of Taò from the minds of their possessors. As we should express it, the devotion to worldly wealth is inconsistent with a spiritual life. "To wear fine clothes, to carry sharp swords, to be filled with drink and victuals, to have a superfluity of costly gems, this is to make a parade of robbery (Or, this is "magnificent robbery," O. P., p. 41); truly not to have Taò" (Ch., 53). Moreover, the very pomp of the palace leads to uncultivated fields and empty barns (Ibid). Laò-tsé therefore warns every one not to consider his abode too narrow or his life too confined. If we do not think it too confined, it will not be so (Ch., 72). Nay, he goes further, and asserts that the world is best known by staying at home. The further a man goes, the less he knows (Ch., 47). A truly virtuous and well-governed people will never care to travel beyond its own limits. To such a people its food will be so sweet, its clothing so beautiful, its dwellings so comfortable, and its customs so dear, that it will never visit the territory of its neighbors, even though that territory should lie so close that the cackling of the hens and the barking of the dogs may be heard across the boundary (Ch., 80).

It results from the above exposition of his ethical principles that Laò-tsé insists mainly upon three virtues: Modesty, Benevolencé, and Contentment. "For my part," he says himself, "I have three treasures; I guard them and greatly prize them. The first is called Mercy,* the second is called Frugality, the third is called Not daring to be first in the kingdom. Mercy — therefore I can be brave; Frugality — therefore I can give away; Not daring to be first in the kingdom — therefore I can become the first of the gifted ones" (Ch. 67).

Of all the sacred books, the Taò-te-king is the most philosophical. It stands, indeed, on the borderland between a revelation and a system of philosophy, partaking to some extent of the nature of both. Since, however, it forms the fundamental classic of a religious sect, and since it has engaged in its interpretation a multitude of commentators,† it appears to be fully entitled to a place among Scriptures. Not indeed that the Chinese regard it as a revelation in the same sense in which nations of a more theological cast of mind apply that term to the books composing their Canon. But I see no reason to doubt that the Tao-sse, however little they attend to its precepts, yet treat it as a work of unapproachable perfection and unquestionable truth. Indeed, the writer of a fabulous life of Laò-tsé, who lived many centuries after his death, expressly ascribes to it those peculiar qualities which, as we have seen, are the special attributes of sacred books (L. V. V., pp. xxxi., xxxii).

To the European reader who approaches it for the first time it will probably appear a perplexing study. Participating largely in that disorder and confusedness which characterizes the class of literature to which it belongs, it presents, in addition, considerable difficulties peculiarly its own. The correct translation of many passages is doubtful. The sense of still more is ambiguous and obscure. Laò-tsé is fond of paradox, and his constant employment of paradoxical antithesis seems specially designed to puzzle the reader. If his doctrine was understood by few, it must be confessed that this was partly his own fault. More-

---

* Or Compassionateness. Chalmers translates "compassion," but this term denotes the sentiment rather than the virtue.

† See their names in Le Livre de la Voie et de la Vertu (hereafter abbreviated thus — L. V. V.). Compose dans le VI Siecle avant l'ere chretienne par le Philosophe Lao-Tseu. Traduit en Francais et publie avec le texte chinois par Stanislas Julien. 8vo. Paris, 1872. xxxvi.

over, the reverence with which he speaks of Taò, and the care with which he insists that Taò does nothing, seem at first sight inconsistent. We feel ourselves in an atmosphere of hopeless mysticism. Nevertheless, these superficial troubles vanish, or at least retire into the background, after repeated perusals of the work. There are few books that gain more on continued acquaintance. Every successive study reveals more and more of a wisdom and a beauty which we miss at first in the obscurity and strangeness of the style.

And first, Taò itself turns out to be a less incomprehensible and contradictory being than we originally supposed. For although he may sometimes be spoken of as doing nothing, or even as destitute of all distinct qualities, yet other attributes expressly exclude the notion of absolute inaction. A being which creates, cherishes and loves, and in which all the world implicitly trusts, is not the kind of nonentity that can be described as wholly devoid of "action, thought, judgment, and intelligence."* Moreover, it is to be borne in mind that the sage is to imitate Taò in the quality—for which he is highly lauded—of doing nothing. The two pictures, that of Taò and his follower, must be held side by side in order to be correctly understood. Now what is the peculiar beauty, from a philosophical point of view, of the order of Nature? It is that all its parts harmoniously perform their several offices, without any violent or conspicuous intrusion of the presiding principle which guides them all.

Other teachers, indeed, have seen God mainly in violent and convulsive manifestations, and have appealed to miraculous suspensions of natural order as the best proofs of his existence. Not so Laò-tsé. He sees him in the quiet, unobtrusive, unapparent guidance of the world; in the unseen, yet irresistible power to which mankind unresistingly submit, precisely because it is never thrust offensively upon them. The Deity of Laò-tsé is free from those gross and unlovely elements which degrade his character in so many other religions. He rules by

---

* Such is the description of M. Julien, derived from the most ancient Chinese commentators. I am at a loss to reconcile it even with his own translation, though it would be presumptuous in me to deny that the learned Sinologue may have reasons for it of which I am not aware.—See L. V. V., p. xiii.

gentleness and love, not by vindictiveness and anger. So should it be with the holy man who takes him for his model. Assuredly we are not to understand those passages which enjoin quiescence so earnestly upon him as a meaning that he is to lead a life of absolute indolence. Like Taò, he is to guide his fellow-creatures rather by the beauty of his conduct than by positive commands laid imperatively upon them. Let him but be a shining example; they will be drawn towards him. The activity from which a wise ruler is to abstain is the vexatious multiplication of laws and edicts, which do harm rather than good. But neither ruler nor philosopher is told to do nothing; for benevolence, love, and the requital of good for evil, to say nothing of other positive virtues, are most strictly enjoined on all. Laò-tsé himself no doubt lived, and loved, a retired contemplative life. This is the kind of existence which he evidently considered the most perfect and the most godlike. He counsels his followers to be wholly unambitious, and to abstain from all active pursuit of political honor. Such counsel might possibly be well adapted to the time in which he lived. But none the less does he lay down rules for the guidance of kings, statesmen, and warriors, in their several spheres. Nor is the book wanting in pithy apothegms applicable to all, and remarkable alike for the wisdom of their substance and the neatness of their form. Whether, in short, we look to the simplicity and grandeur of its speculative doctrine, or to the unimpeachable excellence of its moral teaching, we shall find few among the great productions of the human mind that evince, from beginning to end, so lofty a spirit and so pure a strain.

APPENDIX TO SECTION II.

Translations of the Tao-te-King, ch. 25.

ABEL RÉMUSAT.—"Avant le chaos qui a précédé la naissance du ciel et de la terre, un seul être existait, immense et silencieux, immuable et toujours agissant sans jamais s'altérer. On peut le regarder comme la *mere* de l'univers. J'ignore son nom, mais je le désigne par le mot de *raison*.

Forcé de lui donner un nom, je l'appelle *grandeur, progression, éloignement, opposition*. Il y a dans le monde quatre grandeurs; celle de la raison, celle du ciele, cell de la terre, celle du roi, qui est aussi une des quatre. L'homme a son type et son modèle dans la terre, la terre dans le ciel, le ciel dans la raison, la raison en elle-même."*

STANISLAS JULIEN.—"Il est un être confus qui existait avant le ciel et la terre.

O qu'il est calme! O qu'il est immatériel!

Il subsiste seul et ne change point.

Il circule partout et ne périclite point.

Il peut être regardé comme la mère de l'univers.

Moi, je ne sais pas son nom.

Pour lui donner un titre, je l'appelle *Voie* (Tao).

En m'efforçant de lui faire un nom, je l'appelle *grand*.

De *grand*, je l'appelle *fugace*.

De *fugace*, je l'appelle *éloigné*.

D'*éloigné*, je l'appelle (l'être) *qui revient*.

C'est pourquoi le Tao est *grand*, le ciel est *grand*, la terre est *grande*, le roi aussi est *grand*.

Dans le monde, il y a quatre grandes choses, et le roi en est une.

* Memoire sur la Vie et les Opinions de Lao-tseu, par M. Abel Remusat. Paris, 1823, p. 27.

L'homme imite la terre; la terre imite le ciel; le ciel imite le Tao ; le Tao; le Tao imite sa nature " (L. V. V., p. 35).

JOHN CHALMERS. — "There is something chaotic in nature which existed before heaven and earth. It was still. It was void. It stood alone and was not changed. It pervaded everywhere and was not endangered. It may be regarded as the Mother of the Universe. I know not its name, but give it the title of Tau. If I am forced to make a name for it, I say it is *Great;* being great, I say that it *passes away;* passing away, I say that it is *far off;* being far off, I say that it *returns.*

Now Tau is great; Heaven is great; Earth is great; a king is great. In the universe there are four greatnesses, and a king is one of them. Man takes his law from the Earth; the Earth takes its law from Heaven; Heaven takes its law from Tau; and Tau takes its law from what is in itself " (O. P., p. 18).

REINHOLD VON PLÄNCKNER.—"Es existirt ein das All erfüllendes, durchaus vollkommenes Wesen, das früher war denn der Himmel und die Erde. Es existirt da in erhabener Stille, es ist ewig und unveränderlich, und ohne Anstoss dringt es überall hin, überall da.

Man möchte es als den Schöpfer der Welt ansehen. Seinen Namen weiss ich nicht, ich nenne es am liebsten das Tao; soll ich diesem eine bezeichnende Eigenschaft beilegen, so würde es die der höchsten Erhabenheit sein.

Ja, erhaben ist das Wesen, um das sich das All und Alles im All bewegt, als solches muss es ewig sein, und wie es ewig ist, ist es folglich auch allgegenwärtig.

Ja das Tao ist erhaben, erhaben ist auch der Himmel, erhaben die Erde, erhaben ist auch das Ideal des Menschen. So sind denn vier erhabene Wesen im Universum, und das Ideal des Meschen ist ohne Zweifel eins derselben.

Denn der Mensch stammt von der Erde, die Erde stammt vom Himmel, der Himmel stammt vom Tao.—Und das Tao stammt ohne Frage allein aus sich selbst " (L. T., p. 113).

Section III.—The Veda.*

The word *Veda* is explained by Sanskrit scholars as meaning *knowing* or *knowledge*, and as being related to the Greek οἶδα. Tho works comprised under this designation are manifold, and appertain to widely different epochs. In the first place they fall into two main classes, the *Sanhitâ* and the *Brâhmana*. The Sanhitâ portion of the Veda consists of hymns or metrical compositions addressed to the several deities worshiped by their authors, and expressing religious sentiment; the Brâhmana portion, of theological treatises in prose of an expository, ritualistic and didactic character. Across this subdivision into two classes there runs another of the whole Veda into four so-called Vedas, the Rig-Veda, the Yajur-Veda, the Sâma Veda, and the Atharva-Veda. Each of these has its own Sanhitâs, and its own Brâhmanas; but the Sanhitâ, or hymns, of the three other

* The literature of the Veda is now copious. To mention only a few works, H. H. Wilson published a translation of the first five Ashtakas of the Rig-Veda-Sanhita, but I have forborne to make use of it, from a conviction that the advance of Vedic scholarship has to a great degree, if not wholly, superseded the methods of interpretation employed by him. Benfey has translated the whole of the Sama-Veda-Sanhita into German, and I have studied his translation, but have preferred to rely mainly on the labors of English scholars, both because the inherent obscurity of these ancient hymns might be increased by the process of re-translation, and also because I might possibly fail to catch the exact shade of meaning of the German words. His work should, however, be consulted by those who desire to acquaint themselves with the style of the Veda. Max Muller has unhappily published but one volume of his translation of the Rig-Veda-Sanhita, which is doubtless destined (if completed) to become the standard English version of that portion of the text. The same eminent scholar has translated many of the hymns in his "Ancient Sanskrit Literature." Another source from which I have derived valuable assistance is Dr. Muir's laborious work entitled "Original Sanskrit Texts." Such are the principal authorities on the hymns. Of the Brahmanas, the whole of the Aitareya Brahmana has been translated by Haug, and portions of others by Roer and by Rajendralal Mitra.

Vedas are not materially different from those of the Rig-Veda. On the Rig-Veda they are all founded; this is the fundamental Veda, or great Veda; and in knowing this one we should know all. The other three, according to Max Müller, contain "chiefly extracts from the Rig-Veda, together with sacrificial formulas, charms, and incantations" (Chips, vol. i. p. 9). It must not therefore be imagined that we have in these four Vedas four different collections of hymns. They are rather four different versions of the same collection, the Sâma-Veda, for instance, containing but seventy-one verses which are wanting in the Rig-Veda (S. V., p. xxviii), and being otherwise "little more than a repetition of the Soma Mandala of the Rich" (Wilson, vol. i. p. xxxvii), or of that book of the Rig-Veda which is devoted to the god Soma. The Atharva-Veda-Sanhitâ is indeed to a certain extent an exception; belonging to a later age, it has some hymns altogether peculiar to itself, and its fifteenth book "has something of the nature of a Brâhmana" (O. S. T., vol. i. p. 2). It must be noted, moreover, that of the Yajur-Veda there are two different versions, the Black and the White Yajur-Veda, said to have descended from two rival schools. The hymns of the first are termed the Taittiriya-Sanhitâ, those of the second the Vâjasaneyi-Sanhitâ.

The origin of those four distinct, yet not different Vedas, is thus explained. In certain sacrifices, formerly celebrated in India, four classes of priests were required, each class being destined for the performance of distinct offices. To such of these classes was assigned one of the Vedas, which contained the hymns required by that class. Thus the Sâma-Veda was the prayer-book of the Udgâtri priests, or choristers, who chant the hymns. The Yajur-Veda was the prayer-book of the Adhvaryu priests, or attendant ministers, who prepare the ground, slay the victims, and so forth. The Atharva-Veda was said to be intended for the Brahman who was, according to one of the Brâhmanas, the "physician of the sacrifice;" the general superintendent who was to tell if any mistake had been committed in it (A. B., 5. 5.—vol. ii. p. 376). For the fourth class, the Hotri priests, or reciters of hymns, no special collection was made in the form of a liturgy. They used the Rig-Veda, a collection of the hymns in general without any special object, and they were supposed to know the sacred poetry without the help of a prayer-book (A. S. L., pp 175, 473, and Chips, vol. i. p. 9).

Originally preserved by scattered individuals (for the Mantra part of the Vedas, [or their Sanhitâ] was composed in an age when writing was not in use), the hymns were subsequently collected and arranged in their present form : a task which Indian tradition assigns to Vyâsa, the Arranger, but which was probably the work of many different scholars, possibly during many generations. The same tradition asserts that each Veda was collected, under Vyâsa's superintendence, by a different editor; and that the collections, transmitted from these primary compilers to their disciples, were, in the course of transmission, rearranged in various ways, until the number of Sanhitâs of each Veda in circulation was very considerable. Each school had its own version, but the differences are supposed by Wilson to have concerned only the order, not the matter of the Sûktas.

The extreme antiquity of our extant Veda is guaranteed by the amplest testimony. In the indexes compiled by native scholars 500 or 600 years before Christ, "we find every hymn, every verse, every word and syllable of the Veda accurately counted " (Chips, vol. i. p. 11). Before this was done, not only was the whole vast collection complete, but it was ancient; for had it been a recent composition it would not have enjoyed the preëminent sanctity which rendered it the object of this minute attention. And not only is the Veda ancient, but it has been shown that, from the variety of its component strata, it must have been the growth of no small period of time, its earliest elements being of an almost unfathomable antiquity. Max Müller, who has elaborately treated this question, divides the Vaidik age — the age during which the Veda was in process of formation — into four great epochs. The most primitive hymns of the Rig-Veda he attributes to what he terms *the Chhandas period* (from Chhandas, or metre), the limits of which cannot be fixed in the ascending direction, but which descends no later than 1000 B.C. And he thinks that "we cannnot well assign a date more recent than 1200 to 1500 before our era " (Ibid., vol. i. p. 13.) for the composition of these hymns. The ten books of the Rig-Veda, however, comprise the poetry of two different ages. Some of the hymns betray a more recent origin, and must be assigned to the second, or *Mantra period*. These comparatively modern compositions belong to a time which may have extended from about 1000 to about 800 B.C. After this we enter on the *Brahmana period*, in which the Rig-Veda-Sanhitâ not only existed, but had reached the stage of being misinterpreted, its original sense having been forgotten. During this period — which we may place from B.C. 800 to 600 — the national thought took the form of prose, and the Brâhmanas were written. Here the age of actually-inspired literature terminates, and we arrive at the *Sutra period*, which may have lasted till 200 B.C. Works of high authority, but not in the strict sense revealed works, were produced during these four hundred years (A. S. L., *passim*). An equal, or greater antiquity is usually claimed by other Sanskritists for these several classes of sacred literature. Wilson would place Manu (who belongs to the Sûtra period) not lower than the fifth or sixth century; the Brâhmana literature in the seventh or eighth; and would allow at least four or five centuries before this for the composition and currency of the hymns, thus reaching the date of 1200 or 1300 before the Christian era (Wilson, vol. i. p. xlvii).

Haug, who believes that "a strict distinction between a Chhandas and Mantra period is hardly admissible," and that certain sacrificial formulas, considered by Max Müller to be more recent, are in fact some centuries older than the finished hymns ascribed by that scholar to the Chhandas age, carries back the composition of both Sanhitâ and Brâhmana to a much earlier date. "The bulk of the Brâhmanas" he assigns to B.C. 1400–1200; and "the bulk of the Sanhitâs" to B.C. 2000–1400; while "the oldest hymns and sacrificial formulas may be a few hundred years more ancient still," and thus "the very commencement of Vedic literature" might be between B.C. 2400 and 2000 (A. B., vol. i. pp. 47. 48). While Benfey, considering that the Prâtisâkhyas (a branch of the Sûtras) must have been composed from B.C. 800 to 600, observes that the text of the Sâma-Veda must extend beyond this epoch (S. V., p. xxix.

Of the several Sanhitâs, that of the Rig-Veda (whose name is derived from a word *rich*, praise) is usually considered the most ancient, though Benfey expresses the opinion that the text of the Sâma-Veda may possibly be borrowed from an older version of the Rig-Veda than before us (Ibid., p. xxix). Max Müller, on the other hand, conceives the Sâma and Yajur-Vedas to have been probably the production of the Brâhmana period (A. S. L. p. 457). He even denies to any but the Rich the right to be called Veda at all (Chips, vol. i. p. 9). Whatever claim, or want of claim, they may possess to the honor, it is certain that they have for more than 2,000 years invariably received it at the hands of the Hindus themselves. So far from admitting the preëminence of the Rich, the ancient Hindus, according to one of their descendants, held the Sâma in the highest veneration (Chhand. Up., introduction, p. 1). If a doubt can exist as to the canonicity of any one of them, it can only apply to the Atharva-Veda; for in certain texts we find mention made of three Vedas only, the Atharva, from its comparatively late origin, having apparently been long denied the privilege of admission to an equal rank with its compeers.

Whatever their antiquity, the sanctity of these works in Indian opinion is of the highest order. Never has the theory of inspiration been pushed to such an extreme. The Veda was the direct creation of Brahma; and the Rishis, or Sages, who are the nominal authors of the hymns, did not compose them, but simply "saw" them. Although, therefore, the name of one of these seers is coupled with each hymn, it must not be supposed that he did more than perceive the divine poem which was revealed to his privileged vision. And the Veda is distinguished as *Sruti*, Revelation, from the *Smriti*, Tradition, under which term is included a great variety of works enjoying a high, but not an independent, authority. They are to be accepted, in theory at least, only when they agree with the Veda, and to be set aside if they happen to differ from it; while no such thing as a contradiction within the body of the Veda is for a moment to be thought of as possible, apparent inconsistencies being only due to our imperfect interpretations. The Sruti class comprises only the Mantra of each Veda and its Brâhmahas; the Smriti consists of the great national epics, namely the Râmâyana and Mahâbhârata; the Mânava-Dharma-Sastra, or Menu; the Purânas; the Sûtras, or aphorisms; and the so-called six Vedângas, a term indicating six branches of study carried on by the help of treatises on the pronunciation, grammar, metre,

explanation of words, astronomy, and ceremonial of the Veda.
How thoroughly the Veda was analyzed, how minutely every
word of it was investigated, is shown by the fact that these
Vedângas all have direct reference to it, and were intended to
assist in its comprehension. And in ancient times it was the
duty of Brahmans to be well acquainted both with the Sûktas
(hymns), and with their application to ritual. A Brahman,
indeed, who wanted to marry was not obliged to devote more
than twelve years to learning the Veda, but an unmarrying
Brahman might spend forty-eight years upon it (A. S. L., p. 503).

SUBDIVISION 1. — The Sanhita.

Passing now to a more detailed consideration of the Mantra
division, we find that the Rig-Veda-Sanhitâ — the most comprehensive specimen of this division — comprises more than a
thousand short poems, of which the vast majority are addressed
to one or more of the Indian gods. A few only, and those believed to be of later origin, are of a different character. This
collection is divided in two ways; into ten Mandalas, or eight
Ashtakas, the two divisions being quite independent of one
another. Under each of these greater heads are several lesser
ones, which it is needless to enumerate. The deities to whom
the hymns are devoted are exceedingly various and numerous,
but as this is not an essay specially intended to elucidate the
Veda, but aiming only at a general comparison of this with
other sacred books, it would be going beyond our scope to
attempt a full account of their several names, attributes, and
honors. A few only of the more conspicuous gods need be
noticed.

Of these, Agni, as the one with whose praises the Rig-Veda
opens, and who, next to Indra, is the principal character in the
Vedic hymnology, claims our attention first. He is the god of
fire, or more literally, he is the fire itself, and a god at the
same time. His name is almost identical with the Latin Ignis.
He is frequently spoken of as generated by the rubbing of
sticks, for in this manner did the Rishis kindle the fire required
for their sacrifices. The sudden birth of the fiery element in
consequence of this process must have impressed them as pro-

foundly mysterious.   They allude to it under various images.
Thus, the upper stick is said to impregnate the lower, which
brings forth Agni.   He is the bearer of human sacrifices to the
gods; a kind of telegraph from earth to heaven.   Many are the
blessings asked of him.   But let the Rishis speak for themselves.   Here is the first Sûkta of the Rig-Veda-Sanhitâ:—

1. "I praise Agni, the household priest, the divine offerer of the
sacrifice, the inviter who keeps all treasures.   2. Agni, worthy of the
praises of the ancient Rishis, and also of ours, do thou bring hither the
gods.   3. By Agni, *tho sacrificer* enjoys wealth, that grows from day to
day, confers renown, and surrounds him with heroes.   4. Agni, the
sacrifice which thou keepest from all sides uninvaded, approaches surely
the gods.   5. Agni, inviter, performer of gracious deeds, thou who art
truthful, and who shinest with various glories, come thou, O God,
with the gods.   6. The prosperity, which thou, O Agni, bestowest upon
the worshiper, will be in truth *a prosperity* to thee, O Angiras.   7. We
approach thee in our minds, O Agni, day after day, by night and day, to
offer thee our adoration.   8. Thee the radiant guardian of the meet
reward of the sacrifices, who is resplendent and increasing in his sacred
house.   9. Be thou, O Agni, accessible to us, as a father is to the son;
be near us for our welfare" (Roer, p. 1).

Even more important than Agni is Indra, the great national
god of the Hindus.   He is above all things a combative god.
His strength is immense, and his worshipers implore him to
give them victory and power.   He slays the demon Vrittra,
a myth symbolizing the dispersion of clouds by the sun.
Above all, he loves the juice of the Soma plant (*Asclepias
acida*), which is poured out to him abundantly in sacrifice, which
he consumes with avidity, and from which he derives renewed
force and energy.   These two stanzas, taken from the Sâma-
Veda, express some of his attributes:—

"Thou, O Indra, art glorious, thou art victorious, thou art the lord
of strength; thou conquerest the strong enemies singly and alone, thou
unconquered refuge of men.   To thee, living One, we pray; to thee
now the very wise, for treasures, as for our share; may thy blessing be
granted us" (S. V., ii. 6. 2. 12).

The following hymn brings into especial prominence the more warlike functions of Indra, and may be regarded as a prayer "in the time of war and tumults:"—

8. "May Indra be the leader of these (our armies); may Brihaspati, Largess, Sacrifice and Soma march in front; may the host of Maruts precede the crushing, victorious armies of the gods. May the fierce host of the vigorous Indra, of King Varuna, of the Adityas, and the Maruts (go before us); the shout of the great-souled, conquering, world-shaking gods, has ascended. . . . 10. Rouse, O opulent god, the weapons, rouse the souls of our warriors, stimulate the power of the mighty men; may shouts arise from the conquering chariots. 11. May Indra be ours when the standards clash; may our arrows be victorious ; may our strong men gain the upper-hand; preserve us, O gods, in the fray. 12. Bewildering the hearts of our enemies, O Apvâ (Apvâ is explained as a disease or fear), take possession of their limbs and pass onward; come near, burn them with fires in their hearts; may our enemies fall into blind darkness" (O. S. T., vol. v. p. 110.—Rig-Veda, x. 103).

Indra's Soma-drinking propensities are not particularly alluded to in these verses: elsewhere they form the ever-recurring burden of the chants of which he is the hero. Thus, to take but one specimen, which, by its resemblance to others, may fitly stand for all, he is thus lauded:—

1. "May the Somas delight thee! bestow grace, O hurler of lightning! destroy him who hates the priest. 2. Thou who art praiseworthy, drink our drink! thou art sprinkled with streams of honey! from thee, O Indra, glory is derived. . . . 4. The Indus (the Somas) stream into thee, like rivers, Indra! into the sea, and never overfill thee" (S. V., i. 1. 1).

Indra is, in fact, the Zeus of Indian mythology; the thunderer, the god of the sky, the all-powerful protecter of men and destroyer of the demons of darkness. His functions are easily understood, but it is curious that the Soma, which is offered to him in sacrifice, and which he drinks with all the avidity of a confirmed toper, is itself celebrated as a god of very considerable powers. Soma appears to be regarded as a sort of mediator between the greatest gods and men, especially between man and

Indra. He is repeatedly entreated to go to Indra, to flow around him, and thus to conciliate and delight him. But Soma can confer benefits independently. One poet implores him to stream forth blessing "on the ox, the man, and the horse; and, O king, blessings on plants" (S. V., ii. 1. 1. 1). In the hymns devoted to him he is raised to an exalted station among the celestial beings, while the sacrifice in which he is drunk by the priests is the capital right in the Brahmanical liturgy (A. B., vol, i. p. 59). The most eminent virtues are inherent in this divine beverage, when taken with all the ceremonies prescribed by traditional law. The Soma juice has, in the opinion of Hindu theologians, "the power of uniting the sacrificer on this earth with the celestial King Soma," and making him " an associate of the gods, and an inhabitant of the celestial world" (Ibid., vol. i. pp. 40, 80). Such was the excellence of this juice, that none but Brahmans were permitted to imbibe it. Kings, at their inaugural ceremonies, received a goblet which was nominally Soma, but on account of their inferior caste they were in fact put off with some kind of spirituous liquor which was supposed, by a mystical transformation, to receive the properties of that most holy divinity (Ibid., vol. ii. p. 522). Agreeably to this theory of Soma's extensive powers, he is invoked in such terms, for instance, as these:—

7. "Place me, O purified god, in that everlasting and imperishable world where there is eternal light and glory. O Indu (Soma), flow for Indra. 8. Make me immortal in the world where king Vaivasvata (Yama, the son of Vivasvat) lives, where is the innermost sphere of the sky, where those great waters flow" (O. S. T. vol. v. p. 266.— Rig-Veda, ix. 113).

Singular as it may seem that the juice of the Soma-plant should be at once an object sacrificed on the altar to other gods and a god himself, such a confusion of attributes will be less surprising to those who are familiar with the Christian theory of the Atonement, in which the same God is at once the person who decrees the sacrifice, the person who accepts it, and the victim. At least the double function of Soma is less perplexing than the triple function of Christ.

Considerable among Vedic deities are the Maruts, or gods of

tempest. They are in intimate alliance with **Indra**, to whom their violent nature is closely akin. Their attributes are simple. A notion of them may perhaps be gained from these verses: —

1. "What then now? When will you take (us) as a dear father takes his son by both hands, O ye gods, for whom the sacred grass has been trimmed? 2. Whither now? On what errand of yours are you going, in heaven, not on earth? Where are your cows sporting? 3. Where are your newest favors, O Maruts? Where the blessings? Where all delights? . . . 6. Let not one sin after another, difficult to be conquered, overcome us; may it depart together with lust. 7. Truly they are furious and powerful; even to the desert the Rudriyas bring rain that is never dried up. 8. The lightning lows like a cow, it follows as a mother follows after her young, that the shower (of the Maruts) may be let loose. 9. Even by day the Maruts create darkness with the water-bearing cloud, when they drench the earth. 10. From the shout of the Maruts over the whole space of the earth, men reeled forward. 11. Maruts on your strong-hoofed steeds go on easy roads after those bright ones (the clouds) which are still locked up. 12. May your felloes be strong, the chariots, and their horses; may your reins be well fashioned. 13. Speak out forever with thy voice to praise the Lord of prayer, Agni, who is like a friend, the bright one. 14. Fashion a hymn in thy mouth! Expand like a cloud! Sing a song of praise. 15. Worship the host of the Maruts, the brisk, the praiseworthy, the singers. May the strong ones stay here among us" (R. V. S., vol. i. p. 65.—Rig-Veda, i. 38).

The most charming member of the Vedic pantheon, and the one who seems to have called forth from the Rishis the deepest poetical feeling, is Ushas ('Εως), the Dawn. Her continual reappearance, or birth, morning after morning, seems to have filled them with delight and tenderness. The hymn now to be quoted — too long to be extracted in full — gives expression to the feelings with which they gazed upon this ever-recurring mystery: —

2. "The fair and bright Ushas, with her bright child (the Sun), has arrived; to her the dark (night) has relinquished her abodes; kindred to one another, immortal, alternating Day and Night go on changing color. 3. The same is the never-ending path of the two sisters, which they

travel, commanded by the gods. They strive not, they rest not, the prolific Night and Dawn, concordant, though unlike. 4. The shining Ushas, leader of joyful voices (or hymns) has been perceived; she has opened for us the doors (of the sky); setting in motion all moving things, she has revealed to us riches. Ushas has awakened all creatures. . . . 6. (Arousing) one to seek royal power, another to follow after fame, another for grand efforts, another to pursue as it were his particular object, — Ushas awakes all creatures to consider their different modes of life. 7. She, the daughter of the sky, has been beheld breaking forth, youthful clad in shining attire: mistress of all earthly treasures. Auspicious Ushas, shine here to-day. 8. Ushas follows the track of the Dawns that are past, and is the first of the unnumbered Dawns that are to come, breaking forth, arousing life and awaking every one that was dead. . . . 10. How great is the interval that lies between the Dawns which have arisen, and those which are yet to arise! Ushas yearns longingly after the former Dawns, and gladly goes on shining with the others (that are to come). 11. Those mortals are gone who saw the earliest Ushas dawning; we shall gaze upon her now; and the men are coming who are to behold her on future morns. . . . 13. Perpetually in former days did the divine Ushas dawn; and now to-day the magnificent goddess beams upon this world: undecaying, immortal, she marches on by her own will" (O. S. T., vol. v. p. 188.—Rig-Veda. i. 113).

Hardly a trace of a moral element is to be found in those productions of the Rishis which have hitherto been quoted. And such as these are is the general character of the Rig-Veda-Sanhitâ. It consists in petitions for purely material advantages, coupled with unbounded celebrations of the power of the god invoked, often under the coarsest anthropomorphic images. But while it must be admitted that the sentiment expressed is rarely of a high order, it must not be supposed that the old Hindu gods are altogether destitute of ethical attributes. Marked exceptions to the general tenor of the supplications offered to them certainly occur. There are passages which betray a decided consciousness of sin, a desire to be forgiven and a conviction that certain kinds of conduct entail divine disapprobation, while other kinds bring divine approbation. Thus, in the hymns addressed to the Adityas, a class of gods generally

reckoned as twelve in number, and to Mitra and Varuna, two
of these Adityas, such feelings are plainly expressed (O. S. T.,
vol. v. p. 56 ff). Of these two, Mitra is sometimes explained as
the Sun, or the god of Day, Varuna as the god of Night.
Varuna—whose name corresponds to that of Ouranos—is a
very great and powerful divinity, who is endowed by his adorers
with the very highest attributes. He is said to have meted
out heaven and earth, and to dwell in all worlds as their
sovereign, embracing them within him (Ibid., vol v. p. 61). He
is said to witness sin, and is entreated to have mercy on sinners. One penitent poet implores Varuna to tell him for what
offense he seeks to kill his worshiper and friend, for all the
sages tell him that it is Varuna who is angry with him. And
he pleadingly contends that he was not an intentional culprit;
he has been seduced by "wine, anger, dice, or thoughtlessness."
Another begs the god that, in whatever way mortals may have
broken his laws, he will be gracious. A third admits that he,
who was Varuna's friend, has offended against him, but asks
that they who are guilty may not reap the fruits of their sin;
concluding with this amicable hint: " Do thou, a wise god,
grant protection to him who praises thee" (O. S. T., vol. v. pp.
66, 67). "The attributes and functions ascribed to Varuna,"
observes Dr. Muir, "impart to his character a moral elevation
and sanctity far surpassing that attributed to any other Vedic
deity " (Ibid., vol. v. p. 66). And while even in the earlier portion of the Rig-Veda — from which the above expressions have
been collected by Dr. Muir—such qualities are ascribed to
Varuna, we shall find a still higher conception of his character
in a later work, the Atharva-Veda. Here is the description of
the Lord of Heaven from the mouth of the Indian Psalmist:—

1. " The great lord of these worlds sees as if he were near. If a
man thinks he is walking by stealth, the gods know it all. 2. If a man
stands or walks or hides, if he goes to lie down or to get up, what two
people sitting together whisper, King Varuna knows it, he is there as
the third. 3. This earth, too, belongs to Varuna, the king, and this
wide sky with its ends far apart. The two seas (the sky and the ocean)
are Varuna's loins; he is also contained in this small drop of water.
4. He who should flee far beyond the sky, even he would not be rid of

Varuna, the king. His spies proceed from heaven towards this world; with thousand eyes they overlook this earth.   5. King Varuna sees all this that is between heaven and earth, and what is beyond. He has counted the twinklings of the eyes of men. As a player throws the dice he settles all things. 6. May all thy fatal nooses, which stand spread out seven by seven and threefold, catch the man who tells a lie; may they pass by him who tells the truth " (A. S. L.—Atharva-Veda, iv. 16).

A consciousness of the unity of Deity, under whatever form he may be worshiped, adumbrated here and there in earlier hymns, becomes very prominent in the later portions of the Veda. From the most ancient times, possibly, occasional sages may have attained the conception so familiar to the Hindu thinkers of a later age, that a single mysterious essence of divinity pervaded the universe. And in the tenth book of the Rig-Veda, which is generally admitted to belong to a more recent age than the other nine books, as also in the Atharva-Veda, this essence is celebrated under various names; as Purusha, as Brahma, as Prajâpati (Lord), or Skambha (Support). The hymns in which this consciousness appears are extremely mystical, but a notice of the Veda, however slight, would be very imperfect without a due recognition of their presence. They form the speculative element partly in the midst of, partly succeeding to, the simple, practical, naked presentation of the common-place daily wants and physical desires of the early Rishis. Take the following texts from the first book of the Rig-Veda. They give utterance to an incipient sentiment of divine unity. The first celebrates a goddess Aditi: "Aditi is the sky, Aditi is the air, Aditi is the mother and father and son. Adita is all the gods and the five classes of men. Aditi is whatever has been born. Aditi is whatever shall be born" (O. S. T., vol. v. p. 354.— Rig-Veda, i. 89. 10). More remarkable than this—for we may suspect here a sectarian desire to glorify a favorite goddess— is this assertion: "They call him Indra, Mitra, Varuna, Agni; and he is the celestial (well-winged) Garutmat. Sages name variously that which is but one: they call it Agni, Yama, Mâtarisvan" (O. S. T., vol. v. p. 353.—Rig-Veda, i. 164, 46). In the tenth book of the Rig-Veda, the presence of the speculative element in the theology of the Rishis,—their longing to find a universal Being whom they could adore,—is much, more marked. Thus do they express this sentiment:—"Wise poets make the beautiful-winged, though he is one, manifold by words" (Chips. vol. i. p. 29 —Rig-Veda, x. 114. 5). Or more elaborately thus:—

1. "In the beginning there arose the golden Child—He was the one born lord of all that is. He established the earth and this sky;—Who is the God to whom we shall offer our sacrifice? 2. He who gives life, He who gives strength; whose command all the bright gods revere; whose shadow is immortality, whose shadow is death;—Who is the God to whom we shall offer our sacrifice? 3. He who through his power is the one King of the breathing and awakening world; He who governs all man and beast; Who is the God to whom we shall offer our sacrifice? 4. He whose greatness these snowy mountains, whose greatness the sea proclaims, with the distant river—He whose these regions are, as it were his two arms;—Who is the God to whom we shall offer our sacrifice? 5. He through whom the sky is bright and the earth firm—He through whom the heaven was established,—nay, the highest heaven;—He who measured out the light in the air;—Who is the God to whom we shall offer our sacrifice? 6. He to whom heaven and earth, standing firm by His will, took up, trembling inwardly—He over whom the rising sun shines forth;—Who is the God to whom we shall offer our sacrifice? 7. Wherever the mighty water-clouds went, where they placed the seed and lit the fire, thence arose He who is the sole life of the bright gods;—Who is the God to whom we shall offer our sacrifice? 8. He who by his might looked even over the water-clouds, the clouds which gave strength and lit the sacrifice; He who alone is God above all gods;—Who is the God to whom we shall offer our sacrifice? 9. May He not destroy us—He the creator of the earth; or He, the righteous, who created the heaven; He also created the bright and mighty waters;—Who is the God to whom we shall offer our sacrifice?" (Chips, vol. i. p. 29, or A. S. L., p. 569.—Rig-Veda, x. 121).

The same book contains a very important hymn, entitled the Purusha Sûkta. In it we find ourselves transported from the transparent elemental worship of the ancient Aryas into the misty region of Brahmanical subtleties. Purusha appears to be conceived as the universal essence of the world, all existences being but one-quarter of him. The theory of sacrifice occupies, as in the later Indian literature generally, a prominent position. Purusha's sacrifice involved the momentous consequences of the creation of the several Vedas and of living creatures. The four castes sprang from different parts of his person, the parts corresponding to their relative dignity. The purpose of this portion is obvious, namely, to give greater sanctity to the system of caste, a system to which the earlier hymn makes no allusion, and which we may suppose to have grown up subsequently to the era of their composition. Tedious as it is, the Purusha Sûkta is too weighty to be quite passed over.

1. "Purusha has a thousand heads, a thousand eyes, a thousand feet. On every side enveloping the earth, he overpassed (it) by a space of ten fingers. 2. Purusha himself is this whole (universe), whatever has been and whatever shall be. He is also the lord of immortality, since (or when) by food he expands. 3. Such is his greatness, and Purusha is superior to this. All existences are a quarter of him; and three-fourths of him are that which is immortal in the sky. 4. With three-quarters Purusha mounted upwards. A quarter of him was again produced here. He was then diffused everywhere over things which eat and things which do not eat. 5. From him was born Virâj, and from Virâj, Purusha. When born, he extended beyond the earth, both behind and before. 6. When the gods performed a sacrifice with Purusha as the oblation, the spring was its butter, the summer its fuel, and the autumn its (accompanying) offering. 7. This victim, Purusha, born in the beginning, they immolated on the sacrificial grass. With him the gods, the Sâdhyas, and the Rishis sacrificed. 8. From that universal sacrifice sprang the rich and sâman verses, the metnes and the yajush. 10. From it sprang horses, and all animals with two rows of teeth; kine sprang from it; from it goats and sheep. 11. When (the gods) divided Purusha, into how many parts did they cut him up? what was his mouth? what arms (had he)? what (two objects) are said (to have been) his thighs and feet? 12. The Brahman was his mouth; the Râjanya was made his arms; the being (called) the Vaisya, he was his thighs; the Sûdra sprang from his feet. 13. The moon sprang from his soul (manas), the sun from his eye, Indra and Agni from his mouth, and Vâyu from his breath. 14. From his navel arose the air, from his head the sky, from his feet the earth, from his ear the (four) quarters; in this

manner (the gods) formed the worlds. 15. When the gods, performing sacrifice, bound Purusha as a victim, there were seven sticks (stuck up) for it (around the fire), and thrice seven pieces of fuel were made. 16. With sacrifice the gods performed the sacrifice. These were the earliest rites. These great powers have sought the sky, where are the former Sâdhyas, gods" (O. S. T., vol. i. p. 9.—Rig-Veda, x. 90).

The wide interval which separates theological theories of this kind from the primitive hymns to the old polytheistic gods, is also marked by a tendency to personify abstract intellectual conceptions, and to confer exalted attributes upon them. Skambha, or Support, mentioned above; Kâla, Time, celebrated in the Atharva-Veda; Speech, endowed with personal powers in the tenth book of the Rig-Veda; Wisdom, to whom prayer is offered in the Atharva-Veda, are instances of this generalizing tendency. As a specimen, the hymn to Wisdom may be taken, and readers may console themselves with the reflection that it is our last quotation from the Mantra part of the Veda:—

1. "Come to us, wisdom, the first, with cows and horses; (come) thou with the rays of the sun; thou art to us an object of worship. 2. To (obtain) the succor of the gods, I invoke wisdom the first, full of prayer, inspired by prayer, praised by rishis, imbibed by Brahmachârins. 3. We introduce within me that wisdom which Ribhus know, that wisdom which divine beings (asurâh) know, that excellent wisdom which rishis know. 4. Make me, O Agni, wise to-day with that wisdom which the wise rishis—the makers of things existing—know. 5. We introduce wisdom in the evening, wisdom in the morning, wisdom at noon, wisdom with the rays of the sun, and with speech" (O. S. T., vol, i. p. 255 note.—Atharva-Veda, vi. 108).

Interesting as the Mantra of the Vedas is from the fact of its being the oldest Bible of the Aryan race, it is impossible for modern readers to feel much enthusiasm for its contents. The patient labor of these scholars who have engaged in translations of some parts of it for the benefit of European readers is highly commendable, but it is probable that few who have read any considerable number of these hymns will be desirous of a further acquaintance with them, unless for the purpose of some special researches. Indeed, it may be said that the

devoted industry of Benfey, Muir, Max Müller, and others, has
placed more than a sufficient number of them within reach of
the general public to enable us all to judge of their literary
value and their religious teaching. With regard to the former, it
would be difficult to concede to them anything but a very
modest place. In beauty of style, expression, or ideas, they
appear to me to be almost totally deficient. Assuming, as we
are entitled to do, that all the best specimens have been already
culled by scholars eager to find something attractive in the
Veda, it must be confessed that the general run of the hymns
is singularly monotonous, and their language by no means
conspicuous for poetical coloring. No doubt, poetry always loses
in translation; but Isaiah and Homer are still beautiful in a
German or English dress; the Sûktas of the Rig-Veda are not.
A few exceptions no doubt occur, as in the stanzas to Ushas, or
Dawn, quoted above, but the ordinary level is not a high one.

Although, however, the literary merit of the Veda cannot be
ranked high, its value to the religious history of humanity at
large, and of our race in particular, can hardly be overrated.
To the comparative mythologist, above all, it possesses illimit-
able interest, from the new light it sheds upon the origin and
significance of many of those world-wide tales which, in their
metamorphosed Hellenic shape, could not be effectually brought
under the process of dissection by which their primitive elements have now been laid bare. Mythology is beyond the
province of this work, and therefore I purposely refrain from
entering upon any explanation of the physical meaning of the
old Aryan gods, or of the stories in which they figure.* All
that I have to do with here is the grade attained in the development of religious feeling among those who worshiped them.
And this, it is plain, was at first a very elementary one. The
more striking phenomena of nature—the sun, the moon, the
sky, the storms, the dawn, the fire—at first attracted their
attention, and absorbed their adoration. To these personal
beings, as they seemed to the awe-struck Rishis, petitions of
the rudest type were confidently addressed. Very little allusion,
if any, was made to the necessities of the moral nature; the

* All this will be found admirably treated in Mr. Cox's "Mythology of
the Aryan Nations."

craving for spiritual knowledge was scarcely felt; but great stress was laid on temporal prosperity. Boons of the most material kind were looked for at the hands of the gods. Plenty of offspring, plenty of physical strength, plenty of property, especially in cattle, and victory over enemies; such are the requests most commonly poured into the ears of Indra, or Agni, or the Maruts. These gods are regarded as the sympathizing friends of men, and if they should fail to do what may reasonably be expected of a god, are almost upbraided for their negligence. The conception of their power is a high one, though that of their moral nature is still rudimentary. Their greatness and their glory, their victories, their splendor, are described in vigorous and high-sounding phrases. The changes are rung upon their peculiar attributes or their famous exploits. Each god in his turn is a great god; but all are separate individuals; there appears in the crude Aryan mind to be as yet no dawning of the perplexing questions on the unity of the Divine which troubled its later development. For as it progresses, the Hindu religion gradually changes. External calm, succeeding the wars of the first settlers, promotes internal activity. The great problem of the Universe is no longer solved, five or six centuries after the older Rishis had passed away, in the simple fashion which satisfied their curiosity. Multiplicity is now resolved into unity; mystical abstractions take the place of the elementary powers of nature. Speech is a goddess; the Vedas themselves — as in the Purusha hymn — acquire a quasi-divinity; the Brahmachârin, or student of theology, is endowed with supernatural attributes, due to the sacred character of his pursuits. Sacrifice, fixed and regulated down to the smallest minutiæ, has a peculiar efficacy, and becomes something of far deeper meaning than a merely acceptable present to the gods. Every posture, every word, every tone acquires importance. There are charms, there are curses, there are incantations for good and evil purposes, for the acquisition of wealth or the destruction of an enemy. It is by its collection of such magical formulæ that the Atharva-Veda is distinguished from its three predecessors. It forms the last stone laid upon the edifice of the genuine Veda, an edifice built up by the labor of many centuries, and including the whole of that original revelation to which the centuries that succeeded it bowed down in reverence and in faith.

SUBDIVISION 2.—*The Brâhmanas.*

Attached to this edifice as an outgrowth rather than an integral part, the treatises known as Brâhmanas took their place as appendages of the Sanhitâ. Although they are reckoned by the Hindus as belonging to the Sruti, although their nominal rank is thus not inferior to that of the true Veda, yet it must have taken them many generations to acquire a position of honor to which nothing but tradition could possibly entitle them. For any gleams of poetical inspiration, of imaginative religious feeling, of naturalness or simple earnestnesss that had shone athwart the minds of devout authors in preceding ages, had apparently passed away when the Brâhmanas were composed. They are the elaborate disquisitions of scholars, not the outpourings of men of feeling. Religion was cut and dried when they were written; every part of it has become a matter of definition, of theory, of classification. If in the Vedic hymns we are placed before a stage where religious faith is a living body, whose movements, perhaps uncouth, are still energetic and genuine, the Brâhmanas, on the other hand, take us into the dissecting-room, where the constituent elements of its corpse are exposed to our observation. Not indeed that a true or deep faith had ceased in the Brâhmana period; such an assertion would no doubt be extravagant; but the Brâhmanas themselves are the products of minds more given to analysis than to sentiment, and of an age in which the predominant tendency, at least among cultivated Brahmans, was not so much to feel religion as to think about it. It is so everywhere. The Hebrew Bible, once fixed and completed, gives rise to the Mishnah. The Apostles and Fathers of the Christian Church are followed by a race of schoolmen. The simple Sûtras of Buddhism, replete with plain, world-wide lessons of moral truth, give place to the abstruse developments of incomprehensible theology. Thus the Brâhmanas mark the epoch when the Veda had finally ceased to grow, and its every word and letter had become the object of an unquestioning adoration as the immediate emanation of God.

But among a people so subtle and so inquisitive in all matters of religious belief as the Hindus, opinion could not rest unmoved upon the original foundation. Their minds did not, like those of the Jews, stop short for ever in their intellectual progression, chained to the unshakeable rock of a god-given Revelation. Ever active, ever attracted to the enigmas of life, the Brahmans pushed their speculations into new regions of thought, pondered upon new problems, and invented new solutions. Not that we are to expect to find in the literature of this period any valuable discoveries or any very striking philosophy. The true philosophical systems came later. But still we do find a restless spirit of inquiry, ever prompting fresh efforts to conceive the significance of the gods or to penetrate the mysteries of nature, though the questions discussed are often trifling, and the results arrived at frivolous.

Every Veda has, as already stated, its own Brâhmana or Brâhmanas. Thus, two of these treatises appertain to the Rig-Veda; three to the Sâma-Veda, one to the Black and one to the White Yajur-Veda, and one to the Atharva-Veda (O. S. T., vol. i. p. 5). Appended to the Brâhmanas, and forming, according to Dr. Muir, their "most recent portions," are the Âranyakas and Upanishads, a kind of supplementary works devoted to the elucidation of the highest points of theology. The Brâhmanas present an example of Ritualism in all its glory. They fix the exact nature of every part of every ceremony; describe minutely the mode in which each sacrifice is to be offered; mention the Mantras to be recited on each occasion; declare the benefits to be expected from the several rites, and explain the reasons — drawn from the history of the gods — why they are all to be performed in this particular way and order, and in no other. They are in fact liturgies, accompanied by exposition. Hence they are totally unfit for quotation in a general work, for they would be incomprehensible without an accompanying essay on the Vedic sacrifices, entering into details which would interest none but professional students of the subject.

Thus, the Aitareya Brâhmana occupies itself entirely with the duties of the Hotri priests; for the recitation of the Rig-Veda, to which this Brâhmana belonged, was their province.

Occasionally, however, the Brâhmanas, Upanishads, and Âran-yakas are enlivened by the introduction of apologues, intended to illustrate the point of theological dogma to which the author is addressing himself. Some of these apologues are curious, though the style in which they are related is generally so pro-lix as to preclude extraction. A notion of them may be gathered from condensed statements. Thus, in the Brihad Âranyaka Upanishad a story is told of a dispute among the vital organs as to which of them was "best founded," i. e., most essential to life. To obtain the decision of this controversy they repaired to Brahma, who said, "He amongst you is best founded by whose departure the body is found to suffer most." Hereupon Speech departed, and returning after a year's absence, inquired how the others had lived without it. "They said, 'As dumb people who do not speak by speech, breathing by the vital breath, seeing by the eye, hearing by the ear, thinking by the mind, and begetting children, so have we lived.'" The eye, the ear, the mind, the organ of generation, each departed for a year, and, *mutatis mutandis*, with similar results; blindness, deafness, idiocy, impotence, were all compatible with life. Lastly, "the vital breath being about to depart, as a great, noble horse from the Sindhu country raises its hoofs, so it shook those vital organs from their places. They said, 'Do not depart, O Ven-erable. We cannot live without thee.' 'If I am such, then offer sacrifice to me." (They answered)—'Bo it so.'" All the other organs hereupon admitted that their own existence depended on that of the vital breath (B. A. U., ch. vi. p. 2,9).

Several narratives in various Brâhmanas point to the fact that theological knowledge was not in these early days confined to the single caste by which it was afterwards monopolized, for they speak of well-read kings by whom Brahmans were in-structed. In the Chhândogya Upanishad, for example, five mem-bers of the Brahmanical caste engaged in a debate upon the question "Which is our soul, and which is Brahma?" Unable to satisfy themselves, they repaired, accompanied by another theologian who had been unable to answer them, to a monarch named Asvapati, and declining his proffered gifts, requested him to impart to them the knowledge he possessed of the Universal Soul. He accordingly asked each of them in turn which soul he adored. The first replied that he adored the heaven; the second, the sun; the third, the winds; the fourth, the sky; the fifth, water; the sixth, the earth. To each of them in turn the king admitted that it was indeed a partial manifestation of the Universal Soul which he worshiped, and that its adoration would confer some advantages. But, he finally added, "You consume food, knowing the Universal Soul to be many; but he who adoreth that Universal Soul which pervadeth the heaven and the earth, and is the principal object indicated by (the pronoun) *I*, consumeth food everywhere and in all regions, in every form and in every faculty." Of that all-pervading Soul the several phenomena of the visible Universe worshiped by the Brahmans in their ignorance are but parts (Chhand. Up., ch. v. section 11–18, p. 92–97). Other Brâhmanas tell similar stories of the occasional preëminence of the Kshattriya caste in the rivalry of learning. Thus, the Satapatha Brâhmana, the Brihad Âranyaka Upanishad, and the Kaushîtaki Brâhmana Upanishad, all refer to a certain king Ajâtasatru, who proved himself superior in theological disputation to a Brahman named Bâlâki, "renowned as a man well-read in the Veda." Let us take the version of the last-named Upanishad. Bâlâki proposed to "declare divine knowledge" to the king, who offered to give him a thousand cows for his tuition. But after he had propounded his views on the Deity, and had been put to shame by the king's answers, the latter said, "Thou hast vainly proposed to me; let me teach thee divine knowledge. He, son of Balaka, who is the maker of these souls, whose work that is,—he is the object of knowledge." Convinced of his ignorance, Bâlâki proposed to become the king's pupil. "The king replied, ·I regard it as an inversion of the proper rule that a Kshattriya should initiate a Brahman. But come, I will instruct thee'" (O. S. T., vol. i. p. 431).

Both these stories illustrate the striving towards conceptions of the unity of the divine essence which is characteristic of this speculative age. The next, from the Satapatha Brâhmana, has reference to another important point,—the future of the soul. A young Brahman, called Svetaketu, came to a monarch who inquired whether he had received a suitable education from his father. The youth replied that he had. Hereupon the king proceeded to put him through an examination, in which he completely broke down. One of the question was this:—"Dost thou know the means of attaining the path which leads to the gods, or that which leads to the Pitris (Ancestors (*patres*); by what act the one or the other is gained?" In other words did he know the way to heaven? The student did not. Vexed at his failure, the young man hastened to his father, reproached him with having declared that he was instructed, and complained that the Râjanya had asked him five questions, of which he knew not even one. Gautama inquired what they were, and on hearing them, assured his son that he had taught him all he himself knew. "But come, let us proceed thither, and become his pupils." Receiving his guest with due respect, the king offered Gautama a boon. Gautama begged for an explanation of the five questions. "That," said the king, "is one of the divine boons; ask one of those that are human." But Gautama protested that he had wealth enough of all kinds, and added, "Be not illiberal towards us in respect to that which is immense, infinite, boundless." The king accordingly accepted them as his pupils, saying, "Do not attach any blame to me, as your ancestors (did not). This knowledge has never heretofore dwelt in any Brahman; but I shall declare it to thee. For who should refuse thee when thou so speakest?" (O. S. T., vol. i. p. 434.)

Unhistorical as they probably are in their details, these traditions are curious both as illustrating the predominant inclination to speculative inquiries, and the fact that in those inquiries the priestly caste was sometimes outshone by their more secular rivals. The following quotation bears upon another doctrine, the transcendent merit of patience under trials, even of the severest kind. Manu, the typical ancestor of mankind, is represented as resigning his most precious possessions to enable impious priests to perform a sacrifice:—

"Manu had a bull. Into it an Asura-slaying, enemy-slaying voice had entered. In consequence of this (bull's) snorting and bellowing, Asuras and Râkshasas (these are species of demons) were continually destroyed. Then the Asuras said, 'This bull, alas! does us mischief; how shall we overcome him?' Now there were two priests of the Asuras called Kilâtka and Akuli. They said, 'Manu is a devout believer: let us make trial of him.' They went and said to him, 'Let us sacrifice for thee.' 'With what victim?' he asked. 'With this bull,' they replied. 'Be it so,' he answered. When it had been slaughtered, the voice departed out of it, and entered into Manu's wife Mânavî. Wherever they hear her speaking, the Asuras and Râkshasas continue to be destroyed in consequence of her voice. The Asuras said, 'She does us yet more mischief; for the human voice speaks more.' Kilâta and Akuli said, 'Manu is a devout believer: let us make trial of him.' They came and said to him, 'Manu, let us sacrifice for thee.' 'With what victim?' he asked. 'With this (thy) wife,' they replied. 'Be it so,' he answered" O. S. T., vol. i. p. 188).

Sometimes, though not often, the Brâhmanas contain references to moral conduct. A very theological definition of Duty is given in the Chhândogya Upanishad, where it is stated, "Threefold is the division of Duty. Sacrifice, study, and charity constitute the first; penance is the second; and residence by a Brahmachârin (a student of theology) exclusively in the house of a tutor is the third. All those [who attend to these duties] attain virtuous regions; the believer in Brahma alone attains to immortality" (A. B., vii. 2. 10). In another Brâhmana it is asserted that "the marriage of Faith and Truth is a most happy one. For by Faith and Truth joined they conquer the celestial world" (Chhand. Up., ch. ii. sec. 23). And the the story of Sunahsepa, which contains an emphatic repudiation of human sacrifice, has a moral bearing. As a rule, however, the Brâhmanas do not concern themselves with ethical questions. The rules of sacrifice, and the doctrines of a complicated theology, are their main business; and the topics they are thus led to debate in elaborate detail must frequently impress the European reader as not only uninteresting, but unmeaning.

Section IV.—The Tripitaka.*

* No complete translation of the Tripitaka exists, or is ever likely to exist in any European language. Its vast extent, and the comparative worthlessness of many of its parts, would preclude its publication as a whole. But complete treatises, or portions of treatises, have been translated by Burnouf, in his "Histoire du Buddhisme Indien," and "Lotus de la Bonne Loi;" by Beal, in his "Chinese Buddhist Scriptures;" by Schmidt, in "Der Weise und der Thor;" by Hardy, in his "Manual of Buddhism," and by Ala-

When the master-mind who, by oral and personal instruction, has led his disciples to the knowledge of new and invaluable truths passes away — when the lips that taught them are closed forever, and the intellect that solved the problems of human life is at rest, when the soul that met the spiritual cravings of their souls is no more near them — a necessity at once arises for the collection of the sayings, the apologues, or the parables which can now be heard no more, and which only live in the memories of those who heard them. The precious possession must not be lost. The light must not be suffered to die out. Either the words of the Departed One must be transmitted orally from disciple to disciple, from generation to generation (as happens in countries where writing is uncommon or unknown), or they must be rendered imperishable by being once for all recorded in books.

Such was the course of events upon the death of Gautama Buddha. Tradition tells us that immediately after that great Teacher had entered into Nirvana, his disciples assembled in council to collect his λόγια, and to fix the Canons of the Faith. This Canon consisted of three portions, and is therefore called the *Tripitaka*, or Three Baskets. Of these baskets, his disciple Upali was appointed to recall to memory, and edit, the one termed *Vinaya*, or the Buddha's instructions on discipline; Ananda (the intimate friend of Gautama), the Sutras, or practical teachings; and Kasyapa, the Abhiddharma, or metaphysical lectures. Into these three classes the Buddhist Canon remains still divided. But the text, as thus established, did not escape the necessity of further revision. One hundred and ten years after Sakyamuni's decease, certain monks brought considerable scandal on the Church by disregarding his precepts. To meet the difficulty, a council was held under the Buddhist king Asoka, the orthodox faith was determined, and a new edition of the Canonical Works compiled by seven hundred "accomplished priests." Divisions and heresies, however, could not be pre-

baster, in his " Modern Buddhist." An exact analysis of the contents of the hundred volumes of the great collection called the Kah-gyur is supplied by Csoma Korosi in the 20th vol. of the "Asiatic Researches." The leading features of the books, and parts of books thus translated, are so well marked and uniform, that nothing further is needed to enable us to estimate the general character of each division of the whole Tripitaka.

vented. In Kanishka's reign, four hundred years after Buddha, the Church was split up into eighteen sects, and a third council had to issue a third Revision of the Sacred Texts.*

All this is not to be taken as literally true. Especially is it impossible to accept the story that a Text of the Buddha's precepts and lectures was formed immediately after his death. It is probable that not even the earliest parts of the Tripitaka were committed to writing till long after that event, and it is quite certain that its later elements could not have been added till some centuries after it. Nevertheless, they may be, and indeed it is almost beyond doubt that there are, some works in this Canon which were already current as the Word of Buddha in the time of Asoka, who reigned in the third century before Christ. In an inscription quoted by Burnouf, and indisputably emanating from that monarch, it is stated that the law embraces the following topics:—"The limits marked by the Vinaya, the supernatural faculties of the Ariyas, the dangers of the future, the stanzas of the hermit, the Sutra of the hermit, the speculation of Upatisa (Sariputtra) only, the instruction of Laghula (Rahula), rejecting false doctrines. This," adds the proclamation, "is what has been said by the blessed Buddha" (Lotus, p. 725). In this enumeration we recognize, as Burnouf has observed, the classes Vinaya and Sutra, which still form two out of the three baskets, and we find also that certain texts were accepted by the Church as containing the genuine teaching of the Buddha. We must suppose, therefore, that at the epoch of the Council held under Asoka in B. C. 246, there were already many unquestioned works in circulation. Nor is there any reason to doubt that some of these have descended to our times. Burnouf divides the Sutras (in the more general sense of instructions or sermons) into two kinds: simple, and developed Sutras, of which the simple ones bear marks of antiquity and of fairly representing primitive Buddhism, while the developed Sutras contain the fanciful speculations of a later age.

Two most fortunate discoveries, the one made by Mr. Hodgson in Nepaul, the other by Csoma Körösi in Thibet, have placed the vast collection forming the Canon of Buddhism

---

* Southern Buddhists fix the dates of these General Counsels somewhat differently.

within the reach of European scholars. Brian Houghton Hodgson was the British Resident in Nepaul in the early part of the present century, and he there succeeded in obtaining a large number of volumes in Sanskrit which he presented to the Asiatic Societies of London and Paris. To the latter he presented first twenty-four works, and subsequently sixty-four MSS,, being copies of works he had sent to the Asiatic Society in London. These books happily fell into the hands of one of the greatest of Sanskrit scholars, Eugené Burnouf, who, in his "History of Indian Buddhism," translated a sufficient number of them to serve as specimens. About the same time a zealous Hungarian, Csoma Körösi, undertook an adventurous journey into the heart of Asia, with a view of discovering the original stock of the Hungarian race. Failing in this object, he achieved another of greater value, that of unearthing the whole of the sacred books known in Thibet under the name of the *Kahgyur*. or *Kan-gyur* (properly b*kah*-h*gyur*), which is the Thibetan translation, in one hundred volumes, of the very works of which Hodgson in Nepaul had discovered the Sanskrit originals. Such is the nature of our guarantees for the authenticity of the text.

Subdivision 1. — *The Vinaya-Pitaka.*

Let us proceed to consider in detail the division which stands first in the Buddhist classification, the Vinaya-Pitaka, or basketful of works on Discipline. These, according to Burnouf, are of very different ages, some being, from the details they furnish with reference to Sâkyamuni, his institutions and his surroundings, of very ancient date, and others, which relate events that did not occur till two hundred years or more after his death, belonging to a more recent period. One of the most instructive of the legends which form the staple of the works on Discipline, is that of Pûrna. Only a brief extract of it can be attempted here.

Bhagavat (that is, the Lord, or Buddha) was at Srâvasti, in the garden of Anâthapindika. (Anâthapindika was a householder who had embraced the religion of the Buddha, and in whose garden he was accustomed to preach.) There resided at this time in the town of Surparaka a very wealthy house-

holder, named Bhava. This Bhava had three sons by his legitimate wife, who were christened respectively Bhavila, Bhava-
trata, and Bhavanandin. After some years he fell into an illness
which led to his using language of extraordinary violence.
His wife with her three sons deserted him in consequence, but
a young female slave, reflecting that he had immense wealth,
and that it would not be suitable for her to desert him,
remained in the house and nursed him throughout his malady.
Seeing that he owed her his life, Bhava on his recovery told her
that he would give her a reward. The young woman begged
that if satisfied she might be admitted to her master's bed.
Bhava endeavored to get off, promising a handsome sum of
money and her liberty instead, but the girl was determined, and
obtained her wish. The result was that "after eight or nine
months" she gave birth to a beautiful boy, to whom the name
of Pûrna (the Accomplished) was given. The infant Pûrna was
confided to eight nurses, and subsequently received a first-rate
education. In due time, the three elder sons were married by
their father's desire, but the father, seeing them absorbed in
mere uxoriousness, reproved their indolence, telling them that
he had not been married until he had amassed a lac (100,000) of
Suvarna (representing about twenty-eight shillings). Struck by
this reproof, the three sons went to sea on a mercantile expedition, and returned after having each made a lac of Suvarnas.
But Pûrna, who had remained at home to manage the shop,
was found to have gained an equal sum in the same time.
Bhava, perceiving Pûrna's talents, impressed on his sons the
importance of union, and the duty of disregarding what was
said by their wives; women being the destroyers of family
peace. He illustrated his remarks by a striking expedient.
Having desired his sons to bring some wood, and to kindle it,
he then ordered them all to withdraw the brands. This being
done, the fire went out, and the moral was at once understood
by the four young men. United the fuel burns; and thus the
union of brothers makes their strength. Bhavila in particular
was warned by his father never to abandon Pûrna. In course
of time Bhava died, and the three legitimate sons undertook
another voyage. During their absence, the wives of the two
younger sons fancied themselves ill-treated by Pûrna, who, in

the midst of his business in the shop, did not supply their maids fast enough with all they sent for. On the return of their husbands these two complained to them that were treated as happens to those in whose family the son of a slave exercises the command. The two brothers merely reflected that women sowed divisions in families. Unhappily, however, some trifling incidents, in which Bhavila's child appeared to have been treated by Pûrna with undue partiality, gave the sister-in-law a more plausible pretext for their complaints. Such was the effect of their jealousy, that the younger brothers determined to demand a division of the property, in which Pûrna (as a slave) was to form one of the lots. Bhavila, as eldest brother, had first choice, and remembering his father's advice, chose Pûrna. One of the other brothers took the house and land, and ejected Bhavila's wife; the other took the shop and the property in foreign parts, and ejected Purna. Bhavila, his wife, and Pûrna, retired penniless to the house of a relative. The wife in distress sent out Pûrna with nothing but a brass coin, which had been attached to her dress, to buy provisions. Pûrna met a man who had picked up some stranded sandal-wood on the sea-shore, and buying it of him (on credit) for five hundred Kârshâpanas, sold a portion of it again for one thousand. With this sum he first paid the man who had sold the wood, and then obtained provisions for the household. He had still in his possession some pieces of the sandal-wood, which was of a very valuable species called Gosirsha. Shortly after this, the king fell ill, and his doctors having prescribed an ungent of this very wood, it was found that no one but Pûrna had any in his possession. Pûrna sold a piece of it to the Government at one thousand Kârshâpanas, and the king recovered. Hereupon he reflected that he was but a poor sort of king who had no Gosirsha sandal-wood in his establishment, and sent for Pûrna. Pûrna, guessing his object, approached him with one piece in his hand, and three in his robe. The king, after ascertaining that the price of the one piece would be a lac of Suvarnas, inquired if there was more. Pûrna then showed him the three other pieces, and the king would have given him four lacs of Suvarnas. The wily merchant, however, offered to present him with one piece, and when the grateful monarch offered him a boon, requested that he might henceforth be protected against all insults, which was at once accorded.

About this time five hundred merchants arrived at Surparaka with a cargo of goods. The Merchants' Company passed a resolution that none of them should act independently of the rest in buying any of these goods; in short, that there should be no competition. Any one dealing with the merchants alone was to pay a fine. Pûrna, however, at once went to the vessel and bought the whole cargo at the price demanded, eighteen lacs of Suvarnas, paying the three lacs he had received as security. The Merchants' Company, finding themselves anticipated, seized Pûrna and exposed him to the sun to force him to pay the fine. No sooner was the king informed of this than he sent for the Merchants' Company to learn the cause of their proceedings. They told him; but being obliged to confess that they had never informed Pûrna or his brother of the resolution passed, they had to release him with shame. Fortune still favored him. Soon after this, the king happened to require the very articles which Purna had purchased, and desired the Merchants' Company to purchase them. Pûrna hereupon sold them at double the price he had paid. His next step was to undertake a sea-voyage for commercial purposes, and the first having been successful, it was followed by five others, all equally so. His seventh was undertaken at the instance of some Buddhist merchants from Srâvasti, where Gautama was teaching. During the voyage he was profoundly impressed with their religious demeanor. "These merchants, at night and at dawn, read aloud the hymns, the prayers which lead to the other shore, the texts which disclose the truth, the verses of the Sthaviras, those relating to the several sciences, and those of the hermits, as well as the Sûtras containing sections about temporal interests. Pûrna, who heard them, said to them, 'Gentlemen, what is that fine poetry which you sing?' 'It is not poetry, O prince of merchants; it is the very words of the Buddha.' Pûrna, who had never till now heard this name of Buddha mentioned, and who felt his hair stand up all over his body, inquired with deep respect, 'Gentlemen, who is he whom you call Buddha?' The merchants replied, 'The Sramana Gautama, descended from the Sâkya family, who

having shaven his hair and beard, having put on garments of
yellow hue, left his house with perfect faith to enter upon a
religious life, and who has reached the supreme condition of
an all-perfect Buddha; it is he, O prince of merchants, who is
called the Buddha.' 'In what place, gentlemen, does he now
reside?' 'At Srâvasti, O prince of merchants, in the wood of
Jetavana, in the garden of Anâtha-pindika.'" The result of
this conversation was that Pûrna, on his return, announced to
his brother his intention of becoming a monk, and advised him
never to go to sea, and never to live with his two brothers.
After this he went straight to Anâtha-pindika, and was by him
presented to the Buddha, who received him with the remark
that the most agreeable present he could have was a man to
convert. Pûona then received the investiture and tonsure by
miracle, and was instructed in the law (in an abridged version)
by his master. A beautiful, and very characteristic conversation follows the reception of the new doctrine. The Buddha
inquired of Pûrna where he would now reside, and the latter
(who intended to lead an ascetic life) replied that he would reside "in the land of the Sronaparantakas.* 'O Pûrna,' says
Gautama, 'they are violent, these men of Sronaparanta: they
are passionate, cruel, angry, furious, and insolent. When the
men of Sronaparanta, O Pûrna, shall address thee to thy face
in wicked, coarse, and insulting language, when they shall become enraged against thee and rail at thee, what wilt thou
think of that?' 'If the men of Sronaparanta, O Lord, address
me to my face in wicked, coarse, and insulting language, if they
become enraged against me and rail at me, this is what I shall
think of that: They are certainly good men, these Sronaparantakas, they are gentle, mild men, they who address me to my
face, in wicked, coarse and insulting languge, they who become
enraged against me and rail at me, but who neither strike me
with the hand nor stone me.'" The rest must be given in an
abridged form. "But if they do strike thee with the hand or
stone thee?" "I shall think them good and gentle for not
striking me with swords or sticks." "And if they do that?"
"I shall think them good and gentle for not depriving me

* Apparently a people living beyond the frontiers (of the civilized
world). See H. B. I., p. 252, *n.*

entirely of life." "And if they do that?" (what follows is literal.) "If the men of Sronaparanta, Ọ Lord, deprive me
entirely of life, this is what I shall think: There are hearers
of Bhagvat [the Lord] who by reason of this body full of
ordure, are tormented, covered with confusion, despised, struck
with swords, who take poison, who die of hanging, who are
thrown down precipices. They are certainly good people, these
Sronaparantakas, they are gentle people, they who deliver me
with so little pain from this body full of ordure." "Good, good,
Pûrna; thou canst, with the perfection of patience with which
thou art endowed, yes, thou canst live, thou canst take up thy
abode in the land of the Sronaparantakas. Go, Pûrna; delivered thyself, deliver; arrived thyself at the other shore, cause
others to arrive there; consoled thyself, console; having come
thyself to complete Nirvâna, cause others to arrive there."

Hereupon Pûrna took his way to Sronaparanta, where he
converted a huntsman who had intended to kill him, and
obtained five hundred novices composed of both sexes.

After a time, Bhavila, his brother, was requested by Bhava-
trata and Bhavanandin to enter into partnership with them; and
his repugnance to the proposal was overcome by the reproaches
of his younger brothers, who said that he would never have
dared to go to sea as Pûrna had done. Stung by this taunt, he
engaged with them in a sea-voyage. The vessel was attacked
by a furious storm, raised by a demon in consequence of the
merchants having cut some sandal-wood which was under this
demon's protection. Bhavila stood dumbfounded; and when
the passengers inquired the reason, informed them that he was
thinking of his brother's advice never to go to sea. It turned
out that the merchants on board knew of Pûrna's great sanctity,
and they addressed their prayers to him. He came through the
air, after the manner of Buddhist ascetics, appeared sitting
cross-legged over the vessel, and allayed the tempest. The
vessel, loaded with sandal-wood, was brought safely back to
Surparaka. The sandal-wood Pûrna took possession of in order
to make a palace for the Buddha, and desired his brothers to
invite that personage and his disciples to a repast. The invitation was miraculously conveyed to the Buddha (who was a long
way off, at Srâvasti), and he told his followers to prepare to

accept it. Pûrna returned suddenly to the Assembly (around Buddha) and performed a miracle. The king of Surparaka, on his side, made preparations on the grandest scale for the reception of the Buddhist hierarchy, which came to his city by all kinds of supernatural means. Pûrna, standing by him, explained the various prodigies as they occurred. Omitting some marvelous conversions wrought by the Buddha on his way, it may be mentioned that he descended into the middle of the town of Surparaka from the air, and there taught the law, by which hundreds of thousands of living beings attained the several degrees of knowledge which lead, sooner or later, to salvation.

Passing over a passage in which two royal Nâgas (or serpent-kings) make their appearance to receive the law, and another in which Gautama proceeds to another universe to instruct the mother of his disciple Maudgalyâyana, we arrive at the moral which always forms the conclusion of these Buddhist tales. The monks surrounding the Buddha inquired what actions Pûrna had performed in order, first, to be born in a rich family; secondly, to be the son of a slave; and lastly, "when he had entered on a religious life, to behold the condition of an Arhat * face to face, after having annihilated all the corruptions of evil?" Buddha replied, that in the very age in which we live, but at a period of it when men lived twenty thousand years, there was a venerable Tathâgata, or Buddha, named Kâsyapa, who resided near Benares. Pûrna, who had adopted a religious life under him, "fulfilled among the members of the Church † the duties of servant of the law." The servant of a certain Arhat set himself to sweep the monastery, but the wind blowing the dirt from side to side, he gave up the attempt, intending to proceed when the wind should have abated. The servant of the law coming in, and finding the monastery unswept, allowed himself to be carried away by rage, and to utter these offensive words: "This is the servant of some slave's son."

---

* The state of an "Arhat" is the highest of four degrees which the hearers of the Buddha used to attain; i. e., the one which led most directly to Nirvana. The other three degrees were those of Srotapatti, of Sakridagamin, and Anagamin. The Arhat was not born again; each of the other three had a smaller or greater number of existences to undergo before Nirvana.

† I translate "l'Assemblee" by this phrase, which appears to render its meaning more precisely than a more literal translation.

When he had had time to recover his calmness, the Arhat's servant presented himself, and asked if he knew him. The servant of the law replied that he did, and that they both had entered into a religious life under the Buddha Kâsyapa. The other rejoined that while he had fulfilled all his duties, the servant of the law had been guilty of a fault in giving way to his temper, and exhorted him to diminish that fault by confession. The latter repented, and was thereby saved from re-birth in hell; but he was doomed to be re-born for five hundred generations in the womb of a slave. In this last existence he was still the offspring of a slave; but because he had formerly served the members of the Church, he was born in a rich and prosperous family; and because he had formerly read and studied Buddhist theology, he now became an Arhat under Gautama Buddha, after annihilating evil (H. B. I., p. 235 ff).

Such is a favorable specimen of a vast number of legends contained in the Buddhist Canon. The following fragment is of a rather different kind. It illustrates the extravagant adoration paid to the person of Buddha some generations after his death. A king named Rudrayana had sent to another, named Bimbisâra, an armor of marvelous properties and priceless value. Bimbisâra, at a loss what present he could send back which would be a fitting return for such a gift, determined to seek out Buddha and consult him on the point:—

"King Bimbisara addressed him thus:—'In the town of Rôruka, Lord, there lives a king called Rudrayana; he is my friend; though I have never seen him, he has sent me a present of an armor composed of five pieces. What present shall I give him in return?' 'Have the representation of the Tathagata traced on a bit of stuff,' answered Bhagavat, 'and send it him as a present.'

"Bimbisâra sent for some painters, and said—'Paint on a bit of stuff the image of the Tathâgata.' The blessed Buddhas are not very easy to get at, which is the reason why the painters could find no opportunity of [painting] Bhagvate. So they said to Bimbisâra—'If the king would give a feast to Bhagavat in the interior of his palace, it would be possible for us to seize the occasion of [painting] the blessed one. King Bimbisâra having accordingly invited Bhagavat to his palace, gave him a feast. The blessed Buddhas are beings that people are never weary of looking at. Whichever limb of Bhagavat the painters looked at they could not leave off contemplating it. So they could not seize the moment to paint him. Bhagavat then said to the king—'The painters will have trouble, O great king; it is impossible for them to seize the moment to [paint the] Tathâgata, but bring the canvass.' The king having brought it, Bhagavat projected his shadow on it, and said to the painters—'Fill that outline with colors; and then write over it the formulas of refuge as well as the precepts of instruction; you will have to trace both in the direct order, and in the inverse order the production of the [successive] causes [of existence], which is composed of twelve terms; and on it will be written these two verses:

"'Begin, go out [of the house]; apply yourself to the law of Buddha; annihilate the army of death, as an elephant upsets a hut of reeds.

"'He who shall walk without distraction under the discipline of this law, escaping birth and the revolution of the world, will put an end to sorrow.*

"'If any one asks what these verses are, you must answer: The first is the introduction; the second, the instruction; the third, the revolution of the world; and the fourth, the effort.'" (H. B. I., p. 341).

Bimbisâra, acting under Bhagavat's dictation, then wrote to Rudrayana that he was about to send him the most precious object in the three worlds, and that he must adorn the way by which it would arrive for two and a half yojanas. Rudrayana was rather irritated by this message, and proposed immediate war, but was dissuaded by his ministers. The picture therefore was received with all honor, and not uncovered till after it had been duly adored. Certain foreign merchants who happened to be on the spot, on seeing the portrait, cried out altogether: "Adoration to Buddha." At this name the king felt his hair stand on end, and inquired who Buddha was. His position, and the meaning of the inscription, was explained to him by the merchants. The consequence, as may be supposed, was his conversion to Buddhism. He reflected on the causes of existence, and attained the degree of Srotâpatti (H. B. I., p.)

Very little allusion is made in these legends to the immediate subject of the Vinaya-pitaka, namely, Discipline. But a

* These two verses are a standing formula by which the Buddha of the Canon summons the world to receive his law.

reference to Csoma's Analysis of the Dulva (the Tibetan title for the Vinaya) will show that it is in fact largely occupied in laying down rules for the guidance of monks and nuns, these rules being frequently supposed to have arisen out of particular events, while "moral tales" are freely intermingled with the treatment of the main business. The hap-hazard manner in which the regulations needful for the government of the Church were framed — according to the theory of the Scriptures — may be illustrated by a few specimens. Thus, two persons in debt had taken orders, "Shakya (Sâkyamuni) prohibits the admission into the religious order of any one who is in debt" (As. Re., vol. xx. p. 53). This rule entirely agrees with the general spirit of Gautama's proceedings, as narrated in the Buddhist books, and we are warranted in supposing that statements so harmonious rest on a historical foundation. Thus, he is said to have refused to admit young people without the consent of their parents, or servants of a king without their royal master's sanction. Regulations like these may well have been made by Buddha from a cautious anxiety to avoid all conflict with established authorities. Further on in the same volume of the Dulva the reception of hermaphrodites is likewise prohibited (As. Re., vol. xx. p. 55). On another occasion, leave is given to learn swimming. "Indecencies," are then "committed in the Ajirapati river. They are prohibited from touching any woman; — they may not save even one that has fallen into the river" (Ibid., vol. xx. p. 59). Elsewhere we are told of a pious lady who provided the infant community with cloth to make bathing clothes, since she had heard that both monks and nuns bathed without any garments (Ibid., vol. xx, p. 70). A little further on, the dress of the priesthood is prescribed. Some of the disciples wished to wear one thing, and some another; others to go naked. "Shakya tells them the impropriety and indecency of the latter, and prohibits it absolutely: and rebuking them, adds that such a garb, or to go naked, is the characteristic sign of a *Mu-stegs-chan* (Sansk) *Tirthika*" (Ibid., vol. xx. p. 71). Here again we seem to have a historical trait, for it was one of the distinctive features of Buddhism that its votaries were never naked, like the Tîrthikas, or heretical ascetics, but always wore the yellow robe. In other places there are rules on lodging, on bedding, on the treatment of quarrelsome priests, the use of fragrant substances, and many other trivial points of ecclesiastical discipline. The volumes containing all these instructions are followed by one in which the same stories are told, and the same morals deduced from them, concerning the nuns. Then there are some injunctions apparently peculiar to this sex, as, for instance, the restraint imposed on their possession of a multiplicity of garments. Another prohibition was called forth by the following conduct of a nun. A king had sent a piece of fine linen cloth as a present to a brother king. "It comes afterwards into the hands of *G*tsug-*D*gah-Mo (a lewd or wicked priestess); she puts it on, appears in public, but from its thin texture, seems to be naked. The priestesses are prohibited from accepting or wearing such thin clothes" (As. Re., vol. xx. p. 85).

It will be observed from these few quotations that according to the Canon the Buddha's usual mode of proceeding was to lay down rules as occasion required. Some instructive anecdote is related, and the new order follows as a natural consequence of the event. More probably the rules were in fact made first, and the anecdotes subsequently composed to account for them. However this may be, there exist in the Canon some undoubtedly ancient ordinances not called forth by any special circumstances, conformity to which was required of the monks, if not by their founder himself, at least by the rulers of his Church in its most primitive condition. Such, for example, are "the thirteen rules by which sin is shaken," reported by Burnouf, which are also found, with the exception of a single one, in a Chinese work entitled "the sacred book of the twelve observances" (H. B. I., p. 304). These rules belong, according to Burnouf, to an epoch when the organization of the monks under a powerful hierarchy, and their residence in settled monasteries, had scarcely begun. Some of them are even inconsistent with the institution of such monasteries, or Viharis, which are nevertheless very ancient. The fact that the above-named Chinese treatise, the pentaglot Buddhist Vocabulary,* and a

---

* This Vocabulary is a Chinese compilation, forming one of a class of catalogues drawn up in ancient times by Buddhist preachers. Such catalogues are found in the midst of canonical books, and are of high author-ity among Buddhists.

list current among the Singhalese, all contain these articles of
discipline (though with slight variations) proves, moreover, that
they appertain to that common fund on which Northern and
Southern Buddhists drew alike. The first article (following the
order in the Vocabulary) signifies "wearing rags found in the
dust," and refers to an injunction addressed to the monks to
wear vestments composed of rags picked up in heaps of ordure,
in cemeteries, and such places. The second, "he who has
three garments," corresponds to an order found in the Chinese
book forbidding monks to have more than three garments.
Of the third article which is corrupt, Burnouf can give no satisfactory explanation; and the fourth means "he who lives by
alms," a practice at all times imposed on the monastic orders.
Fifthly, the ascetic is described as "he who has but one seat;"
sixthly, as "one who eats no sweetmeats after his meal," all
eating for the day having to be finished by noon. Seventhly,
he "lives in the forest," that is, in lonely places; and eighthly,
he is "near a tree," the Chinese injunction requiring him to
sit near a tree, and to seek no shelter. The ninth order obliges
them to sit on the ground, that is, to live in the open air; the
tenth, to dwell among tombs, which the Singhalese interpret
as an order to visit cemeteries and meditate on the instability
of human affairs; the eleventh, to sit, and not to lie down.
Of the meaning of the twelfth there is some doubt; it may signify that the monk is to remain where he is, or that he is not
to change the position of his mat when once laid down. To
these twelve the Singhalese add a thirteenth article, that the
monk is to live by begging from house to house.

Not less remarkable are the ten commandments of Buddhism, which are doubtless also of considerable antiquity. Burnouf states that he has found them in the sequel of the Prâtimoksha Sûtra in the Pali-Burman copy of that most important
work (to which reference will shortly be made). These are the
ten commandments as given in that authority:—

1. Not to kill any living creature.
2. Not to steal.
3. Not to break the vow of chastity.
4. Not to lie.

5. Not to drink intoxicating liquors.

6. Not to take a meal except at the appointed time.

7. Not to visit dances, performances of vocal or instrumental music, or dramatic representations.

8. Not to wear garlands, or use perfumes and unguents.

9. Not to sleep on a high or large bed.

10. Not to accept gold or silver (Lotus, p. 444).

Of these commandments, some are evidently general, being founded on the fundamental principles of ethics; others are addressed only to those in orders. Such is the case with the last five, all of which bear reference to certain disciplinary laws imposed upon the monks and nuns. Their object is to prohibit luxury of various kinds, such as the use of a large bed, and to restrain the love of sensual enjoyments, such as plays, music, and dancing. Another list of offenses, after enumerating the first five of those contained in the preceeding list, adds five more, namely:—

1. Blasphemy of the Buddha.

2. Blasphemy of the Law.

3. Blasphemy of the Church.

4. Heresy.

5. Violation of a nun (Lotus, p. 445).

Such are the leading points of monastic discipline among the primitive Buddhists. A more elaborate and formal treatise on the subject of the sins to be avoided, and the penalties to be imposed on their commission, is the Prâtimoksha Sûtra, on Sûtra on Emancipation. It is the standard work on this subject, and should be recited before the assembled Vihâra twice in each month, any guilty brother confessing any transgression of its precepts of which he might be conscious. Its antiquity is undoubted, for in a Sûtra known to have been brought to China from India in A.D. 70 (and therefore already of established repute) the Prâtimoksha is referred to as the "two hundred and fifty rules" (C. B. S., p. 189). It does, in fact, contain two hundred and fifty rules in its Chinese form, while the Thibetan version contains two hundred and fifty-three, and the Pali version but two hundred and twenty-seven (H. B. I., p. 303). While the

Prâtimoksha Sûtra now to be quoted is destined for monks, or Bhikshus, it is to be noted that there exists likewise a "Bhikshunî Prâtimoksha Sûtra," or Treatise on Emancipation for Nuns (As. Re., vol. xx. pp. 79, 84). The rules are, *mutatis mutandis*, the same for both sexes.

It will be interesting to glance rapidly at the nature of the faults and crimes the confession of which is here imposed on Bhikshus and Bhikshunîs.*

The Sûtra opens with certain stanzas designed to celebrate the Buddhist Trinity, — the Buddha, the Law, and the Church. Then follow some "preparatory questions:"—

"Are the priests assembled? (They are.) Are all things arranged? (seats, water, sweeping, &c.) (They are.) Let all depart who are not ordained. (If any, let them go; if none are present, let one say so.) Does any Bhikshu here present ask for absolution ? (Let him answer accordingly.) Exhortation must be given to the priestesses (but if there are none present, let one say so). Are we agreed what our present business is? It is to repeat the precepts in this lawful assembly.

"Venerable brethren, attend now! On this . . . day of the month . . . . let the assembled priests listen attentively and patiently, whilst the precepts are distinctly recited.

COMMENCEMENT.

"Brethren! I desire to go through the Pratimoksha. Bhikshus! assembled thus, let all consider and devoutly reflect on these precepts. If any have transgressed, let him repent! If none have transgressed, then stand silent! silent! Thus, brethren, it shall be known that ye are guiltless.

"Now if a stranger ask one of us a question we are bound to reply truthfully: so, also, Bhikshus, we who reside in community, if we know that we have done wrong, and yet decline to acknowledge it, we are guilty of prevarication. But Buddha has declared that prevarication effectually prevents our religious advancement. That brother, therefore, who is conscious of transgression, and desires absolution,

---

* The translation of this Sutra is due to Mr. Beal, to whose most useful labors on Buddhism I am much indebted.—C. B. S., p. 206.

ought at once to declare his fault, and after proper penance he shall have rest and peace.

"Brethren! having repeated this preface, I demand of you all—Is this assembly pure or not? (Repeat this three times.) Brethren! this assembly is pure; silent! silent! ye stand! So let it be! Brethren, I now proceed to recite the four parajika laws, ordered to be recited twice every month."

These four laws are then repeated, and the penalty of excommunication, which attaches to a breach of any of them, is enunciated. The first of the four prohibits impure conduct; the second, theft. The third runs as follows:—

"If a Bhikshu cause a man's death, or hold a weapon and give it a man (for the purpose), or if he speak of the advantages of death, or if he carelessly exhort one to meet death (saying), 'Tush, you are a brave man,' or use such wicked speech as this, 'It is far better to die and not to live,' using such considerations as these, bringing every sort of expedient into use, praising death, exhorting to death: this Bhikshu ought to be excluded and cut off."

The fourth rule is against pretending to a perfect knowledge of the Truth which the Bhikshu does not in fact possess.

At the end of the recitation of these four rules it is declared that a brother who has transgressed any one of them "has acquired the guilt which demands exclusion, and ought not to live as a member of the priesthood." The question as to the purity of the Assembly is then again put, and the priest (after declaring it pure) proceeds to thirteen rules, the breach of which is punished by suspension. The first restrains a monk from pampering lustful thoughts, the second from bringing any part of his body in contact with that of a woman, the third from lewd talk with a woman, the fourth from obtaining a woman to minister to him. For a violation of this last injunction the highest penance, as well as suspension, is appointed. There follow rules against building a residence of illegal size, or without due consecration, or on an inconvenient site; against building a Vihâra on an inconvenient site; against slander of a Bhikshu (two rules), against causing disunion in a community, against forming a cabal for mutual protection against just censure, against disorderly conduct when living in a house, against a refusal to listen to expostulation or reproof. Solitary confinement, and six days of penance, are the penalties imposed on these offenses; after the infliction of the sentence absolution is to be given. Next we have two rules "not capable of exact definition," but relating to licentious talk with "a faithful laywoman." Thirty rules relating to priests' robes and the like matters are now recited. They seem to be aimed at covetousness in receivi g or asking gifts. After the usual inquiry as to the purity of the brethren, ninety rules against offenses requiring "confession and absolution" are to be read. Some of these seem to be repetitions of previous ones belonging to a more serious category, as the first two, on lying and slander, and the eighth, against pretended knowledge. Then the Prâtimoksha proceeds to say that if a Bhikshu use hypocritical language, if he occupy the same lodging as a woman, or the same as a man not yet ordained above two nights, if he chant prayers with a man not yet ordained, if he rail at a priest, if he use water containing insects (so as to destroy life), if he give clothes to a Bhikshuuî, or nun, if he go with a Bhikshunî in any boat except a ferry-boat, if he agree to walk with a Bhikshuî along the road, if he gambol in the water while bathing, if he drink distilled or fermented liquor, or commit any of the many other faults, partly against morality in general, partly against conventual rule, he is guilty of a transgression of this class. Four rules follow against receiving food from a nun, against allowing a nun in a layman's house to point out certain dishes, and have them given to certain monks; against going to dinner uninvited; against the omission on the part of a monk residing in a dangerous place to warn those who may bring him victuals of the risk they run. A hundred rules, mostly trifling, are now entered on. They are such as these: "Not to enter a layman's house in a bouncing manner." "Not to munch or make a munching noise in eating rice," and likewise, "not to make a lapping noise." "Not to clean the teeth under a pagoda;" with many other minute regulations on a multitude of trivial points. The seven concluding laws refer simply to the mode of deciding cases.

SUBDIVISION 2.— *The Sutra-Pitaka.*

We have thus concluded our notice of the Prâtimoksha Sûtra, and may pass on to the Sûtra-pitaka, the second of the three baskets into which the Canon is divided. Sûtra is a term signifying a discourse, or lecture, and the Sûtras of Buddhism are frequently moral stories, supposed to emanate from Gautama Buddha himself, and embodying the great features of his gospel, as the Sermon on the Mount and the Parables do those of the gospel of Jesus. A very interesting collection of such stories belonging to the Sûtra-pitaka is contained in a work translated from the Thibetan by a Russian scholar, and forming, under the title of the *H*dsangs-*b*lun, or the Wise Man and the Fool, a portion of the twenty-eighth volume of the *M*do, or Sûtra-pitaka. From Csoma's Ananysis it appears that many other narratives of a similar nature are embodied in this section of the Canon, though much of it also consists of more direct dogmatic instruction. From "The Wise Man and the Fool" I select a chapter which affords a good illustration of the boundless charity which Buddhism inculcates.

The victoriously-perfect One was living at Srâvasti. When the time came to receive alms, he set out with his disciple Ânanda, alms-bowl in hand, along the road. It so happened that he met two men who had been condemned to death for repeated robberies, and were being led to execution. Their mother, seeing the Buddha, thus addressed him:— "O chief of gods, think of us with mercy, and vouchsafe to take under thy protection these my sons who are going to execution." Buddha accordingly interceded with the king, who gave them a free pardon. Touched with gratitude, the two men asked leave to become monks, and on Buddha's consenting to receive them, their hair at once fell off from head and face, and their garments assumed the yellow hue of the order.[*] Both mother and sons attained high spiritual grades. Ânanda marveled what good deeds these three could have performed to meet with the victoriously-perfect One, to be saved from such great evils, and to obtain the prospect of Nirvâna. Buddha thereupon informed

---

[*] This is a standing miracle on the reception of novices by Buddha.

him that this was not the first occasion on which he had saved
their lives, and on Ânanda's request for a further explanation,
related the following circumstances. Countless years ago, there
lived in Jumbudwîpa (India) a certain king who had three sons.
The youngest son was mild and merciful from his childhood
upwards. One day, when the king, with his ministers, wives
and sons, was at a picnic outside the town, the three sons went
into a wood, where they found a tigress, with young recently
littered, so nearly starved that she was almost on the point of
devouring her own brood. The youngest asked his brothers
what food a tigress would eat. "Newly-killed meat and warm
blood." "Is there any one who would support its life with his
own body?" "No one," replied the elder brothers; "that
would be too difficult" (I give only the substance of this colloquy). Then the youngest prince thought within himself:
"For a long time I have been driven about in the circle of
births, and have thrown away my body and my life innumerable times; often have I sacrificed it for the passion of the desires, often for that of rage, often too for folly and ignorance;
what value then has this body, which has not one single time
trodden the field of meritorious actions for the sake of religion!"
Meantime, all three had walked on; but the youngest, pleading
some business of his own, desired them to go on, leaving him
to follow. Having returned to the cave of the tigress, he laid
himself down beside her, but found her too weak to open her
mouth. Hereupon the prince contrived to bleed himself with a
sharp splinter of wood, and the tigress, after licking the blood
that flowed from him, was sufficiently refreshed to consume him
altogether. The two elder brothers, wondering at his long absence, returned to the tiger's hole, where, on finding his remains,
they rolled upon the ground and fainted, overcome with grief.
The queen, who had had an alarming dream, questioned them
anxiously on their return as to their brother, and she too on
learning the sad event, which their choking voices for some time
prevented them from telling, fell senseless to the ground. Soon
after, both king and queen visited the den, but could find nothing but bones. Meantime, the prince had been born again in
the Tushita heaven. Looking about to discover what good
action of his had brought him to this place, he saw the bones

of his former body in the tigress's den, and his parents sighing and groaning around them. He returned from his heavenly abode to give them some consolation and some good advice. They were at length somewhat comforted, and collecting his bones, buried them in a costly sarcophagus.

Buddha then turns to Ananda and asks him whom he supposes the actors in this tragedy to have been. He tells him, without waiting for an answer, that the king was his present father, the queen his present mother, the elder princes certain personages named Maitreya and Vasumitra, and the youngest prince no other than himself. The young tigers were, it need hardly be said, the condemned felons whom he had now again delivered from death.

While this anecdote inculcates charity in its fullest extent, the one which is now to be quoted illustrates another most conspicuous point in the ethics of Buddhism, — the regard paid by it to personal purity and the deadening influence it exercised on the senses. The translation of this curious legend is due to Burnouf: —

"There was at Mathurâ a courtesan called Vâsavadattâ. Her maid went one day to Upagupta to buy her some perfumes. Vâsavadattâ said to her on her return: 'It seems, my dear, that this perfumer pleases you, as you always buy from him.' The maid answered her: 'Daughter of my master, Upagupta, the son of the merchant, who is gifted with beauty, with talent, and with gentleness, passes his life in the observance of the law.' On hearing these words Vâsavadattâ conceived an affection for Upagupta, and at last she sent her maid to say to him: 'My intention is to go and find you; I wish to enjoy myself with you.' The maid delivered her message to Upagupta; but the young man told her to answer her mistress: 'My sister, it is not yet time for you to see me.' Now it was necessary in order to obtain the favors of Vâsavadattâ to give five hundred Purânas. Thus the courtezan imagined that [if he refused her, it was because] he could not give the five hundred Purânas. For this reason, she sent her maid to him again to say, 'I do not ask a single Kârchâpana from the son of my master; I only wish to enjoy myself with him.' The maid again delivered this new message, and Upagupta answered her in the same way: 'My sister, it is not time yet for you to see me.'

"However, the son of a master-workman had come to settle with Vâsavadattâ, when a merchant, who was bringing from the north five hundred horses which he wished to sell, came to the town of Mathurâ, aud asked who was the most beautiful courtezan. He was answered that Vâsavadattâ was. Immediately, taking 500 Purânas and a great number of presents, he went to the courtezan. Then Vâsavadattâ, urged by covetousness, assassinated the son of the master-workman, who was at her house, threw his body into the middle of the filth of the town, and gave herself up to the merchant. After some days, the young man was extricated from the filth by his parents, who denounced the murder. The king at once gave orders to the executioners to go and cut off Vâsavadattâ's hands, feet, ears, and nose, and to leave her in the cemetery. The executioners carried out the orders of the king, and left the courtezan in the place named.

"Now Upagupta heard of the punishment that had been inflicted on Vâsavadattâ, and at once this idea came into his mind: 'Some time ago, this woman wished to see me for a sensual object, and I did not consent that she should see me. But now that her hands and feet, ears and nose, have been cut off, it is time she should see me,' and he pronounced these verses:

"'When her body was covered with beautiful attire, when she shone with ornaments of different sorts, the best thing for those who aspired to deliverance and who wished to escape the law of renewed birth was not to go and see this woman.

"'To-day, when she has lost her pride, her love and her joy, when she has been mutilated by the edge of the knife, when her body is reduced to its true nature, it is time to see her.'

"Then sheltered by a parasol carried by a young man who accompanied him as a servant, he went to the cemetery with a measured step. Vâsavadattâ's maid had stayed with her mistress out of gratitude for her past kindness, and she prevented the crows from approaching her body. [Seeing Upagupta] she said to her: 'Daughter of my master, he to whom you sent me several times, Upagupta, is coming this way. No doubt he comes attracted by the desire for pleasure.' But Vâsavadattâ, hearing these words, answered:

"'When he sees me deprived of beauty, racked with grief, lying on the ground all covered with blood, how can he feel love of pleasure?'

"Then she said to her maid; 'Friend, pick up the limbs that have been severed from my body.' The maid picked them up at once, and hid them under a bit of linen. At this moment Upagupta arrived, and he stood up before Vâsavadattâ. The courtezan, seeing him standing up before her, said to him: 'Son of my master, when my body was whole, when it was made for enjoyment, I several times sent my maid to you, and you answered me: "My sister, it is not time for you to see me." To-day, when the knife has carried off my hands and feet, my ears and nose, when I am thrown in the dirt and in blood, why do you come?' And she uttered the following verses:

"'When my body was soft like the lotus flower, when it was adorned with ornaments and rich clothes, when it had all which attracted the eye, I was so unhappy as not to see you.

"'To-day why do you come to contemplate a body, the sight of which the eyes cannot bear, which games, pleasure, joy, and beauty have abandoned, which inspires horror, and is stained with blood and dirt?'

"Upagupta answered her: 'I have not come to you, my sister, attracted by the love of pleasure; but I am come to see the real nature of the miserable objects of the enjoyments of man'" (H. B. I., p. 146 ff).

Such is the character of the more ancient portions of the Sûtra-pitaka. It consists largely of tales, most of which have much the same outward form, the details only being varied; and all of which are intended to impress some kind of moral upon their hearers. But the Sûtra collection is composed of two different classes of works, the one class being named by Burnouf simple Sûtras, the other developed Sûtras. The developed Sûtras belong, according to the same authority, to a much later period, and are marked off from the simple Sûtras by certain well-defined characters. They are indeed of a kind which absolutely precludes the notion that they can emanate in any way whatever from Sâkyamuni, or that they could have been composed during the modest beginnings of his Church, when his followers were rather intent on practical goodness than on pompous and high-flown descriptions of their Master's magnificence. Not that all the Sûtras classed by Burnouf as simple must needs belong to a very early age; but that the developed Sûtras certainly could not have been written until some centuries after Sâkyamuni's death, when his disciples, instead of using their voices in actual conversation, enjoyed the leisure and the means to employ their pens in attempted fine writing. Burnouf has given the public a single specimen of a Sûtra of this class, and they must be very devoted students of Oriental literature who wish for another. Here is a sample of its style:—

"Then the Bodhisattva Mahâsattva Akshayamati having risen from his seat, after throwing his upper garment over his shoulder, and placing his right knee on the ground, directing his joined hands, in token of respect, to the quarter where Bhagavat was, addressed him in these words: 'Why, O Bhagavat, does the Bodhisattva Mahâsttva Avalokitesvara bear that name?' This having been said, Bhagavat spoke thus to the Bodhisattva Akshayamati: 'O son of a family, all the hundreds of thousands of myriads of creatures existing in the world who suffer pains, have but to hear the name of the Bodhisattva Avalokitesvara to be delivered from this mass of pains'" (Lotus, p. 261).

The extraordinary diffuseness of this kind of composition is scarcely credible. Not only is every doctrine elaborated in the utmost number of words possible, but its exposition in prose is regularly followed by a second exposition in verse. Add to this peculiar feature of developed Sûtras another, namely, that innumerable crowds of supernatural auditors (especially Bodhisattvas, or future Buddhas) are present at their delivery by the Buddha, and take part in the dialogue, or demand explanations on knotty points, and some conception may be formed of their wholly unreal and unnatural character. Thus, the Lotus concludes with the statement that innumerable Tathâgatas (Buddhas) come from other universes, seated on thrones near diamond trees, innumerable Bodhisattvas, and the whole of the four assemblies of the universe, with Devas (gods), men, Asuras, and Gandharvas, transported with joy, praised what Bhagavat had said. Although the simple Sûtras mention the presence of gods at the Buddha's teaching, yet they do not (so far as I am aware) introduce these hosts of Bodhisattvas and Buddhas belonging to other worlds than ours. Their horizon had not extended itself to such vast limits, and they confined themselves to the universe in which we live.

SUBDIVISION 3.—*The Abhidharma-pitaka.*

A third section of the Canon remains, the Abhidharma, or Metaphysics. Buddhist metaphysics are so absolutely mystical that it would be a waste of time to enlarge upon them in a work not specially consecrated to Oriental subjects. The subtleties of the Indian mind would require far more space to explain than would be consistent with the objects in view here, even if the writer were competent to explain them. The impression left on the mind by the perusal of the Adhidharma is that we delude ourselves if we believe in the reality of anything whatever. There is no material world; all we see, hear, feel or believe, is illusion; our thoughts themselves are no-thoughts; this doctrine is that of wisdom and truth, but there is no wisdom and no truth. The Buddha arrives by his meditations at this sublime knowledge; but there is no meditation and no knowledge. He conducts living creatures to Nirvâna: but there are neither creatures to be conducted, nor a Buddha to conduct them. All is nothingness, and nothingness is all. That this nihilism is common to all the schools into which Buddhists are divided, I do not mean to assert. There are in Nepaul certain schools which hold a peculiar modification of theism, and they probably may not embrace these strange and unintelligible systems. But the views—if views they can be called—which have just been described, do mark the canonical books of the Abhidharma with which I am acquainted; such as the so-called Pradjnâ Pârmamitâ, or Perfection of Wisdom. There is, however, one metaphysical theory which is not a mere series of contradictions, and which, from its close connection with the deepest roots of the Buddhistic faith, deserves more than a mere cursory mention. It is the dogma known as that of the twelve Nidânas, or successive causes of existence.

It has already been explained that the original aim of Buddhism—the salvation offered by Sakyamuni—was deliverance from this painful existence. The four truths which formed the foundation of his system have also been spoken of. It may be well to remind the reader that they are these:—1. The existence of Pain; 2. The production of Pain; 3. The annihilation of

Pain; 4. The way to the annihilation of Pain. Now if existence was, as the Buddhists believed, the source of pain, it was important to discover the source of existence. This the theory of the Nidânas professes to do. It is therefore not only intimately related to the four great truths, but forms an essential supplement to them. A very ancient formula, discovered not only in books but on images, declares that, "Of all things proceeding from cause, the cause of their procession hath the Tathagata explained. The great Sramana has likewise declared the cause of the extinction of all things." Whether this formula refers to the four truths, or to the Nidânas, it is impossible to say. The Nidânas, however, might well be referred to in these terms. They are described in a passage which Burnouf has quoted from the Lalitavistara, in which the Bodhisattva (afterwards Buddha) is stated to have risen through prolonged meditation from the knowledge of each successive consequent to that of its antecedent. The Bodhisattva, we are told, collected his thoughts and fixed his intelligence in the last watch of night, just before the dawn appeared. "Then this thought came into his mind: The existence of this world, which is born, grows old, dies, falls, and is born again, is certainly an evil. But he could not recognize the means of quitting this world, which is nothing but a great accumulation of sorrows, which is composed but of decrepitude, illness, death, and other miseries, which are altogether formed of them.

"This reflection brought the following thought into his mind: What is the thing the existence of which leads to decrepitude and death, and what cause have decrepitude and death? This reflection came into his mind: Birth existing, decrepitude and death exist; for decrepitude and death have birth as their cause."

A similar process of reasoning led him to see that the cause of birth was existence; that of existence, conception; that of conception, desire; that of desire, sensation; that of sensation, contact; that of contact, the six seats of sensible qualities; that of the six seats, name and form; that of name and form, knowledge; that of knowledge, the concepts; that of the concepts, ignorance. "It is thus," exclaims the Bodhisattva when this great light had burst upon him, "it is thus that the production

of this world, which is but a mass of sorrows, takes place."
And by an inverse process he went on to reflect that if ignorance did not exist, neither would the concepts, and so on
through every link of the chain. Until at length, "from the
annihilation of birth results the annihilation of decrepitude, of
death, of sufferings, of lamentations, of sorrow, of regret, of
despair. It is thus that the annihilation of this world, which is
but a mass of sorrows, takes place" (H. B. I., p. 487).

This speculation is by no means easy to understand. Apparently it means that ignorance, in the sense of a mistaken
notion of the reality of the material world, leads to a whole
series of blunders, ending inevitably in birth. From this fundamental error or belief in the existence of sensible objects
spring certain other false conceptions. Knowledge, which next
ensues, may mean not merely cognition but consciousness,
knowledge of our existence; and in this sense, or in something
like it, it must be taken in order to explain the apparent paradox of a deduction of the pedigree of knowledge directly from
ignorance. Hence name and form, a still further distinction of
the individual — a specialization of the vague knowledge of
himself which the last stage brought him to. The next step
carries us on to the six seats of sensible qualities; a phrase
expressing the organs by which sensible qualities are perceived
—the five senses, and *Manâs*, the heart, which the Indians considered as a sixth sense. It appears also from Burnouf's remarks that the Sanskrit term includes along with the organs
the qualities they perceive, the Law being assigned to the heart
or internal sense as the object of its perception. The six
seats being given, contact follows; contact implies sensation,
and sensation naturally leads to desire. Conception is represented as the effect of desire, but another translation of this
term by attachment, fondness for material things, renders the
sequence easier to understand. Attachment to anything but the
three gems — the Buddha, the Law, and the Church — is, however, a fatal error, and leads to the melancholy result of existence. Evidently, however, the being whose downward progress
has thus been described must have existed before, and the
event here alluded to must probably be the passage into the
definite condition of the human embryo. And this is rather

confirmed by the fact that the next step is that of birth, followed, as a matter of course, by the miseries of human life, terminating in death.* And death, unless every remnant of attachment to, and desire for, all worldly things has been purged away, unless every trace of sinful tendencies has been obliterated, is but a fresh beginning of the same weary round.

Subdivision 4. — *Theology and Ethics of the Tripitaka.*

Thus we have examined in succession the three great divisions of the Buddhist Canon. We may pass over a comparatively late and spurious addition to it, the Tantras—full of the worship of strange gods and goddesses, and of magical formularies —to consider the general features of these sacred works in reference to their theological teaching and to their moral tendency. Theology is perhaps a term that will be held to be misplaced in speaking of a system which acknowledges no God. Yet Buddhism is so full of supernatural creatures, and the Buddha himself occupies a position so nearly divine, that it would be hard to find a more appropriate word. Buddha himself is the central figure of the whole of his system, far more completely than Christ is the central figure of Christianity, or Mahomet of Islam. There is no Deity above him; he stands out alone, unrivaled, unequaled, and unapproachable. The gods of the Hindu pantheon are by no means annihilated in the Buddhist Scriptures. On the contrary, they play a certain part in them, as when some of the greatest among their number assist at the delivery of Mâyâ. But the part assigned to them is always a subordinate one; they are practically set aside, not by the skeptical process of questioning their existence, but by the more subtle one of introducing them as humbly seated at the Buddha's footstool, and devout recipients of his instructions. Hostility to Gautama Buddha there may be, but not from them. It proceeds from heretical Brahmans—rivals in trade—and from those whom they may for a time deceive. The gods are among the most docile of his pupils, and display a praiseworthy

* I do not pretend to any certainty that the above interpretation is correct, but I have in the main followed a trustworthy guide, Burnouf. See H. B. I., p. 491-507.

eagerness to acquire the knowledge he may condescend to impart. Infinitely above gods and men, because possessing infinitely deeper knowledge and infinitely higher virtue, stands the Tathâgata, the man who walks in the footsteps of his predecessors. His position is the greatest to which any mortal creature can attain. But it has been attained by many before, and will be by many hereafter. Far away into ages separated from ours by millions of millions of years stretches the long list of Buddhas, for every age has received a similar light to lighten up its darkness. All have led lives marked by the same incidents, and have taught the same truths. But by and by the darkness has returned; the doctrines of the former Buddha have been forgotten, and a new one has been needed. Then in due season he has appeared, and has again opened to mankind the path of salvation. Thus Kâsyapa Buddha preceded Gautama Buddha, and Maitreya (now a Bodhisattva) will succeed him. The Buddha is an object of the most devout adoration. Prayers are addressed to him; his relics are enshrined in Stûpas, or buildings erected by the piety of believers to cover them; his footprints are viewed with reverential awe, and his tooth, preserved in Ceylon, receives the constant homage of that pious population. Thus his position is not unlike that of a true Deity, though the theory of Buddhism would require us to suppose that he is non-existent, and therefore wholly unable to aid his worshipers. But this theory is not acted upon, and is probably not held in all its strictness; for Buddha—though to some extent superseded in Northern Buddhsim by other divinities—is the object of a decided worship in both its elements of prayer and praise.

But the preëminent station occupied by a Buddha is not reached without a long and painful education. Through ages, the length of which is scarcely to be expressed by numbers, they are qualifying themselves for their glorious task. During this period they are termed Bodhisattvas, that is, beings who have taken a solemn resolution to become Buddhas, and are practicing the necessary virtues. The very fact of taking this resolution is an exercise of exalted benevolence, for their excellence is such that they might, if they pleased, enter at once into Nirvâna. But such is their love for the human race, that they prefer to be born again and again in a world of woe, in order to throw open Nirvâna to others besides themselves. To attain their end, they must make an offering to some actual Buddha, wishing at the same time that by virtue of this act they may become Buddhas themselves; and they must receive an assurance from the object of their gift that this wish will be fulfilled. Thus Gautama, who happened at the time to be a prince, presented a golden vessel full of oil to a Buddha named Purana Dîpankara, with the wish alluded to, and was assured by him that he would in a future age become a supreme Buddha (M. B., p. 92). The tales of the pains endured, the sacrifices made, the virtues practiced by Gautama during this probationary period are numerous and varied. He himself, by virtue of his faculty of knowing the past, related them to his disciples. He had sacrificed wife, children, property, even his own person, for the good of other living creatures; he had endured all kinds of sufferings; he had shown himself capable of the rarest unselfishness, the most perfect purity, the most unswerving rectitude. The tale of his endurances might move compassion, had it not been crowned at last with the highest reward to which a mortal can aspire.

While the Buddha occupies the first rank among human and superhuman beings, and a Bodhisattva the second, the Scriptures introduce us to others holding very conspicuous places among the spiritual nobility. Such, for instance, are the Pratyeka Buddhas. These are persons of very high intelligence and very extraordinary merit. But they are unable to communicate their knowledge to others. They can save themselves; others they cannot save. Herein lies their inferiority to supreme Buddhas,—that while their spiritual attainments are sufficient to ensure their entry into Nirvâna, they are inadequate to enable them to obtain the same privilege for any other person.

In addition to these not very interesting Buddhas, the legends speak of certain grades of intelligence attained by Gautama's hearers. Thus, we are often told that many of the audience — perhaps hundreds of thousands — after hearing a sermon from him, became Arhats; others are said to have become Anâgâmin, Sakridâgâmin, or Srotâpanna. These degrees are based upon the reception of the four truths. According to the manner in which a man received these truths, he entered one of eight paths, each of the four degrees having two classes, a higher and a lower one. Sometimes these paths are called "fruits;" a disciple is said to obtain the fruits of such and such a state. An Arhat is a person of very high station indeed. Excepting a Buddha, none is equal to him, either in knowledge or miraculous powers, both of which he possesses to a preëminent extent. The Arhat after his death enters at once into Nirvâna. The Anâgâmin enters the third path (from the bottom), and is exempt from re-birth except in the world of Devas, or gods. He who obtains or "sees" the fruit of the second path is born once more in the world of gods or in that of men. Finally, the Srotâpanna undergoes re-birth either among gods or men seven times, and is then delivered from the stream of existence.*

Below the fortunate travelers along the path stands the mass of ordinary believers. All of these, of course, aim ultimately— or should aim—at that perfection of knowledge and of character which ensures Nirvâna; but in popular Buddhism at the present day this distant goal appears to be well-nigh forgotten, and to have given place to some heaven, or place of enjoyment, above which the general hope does not rise.

Believers in general are divided into two classes, Bhikshus and Bhikshunîs, or monks and nuns; and Upâsakas, lây disciples. The distinction between these classes is well illustrated by the following extract from a sacred book, the consideration

---

* The authorities do not entirely agree in the accounts they give of the speed with which these paths lead to Nirvana. The above statement appears to me unquestionably the oldest and most authentic. It is in agreement with Eitel, Sanskrit-Chinese Dictionary, *sub vocibus* (Sakridagamin, however, is omitted), and with Hardy, E. M., p. 280.

Eitel indeed adds that an Arhat, if he does not enter Nirvana, may become a Buddha, but this is probably a Northern perversion of the original notion. In the genuine authorities, a Bodhisattva is quite distinct from an Arhat. The account derived by Burnouf (H. B. I. p. 291 ff.) from Northern sources is palpably a corruption of the oldest doctrine, proceeding from that unbounded love of exaggerated numbers which is the besetting sin of Buddhist writers. According to this version, the Srotapanna must pass through 80,000 ages before his seven births; the Sakridagamin, after 60,000 ages, is to be born once as a man and once as a god; the Anagamin, after 40,000 ages, is exempted from re-birth in the world of desire, and arrives at supreme knowledge; which the Arhat reaches after 20,000 ages. Poor comfort this to souls longing for their eternal rest. Cf. Koppen, R. B., vol. i. p. 498.

of which will lead us from the domain of theology into that of
morality:—"What is to be done in the condition of a mendicant?—The rules of chastity must be observed during the whole
of life.—That is not possible; are there no other means?—
There are others, friend; namely, to be a devotee (Upâsaka).—
What is to be done in this condition?—It is necessary during
the whole of one's life to abstain from murder, theft, pleasure,
lying, and the use of intoxicating liquors." The injunctions
thus stated to be binding on the laity are in fact the first five
of the ten commandments, pleasure being simply a designation
of unchastity, which the layman as well as the monk is here
ordered to eschew. The first five commandments are in fact
general, referring to universal ethical obligations, not merely
to monastic discipline, like the other five. But Buddhist morality is by no means merely negative. It enjoins not only abstinence from such definite sins as these, but the practice of positive virtues in their most exalted forms. In no system is benevolence, or, as it is termed in the English New Testament, charity, more emphatically inculcated. Exhibited, as we have seen
it is, in the highest degree by Buddha himself, it should be
illustrated to the extent of their capabilities by all his followers.
Chastity is the subject of almost equal praise. And the other
virtues come in for their share of recognition, the general object
of the examples held up to admiration being to exhort the
faithful to a life spotless in all its parts, like that of their master. With this aim the legends related generally fall into some
such form as this: Characters appear who undergo some suffering, but receive also some great reward, such as meeting
with Buddha, and embracing his religion. It is then explained
by Buddha that the sufferings were the result of some bad action
done in a former life, and the benefit received the result of
some good action; while he will probably add that he himself
in that bygone age stood in the relation of a benefactor to the
recipient of his faith. Or a number of persons are introduced
playing various parts, good and evil, and receiving blessings or
misfortunes. One of these is conspicuous by the excellence of
his conduct. Then, at the end of the story, the disciples are
told not to imagine that this model of virtue is any other than
Sâkyamuni himself, while the other characters are translated,

according to their special peculiarities, each into some individual living at the time, and forming either one of Buddha's retinue, or connected with him by ties of kindred, or (if wicked) marked by hostility to his person or doctrine. Thus, the bad parts in these dramas are often allotted to his cousin Devadatta, who figures in these Scriptures as his typical opponent.

The essential doctrine of all these moral fictions — the corner-stone of Buddhist ethics — is that every single act of virtue receives its reward, every single transgression its punishment. The consequences of our good deeds or misdeeds, mystically embodied in our Karma, follow us from life to life, from earth to heaven, from earth to hell, and from heaven or hell to earth again. Karma expresses an idea by no means easily seized. Perhaps it may be defined as the sum total of our moral actions, good and bad, conceived as a kind of entity endowed with the force of destiny. It is our Karma that determines the character of our successive existences. It is our Karma that determines whether our next birth shall be in heaven or hell, in a happy or miserable condition here below. And as Karma is but the result of our own actions, each of which must bear its proper fruit, the balance, either on the credit or debit side of our account, must always be paid; to us or by us, as the case may be.

Let us illustrate this by an instance or two. A certain prince, named Kunâla, remarkable for his personal beauty, had been deprived of his eyes through an intrigue in his father's harem. Sâkyamuni, in pointing the moral, informs his disciples that Kunâla had formerly been a huntsman, who finding five hundred gazelles in a cave, had put out their eyes in order to preclude their escape. For this cruelty he had suffered the pains of hell for hundreds of thousands of years, and had then had his eyes put out in human existences. But Kunâla also enjoyed great advantages. He was the son of a king, he possessed an attractive person, and, above all, he had embraced the truths of Buddhism. Why was this? Because he had once caused a Stûpa of a former Buddha, which an unbelieving monarch had suffered to be pulled to pieces, to be rebuilt, and had likewise restored a statue of this same Buddha which had been spoilt (H. B. I., p. 414). The truly Buddhistic spirit of this young prince is evinced by the circumstance that he interceded earnestly with his father for the pardon of his step-mother who had caused him to be so cruelly mutilated.

In another case, a poor old woman, who had led a miserable existence as the slave of an unfeeling master and mistress, was re-born in one of the heavens, known as that of the three-and-thirty gods. Five hundred goddesses descended to the cemetery where she had been heedlessly thrown into the ground, strewed flowers on her bones, and offered them spices. The reason of all this honor was, that on the previous day she had met with Kâtyâyana, an apostle of Buddhism, had drawn water and presented it to him in his bowl, and had consequently received a blessing from him, with an exhortation to enter her mistress's room after she had gone to sleep, and sitting on a heap of hay to fix her mind exclusively upon Buddha. This advice she had attended to, and had consequenty received the above-named reward (W. u. T., p. 153).

Good and evil, under this elaborate system, are thus the seeds which, by an invariable law, produce their appropriate fruits in a future state. The doctrine may in fact be best described in the words attributed to its author:—"A previous action does not die; be it good or evil, it does not die; the society of the virtuous is not lost; that which is done, that which is said, for the Aryas,* for these grateful persons, never dies. A good action well done, a bad action wickedly done, when they have arrived at their maturity, equally bear an inevitable fruit" (H. B. I., p. 98).

SECTION V. — THE ZEND-AVESTA.†

Persia was once a great power in the world; the Persian

---

* Aryas is a term comprehending the several classes of believers.

† There is a complete translation of the Zend-Avesta by Spiegel. It contains useful introductory essays; but in the present state of Zend scholarship the translation cannot be regarded as final. Dr. Haug, in a German treatise, has elucidated as well as translated a small, but very important, portion, of the Zend-Avesta, termed the five Gathas. The same scholar has also published a volume of Essays on the Parsee language and religion, which contains some translated passages, and may be consulted with advantage, though Dr. Haug's English stands in great need of revision. Burnouf has translated but a very small part of the Zend-Avesta, in a work entitled

religion, a conquering and encroaching faith. The Persian Empire threatened to destroy the independence of Greece. It held the Jews in actual subjection, and its religious views profoundly influenced the development of theirs. Through the Jews, its ideas have penetrated the Christian world. and leavened Europe. It once possessed an extensive and remarkable sacred literature, but a few scattered fragments of which have descended to us. These fragments, recovered and first translated by Anquetil du Perron, have been but imperfectly elucidated as yet by European scholars; and there can be no doubt that much more light remains to be cast upon them by philology as it progresses. Such as they are, however, I shall make use of the translations already before us to give my readers an imperfect, account of the character of the Parsee Scriptures.

These compositions are the productions of several centuries and are widely separated from one another in the character of their thought, and in the objects of worship proposed to the faithful follower of Zarathustra. The oldest among them, which may belong to the time of the prophet himself, are considered by Haug to be as ancient as B.C. 1200, while the youngest were very likely as recent as B.C. 500.

Haug considers the Avesta to be the most ancient text, while the Zend was a kind of commentary upon this already sacred book.

Taking the several portions of the Zend-Avesta in their chronological order (as far as this can be ascertained), we shall begin with the five Gâthâs, which are pronounced by their translator to be "by far the oldest, weightiest, and most important pieces of the Zend-Avesta" (F. G., xiii). Some portions of these venerable hymns are even attributed by him to Zarathus-

---

"Le Yacna." Unfortunately Dr. Haug and Dr. Spiegel—both very eminent Zend scholars—are entirely at variance as to the proper method of translating these ancient documents; and pending the settlement of this question, any interpretation proposed must be regarded by the uninstructed reader as uncertain. I cannot refrain from adding an expression of regret that Dr. Haug, to whose labors in the interpretation of these obscure fragments of antiquity we owe so much, should have so far forgotten himself as to fall foul of Dr Spiegel in a tone wholly unbecoming a scholar and inappropriate to the subject. It is not by this kind of learned Billingsgate that the superiority of his translation to that of his rival, as he evidently considers him or his fellow-laborer as I should prefer to call him, can be established.

tra himself; but this—except where the prophet is in some way named as the author — must be considered only as an individual opinion, which can carry no positive conviction to other minds until it is supported by stronger evidence than any at present accessible. Meantime, we may rest assured that we possess among these hymns some undoubted productions of the Zarathustrian age.

SUBDIVISION I. — *The Five Gâthâs.*

Proceeding to the individual Gâthâs, we find that the first, which begins with the 28th chapter of the Yaçna, bears the following heading: "The revealed Thought, the revealed Word, the revealed Deed of the truthrul Zarathustra.—The immortal saints chanted the hymns."*

The Gâthâ Ahunavaiti—such is its title — then proceeds: —

1. "Adoration to you, ye truthful hymns!

2. "I raise aloft my hands in devotion, and worship first all true works of the wise and holy Spirit, and the Understanding of the pious Disposition, in order to participate in this happiness.

3. "I will draw near to you with a pious disposition, O Wise One! O Living One! with the request that you will grant me the mundane and the spiritual life. By truth are these possessions to be obtained, which he who is self-illuminated bestows on those who strive for them" (F. G., vol. i. p. 24.—Yaçna, xxviii. 1–3).

The most important portion of this Gâthâ is the 30th chapter, because in it we have a vivid picture of the conflict in which the religion of Ahura-Mazda was born. Philological inquiry has rendered it clear beyond dispute, that Parseeism took its rise in a religious schism between two sections of the great Aryan race, at a period so remote that the occupation of Hindoostan by an offshoot of that race had not yet occurred. The common ancestors of Hindus and Persians still dwelt together in Central Asia, when the great Parsee Reformation

---

* Throughout the Gathas I follow Haug; and I need make no apology for neglecting Spiegel's translation, because that scholar himself admits, with creditable candor, that even his indefatigable perseverance was baffled by the difficulties of this portion of the Yacna.—Av., 2. xi.

disturbed their harmony; the one section adopting, or adhering to, the Vedic polytheism which they subsequently carried to India; the other embracing the more monotheistic creed which afterwards became the national religion of Persia.

The following hymn of the reformers carries us into the very midst of the strife: —

1. "I will now tell you who are assembled here, the wise sayings of the most wise, the praises of the living God, and the songs of the good spirit, the sublime truth which I see arising out of these sacred flames.

2. "You shall, therefore, hearken to the soul of nature (*i. e.*, plough and cultivate the earth); * contemplate the beams of fire with a most pious mind! Every one, both men and women, ought to-day to choose his creed (between the Deva and the Ahura religion). Ye offspring of renowned ancestors, awake to agree with us (*i. e.*, to approve of my lore, to be delivered to you at this moment)!"

(The prophet begins to deliver the words, revealed to him through the sacred flames.)

3. "In the beginning there was a pair of twins, two spirits, each of a peculiar activity; these are the good and the base, in thought, word, and deed. Choose one of these two spirits! Be good, not base!

4. "And these two spirits united created the first (material things); the one, the reality, the other, the non-reality. To the liars (the worshipers of the devas, *i, e.*, gods) existence will become bad, whilst the believer in the true god enjoys prosperity.

5. "Of these two spirits you must choose one, either the evil, the originator of the worst actions, or the true holy spirit. Some may wish to have the hardest lot (*i. e.*, those who will not leave the polytheistic deva-religion), others adore Ahura-Mazda by means of sincere actions.

6. "You cannot belong to both of them (*i. e.*, you cannot be worshipers of the one true God and of many gods at the same time). One of the devas, against whom we are fighting, might overtake you, when in deliberation (what faith you are to embrace), whispering you to choose the no-mind. Then the devas flock together to assault the two

---

* The sentences enclosed in parentheses are Haug's explanations of the sense of the text.

lives (the life of the body, and that of the soul), praised by the prophets"
(Parsees, pp. 141, 142.—Yasna, 30).

In another portion of this Gâthâ it is interesting to observe
the spirit of religious zeal breaking out, as it so generally does,
into the language of persecution:—

xxxi. 18. "Do not listen to the sayings and precepts of the wicked
(the evil spirit), because he has given to destruction house, village, district, and province. Therefore kill them (the wicked) with the sword!"

The wicked, as appears from the context, are those who did
not accept the Zarathustrian revelation.

In the second Gâthâ, or Gâthâ Ustavaiti, there are some very
curious passages. A few have been quoted in the notice of
Zarathustra. The following verses indicate the nature of the
worship addressed to Ahura-Mazda in the most ancient period
of the Parsee religion:—

xliii. 2. "I believe thee to be the best thing of all, the source of
light for the world. Everybody shall choose thee (believe in thee) as
the source of light, thee, thee, holiest spirit Mazda! Thou createst all
good true things by means of the power of thy good mind at any time,
and promisest us (who believe in thee) a long life.

4. "I will believe thee to be the powerful, holy (god) Mazda! For
thou givest with thy hand, filled with helps, good to the pious man, as
well as to the impious, by means of the warmth of the fire strengthening
the good things. For this reason the vigor of the good mind has fallen
to my lot.

5. "Thus I believe in thee as the holy God, thou living Wise One!
Because I beheld thee to be the primeval cause of life in the creation.
For thou hast made (instituted) holy customs and words, thou hast given
a bad fortune (emptiness) to the base, and a good one to the good man.
I will believe in thee, thou glorious God! in the last (future) period of
creation" (Parsees. p. 149).

xliv. 3. "That which I shall ask thee, tell it me right, thou living
God! Who was in the beginning the father and creator of truth? Who
made the way for the sun and stars? Who causes the moon to increase
and wane, if not thou? This I wish to know besides what I already
know.

4. "That I will ask thee, tell it me right, thou living God! Who is holding the earth and the skies above it? Who made the waters and the trees of the field? Who is in the winds and storms that they so quickly run? Who is the creator of the good-minded beings, thou Wise One?

5. "That I will ask thee, tell it me right, thou living God! Who made the lights of good effect and the darkness? Who made the sleep of good effect and the activity? Who made morning, noon and night, always reminding the priest of his duties?" (Ibid., p. 150.)

xlvi. 7. "Who is appointed protector of my property, Wise One! when the wicked endeavor to hurt me? Who else, if not thy fire, and thy mind, through which thou hast created the existence (good beings), thou living God! Tell me the power necessary for holding up the religion" (Ibid,, p. 156).

The third Gâthâ is termed Çpeñta-Mainyus. It begins with praise of Ahura-Mazda as the giver of the two forces of perfection and immortality. From this hollest spirit proceeds all the good contained in the words uttered by the good mind. He is the father of all truth. Of such a spirit is he who created this earth with the fire resting in its lap. Ahura-Mazda placed the gift of fire in the sticks that are rubbed together by the duality of truth and piety. The following verse refers to Mazda's prophet, Zarathustra:—

xlviii. 4. "He who created, by means of his wisdom, the good and the no-mind in thinking, words, and deeds, rewards his obedient followers with prosperity. Art thou (Mazda) not he in whom the last cause of both intellects (good and evil) is *hidden?*" (Parsees, p. 159).

The concluding chapter of this Gâthâ is a hymn of praise supposed to emanate from the Spirit of Earth and to be addressed to the highest genii. It is not without beauty and sublimity, but I forbear to make quotations from it, as some of its most interesting verses are noticed elsewhere.

The fourth and fifth Gâthâ are much shorter, and are considered by Haug as an appendix. The following verse may serve as a specimen of the former:—

lii. 20. "May you all together grant us this your help, truth through the good mind, and the good word in which piety consists. Be lauded and praised. The Wise One bestows happiness.

21. "Has not the Holy One, the living wise one, created the radiant truth, and possession with the good mind by means of the wise sayings of Ârmaiti, by her actions and her faith?

22. "The living Wise One knows what is always the best for me in the adoration of those who existed and still exist. These I will invoke with mention of their names, and I will approach them as their panegyrist" (F. G., vol. ii. p. 56).

Of the first three verses of the fifth Gâthâ I have spoken above (p. 184). The fourth and fifth run thus:—

liii. 4. "I will zealously confess this your faith, which the blessed one destined to the landlord for the country people, to the truthful householder for the truthful people, ever extending the glory and the beauty of the good mind, which the living Wise One has bestowed on the good faith for ever and ever.

5. "I proclaim formulæ of blessing to girls about to be married: Attend! attend to them! You possess by means of those formulæ the life of the good mind. Let one receive the other with upright heart; for thus only will you prosper" (F. G., vol. ii. p. 57).

SUBDIVISION 2.—*Yacna 35–41, or the Yacna of seven chapters.*

The Yaçna of seven chapters, which in the present arrangement of the text is inserted between the first and second Gâthâs, is of more recent date than the Gâthâs, but more ancient than the rest of the Zend-Avesta. "It appears to be the work of one of the earliest successors of the prophet, called in ancient times *Zarathustra* or *Zarathustrotema*, who, deviating somewhat from the high and pure monotheistic principles of Çpitama, made some concessions to the adherents of the ante-Zoroastrian religion by addressing prayers to other beings than Ahura-Mazda" (Parsee, p. 219). The seven chapters may be most accurately described as Psalms of praise, in which a great variety of objects, spiritual and natural, receive a tribute of pious reverence from the worshiper. They are not, however, on that account to be considered as gods, or as in any way the equals of Ahura-Mazda, who is still supreme. The beings thus addressed are portions of the "good creation," or of the things created by the good power, Ahura-Mazda; and they are either subjects of his spiritual kingdom, such as the Amesha-çpentas (seven very important spirits), or they are simply portions of the material universe treated as semi-divine, and exalted to objects of religious worship. Thus in the last chapter of this section, the author directs his laudations to the following, among other, genii and powers: the dwelling of the waters, the parting of the Ways, mountains, the wind, the earth, the pure ass in Lake Vouru-Kasha, this lake itself, the Soma, the flowing of the waters, the flying of the birds. It is plain from this enumeration that we are already a step beyond the simple adoration of Ahura-Mazda so conspicuous in the Gâthâs, and that the door is opened to the multitude of spirits and divinities that make their appearance in other parts of the Parsee ritual.

This section of the Yaçna opens, however, with a striking address to Ahura-Mazda:[*]—

xxxv. I. "We worship Ahura-Mazda the pure, the master of purity. We worship the Amesha-çpentas (the archangels), the possessors of good, the givers of good. We worship the whole creation of the true spirit, both the spiritual and terrestrial, all that supports (raises) the welfare of the good creation, and the spread of the good Mazdayaçna religion.

2. "We praise all good thoughts, all good words, all good deeds,

* It is a satisfaction to find that Spiegel's translation does not differ so widely from Haug's after we leave the territory of the Gathas. As a specimen, I quote the following verses from his Avesta, vol. ii. p. 135, which the reader may compare with the English rendering of the same passage in the text:—

Yacna Haptaghati.

XXXV I.

1. "(Racpi). Den Ahura-Mazda, den reinen Herrn des Reinen, preisen wir. Die Amesha-cpenta, die guten Herrscher, die weisen, preisen wir. 2. Die ganze Welt des Reinen preisen wir, die himmlische wie die irdische, 3. mit Verlangen nach der guten Reinheit, mit Verlangen nach dem guten mazdayacnischen Gesetze. 4. (Zuota.) Der guten Gedanken, Worte und Werke, die hier und anderswo 5. gethan worden sind oder noch gethan werden, 6. Lobpreiser und Verbreiter sind wir, damit wir zu den Guten gehoren mogen. 7. Das glauben wir, Ahura-Mazda, Reiner, Schoner, 8. Das wollen wir denken, sagen und thun: 9. was das Beste ist unter den Handlungen der Menschen fur beide Welten. 10. Durch diese Thaten nun erbitten wir, dass fur das Vieh 11. Annehmlichkeit und Futter gespendet werden moge 12. den Gelehrten wie den Ungelehrten, den Machtigen wieden Unmachtigen."

which are and will be (which are being done and which have been done) and we likewise keep clean and pure all that is good.

3. "O Ahura-Mazda, thou true happy being! we strive to think, to speak, and to do only those of all actions which might be best fitted to promote the two lives (that of the body and of the soul).

4. "We beseech the spirit of earth by means of these best works (agriculture) to grant us beautiful and fertile fields, to the believer as well as to the unbeliever, to him who has riches as well as to him who has no possession" (Parsees, p. 163).

The following invocation of fire deserves to be mentioned before we quit this portion of the Yaçna:—

xxxvi. 4. "Happy is the man to whom thou comest in power, O Fire, Son of Ahura-Mazda.

5. "Friendlier than the friendliest, more deserving of adoration than the most adorable.

6. "Mayest thou come to us helpfully to the greatest of transactions. . . .

9. "O Fire, Son of Ahura-Mazda, we approach thee

10. "with a good spirit, with good purity" (Av., ii. 137).

SUBDIVISION 3. — *Yacna, Chapter XII.*

This chapter is stated by Haug to be written in the Gâthâ dialect; it is therefore extremely ancient, and as it contains the Confession of Faith made by Zarathustrian converts on their abandonment of idolatry, or worship of the Devas, it is of sufficient importance to be quoted at length:—

xii. 1. "I cease to be a Deva *worshiper*. I profess to be a Zoroastrian Mazdayaçna (worhiper of Ahura-Mazda), an enemy of the Devas, and a devotee to Ahura, a praiser of the immortal saints (Amesha-çpentas), a worshiper of the immortal saints. I ascribe all good things to Ahura-Mazda, who is good, and has good, who is true, lucid, shining, who is the originator of all the best things, of the spirit in nature (gâus), of the growth in nature, of the luminaries and the self-shining brightness which is in the luminaries.

2. "I choose (follow, profess) the holy Armaiti, the good; may she be mine! I abominate all fraud and injury committed on the spirit of

earth, and all damage and destruction of the quarters of the Mazday-açnas.

3. "I allow the good spirits who reside on this earth in the good animals (as cows, sheep, &c.), to go and roam about free according to their pleasure. I praise, besides, all that is offered with prayer to promote the growth of life. I shall cause neither damage nor destruction to the quarters of the Mazdayaçnas, neither with my body nor my soul.

4. "I forsake the Devas, the wicked, bad, false, untrue, the originators of mischief, who are most baneful, destructive, the basest of all beings. I forsake the Devas and those who are Devas-like, the witches and their like, and any being whatever of such a kind. I forsake them with thoughts, words and deeds: I forsake them hereby publicly, and declare that every lie and falsehood is to be done away with.

5, 6. "In the same way as Zarathustra at the time when Ahura-Mazda was holding conversations and meetings with him, and both were conversing with each other, forsook the Devas; so do I forsake the Devas, as the holy Zarathustra did.

7. "To that party to which the waters belong, to whatever party the trees, and the animating spirit of nature, to that party to which Ahura-Mazda belongs, who has created this spirit and the pure man; to that party of which Zarathustra, and Kavâ Vistâçpa and Frashaostra and Jâmâçpa were, of that party of which all the ancient fire-priests (Sosh-yañto) were, the pious, who were spreading the truth: of the same party and creed *am* I.

8. "I am a Mazdayaçna, a Zoroastrian Mazdayaçna. I profess this religion by praising and preferring it to others (the Deva religion). I praise the thought which is good, I praise the word which is good, I praise the work which is good.

9. "I praise the Mazdayaçna religion, and the pure brotherhood which it establishes and defends against enemies, the Zoroastrian Ahura religion, which is the greatest, best, and most prosperous of all that are, and that will be. I ascribe all good to Ahura-Mazda. This shall be the praise (profession) of the Mazdayaçna religion."

SUBDIVISION 4. — *The Younger Yacna, and Vispered.*

While the Gâthâs and the confession just quoted represent the most ancient phase of the Mazdayaçna faith, we enter, in the remaining portion of the Yaçna, on a much later stage of the growing creed. So many new divinities, or at any rate, objects of reverential addresses, now enter upon the scene, that we almost lose sight of Ahura-Mazda in the throng of his attendants. We seem to be some ages away from the days when Zarathustra bade his hearers choose between the one true God and the multitude of false gods worshiped by his enemies. Ahura-Mazda is safely enthroned, and Zarathustra shines out gloriously as his prophet; but Zarathustra's creed is overloaded with elements of which he himself knew nothing. The first chapter of the Yaçna, a liturgical prayer, brings these elements conspicuously before us. It is an invocation and celebration of a great variety of powers belonging to what is termed the good creation, or the world of virtuous beings and good things, as opposed to the malicious beings and bad things who form the realm of evil.* Thus it opens:—

"I invoke and I celebrate the creator Ahura-Mazda, luminous, resplendent, very great and very good, very perfect and very energetic, very intelligent and very beautiful, eminent in purity, who possesses the excellent knowledge, the source of pleasure; him who has created us, who has formed us, who has nourished us, the most accomplished of intelligent beings."†

Every verse, until we approach the end, commences with the same formula:—"I invoke and I celebrate;" or, as Spiegel translates it, "I invite and announce it;" the sole difference is in the beings invoked. Many of these are powers of more or less eminence in the Parsee spiritual hierarchy, but it would be going beyond our object here to enumerate their names and specify their attributes. To a large proportion of them the epithets "pure, lord of purity," are added, while some are dignified with

---

* I follow Burnouf's translation, because the strict accuracy of his method is acknowledged by both Haug and Spiegel. There are considerable differences in the text followed by Burnouf and Spiegel, which I need not weary the reader by particularizing in detail.

† Y., p. 146.—Cf. Spiegel: 1. "Ich lade ein und thue es kund: dem Schopfer Ahura-Mazda, dem glanzenden, majestatischen, grossten, besten schonsten, 2. dem starksten, verstandigsten, mit bestem Korper versehenen, durch Heiligkeit hochsten. 3. Der sehr weise ist, der weithin erfreut, 4. welcher ans schuf, welcher uns bildete, welcher uns erhielt, der Heiligste unter den Himmelischen."- Av., ii. 35.

more special titles of honor. After the above homage to Ahura-
Mazda, the writer invokes and celebrates, among others: Mithra
(a very famous god), who increases oxen, who has one thousand
ears, and ten thousand eyes; the fire of Ahura-Mazda; the
water given by Ahura-Mazda; the Fravashis (angels or guardian
spirits) of holy men and of women who are under men's protection; energy, with a good constitution and an imposing figure; victory given by Ahura; the months; the new moon; the
full moon; the time of fecundation; the years; all the lords of
purity, and thirty-three genii surrounding Hâvani, who are of
admirable purity, whom Mazda has made known, and Zarathustra has proclaimed; the stars, especially a star named Tistrya;
the moon, which contains the germ of the ox; the sun, the eye
of Ahura-Mazda; the trees given by Mazda; the Word made
known by Zarathustra against the Devas; the excellent law of
the Mazdayaçnas; the perfect benediction; the pure and excellent man; these countries and districts; pastures and houses;
the earth, the sky, the wind; the great lord of purity; days,
months, and seasons; the Fravashis of the men of ancient law;
those of contemporaries and relations, and his own; all genii
who ought to be invoked and adored. It is manifest from this
invocation, in which I have omitted many names and many
repetitions, how far we are from the stern and earnest simplicity of the Gâthâs. Regular liturgical forms have sprung up, and
these express the more developed and complicated worship which
the Parsee priesthood has now engrafted on the Zarathustrian
monotheism.

The concluding verses run as follows:—

"O thou who art given in this world, given against the Deves, Zarathustra * the pure, lord of purity, if I have wounded thee, either in
thought, word, or deed, voluntarily or involuntarily, I again address
this praise in thine honor; yes, I invoke thee if I have failed against
thee in this sacrifice and this invocation.

"O all ye very great lords, pure, masters of purity, if I have
wounded you, &c. [as above].

"May I, a worshiper of Mazda, an adherent of Zarathustra, an
enemy of the Devas, an observer of the precepts of Ahura, address my

* No mention of Zarathustra here in Spiegel.—Av. ii. 44.

homage to him who is given here, given against the Devas; to Zarathustra, pure, lord of purity, for the sacrifice, for the invocation, for the prayer that renders favorable, for the benediction. (May I address my homage) to the lords (who are) the days, the parts of days, &c., for the benediction; that is to say: (may I address my homage) to the lords (who are) the days, the parts of days, the months, the seasons of the year (Gahanbârs), the years; for the sacrifice, for the invocation, for the prayer that renders favorable,·for the benediction."*

The rest of the Yaçna consists mainly of praises or prayers addressed to the very numerous objects of Parsee adoration, and most of it is of little interest. The following short section however, deserves remark:—

Yacna 12.

1. " I praise the thoughts rightly thought, the words rightly spoken, and the deeds rightly done.

2. "I seize upon (or resort to) all good thoughts, words and deeds.

3. "I forsake all bad thoughts, words, and deeds.

4. "I bring you, O Amesha-çpentas,

5. "Praise and adoration,

6. "With thoughts, words, and deeds, with heavenly mind, the vital force from my own body."†

In the following verses again there is some excellence:—

1. "May that man attain that which is best who teaches us the right way to our profit in this world, both the material and the spiritual world, the plain way that leads to the worlds where Ahura is enthroned, and the sacrificer, resembling thee, a sage, a saint, O Mazda.

2. "May there come to this dwelling contentment, blessing, fidelity, and the wisdom of the pure."

8. "In this dwelling may Çraosha‡ (obedience) put an end to disobedience, peace to strife, liberality to avarice, wisdom to error, truthful speech to lying, which detests purity " (Av. ii. 186, 187.—Yaçna 59).

---

* Y. pp. 585, 588, 592. The concluding stanza is simpler and more intelligible in Spiegel.—Av., ii. 44.

† Av., vol. ii. p. 85.—Yacna, 12. The ch. xii. quoted above is No. 13, in Spiegel.

‡ Craosha is an important divinity in Parsee worship, who is considered by Spiegel to express the moral quality of obedience.

The prominent position occupied by fire in the Parsee faith is well known. The presence of fire is indeed an essential part of their ritual, in which it is treated with no less honor than the consecrated wafer in that of Catholic Christians. Not only, however, is it employed in their rites, but it is addressed as an independent being, to whom worship is due. Not that its place in the hierarchy is to be confounded with that of Ahura-Mazda. It is not put upon a level with the supreme being, but it is addressed as his son, its rank being thus still more closely assimilated to that of the host, which is in like manner a part of the liturgical machinery and an embodiment of the son of God. A special chapter of the Yaçna — the 61st — is devoted to Fire, and a summary of its contents will help us to understand the light in which this deity was regarded.

The sacrificer begins by vowing offerings and praise and good nourishment to "Fire, son of Ahura-Mazda." He trusts that Fire may ever be provided with a proper supply of wood, and may always burn brightly in this dwelling, even till the final resurrection. He beseeches Fire to give him much property, much distinction, holiness, a ready tongue, wit and understanding, activity, sleeplessness, and posterity. Fire is said to await nourishment from all; whoever comes, he looks at his hands, saying: "What does the friend bring his friend, the coming one to him who sits alone?" And this is the blessing he bestows on him who brings him dry wood, picked out for burning: "Mayest thou be surrounded with herds of cattle, with abundance of men. May it be with thee according to the desire of thy heart, according to the desire of thy soul. Be joyous, live thy life the whole time that thou shalt live."[*]

The last chapter but one of the Yaçna is a hymn in universal praise of the good creation. All the objects belonging to that creation — that is, made by Ahura-Mazda, and standing in contrast with the bad creation of Agra-Mainyus — are enumerated, and as a catalogue of these the hymn is interesting. Ahura-Mazda himself is named first; then Zarathustra; after this follows the Fravashi (angel) of Zarathustra, the Amesha-çpentas, the Fravishis of the pure, and so forth, through a long list of

* Av., vol. ii. p. 191.—Yacna, 61. This blessing is repeated, Khorda-Avesta, 11.

animate and inanimate beings. Each is named with the formula "we praise" following the title, as: "The whole earth we
praise" (Av., vol. ii. p. 202.—Yaçna, 70).

So close is the resemblance between the Vispered and that
portion of the Yaçna which we have just examined, that it will
be needless to dwell upon the contents of the former. We may
therefore at once pass on to a very important section, for theological purposes, of the Zend-Avesta, namely—

Subdivision 5.— *Vendidad.*

Totally unlike either the Yaçna, the Vispered, or the Yashts,
the Vendidad is a legislative code—dealing indeed largely with
religious questions, but not confining itself exclusively to them.
It differs from the remainder of the sacred volume much as
Leviticus differs from the Psalms, or as the Institutes of Menu
differ from the hymns of the Rig-Veda. It is regarded as
equally holy with the rest of the Avesta, and is recited in
divine service along with Vispered and Yaçna, the three together forming what is termed the Vendidad-Sade (Av., ii. lxxv).
Its abrupt termination indicates that the code is not before us
in its entirety; the portion which has been preserved, however,
does not appear to have suffered great mutilation. Let us
briefly summarize its contents, first premising that the form
they assume (with trifling exceptions) is that of conversations
between Ahura-Mazda and his prophet.

The first Fargard (or chapter) is an enumeration of the good
countries or places created by Ahura-Mazda, and of the evils—
such as the serpent, the wasp, and various moral offenses,
including that of doubt—created in opposition to him in each
case by the president of the bad creation, Agra-Mainyus. The
second Fargard is a long narrative of the proceedings of a
mythological hero named Yima (the Indian Yama), to whom
Ahura-Mazda is stated to have once committed the government
of the world, or of some part of it. Thus far we have not
entered on the proper subject-matter of the Vendidad. The
third Fargard, while still introductory, approaches more nearly
to the subsequent chapters, alike in its form and its contents.

In it Zarathustra lays certain queries before Ahura-Mazda, and the replies given by that deity are of high importance for the comprehension of both the social and moral status of the Parsees at the time when this dialogue was written. The stress laid upon the virtue of cultivating the soil is especially to be noticed. Similar sentiments are frequently repeated in the Vendidad, and indicate a people among whom agriculture was still in its infancy, the transition from the pastoral state to the more settled condition of tillers of the soil being still incomplete. The compilers of this code evidently felt strongly the extreme value to their youthful community of agricultural pursuits, and therefore encouraged them at every convenient opportunity by representing them as peculiarly meritorious in the sight of God.

Zarathustra begins his inquiries by asking what is in the first place most agreeable to this earth, and successively ascertains what are the five things which give it most satisfaction, and what the five which cause it the most displeasure, Ahura-Mazda answers that, in the first place, a holy man with objects of sacrifice is the most agreeable; then a holy man making his dwelling-place, and storing it with all that pertains to a happy and righteous life; then the production of grain and of fruit trees, the irrigation of thirsty land, or the drainage of moist land; fourthly, the breeding of live-stock and draught-cattle: fifthly, a special incident connected with the presence of such animals on the land. The five displeasing things are, the meetings of Daevas and Drujus (evil spirits), the interment of men or dogs (which was contrary to the law), the accumulation of Dakhmas, or places where the bodies of the dead were left exposed, the dens of animals made by Agre-Mainyus, and lastly, unbecoming conduct on the part of the wife or son of a holy man. Further questions are then put as to the mode of conduct which wins the approbation of the earth, and it is stated to consist in actions which tend to counteract the evils above enumerated. In the course of these replies occasion is again taken to eulogize the man who vigorously cultivates the soil, and to censure him who idly leaves it uncultivated. Certain penalties are then imposed on those who bury dogs or men, but the sin of leaving them underground for two years is declared to be inexpiable, except by the Mazdayaçna Law, which can purify the worst offenders:—

" For it (the Law) will take away these (sins) from those who praise the Mazdayaçna Law, if they do not again commit wicked actions. For this the Mazdayaçna Law, O holy Zarathustra, takes away the bonds of the man who praises it. It takes away deceit. It takes away the murder of a pure man. It takes away the burial of the dead. It takes away inexpiable actions. It takes away accumulated guilt. It takes away all sins which men commit" (Av., vol. i. p. 87, 88.—Vendidaâ, iii. 140-148).

We see from this that the power of the Law to deliver sinners from the burden of their offenses was in no way inferior to that of the Atonement of Christ.

It is unnecessary to dwell upon the fourth Fargard, which deals with the penalties—consisting mainly of corporal punishment—for breach of contract and other offenses. The fifth and sixth, being concerned with the regulations to be observed in case of impurity arising from the presence of dead bodies, are of little interest. A large part of the seventh is occupied with the same subjects, but its course is interrupted by certain precautions to be attended to in the graduation of students of medicine, which may be commended to the notice of other religious communities. Should a Mazdayaçna desire to become a physician, on whom, inquires Zarathustra, shall he first try his hand, the Mazdayaçna (orthodox Parsees), or the Daevayaçnas (adherents of a false creed)? Ahura-Mazda replies that the Daevayaçnas are to be his first patients. If he has performed three surgical operations on these heretics, and his three patients have died, he is to be held unfit for the medical profession, and must on no account presume to operate on the adherents of the Law. If, however, he is successful with the Daevayaçnas, he is to receive his degree, and may proceed to practice on the more valuable bodies of faithful Parsees. So careful a contrivance to ensure that none but infidels shall fall victims to the knife of the unskilful surgeon evinces no little ingenuity.

The eighth Fargard relates chiefly to the treatment of dead bodies, while the ninth proceeds to narrate the rites for the purification of those who have come in contact with them. A terri-

ble penalty — that of decapitation — is enacted against the man
who ventures to perform this rite without having learnt the
law from a priest competent to purify. The tenth Fargard prescribed the prayers by which the *Drukhs*, or impure spirit supposed to attach itself to corpses, and to come from them upon
the living, is to be driven away: and the subject is continued
in the eleventh, which contains formularies for the purification of
dwellings, fires, and other objects. Along with injunctions as to
the purification of houses where a death has occurred, the
twelfth Fargard informs its hearers how many prayers they
are to offer up for deceased relatives. The number varies both
according to their relationship, being highest for those that are
nearest akin, and according to their purity or sinfulness, double
as many being required for the sinful as for the pure. After a
short introduction expounding the merit of killing a certain
species of animal and the demerit of killing another (what they
are is uncertain), the thirteenth Fargard proceeds to enumerate
in detail the various kinds of offenses against dogs, and the corresponding penalties. Dogs were evidently of the utmost importance to the community, and their persons are guarded with
scarcely less care than those of human beings. They are held
to have souls, which migrate after their decease to a canine
Paradise. It seems, too, that shades of departed dogs are
appointed to watch the dangerous bridge over which men's
souls must travel on the road to felicity, and which the wicked
cannot pass; for we are informed of the soul of a man who has
killed a watch-dog, that "the deceased dogs who guard against
crime and watch the bridge do not make friends with it on
account of its abominable and horrible nature" (Av., vol. i. p.
192.—Vendidad, xiii, 25); while a man who has killed a water-
dog is required to make "offerings for its pious soul for three
days and three nights" (Av., vol. i. p. 201.—Vendidad, xiii, 173).
The place to which the souls of these animals repair is termed
"the water-dwelling," and it is stated that two water-dogs
meet them on their arrival, apparently to welcome them to
their aqueous heaven (Av,, vol. i. p. 200.—Vendidad, xiii. 167). Not
only killing dogs, but wounding them or giving them bad food,
are crimes to be severely punished; and even in case of madness the dog's life is on no account to be taken. On the con-

trary, the utmost care is to be taken, by fastening him so as to prevent escape, that he should do himself no injury, for if he should happen in his madness to fall into water and die, the community will have incurred sin by the accident.* The following verses convey an interesting notion of the esteem in which the dog was held among the early Parsees. The speaker is Ahura-Mazda:—

"I have created the dog, O Zarathustra, with his own clothes and his own shoes; with a sharp nose and sharp teeth; attached to mankind, for the protection of the herds. Then I created the dog, even I Ahura-Mazda, with a body capable of biting enemies. When he is in good health, when he is with the herds, when he is in good voice, O holy Zarathustra, there comes not to his village either thief or wolf to carry off property unperceived from the villages " (Av., vol. i. p. 197.—Vendidad, xiii. 106–113).

In the fourteenth Fargard, water-dogs are further protected against wounds; while in the fifteenth, the preservation of the canine species at large is ensured by elaborate enactments. To give a dog bones which he cannot gnaw, or food so hot as to burn its tongue, is a sin; to frighten a bitch in pup, as by clapping the hands, is likewise to incur guilt; and they are gravely criminal who suffer puppies to die from inattention. If born in camel-stalls, stables, or any such places, it is incumbent on the proprietor to take charge of them; or, if the litter should be at large, at least the nearest inhabitant is bound to become their protector. Strangely intermingled with these precautions are rules prohibiting cohabitation with women in certain physical conditions, and enactments for the prevention of abortion, and for ensuring the support of a pregnant girl by her seducer, at least until her child is born. The crime of abortion is described in a manner which curiously reveals the practices occasionally resorted to by Parsee maidens. Should a single woman be with child, and say, "The child was begotten by such and such a man "—

* There is, indeed, a passage which permits the mutilation of a mad dog by cutting off an ear, or a foot, or the tail; Spiegel, however, regards it as interpolated, and it is palpably at variance with the remainder of the chapter.

"If then this man says, 'Try to make friends with an old woman and inquire of her; if then this girl does not make friends with an old woman, and inquire of her, and this old woman brings Baga, or Shaêta, or Ghnâna, or Fracpâta, or any of the vegetable purgatives, saying, 'Try to kill this child;' if then the girl does try to kill the child, then the girl, the man, and the old woman are equally criminal."

Neither the sixteenth nor the seventeenth Fargard need detain us. They relate, the one to the above-mentioned rules to be observed towards women, the other to the disposal of the hair and nails, which are held to pollute the earth. The eighteenth Fargard begins, as if in the middle of a conversation, with an address by Ahura-Mazda, on the characteristics of true and false priests, some, it appears, having improperly pretended to the priesthood. After some questions on other points of doctrine put by Zarathustra, we are suddenly introduced to a conversation between the angel Çraosha and the Drukhs, or evil spirit, in which the latter describes the several offenses that cause her to become pregnant, or, in other words, increase her influence in the world. After this interlude, we return to Ahura-Mazda and Zarathustra. The prophet, having been exhorted to put questions, inquires of his god who causes him the greatest annoyance. Ahura-Mazda replies that it is "he who mingles the seed of the pious and the impious, of Daeva-worshipers and of those who do not worship the Daevas, of sinners and non-sinners." Such persons are "rather to be killed than poisonous snakes." Hereupon Zarathustra proceeds to ascertain what are the penalties for those who cohabit with women at seasons when the law requires them to be separate. At the beginning of the nineteenth Fargard, we have an account of the temptation of the prophet by the evil one, to which allusion has been made in another place. Zarathustra seeks for information as to the means of getting rid of impurities, and is taught by Ahura-Mazda to praise the objects he has created. In the latter part of the chapter we have a remarkable account of the judgment of departed souls. In conclusion, we have a psalm of praise recited by the prophet in honor of God, the earth, the stars, the Gâthâs, and numerous other portions of the good creation. There is little in the twentieth Fargard be-

yond the information that Thrita was the first physician, and a
formula of conjuration, apparently intended to be used in order
to drive away diseases. In the twenty-first, we find praises of
the cloud, the sun, and other heavenly bodies. The last Fargard of the Vendidad differs widely from the rest in its manner of representing Ahura Mazda. It is, no doubt, as Spiegel
observes, of late origin. Ahura-Mazda complains of the opposition he has encountered from Agra-Mainyus, who has afflicted
him with illness (whether in his own person, or in that of
mankind, is not clear). He calls upon Manthra-Çpenta, the
Word, to heal him, but that spirit declines, and a messenger is
accordingly sent to Airyama to summon him to the task.*
Airyama commences his preparations on an extensive scale, but
at this point the Vendidad breaks off, and we are left in doubt
as to the result of his efforts.

SUBDIVISION 6. — *The Khorda-Avesta, with the Homa Yasht.*

The term Khorda-Avesta, or little Avesta, is applied, according to Spiegel, to that part of the Zend-Avesta which includes
the Yashts, and certain prayers, some of them of extreme sanctity, and constantly employed in Parsee worship. He informs
us that, while the remainder of the sacred texts serve more
especially for priestly study and for public reading, the Khorda-
Avesta is mainly used in private devotion (Av., vol. iii. p. 1).
Some of its prayers belong to a comparatively recent period,
being composed no longer in the Zend language, but in a
younger dialect; and we meet in them with the Persian forms
of the old names — Ormazd standing for Ahura-Mazda, Ahriman
for Agra-Mainyus, and Zerdoscht for Zarathustra. The names
of the genii have undergone corresponding alterations. We find
ourselves in these prayers, and indeed throughout the Yashts,
many centuries removed from the age of Zarathustra and his
immediate followers. Some of the more celebrated prayers,
however (not belonging to the class of Yashts), must be of considerable antiquity, if we may judge from the fact of their being
mentioned in the Yaçna. Thus, in the 19th chapter of the

* Spiegel holds that Airyama is only a certain prayer hypostatized.—Cf.
Av., vol. iii. p. 34.

Yaçna, we find an elaborate exaltation of the powers of the Ahuna-Vairya, which stands second in the Khorda-Avesta. Zarathustra is represented as asking Ahura-Mazda, "What was the speech which thou spokest to me, as existing before the sky, before the water, before the earth, before the ox, before the trees, before the fire, son of Ahura-Mazda, before the pure men, before the Daevas with perverted minds, and before men, before the whole corporeal world, before all things created by Mazda which have a pure origin?" This speech, existing prior to all created objects, is declared to have been a part of the Ahuna-Vairya. The immenso benefits of repeating this prayer, which is stated to ensure salvation, are then recounted to the prophet. The 20th chapter is occupied with the merits of another of these short formularies, the Ashem-vohû. These prayers are in continual use, not only in the liturgy, but among the laity. They are sometimes required to recite great numbers of Ahuna-Vairyas at one time, and at the commencement of sowing, or of any good work, it is proper to repeat it. The Ashem-vohû is to be said on various occasions, particularly on waking and before going to sleep (Av., vol. ii. pp. lxxxii., lxxxiii). The higher sanctity, as well as greater antiquity, of these prayers is evinced by the fact that we find them constantly introduced in the course of others, to which they form a necessary supplement. There are often several Ashem-vohûs in a single brief prayer. The Ashem-vohû, in fact, fulfills a function much like that of the Lord's prayer in the liturgies of some Christian Churches.

Let us now see what these most sacred forms of adoration contain. The Ashem-Vohû is to this effect:—

> " Purity is the best possession.
> Hall, hail to him:
> Namely, to the pure man best in purity "*

It is strange that, in a formulary occupying so conspicuous a place in Parsee devotion, there should be no acknowledgment of God. But this want is supplied in the Ahuna-Vairya, or Yathâ-ahû-vairyo, which follows it.

* Av., vol. iii. p. 3. — Khorda-Avesta, 1.

Yathâ-ahû-vairyo:—

" As it is the Lord's will, so (is he) the ruler from purity.

(We shall receive) gifts from Vohu-mano for the works (we do) in the world for Mazda.

And (he gives) the kingdom to Ahura who protects the poor" (Av., vol. iii.—Khorda-Avesta, 2).

Certainly this is not very intelligible, but the last clause is remarkable, as implying that the way to advance God's kingdom on earth is to confer benefits on the poor.

Passing over a number of other prayers, we enter upon the Yashts, which are distinguished from all other parts of the Avesta by the fact that each of them is written in celebration of some particular god or genius.   Ahura-Mazda, indeed, still retains his supremacy, and every Yasht begins with a formula, of which the first words are "In the name of the God Ormazd," while the first Yasht is devoted exclusively to his praise. Subject to this recognition, however, the inferior potentates are each in turn the object of panegyrics in that exaggerated style in which Oriental literature delights.   We need not stop to recount the particular honors rendered to each.   One Yasht, however, is sufficiently curious to merit our attention, the more so as we possess a translation of it by Burnouf.*   It is termed the Homa Yasht, and is intended to extol the brilliant qualities of the god whose name it bears.   At that period of the day which is termed Hâvani—so it begins—Homa came to find Zarathustra, who was cleaning his fire, and singing the Gâthâs.   "Zarathustra asked him: 'What man art thou who in all the existing world appearest to my sight as the most perfect, with thy beautiful and immortal person?'   Then Homa, the holy one, who banishes death, answered me: 'I am, O Zarathustra, Homa, the holy one, who banishes death. Invoke, O Çpitama,* extract me to eat me, praise me to cele-

---

* In the "Journal Asiatique," 4me Serie, tom. 4, 5, 6, 7, 8. I have followed it exclusively. The Homa Yasht is not formally included in the Khorda-Avesta; it forms the 9th chapter of the Yacna. But the fact that, while utterly alien to the rest of the Yacna, it is truly a Yasht—being in honor of a special personage—induced me to defer its consideration till now.

* The term Çpitama, usually coupled with the name of Zarathustra, is translated by Spiegel "holy," but is treated by Haug and Burnouf as a proper name. There are indications that it may have been the family name of the prophet. See Av., vol. iii. p. 209, n.

brate me, in order that others, who desire their good, may praise me in their turn.' Then Zarathustra said: 'Adoration to Homa! Who is the mortal, Homa, who first in the present world extracted thee for sacrifice? What holiness did he acquire? What advantage accrued to him thereby?" Homa replies that Vivanghat was the first to extract him for sacrifice, and that he acquired the advantage of becoming father to the glorious Yima, in whose reign "there was neither cold nor (excessive) heat, nor old age nor death, nor envy produced by the Dêva. Fathers and sons alike had the figure of men of fifteen years of age, as long as Yima reigned." Similar questions are then put by Zarathustra regarding the second, third, and fourth mortals who worshiped Homa, and similar replies are given. All had distinguished sons; but the last, Puruchaspa, was rewarded beyond all others by the birth of Zarathustra himself. Homa thereupon magnifies Zarathustra in the usual style of the later parts of the Zend-Avesta, and Zarathustra, who is not to be outdone in the language of compliment, thus addresses him in return: "Adoration to Homa! Homa, the good, has been well made; he has been made just; made good; he bestows health; he has a beautiful person; he does good; he is victorious; of the color of gold; his branches are inclined to be eaten; he is excellent; and he is the most celestial way for the soul. O thou who art of the color of gold, I ask thee for prudence, energy, victory, beauty, the force that penetrates the whole body, greatness which is spread over the whole figure;" and so forth, through several other by no means modest petitions. In a more formal manner Zarathustra then demands of Homa the following favors: 1st, the excellent abode of the saints; 2dly, the duration of his body; 3dly, a long life; 4thly, and 5thly, to be able to annihilate hatred and strike down the cruel man; 6thly, that they (the faithful?) may see robbers, assassins, and wolves before being seen by them. After this, Homa is praised generally. He gives many good gifts, among them posterity to sterile mothers, and husbands to spinsters of advanced years. He is finally requested, if there should be in the village or the province a man who is hurtful to others, to take from him the power of walking, to darken his intelligence, and to break his heart (For another Yasht, see ch. i).

The Yashts are succeeded by various pieces, of which one relates to Parsee eschatology, and the others, celebrating numerous supernatural objects of worship, do not call for any special remark. After these we come to the so-called Patets, which belong to the most recent portions of the book, and indicate a highly developed consciousness of sin, and of the need of divine forgiveness. They correspond in tone and character to the General Confession which has been placed by the Church of England in the forefront of her Liturgy, except that they contain long enumerations of the several classes of offenses for which pardon is to be entreated. One of them, after such a catalogue, thus addresses the Deity:—

"Whatever was the wish of the Creator Ormazd, and I ought to have thought and did not think, whatever I ought to have said and did not say, whatever I ought to have done and did not do,—I repent of these sins, with thoughts, words, and works, both the corporeal and the spiritual, the earthly and the heavenly sin, with the three words (that is, with thoughts, words, and works). Forgive, O Lord; I repent of the sin.

"Whatever was the wish of Ahriman, and I ought to have thought and yet did think, whatever I ought not to have said and yet did say, whatever I ought not to have done and yet did,—I repent of these sins with thoughts, words, and works, both the corporeal and the spiritual, the earthly and the heavenly sins, with the three words. Forgive, O Lord; I repent of the sin" (Av., vol. iii. p. 211.—Khorda-Avesta, xlv. 8, 9).

Another of these Patets contains the following comprehensive formula:—

"In whatever way I may have sinned, against whomsoever I may have sinned, howsoever I may have sinned, I repent of it with thoughts, words, and works; forgive!" (Av., vol. iii. p. 216.—Khorda-Avesta, xlv. 1.

The same Patet contains a confession of faith, which, as it alludes to the several dogmas that were held to be of first-rate importance in the creed of the true disciple of Zarathustra, may be worth quoting before we quit the subject:—

"I believe in the existence, the purity, and the indubitable truth of the good Mazdayaçna faith, and in the Creator Ormazd and the Amschaspands, in the exaction of an account, and in the resurrection of the new body.   I remain in this faith, and confess that it is not to be doubted, as Ormazd imparted it to Zertuscht, Zertuscht to Fraschaostra and Jâmâçp, as Âderbât, the son of Mahresfand, ordered and purified it, as the just Paoiryotkaeshas and the Deçtûrs in family succession have brought it to us, and I thence am acquainted with it" (Av., vol. iii. p. 218.—Khorda-Avesta, xlv. 28).

In more than one respect this confession is interesting. First, it asserts the excellence and the unquestionable infallibility of the traditional faith in terms which a Catholic could hardly improve upon. Secondly, it brings before us in succinct form the leading points included in that faith—the Creator, at the head of all the created world; the seven Amshaspands or Amesha-Çpentas, heavenly powers of whom Ormazd himself was chief; the judgment to be expected after death, and the strict account then to be required; lastly, the general resurrection with its new body.   Proceeding next to the manner in which this faith had been handed down from generation to generation, we have first the cardinal doctrine that God himself was the direct teacher of his prophet; after that, a statement that the prophet communicated it to others, from whom it descended to still later followers, one of whom is declared to have "ordered and purified it."   Thus the consciousness of subsequent additions to the original law is betrayed. Thus amended, the priests, or Deçtûrs, are said to have transmitted it to the time of the speaker, the authority of the ecclesiastical order in the interpretation of the sacred records being thus carefully maintained.

How many generations had elapsed before the transmission of the law could thus become the subject of deliberate incorporation among recognized dogmas, it is impossible to say. Undoubtedly, however, we stand a long way off—not only in actual time, but in modes of thought and forms of worship— from the ancient Iranian prophet. The change from the faith of Peter to that of St. Augustine is not greater than that from the faith of Zarathustra's rude disciples to that of the subtle, self-conscious priests who composed these later formularies, or the laity who accepted them. Still, after all has been said, after it has been freely admitted that subsequent speculation, or imagination, or the influence of neighboring creeds, introduced a host of minor spirits or quasi-gods, of whom Zarathustra knew nothing, it must also be emphatically asserted that the God of Zarathustra never loses, among the multitude of his associates, either his supremacy or his unique and transcendent attributes. While in the Gâthâs Ahura-Mazda alone is worshiped; while in the later chapters of the Yaçna many other personages receive a more or less limited homage along with him; while in the Yashts these personages are singled out one after another for what appears unbounded adoration,—the original God invariably maintains his rank as the Creator; the one Supreme Lord of mankind, as of all his creatures; the instructor of Zarathustra; the Being compared to whom all others stand related as the thing made towards its Maker. Theism does not in the Avesta pass into polytheism. Strictly speaking, its spirit is monotheistic throughout, though we might often be betrayed into thinking the contrary by the extravagance of its language. Nor can I discover in its pages the doctrine which some have held to be contained in it, namely, that above Ahura-Mazda, somewhere in the dark background of the universe, was a God still greater than him, the ultimate Power to which even he must yield, Zrvâna-Akarana, or Infinite Time. The very name of this highly abtract being appears but rarely in the Avesta, and never, so far as I am able to discover, in the character thus assigned to him. Ahura-Mazda remains throughout the God of Gods; his is the highest and most sacred name known to his worshipers, and none can compare with him, the Infinite Creator, in greatness, in glory, or in power.

It is not to be expected that, in the early stage of social progress at which a great part at least of the Avesta was written, its moral doctrines should be altogether faultless. Nevertheless, it may well sustain a comparison in this respect with the codes which have been received as authoritative by other nations. Subject to the drawback, common to all theologically-influenced systems of ethics, of laying as much stress upon

correct belief and the diligent performance of the customary
rites as upon the really fundamental duties of men, the Zend-
Avesta upholds a high standard of morality, and honestly seeks
to inculcate upon believers the immense importance of leading
an upright and virtuous life. Such a life alone is pleasing to
God; such a life alone can insure a safe passage over the hazardous bridge by which the soul must pass to Paradise. Not
only are the more obvious virtues—respect for life, careful
observance of promises, industrious conduct—sedulously enjoined on the faithful Parsee, but some others, less obvious and
too frequently overlooked, are urged upon them. The seducer
is bound to provide both for the infant he has called into existence, and for its mother, at least for a certain period. Domestic
animals are not forgotten, and humanity towards these dependent creatures is commanded in a series of precepts, the spirit of
which would do honor to any age. And, in general, the blame-
lessness required in thoughts, words, and works imposed on the
devout Mazdayaçna a comprehensive attention to the many
ways in which he might lapse from virtue, and held before him
an exalted conception of moral purity.

Yet, when all this has been said, it must still be admitted
that the Zend-Avesta hides its light, such as it is, under a
bushel. Such is the number of supra-mundane spirits to be
lauded, such a mass of ceremonies to be attended to, so great
the proportion of space devoted to guarding against legal impurities as compared with that consigned to preventing moral
evil, that the impression left upon the minds of unbelieving
readers is on the whole far from favorable. Morality has, in
fact, got buried under theology. The trivialities, inanities, and
repetitions that abound in the sacred text draw off the mind
from the occasional excellences of thought and expression which
it contains. Thus he who toils through the verbose Fargards
of the Vendidad, the obscure chapters of the older and younger
Yaçna, or the panegyrical rhapsodies of the Yashts, will find
but little to reward his search. With the Gâthâs indeed it is
otherwise. These are full of interest, and not quite devoid of a
simple grandeur. But as a whole, the Avesta is a mine which,
among vast heaps of rubbish, discloses but here and there a
grain of gold.

SECTION VI.— THE KORAN.*

Alone among the Scriptures of the several great religions, the Koran is the work of a single author. It is, therefore, characterized by greater uniformity of style, subject, and doctrine than the sacred collections of other nati ns. Considerable as the difference is between its earlier and its later Suras, a consistent line of thought is visible throughout, and pious Moslems are free from the difficulty that has always beset Christian theologians of "harmonizing" contradictory passages both supposed to emanate from God. There are, indeed, earlier revelations inconsistent with later ones; but in this case, the former are held to have been abrogated by the latter. Mediocre in the order of its thought, diffuse in style, abundant in repetitions, there are few books more calculated to task the patience of a conscientious reader. But we must recollect, in judging it, that its author did not write it, and very possibly never contemplated its existence as a complete work. He published it from time to time as occasion required, much as a modern statesman would announce his views by means of speeches, pamphlets, or election addresses.

When a revelation arrived, Mahomet in the first instance dictated it to his secretary Zaid, who wrote it on palm-leaves or skins, or tablets of any kind that might be at hand. Of the remaining Moslems, some took copies, but many more committed the revelations to memory; the Arab memory being remarkably retentive. Under the reign of Abu Bekr, the prophet's successor, Omar, finding that some one who knew a piece of the Koran had been killed, suggested that the whole should be collected. The suggestion was adopted, and Abu Bekr intrusted the work of collection to the secretary Zaid. The Koran was then put together, not only from the leaves that had been left by Mahomet, and thrown without any regard to order into a chest, but also from the fragments, either writ-

* Complete translations of the Koran into English have been made by Sale and by Rodwell. Considerable portions have been rendered into German by Springler, " Das Leben und die Lehre des Mohammed;" and by Gustav Weil, "Mohammed der Prophet;" and into English by Dr. Muir, in his "Life of Mahomet."

ten or preserved in the memory, that were contributed by individual believers. The copy thus made was not published, but was committed for safe custody to Hafsa, daughter of Omar, and one of the widows of the prophet. She kept it during the ten years of her father Omar's caliphate. But as there were no official and authorized copies of this genuine Koran, it came to pass that the various missionaries who were sent as teachers to the newly-conquered countries repeated it differently, and that various readings crept into the transcripts in use. Hence serious threatenings of division and scandal among the Moslems. The caliph Othman, foreseeing the danger, appointed a commission, with the secretary Zaid at its head, to copy the copy of Hafsa and return it to her, their duty being to determine on differences of reading, and to be careful to restore the Meccan idiom where it had been departed from in any of the versions. Several copies were made by the commissioners, of which one was kept at Medina, and the others sent to the great military stations. This was the official text, prepared about A. H. 25–30; and after its establishment, all private copies or fragments of the Koran were ordered by Othman to be destroyed.* The original Koran, which Mahomet did but reproduce, is supposed by those who accept it as divine to be preserved in heaven, in the very presence of its original author, on an enormous table.

In the Koran, as arranged by Zaid, there is apparently no fixed principle in the order of the Suras or chapters. In the main, the longest Suras come first, but even this rule is not adhered to consistently. Of chronological arrangement there is not a trace, and it has been left to the ingenuity of European scholars to endeavor to discover approximately the date of the several revelations. Of some, the occasions of their publication are known, but in the case of the great majority, nothing beyond a conjectural arrangement can be attained.

The principal themes with which the Koran is occupied are the unity of God; his attributes; the several prophets preceding Mahomet, whom he has sent to convert unbelievers; the joys of Paradise and the terrors of hell; and the legislative edicts promulgated for the government of the Arabs under the

* L. L. M., vol. iii., Vorrede. Sale preliminary discourse, p. 46.—K., p. vii.

new religion. Of these several subjects, the first two occupy a
predominant place in the earliest revelations. Legends of
prophets, of whom Mahomet recognized a considerable number,
form one of the standing dishes set before the faithful during
all but the very beginning of his career. He was also fond of
speaking of the contrast between the position of believers and
skeptics in a future state; but he seems at first to have expected
a temporal judgment on his Meccan opponents, and afterwards
to have been contented with awaiting the divine vengeance in
another world. Legislation, of course, belongs only to that portion of the Koran which was revealed after the Hegira.

A few specimens will be quite sufficient to give a notion both
of the earlier and later style of this sacred volume. Here is a
Sura revealed at Mecca during the first struggles of the prophet's mind, when it was completely possessed with the awfulness
of the new truth : —

"O thou enfolded in thy mantle, stand up all night, except a small
portion of it, for prayer. Half; or curtail the half a little,—or add to it:
and with measured tone intone the Koran, for we shall devolve on thee
weighty words. Verily, at the coming of night are *devout* (Italics, here
and elsewhere, in Rodwell) impressions strongest, and words are most
collected; but in the daytime thou hast continual employ—and commemorate the name of thy Lord, and devote thyself to him with entire
devotion. . . . Of a truth, thy Lord knoweth that thou prayest
almost two-thirds, or half, or a third of the night, as do a part of thy
followers" (K., p. 7.—Sura, 73).

This is the opening Sura of the Koran : —

"Praise be to God, Lord of the worlds! the compassionate! the
merciful! King on the day of reckoning! Thee *only* do we worship, and
to thee do we cry for help. Guide thou us on the straight path, the
path of those to whom thou hast been gracious; with whom thou art not
angry, and who go not astray " (K., p. 11.—Sura, 1).

In the Sura now to be quoted we find an allusion to one of
the prophets whom Mahomet regarded as precursors —the
prophet Saleh, who had sent them to a people called Themoud
to bid them worship God. The legend associated with his name

is, that he appealed to a she-camel as a proof of his divine
mission, commanding the people to let her go at large and do
her no hurt. Some of the Themoudites believed; but they were
ridiculed by the skeptical chiefs of the nation, whose wickedness
went so far as actually to hamstring the apostolic camel. Hereupon an earthquake overtook them by night, and they were all
found dead in the morning (K., p, 376.—Sura, 7. 71–77). Such
things were Mahomet's stock-in-trade; and the following Sura
exemplifies the mixture of his early poetic thoughts with the
prosaic narratives which did duty so constantly during the
maturity of his apostleship:—

"By the Sun and his noonday brightness! by the Moon when she
followeth him! by the Day when it revealeth his glory! by the Night
when it enshroudeth him! by the Heaven and him who built it! by the
Earth and him who spread it forth! by a Soul and him who balanced it,
and breathed into it its wickedness and its piety! blessed now is he who
hath kept it pure, and undone is he who hath corrupted it!

"Thomoud in his impiety rejected the message of the Lord, when
the greatest wretch among them rushed up:—Said the apostle of God to
them,—The camel of God! let her drink. But they treated him as an
imposter and hamstrung her. So their Lord destroyed them for their
crime, and visited all alike; nor feared he the issue" (K., p. 24.—Sura, 91).

The same Sura which contains the history of Saleh, prophet
of Themoud, refers also to various other divine messengers who
had fulfilled the same office of announcing the judgments of
God. Mahomet's general view of the prophetic function seems
to be expressed in these words:—

"Every nation hath its set time. And when their time is come they
shall not retard it an hour; and they shall not advance it. O children
of Adam! there shall come to you Apostles from among yourselves,
rehearsing my signs to you; and whoso shall fear God and do good
works, no fear shall be upon them, neither shall they be put to grief.
But they who charge our signs with falsehood, and turn away from them
in their pride, shall be inmates of the fire; for ever shall they abide
therein " (K., p. 371.—Sura, 7. 32–34).

The prophets whom he mentions in this Sura are Noah, who
was sent to warn his people of the Deluge; Houd, sent to Ad,

an unbelieving nation whom God cut off, with the exception of
those who had accepted Houd; Saleh, sent to Themoud as
above related; Lot, sent to Sodom to warn it against sin;
Shoaib, sent to Madian, a people of which the unbelieving
members were destroyed by earthquakes; Moses, sent with
signs to Pharaoh and his nobles, as also to the Israelites, of
whom some worshiped the calf, and were overtaken by the
wrath of their Lord (K., p. 375–386. — Sura, 7. 57–154). In another
Sura he makes mention of other prophets besides these: namely,
of John the Baptist, Jesus of Nazareth, Abraham, Ishmael, and
Enoch (K., p. 127 ff. —Sura, 19).

His view of Jesus Christ is peculiar and interesting. He invariably treats him with the highest respect as a servant of
God and his own precursor, but he is careful to protest that the
ópinion of his divinity was not held by Jesus, and was a baseless invention of his followers. The notion that God could have
a son seems to him a gross profanation, and he often recurs to
it in terms of the strongest reprobation. Thus he endeavors to
claim Christ as a genuine Moslem, and to include Christianity
within the pale of the new faith. A Christian who adopted it
might continue, indeed must continue, to believe everything in
the Old and New Testaments, except such passages as expressly
assert the incarnation and divinity of Jesus. Yet Mahomet's
own version of this prophet's conception involves a supernatural
element, and only differs from that of Luke in not asserting the
paternity of God.

"And make mention in the Book," he says, "of Mary when
she went apart from her family, eastward, and took a veil *to
shroud herself* from them, and we sent our spirit to her, and he
took before her the form of a perfect man. She said: 'I fly for
refuge from thee to the God of Mercy! If thou fearest him
begone from me.' He said : 'I am only a messsenger of thy
Lord, that I may bestow on thee a holy son.' She said: 'How
shall I have a son, when man hath never touched me, and I am
not unchaste.' He said: 'So shall it be. Thy Lord hath said:
easy is this with me, and we will make him a sign to mankind
and a mercy from us. For it is a thing decreed.' And she conceived him, and retired with him to a far-off place " (K., p. 128.
—Sura, 19. 16–22).

Her virginity is expressly asserted in another place, where she is described as "Mary, the daughter of Imran, who kept her maidenhood, and into whose womb we breathed of our spirit."*

When the child was born the woman was accused of unchastity, but the infant prophet at once opened his mouth and declared his prophetic character. From this narrative it appears that, in Mahomet's opinion, Jesus was neither begotten by a human father, nor was the son of God. He finds a *via media* in the doctrine that he was created, like Adam, by an express exertion of the power of the Almighty. "He created him of dust: He then said to him, 'Be,' and he was" (K., p. 502.—Sura, 3. 52). And again, in the Sura above quoted: "It beseemeth not God to beget a son, Glory be to him ! when he decreeth a thing, he only saith to it, Be, and it is" (K., p. 130.—Sura, 19. 36).

He is very indignant against those who hold the doctrine of the incarnation, which he apparently considers as equivalent to that of physical generation by the Deity, and which, under any aspect, is certainly shocking to a genuine monotheist.

"They say: 'The God of Mercy hath gotten offspring.' Now have ye done a monstrous thing! Almost might the very heavens be rent thereat, and the earth cleave asunder, and the mountains fall down in fragments, that they ascribe a son to the God of Mercy, when it beseemeth not the God of Mercy to beget a son!" (K., p. 135.—Sura, 19. 91-93.) "And they say, 'God hath a son:' No! Praise be to him! But his whatever is in the heavens and the earth! All obeyeth him, sole Maker of the heavens and of the earth! and when he decreeth a thing he only saith to it, Be, and it is" (K., p. 445.—Sura, 2. 110-111).

Mahomet's conception of his own character is most clearly expressed in the seventh Sura, where, after enumerating some of the prophets who had gone before him (as already related), he proceeds to describe a supposed dialogue between Moses and God, in which the Deity speaks thus:—

"My chastisement shall fall on whom I will, and my mercy embraceth all things, and I write it down for those who shall fear me, and

---

* K., p. 604.—Sura, 66. 12. She is called the daughter of Imran, by a confusion between Mary, mother of Jesus, and Mariam, sister of Moses.

pay the alms, and believe in our signs, who shall follow the Apostle, the unlettered Prophet—whom they shall find described with them in the Law and Evangel. What is right will he enjoin them, and forbid them what is wrong, and will allow them healthful viands and prohibit the impure, and will ease them of their burden, and of the yokes which were upon them; and those who shall believe in him, and strengthen him, and help him, and follow the light which hath been sent down with him,—these are they with whom it shall be well."

The revelation to Moses now ceases, and God continues to address Mahomet with the usual preliminary "say:"—

"Say to them: O men! Verily I am God's apostle to you all: whose is the kingdom of the Heavens and of the Earth! There is no God but he! He maketh alive and killeth! Therefore believe on God and his apostle—the unlettered Prophet—who believeth in God and his word. And follow him that ye may be guided aright" (K., p. 386.—Sura, 7. 155–158).

Mahomet liked to describe himself as unlettered, and thus to obtain for the scriptural knowledge and literary skill displayed in the Koran the credit of its being due to inspiration.

In another place he again describes his prophetic character in the following strain:—

"Muhammed is not the father of any man among you, but he is the Apostle of God and the seal of the prophets: and God knoweth all things. . . . O Prophet! we have sent thee to be a witness, and a herald of glad tidings, and a warner; and one who, through his own permission, summoneth to God, and a light-giving torch" (K., p. 567.—Sura, 33, 40, 44, 45).

A conspicuous feature of the Koran to which allusion has not yet been made is its frequent reference to the pleasures of Paradise to be enjoyed by the faithful, and the pains of hell to be suffered by the infidels. The day of judgment is continually held out as an encouragement to the former, and a terror to the latter. The fifty-sixth Sura contains a description of heaven which is enough to make the mouth of good Moslems water. "The people of the right hand" are to be happy; those of the left hand, wretched. The former are to have "gardens of delight," with "inwrought couches," whereon reclining, "aye-blooming youths" are to bring them "flowing wine" of the best celestial vintage. They are to enjoy their favorite fruits, and to eat whatever birds they long for. "Houris with large dark eyes," and "ever virgins," never growing old, are to supply them with the pleasures of love, so strangely overlooked in the Christian pictures of heavenly life. On the other side, we have "the people of the left hand," who are to be tormented with "pestilential winds" and "scalding water," and are to live "in the shadow of a black smoke," with the fruit of a bitter tree to eat and boiling water to drink (K., p. 60.—Sura, 56). The prophet delights in warning his enemies of their coming fate. "Verily," says God in another place, "we have got ready the flame for the infidel" (K., p. 598.—Sura, 48. 13). "O Prophet!" we read elsewhere, "make war on the infidels and hypocrites, and deal rigorously with them. Hell shall be their abode! and wretched the passage to it!" (K., p. 606.—Sura, 66 9). "God promiseth the hypocritical men and women, and the unbelievers, the fire of hell—therein shall they abide—this their sufficing portion!" (K., p. 621.—Sura, 9, 69). Some, who had declined to march with the Prophet from Medina on account of the heat, are sternly reminded that "a fiercer heat will be the fire of hell" (K., p. 623.—Sura, 9. 82).

In contradistinction to the deplorable state of the hypocrites and unbelievers—blind in this world and destined to suffer eternally in the next—we have a pleasing picture of the condition of the faithful Moslems:—

"Muhammed is the apostle of God; and his comrades are vehement against the infidels, *but* full of tenderness among themselves. Thou mayst see them bowing down, prostrating themselves, imploring favors from God, and his acceptance. Their tokens are on their faces, the marks of their prostrations. This is their picture in the Law and their picture in the Evangel; they are as the seed which putteth forth its stalk; then strengtheneth it, and it groweth stout, and riseth upon its stem, rejoicing the husbandman—that the infidels may be wrathful at them. To such of them as believe and do the things that are right, hath God promised forgiveness and a noble recompense" (K., p. 601.—Sura, 48. 29).

Section VII. — The Old Testament.

Before entering upon the comparative examination of the
Hebrew Canon, it is necessary to say a few words of the extraordinary race who were its authors. There is probably no other
book of which it may be said, with the same depth and fulness
of meaning, that it is the work of a nation and the reflection
of a nation's life. The history of the Bible and the history of
the Jews are more intimately bound up together than is that
of any other nation with that of any other book. During the
period of their political existence as a separate people they
wrote the Canon. During the long period of political annihilation which has succeeded, they have not ceased to write commentaries on the Canon. This one great production has filled
the imaginations, has influenced the intellect, has fed the religious ardor of each succeeding generation of Jews. To name
the canonical Scriptures, and the endless series of writings suggested by them or based upon them, would be almost to sum
up the results of the literary activity of the Hebrew race.

Our first historical acquaintance with the Hebrews brings
them before us as obtaining by conquest, and then inhabiting,
that narrow strip of territory bordering the Mediterranean Sea
which is known as Palestine. Their own legends, indeed, carry
us back to a still earlier period, when they lived as slaves in
Egypt; but on these, from the character of the narrative, very
little reliance can be placed. The story, gradually becoming
less and less mythical, tells us, what is probably true, that
they overcame the native inhabitants of Palestine in war, and
seized upon their land; that they then passed through an anarchial period, during which the centre of authority seems to
have been lost, and the national unity was in no small danger
of being destroyed, had not vigorous and able leaders interposed
to save it; that, under the pressure of these circumstances, they
adopted a monarchial constitution, by which the dangers of this
time of anarchy were at least to a large extent averted, and the
discordant elements brought into subjection to a common centre.
Thus united, the Jewish monarchy rapidly attained a considerable height of splendor and of power. Surrounding nations fell

under its sway, and it took rank as one of the great powers which divided Western Asia. But this glory was not to last long. The monarchy, broken up into two hostile parts by the folly of Rehoboam, lost alike its unity and its strength; and after a long series of kings, whom it is needless to enumerate, both its branches fell victims, at separate times, the one to Shalmaneser, king of the Assyrians, the other to Nebuchadnezzar, king of the Chaldees. The latter event, while it put an end to the very existence of the Jewish nation as an independent political power — for it was but a fitful independence which was recovered under the Asmoneans — marks an epoch which severs the history of the Jews into two periods, distinguished from one another by the completely different character borne by the people in each. It is customary, for theological purposes, to represent the religious development of the Jews as pervaded by a fundamental unity. They are supposed to have known and worshiped the true God from the beginning, to have been sharply marked off from the rest of the world by their strict monotheism, and to have been unfaithful to their inherited creed only when they refused to recognize Christ and his apostles as its authorized interpreters. Their own records tell a very different story. According to these, the religion of the Jews, like that of other nations, progressed, changed, improved, underwent purification and alteration, and was, in its earlier forms, not much unlike that of the surrounding heathens. Their leaders, indeed, and all those whom their Scriptures uphold as examples of excellence, worshiped a national God, Jehovah, whom they may have considered the only god who enjoyed actual existence and possessed actual power. But whether or not this were the case, he was, for all practical purposes, simply the tutelary deity of the Hebrews. In his name the conquerors of Palestine pillaged, murdered, and inflicted cruelties on the vanquished; to him they looked for aid in their belligerent undertakings; to him they offered the first fruits of victory. It was under his direct leadership that they professed to subdue the heathens, and to attain national security. The ark was his dwelling, and it could only bring destruction to the Philistines, who were not under the protection of its inmate. And when the Jews asked to be placed under the rule of a monarch, they were told by the mouthpiece of Jehovah that it was his divine government which they were rejecting. The morality of the chiefs who conducted the invasion and subjugation of Palestine was not one whit superior to that of their enemies, nor was the god on whose power they relied of an essentially higher nature than many other national or local divinities who were worshiped by other nations. They were the rude leaders of a rude people worshiping a rude deity. His character was such as we might expect the tutelary divinity of a tribe of wandering and unsettled Bedouins to be. Having to establish their right to a permanent home and an organized government by force of arms, it was only natural that they should represent their God as favoring the exploits of those arms, and even urging them on to the most ruthless exercise of the rights of conquerors. It was natural that even their most revolting acts should be placed under the especial patronage of this approving god. It was natural, too, that when the conquest had been at least in great part effected, while yet the anarchial and semi-savage condition of the victors continued (as it did more or less until after the accession of David), and internal strife took the place of external warfare, the national god should become to some extent a party-god; should favor one section against another, and even excite the ferocious passion of those to whose side he inclined. The god of Moses, of Joshua, and the Judges was thus a passionate, relentless, and cruel partisan. No doubt the facts were not precisely such as they are represented to us by the writers in the Old Testament, since in the internecine conflicts which occasionally broke forth we may assume that each side claimed for itself the approbation of Jehovah. But still the story of the Hebrew annals is clear enough to show us the semi-savage character of the people in these early days, and their utter failure to form that lofty conception of the deity with which they have been so largely credited by believers in the supernatural inspiration of their historical records.

The primitive conception entertained at this period, which corresponded with that generally found among uncivilized nations, was improved and elevated to some extent during the age of comparatively settled government which succeeded. As the Israelites advanced in the practice of the arts, in the possession of wealth, in the cultivation of the literary or musical attainments that refine domestic life, in the peaceful organization of a society that had become more industrial and less warlike, their idea of Jehovah underwent the modifications which these changes imply. The god of Samuel is widely different from the god of Isaiah or Jeremiah. Whether the popular notion had risen to the height attained by these prophets may indeed be doubted; but this too must have altered in order to make such prophets possible. Yet, in spite of the comparative improvement, there are abundant indications during the kingly period that the old Hebrew deity still retained the ferocious characteristics by which he had formerly been distinguished. Elijah's patron is gracious enough to his own adherents, but the attributes of mercy or gentleness towards human beings generally are undiscoverable in his character. And the deeds of blood which pious monarchs from time to time were guilty of in his honor, and which received his approbation, show that if the process of his civilization had begun, it was still very far from being completed.

But the special glory of the Jewish race is supposed to consist even more in the fact that this God, such as he was, stood alone, than in the excellence of the manner in which they conceived of his nature. The constancy of their monotheism, amid the polytheism of surrounding nations, has appeared to subsequent generations so marvelous as to require a revelation to account for it. The facts, however, as related to us by the Jews themselves, do not warrant the supposition that monotheism actually was the creed of the people until after the Captivity. It appears, indeed, that that form of belief was held by those who are depicted to us as the most eminent and the most virtuous among them, and it would seem that there was generally a considerable party who adhered to the worship of Jehovah, and at times succeeded in forcing it upon the nation at large. But that Jehovism was the authorized and established national religion, and that every other form and variety of faith was an authorized innovation, is a far wider conclusion than the facts will warrant us in drawing. This, no doubt, and nothing less than this, is the contention of the historical writers of the Old Testament; but even their own statements, made as they are under the influence of the strongest Jehovistic bias, point with tolerable clearness to a different conclusion. They inform us that while the most ancient leaders of the Israelites who conducted them to the promised land, the distinguished Judges who from time to time arose, and all the most virtuous kings, belonged to the religion of Jehovah, the people, notwithstanding these great examples, were continually guilty of relapses into idolatry of the most flagrant kind. This tendency manifested itself so early, and reappeared with such persistence during the whole history of the Israelites of both branches up to the destruction of their respective monarchies, that we cannot, consistently with the admitted facts, suppose that Jehovism had at any time taken very deep root in the mind of the people. They seem, on the contrary, to have been readily swayed to and fro by the example of the reigning monarch. Whether indeed they sincerely adopted monotheism under a monotheistic sovereign, may perhaps be doubted; but the emphatic denunciations of the Biblical writers leave us no room to question the perfect sincerity of their idolatry. All therefore that we can be justified in inferring from what they tell us is, that a succession of priests and prophets maintained the faith of Jehovah from age to age, and that from time to time a sovereign arose who favored their views, and did all in his power, sometimes by fair means and not unfrequently by foul, to advance the interests of the Jehovistic party. Indian history acquaints us with very similar fluctuations in the religion of a province, according as the priests of one or the other contending sect succeeded in obtaining influence over the mind of the reigning Rajah. But although we maintain that monotheism was not, previous to the captivity, the popular religion of the Jews, we need not go the length of asserting that there was no difference in their minds between Jehovah and the other deities whom they adopted from surrounding nations. Jehovah was unquestionably the national god, who was held to extend a peculiar protection over the Hebrew race. Nor does it follow that those who betook themselves to some idolatrous *cultus* necessarily abandoned that of Jehovah. Both might well have been carried on together, and there is abundant evidence that the Jews of this period had much of that elasticity which characterizes polytheism, and makes it ever ready to add new members to its pantheon without discarding old favorites. So far as there was a national worship carried on by a national priesthood, Jehovah must have been its object. But we are not therefore compelled to imagine that the nation had adopted Jehovism in so solemn and binding a manner as to render its abandonment a gross violation of their fundamental institutions. No doubt, according to the Scriptural writers, it was a deliberate breach of the orignal constitution to forsake, even for a moment, the exclusive service of the national god for that of any other deity whatsoever. But the supernatural origin assigned by them to this original constitution throws a doubt on their assertions, while the facts they report serve to increase it. For while we learn that Jehovah was deserted by one generation after another in favor of more popular rivals, much to the indignation of his priests and prophets, we do not perceive any traces of a consciousness on the part of the idolaters that they were guilty of infidelity to fundamental and unchangeable laws. They rather appear to have acted in mere levity, and the repeated objurgations of the Jehovistic party would tend to the conclusion that the people were not aware of any binding obligation to adhere to the worship of this deity to the exclusion of that of every other. The efforts of the Jehovists may indeed show that *they* believed such an obligation to exist: but not that their opponents were equally aware of it. Moreover, we are not without some more positive testimony which strongly favors this view of their mutual relations. Under the reign of the pious, and no doubt credulous, Josiah, a certain priest professed to have discovered a "book of the law" mysteriously hidden in the temple. Without discussing in this place what book this may have been, it is plain that it inculcated Jehovism under the penalty of curses similar to those found in Deuteronomy, and it is plain too that its contents caused the monarch a painful surprise, which expressed itself by his rending his clothes and sending a commission to "inquire of the Lord" "concerning the words of this book that is found." Now is it possible to suppose that the words of such a book as this could have inflicted on Josiah so great a shock, or have required the appointment of a special commission to inquire concerning them, if it had been a mat-

ter of familiar and general knowledge among the Jews that
their forefathers had solemnly adopted Jehovism as the only
lawful national creed, invoking upon themselves those very
curses which the most devout of monarchs was now unable to
hear without astonishment and alarm ?· And how are we to explain the production of this book by the priests as a new discovery? If it had been merely the re-discovery of a lost volume
would the language of the narrative have been at all appropriate? Must not Josiah in that case have rejoiced at the restoration to Judah of so precious a treasure, however much he
might have regretted the failure of the nation to observe its
precepts? The difficulty of supposing such facts to have been
forgotten is equally great. It would be scarcely possible to imagine that not only the people, but the priests, could at any
period have lost all memory of the fact that they were bound,
under the most terrible penalties, to adhere to the faith of Jehovah. At least the spiritual advisers of so religious a monarch
must have been well aware that their own creed formed an
essential part of the Jewish constitution; and we cannot doubt
that they would carefully have impressed this fact on their willing pupil, not as a startling disclosure made only after he had
been seventeen years on the throne and had attained the age of
twenty-five, but as one of his earliest and most familiar lessons.
In fact, this sudden discovery, in some secret recess of the temple, of a hitherto unknown volume, concerning whose claims to
authority or antiquity the writers preserve a mysterious silence,
rather suggests the notion of a Jehovistic *coup d'etat*, prepared
by the zeal of Hilkiah the priest and Shaphan the scribe. A
long time had passed since the accession of the king. His
favorable dispositions were well known. Since the eighth year
of his reign at least he had been under the influence of the
priests, and in the twelfth he had entered (no doubt under their
directions) upon that career of persecuting violence which was
usual with pious monarchs in Judea.* His mind was undoubtedly predisposed to receive with implicit confidence any statements they might make. Hence, if Hilkiah and his associates
had conceived the idea of compiling, from materials at their

---

* So in 2 Chron. xxiv. 3-7. But in 2 Kings xxii. 1, 2, there is no
mention of the period at which "he began to seek after the God of David."

command, a book which, while recapitulating some events in the ancient history of Israel, should represent those events in a light favorable to their designs, they could hardly have chosen a better moment for the execution of such a scheme. That they actually did this, it would be going beyond the evidence in our possession to assert, It may be that the book was an old one; and in any case, it is unnecessary to suppose that it was an original composition of Hilkiah's, palmed off upon the king as ancient. All that appears to me clearly to follow from the terms of the narrative is, that the law which this book contained (evidently the law of Jehovah) had not hitherto been regarded as the established law of the country, and that the production of this volume, in which its claims to that dignity were emphatically asserted, and its violation represented as entailing the most grievous curses, was one of the plans taken by the priestly party to procure for it the recognition of that supremacy which they declared it had actually enjoyed in the days of their forefathers. But although the history of Israel has been written by adherents of this party, and we are unfortunately precluded from checking their statements by any document recounting the same events from the point of view of their opponents, their records, biased as they are, clearly show us a nation whose favorite and ordinary creed was not monotheism; which was ever ready to adopt with fervor the idolatrous practices of its neighbors; and which was not converted to pure and exclusive monotheism till after the terrible lesson of the Captivity in Babylon.

This great event was turned to excellent account by the priests and prophets of Jehovah. Instead of regarding it as a natural consequence of the political relations of Judea with more powerful empires, they represented it as the fulfillment of the penalties threatened by Jehovah for infidelity towards himself. And as this view offered a plausible explanation of their unparalleled misfortunes, it was naturally accepted by many as the true solution of sufferings so difficult to reconcile with the protection supposed to be accorded by their national god. Under these circumstances a double process went on during their compulsory residence in heathendom. Great numbers, who were either not Jehovists, or whose Jehovism was but lukewarm, gradually adapted themselves to their situation among idolaters, and became at length indistinguishably fused, as the ten scribes had been, with the alien races. But a few remained faithful to their God. These few it was who formed the whole of the nation which, when return was possible, returned to their native soil. Those who were not inspired by a deep sense of the sanctity of their national religion; those to whom the restoration of their national rites was not the one object of overwhelming importance; those whose hopes of national restoration were of a temporal rather than a spiritual nature, had no sufficient motive to return to their native soil. Jerusalem could have no attractions for them which Babylon did not possess. Thus, by a natural process, the most ardent, the most spiritual, the most unbending monotheists were weeded out from the mass of the community, and it was they who accompanied Zerubbabel or Ezra on his sacred mission. Misfortune, which had not shaken their faith, had deepened and purified it. Not only were they Jehovists, but they were Jehovists of the sternest type. There was among them none of that admixture of levity, and none of that facile adaptability to foreign rites, which characterized the oldest Jews. From this time forward their monotheism has never been broken by a single relapse.

Thus the Captivity forms the turning-point in the character of the Jews; for, in fact, the nation which was conquered by Nebuchadnezzar was not the nation which, in the days of Kyros and Artaxerxes returned to re-colonize and rebuild Jerusalem. The conquered people belonged to a monarchy which, if it was now feeble and sunken, was directly descended from one which had been glorious and mighty, and which had aimed at preserving for Judea the status and dignity of an independent power. Under its influence the Jews had been mobile, idolatrous, deaf to the voice of Jehovistic prophets, neglectful of Jehovistic rites; desirous of conquest, and, when that was impossible, unwilling on political grounds to submit to foreign domination; rude if not semi-barbarous in morals, and distracted by the contention of rival religious parties. But this polity, of which the ruling motives were mainly political, was succeeded after the return of the exiles by a polity of which the ruling motives were exclusively religious. All were now adherents of Jehovah;

all were zealous performers of the rites conceived to be his due.

This change must be borne in mind if we would understand Jewish history; for the same language is not applicable to the Jews before and after the Captivity, nor can we regard in the same light a struggling and feeble race upholding its unanimous faith in the midst of trials, and an independent nation in which a party, from time to time victorious, endeavors to impose that faith by force. We may without inconsistency censure the violence of the Jehovistic sectaries, and admire the courage of the Jehovistic people. But although there is much in this change that is good, it must be admitted that it has its bad side. While becoming more conscientious, more scrupulously true to its own principles, and more penetrated with a sense of religion, Judaism became at the same time more rigid, more formal, more ritualistic, and more unsocial. Ewald has remarked that the constitution established after the return from captivity is one that lays undue stress upon the exterior forms of religion, and may in time even become hostile to what is truly holy. As it claims to be in possession of something holy which temporal governments do not possess, it cannot submit to their dominion; hence, he observes, Israel could never become an independent nation again under this constitution.[*] Nor was this all. Even apart from its tendency to magnify external forms, which was perhaps not of its essence, the religion of Jehovah had inherent vices. The Jews, believing their god to be the only true one, and insisting above all on the supreme importance of preserving the purity of his *cultus*, were necessarily led to assume a haughty and exclusive attitude towards all other nations, which could not fail to provoke their hostility. This unloveable spirit was shown immediately after their return by their contumelious rejection of the Samaritan proposals to aid in building the temple—proposals which seem to have been made in good faith; by the Sabbatarian legislation of Nehemiah; and even more by the exclusively harsh measures taken by Ezra for the purification of the race. It was simply inevitable that all heathen nations who came in contact with them should hate a people who acted on such principles.

[*] Ewald, Geschichte des Volkes Israel, vol. iv.—Die Heilgherrschaft, 3 Die bestimmtere Gestaltung der Zeit der neuen Wendung.

Nor were the fears of the heathen altogether without foundation. When the Jews recovered a temporary independence under
the Maccabees, their intolerance, now able to vent itself in acts
of conquest, became a source of serious danger. Thus, John
Hyrcanus destroyed the temple of the Samaritans (who also
worshiped Jehovah) on Mount Gerizim, and the Jews actually
commemorated the event by a semi-festival. Alexander Janna-
sus, too, carried on wars of conquest against his neighbors. In
one of these he took the town of Gaza, and evinced the treatment to be expected from him by letting loose his army on the
inhabitants and utterly destroying their city. It was no doubt
their unsocial and proud behavior towards all who were not
Jews that provoked the heathens to try their temper by so
many insults directed to the sensitive point—their religion.
Culpable as this was, it must be admitted that it was in some
degree the excessive scrupulosity of the Jews in regard to things
indifferent in themselves that exposed them to so much annoyance. Had they been content to permit the existence of Hellenic or Roman customs side by side with theirs, they might have
been spared the miseries which they subsequently endured.
But the Scriptures, from beginning to end, breathed a spirit of
fierce and exclusive attachment to Jehovah; he was the only
deity; all other objects of adoration were an abomination in
his sight. Penetrated with this spirit, the Jews patiently sub-
mitted to the yoke of every succeeding authority—Chaldeans,
Syrians, Egyptians, Romans—until the stranger presumed to
tamper with the national religion. Then their resistance was
fierce and obstinate. The great rebellion which broke out in
the reign of Antiochus Epiphanes, under the leadership of Mattathias, was provoked by the attempt of that monarch to force
Greek institutions on the Jewish people. The glorious dynasty
of the Asmoneans were priests as well as kings, and the royal
office, indeed, was only assumed by them in the generation
after that in which they had borne the priestly office, and as a
consequence of the authority derived therefrom. Under the
semi-foreign family of the Herods, who supplanted the Asmoneans, and ruled under Roman patronage, as afterwards under
the direct government of Rome, it was nothing but actual or
suspected aggressions against the national faith that provoked

the loudest murmurs or the most determined opposition. It was this faith which had upheld the Jews in their heroic revolt against Syrian innovations. It was this which inspired them to support every offshoot of the Asmonean family against the odious Herod. It was this which led them to entreat of Pompey that he would abstain from the violation of the temple; to implore Caligula, at the peril of their lives, not to force his statue upon them; to raise tumults under Cumanus, and finally to burst the bonds of their allegiance to Rome under Gessius Florus. It was this which sustained the war that followed upon that outbreak—a war in which even the unconquerable power of the Roman Empire quailed before the unrivaled skill and courage of this indomitable race; a war of which I do not hesitate to say that it is probably the most wonderful, the most heroic, and the most daring which an oppressed people has ever waged against its tyrants.

But against such discipline as that of Rome, and such generals as Vespasian and Titus, success, however brilliant, could be but momentary. The Jewish insurrection was quelled in blood, and the Jewish nationality was extinguished—never to revive. One more desperate effort was indeed made; once more the best legions and the best commanders of the Empire were put in requisition; once more the hopes of the people were inflamed, this time by the supposed appearance of the Messiah, only to be doomed again to a still more cruel disappointment. Jerusalem was razed to the ground; Aelia Capitolina took its place; and on the soil of Aelia Capitolina no Jew might presume to trespass. But if the trials imposed on the faith of this devoted race by the Romans were hard, they were still insignificant compared to those which it had to bear from the Christian nations who inherited from them the dominion of Europe. These nations considered the misfortunes of the Jews as proceeding from the divine vengeance on the crime they had committed against Christ; and lest this vengeance should fail to take effect, they made themselves its willing instruments. No injustice and no persecution could be too bad for those whom God himself so evidently hated. Besides, the Jews had a miserable habit of acquiring wealth; and it was convenient to those who did not share their ability or their industry to plunder them from time to time. But the Jewish race and the Jewish religion survived it all. Tormented, tortured, robbed, put to death, hunted from clime to clime; outcasts in every land, strangers in every refuge, the tenacity of their character was proof against every trial, and superior to every temptation. In this unequal combat of the strong against the weak, the synagogue has fairly beaten the Church, and has vindicated for itself that liberty which during centuries of suffering its enemy refused to grant. Eighteen hundred years have passed since the soldiers of Titus burned down the temple, laid Jerusalem in ashes, and scattered to the winds the remaining inhabitants of Judea; but the religion of the Jews is unshaken still; it stands unconquered and unconquerable, whether by the bloodthirsty fury of the legions of Rome, or by the still more bloodthirsty intolerance of the ministers of Christ.

SUBDIVISION I. — *The Historical Books.*

It is scarcely necessary to say that no complete account of the contents of the Old Testament can be attempted here. To accomplish anything like a full description of its various parts, and to discuss the numerous critical questions that must arise in connection with such a description, would in itself require a large volume. In a treatise on comparative religion, anything of this kind would be out of place. It is mainly in its comparative aspect that we are concerned with the Bible. Hence many very interesting topics, such, for instance, as the age or authorship of the several books, must be passed over in silence. Tempting as it may be to turn aside to such inquiries, they have no immediate bearing on the subject in hand. Whatever may be the ultimate verdict of Biblical criticism respecting them, the conclusions here reached will remain unaffected. All that I can do is to assume without discussion the results obtained by the most eminent scholars, in so far as they appear to me likely to be permanent. That the Book of Genesis, for example, is not the work of a single writer, but that at least two hands may be distinguished in it; that the Song of Solomon is, as explained both by Renan and Ewald, a drama, and not an effusion of piety; that the latter part of Isaiah is not written by the same prophet who composed the former, — are conclusions of criticism which I venture to think may now be taken for granted and made the basis of further reasoning. At the same time I have taken for granted — not as certain, but as likely to be an approximation to the truth — the chronological arrangement of the prophets proposed by Ewald in his great work on that portion of Scripture. Further than this, I believe there are no assumptions of a critical character in the ensuing pages.

First, then, it is to be observed that the problems which occupied the writers of the Book of Genesis, and which in their own fashion they attempted to solve, were the same as those which in all ages have engaged the attention of thoughtful men, and which have been dealt with in many other theologies besides that of the Hebrews. The Hebrew solution may or may not be superior in simplicity or grandeur to the solutions of Parsees, Hindus, and others; but the attempt is the same in character, even if the execution be more successful. The authors of Genesis endeavor especially to account for: —

1. THE CREATION OF THE UNIVERSE.
2. THE ORIGIN OF MAN AND ANIMALS.
3. THE INTRODUCTION OF EVIL.
4. THE DIVERSITY OF LANGUAGES.

Although the fourth of these questions is, so far as I am aware, not a common subject of consideration in popular mythologies, the first three are the standard subjects of primitive theological speculation. Let us begin with the Creation.

One of the earliest inquiries that human beings address themselves to when they arrive at the stage of reflection is: — How did this world in which we find ourselves come into being? Out of what elements was it formed? Who made it, and in what way? A natural and obvious reply to such an inquiry is, that a Being of somewhat similar nature to their own, though larger and more powerful, took the materials of which the world is formed and moulded them, as a workman moulds the materials of his handicraft, into their present shape. The mental process gone through in reaching this conclusion is simply that of pursuing a familiar analogy in such a manner as to bring the unknown within the range of conceptions applicable to the known. The solution, as will be seen shortly, contrives to satisfy one-half of the problem only by leaving the other half out of consideration. This difficulty, however, does not seem to have occurred to the ancient Hebrew writers who propounded the following history of the Creation of the Universe:—

"In the beginning," they say, "God created the heavens and the earth. And the earth was desolate and waste, and darkness on the face of the abyss, and the Spirit of God hovering on the face of the waters. And God said: Let there be light, and there was light. And God saw the light that it was good, and God divided between the light and the darkness. And God called the light Day, and the darkness he called Night. And it was Evening, and it was Morning: one day.

"And God said: Let there be a vault for separation of the waters, and let it divide between waters and waters." Hereupon he made the vault, and separated the waters above it from those below it. The vault he called Heavens. This was his second day's work. On the third, he separated the dry land from the sea, "and saw that it was good;" besides which he caused the earth to bring forth herbs and fruit-trees. "And God said: Let there be lights in the vault of the heavens to divide between the day and between the night, and let them be for signs and for times and for days and for years." Hereupon he made the sun for the day, the moon for the night, and the stars. "And God put them on the vault of the heavens to give light to the earth, and to rule by day and by night, and to separate between the light and the darkness; and God saw that it was good. And it was evening, and it was morning; the fourth day" (Gen. i. 1–19).

Let us pause a moment here before passing on to the next branch of the subject: the creation of animals and man. The author had two questions before him; how the materials of the universe came into being, and how, when in being, they assumed their present forms and relative positions. Of the first he says nothing, unless the first verse be taken to refer to it. But this can scarcely be; for the expression, "God made the heavens and the earth," cannot easily be supposed to refer to the original production of the matter out of which the heavens and the earth were subsequently made. Rather must we take it as a short heading, refering to the creation which is about to be described. And in any case, the manner in which there came to be anything at all out of which heavens and earth could be constructed is not considered. We are left apparently to suppose that matter is coeval with the Deity; for the author never faces the question of its origin, which is the real difficulty in all such cosmogonies as his, but hastens at once to the easier task of describing the separation and classification of materials already in existence.

Somewhat similar to the Hebrew legend, both in what it records and in what it omits, is the story of creation as told by the Quichés in America:—

"This is the first word and the first speech. There were neither men nor brutes, neither birds, fish, nor crabs, stick nor stone, valley nor mountain, stubble nor forest, nothing but the sky; the face of the land was hidden. There was naught but the silent sea and the sky. There was nothing joined, nor any sound, nor thing that stirred; neither any to do evil, nor to rumble in the heavens, nor a walker on foot; only the silent waters, only the pacified ocean, only it in its calm. Nothing was but stillness, and rest, and darkness, and the night; nothing but the Maker and Moulder, the Hurler, the Bird-Serpent" (M. N. W., p. 196. —Popol Vuh, p. 7).

Another cosmogony is derived from the Mixtecs, also aborigines of America:—

"In the year and in the day of clouds, before ever were either years or days, the world lay in darkness; all things were orderless, and a water covered the slime and the ooze that the earth then was" (M. N. W., p. 196).

Two winds are in this myth the agents employed to effect the subsidence of the waters, and the appearance of dry land. In another account, related by some other tribes, the muskrat is the instrument which divides the land from the waters. These myths, as Mr. Brinton, who has collected them, truly remarks, are "not of a construction, but a reconstruction only, and are in that respect altogether similar to the creative myth of the first chapter of Genesis."

In the Buddhistic history of the East Mongols, the creation of the world is made, as in Genesis, the starting-point of the relation. But the creative forces in this mythology are apparently supposed to be inherent in primeval matter. Hence we have a Lucretian account of the movements of the several parts of the component mass without any consideration of the question how the impulse to these movements was originally given. "In the beginning there arose the external reservoir from three different masses of matter; namely, from the creative air, from the waving water, and from the firm, plastic earth." A strong wind from ten-quarters now brought about the blue atmosphere. A large cloud, pouring down continuous rain, formed the sea. Dry land arose by means of grains of dust collecting on the surface of the ocean, like cream on milk."*

Although the sacred writings of the Parsees contain no connected account of the creation, yet this void is fully supplied by traditions which have acquired a religious sanction, and have entered into the popular belief. These traditions are found in the Bundehesh and the Shahnahmeh, works of high authority in the Parsee system. According to them, Ahura-Mazda, the good principle, induced his rival, Agra-Mainyus, the evil principle, to enter into a truce of nine thousand years, foreseeing that by means of this interval he would be able to subdue him in the end. Agra-Mainyus, having discovered his blunder, went to the darkest hell, and remained there three thousand years. Ahura-Mazda took advantage of this repose to create the material world. He produced the sky in forty-five days, the water in sixty, the earth in seventy-five, the trees in thirty, the cattle in eighty, and human beings in seventy-five; three hundred and sixty-five days were thus occupied with the business of creation. It will be observed that, though the time taken is longer, the order of production is the same in the Parsee as in the Hebrew legend. This fact tends to confirm the supposition, which will hereafter appear still more probable, of an intimate relation between the two.

* Geschichte der Ost-Mongolen und ihres Furstenhauses verfasst von Ssanang Ssetsen Chungtaidschi. Aus dem Mongolischen ubersetzt von J. J. Schmidt, St. Petersburg. 1829. 4to. p. 3.

This work will, in the following pages, always be referred to under "G. O. M."

Always prone to speculation, the Hindus were certain to find in the dark subject of creation abundant materials for their mystic theories. Various explanations are accordingly given in the Rig-Veda. Thus, the following account is found in the tenth Book:—

"Let us, in chanted hymns, with praise, declare the births of the gods,—any of us who in this latter age may behold them. Brahmanaspati blew forth these births like a blacksmith. In the earliest age of the gods, the existent sprang from the non-existent: thereafter the regions sprang from Uttānapad. The earth sprang from Uttānapad, from the earth sprang the regions: Daksha sprang from Aditi, and Aditi from Daksha. Then the gods were born, and drew forth the sun, which was hidden in the ocean" (O. S. T., vol. v. p. 48.—Rig-Veda, x. 72).

With higher wisdom, another Vaidik Rishi declares it impossible to know the origin of the universe:—

"There was then neither non-entity nor entity: there was no atmosphere, nor sky above. What enveloped [all]? Where, in the receptacle of what, [was it contained]? Was it water, the profound abyss? Death was not then, nor immortality; there was no distinction of day or night. That One breathed calmly, self-supported; there was nothing different from, or above, it. In the beginning darkness existed, enveloped in darkness. All this was undistinguishable water. That One which lay void, and wrapped in nothingness, was developed by the power of fervour. Desire first arose in It, which was the primal germ of mind; [and which] sages, searching with their intellect, have discovered in their heart to be the bond which connects entity with non-entity. The ray [or cord] which stretched across these [worlds], was it below or was it above? There were there impregnating powers and mighty forces, a self-supporting principle beneath, and energy aloft. Who knows, who here can declare, whence has sprung, whence, this creation? The gods are subsequent to the development of this [universe]; who then knows whence it arose? From what this creation arose, and whether [any one] made it or not, he who in the highest heaven is its ruler, he verily knows, or even he does not know" (O. S. T., vol. v. p. 356.—Rig-Veda, x. 129).

A later narrative ascribes creation to the god Prajâpati, who, it is said, having the desire to multiply himself, underwent the requisite austerities, and then produced earth, air, and heaven (A. B., vol. ii. p. 372).

We now return to Genesis, which proceeds to its second problem: the creation of living creatures and of man. This is solved in two distinct fashions by two different writers. The first relates that on the fifth day God said, "Let the waters swarm with the swarming of animals having life, and let birds fly to and fro on the earth, on the face of the vault of the heavens." Having thus produced the inhabitants of the ocean and air on the fifth day, he produced those of earth on the sixth. On this day too he made man in his own image, and created them male and female. The whole of his work was now finished, and on the seventh day he enjoyed repose from his creative exertions, for which reason he blessed the seventh day (Gen. 1–ii. 3).

Here the first account of creation ends; the second begins with a descriptive title at the fourth verse of the second chapter. The writer of this version, unlike his predecessor, instead of ascribing the creation of man to the immediate fiat of Elohim, describes the process as resembling one of manufacture. God formed the human figure out of the dust of the earth, and then blew life into it, a conception drawn from the widespread notion of the identity of breath with life. Again the narrator of the second story varies from the narrator of the first about the creation of the sexes. In the first, the male and female are made together. In the second, a deep sleep falls upon the man, during which God takes out a rib from his side and makes the woman out of it. Generally speaking, it may be remarked that the former writer moves in a more transcendental sphere than the latter. He likes to conceive the origin of the world, with all its flora and all its fauna, as arising from the simple power of the word of God. How they arise he never troubles himself to say. The latter is more terrestrial. God with him is like a powerful artist; extremely skilled indeed in dealing with his materials, but nevertheless obliged to adapt his proceedings to their nature and capabilities. This author delights in the concrete and particular; and not only does he aim at relating the order of the creation, but also at making the *modus operandi* more or less intelligible to his hearers.

A somewhat different account of the origin of man is given in the traditions of Samoa, one of the Fiji islands. These traditions also describe an epoch when the earth was covered with water. "Tangaloa, the great Polynesian Jupiter," sent his daughter to find a dry place. After a long time she found a rock. In subsequent visits she reported that the dry land was extending. "He then sent her down with some earth and a creeping plant, as all was barren rock. She continued to visit the earth and return to the skies. Next visit, the plant was spreading. Next time, it was withered and decomposing. Next visit, it swarmed with worms. And the next time, the worms had become men and women! A strange account of man's origin!" On which it may be remarked, as a curious psychological phenomenon, tending to illustrate the effects of habit, that the missionary considers it "a strange account of man's origin" which represents God as making him from worms, but readily accepts another in which he is made out of dust.

The third question dealt with in Genesis is that of the origin of evil. This is a problem which has engaged the attention and perplexed the minds of many inquirers besides these ancient Hebrews, and for which most religions provide some kind of solution. The manner in which it is treated here is as follows :—

When God made Adam, he placed him in a garden full of delights, and especially distinguished by the excellence of its fruit-trees. There was one of these trees, however, the fruit of which he did not wish Adam to eat. He accordingly gave him strict orders on the subject in these words: "Of every tree of the garden thou mayst eat; but of the tree of knowledge of good and evil, of that thou mayst not eat, for on what day thou eatest thereof, thou diest the death" (Gen. ii. 16, 17). This order we must suppose to have been imparted by Adam to Eve, who was not produced until after it had been given. At any rate, we find her fully cognizant of it in the ensuing chapter, where the serpent appears upon the scene and endeavors, only too successfully, to induce her to eat the fruit. After yielding to the temptation herself, she induced her husband to do the like; whereupon both recognized the hitherto unnoticed fact of their nudity, and made themselves aprons of fig-leaves. Shortly after this crisis in their lives God came down to enjoy the cool of the evening in the garden; and Adam and Eve, feeling their guilt, ran to hide themselves among the trees. God called Adam, and the latter replied that he had hidden himself because he was naked. But God at once asked who had told him he was naked. Had he eaten of the forbidden tree ? Of course Adam and Eve had to confess, and God then cursed the serpent for his gross misconduct, and punished the man by imposing labor upon him, and the woman by rendering her liable to the pains of childbirth. He also condescended so far as to become the first tailor, making garments of skins for Adam and Eve. But though he had thus far got the better of them by his superior strength, he was not without apprehension that they might outwit him still. "And God, the Everlasting, spoke: See, the man is become as one of us, to know good and evil; and now, lest he should stretch out his hand and take also of the tree of life, and eat and live forever! Therefore God, the Everlasting, sent him out of the garden of Eden, to cultivate the ground from which he had been taken " (Gen. iii. 22, 23). And in order to make quite sure that the man should not get hold of the tree of life, a calamity which would have defeated his intention to make him mortal, he guarded the approach to it by means of Cherubim, posted as sentinels with the flame of a sword that turned about. In this way he conceived that he had secured himself against any invasion of his privilege of immortality on the part of the human race.

Like the myth of creation, the myth of a happier and brighter age, when men did not suffer from any of the evils that oppress them now, is common, if not universal. Common too, if not equally common, is the notion that they fell from that superior state by contracting the stain of sin. I need scarcely refer to the classical story of a golden age, embodied by Hesiod in his "Works and Days," nor to the fable of Pandora allowing the ills enclosed in the box to escape into the world. But it may be of interest to remark, that the conception of a Paradise was no less familiar to the natives of America than to those of Europe. "When Christopher Columbus," observes Brinton, "fired by the hope of discovering this terrestrial paradise, broke the enchantment of the cloudy sea and found a new world, it was but to light upon the same race of men, deluding themselves with the same hope of earthly joys, the same fiction of a long-lost garden of their youth " (M. N. W., p. 87). Elsewhere he says: "Once again, in the legends of the Mixtecas, we hear the old story repeated of the garden where the first two brothers dwelt. . . . 'Many trees were there, such as yield flowers and roses, very luscious fruits, divers herbs, and aromatic spices'" (M. N. W., p. 90). Corresponding to the golden age among the Greeks was the Parsee conception of the reign of Yima, a mythological monarch who was in immediate and friendly intercourse with Ahura-Mazda. Yima's kingdom is thus described in the Vendidad: "There was there neither quarreling not disputing; neither stupidity nor violence; neither begging nor imposture; neither poverty nor illness. No unduly large teeth; no form that passes the measure of the body; none of the other marks, which are marks of Agra-Mainyus, that he has made on men" (Av., vol. i. p. 76. —Vendidad, Fargard, ii. 116 ff). In another passage, found in the Khorda-Avesta, not only is the happiness of Yima's time depicted, but it is also distinctly asserted that he fell through sin. "During his rule there was no cold, no heat, no old age, no death, no envy created by the Devas, on account of the absence of lying, previously, before he (himself) began to love lying, untrue speeches. Then, when he began to love lying, untrue speeches, Majesty fled from him visibly with the body of a bird" (Av., vol. iii. p. 175—Khorda-Avesta, xxxv 32, 34).

More elaborately than in any of these systems is the fall of man described in the mythology of Buddhism. In this religion, as in that of the Jews, man is of divine origin, though after a somewhat different fashion. A spiritual being, or god, fell from one of the upper spheres, to be born in the world of man. Through the progressive increase of this being arose " the six species of living creatures in the three worlds." The most eminent of these species, Man, enjoyed an untold duration of life (another point in which Buddhistic legends resemble those of

the Hebrews). Locomotion was carried on through the air;
they did not consume impure terrestrial food, but lived on
celestial victuals; and propagation, since there was no distinction of sex, was carried on by means of emanation. They did
not require sun or moon, for they saw by their own light.
Alas! one of these pure beings was tempted by a fool called
earth-butter and ate it. The rest followed its example. Hereupon the heavenly food vanished; the race lost their power of
going about the sky, and ceased to shine by their own light.
This was the origin of the evil of the darkening of the mind.
As a consequence of these deeds, sun, moon, and stars appeared.
Still greater calamities were in store for men. Another, at another time, ate a different kind of food, an example again followed by the rest. In consequence of this, the distinctions of
sex were established in them; passion arose; they began to beget children. This was the origin of the evil of sensual love.
On a further occasion, one of them ate wild rice, and all lived
for a time on wild rice, gathered as it was needed for immediate consumption. But when some foolish fellow took it into his
head to collect enough for the following day, the rice ceased to
grow without cultivation. This was the origin of the evil of
idle carelessness. It being now necesssary to cultivate rice,
persons began to appropriate and quarrel about land, and even
to kill one another. This was the origin of the evil of
anger. Again, some who were better off. hid their stores from
those who were not so well off. This was the origin of the evil
of covetousness. In course of time the age of men began to
decline so as to be expressible in numbers. It continues gradually to decline until a turning-point arrives, at which it again
increases (G. O. M., p. 5–9).

Several points of similarity between the Hebrew myth and
that just narrated will doubtless occur to the reader. The fall
of man is due, in this, as in Genesis, to the eating of a peculiar
food by a single person; and this example is followed, in the
one case, by the only other inhabitant; in the other, by all.
The calamity thus entailed does not terminate in the loss of
former pleasures, but extends to the introduction of crime and
sexual relations. Eve is cursed by having to bear children; the
same misfortune happened to the Buddhist women. Cain quar-

reled with Abel and killed him; so did the landed proprietors in the Indian legend quarrel with and kill one another.

The fourth question which appeared to have engaged the attention of the authors of Genesis was that of the variety of languages. How was it, if all mankind were descended from a single pair, and if again all but the Noachian family had been drowned, that they did not all speak the pure language in which Adam and Eve had conversed with their Creator in Paradise? Embarrassed by their own theories, the writers attempted to account for the phenomenon of the diverse modes of speech in use among men by an awkward myth. Men had determined to build a town, with a tower which should reach to heaven. Jehovah, however, came down one day to see what they were about, and was filled with apprehension that, if they succeeded in this undertaking, he might find it impossible to prevent them from carrying out their wishes in other ways also, whatever those wishes might be. So he determined to confound their language, that they might not understand one another, and by this happy contrivance put an end to the construction of the dangerous tower (Gen. xi. 1–9).

We have anticipated the course of the narrative in order to consider the solutions offered in Genesis of the four principal problems with which it attempts to deal. We must now return to the point at which we left the parents of the race, namely, immediately after their expulsion from Eden. They now began to beget children rapidly; and Adam's eldest son, Cain, afterwards killed his second son, Abel, for which Jehovah cursed him as he had previously cursed his parents. Adam and Eve had several other children, and (though this is nowhere expressly stated, but only implied) the brothers and sisters united in marriage to carry out the propagation of the species. In course of time, however, the "sons of God" began to admire the beauty of the "daughters of men," and to take wives from among them. Jehovah, indignant at such a scandal, fixed the limits of man's life—which had hitherto been measured by centuries—at 120 years. At the same time there were giants on earth. Now Jehovah saw that the human race was extremely wicked, so much so, that he began to wish he had never created it. To remedy this blunder, however, he determined to destroy it; and in order that the improvement should be thorough, to destroy along with it all cattle, creeping things, and birds, who had not (so far as we are aware,) entered into the same kind of irregular alliances with other species as men. Nevertheless, he had still a lingering fondness for his handiwork, badly as it had turned out; and therefore determined to preserve enough of each kind of animal, man included, to carry on the breed without the necessity of resorting a second time to creation. Acting upon this resolve, he ordered an individual named Noah to build an ark of gopher-wood, announcing that he would shortly destroy all flesh, but wished to save Noah and his three sons, with their several wives. He also desired him to take two members of each species of beasts and birds, or, according to another account, seven of each clean beast and bird, and two of each unclean beast; but in any case taking care that each sex should be represented in the ark. When Noah had done all this, the waters came up from below and down from above, and there was an increasing flood for forty days. All terrestrial life but that which floated in the ark was destroyed. At last the waters began to ebb, and finally the ark rested on the 17th day of the 7th month on Mount Ararat. After forty more days Noah sent out a raven and a dove, of which only the dove returned. In seven days he sent the dove again, and it returned, bringing an olive-leaf; and after another week, when he again sent it out, it returned no more. It was not, however, till the 27th of the 2d month of the ensuing year (these chroniclers being very exact about dates) that the earth was dried, and that Noah and his party were able to quit the ark. To commemorate the goodness of God in drowning all the world except himself and his family, Noah erected an altar and offered burnt-offerings of every clean beast and every clean fowl. The effect was instantaneous. So pleased was Jehovah with the "pleasant smell," that he resolved never to destroy all living beings again, though still of opinion that "the imagination of man's heart is evil from his youth" (Gen. vi. 7, 8).

The myth of the deluge is very general. The Hebrews have no exclusive property in it. Many different races relate it in different ways. We may easily suppose that the partial deluges to which they must often have been witnesses suggested the notion of a universal deluge, in which not only a few tribes or villages perished, but all the inhabited earth was laid under water; or the memory of some actual flood of unusual dimensions may have survived in the popular mind, and been handed down with traits of exaggeration and distortion such as are commonly found in the narratives of events preserved by oral tradition. Let us examine a few instances of the flood-myth.

The Fijians relate that the god "Degei was roused every morning by the cooing of a monstrous bird," but that two young men, his grandsons, one day accidentally killed and buried it. Degei having, after some trouble, found the dead body, determined to be avenged. The youths "took refuge with a powerful tribe of carpenters," who built a fence to keep out the god. Unable to take the fence by storm, Degei brought on heavy floods, which rose so high that his grandsons and their friends had to escape in "large bowls that happened to be at hand." They landed at various places; but it is said that the two tribes became extinct (Viti, p. 394).

The Greenlanders have "a tolerably distinct tradition" of a flood. They say that all men were drowned excepting one. This one beat with his stick upon the ground and thereby produced a woman (Grönland, p. 246).

Kamtschatka has a somewhat similar legend, except that it admits a larger number of survivors. Very many, according to this version, were drowned, and the waves had sunk those who had got into boats; but others took refuge in rafts, binding the trees together to make them. On these they saved themselves with their provisions and all their property. When the waters subsided, the rafts remained on the high mountains (Kamtschatka, p. 273).

Among the North Americans "the notion of a universal deluge" was, in the time of the Jesuit De Charlevoix, "rather wide-spread." In one of their stories, told by the Iroquois, all human beings were drowned; and it was necessary, in order to re-populate the earth, to change animals into men (N. F., vol. iii. p. 345).

The Tupis of Brazil are supposed to be named after Tupa, the first of men, "who alone survived the flood" (M. N. W., p. 185). Again, "the Peruvians imagined that *two* destructions had taken place, the first by a famine, the second by a flood; according to some a few only escaping, but, after the more widely accepted opinion, accompanied by the absolute extirpation of the race." The present race came from eggs dropped out of heaven (Ibid., p. 213). Several other tribes relate in diverse forms this world-wide story. In one of the versions, found in an old Mexican work, a man and his wife are saved, by the directions of their god, in a hollow cypress. In another, the earth is destroyed by water, because men "did not think nor speak of the Creator who had created them, and who had caused their birth." "Because they had not thought of their Mother and Father, the Heart of Heaven, whose name is Hurakan, therefore the face of the earth grew dark, and a pouring rain commenced, raining by day, raining by night" (Ibid., p. 206 ff).

The diluvian legend appears in a very singular form in India in the Satapatha Brâhmana. There it is stated, that in the basin which was brought to Manu to wash his hands in, there was one morning a small fish. The fish said to him, "Preserve me, I shall save thee." Manu inquired from what it would save him. The fish replied that it would be from a flood which would destroy all creatures. It informed Manu that fishes, while small, were exposed to the risk of being eaten by other fishes; he was therefore to put it first into a jar; then when it grew too large for that, to dig a trench and keep it in that; that when it grew too large for the trench, to carry it to the ocean. Straightway it became a large fish, and said: "Now in such and such a year, then the flood will come; thou shalt therefore construct a ship, and resort to me; thou shalt embark in the ship when the flood rises, and I shall deliver thee from it." Manu took the fish to the sea, and in the year that had been named, "he constructed a ship and resorted to him. When the flood rose, Manu embarked in the ship. The fish swam towards him. He fastened the cable of the ship to the fish's horn. By this means he passed over this northern mountain. The fish said, 'I have delivered thee; fasten the ship to a tree. But lest the water should cut thee off whilst thou art on the mountain, as much as the water subsides, so much shalt thou descend after it.' He accordingly descended after it as much (as it subsided). . . . Now the flood had swept away all these creatures; so Manu alone was left here'' (O. S. T., vol. i. p. 183). The story goes on to relate that Manu, being quite alone, produced a woman by "arduous religious rites," and that with this woman, who called herself his daughter, "he begot this offspring, which is this offspring of Manu," that is, the existing human race.

After the flood, the history proceeds for some time to narrate the lives of a series of patriarchs, the mythological ancestors of the Hebrew race. Of these the first is Abram, afterwards called Abraham; to whom a solemn promise was made that he was to be the progenitor of a great nation; that Jehovah would bless those who blessed him, and curse those who cursed him; and that in him all generations of the earth should be blessed (Gen. xii. 1–3). When Abraham visited Egypt, he desired his wife Sarah to call herself his sister, fearing lest the Egyptians should kill him for her sake. She did so, and was taken into Pharaoh's harem in consequence of her false statement; but Jehovah plagued Pharoah and his house so severely that the truth was discovered, and Sarah was restored to her lawful husband. It is remarkable that Abraham is stated to have subsequently repeated the same contemptible trick, this time alleging by way of excuse that Sarah really was his stepsister; and that Abraham's son, Isaac, is said to have done the same thing in reference to Rebekah (Gen. xii. 10–20, xx., xxvi 6–11). Abimelech, king of Gerar, who was twice imposed upon by these patriarchs, must have thought it a singular custom of the family thus to pass off their wives as sisters. Apparently, too, both of them were quite prepared to surrender their consorts to the harems of foreign monarchs rather than run the smallest risk in their defense.

Abraham, at ninety-nine years of age, was fortunate in all things but one: he had no legitimate heir. But this too was to be given him. Jehovah appeared to him, announced himself as Almighty God, and established with Abraham a solemn covenant. He promised to make him fruitful, to give his posterity the land of Canaan, in which he then was, and to cause Sarah to have a son. At the same time he desired that all males should be circumcised, an operation which was forthwith per-

formed on Abraham, his illegitimate son Ishmael, and all the
men in his house (Gen. xvii). In due time Sarah had a son
whom Abraham named Isaac.   But when Isaac was a lad, and
all Abraham's hopes of posterity were centered in him as the
only child of Sarah, God one day commanded him to sacrifice
him as a burnt-offering on a mountain in Moriah.   Without a
murmur, without a word of inquiry, Abraham prepared to obey
this extraordinary injunction, and was only withheld from
plunging the sacrificial knife into the bosom of his son by the
positive interposition of an angel.   Looking about, he perceived
a ram caught in a thicket, and offered him as a burnt offering
instead of Isaac.   For this servile and unintelligent submission,
he was rewarded by Jehovah with further promises as to the
amazing numbers of his posterity in future times (Gen. xxi. 1–8;
xxii. 1–19).

The tradition of human sacrifice, thus preserved in the story
of Abraham and Isaac, is found also in a curious narrative of
the Aitareya Brahmana.   That sacred book also commemorates
an important personage, in this instance a king, who had no
son.   Although he had a hundred wives, yet none of them bore
him a male heir.   He inquired of his priest, Narada, what were
the advantages of having a son, and learned that they were
very great.   "The father pays a debt in his son, and gains immortality," such was one of the privileges to be obtained by
means of a son.   The Rishi Narada therefore advised King
Harischandra to pray to Varuna for a son, promising at the
same time to sacrifice him as soon as he was born.   The king
did so.   "Then a son, Rohita by name, was born to him.
Varuna said to him, 'A son is born to thee, sacrifice him to me.'
Harischandra said, 'An animal is fit for being sacrificed, when
it is more than ten days old.   Let him reach this age, then I
will sacrifice him to thee.   At ten days Varuna again demanded
him, but now his father had a fresh excuse, and so postponed
the sacrifice from age to age until Rohita had received his full
armor."   Varuna having again claimed him, Harischandra now
said, "Well, my dear, to him who gave thee unto me, I will
sacrifice thee now."   But Rohita, come to man's estate, had no
mind to be sacrificed, and ran away to the wilderness.   Varuna
now caused Harischandra to suffer from dropsy.   Rohita, hear-

ing of it, left the forest, and went to a village, where Indra, in disguise, met him and desired him to wander. The advice was repeated every year until Rohita had wandered six years in the forest. This last year he met a poor Rishi, named Ajigarta, who was starving, to whom he offered one hundred cows for one of his three sons as a ransom for himself in the sacrifice to be offered to Varuna. The father having objected to the eldest, and the mother to the youngest, the middle one Sunahsepa, was agreed upon as the ransom, and the hundred cows were paid for him. Rohita presented to his father the boy Sunahsepa, who was accepted by the god with the remark that a Brahman was worth more than a Kshattriya. "Varuna then explained to the king the rites of the Rajasuya sacrifice, at which on the day appointed for the inauguration he replaced the (sacrificial animal) by a man."

But at the sacrifice a strange incident occurred. No one could be found willing to bind the victim to the sacrificial post. At last his father offered to do it for another hundred cows. Bound to the stake, no one could be found to kill him. This act also his father undertook to do for a third hundred. "He then whetted his knife and went to kill his son. Sunahsepa then got aware that they were going to butcher him just as if he were no man (but a beast). 'Well,' said he, 'I will seek shelter with the gods.' He applied to Prajapati, who referred him to another god, who did the same; and thus he was driven from god to god through the pantheon, until he came to Ushas, the dawn. However, as he was praising Ushas, his fetters fell off, and Harischandra's belly became smaller; until at the last verse he was free, and Harischandra well." Sunahsepa was now received among the priests as one of themselves, and he sat down by Visvamitra, an eminent Rishi. Ajigarta, his father, requested that he might be returned to him, but Visvamitra refused, "for," he said, "the gods have presented him to me." From that time forward he became Visvamitra's son. At this point, however, Ajigarta himself entreated his son to return to his home, and the answer of the latter is remarkable. "Sunahsepa answered, 'What is not found even in the hands of a Shudra, one has seen in thy hand, the knife (to kill thy son); three hundred cows thou hast preferred to me, O Angiras.

Ajigarta then answered, 'O my dear son! I repent of the bad deed I have committed; I blot out this stain! one hundred of the cows shall be thine!' Sunahsepa answered, 'Who once might commit such a sin, may commit the same another time. Thou art still not free from the brutality of a Shudra, for thou hast committed a crime for which no reconciliation exists.' 'Yes, irreconcilable (is this act),' interrupted Visvamitra!" (A. B., p. 460–469.)

On the likeness of this story to the Hebrew legend of the intended sacrifice of Isaac, and on the difference between the two, I shall comment elsewhere. From the days of Abraham the history proceeds through a series of patriarchal biographies — those of Isaac and Rebekah, of Jacob and Rachel, of Joseph and his brothers — to the captivity of the Israelites in Egypt under the successor of the monarch whose prime minister Joseph had been. It is at this point that the history of the Hebrews as a distinct nation may be said to begin. The patriarchs belong to universal history. But from the days of the Egyptian captivity it is the fortunes of a peculiar tribe, and afterwards of an independent people that are followed. We have their deliverance from slavery, their progress through the wilderness, their triumphant establishment in their destined home, the rise, decline, and fall of their national greatness, depicted with much graphic power, and intermingled with episodes of the deepest interest. It would not be consistent with the plan or limits of this work to follow the history through its varied details; all we can do is to touch upon it here and there, where the adventures, institutions, or imaginations of the Hebrews present points of contact with those of other nations as recorded in their authorized writings.

It was only by the especial favor of Jehovah that the Hebrew slaves were enabled to escape from Egypt at all. That deity appointed a man named Moses as their leader; and, employing him as his mouthpiece, desired Pharaoh to let them go. On Pharaoh's refusal, he visited Egypt with a series of calamities; all of them inadequate to the object in view, until at length Pharaoh and all his army were overwhelmed in the Red Sea, which had opened to allow the Israelites to pass. These last now escaped into the wilderness, where, under the guidance of

Moses, they wandered for forty years, undergoing all sorts of hardships, before they reached the promised land. During the course of their travels, Jehovah gave Moses ten commandments, which stand out from a mass of other injunctions and enactments, by the solemnity with which they were delivered, and by the extreme importance of their subject-matter. They are reported to have been given to Moses by Jehovah in person on Mount Sinai, in the midst of a very considerable amount of noise and smoke, apparently intended to be impressive. By these laws the Israelites were ordered—

   1. To have no other God but Jehovah.
   2. To make no image for purposes of worship.
   3. Not to take Jehovah's name in vain.
   4. Not to work on the Sabbath day.
   5. To honor their parents.
   6. Not to kill.
   7. Not to commit adultery.
   8. Not to steal.
   9. Not to bear false witness against a neighbor.
  10. Not to covet.

Concerning these commandments, it may be observed that the acts enjoined or forbidden are of very different characters. Some of the obligations thus imposed are universally binding, and the precepts relating to them form a portion of universal ethics. Others again are of a purely special theological character, and have no application at all except to those who hold certain theological doctrines. Lastly, others command states of mind only, which have no proper place in positive laws enforced under penalties. To illustrate these remarks in detail: the four commandments against killing, stealing, adultery, and calumny are of universal obligation, and though they are far from exhausting the list of actions which a moral code should prohibit, yet properly belong to it and are among its most important constituents. But the first, second, third, and fourth commandments presuppose a nation believing in Jehovah as their God; and even with that proviso the fourth, requiring the observance of a day of rest, is purely arbitrary; belonging only to ritual, not to morals. To place it along with prohibitions of murder and theft, is simply to confuse in the minds of hearers the all-important distinction between special observances and universal duties. Again, the fifth and tenth commandments require mere emotional conditions; respect for parents in the one case, absence of covetousness in the other. No doubt both these mental conditions have actions and abstinences from action as their correlatives; but it is with these last that law should deal, and not with the mere states of feeling over which no commandment can exercise the smallest control. Law may forbid us to annoy our neighbor, or do him an injury on account of his wife whom we love, or his estate which we desire to possess; but it is idle to forbid us to wish that the wife or the estate were ours.

These errors are avoided in the five fundamental commandments of Buddhism, which relate wholly to matters that, if binding upon any, are binding upon all. They are these:—

1. Not to kill.
2. Not to steal.
3. Not to indulge in illicit pleasures of sex.
4. Not to lie.
5. Not to drink intoxicating liquors.*

No doubt the fifth is not of equal importance with the rest; yet its intention is simply to put a stop to drunkenness, and this it accomplishes, like teetotal societies, by requiring entire abstinence. Probably in hot climates, and with populations not capable of much self-control, this was the wisest way. The third commandment, as I have presented it, is somewhat vague, but this is because the form in which it is given by the authorities is not always the same. Sometimes it appears as a mere prohibition of all unchastity; but the more probable view appears to be that of Burnouf, who interprets it as directed against adultery, in substantial accordance with Alabaster, who renders it as an injunction "not to indulge the passions, so as to invade the legal or natural rights of other men."

In the eight principal commandments of the Parsees, the

* R. B., vol. i. p. 434.—Lotus, p. 447.—Wheel, p. xliii,

breach of which was to be punished with death, there is the
the same confusion of theological and natural duties as in the
Hebrew Bible. The Parsees were forbidden —

1. To kill a pure man (*i. e.*, a Parsee).
2. To put out the fire Behram.
3. To throw the impurity from dead bodies into fire or water.
4. To commit adultery.
5. To practice magic or contribute to its being practiced.
6. To throw the impurity of menstruating women into fire or water.
7. To commit sodomy with boys.
8. To commit highway-robbery or suicide (Av., vol. ii. p. lx).

Besides these commandments, Jehovah gave his people a
vast mass of laws, amounting in fact to a complete criminal
code, through his mouthpiece Moses. Among these laws were
those which were written on the two tables of stone, commonly
though erroneously supposed to have been the ten commandments of the twentieth chapter. The express statement of
Exodus forbids such a supposition. It is there stated that when
God had finished communing with Moses he gave him "two
tables of testimony, tables of stone, written with the finger of
God." This most valuable autograph Moses had the folly to
break in his anger at finding that the Israelites, led by his
brother Aaron, had taken to worshiping a golden calf in his
absence (Ex., xxxi. 18, and xxxii, 19). God, however, desired him
to prepare other tables like those he had destroyed, and kindly
undertook to write upon them the very words that had been on
the first. Apparently, however, he only dictated them to Moses,
who is said to have written upon the tables "the words of the
covenant, the ten commandments." What these words were
there can be no doubt, for he had begun his address to Moses
by saying, "Behold, I make a covenant;" and had concluded
it by the expression, "Write thou *these* words: for after the
tenor of these words have I made a covenant with thee and
with Israel" (Ex. xxxiv. 1-28). Now the commandments thus
asserted to have been written on the tables of stone were very
different from the ten given before on Mount Sinai, and resemble more closely still the style of those quoted from the Parsee

books. Yet they were evidently deemed by the writers of great importance, from the honor ascribed to them of having been originally written in God's own handwriting on stone. Their purport is:—1. To forbid any covenant with the inhabitants of the land to which the Israelites were going, and to enjoin them to "destroy their altars, break their images, and cut down their groves;"—2. To require the observance of the feast of unleavened bread;—3. To lay claim to firstlings for Jehovah, and demand their redemption;—4. To command the Sabbatical rest;—5. To enjoin the observance of the feast of weeks;—6. To desire that all males should appear thrice yearly before the Lord;—7. To forbid the sacrifice of blood with leaven;—8. To forbid leaving the sacrifice of the feast of the passover till morning; —9. To demand the first-fruits for Jehovah;—10. To forbid seething a kid in its mother's milk.*

Eminent as Moses was, and high as he stood in the favor of his God, he was not permitted to lead his people to Canaan. Jehovah punished him for a momentary weakness by depriving him of that privilege, which was reserved for Joshua. Just as the waters of the Red Sea were cleft in two to allow the Israelites to quit Egypt, so were those of the Jordan cleft in two to allow them to enter Canaan. No sooner did the feet of the priests bearing the ark touch the water, than the portion of the river below was cut off from that above, the upper waters rising into a heap (Josh. iii). Striking as this miracle is, it is not more so than that performed by Visvamitra, an Indian sage. When he arrived at a river which he desired to cross, that holy man said: "Listen, O sisters, to the bard who has come to you from afar with wagon and chariot. Sink down; become fordable; reach not up to our chariot-axles with your streams. (The rivers answer): We shall listen to thy words, O bard; thou hast come from far with wagon and chariot. I will bow down to thee like a woman with full breast (suckling her child), as a maid to a man will I throw myself open to thee. (Visvamitra says): When the Bharatas, that war-loving tribe, sent forward, impelled by Indra, have crossed thee, then thy headlong current

* My attention was drawn to the fact that these were the contents of the tables by Goethe's interesting essay: "Zwei wichtige, bisher unerorterte biblische Fragen."

shall hold on its course. I seek the favor of you the adorable. The war-loving Bharatas have crossed; the Sage has obtained the favor of the rivers. Swell on, impetuous and fertilizing; fill your channels; roll rapidly " (O. S. T., vol. i. p. 340).

So that the very same prodigy which, according to the Book of Joshua, was wrought for the benefit of the Hebrew people in Palestine, was, according to the Rig-Veda, wrought for the benefit of a warlike tribe in India.

After their arrival and settlement in Palestine the Israelites passed through a period of great trouble and disturbance. The government was a direct theocracy; men appointed by God, that is, self-appointed, put themselves at the head of affairs and governed with more or less success under the inspiration, and in the name of Jehovah. During this time the people were exposed to great annoyance from their enemies the Philistines, by whom they were for a certain space held in subjugation. The legend of the national hero and deliverer, Samson, falls within this period of depression under a foreign yoke. Samson in the Jewish Herakles, and his exploits are altogether as fabulous as those of his Hellenic counterpart; though it is not impossible that such a personage as Samson may have lived and may have led the people with some glory against their hereditary enemies. Many internal disturbances contributed to render the condition of the Israelites under their theocracy far from enviable; and at length, under the government of Samuel, the last representative of this state of things, the people could bear their distress no longer and united to demand a king. The request was undoubtedly a wise one; for the authority of a monarch was eminently needed to give internal peace and protection against external attacks to the distracted nation. Samuel, however, was naturally opposed to such a change. His feelings and his interests were alike concerned in the maintenance of the direct government of Jehovah, whose plenipotentiary he was. But all his representations that the proposal to elect a king was a crime in the eyes of God, were unavailing. He was compelled to yield, and selected, as the monarch appointed by Jehovah himself, a young man named Saul. Before long, however, Jehovah discovered that he had made a mistake, and that Saul was not the kind of man he had hoped to find him, Samuel was therefore desired to anoint David to supplant him. In other words, Saul did not prove the obedient instrument which Samuel had hoped to make of him, and he therefore entered into a secret conspiracy to procure his deposition. The conduct of Saul, and his relations to David, have probably been misrepresented by the ecclesiastical historians, who persistently favor David. Nevertheless, they cannot wholly disguise the lawless and savage career of this monarch before his accession to the throne, of which at length he obtained possession. Nor was his conduct during his occupation of it altogether exemplary. He, however, promoted the views of the priestly party, and this was enough to cover a multitude of sins.

His son Solomon who succeeded him was the most magnificent of the monarchs of Israel and the last who ruled over the undivided kingdom. He was especially renowned for his wisdom, which is exemplified by a famous decision. Two women came before him to dispute the ownership of an infant. One of them stated that the other, who was alone in the same house with her, had killed her own child by lying upon it during the night, and taken the living child from its mother while that mother was asleep. The other asserted that the living child was hers. Having heard the two statements, the king ordered the living child to be cut in two and half given to each woman. Hereupon the one declared that she would prefer to resign it altogether; but the other professed her acquiescence in the judgment. The king at once awarded it to her who had been willing to resign it rather than see it divided (1 Kings, iii. 16-28). Equal, or perhaps even greater wisdom, was displayed by a monarch whose history is recorded in one of the sacred books of Buddhism. Two women were contending before him about their right to a boy. He desired each of them to take hold of it by one of its hands and to pull at it; the one who succeeded in getting it to keep it. She who was not the mother pulled unmercifully; whereas the true mother, though stronger than her rival, only pulled gently in order to avoid hurting it. The king perceived the truth, and adjudged it to the one who had pulled it gently (G. O. M., p. 344).

Rehoboam, the son and successor of Solomon, failing to conciliate the people at his accession, brought about the schism between Samaria and Judea, between the ten tribes and the two, which was never afterwards healed. After this the government in each kingdom may be described as absolute monarchy tempered by prophetical admonition. The prophets, who formed a kind of professional body of advisers in the interest of Jehovah, made it their business to reprove the crimes, and especially the idolatries of the kings. They exercised the kind of influence which a *corps diplomatique* may sometimes exercise on a feeble court. The monarchs sometimes attended to their advice; sometimes rejected it; and they receive commendation or reproof at the hands of the historians according to their conduct in this respect. Two of these prophets, Elijah and Elisha, were men of great eminence, and their actions are recorded at length. Such was the power of Elisha that when, on one occasion, he cursed some children who had called him bald head, she-bears came out of the wood and ate forty-two of them (2 Kings ii. 23-25). Respect for ecclesiastics or prophets is sometimes inculcated by such decided measures as these. A young Buddhist monk once laughed at another for the alacrity with which he leapt over a grave, saying he was as active as a monkey. The man whom he had ridiculed told him that he belonged to the highest rank in the Church; that is, that he was an Arhat. Upon hearing this the young monk was so alarmed that all his hair stood on end, and he begged for forgiveness. His repentance saved him from being born in hell; but because he had laughed at an Arhat he was condemned to be born 500 times as a monkey (G. O. M., p. 351).

Elisha's powers in other respects were not less wonderful. He could cause iron to swim, could foretell the course of events in a war, could restore the dead to life, and could smite the king's enemies with blindness (2 Kings vi. 7). In this last accomplishment he has rivals, as Canon Callaway has correctly noted, among the Amazulu priests. The Amazulus have a word in their language to describe the practice. "It is called an *umlingo*," they say, if, when a chief is about to fight with another chief, his doctors cause a darkness to spread among his enemies, so they are unable to see clearly (R. S. A., vol. iii. p. 338).

The kingdom of Israel, unfaithful to the worship of Jehovah, fell under the yoke of Shalmaneser, King of Assyria; while

Judah, though attacked and summoned to submit, by his successor, Sennacherib (or more correctly Sanherib), remained independent some time longer. The King of Judah was at this time Hezekiah, a man thoroughly imbued with the principles of the Jehovistic party, and therefore much lauded by the historians. The prophet of the day was Isaiah, one of the most eminent of those who have filled the prophetic office. Isaiah warmly encouraged Hezekiah to resist the designs of conquest cherished by Sanherib, and promised a successful issue. The messengers of the Assyrian monarch had insultingly reproached Jehovah with his inability to deliver the land, alleging that none of the gods of the territories which he had conquered had availed them anything. But a signal confutation of this profane belief in large armies as against deities was about to be given, and that in a manner which gave an equally signal triumph to Jehovah, the god of the Jews, and Ptah, the god of the Egyptians. Sanherib was engaged in an expedition against Egypt, which was governed at this time by a priest-king, resembling Hezekiah in the piety of his character. This priest was in bad odor with his army, who refused to assist him against the invaders. During his trouble on this account, the god whom he served appeared to him in his sleep and promised that he should suffer nothing, for he would send him his divine assistance, just as Jehovah promised deliverance through the mouth of Isaiah. He therefore went with some followers to Pelusium, and when there, a number of field-mice, pouring in upon the Assyrians, devoured their quivers, their bows, and the handles of their shields, so that on the next day they fled defenseless, and many were killed. Herodotus tells us that in his day there was still to be seen the statue of the king in the temple of Ptah, a mouse in his hand, and this inscription: "Whoever looks on me, let him revere the gods" (Herod., ii. 141). In the Hebrew version of this catastrophe, the field-mice are converted into the angel of the Lord, and the destruction of the weapons into the slaughter by that angel of 185,000 men. Sanherib, it is added, returned to Nineveh, where he was assassinated by his two sons (2 Kings xix. 35-37). But Sanherib himself, in a deciphered inscription, declares that he had beaten the Egyptians, subjected Judea, carried off many of its inhabitants, and only left Jerusalem to the king (R. I., p. 328). Certainly this statement is strongly confirmed, so far as Judea is concerned, by the admission of the historians themselves, that Sanherib had taken the fenced cities of the country; that Hezekiah had made an unreserved submission to him, and had even sent him, by way of tribute, not only all the treasures in his own palace and in the temple, but the very gold from the doors of the temple, and from the pillars which he himself had overlaid (2 Kings xviii. 13-16). So humiliating a position went far to justify the taunts of the Assyrian ambassadors, that the god of Judea was no more to be trusted as a defense against material weapons than the gods of the subjugated nations.

A remarkable instance of the favor of Heaven towards Hezekiah was subsequently evinced. The king fell dangerously ill, and was warned by Isaiah to make the necessary arrangements in view of his death, which was about to happen. Hezekiah did not bear the announcement with much dignity. He passionately implored Jehovah to remember his piety and good deeds, and then "wept sore." Moved by this pitiable supplication, Jehovah sent Isaiah back again to promise him fifteen years' more life. On Hezekiah's asking for a sign that he would be healed, Isaiah asked him whether he would prefer that the shadow on the dial should advance or go back ten degrees. Hezekiah, thinking that it was a mere trifle for a god to cause it to advance, desired that it might turn backwards (2 Kings, xx. 1-11).

A similar grace was shown towards King Woo in China, but in this case it was the prayer of others, not his own, that effected his recovery. His brother, the Duke of Chow, erected four altars, put certain symbols upon them, and addressed himself to three departed kings. "The *grand* historian *by his order wrote* on tablets his prayer to the following effect:—"A. B., your chief descendant, is suffering from a severe and dangerous sickness;—if you three kings have in heaven the charge of *watching over* him, *Heaven's* great son, let me, Tan, be a substitute for his person. I have been lovingly obedient to my father; I am possessed of many abilities and arts which fit me to serve spiritual beings. Your chief descendant, on the other hand, has not so many abilities and arts as I, and is not so

capable of serving spiritual beings. And, moreover, he was
appointed in the hall of God to extend his aid to the four quarters *of the empire,* so that he might establish your descendants
in this lower world. The people of the four quarters stand in
reverent awe of him. Oh! do not let that precious heaven-con-
ferred appointment fall to the ground, and all our former kings
will also have a perpetual reliance and resort. I will now seek
for your orders from the great tortoise " (C. C., vol. iii. p. 353.—
Shoo King, part 5, book 6). After this prayer, the Duke divined
with the tortoises, which gave favorable indications. "The orac-
ular responses" were favorable too. Accordingly the king recovered, but the devoted brother, though he did not die, suffered
for some time from unjust suspicions, and retired from court.
This was after the decease of King Woo. The discovery of the
tablets by Woo's successor led to his restoration to favor. The
relation of the reign of Hezekiah, one of the most inglorious
of Judah's rulers, is an example of the use made of a theory
which pervades and colors the whole history of the kings from
beginning to end. That theory is, that God favored and protected those monarchs who worshiped and obeyed his prophets,
while he punished those who worshiped other gods and neglected his orders. The deposition of Saul, the glory of David,
the destruction of the families of Jeroboam and Baasha, the
miserable fate of Ahab and his seventy sons, the exaltation of
Jehu and his milder punishment proportioned to his mitigated
idolatry, are all examples of the prevalence of this theory.
Some of the facts indeed were rather difficult to deal with; such,
for instance, as the palpable decline of Judea under Hezekiah,
and the continuance of its previous misfortunes under Josiah,
the most praiseworthy of the kings, who, in spite of his unrivaled piety, was slain in a battle against a mere pagan. But
inconsistencies like these might be glossed over or explained
away. The best kings might meet with the greatest calamities,
and the people of Jehovah might prove even more unfortunate
than the heathen. It mattered not. They were still under his
protection; and if they suffered, it was because they had not
worshiped him enough, or not worshiped him exclusively. With
this elastic hypothesis the key to all historical events was
found.

Traces of a similar theory are to be found in the sacred books of China, though in one instance it is placed in the mouth of a successful sovereign desirous of vindicating his supersession of a former dynasty. It is, however, precisely in such cases, where some David or Jehu has deposed a former monarch and taken his throne, that this theory is useful, transferring, as it does, the responsibility of the issue to a higher power. Thus speaks the Chinese king:—"I have heard the saying—'God leads men to tranquil security,' but the sovereign of Hea would not move to such security, whereupon God sent down *corrections*, indicating his mind to him. Kёe, however, would not be warned by God, but proceeded to greater dissoluteness and sloth and excuses for himself. Then Heaven no longer regarded nor heard him, but disallowed his great appointment, and inflicted extreme punishment. Hereupon it charged your founder, T'ang the Successful, to set Hea aside, and by means of able men to rule the empire. From T'ang the Successful down to the Emperor Yih, every sovereign sought to make his virtue illustrious, and duly attended to the sacrifices. And thus it was that while Heaven exerted a great establishing influence, preserving and regulating the house of Yin, but its sovereigns on their part were humbly careful not to lose the favor of God, and strove to manifest a good-doing corresponding to that of Heaven. But in those times, their successor showed himself greatly ignorant of *the ways of* Heaven, and much less could it be expected of him that he would be regardful of the earnest labors of his fathers for the country, Greatly abandoned to dissolute idleness, he paid no regard to the bright principles of heaven, nor the awfulness of the people. On this account God no longer protected him, but sent down the great ruin which we have witnessed. Heaven was not with him because he did not seek to illustrate his virtue. *Indeed*, with regard to all states, great and small, throughout the four quarters of the empire, in every case there are reasons to be alleged for their punishment. . . The sovereigns of our Chow, from their great goodness, were charged with the work of God. There was the charge to them, Cut off Yin. *They proceeded to perform it*, and announced the correcting work of God. . . . The thing was from the decree of Heaven; do not resist me; I dare not have any further change for you'" (C. C., vol. iii. p. 460.—Shoo King, part 5, b. 14, ii. 1–18).

But it was not only by interested parties that this doctrine was proclaimed in China. The She King, a sacred book corresponding in character to the Psalms, distinctly adopts it, and thus gives it the highest sanction. This is the language of one of the Odes:—

" Great is God,

   Beholding this lower world in majesty.

   He surveyed the four quarters [of the kingdom],

   Seeking for some one to give settlement to the people.

   Those two [earlier] dynasties

   Had failed to satisfy him with their government;

   So throughout the various States

   He sought and considered

   For one on which he might confer the rule.

   Hating all the great [States],

   He turned his kind regards on the west,

   And there gave a settlement [to king T'æ]. . . .

   God having brought about the removal thither of this Intelligent
      ruler,

   The Kwan hordes fled away; . . .

   God, who had raised the State, raised up a proper ruler for it. . . .

   This King Ke

   Was gifted by God with the power of judgment,

   So that the fame of his virtue silently grew.

   His virtue was highly intelligent,

   Highly intelligent and of rare discrimination ;

   Able to lead; able to rule,—

   To rule over this great country;

   Rendering a cordial submission, effecting a cordial union.

   When the sway came to King Wăn,

   His virtue left nothing to be dissatisfied with.

   He received the blessing of God,

   And it was extended to his descendants."

The Ode proceeds to relate how completely victorious this virtuous king was over his enemies, and how perfect was the security from invasion enjoyed by the country while he governed it (C. C., vol. iv. p. 448. — She King, part 3, b. 1, ode 7).

Feelings like those that inspired the Jewish chroniclers are still more clearly visible in the history of Thibet than in that of China. Here the orthodox compilers frequently inform us that the reign of a king who observed the law and honored the clergy was distinguished in a peculiarly high degree by the prosperity of the land and the happiness of its people. Of one, for instance, who "entered the portals of religion" at thirty-eight years of age, it is noted that "he founded the constitution of the whole great nation on order, and furthered its welfare and peace" (G. O. M., p. 201). His son made the whole great nation happy by promoting religion and the laws" (Ibid., p. 203). Another monarch receives a still higher panegyric. 'by the unbounded honor he showed towards the clergy, he exalted religion, so that by the religious care which he bestowed on the inhabitants of the snow-kingdom, the welfare of the people of Thibet equaled that of the Tegri" (gods or spirits). A painful contrast is presented by his successor on the throne, Lang-Dharma, who belonged to the heretical "black religion," who destroyed the temples of Buddhism, persecuted its adherents, burnt its books, and degraded its ministers. So impious was he, that the very names of the three gems and of the four orders of clergy ceased to be mentioned in the land. He met, however, with his well-deserved punishment at the hands of a faithful Buddhist, who assassinated him with a bow and arrow, at the same time using words to the effect that, as Buddha overcame the unbelievers, so he had killed the wicked king (Ibid., p. 49). Another king "showed respect to the hidden sanctuaries, whereby his power and the welfare of the land increased" (Ibid., p. 321). Comparable to Josiah in his piety and reverence for the true religion was a king whose reign is described in glowing language by his admiring historians. "This powerful ruler," they say, "who regarded the religion of Buddha as the most precious gem, gave great freedoms and privileges to the clergy." He honored temples and respected the pious endowments of his ancestors. Not only did he punish thieves, robbers, and similar criminals, but if any man, of high or low position, was inimical or ill-disposed towards the faith he was

deprived of his property and reduced to the greatest distress.
Some of those whose heresy was visited with this severe chastisement were so unreasonable as to grumble, and pointed out
that it was only the clergy who were fattening on their misery
and oppression. In saying this they pointed at the spiritual
men who passed by; whereupon the faithful king issued a
decree, saying, "It is strictly prohibited to look contemptuously
at my clergy and to point at them with the finger;" whoever
dared to do so was to have his eyes put out and his finger cut
off. Unfortunately "these orders of the pious king" led to the
formation of a party of malcontents, by two of whom he was
strangled in his sleep. The lamentations of the historian at
this untoward event are unmeasured. The power and strength
of the Thibetan kingdom ran away like the stream of spring
waters; the happiness and welfare of the people were extinguished like a lamp whose oil is exhausted; the royal power
and majesty vanished like the colors of the rainbow; the black
religion began to prevail like a destructive tempest; the inclination to good dispositions and good deeds was forgotten like a
dream. Moreover, the translation of religious writings remained
unfinished—for this king had also resembled Josiah in his
interest in sacred books;—and those great men who adhered
to the true religion could only weep over its decline and fall (G.
O. M., p. 361).

Not less pitiable was the fate of Judea under the irreligious
monarchs who followed upon Josiah. One was taken prisoner
by the king of Egypt; two others were carried off to Babylon
by Nebuchadnezzar; under the fourth, the national independence was finally extinguished, and the people reduced to a condition of captivity in a foreign land. This calamity is distinctly
ascribed to their neglect of the true religion, and their contempt
for the messengers of God (2 Chron. xxxvi. 14-17).

Strictly speaking, the history of the Jewish nation ends with
the Captivity. But there are still three books of a historical
character in the Old Testament, Ezra and Nehemiah, relating
the fortunes of a small number of Jews who returned to the
land of their forefathers, when a change of policy in their
rulers rendered this return possible; and Esther, containing the
account of the reception of a Jewish woman into the harem of

a heathen king, and showing how ably she contrived to use her influence in favor of the interests of her race.

Subdivision 2.—*Job, Psalms, Proverbs, and Ecclesiastes.*

The Book of Job, the Psalms attributed to David, and the Proverbs and Ecclesiastes attributed to Solomon, resemble one another in teaching religion and morality by the method of short sentences or maxims. They do not, like the books we have just examined, convey their moral by means of historical narrative; nor do they, like the prophets, impress it in flowing and continuous rhetoric. Between the sober and even course of the history, and the impassioned emotional torrents poured out by the prophets, they occupy a medium position. They are more introspective, more occupied with feelings and reflections, than the first; more heedful of external nature, more able to contemplate facts, apart from their peculiar construction of those facts, than the last.

Job is the story of a wealthy land-owner, concerning whom God and Satan enter into a sort of wager; God, in the first instance, challenging Satan to consider his piety and general good character, and Satan replying that, if only his prosperity were destroyed, he would curse God to his face. God then gives Satan leave to put his theory to the test by attacks directed against Job's property, desiring at the same time that his person may be spared. Job bears the loss of his wealth with resignation; but at a second colloquy Satan insinuates that his virtue would give way if his misfortunes extended to his person. Hereupon God gives Satan leave to attack him in every respect so long as he spares his life. Poor Job is accordingly covered with boils from head to foot, and his patience, proof against poverty, breaks down under this terrible infliction. He loudly curses the day of his birth, and wishes he had died from the womb. After this introduction, which, in its familiar conversations between Jehovah and the devil, resembles the grotesque legends of the middle ages, the bulk of the book is occupied with the complaints of Job, the discourses of his three friends who come to comfort him, the reproaches directed against his self-righteousness by a person named

Elihu, and, finally, a long address — containing as it were the moral of the tale — from the Almighty himself. At the close of the book Job expresses his abhorrence of himself and his profound repentance, and his former prosperity is then not only restored but amplified to a high degree. He has seven sons and three beautiful daughters, and dies one hundred and forty years after the events narrated, having seen four generations of his descendants. What was the effect on the mind of Satan of this result, whether he considered himself defeated, or whether he was confirmed in his malicious opinion that Job did not "fear God for nought," is nowhere stated. But one of the most curious features of this book is the picture it gives of that person, as a being not altogether bad, though fond of mischief, taking a somewhat cynical view of the motives of human conduct, and anxious, in the interests of his theory, to try experiments upon a subject selected for him by his antagonist, and therefore peculiarly likely to disappoint his expectations. It does not appear that he had any desire to hurt Job further than was necessary for his purpose, nor is there a trace of the bad character he subsequently obtained as a mere devil, longing to involve men's souls in eternal destruction.

In the Psalms we have a series of religious songs of varying character— praising, blessing, supplicating, complaining, lamenting, invoking good or evil upon others, according to the mood of the several writers, or of the same writer at different seasons. Some of them are of considerable beauty, and express much depth of religious feeling. Others, again, are inspired by sentiments of malevolence, and merely appeal to God in support of national or private animosities. As examples of the latter class, take the 110th Psalm, supposed to have been addressed to David, where it is predicted that "the Lord at the right hand shall strike through kings in the day of his wrath," and that "he shall fill the places with the dead bodies; he shall wound the heads over many countries." In the immediately preceding Psalm, the 109th, the writer is still more vindictive, and his enemy is more exclusively his own. He begins by calling him "wicked," and says he has spoken against him with a lying tongue, Premising that he is altogether in the act of prayer, he prays against the adversary in somewhat emphatic language:—

" Set thou a wicked man over him, and let the accuser stand at his right hand. When he shall be judged, let him be found guilty, and let his prayer become sin. Let his days be few, and let another take his office. Let his children be fatherless, and his wife a widow. Let his children wander about and beg, and seek food far from their desolate places. Let the creditor catch all that he hath, and strangers rob the fruit of his industry. Let there be none to extend mercy to him, and let none be merciful to his fatherless children. Let his posterity be cut off, and in the following generation let their name be blotted out. Let the iniquity of his fathers be remembered with the Lord, and let not the sin of his mother be blotted out. Let them be before the Lord continually, and let him cut off the memory of them from the earth " (Psalms cix. 1–15).

In the following verse the enemy is declared to have persecuted the poor and needy, and this is put forward as the excuse for imprecations evidently inspired by personal ill-will. In another of these Psalms, Jehovah is entreated to persecute the enemies of Israel with storm and tempest, as fires burn up woods and flames set mountains on fire (Psalms lxxxiii. 14, 15). Elsewhere the king is said to trust in the Lord, and he therefore hopes that the Lord will find out his enemies, and will make them as a fiery oven in the time of his anger; that the fire will devour them ; and that he will destroy their fruit from the earth and their seed from among the children of men (Ps. xxi. 8–10).

Parallels to these Psalms of cursing may be met with in the Veda, just as the Psalms in general are more nearly paralleled by the Vedic hymns than by those of any other sacred book. One poet writes as follows : —

" Blinded shall ye be, O enemies, like headless snakes, and thus plagued by Agni, may Indra always kill the best of you. Whatever relation troubles us, whatever stranger wishes to kill us, him may all the gods destroy; prayer is my powerful protection, my refuge and powerful protection " (S. V., p. 297.—Sama Veda, 2. 9. 3. 8).

Remarkably close is the similarity between the assertion of the Hindu Rishi that prayer is his powerful protection, and that of the Hebrew Psalmist that he is, or gives himself to, prayer. In another hymn the aid of a goddess Apvā (said to mean "disease or fear") is invoked against the enemies of the singer:—

" Bewildering the hearts of our enemies, O Apvu, take possession of their limbs and pass onwards; come near, burn them with fires in their hearts; may our enemies fall into blind darkness (O. S. T. vol. v. p. 110). . . . Attack, ye heroes, and conquer; may Indra grant you protection; may our arm be productive of terror, that ye may be unconquerable. Arrow-goddess, sharpened by prayer; fly past as when shot off; reach the enemies; penetrate into them ; let not even one escape thee" (S. V., p. 297.—Sama Veda, 2. 9. 3. 5).

But these expressions of hostility, directed apparently against enemies who were engaged in actual war with the friends of the writer, make no approach in the bitterness of their curses to the language of the Psalmist when dealing with his personal foes. A parallel to this more private enmity may be found in the Atharva-Veda, where the god Kama is invoked to bring down the severest evils upon the objects of the imprecation:—

" With oblations of butter I worship Kama, the mighty slayer of enemies. Do thou, when lauded, beat down my foes by thy great might. The sleeplessness which is displeasing to my mind and eye, which harrasses and does not delight me, that sleeplessness I let loose upon my enemy. Having praised Kama, may I rend him. Kama, do thou, a fierce lord, let loose sleeplessness, misfortune, childlessness, homelessness, and want upon him who designs us evil. . . . May breath, cattle, life, forsake them. . . . Indra, Agni, and Kama, mounted on the same chariot, hurl ye down my foes; when they have fallen into the nethermost darkness, do thou, Agni, burn up their dwellings. Kama, slay my enemies; cast them down down into thick [literally, blind] darkness. Let them all become destitute of power and vigor, and not live a single day. . . . Let them (my enemies) float downwards like a boat severed from its moorings. . . . Do thou, Kama, drive my enemies from this world by that [same weapon or amulet] wherewith the gods repelled the Asuras, and Indra hurled the Dasyus into the nethermost darkness" (O. S. T., vol. v. p. 404).

As corresponding to the many expressions to be found in the

Psalms of trust in God, of pious belief in his protection, and of sensibility to his all-embracing knowledge, we may quote the language of a Chinese monarch in one of the Odes of the She King. The first six lines are, it appears, held by the current interpretation in China to contain the admonition addressed by the ministers to the king, and the last six the king's reply. But we may more reasonably suppose, with Dr. Legge, that the whole Ode is spoken by the king himself:—

" Let me be reverent, let me be reverent [in attending to my duties];
  [The way of] Heaven is evident,
  And its appointment is not easily [preserved].
  Let me not say that It is high aloft above me.
  It ascends and descends about our doings;
  It daily inspects us wherever we are.

  I am [but as] a little child,
  Without intelligence to be reverently [attentive to my duties];
  But by daily progress and monthly advance,
  I will learn to hold fast the gleams [of knowledge], till I arrive at
    bright intelligence.
  Assist me to bear the burden [of my position],
  And show me how to display a virtuous conduct." *

We may fairly place this simple expression of the author's desire to do his duty, and of his reverential consciousness that Heaven is ever about us and " inspects us wherever we are," beside the words attributed to David :—

" O Jehovah, thou hast searched me, and known me. Thou knowest my down-sitting and mine uprising, thou understandest my thought afar off. Thou winnowest my path and my lying down, and art acquainted with all my ways " (Psalm cxxxix. 1-3).

We need not dwell upon the Proverbs, traditionally ascribed to Solomon, but scarcely worthy of the renowned wisdom of that monarch. Some of them are indeed shrewd and well expressed; others are commonplace; and others again display

* C. C., vol. iv. p. 598.—She King, part 4, b. i. [iii.] 3.

more worldly wisdom than religion or virtue. Such is the recommendation of bribery: "A gift in secret pacifieth anger, and a reward in the bosom strong wrath" (Prov. xxi. 14); which, if written by a king and dispenser of justice, would be a tolerably broad hint to his loving subjects. It is noteworthy that Christ had studied this book, and that it had sunk deep into his mind" (E. g., Prov. xxv. 21, 22, and xxvii. 1). The two concluding chapters are not by the same author, at least if we may believe in their superscriptions. In the last of all, a king named Lemuel repeats for the benefit of posterity the advice given him by his mother, and no doubt by many mothers to many sons both before and after him, to be careful about women and not to drink wine or spirituous liquors.

Ecclesiastes, or Koheleth, composed (according to Ewald) in the latter end of the Persian dominion, is the work of a cynic who has had much experience of the world, and has found it hollow and unsatisfactory. He is not a man of very devout mind, and can find no comfort in the ordinary commonplaces about the goodness of God, or the manner in which misfortunes are sent as punishments for sin. There is much good sense mixed with his lamentations over the vanity of life. He has seen all the works done under the sun, and all are in his opinion "vanity and vexation of spirit."

"Wisdom and knowledge do but bring more grief. Koheleth tried various kinds of pleasure and found them vain too. He built, he planted, he made pools of water. He procured men-servants and maid-servants, and (as a natural consequence) had servants born in his house. All was equally fruitless. But whatever a man does, he has nothing but sorrow and grief. Even wisdom is of little use, for a dolt may inherit the fruit of the wise man's labors. Men are no better than animals; they all die equally; all return to the dust. Who can say that man's spirit goes upwards, and the animal's downwards? Just men are often rewarded like wicked men, and wicked men like just ones; this is one of the many vanities on earth. So then the best thing a man can do is to eat, drink, and enjoy life with an agreeable wife; for this life is all he has. Once dead, there is no further consciousness, or participation in anything that is going on. Whatever a man's hand finds to do, let him do it with all his might; for there is neither action nor knowledge in the grave. It is well to remember God in youth before the evil days come. Words of the wise are as goads, but book-making and preaching are both of them a bore." Lastly, Koheleth concludes with the pious advice to the young man whom he is addressing, to fear God and keep his commandments, for that God will judge every action, be it good or be it bad.

SUBDIVISION 3. — *The Song of Solomon.**

It is a singularly fortunate circumstance that the Song of Songs, a little work of an altogether secular nature and wholly unlike any other portion of the Hebrew Scriptures, should have been admitted into the Canon. Whatever may have been the delusion, whether its reputed Solomonian authorship or some other theory about it, under which it obtained this privilege, we owe it to this mistake that the solitary example of the Jewish drama in existence should have been preserved for the instruction of modern readers. I say modern readers, because it is not until quite recently that the dramatic character of this piece has been ascertained and established beyond reasonable doubt. Thanks to the scholarship of Germany and France, we are now able to read the Song in the light of common sense. The stern theology of Judaism is for once laid aside, and we have before us a common love-story such as might happen among any Gentile and unbelieving race. A young girl, called a Sulamite, who is attached to a young man of her own rank in life, has been carried off to the harem of Solomon against her will. She is indifferent to the splendor of the royal palace, and resists the amorous advances of the king. Thus she succeeds in "keeping her vineyard;" and is rewarded by rejoining her shepherd lover in her native village. The play is not without beauty, although it evinces a somewhat primitive condition of the drama at the time of its composition.

SUBDIVISION 4. — *The Prophets.*

We have in the prophetical books a class of writings alto-

---

* For information on the character and signification of this book, see "Le Cantique des Cantiques," par Ernest Renan.

gether peculiar to the Hebrew Scriptures. The prophets were men who during the whole course of the Hebrew monarchy, and even long after its close, acted as the inspired organs of the Almighty; admonishing, reproving, warning, or counseling in his name. At first the method by which the revelations they received were made known by them, was oral communication. Writing was not employed by them as an instrument of prophetic discourse until after the earliest and most flourishing stage of the monarchy was past. Perhaps they were the most powerful of the prophets who addressed their exhortations directly to those for whom they were intended in eloquent discourse or timely parable. Such prophets were Samuel, Nathan, Elijah, and Elisha, at the courts of the several kings in whose days they lived. Prophecy had declined a little in its influence on the people when its representatives betook themselves to the calmer method of written composition. Nevertheless, some of the prophets who have left us their works in writing continued at the same time to employ the older instrument of spoken addresses. Isaiah and Jeremiah are conspicuous instances of this employment of the two organs of communication downwards. During this same period there were many prophets who trusted exclusively to writing; while in the latest stage of prophetical inspiration, oral instruction was altogether dropped, and literary means alone were employed to make known the mind of Jehovah to his chosen people.

The constant theme of all the prophets whose works have come down to us is the future greatness of the Hebrew race; their complete triumph over all their enemies; the glory of their ultimate condition, and the confusion or destruction of those who have opposed their march to this final victory. The human agent by whom this great revolution is to be effected is the Messiah. He is the destined weapon in the hand of God by whom Jewish religion, Jewish institutions, and Jewish rulers are to attain that supremacy over heathen religion, heathen institutions, and heathen rulers which is their natural birthright. Continual disappointment had no effect upon these sanguine expectations. The Messiah *must* come, Israel *must* be victorious over every other nation that came in the way: this was the word of God, and it could not fail to be fulfilled.

Troubles of many kinds might beset the people in the mean-time; but of the attainment of the goal at last there could be no doubt.

Of course this ever-recurring burden of the prophetic song is varied by many strains on subordinate or outlying topics. The prophets constantly refer to the events of the day, and use them for their own purposes. They reprove the sins of kings and people, endeavoring to show that these bring upon them the misfortunes from which they suffer and which postpone the day of their triumph over the Gentiles. They connect special calamities with special offenses. They indicate the conduct which under existing circumstances ought to be pursued. They draw eloquent and beautiful pictures of the state of their own and of foreign countries. And they endeavor to raise the popular conceptions of the majesty of God, of his character, and his requirements, to the level they have themselves attained.

Turning now to the individual books which have come down to us in the Canon, and which must by no means be taken as comprehending all the works of the prophets who wrote their prophecies, we find that the oldest of these is that of Joel, the son of Pethuel.* Joel is supposed by the highest authority to have lived in the time of King Jehoash, or Joash, who is praised for his devout obedience to Jehoiada, the priest (2 Kings, xii). His prophecy was occasioned by a devastation of locusts. Locusts had wasted the land for some years, and there had been drought at the same time. On the occasion of a long drought Joel feared a fresh invasion of locusts, and therefore summoned his people to a festival of repentance at the temple. This festival occurred, and rain soon followed (P. A. B., vol. i. p. 87 ff). Here the old notion of a direct connection between the attention paid by the people to Jehovah and his care for them is almost grotesquely manifested. Locusts are to be averted by fasting; rain obtained by rather more than usual devotion to God. On the other hand, the more spiritual view of religion to which the prophets generally tend, is shown in the order to the people to rend their hearts and not their garments. After thus attending to immediate necessities, Joel in stirring language ex-

---

* Throughout these descriptions of the prophetic books, I follow the chronological arrangement of Ewald.

horts the people to war, hoping that they would thus get rid of the foreign oppressors who had broken into the sunken kingdom of David. He bids them beat their plough-shares into swords, and their pruning hooks into spears, and desires the weak to say that they are strong. He promises his people revenge over their enemies, and holds out the cheering prospect of a time when, instead of their sons and daughters being sold as slaves to strangers, they will themselves make slaves of the sons and daughters of the heathen.

Some short passages subsequently embodied by Isaiah in his works are considered by Ewald to belong to the same early age as Joel. The next complete prophet, however, in order of time, was Amos, whose revelations applied to the northern kingdom and threatened it with invasion by the Assyrians. Amos in fact utters a series of threatening predictions against various peoples, and his tone is mainly that of reproof. While, however, he foretells the captivity of Israel, and holds out nothing but the most depressing prospects of ruin and misery throughout the bulk of his book, he falls at the end into the accustomed strain of hopeful exultation. "The tabernacle of David" is to be raised up; Israel is to be supreme over the heathen; and the Israelites are not to be disturbed again from the land which God has given them, where exuberant prosperity is to be their lot. Incidentally, Amos tells us a little of his personal history, which is not without interest. He attributes his consecration to the prophetic office to the direct intervention of Jehovah. He had originally no connection with other prophets, but was a simple herdsman, and was employed to gather sycamore fruit. But Jehovah took him while he was following the flock, and said, "Go, prophecy unto my people Israel." His is thus a typical case of the belief in immediate inspiration, and he is an example of the kind of character which led to the existence among the Israelites of the peculiar and powerful class who were holy, but not consecrated. Amos also tells us of a quarrel he had had with Amaziah, a priest at the court of Jeroboam. This priest had complained of his dismal predictions to the king, and had bidden him go to Judah and prophecy there. In return for this evidence of hostility Amos informs the priest that his wife is to become a prostitute in the town, that his sons and his daughters are to fall by the sword, that his land is to be divided by lot, and that he himself is to die on polluted soil (Amos vii. 10–17). Such were the courtesies that passed between rival teachers of religion at the court of Jeroboam.

Hosea also tells us something of his personal affairs, more especially of his matrimonial relations, in which he was far from fortunate. We feel, in his opening chapters, the soreness of a husband whose wife has contemned his company and sought the amusement of a troop of lovers. Gomer, in fact, was shockingly unfaithful, and Hosea uses her as a type of the infidelity of Israel to Jehovah. At length she deserted him altogether, and went to another house, but he brought her back as a slave and put her under strict conjugal discipline. In like manner is Israel to return to her God, whom she has deserted for a time, and under the influence of God's love, freely bestowed after his anger has passed away, is to enjoy a period of great prosperity. Hosea, it will be observed, belonged to the northern kingdom, and his book is preëminently the Ephraimitic book of prophecy. But he wrote it in Judah. He worked in the north at two distinct epochs, first towards the close of Jeroboam II.'s reign, afterwards in the time of Zachariah, Shallum, and Mena-hem (P. A. B., vol. i. p. 171 ff).

An anonymous prophet, contemporary with Isaiah, stands next in order of time. He is the author of Zechariah ix.–xi. inclusive, and of Zechariah chap. xiii. ver. 7–9 (P. A. B., vol i. p. 247 ff). These chapters contain the first distinct announcement of the advent of the Messiah, who is described in the famous prediction of a King coming to Jerusalem on an ass, and on a colt, the foal of an ass. Here too we find the curious allegory of the two staves, Beauty and Bands, whereof one was broken by the prophet in token of the breach of his covenant with all the nations; the other, in token of the rupture of fraternal relations between Israel and Judah. In the course of this allegory, the prophet demands his price, thirty pieces of silver, and throws it into the temple treasure; a passage which, by an accidental obscurity in the Hebrew, has been mistranslated as referring, not to the treasure, but to "the potter in the house of Lord," and then misapplied to the betrayal of Christ and the purchase of the potter's field.

In the concluding words of this prophet it is announced that
two-thirds of the people will perish, but that the remaining
third will, after refining and trial, be accepted by God as his
own people.

We enter now upon the consideration of a prophet who
\ stands in the foremost rank of those distinguished leaders of
opinion whose works have been included in the Canon. There
is no greater name among the prophets of Israel than that of
Isaiah. But in speaking of Isaiah we must not fall into the
confusion of including under his writings the compositions of a
prophet of far later date, which have been mistakenly bound
up with his. Isaiah himself cannot receive credit for all that
is published in his name. But that which he has actually left
us is enough to entitle him to admiration as a master of
rhetoric.

Isaiah lived in the reign of Hezekiah, and enjoyed a position
of high public consideration. Some of his prophetic sayings he
wrote down soon after he had uttered them; others not till
long after. He had begun to come forward as a prophet in the
last year of the reign of Uzziah. When he had labored a long
time in his vocation of teacher, he determined to collect his
sayings in a book. His oldest work was written about the year
740 B. C., just after the accession of the young and weak Ahaz
at Jerusalem, when the Assyrians had rendered the northern
kingdom tributary but had not yet come to Judea. His second
was written apparently in the reign of Hezekiah, in 724; and
his third in the days of the same king, when the service of
Jehovah had been restored. Such at least are the conclusions
of the highest living authority on the literature of the Hebrew
race (P. A. B., vol. i. p. 271 ff).

The earliest stratum discernible (according to that authority)
in the Book of Isaiah is from chap. ii. 2 to chap. v. inclusive,
and chap ix. 7-x. 4. The last five verses of chap. v. should not
be taken along with the rest of the chapter, but should follow
upon chap. x. 4 (Ibid., vol. i. p. 286 ff). These passages begin
with a beautiful description of the happiness of the Israelites
in the days of their coming glory, when the mountain of the
Lord's house will be established on the top of the mountains,
and exalted above the hills; and when all nations will flow to

it, to worship and to learn the true faith. It is remarkable as evidence of the wide distinction between the view of Joel and that of Isaiah, that Isaiah exactly reverses the image of his predecessor, declaring that swords will be beaten into ploughshares and spears into pruning-hooks. Joel was looking to the necessities of the immediate present; Isaiah to the prospects of the future. These chapters also contain an amusing ironical account of the finery of the Jerusalem ladies, which might apply with slight alterations to the rich women of all ages and countries. No doubt it was very offensive to Isaiah that they should go about with necks erect and wanton eyes, walking with a mincing gait; but a prophet who should threaten the women of London or Paris with scab on the head and the exposure of their persons on account of sins like these, would certainly bring more reprobation on himself than on them. But manners in Isaiah's days were not so delicate. A time is predicted when Jehovah will wash away the filth of Zion's daughters, and when all in Jerusalem shall be called holy.

In the second part of his book (chap. vi. 1. chap. ix. 6, and chap. xvii. 1–11) Isaiah gives an interesting, though only figurative, account of his consecration to the prophetic office. In the year of King Uzziah's death he says he saw the Lord sitting on his throne with a train so long as to fill the temple. When he cried out that he was undone, for that he, a man of unclean lips, had seen the King, the Lord of hosts, a seraph flew up to him with a live coal in a pair of tongs, laid the coal on his mouth, and told him that his iniquity was now taken away and his sin purged. After this the voice of the Lord was heard inquiring whom he should send, and Isaiah offered to take the post of his ambassador: "Here am I, send me." The proposal was accepted, and he at once received his instructions from headquarters. The prophet began to preach in the manner desired, and among much discouraging matter he uttered the magnificent description of the Messiah, which is familiar to all : —

" For unto us a child is born, unto us a son is given: and the government shall be upon his shoulder: and his name shall be called Wonderful, Counselor, the mighty God, the everlasting Father, the Prince of Peace."

Isaiah's third work (composed in the reign of Hezekiah) begins at the first chapter of the canonical book. It opens with a pathetic lamentation over the infidelity of the children of Israel to their God, and proceeds at chap. xiv. 28 to recount a "burden" which came in the death-year of King Ahaz. A prophecy by which a much older prophet (belonging, as is supposed, to the time of Joel) is embodied in "the burden of Moab," and extends through chap. xv. and chap. xvi. 7–12, after which Isaiah, having mentioned that this was formerly the word of the Lord about Moab, proceeds to say that his present word is that within three years the glory of Moab shall be contemned. The latter part of chap. xxi. (ver. 11–17), dealing with Dumah and Arabia, also belongs to this period.

Further divisions are distinguishable in the writings of Isaiah after these three parts have been separated from the rest. Thus, we have a fourth division consisting of the 22d and 23d chapters, and containing a personal attack on Shebna and a prediction of the fall of Tyre. A fifth division, from chap. xxviii. to xxxii. inclusive, ends with a beautiful description of the happier time that is to come, when the fruit of justice will be peace, and the result of justice quietness and security, when the people will dwell in sure habitations and untroubled abodes. There is another writing, the sixth in order, which begins at chap. x. 5, and extends, in the first instance, to the end of chap. xii. This prophecy is remarkable, even in this eloquent book, for the marvelous eloquence with which, in his visions of future glory, the inspired seer depicts the government of the "rod out of the stem of Jesse," the "Branch" that is to "grow out of his roots," in whose reign the wild beasts will no longer persecute their prey, nor Ephraim and Judah keep up the memory of their ancient feud; who will cause his beloved people to put the Philistines to flight, to conquer Edom and Moab, and reduce the children of Ammon to submission. Prophecies directed against Ethiopia and Egypt (chap. xvii. 12–xviii. 7, and chap. xx.) belong to the same portion of Isaiah's collected works. Threats against the Assyrians are contained in additional chapters, namely, chap. xxxiii. and chap. xxxvii. 22–35. Lastly, a seventh portion of Isaiah consists of chap. xix., which, after holding out the prospect of great misfortunes to Egypt, ends in a somewhat unusual strain by admitting both Egyptians and Assyrians to be equal sharers with the Israelites in the ultimate prosperity of the earth, and declaring that the Lord himself will bless them all, saying, "Blessed be Egypt my people, and Assyria the work of my hands, and Israel mine inheritance."

It should be noted that, if Ewald's supposition be correct, the first four sections of the work, thus decomposed into its several constituents, were edited by Isaiah himself, while the fifth, sixth, and seventh were added by subsequent compilers to the collection he had left behind (P. A. B., vol. i. p. 48:).

A very short prophecy called by Obadiah's name follows upon the genuine writings of Isaiah in chronological order. It is in fact anonymous. In its present form it belongs to the time of the Captivity. The object of the unknown prophet was to reprove the Idumeans for rejoicing in and profiting by the destruction of Jerusalem. In his writing he embodied an older prophecy by the actual Obadiah, referring to a calamity that had befallen Edom, when a part of its territory had been surprised and completely plundered by a people with whom it had just been in alliance. The same old piece was used by Jeremiah (chap. xlix. 7) in his prophecy upon Edom (Ib., vol. i. p. 489 ff).

Micah, the next prophet, was a younger contemporary of Isaiah, but lived in the country. When he wrote the northern kingdom was approaching its end, and he threatens Judah with chastisement and destruction. He foresaw the fulfillment of Messianic hopes as arising only from the ruin of the existing order of things. No more than the first five chapters are by Micah himself (Ib., vol. i. p. 498 ff). His book is remarkable for the extremely warlike description he gives of Messianic happiness. Many other prophets conceive it as an important element in that happiness that the Israelites shall be victorious over their enemies; but few, if any, have come up to Micah in the fervor with which he foretells the desolation, the carnage, the utter suppression of rival nations, which will accompany that age. The author of the scenes of blood will be the ruler who is to come from Bethlehem-Ephratah. The prophet who has added the last two chapters also looks forward to an age when

Jehovah will at length perform his promises to Abraham and Jacob, to the terror of the unbelieving nations.

Next after Micah stands Nahum. The occasion of his prophecy was a hostile attack directed against Nineveh. He must have seen the danger with his own eyes, and he was therefore a descendant of one of the Israelites who had been carried off to Assyria. He evidently lived far from Palestine, and was familiar with Assyrian affairs. Elkosh, where the inscription places his residence, was a little town on the Tigris. His book may refer to the siege of Nineveh by the Median king Phraortes about six hundred and thirty-six (P. A. B., vol. ii. p. 1). The interest of Nahum's prophecy is merely local; he does not rise beyond the politics of the hour, and we need not therefore stop to examine his utterances in detail. It may be noted, however, that an expression which has become famous through its adoption by a much later prophet, "Behold, upon the mountains the feet of him that bringeth good tidings, that publisheth peace," is first found in Nahum.

Zephaniah's prophecy arose out' of a great movement of nations. He lived in the reign of Josiah, but wrote before the reformation effected by that monarch. The movement alluded to by him must have been the great irruption of the Scythians mentioned by Herodotus as having interrupted the siege of Nineveh by Kyaxares, King of the Medes (Herod., i. 103). These last days of the Assyrian kingdom gave rise to long disturbances in which the Chaldeans became conquerors (P. A. B., vol. ii. p. 14). After various threatenings against divers people, the prophecy of Zephaniah ends with a beautiful vision of the age to come, when the suppliants of Jehovah will come from beyond the rivers of Ethiopia; and when a virtuous and happy remnant will be left in Israel.

When Habakkuk, the next prophet, wrote his thoughts, and composed the public prayer or psalm which forms his concluding chapter, the Chaldeans were already in the land. This "bitter and hasty nation" was quite a new phenomenon there. Habakkuk lived after the reformation of Josiah, and therefore in the reign of Jehoiakim (Ib., vol. ii. p. 29). He seems to have written to plead with the Almighty for deliverance, and to express unabated confidence in him; and he hoped that his words, set to music and sung in public worship, would induce him to abate his anger as manifested in the Chaldean scourge.

An anonymous prophet (Ib., vol. ii. p. 52) (Zechariah xiii. 1–xiii. 6, and xiv.) predicts the siege and capture of Jerusalem, with all the miserable incidents of conquest: the rifling of her houses, the ravishing of her women, the condemnation to captivity of half her inhabitants. Like other prophets, however, he looks forward in sanguine anticipation to a day when the heathen nations who now make war upon Jerusalem will regularly go up there every year to worship Jehovah, and keep the feast of tabernacles. At least if any of them do not, they will have no rain. In that glorious age the very pots in the Lord's house will be like the bowls for offerings; nay, every pot in Judah and Jerusalem will be holy to the Lord of hosts.

We pass now to the consideration of a prophet who stands second in eminence only to Isaiah, and to the unknown author of the later work which in the Canon is included in the Book of Isaiah. Jeremiah began to prophesy in the thirteenth year of Josiah, and continued to do so during the reigns of Jehoiakim and Zedekiah. His active life, like that of Isaiah, extended over a period of half a century (P. A. B., vol. ii. p. 63 ff). It is noteworthy that Jeremiah was a priest, and therefore combined in his person the double qualification of consecration and of exceptional holiness: that is, he was consecrated to Jehovah, and also appointed expressly by Jehovah. The manner of his appointment to be a holy person resembles the manner of the appointment of Isaiah. The word of the Lord came to him, saying, that before God had formed him in the belly he had known him, and before he had come forth from the womb he had sanctified him, and ordained him a prophet unto the nations. Jeremiah objected that he was but a child. But Jehovah told him not to say he was a child, for that he was to go where he was sent, and speak what he was commanded. He was not to be afraid of men's faces, for he, the Lord, would deliver him. Then he touched Jeremiah's mouth with his hand, and said: "Behold, I put my words in thy mouth. See, I appoint thee this day over the nations and over the kingdoms, to root out, and to pull down, and to destroy, and to throw down, to build and to plant." After this solemn dedication to his duties Jeremiah was certainly endowed with the fullest qualifications for the prophetic office. He immediately began to see images; namely, a rod of an almond-tree and a seething pot, and it continued afterwards to be one of his characteristics to employ material imagery of this nature for the purpose of illustrating the truths he had to communicate.

After this introduction, we have a long section of the work, namely, from the second chapter to the twenty-fourth, beginning with the prophecies of the thirteenth year of Josiah. Among other things this portion includes Jeremiah's bitter imprecation upon his personal enemies, the "men of Anathoth," on whom he begs to be permitted to witness the vengeance of God, and concerning whom he receives the consoling assurance that their young men will die by the sword, and their sons and daughters by famine, and that there will not be a remnant left. This section contains also the terrible prayer against those who "devised devices" against Jeremiah, in other words, did not believe in his predictions. In its intense intolerance, in its unblushing disclosure of private malignity, in its unscrupulous enumeration of the ills desired for these opponents of the prophet, it is perhaps unrivaled in theological literature. To do Jeremiah justice it ought to be quoted at length:—

" Give heed to me, O Jehovah, and listen to the voice of my opponents. Shall evil be recompensed for good, that they dig a pit for my life? Remember how I stood before thee, to speak a good word for them, to turn away thy wrath from them. Therefore give their sons to famine, and deliver them into the power of the sword; and let their wives be bereaved of their children and widowed, and let their men be put to death; let their young men be slain by the sword in battle. Let a cry be heard from their houses, when thou suddenly bringest troops upon them; for they have digged a pit to take me, and hid snares for my feet. Yet thou, Jehovah, knowest all their counsel against me to slay me; and blot not out their sin from thy sight, and let them be overthrown before thee; deal with them in the time of thine anger" (Jer. xviii. 19–23).

In another chapter there is a curious account of an incident with Pashur, superintendent of the Temple, who had caused

Jeremiah to be put in stocks for a day. Jeremiah complains bitterly of the treatment he meets with on account of his prophesying, and wishes to resign the office, but the impulse proves too strong for him. He consoles himself with a pious hope that Jehovah will let him see his vengeance on his enemies (Jer. xx. 1–12). He continues to predict misfortunes, but intermingles with his gloomier forebodings a fine vision of the time when God shall gather together the remnant of his flock from the countries to which he has driven them, and raise up "a righteous Branch" of the house of David, who will reign and prosper, who will execute justice and equity, in whose days Judah will be saved, and Israel dwell secure (Jer. xxiii. 2–6).

In a third section of his work (chap. xlvi. 1–12, and chap. xlvii. 49) Jeremiah deals with foreign nations, and then (in chap. xxv.) declares that he has been prophesying a long time without being able to get the Jews to listen to him, foretells their subjugation by Nebuchadnezzar, and (rather unfortunately for his own and Jehovah's reputation for correct foresight) commits himself to the definite term of seventy years as the duration of the coming captivity. A wise prophet would have kept within the safe region of vagueness, where he could not come into collision with awkward dates nor drive orthodox interpreters into such pitiable straits as those in which Ewald, for example, finds himself, when he is compelled to say that seventy years is a perfectly general indication of a future that cannot be more precisely fixed, and that it merely refers to the third generation from the writer (P. A. B., vol. ii. p. 230). The remainder of this section (chap. xxvi.–xxix.) relates certain cencounters with other prophets whose predictions had turned out false, and one of whom, as Jeremiah exultingly relates, died during the year, exactly as Jeremiah had declared he would. Interesting evidence is supplied by these chapters of the existence of numerous prophets who differed from each other, and between whose claims only the event could decide.

In the fourth section (chap. xxx.–xxxv.) Jeremiah prophesies the restoration of Israel, and tells his readers how he bought a field from his cousin on the strength of his hopes that the captivity would have an end. A fifth part (chaps. xxxvi., xlv.) relates to Baruch, Jeremiah's secretary; and an appendix (chap.

xxxvii.-xliv., and chap. xlvi. 13-28) contains historical matter, and predictions about Egypt, but concludes with the usual promise of the ultimate return of the Jewish nation to its ancestral home.

The last chapter of Jeremiah is purely historical, and, like the historical portions of Isaiah, need not be considered under the prophets; but it must be noted that chaps. l. and li. are not by Jeremiah, being the work of a much later writer, who lived in Palestine, and who composed them to show that the words of the genuine Jeremiah were fulfilled in the destruction of Babylon by the Medes, which was taking place at this time (P. A. B., vol. iii. p. 140 ff). The small Book of Lamentations over the unhappy fate of Jerusalem, ascribed to Jeremiah, is an artistic attempt to embody the grief of the writer in a song of which each verse begins with a new letter, in alphabetical order.

We pass now to the prophet Ezekiel, a Jew who was taken into captivity with Jehoiachin, and lived at a small town of Mosopotamia. He felt the first prophetic impulses in the fifth year of the Captivity (Ib., vol. ii. p. 322 ff). At this time the heavens were opened; he saw visions, and the word of the Lord came expressly to him. Such was the nature of his consecration. The first section of Ezekiel extends from chap. i. to xxiv., and contains utterances about Israel before the destruction of Jerusalem. The second section (chap. xxv.-xxxii.) deals with foreign nations, and the third (chap. xxxiii.-xlviii.) holds out promises of restoration.

Ezekiel is very inferior to his great predecessors, Isaiah and Jeremiah. He has neither the fervid, manly oratory of the first nor the pathetic, though rather soft and feminine flow of the second. He takes pleasure in rather course images, such as that of the bread baked with human dung (Ezek. iv), that of Jehovah with his two concubines, who bore him sons and vexed him with their licentious conduct (Ezek. xxiii), or that of the child whose naval was not cut, who grew up into a woman, over whom Jehovah spread his skirt and covered her nakedness (Ezek. xvi. 8). And in general, Ezekiel is particularly prone to teaching by means of similes and illustrations. Sometime he sees visions in which God explains his meaning; at other times he acts in a manner which is designed to be typical of coming events. Thus, on one occasion, he openly brings out his furniture for removal, as a sign to the rebellious house of Israel (Ezel. xii. 1–7).

As in Jeremiah, so in Ezekiel we find traces of hostility towards rival prophets, whom he denounces in no measured terms. It is interesting, too, to observe that there were female prophets in his day, who prophesied out of their own hearts. To them also he conveys the reprobation of the Almighty (Ezek. xiii). The form in which he looks forward to the restoration of Israel and Judah to their homes, is somewhat different from that in which it was expected by his predecessors. In a very singular vision, he relates that his God took him into a valley which was full of bones, and told him that these were the bones of the whole house of Israel. Ezekiel is then informed that God will open the graves of the dead, and cause these bones to live again, and will bring them to the land of Israel. Afterwards, he is told to join two sticks into one, this junction representing the future union of Ephraim and Judah, who are to be gathered from among the heathen, and are to form one nation governed by one king. That king is to be David, who will be their prince forever. God will make an everlasting covenant of peace with them, and put his sanctuary in their midst for evermore. Here the resurrection of the dead, and the return of David, instead of the appearance of a new king, are peculiar features.

An anonymous prophet is supposed to have written Isaiah xxi. 1–10, and another Isaiah xiii. 2–xiv. 23, the latter referring to Babylon, and containing the imaginary exultation of the restored Israelites over the fallen Babylonians. After these fragments we have the work of one who is perhaps the greatest of all the prophets, but who also is unknown to us by name. As the most fitting description we may perhaps call him the anonymous prophet. The whole of the latter portion of Isaiah, from chap. xl. to the end, is his work. The anonymous prophet lived in Egypt. His peculiar conception was that Israel was the servant of the Lord for the peace and the salvation of nations, as Kyros was his servant in war (P. A. B., vol. iii. p. 20 ff). Alike in beauty of language and sublimity of thought he is supreme among the writers of the Hebrew Bible. He is the prophet of sorrow: yet also the prophet of consolation. Whether by a curious accident, or whether by virtue of a tendency (not uncommon among truly great writers) to withdraw his personality from observation and confine himself wholly to the message he had to deliver, he tells us nothing of himself. Hence he has for centuries been hidden behind the figure of Isaiah, whom nevertheless he surpasses in the purity of his ideal. To him we owe the beautiful passage beginning "Comfort ye, comfort ye, my people," with the description afterwards applied by Jesus Christ to John the Baptist. From him also we have the most exalted conceptions of the Messiah, the moral element in his character being raised as compared with the element of material power, to a height hitherto unexampled in prophetic vision. Take, for instance, this description of his mildness combined with indomitable perseverence:—

"He shall not cry, nor lift up, nor cause his voice to be heard in the street. A bruised reed shall he not break, and the smoking flax shall he not quench; he shall bring forth judgment unto truth. He shall not fail nor be discouraged, till he have set judgment in the earth, and the isles shall wait for his law" (Is. xlii. 2–4).

It is the anonymous prophet, too, who has given us the familiar passage, "He is despised and rejected of men;" a passage describing the career of a great man whose teachings involved him in persecution and ultimately in martyrdom, but nowise applicable to the Messiah. That a historical incident, known to the writer, is alluded to in this touching account of suffering goodness, admits of no reasonable doubt.

The anonymous prophet is preëminently the prophet of consolation. Living in the days of Kyros and of the restoration of the Temple, he had the elements of soothing speech ready to his hand; and as his predecessors had prophesied destruction and woe, occasionally varied with strains of hope, so he prophesies in strains of hope, occasionally varied with sterner language. It is his especial mission to heal the wounds that have been made in the spirit of Judah. God had indeed forsaken her for a while; but he will now take her back as a deserted wife,

who had suffered her punishment. He had hidden his face in
a little wrath for a moment; but with everlasting kindness will
he now have mercy upon her (Is. liv. 5-7). The concluding
chapter of the anonymous prophet contains a magnificent description of the ultimate gathering of all nations and tongues,
when Jerusalem will be the central point of human worship,
and the glory of God will be seen by all. The picture is not
indeed unmingled with darker shades, for great numbers are to
be destroyed by Jehovah in his indignation. On the other hand,
there is a trait exhibiting the superiority of this prophet to his
predecessors in toleration for the Gentiles: namely, the remarkable prediction that some of them also are to be priests and
Levites (Is. lxvi. 12-24). The man who could utter this sentiment had made a signal advance upon the ordinary narrow and
exclusive notions of the prerogatives of the Jewish race.

It was mentioned that the fiftieth and fifty-first chapters of
Jeremiah were added by a later hand. The same hand (in
Ewald's opinion) composed the thirty-fourth and thirty-fifth
chapters of Isaiah, of which the second describes in very eloquent terms the coming glory, when "the ransomed of the
Lord shall return, and come to Zion with songs, and everlasting
joy upon their heads; they shall obtain joy and gladness, and
sorrow and sighing shall flee away" (Is. xxxv. 10). Another
unknown writer (Isaiah xxiv.-xxvii.) predicts in the first place
the desolation which the Lord is about to effect, and then the
happiness of the Jews who will be brought to their own land
again, to worship Jehovah in the holy mount at Jerusalem.
One of his expressions, "He will swallow up death in victory,"
has been adopted by St. Paul; another, "The Lord God will
wipe away tears from off all faces," by the author of the Apocalypse.

The interest of Haggai's prophecy is purely special: it refers
to the building of the temple at Jerusalem in the reign of
Darius. It was the unexpected obstacles by which the building
was hindered that kindled his zeal; he made his five speeches
in three months of the same year. Probably he had not seen
the first temple, and he left his prophetic work to his younger
contemporary Zechariah (P. A. B., vol. iii. p. 177 ff).

Zechariah also lived in the time of Darius, and dealt principally with the building of the temple (Ib., vol. iii. p. 187 ff). A series of visions which he professes to see shows how his mind was running upon this absorbing theme; and he even expects the Messiah, whom Isaiah and Jeremiah had called a Branch of David, and whom he more emphatically terms *the* Branch, to appear at the head of affairs and to carry the works to their completion (Zech., 8, and vi. 12). He supposes that he will then sit and rule upon his throne; a priest will be beside him, and there will be a counsel of peace between these two — the monarch and his ecclesiastical minister (Zech., vi. 13).

It was probably more than half a century later that the short book bearing the title of Malachi was written. The true name of its author is unknown, and that of Malachi, my messenger, was taken by its editor from the first verse of the third chapter (P. A. B., vol. iii. p. 214 ff). He is not a prophet of a high calibre, as is shown by his denunciation, already quoted, of those among the Jews who offered Jehovah their least valuable cattle. Nor is his conception of the Messianic epoch in any way comparable to that of the great prophets whose works he might have studied. He says indeed that the Sun of righteousness will arise with healing in his wings; but it appears that this healing is to consist in the Israelites treading down the wicked, who will be as dust under their feet. He concludes by announcing the return of Elijah, before "the great and dreadful day of the Lord," and says, in his threatening tone, that this prophet will turn the hearts of the fathers to the children, and of the children to the fathers, lest God should come and smite the earth with a curse.

The Book of Jonah, which may have been written in the fifth or sixth century B. C. (P. A. B., vol. iii. p. 233 ff), is a story with a moral rather than a prophecy, Jonah was desired by Jehovah to preach against Nineveh, but fled from his duty, and took passage in the ship to Tarshish, duly paying his fare. However, when a storm arose, Jonah knew that it was sent as a penalty for his disobedience, and told the sailors to throw him overboard. This they did, but he was swallowed alive by a large fish prepared for the purpose, and remained within it three days. By this lesson he was prepared to execute God's commands, and was accordingly thrown up by the fish on dry land.

He preached to the people of Nineveh, as desired, the coming destruction of their city; but when they repented, Jehovah changed his mind, much to the annoyance of his prophet, who represented that his unfortunate tendency to clemency was the very reason why he had not wished to enter his service. But Jehovah, by causing him to regret the destruction of a gourd which had sheltered him, showed him that there would be much more reason to spare so large a city as Nineveh, which contained, not only a vast population, but also a great deal of cattle.

If Malachi and Jonah stand in unfavorable contrast to the works composed during the golden age of Hebrew literature, Daniel, the latest book of the Old Testament, represents the complete degeneracy of prophecy. It is from beginning to end artificial; professing to be written at one time and by an author whose name and personality are given; in reality written at another time, and by an author whose name and personality are concealed. Hence it contains pseudo-prophecies, which are comparatively clear, extending from the imagined date of the supposed prophet to the actual date of the real prophet; and it contains genuine prophecies which are obscure, and which extend from the actual date into the actual future. It contains also much that relates to the politics of the day, and which, for obvious reasons, is cast into an enigmatic form. Daniel was written about the year B. C. 168, a little before the death of Antiochus Epiphanes, and the allusions to that monarch are of course made under the veil of prophecy, in a style designed to be intelligible, without being direct. The predictions of the eleventh chapter refer to the wars of the Syrian and Egyptian kings, and especially to Antiochus Epiphanes, who is the "vile person" mentioned in the twenty-first verse. The purpose of the work was to set an example of fidelity to Jehovah to the powerful Jews who were connected with the Syrian court, and especially to the younger members of the great Jewish families, who were in danger of being corrupted by its seductions (P. A. B., vol. iii. p. 298 ff).

The form chosen to effect the writer's object is autobiographical. In this way he was able to utter his political views — which, directly expressed, would have been dangerous to his

safety — under the guise of sentiments uttered by Daniel, the
fictitious narrator of the story. Daniel was taken as a captive
child along with other children of Jewish race to serve at the
court of Nebuchadnezzar, and remained at the Chaldean court
until the death of Nebuchadnezzar's son, Belshazzar, and the
subjugation of his empire by the Medes and Persians. He continued to hold an honorable position at the Persian court under
Darius and Kyros. He first rose to distinction by relating and
interpreting to Nebuchadnezzar a dream which the king had
himself forgotten. Thus, from being a mere page he rose to be
a sort of astrologer royal. His life was not, however, free from
trouble. Among the children who had been brought with him
from Judea he had three friends, Hananiah, Mishael, and Aza-
riah, whom the Chaldeans called Shadrach, Meshach, and Abednego. When Daniel had successfully interpreted the king's
dream, he contrived to obtain lucrative situations in the province
of Babylon for Shadrach, Meshach, and Abednego. But these
three having refused to worship a golden image which the king
had set up in that province were by the king's orders cast into
a burning fiery furnace, heated beyond its usual temperature.
But though they fell bound in the midst of it, they were not
burnt, and were seen walking about at their ease in it, accompanied by a fourth, who looked like the Son of Man (Dan. iii).

It is remarkable that a precisely similar prodigy occurred in
one of the innumerable previous existences of the Buddha
Sakyamuni. He was at this time the son and heir of a great
king, and to prove his devotion to the true doctrine he literally
obeyed the instructions of a Brahman, who desired him to fill
a ditch ten yards deep with glowing coals and jump into it. On
this condition the Brahman had consented to teach him the
holy doctrine. Resisting all entreaties to preserve his life, the
prince caused the pool of fire to be prepared and leapt into it
without shrinking for a moment. On the instant it was converted into a basin of flowers, and he appeared sitting on a
lotus-flower in its midst, while the gods caused a rain of flowers,
that rose knee-deep to fall upon the assembled people (G. O.
M., p. 14).

Nor is this the only other example of a wise discrimination
being exercised by the fiery element. During the reign of the

Indian king Asoka, who in the early part of his career was
ferocious and irreligious, the public executioner enjoyed the singular privilege of being entitled to retain in his house every
one, whatever his position or character, who might cross the
threshold of his door. Now the outside of the executioner's
house was beautiful and attractive, though within it was full of
instruments of torture, with which he inflicted on his victims
the punishments of hell. One day a holy monk, named Samu-
dra, arriving at this apparently charming house, entered it, but
on discovering the nature of its interior wished to make his
exit. But it was too late. The executioner had seen him, and
told him that he must die. After seven days' respite; he threw
the monk into an iron caldron filled with water mixed with
loathsome materials, and kindled a fire below it. But the fire
would not burn. Far from experiencing any pain, the holy
man appeared calmly seated on a lotus. The executioner having
informed Asoka of this fact, the king arrived with a suite of
thousands of persons. Seeing this crowd, the monk darted into
the air, and there produced miraculous appearances. The king,
struck by the extraordinary sight, requested the ascetic to say
who he was, declaring that he honored him as a disciple. Sa-
mudra, perceiving that the moment had arrived at which the
king was to receive the grace of instruction in the law, replied
that he was a son of Buddha, that merciful Being, and that he
was delivered from the bonds of existence. And thou, O great
king, thy advent was predicted by Bhagavat, when he said: A
hundred years after I shall have entered into complete Nirvana,
there will be in the town of Pataliputtra a king called Asoka, a
king ruling over the four quarters of the world, a just king,
who will distribute my relics," and so forth. He proceeded to
point out to Asoka the wickedness of establishing a house of
torment like that he was in, and entreated him to give security
to the beings who implored his compassion. Hereupon the king
accepted the law of Buddha, and determined to cover the earth
with monuments for his relics. But when the royal party were
about to leave the place, the executioner had the audacity to
remind Asoka of his promise that no one who had once entered
his doors might ever go out. "What," cried Asoka, "do you
wish then to put me also to death?" "Yes," replied the man.

On this he was seized and thrown into the torture-room, where he died in the flames, and his house was destroyed (H. B. I., p. 365–372).

Daniel himself met with an adventure of the same perilous nature as that which had befallen his three friends, though under another government. Darius, by the advice of some counselors who desired to destroy Daniel, had made an order that no one should ask a petition of any god or man save himself for thirty days. But Daniel of course continued to worship Jehovah as before, and was sentenced in the terms of the edict to be thrown into a lions' den. But the lions would no more eat Daniel than the fire would burn his co-religionists; and just as Asoka, when he had witnessed the escape of the ascetic, worshiped Buddha, so Darius, having discovered Daniel uninjured in the lions' den, immediately ordered that in all parts of his dominions people should tremble and fear before the God of Daniel (Dan. vi).

Of the prophecies contained in this book the most remarkable is that concerning the Messiah, who is announced as destined to come at a time fixed by a mystical calculation expressed in weeks. The object of the writer was to fix a date for the Messiah's appearance, without expressing himself in such unambiguous terms as would be universally understood. Such is the true method of prophecy in all religions, for a prophet who utters his forecast of the future in such a manner as to render his meaning unmistakable, exposes himself to the hazardous possibility that the event in history may turn out altogether unlike the event foretold.

SUBDIVISION 5.—*The God of Israel.*

One great question has hitherto been left untreated — that of the theology and morals of the Hebrew Bible. Theology and morals are so intimately blended in its pages that the one can scarcely be discussed without involving the other. The character of Jehovah is the pattern of morality; his will is its fundamental law; his actions its exemplification. Hence to consider the character of Jehovah is of necessity to consider also the Hebrew notions of ethics; while to inquire into the Hebrew

standard of ethics is to enquire into the commands of Jehovah.
Let us try then to ascertain what manner of deity Jehovah is.
To do so, our best course will be to select the salient features
of his history, as related by the sacred writers.

Now, at the very outset of his proceedings we observe that
he takes up towards mankind a very definite attitude: that of a
superior entitled to demand implicit obedience. Whether the
fact that he was man's creator justified so extensive a claim it
is needless in this place to discuss. Suffice it that he had the
power to enforce under the severest penalties the submission he
demanded. But it might have been expected that a divine
being, who assumed such unlimited rights over a race so vastly
his inferiors in knowledge and in strength, should at least exercise them with discretion and moderation. It might have been
expected that where he claimed obedience it would be with a
view to the well-being of his creatures; not merely as an arbitrary exercise of his enormous power. What, on the contrary, is
the conduct he pursued? His very first act after he had created
Adam and Eve and placed them in Paradise was to forbid them,
under penalty of death, to eat the fruit of a certain tree which
grew in their garden. There is not even a vestige of a pretense
in the narrative that the fruit of this tree would in itself, and
apart from the divine prohibition, have done them any harm.
Quite the contrary; the fact of eating it enlarged their faculties;
making them like gods, who know good and evil. And Jehovah
was afraid that they might, after eating the fruit of the tree of
knowledge, eat also that of the tree of life, after which he
would be unable to kill them. So that it was his deliberate
purpose in issuing this injunction to keep mankind feeble,
ignorant and dependent. Nor is this by any means the whole
extent of his misconduct. One of two charges he cannot escape.
Either he knew when he created Adam and Eve that their
nature was such that they would disobey, or he did not. In the
first case, he knowingly formed them liable to fall, knowingly
placed them amid conditions which rendered their fall inevitable; and then punished them for the castastrophe he had all
along foreseen as the necessary result of the character he had
bestowed upon them. In the second case, he was ignorant and
short-sighted, being unable to guess what would be the nature

of his own handiwork; and should not have meddled with tasks which were obviously beyond the scope of his faculties. And even in this latter case, the most favorable one for Jehovah, he acted with unpardonable injustice towards the man and woman in first creating them with a nature whose powers of resistance to temptation he could not tell, then placing temptation, raised to its utmost strength by a mysterious order, continually under their noses, then allowing a serpent to suggest that they should yield to it, and lastly punishing the unhappy victims of this chain of untoward circumstances by expulsion from their garden. A human parent who should thus treat his children would be severely and justly censured. It is a striking proof how rudimentary were the Hebrew conceptions of justice, that they should have accepted, in reference to their deity, a story which evinces so flagrant a disregard of its most elementary requirements (Gen. ii. 8, and iii). Just as in the case of Adam and Eve, he required implicit obedience to an arbitrary command, so in the case of Abraham he required implicit obedience to an immoral one. There was with him no fixed system of morality. Submission to his will was the alpha and omega of virtue. Observe now how superior is the feeling shown in the Hindu legend which has been quoted as a parallel to that of the projected sacrifice of Isaac. Although in that story the father was bound by a solemn promise to sacrifice his son, yet he is never blamed for his reluctance to do so, though Abraham is praised for his willingness; while the Brahman who is actually prepared to plunge the sacrificial knife into his child's breast is treated with scorn and reprobation for his unfeeling behavior. Even the service of the gods is not made supreme over every human emotion. But the conception of the existence of duties independent of the divine will seems not to have entered the minds of the Hebrew theologians who wrote these books.

The further proceedings of Jehovah are quite in keeping with his beginning in the garden of Eden. Throughout the whole course of the history he shows the most glaring partiality. In its · earlier period he is partial to individuals; in its later, to the Hebrew race. Let us notice a few cases of this favoritism as shown towards individual favorites. Immediately

after the curse upon Adam and Eve, and their banishment from
Eden, we have the instructive story of Cain and Abel, so mag-
nificently dramatized by Byron. These two brothers, sons of
the original couple, both brought offerings to Jehovah; Cain,
the fruit of the ground; Abel, the firstlings of his flock. But
the Lord had respect to Abel and his offering, but not to Cain
and his offering. Why was this difference made? Absolutely
no reason is assigned for it, and it is not surprising, however
lamentable, that it should have excited the jealousy of the
brother who was thus ill-treated (Gen. iv. 1-8). Again, it has
been remarked above that Abraham and Isaac had a singular
way of passing off their wives as their sisters. Pharaoh was
once deceived in this way about Sarah; Abimelech of Gerar,
once about Sarah, and once about Rebekah. These two monarchs were plagued by Jehovah on account of their innocent
mistake; the patriarchs were not even reproved for this cow-
ardly surrender of their consorts to adulterous embraces (Gen.
xii. 11-20, xx., xxvi. 7-11). Jacob is another favorite, while his
brother Esau is coldly treated. Yet the inherent meanness of
Jacob's character, and the comparative excellence of Esau's,
are too obvious to escape even a careless reader. What can be
more pitiful than the conduct of Jacob in taking advantage of
a moment of weakness in his brother to purchase his birthright?
(Gen. xxv. 29-34.) What more ungenerous than the odious trick
by which he imposed upon his father, and cheated Esau of his
blessing? (Gen. xxvii.) What again can be more magnanimous
than the long subsequent reception by Esau of the brother
whose miserable subserviency showed his consciousness of the
wrong he had done him? (Gen. xxxiii. 1-15). Yet this is the
man whom Jehovah selects as the object of his peculiar blessing, and whose very deceitfulness towards a kind employer he
suffers to become a means of aggrandizement (Gen. xxx. 41-43).

The same partisanship which in these cases forms so conspicuous a trait in the character of Jehovah distinguishes the
whole course of his proceedings in reference to the delivery of
the Israelites from Egypt and their settlement in Palestine.
Every other nation is compelled to give way for their advantage.
Pharaoh and all the Egyptians are plagued for holding them in
slavery, not in the least because Jehovah was an abolitionist

(for he never troubled himself about slavery anywhere else), but because it was his own peculiar people who were thus in subjugation to a race whom he did not equally affect. Throughout the long journey from Egypt to the promised land, Jehovah accompanies the Israelites as a sort of commander-in-chief, directing them what to do, and giving them the victory over their enemies. As the Red Sea was divided to enable them to escape from their enemies on the one side, so the Jordan was cleft in two to enable them to conquer their enemies on the other (Ex. xiv. 21 22.—Josh. iii. 7-17). The walls of a fortified city were thrown down to enable them to enter (Josh. vi. 20). The sun was arrested in his course to enable them to win a battle (Josh. x. 12-14). Hornets were employed to accomplish the expulsion of hostile tribes without trouble to the Israelites (Josh. xxiv. 12). Thus, as Jehovah afterwards took care to remind them, he gave them a land for which they did not labor, and cities which they did not build (Josh. xxiv. 13).

Nevertheless the lot of the race who were thus highly favored was far from happy. Their God was indeed a powerful protector, but he was also an exacting ruler. His service was at no time an easy one, and he was liable to outbursts of passion which rendered it peculiarly oppressive. Tolerant as he might be towards some descriptions of immorality, he had no mercy whatever for disloyalty towards himself. On one occasion he characterized himself by the name of "Jealous" (Ex. xxxiv. 14), which was but too appropriate, and implied the possession of one of the least admirable of human weaknesses. Now the Israelites were unfortunately prone to lapses of this kind. Such was the severity with which these offenses were treated that it is questionable whether it would not have been a far happier fate to be drowned in the Red Sea with the Egyptians than preserved with the children of Israel. A few instances of what they had to undergo will illustrate this remark.

Moses had impressed upon the people the importance of having no other deity but Jehovah, and had succeeded while he was actually among them in restricting them to his worship alone. But no sooner was he absent for a season than they immediately forsook Jehovah, and took to worshiping a golden calf. Worst of all, this new divinity was set up by Aaron, the brother of Moses, and high priest of the Jehovistic faith. That Jehovah should be rather vexed at such ungrateful behavior, after all the trouble he had taken in plaguing and slaughtering the Egyptians, was only natural; but it was surely an extraordinary want of self-control to propose to consume the whole nation at once, reserving only Moses as the progenitor of a better race. Here, as in other cases, Moses showed himself more merciful than his God. He ingeniously urged as a motive to clemency that the Egyptians would say extremely unpleasant things if the Israelites were destroyed; and after his return to the camp he contrived to appease him by inducing the Levites to perpetrate a fratricidal massacre, whereby three thousand people fell. This measure was described by Moses as a consecration of themselves to the Lord, that he might bestow his blessing upon them. It proved successful, for Jehovah now contented himself with merely plaguing the people instead of exterminating them (Ex. xxxii). Thus, he had scarcely finished plaguing the Egyptians before he began plaguing the Israelites in their turn. Indeed he was at this period peculiarly prone to sending plagues of one kind or another. Some complaints of the Israelites in the wilderness were visited by fire which burnt up those who were at the extremities of the camp (Num. xi. 1–3). When they began to pine for the varied food they had enjoyed in Egypt, and to lament the absence of flesh meat, he sent them quails indeed, but accompanied the gift with a very great plague, of which large numbers perished (Num. xi. 4–34). When they were dismayed by the reports brought them concerning the inhabitants of Palestine, and complained of their God for the position he had brought them into, he again fell into a rage and proposed to destroy them all by pestilence except Moses. But Moses a second time appealed to him on what seems to have been his weak side,— his regard for his reputation among the Egyptians. These had all heard of what he had been doing, and would not they and the other neighboring nations ascribe the destruction of the Isrealites in the wilderness to his inability to bring them into the promised laud? Moved by this reasoning, Jehovah consented to spare the people, but determined at the same time to avenge himself upon them by not permitting any of those that had come from

Egypt (except Joshua and Caleb, who had reported in the proper spirit about Palestine) to set foot within the country to which he had solemnly engaged himself to conduct them (Num. xiv. 1-39). Thus, they were only saved from the Egyptians to perish in the wilderness. Truly, the tender mercies of the Lord were cruel.

But the miseries of these unfortunate wanderers were by no means ended. When, oppressed by the troubles and weariness of the way, they dared to murmur, and inquired of Moses why he had brought them out of Egypt to die in the wilderness, where there was neither tolerable bread, nor water, the resentment of Jehovah was excited by this audacity. They ought to have been only too grateful that they had remained alive. Jehovah had not caused the earth to swallow them as it had done Korah, Datham, and Abiram, with their wives and little children, because they had ventured to complain of the government of Moses; nor had he destroyed them by plague, as he had destroyed 14,700 people because there had been some expressions of dissatisfaction at the sudden death of those seditious men. If then they had hitherto escaped destruction, they were certainly foolish in complaining of the hardships of the desert. At any rate Jehovah soon convinced them that their grumbling was useless. No constitutional opposition was permitted in those days. Fiery serpents were despatched to bite them, and many of them died in consequence. Such was the extent of the calamity that Moses, always more merciful than his God, interceded for his people; and was directed to set up a brazen serpent, by looking at which the bites of the living serpents were healed (Num. xxi. 1-9).

The extraordinary cruelty ascribed by the Hebrews to their national deity is shown in many other instances besides those that have been mentioned. And it is to be noticed that it is cruelty mingled with caprice. No one could tell beforehand precisely what actions he would visit with punishment, nor what would be the punishment with which he would visit them. Everything with him was uncertain. He had no fixed system of laws at all, and he sometimes condemned a criminal in virtue of *ex post facto* legislation. The deluge is an example of all these vices combined. It was an excessively cruel punishment;

it was inflicted capriciously, and once in a way only, because
God had changed his mind as to the propriety of having created
man; and it was the result of a resolution arrived at after the
offenses it was designed to chastize had already been committed. No human being could possibly have guessed beforehand
that his crimes would be punished in that particular way. And
after the crimes of the antediluvians had been thus punished,
the survivors received a promise that no misconduct on their
part would ever be visited upon them in the same way. So that
any conceivable utility which the deluge might have had as a
warning for the future was utterly destroyed. Equal caprice,
though not equal cruelty, was shown towards the builders of
the tower of Babel, who were suffered to begin their labors
without hindrance, but were afterwards stopped by the confusion of their languages. Why it was wrong to erect such a
tower is never stated. Could any of those engaged upon it have
guessed that the attempt was one deserving of punishment?
Still worse was Jehovah's behavior to the prophet Balaam, for
he first ordered him to go with the men who were sent for
him, and then was angry with him because he went (Num. xxii.
20, 22). Such conduct was on a level with that of a pettish
woman. Instances of barbarous severity may be found in
abundance. Nadab and Abihu, sons of Aaron, were devoured
by "fire from the Lord," because they had taken their censers,
and offered strange fire before him (Lev. x. 1, 2). A man who
on the father's side was Egyptian, was ordered to be stoned for
blaspheming and cursing the name of the Lord; Jehovah being
peculiarly eager in avenging personal affronts (Lev. xxiv. 10–16).
On this occasion no doubt a general law was announced affixing
the penalty of stoning to the offense of blasphemy; but the
law was *ex post facto* so far as the individual who suffered by
its operation was concerned. On another occasion the heads of
the people were ordered to be all hung for whoredom with the
daughters of Moab, and for idolatry. Phinehas, Aaron's son,
seeing an Israelite with a Midianitish woman, ran then both
through the body with a javelin; for which heroic exploit
against an unprepared man and a defenseless women he was
specially praised; was declared to have turned away God's
wrath from Israel, and received a "covenant of peace" for

himself and his posterity (Num. xxv. 1–15). At a much later period, when David was causing the ark to be brought back from the Philistines, an unfortunate man who had put out his hand to touch it because the oxen shook it, was immediately slain; an act at which even the pious David was displeased, and which caused him, not unnaturally, to be "afraid before the Lord that day" (2 Sam. vi. 6–9). In the reign of Jeroboam a prophet who had only been guilty of the involuntary error of believing another prophet who had told him a falsehood, was killed by a lion sent expressly for his punishment, while the man who had deceived him escaped scot free (1 Kings xiii. 1–32). Another man suffered for refusing to obey the word of a prophet what this one had suffered for obeying it. Being desired by one of the "sons of the prophets" to smite him so as to cause a wound, and having declined the office, he was informed that for his disobedience to the voice of the Lord he would be slain by a lion, which accordingly happened (1 Kings xx. 35, 36). Mercy towards a conquered enemy was sometimes an actual crime. Because he spared Agag, Saul was rejected from being king over Israel, and the Lord repented that he had appointed so weak-minded a man. Samuel, who was made of sterner stuff, had no scruple in carrying out the behests of his God, for he "hewed Agag in pieces before the Lord" (1 Sam. xv). In like manner Ahab was reproved for sparing the life of Ben-hadad, King of Syria (1 Kings xx. 42, 43). The same monarch whose leniency had thus brought him into trouble was afterwards the victim of a sanguinary fraud practiced upon him by Jehovah. Tired of his reign, and eager to effect his destruction, the Lord put a lying spirit into the mouth of all his prophets, who were thus induced to prophesy victory in an engagement which actually terminated in his defeat and death (1 Kings xxii. 1–40). Observe, that however foolish Ahab may have been in believing the false prophets and disbelieving Micaiah, this does not excuse Jehovah, who according to his own chosen spokesman, deliberately arranged this scheme for the overthrow of the king in the court of heaven. Other barbarous deeds followed upon this. To gratify Elijah, a hundred men who were guiltless of any crime whatever, were consumed by fire (2 Kings i. 9–12). To assuage the wounded vanity of Elisha, forty-two little children were eaten by bears (2 Kings ii. 23, 24). To maintain the glory of the true God, Elijah slaughtered the prophets of Baal to the number of many hundreds (1 Kings xviii. 17–40). To reëstablish the orthodox faith, Jehu got rid of the worshipers of Baal, collected together by an infamous trick, in one indiscriminate massacre; an atrocity for which he was specially praised and rewarded by "the Lord" (2 Kings x. 18–30).

It is needless to prolong the list of cruelties practiced upon private individuals. But the subject would be incompletely treated, did we not observe that the same spirit prevailed in the dealings of Jehovah with nations. Thus, when the Israelites were about to enter the land of Canaan, they were desired utterly to destroy the seven nations who possessed it already (Deut. vii. 2). When they captured Jericho, they slew all its inhabitants, young and old, except the household of the prostitute with whom their messengers had lodged, and who had shamelessly betrayed her countrymen. Her, with her family they saved (Josh. vi. 1–25). All the inhabitants of Ai were utterly destroyed (Josh, viii. 26). All the inhabitants of Makkedah were utterly destroyed (Josh. x. 28). All the inhabitants of many other places were utterly destroyed (Josh. x. 29–43, and xi. 11, 14). One city alone made peace with Israel; all the rest were taken in battle, and that because Jehovah had deliberately and of set purpose hardened the hearts of their inhabitants, that they might be utterly destroyed (Josh. xi. 20).

Such a catalogue of crimes—and the number is by no means exhausted—would be sufficient to destroy the character of any pagan divinity whatsoever. I fail to perceive why the Jews alone should be privileged to represent their God as guilty of such actions without suffering the inference which in other cases would undoubtedly be drawn—namely, that their conceptions of deity were not of a very exalted order, nor their principles of morals of a very admirable kind. There is, indeed, nothing extraordinary in the fact that, living in a barbarous age, the ancient Hebrews should have behaved barbarously. The reverse would rather be surprising. But the remarkable fact is, that their savage deeds, and the equally savage ones attributed to their God, should have been accepted by Christendom as flowing in the one case from the commands, in the other from the immediate action of a just and beneficent Being. When the Hindus relate the story of Brahma's incest with his daughter, they add that the god was bowed down with shame on account of his subjugation by ordinary passion (O. S. T., vol. i. p. 112). But while they thus betray their feeling that even a divine being is not superior to all the standards of morality, no such consciousness is ever apparent in the narrators of the passions of Jehovah. While far worse offenses are committed by him, there is no trace in his character of the grace of shame.

Turning now to the legislation which emanated from him, we shall find evidence of the same spirit which has been seen to mark his daily dealings. It is impossible here to examine that legislation in detail, and it may be freely conceded that much of it was well adapted to the circumstances under which it was delivered. Some of the precepts given are indeed trivial, such as the order to the Israelites not to round the corners of their heads, nor mar the corners of their beards (Lev. xix. 27), and others are [such as are] merely special to the Hebrew religion. But the mass of enactments may very probably have been wise, or, at least, not conspicuously the reverse. Those to which the chief exception must be taken, are such as demonstrate the essentially inhuman character of the authority from whom they emanated, Thus, death is the penalty affixed to the insignificant offense of Sabbath-breaking (Ex. xxxv. 2). If the nearest relation, or even the wife of his bosom, or the friend who is as his own soul, secretly entice a man to go and worship other gods, he himself is to put the tempter to death, his own hand being the first to fling the stones by which he is to perish (Deut. xiii. 6-11). The Inquisition itself could have no more detestable law than this. If it is a city that is guilty of such heresy, it is to be burnt down, and all its inhabitants put to the sword (Deut. xiii. 12-16). The mere worship of pagan divinities, apart from any effort to seduce others, is likewise punished with stoning (Deut. xvii. 2-7). In cities not in Palestine, taken in war, all the males only are to be put to death; but in the cities of Palestine itself, nothing that breathes is to be saved alive (Deut. xx. 13-18). A "stubborn and rebellious son" may be put to death by stoning, and that at the instance of his parents (Deut. xxi. 18-21). In appearance this terrible process for dealing with a naughty boy is less severe than the *patria potestas'* of the Romans, by which the power of life and death was lodged in the father alone. Practically, however, the exercise of this unlimited *legal* right was prevented to a large extent, for a religious curse rested on the father who even sold his married son, and he could not pronounce sentence on any child till after consulting the nearest blood-relations on both sides, without incurring the same anathema (Mommsen, History of Rome, vol. i. p. 65). No doubt the purely legal power of the head of the family was unaffected by these restraints. Human authority still permitted him to expose his children at birth, to sell them, or to sentence them to death. But the difference between Roman and Jewish institutions was, that in Rome, religion sought to mitigate the cruelty of the civil law; in Palestine, religion not only did nothing to soften, but positively sanctioned, by its august commands the most revolting enactments of barbaric legislation. It is true that no instance is known to history of the employment of this law by Jews against their children, but this can only show that their parental morality was superior to the morality of the divine law. At a much later time than that at which this enactment was given, when the Israelites returned from the Captivity, the same harsh and intolerant spirit as we have observed in their earlier legislation broke forth again. By a cruel measure, enacted by Ezra, the representative of Jehovah, and taking the form of a covenant with God, the people were forced to repudiate all their wives who were not of pure Israelitish blood (Ezra. ix, and x). Nehemiah, who was likewise zealous in the service of Jehovah, was no less an enemy to "outlandish women," and took rather strong measures against those who had married them, such as cursing them, smiting them, plucking off their hair, and making them swear not to give their sons or daughters in marriage to foreigners (Neh. xiii. 23-28).

Such being the moral characteristics of the Hebrew God, can it be said that the intellectual ideas of the divine nature found in the Old Testament are of a highly refined and spiritual order? On the contrary, as compared with the gods of other races, Jehovah is remarkably anthropomorphic and materialistic. He does not approach in spirituality to the higher conceptions of the Hindus, nor is he even equal to those of less subtle and speculative nations. He is on a level with the gods of popular mythologies, but not with those more mysterious powers who often stand above them. The evidence of this proposition is to be found in the whole tenor of the historical books. Thus, in the very beginning of Genesis, we find that he "rested on the seventh day," (Gen. ii. 2) as if he were a being altogether apart from the forces of nature, and might leave the world to go on without him. A little later he is found "walking in the garden in the cool of the day" (Gen. iii. 8). He clearly had a body resembling that of man, for on one occasion Moses was so highly favored as to be permitted to see his "back parts," and was covered with his hand while he was passing by. His face Moses was not permitted to behold, as it would have caused his death (Ex. xxxiii. 20-23). In order to pass by he "descended" in a cloud, implying local habitation, and at this time he magniloquently proclaimed his own titles and virtues, which he might more gracefully have employed an angel to do for him. Elsewhere it is stated that Moses and the elders "saw the God of Israel," and that he had some sort of paved work of sapphire stone under his feet. When Moses went up alone into the mount, "the sight of the glory of the Lord was like devouring fire." God was at this time supposed to be on the mount, and there held discourse with Moses (Ex. xxiv. 10-25). In the course of it he says that he will "commune" from above the mercy-seat in the tabernacle, again (as in so many other places) implying occupation of definite space (Ex. xxv. 22). He promises to "dwell among the children of Israel," that is, to be a national and local God (Ex. xxix. 45, 46). Confirmation of the view here taken of his limited nature is found in the fact that he thought it necessary to "go down" to Sodom and Gomorrah, to verify the reports which had reached him concerning the conduct of their inhabitants. And when Abraham appealed to him for mercy for those of them who were righteous, his several answers clearly implied that when he went to those cities he would discover how many of them came under that denomination. "If I find in Sodom fifty righteous," and so forth, is the language of one who does not know a fact, but is going to ascertain it. And accordingly at the end of the colloquy "the Lord went his way" (Gen. xviii. 20–33). So completely anthropomorphic is the conception of deity that, although the expression occurs only in a parable, it is not at variance with the mode in which he is usually spoken of when wine is said "to cheer God and man" (Judg. ix. 13). Evidently there was nothing shocking to the Hebrew mind in such an expression. And when they pictured their God as walking, talking, indignant, angry, repenting, jealous, showing himself to human beings, and generally indulging in the passions of mortals, it was perfectly easy to conceive that wine might exercise the same effect on him as it did on them.

No doubt the Hebrew mythology is free from all that class of stories in which a divine being is represented as making love to or cohabiting with women. Or, to speak more accurately, they never represent Jehovah himself as indulging in such amusements. There is a reminiscence of this form of myth in the statement that before the deluge the sons of God intermarried with the daughters of men (Gen. vi. 2); but their supreme Being was free at least from sexual passion. So far as it goes, this is well; but if I had to choose between a God who was somewhat licentious in his relations with mankind, and one who did not stick at deeds of bloodshed of the most outrageous character, I confess I should see no very powerful reason to prefer the latter.

That, in spite of all these drawbacks, there are some better elements in the Hebrew ideal I do not at all deny. The poetical description of God as a "still small voice" is both eloquent and spiritual; and the prayer of Solomon, with its admission that the heaven of heavens cannot contain the Infinite Power who is entreated to dwell in the Temple, is in many respects beautiful and admirable. So also the views of Jehovah attained and uttered by some of the prophets are far loftier than those generally expressed in the historical books. Many of the Psalms, again, are full of beauty in the manner in which they speak of him to whom they are addressed. In a nation so deeply religious as the Jews, and so much given to meditation on God, it was inevitable that the higher class of minds should conceive him more spiritually than the lower, and it is this class to whom we owe the poetical and prophetic writings. It was inevitable also that as civilization advanced, the grosser elements of the conception, which belonged to a barbarous people, should be eliminated, and that the finer ones should remain. The entire supersession of the older God by the newer was prevented by the fact that the Old Testament was a sacred book, and that hence every one of its statements had to be received as absolutely true. The inconsistency between the wrathful monarch of ancient times and the loving Spirit of more recent ages was sought to be surmounted by those processes of interpretation which have been shown to be invariably adopted when it is desired to bring the infallible Scriptures of any nation into harmony with the opinions of their readers. But happily the language of the historical portions of the Old Testament is singularly plain, and no ingenious manipulation of the text can with the smallest plausibility put aside the obvious meaning of the broad assertions on which is founded the above delineation of the God of Israel.

SECTION VIII.—THE NEW TESTAMENT.

Since a considerable portion of the New Testament has already been dealt with in the life of Jesus, we have only, in the present section, to consider the remaining works of which it is composed. These will not require a very elaborate treatment. They consist of one historical book, continuing the history of the Christian community from the death of its founder till the imprisonment of Paul at Rome, of letters, partly genuine, partly spurious, bearing the names of eminent apostles as their authors, and of one composition somewhat akin in its nature to the writings of the Hebrew prophets. Of these several parts of the New Testament (excluding the Gospels) some of the Epistles are probably the most ancient; but as it would be difficult to establish any precise chronological sequence among the several books, it will be most convenient to begin with that which stands first in actual order.

SUBDIVISION 1.— *The Acts of the Apostles.*

The author of the third gospel, having written the life of Jesus, proceeded to compose, in addition to it, a history of the proceedings of his apostles after his decease. We are greatly indebted to him for having done so, for this book is, notwithstanding some extravagances, of considerable value, and is the most trustworthy of the five historical books in the New Testament. It brought the narrative of events nearer to the date at which it was written that the gospel could do, and it dealt with events concerning which better evidence was accessible to the writer. There was thus not the same scope for fiction as there had been in the life of Christ. Nevertheless the story of the Acts of the Apostles is by no means free from legendary admixture.

Beginning with the ascension, which has been already noticed in connection with the gospel, it proceeds to relate the choice of a new apostle in place of the unfaithful Judas. The ceremony by which the choice was made evinces a singular superstition on the part of the apostles. Having selected two men, Joseph and Matthias, they simply prayed that God would show which he had chosen. They then drew lots, and the lot fell upon Matthias (Acts i. 15-26).

The next important event in the history of the Church thus recruited, was the reception of the Holy Ghost on the day of Pentecost. On this occasion the Christians were all assembled, when suddenly there was a sound like that of strong wind; cloven tongues appeared and sat upon them; they were filled with the Holy Ghost, and suddenly acquired the power of speaking foreign languages (Acts ii. 1-13). Since the "gift of tongues" has not been unknown in certain communities in recent times, we might perhaps form a tolerably correct notion from the reports of modern observers as to what the scene among the disciples was like. Even, however, without this modern experience, we should not be altogether in the dark as to the character of the phenomenon of which the author and of the Acts makes. For although it is indeed stated that some of the strangers who were present heard each his own language spoken by the disciples, it is added that the conviction produced upon others was that the Christians were drunk. It must have been a wild and singular exhibition which could lead to the formation of such an opinion. But if we wanted further explanation we should find it in the words of Paul, whose strong practical judgment led him to depreciate the value of the gift of tongues as compared with that of preaching. Had this gift consisted in the power of speaking their own languages to foreign nations, there is none to whom it would have been of greater service than the apostle of the Gentiles. Yet it is he who tells us that at a meeting he would rather speak five words with his understanding, that he might teach others also, than ten thousand in a tongue. So that the words spoken "in tongues" were not spoken with the understanding; they were mere sounds without a meaning to him who uttered them. Equally clear is the evidence of Paul to the fact that they were without a meaning to him who heard them. His reason for desiring his correspondents to cultivate the gift of prophesying (or preaching) rather than that of tongues is that "he that speaks in a tongue speaks not to men, but to God, for *nobody* understands him, but in the spirit he speaks mysteries. But he that preaches speaks to men edification, and exhortation, and comfort. He that speaks in a tongue edifies himself; but he that preaches edifies the Church" (1 Cor. xiv. 2-4). Tongues, he says further on, are for a sign to unbelievers; that is, they are of use merely to impress the senses of those whose minds cannot yet be appealed to. But if the unbelieving or unlearned should happen to enter a meeting where the disciples were all speaking with tongues, they would consider them mad: a striking testimony to the tumultuous character of scenes like that presented by the ehthusiastic assembly of the Christians at Pentecost. Hence Paul desires that two, or at most three, should speak with tongues at a time, and that there should always be somebody to interpret, in other words, to translate nonsense into sense. Without an interpreter, he would not sanction any exercise of his peculiar faculty on the part of the inspired linguist (1 Cor. xiv. 1-28).

To satisfy the doubts of those who attributed the sudden attainments of the apostles to intoxicating drinks, Peter delivered a discourse, which ended in the addition of 3,000 members to the rising sect. It is remarkable that these new members at once became communists, both they and all the disciples having all things in common; a noteworthy indication of what was required by the religion of Christ as understood by his immedi-

ate disciples (Acts ii. 14–47). Further evidence, if any were
needed, of the communistic character of the Church is contained
at the end of the fourth chapter, while the fifth informs us of
the tolerably severe measures taken to enforce it. "There was
one heart and one soul among the multitude of those who
believed, nor did a single one say that any of the things he
possessed was his own; but they had all things common."
Unhappily the one heart and one mind did not extend to Ananias
or to his wife Sapphira, for this naughty couple "sold a possession and kept back part of the price." But Peter was not
thus to be taken in. It does not appear from the account that
Ananias was asked whether the sum he produced was the
whole price of the land, or that he told any falsehood regarding
it. However, Peter remarked that he might have kept either
the property or its price, had he thought proper, and charged
him with lying to God; whereupon the poor man fell down
dead. About three hours later, Sapphira came in; and she distinctly stated that the sum produced by Ananias was the full
price. Peter told her that the feet of those who had buried her
husband were at the door, and would carry her out too. She
then fell down at his feet, and expired in her turn (Acts. iv.
31–v. 11).

No wonder that "great fear came upon all the Church"
when they heard these things. Peter's proceedings were indeed
alarming, and could we for a moment accept the account of his
historian, we should have no option but to hold him guilty of
the wilful murder of Sapphira. He knew, according to his own
statement, what the effect of his words upon this woman would
be, and he should have abstained from any expression that
could bring about so terrible a catastrophe. Happily, we may
reject the whole story as either a fiction or a perversion of fact.
Had it been true, it would have called for very much sterner
measures than those taken by the Sanhedrim, who, having
already desired Peter and John to keep silence about the new
religion, now merely imprisoned the apostles, and afterwards, on
the prudent advice of Gamaliel, determined to release them;
not indeed till after they had beaten them and again prohibited
their propagandist efforts (Acts v. 17–42). It is interesting to
observe that Luke effects the deliverance of the apostles from

prison by the intervention of an angel, and that at a later period, when Peter had been imprisoned by Herod, he again gets him out by means of an angel who appears to him while sleeping, and at whose presence his chains fall off (Acts xii. 1-19). This is quite in accordance with the proceedings of the same author in the gospel, where his partiality for angels as part of his theatrical machinery has been shown to be characteristic.

The infant community was now increasing in numbers, and along with this increase there arose the customary consequences — dissension and mutual distrust. We are fortunate in possessing in the Acts an account of the very first quarrel in the Church; the earliest symptom of those discords and hostilities, which, since that time, have so incessantly raged within her limits. It was on a question of money; the Greeks murmuring against the Hebrews, because they thought their widows were neglected in the daily ministration. The apostles tided over the immediate difficulty by appointing subordinate officers to attend to matters of business. The plan succeeded; but their peace was soon to be disturbed again by graver questions (Acts vi. 1-8).

Among those appointed to superintend the pecuniary interests of the Church was one named Stephen. This man is reported to have performed great wonders and miracles, but some of the Jews accused him of blasphemy, and after an eloquent defense, which to Jewish ears amounted to an admission of the charge, he was sentenced to death by stoning. Foremost in the execution of the sentence was a man named Saul, who was conspicuous at this time for the bitterness with which he pursued the Christians, entering their private houses, and causing them to be imprisoned (Acts vi. 9-viii. 3).

If any proof were needed of the entire conscientiousness of the Jewish persecutors of Christianity at this time we should find it in the character of Saul. Of the honesty of his religious zeal, of the single-minded sense of duty from which he acted in his anti-Christian period, his subsequent career makes it impossible to entertain a doubt. Men like the apostle Paul are not made out of selfish, dishonest, or cruel natures. He was at the martyrdom of Stephen as honorable and fearless an upholder of the ancient faith as he was afterwards to the new. He himself several times refers in his writings to his persecution of the Church, and always in the tone of a man who had nothing to be ashamed of but a mistake in judgment. As touching the righteousness which is in the law, he tells us he was blameless (Phil. iii. 6). And although in intellectual power he was doubtless above the average of his class, in point of genuine devotion to his creed, he may fairly be taken as a type of the men with whom he consented to act.

Saul had probably been impressed by the conduct of the Christians, whom he had so ruthlessly delivered up to justice. At any rate the subject of the Christian religion had taken great hold upon his mind, for on his way to Damascus he saw a vision which induced him to become himself a follower of Jesus. It is unfortunate that we have no detailed account of the nature of the event which led to his conversion from Paul himself. He often alludes to it, but nowhere describes it.

The most important passage bearing upon the subject is in the Second Epistle to the Corinthians, where he thus mysteriously refers to his experience on this occasion: "I knew a man in Christ above fourteen years ago (whether in the body I do not know, whether out of the body I do not know) such an one caught up to the third heaven. And I knew such a man (whether in the body, whether out of the body, God knows), that he was caught up into paradise, and heard unspeakable words, which it is not lawful for a man to utter" (2 Cor. xii. 2-4). So far as it goes, this account does not very well agree with that of the Acts, since there we are told exactly what were the words Paul heard, and what he answered. We are left in doubt then whether the conversation between Christ and the apostle there related rests on the authority of Paul himself, or represents merely the imagination of others as to what might have passed between them. But that Paul saw some kind of vision, which he himself believed to be a vision of Christ, there can be no doubt.

From Luke we have two versions of this incident, one in the form of historical narrative, the other in that of a speech put into the mouth of Paul. According to these he saw a light, and heard a voice saying, "Saul, Saul, why persecutest thou me?"

On inquiry, he learnt that the voice emanated from Jesus, and he was desired to proceed to Damascus, where further instructions would be given him. Luke has not taken sufficient pains to make his two versions harmonize, for in the first we are told that his companions heard a voice, but saw no man; in the second that they saw the light, but did not hear the voice of him that spoke (Acts ix. 7, and xxii. 9). At Damascus a man named Ananias, directed also by a vision, went to Saul to restore his sight, which had been destroyed for the moment by the brilliancy of the celestial light. After this, Saul, subsequently called Paul, escaping from the pursuit of the Jews who had designs upon his life, began to preach in the name of Jesus (Acts ix. 1–31).

Another convert of some consideration, from his official position and from the fact that he was a heathen, was added to the community about this time. This was Cornelius, the Centurion of the Italian band. Cornelius was a religious man, much given to prayer. Tired perhaps of visions, of which there had been two in the last chapter and was to be another in this, Luke introduces his angel — a sort of supernumerary ever ready to appear when wanted — to effect the conversion of Cornelius. The angel told him to apply to Peter, now at Joppa, for further advice as to what he should do. Meanwhile Peter had on his part been prepared by a vision of unclean beasts, which he was desired to eat, for the reception of the Gentile embassy, and the admission of Gentiles to the flock. He accordingly proceeded to Cæsarea, where Cornelius was, and baptized both him and other heathens, upon whom, to the great astonishment of the Jews, the Holy Ghost was poured out and the gift of tongues conferred. Thus did the Church of Christ begin, timidly and feeling her way with caution, to extend her boundaries beyond the limits of the Hebrew people (Acts x).

Some scandal was created in the congregation at Jerusalem by Peter's violation of Jewish rules in dining with uncircumcised people, but there was no gainsaying a vision like that which he produced in reply. Shortly after these events the apostle James, one of those two brothers whose mother had petitioned that they might sit on two thrones, one on each side of Jesus, when his kingdom came, was executed by Herod, the tetrarch; who also imprisoned Peter, but was unable to keep him on account of the angelic intervention mention above. The death of this monarch from a painful internal diaease, is curiously perverted by the writer into a sudden judgment of God, inflicted upon him because he accepted divine honors at the hands of his flatterers (Acts xi. xii).

The history now proceeds to follow the fortunes of Paul. It is stated that there were at Antioch certain prophets and teachers, who were inspired by the Holy Ghost to appoint Barnabas and Saul to the work whereunto they were called. Having laid their hands upon them, they sent them away. Paul now began to travel from place to place, making converts among the heathen. At Paphos he met with a Jewish sorcerer named Elymas, who he caused to be blind for a season, thereby inducing the Roman proconsul Sergius Paulus to believe in Christianity, which had thus shown itself able to produce more powerful sorcerers than the rival creed (Acts xiii. 1-12).

It is a striking proof of the liberality of the Jews at this period that when Paul and his companions had gone into the synagogue of Antioch in Pisidia, the rulers of the synagogue invited them to speak; a freedom which even in the present day would scarcely be granted in any Christian Church to those who were regarded as heretics. Paul took advantage of the proffered opportunity to deliver a speech which ended in the conversion of some of the Jews. On the following Sabbath great crowds came to hear Paul, but the Jews, as was natural, opposed him and contradicted him. After this they stirred up pious women and the principal men of the city against Paul and Barnabas, and (it is stated) expelled them from their coasts (Acts xiii. 50). These apostles having already determined to go (Acts xiii. 46), it was not a severe treatment that was thus inflicted on them. They, however, left Antioch in no very charitable frame of mind, for they shook off the dust of their feet against its inhabitants (Acts xiii. 14-52).

The cure of an impotent man at Lystra led the multitude of that place to adore Paul and Barnabas as gods. Paul, as the orator, they called Hermes, and Barnabas, Zeus. The priest of Zeus brought oxen and garlands, and intended to sacrifice to them, an intention which the people were barely prevented, by the indignant protests of the two apostles, from carrying into effect (Acts xiv. 8–18). This was not the only occasion on which Paul was taken for a god; for when he was cast by shipwreck on the island of Melita, his escape from injury by a venomous reptile which had fastened on his hand was regarded by the savages of that island as a proof of divinity (Acts xxviii. 1–6).

Extremely similar to these incidents, especially to the first, is a circumstance recounted by Sir Francis Drake in his voyage of circumnavigation. His vessel having sprung a leak, while he was exploring the coast of North America, was brought to anchor to be repaired, and the sailors landed to build tents and make a fort for purposes of defense. The natives approached them in companies, armed, and as if designing an attack, but it appeared that they had "no hostile meaning or intent;" for when they came near, they stood "as men ravished in their minds, with the sight of such things as they never had seen or heard of before that time: their errand being rather with submission and feare to worship us as gods, than to have any warre with us as with mortall men. Which thing, as it did partly show itself at that instant, so did it more and more manifest itself afterwards, during the whole time of our abode amongst them." The General gave them materials for clothing, "withall signifying unto them we were no gods, but men, and had neede of such things to cover our own shame; teaching them to use them for the same ends, for which cause wee did eate and drinke in their presence, giving them to understand that without that wee could not live, and therefore were but men as well as they" ("we also are men of like passions with you") (Acts xiv. 15). "Notwithstanding nothing could persuade them, nor remove that opinion which they had conceived of us, that wee should be gods" (W. E., p. 120).

And, as the heathens of Lystra were eager to sacrifice to Barnabas and Paul, so those of this country actually conferred this mark of divinity upon some of the white men in the company of Drake, nor were the utmost protests of the travelers of avail to put a stop to what appeared to them, just as it did to the apostles, an impious rite, derogating from the honor due to the true God. The people had come in a large body, accompanied by their king, to make a formal presentation of the sovereignty to him, and the king had made over into his hands the insignia of the royal office, when the scene now described by Sir Francis took place.

"The ceremonies of this resigning and receiving of the Kingdome being thus performed," says Sir Francis, "the common sort, both of men and women, leaving the king and his guard about him, with our Generall, dispersed themselves among our people, taking a diligent view or survey of every man; and finding such as pleased their fancies (which commonly were the youngest of us), they presently enclosing them about offred their sacrifices unto thom crying out with lamentable shreekes and moanes, weeping and scratching and tearing their very flesh off their faces with their nails ; neither were it the women alone which did this, but even old men, roaring and crying out, were as violent as the women were.

" We groaned in spirit to see the power of Sathan so farre prevaile in seducing these, so harmlesse soules, and labored by all meanes, both by shewing our great dislike, and when that served not, by violent withholding of their hands from that madnesse, directing them (by our eyes and hands lift up towards heaven) to the living God whom they ought to serve ; but so mad were they upon their Idolatry, that forcible withholding them would not prevaile (for as soon as they could get liberty to their hands againe, they would be as violent as they were before) till such time, as they whom they worshiped were conveyed from them into the tents, whom yet as men besides themselves, they would with fury and outrage seeke to have again " (W. E., p. 129).

We are again rominded of the Acts. "And with these sayings scarce restrained they the people, that they had not done sacrifice unto them " (Acts xiv. 18).

An unfortunate change in the popular mind soon occurred ; for on the arrival of some Jews who stirred them up to hostility against the Apostles, they flew from one extravagance to another, and stoned Paul so severely that he was left by them for dead. But as the disciples stood about him he rose, and was able to continue his journey on the next day.

The Christians at Jerusalem were now required to consider the difficult question of the circumcision of the Gentiles; their decision upon which has already been discussed. After the council Paul (who had returned to Antioch) proposed to revisit the places where he had formerly preached, and Barnabas intended to go with him). But a difference of opinion as to whether they should take Mark with them led to a violent quarrel between these two apostles; as the result of which Paul chose Silas as his companion, and left Barnabas to pursue his own course with his friend Mark (Acts xv).

The writer now follows the fortunes of Paul in his missionary work in various countries, and it is remarkable that in the sixteenth chapter he drops the third person, and begins to speak in the first person plural, implying that he himself was one of the company. The fact that from this point onwards the book becomes practically not the Acts of the Apostles, but the Acts of Paul, who is evidently the hero of the story, indicates an author who belonged to the Pauline section of the Church, and to whom Paul was the chief living embodiment of the Christian faith. Who this author was—whether Silas, or some other companion—it would be hard to say, but he seems to have written under the direct inspiration of Paul himself.

Increased by the addition of Timotheus, the party, guided by a vision seen by Paul of a Macedonian entreating them to come, went into Macedonia. At Philippi they met with some success among women, making particular friends with a purple-seller named Lydia. But the conversion of a divining girl who was a source of profit to her employers, led to the imprisonment of Paul and Silas, from which, however, an opportune earthquake set them free (Acts xvi).

At Athens Paul made a speech on the Areopagos, in which he ingeniously availed himself of an altar he had noticed, inscribed "To an Unknown God," to maintain that this unknown God was no other than the Jehovah of the Jews (Acts xvii. 16–34). At Corinth he was allowed to preach every Sabbath in the synagogue (as he had done at Thessalonica, and did again at Ephesus), another evidence of the tolerant spirit of the Jews as compared with Christians. Not, of course, that the Jews were not bigoted adherents of their narrow creed, or that they had any scruple about supporting it by physical force; but they were willing to allow those who had a reformation to propose to be heard in the sonagogues. The effect, as might be expected, was to embitter those who remained orthodox against

Paul. But an attempt on their part to bring him under the jurisdiction of the civil tribunals failed, and after remaining a long time at Corinth, he went on to Ephesus, and thence continued his course through Galatia and Phrygia (Acts xviii. 1–23). An eloquent and able Alexandrian, Apollos by name, came to Ephesus, after Paul had left it. He was a believer in John the Baptist, and was received into the Church by Paul's friends, Aquila and Priscilla, whom he had left behind.

A singular incident occurred on a subsequent visit of Paul's to Ephesus. He found some disciples there and asked them whether they had received the Holy Ghost. They replied that they did not even know whether there was a Holy Ghost. Such crass ignorance must have astonished Paul, who inquired into what they had been baptized. They said, into John's baptism, and the apostle accordingly baptized them in the name of Jesus, with the striking result that they immediately received the Holy Ghost and began to speak in tongues (Acts xix. 1–7). Curious incidental evidence is thus supplied by the case of Apollos and by that of these Ephesians of the existence of a Johannine sect which Christianity superseded and swept into oblivion; and it is remarkable, as affording a presumption that the Baptist did not regard himself as the mere precursor of Christ, that these Johannists do not appear to have been looking forward to any further development of their principles such as the religion of Jesus supplied.

At Ephesus Paul preached for three months in the synagogue, and then, meeting with much opposition, betook himself to a public room, where he disputed daily. But after he had taught two years, a dangerous riot was excited by the tradesmen who dealt in silver shrines for the Ephesian Artemis, and Paul, after the disturbance had been quelled, determined to go into Macedonia (Acts xix. 8–xx. 1). While he was preaching at Troas, a young man, who had fallen asleep, fell from the window at which he was sitting, and was supposed to have been killed. Paul, however, declared that he was still alive, and told them not to be disturbed. This opinion proved to be correct. To this simple incident the historian, by stating that he was "taken up dead," has contrived to give the aspect of a miracle. The case exactly resembles the supposed miracle of Jesus, discussed above (Supra, vol. i. p. 320–323), and is another illustration of the facility with which natural occurrences may, by the turn of a phrase, be converted into marvels (Acts xx. 7–12).

No arguments were now availing to dissuade the apostle from visiting Jerusalem, where it was well known that peril awaited him. Arrived at the centre of Judaism, his first business was to clear himself from the suspicions entertained of his rationalistic tendencies by taking a vow according to the Mosaic ritual. After this the Asiatic Jews raised a clamor against him which ended in a dangerous tumult. From the violent death which threatened him at the hands of the enraged multitude he was rescued by the Roman troops, under cover of whose protection he made his defense before the people (Acts xxi. 27–xxii. 21). It naturally did not conciliate the Jews; and the Roman officer who had made him prisoner, having been deterred from the application of torture by Paul's Roman citizenship, desired his accusers to appear in court to prefer their charges on the following day (Acts xxii. z2–30). But when the case came on, Paul ingeniously contrived to set the Pharisees against the Sadducees by the assertion that he himself was a Pharisee, and that he was charged with believing in a future state. By this not very candid shift he obtained the support of the Pharisaic party, and produced among his prosecutors a scene of clamor and discord from which it was thought expedient to remove him. Defeated in the courts of law, the more embittered of his enemies formed a scheme of private assassination which was revealed to the captain of the guard by Paul's nephew, and from which he was rescued by being sent by night under a strong military escort to the governor of the province, a man named Felix (Acts xxiii). Ananias, the high priest, and others of the prosecutors, followed Paul to Cæsarea in five days, but the nature of their charges was such that they made little impression upon the mind of the governor. He nevertheless kept Paul in confinement, perhaps hoping (as the narrator suggests) that he would receive a bribe to set him free (Acts xxiv). After two years Festus succeeded Felix, and when this governor visited Jerusalem he was entreated by the priests to send for Paul, which, however, he refused to do, and required the prosecutors to come to him at Cæsarea. They went, and charged Paul with offenses which it is said they could not prove. When Festus asked him whether he would go to Jerusalem to be tried by him, Paul replied that he ought to be tried at Cæsar's judgment-seat, as he had done the Jews no wrong, and that he appealed to Cæsar. The policy of this appeal was questionable, for after a time Festus was visited by King Agrippa, to whom he related the facts of the case; and the king, having heard the statement of the prisoner himself, declared that he might have been set at liberty had he not appealed to Cæsar (Acts xxv. xxvi).

Paul therefore was now sent with a gang of prisoners to Rome, on the way to which the ship he was in was wrecked off the island of Melita, where the winter months were accordingly passed. Here he cured numerous inhabitants of diseases, and received high honors in consequence. After three months an Alexandrine vessel conveyed the shipwrecked company to the capital. Arrived at Rome, Paul summoned the Jews to come to the house where, guarded by a soldier, he was allowed to live, and endeavored to convert them. Meeting with indifferent success, he dismissed them with insulting words drawn from Isaiah, and roundly informed them that the salvation of God was now sent to the Gentiles, and that these would hear it (Acts xxvii. xxviii). What was the ultimate fate of this great teacher of Christianity, whether his case was ever heard, and if so, how it was decided; whether he lived a prisoner, or was set free, or died a martyr, we have no historical information, and it is useless, in the absence of evidence, to attempt to conjecture.

SUBDIVISION 2. — *The Epistles.*

In the epistles which have been preserved to us, and which are no doubt but a few rescued from a much larger correspondence, the apostolic authors enforce upon their respective converts or congregations the doctrines of Christianity as understood by them. They explain the relation of Jesus to the Jewish law; they inculcate morality; they reply to objections; they hold out the prospect of the speedy revolution which they expect. Since their opinions on all the topics upon which they touch cannot, within the limits of a general treatise, be discussed in detail, all that is necessary now is to glance rapidly at the more general characteristics of the several writers.

A letter addressed to the twelve tribes scattered abroad, and traditionally ascribed to the apostle James, may best be taken in connection with an anonymous epistle addressed to the Hebrews. They have these two features in common, that they are written to Jewish Christians, and that they discuss the relation of faith to works. It is true that this question is treated by their authors from opposite points of view. Theological controversy began early in the history of the Christian Church, and its first controversial treatises have been embodied in the Canon of its Sacred Books. It appears, moreover, to be highly probable, not only that the two epistles were written on opposite sides of a disputed question, but that the chapter in the one dealing with that question was designed as an answer to the corresponding chapter in the other. It may be difficult to say which was the original statement, which the reply; but when we find the very same examples chosen by both, the one maintaining that Abraham and Rahab were justified by faith, the other that they were justified by works, it is not easy to believe that so exact a coincidence in the mode of treating their subject was accidental. The more argumentative tone taken by James — as of one answering an opponent — induces me to believe that his epistle was the later of the two. The author of the Hebrews insists upon the paramount necessity of faith; showing by a number of historical examples that the conduct of the great heroes of the Hebrew race, besides that of many inferior models of excellence, was wholly due to this cause. The author of James, on the contrary, strenuously maintains that faith is of no value without works, and, as if endeavoring to set aside the force of the examples produced on the other side, selects for his consideration the history of two persons who had been held up as illustrations of the doctrine that we are justified by faith. Abraham, he says, was not justified by faith only, but by works; for he offered Isaac on the altar, which was a very practical illustration of his faith (James ii. 21-23). Rahab again, who according to you was saved from destruction with the unbelievers by faith, was in reality justified by works, for it was a work to receive the messengers and send them out another way (James ii. 25). Not that we deny the importance of faith altogether; but we do deny the exclusive position which you, in your Epistle to the Hebrews, assign to it. Without works faith is a dead, unproductive thing; like a body without its animating spirit. Indeed a man may say to him who relies upon his faith alone, Show me your faith without works, and I will show you mine by my works. What is the use of a faith unaccompanied by works? can it save any one by itself? Certainly not, answers James; Certainly, says the author of the Hebrews. The whole question turns on those hair-splitting distinctions in which theologians have ever delighted; for while the one party considers faith as the producing cause of good actions, the other treats good actions as the evidence of faith. Neither the one nor the other really meant to question the necessity of either element in the combination.

In other respects there is a broad difference between the two epistles. That to the Hebrews is Judaic in tone and spirit; its main object being to prove that Christ is a sort of high-priest, endowed with authority to set aside the old Jewish institutions and substitute something better. James is more catholic and more practical. He insists upon the necessity of not only hearing, but doing the word; of keeping the whole moral law; of bridling the tongue, and of showing no respect to persons on account of their worldly position. He is extremely hostile to the rich, and draws a very unfavorable picture of their conduct (James ii. 6, 7, and v. 1 6). He encourages the poor Christians to endure patiently till Christ comes, which will be very soon (James v. 7, 8). Lastly, he emphatically urges the duty of proselytism upon his flock; remarking that one who converts another when wandering from the truth, both saves the soul of the wanderer and hides a multitude of his own sins (James v. 19, 20).

Two epistles are attributed to the apostle Peter, the first of which, addressed to the strangers in Pontus, Gallatia, Cappadocia, Asia, and Bithynia, purports to be written from Babylon. He holds out to his correspondents the hope of salvation which they have through Jesus, which is a source of joy, notwithstanding their present troubles. Among other precepts he counsels husbands and wives as to their mutual behavior; exhorting wives to be obedient, and not to care too much for dress; and requiring husbands to honor their wives as the weaker vessels (1 Pet. iii. 1-7). The Second Epistle of Peter would appear to be by a rather later author, for he has read the epistles of Paul. He is troubled obout "false teachers," who introduce "heresies of destruction," and denounces them in no measured terms (2 Pet. ii). Having, as above described, comforted the Christians for the long delay in the second coming of the Savior, he exhorts them not to be led away by the error of the wicked, but to grow in grace and in the knowledge of their Lord (2 Pet. iii. 17, 18).

Of the three epistles bearing the name of John, the first only is of any considerable length. The style of this epistle is extremely simple, and it reads like the kindly talk of an old man to children. He tells his flock not to sin, not to love the world, and to love one another. So much does he keep to these purely general maxims, that it would be difficult to gather any really useful instruction from his benevolent garrulity. It is characteristic of him to insist again and again upon love as the cardinal virtue of a Christian. Besides this, perhaps the most definite advice he gives is to pray for anything desired, and to entreat of God the forgiveness of a brother who has committed a sin not unto death (1 John v. 14-16). With great self-complacency he calmly asserts that he and his friends are of God, and that the whole world lies in wickedness (1 John v. 19); a pleasant mode of putting those towards whom it was impossible to practice the love about which he spoke outside of the pale of brotherhood.

The writer of John's second epistle, addressed to a lady and her children, illustrates the kind of charity resulting from such views as this, when he tells them not to receive into their house, nor bid "farewell" to any one who does not hold correct doctrines (2 John 10). The third epistle, written to Gaius, contains little beyond matters of purely personal interest. The Epistle of Jude, who calls himself brother of James, denounces certain "ungodly men," who have "crept in unawares," and are doing great mischief in the Church. It is principally interesting from its reference to the legend of the contest of Michael the archangel with the devil for the body of Moses, which popular tale the writer seems to accept as unquestionably authentic (Jude 9).

Having thus referred to the writings which bear, whether correctly or not, the names of the original apostles of Jesus, we come to those of one who was far greater than any of these — the apostle who was not converted until after the death of his Master. Paul, to whom the great majority of the epistles preserved in the New Testament are ascribed, and by whom many of them were undoubtedly written, is the central figure of the apostolic age, and the one who redeems it from the somewhat unintellectual character it would otherwise have had. Through him it principally was that Christianity passed from the condition of a Jewish sect to that of a comprehensive religion. What Christ himself had been unable to do, he did. What the apostles of Christ shrunk from attempting, he accomplished. He himself was not unconscious of the magnitude of his labors. Hence there is noticeable now and then in his writings, though veiled under respectful phrases, a sort of intellectual contempt for the older apostles, who were not always prepared for the thorough-going measures which appeared to him so obviously expedient. He is extremely anxious not to be thought one whit inferior to them by reason of his comparatively late appointment to the apostleship. He carefully rebuts the suspicion that he acted in subordination to them, or even in conjunction with them, after his conversion. His course, he is anxious to let every one know, was taken in entire independence of the Church at Jerusalem. Moreover, he insists emphatically upon his personal qualifications. Was any one a Hebrew? so was he. Had others received visions or revelations? so had he. Had others been persecuted? so had he. He is fond of dwelling upon his individual history in order to support his claims. Thus he tells us that in former times he persecuted the Church of God, and that he was more Jewish than the Jews, being even more zealous than they of the traditions of his fathers. It was therefore entirely by special revelation from God, and not by any human agency whatever, that he was consecrated to his present work. Indeed his revelations were so abundant that it needed a " thorn in the flesh " to prevent him from being too proud of them — a work, however, in which the thorn was not entirely successful. His sufferings for the sake of the gospel afforded him another and more legitimate cause of satisfaction. He says of these that he received thirty-nine stripes from the Jews on five occasions; that he was thrice beaten with rods; once stoned; thrice shipwrecked; a day and night in the deep (in an open boat?); often in all sorts of perils, in watchings, cold and thirst, hunger and nakedness. Once too he escaped from arrest at Damascus, which does not seem a very serious calamity (2 Cor. xi. 22-28.—Gal. i. 11-24).

Now the object of all these autobiographical statements is evidently to place himself on a level with other apostles who might seem at first to be more highly privileged than he was. Not so, he contends; if they are ministers of Christ, I am quite as much so; if they saw Christ before his death, I have seen him after it; if they have labored in his cause, I have labored more; if they have suffered for his sake, I have suffered more. Hence my authority is in every respect equal to theirs, and should there be a difference of opinion between us you must believe me, your pastor, rather than them. Nay, even if an angel from heaven should preach any other gospel than that which I have preached, you must not believe him; much more then must you disbelieve an apostle. Besides, appearances are deceptive, and as Satan may appear in the character of an angel of light, so the ministers of Satan may, and do appear in the character of apostles of Christ (2 Cor. xi. 13-15.—Gal. i. 8). There was therefore a section of the Church — probably the Judaic section, under the guidance of one of the original apostles — with whom Paul was at issue, and whom he considered it incumbent upon him to oppose by every argument in his power. These are they whom he refers to as "troubling" the Galatians, and perverting the Gospel of Christ (Gal. i. 7).

Such was the view taken by Paul of his function in the rising sect. Whatever may have been its logical justification, it was fully justified by facts. In power of reasoning, in grasp of principles, in comprehensiveness of view, he was not only "not a whit behind the chiefest apostles," but far before them. His letters are by far the most remarkable of the writings which the New Testament contains. They evince a mind almost overburdened by the mass of feelings struggling for expression. He is profoundly penetrated with the new truth he has discovered, or rather which Christ has discovered to him, and he seems to have scarcely time to consider how he may best express it. His mind, though wealthy in ideas and fertile in applying them to practice, is not always clear. It seems rather to struggle with its thoughts than to command them. Hence a certain confusedness in style, a crowding together of notions in a single sentence, and a want of logical arrangement in his presentation of a subject, which render his epistles not altogether easy reading. It may have been those characteristics which caused another apostle (or one who wrote in that apostle's name) to say that there were some things in the writings of his beloved brother Paul that were "hard to be understood" (2 Pet. iii. 16).

When, however, the uncouth style is surmounted, the thought will be found well worthy of consideration. Of all the writers in the New Testament Paul is the one who presents the largest materials for intellectual reflection. Whether or not we agree in his views, we can scarcely refuse to consider his arguments. And herein he is peculiar among his associates. He is the only one of the canonical writers who has any notion of presenting arguments for consideration at all. While others dogmatize, he reasons. He may reason badly, but he has at least the merit of being able to enter in some degree into the views of his opponents, and of attempting to reply to them on rational grounds.

Another striking feature of the mind of Paul is its robustness. Brought up a Pharisee, a sect devoted to extending the regulations of the law to the utmost minutiæ, he nevertheless rose completely above the domination of trifles. Even matters which in most religions are regarded as of capital importance, he treated as of little moment in themselves. Ceremonies, observances, outward forms of every kind he held in slight esteem in comparison with moral conduct. Not the mere knowledge of the Jewish law or the power of teaching it to others, is of any avail, but the observance of its ethical precepts (Rom. ii. 17-23). Uncircumcision is just as good as circumcision, provided the uncircumcised man keep the law. The true Jew is not he who is a Jew outwardly, nor true circumcision that performed upon the flesh. He is the true Jew who is one inwardly, and that is true circumcision which is in the heart (Rom. ii. 24–29). Indeed, in the renovated condition which is effected by Christianity, there is neither Greek nor Jew; neither circumcision nor uncircumcision; neither barbarian, Scythian, slave, nor freeman; but Christ is everything and in everything (Col. iii. 11.—Gal. iii. 28). In the same rationalistic spirit he lays down the admirable rule that external forms are valuable only to those who think them so. One man believes he may eat everything; another eats only herbs. One man esteems all days alike; another esteems one day above another. The freethinker must not despise the one who holds himself bound by such things, nor must this latter condemn the freethinker. The really important matter is that every one should have a complete conviction of his own. In that case, whatever conduct he pursues in these trivialities, being dictated by his conscience, is religious conduct. On the one side, the more scrupulous must not pass judgment on the less scrupulous, that being the office of Christ; but, on the other side, the less scrupulous must endeavor not to give offense to the more scrupulous. In illustration of this doctrine Paul confesses that to him personally the Jewish distinction between clean and unclean meat is totally unmeaning; yet if his brother were grieved by his eating the so-called unclean meats, he would rather give up the practice than destroy by his meat ones for whom Christ had died. All things, indeed, are pure in themselves, yet it is not well to eat flesh or drink wine if another is scandalized thereby. We who are strong-minded, and have surmounted these childish scruples of our forefathers, must bear the infirmities of the weak rather than please ourselves (Rom. xiv. xv. 1).

Certainly when the things are in themselves totally indifferent, the principle of concession to the superstitions of minds governed by traditional beliefs may sometimes be advantageously adopted. But the importance of protesting against the bondage exercised by such beliefs over human life is also not to be underrated, and Paul seems scarcely to give it sufficient weight in the preceding argument. No doubt on the ground of policy, and in reference to the desirability of keeping the mem-

bers of the nascent sect from internal quarrels, Paul was right;
but a principle which in certain cases may be expedient for a
given end, is not to be set up as a universal rule of ethics. Nor
is it obvious that Paul intended to do this. He himself, if
questioned, would probably have admitted that there were
limits beyond which concession ought not to go, those limits
being fixed by the consideration that such concession, if pushed
too far, must end in the perpetual subordination of the whole
of the Christian body to the weaknesses of its least enlightened
members. The morality expressed in the lines

> "Leave thou thy sister when she prays
> Her early heaven, her happy views,
> Nor thou with shadowed hint confuse
> A life that leads melodious days,"

is good morality under certain conditions, but there is too great
a tendency on the part of those who retain their "early
heaven" to press this conduct upon those whose "faith has
centre everywhere, nor cares to fix itself to form." It ought
not to be forgotten that but for the Christian disregard of
forms, persevered in in despite of the scandal to the Jews,
Christianity must always have remained a branch of Judaism.

A peculiar merit to be set to Paul's account is, that he is the
only one of all the writers in the New Testament who treats
the supremely important question of the relations of the sexes,
a subject so remarkably overlooked by Christ himself. Whether
the guidance he affords his converts on this head is good guidance or not, he does at least attempt to guide them. Let us
notice first what he considers abnormal relations, and then proceed to what he lays down as a normal one. In the first Epistle to the Corinthians he is loud in his denunciations of a man
who cohabited with his father's wife, the father being, I presume, deceased. Whether the son had married his stepmother,
or merely lived with her, is not altogether clear, since, in either
case, the apostle might brand their connection with the title of
fornication. However, he condemns it uttterly and without reference to any accompanying circumstances, desiring the Corin-
thian community to deliver up the man to Satan for the de-

struction of the flesh, in the name and with the power of their Lord Jesus, in order that his spirit might be saved at the day of judgment (1 Cor. v). Here then we have an early example of excommunication, accompanied by the formula to be used in performing the solemnity.

That the severe reproof bestowed by Paul upon the Corinthians for permitting such conduct greatly affected them, we gather from the tenderer language employed in the subsequent epistle, where he admits having at one moment repented that he had caused them so much sorrow, though he soon saw that it had been for their good (2 Cor. vii. 8–13). It is gratifying, also, to find that his tone towards the unfortuate individual who had been excommunicated at his desire is greatly softened, and that he desires the Corinthians to forgive him, and receive him back into their body, lest he should be swallowed up with too much sorrow (2 Cor. ii. 6, 7). It would have been interesting had he informed us why he considered cohabitation with a step-mother so terrible a crime, but such a recurrence to first principles was not to be expected. He, no doubt, acted on a purely instinctive sentiment of repugnance to such an arrangement.

A second kind of relation between the sexes which the apostle condemns is that of prostitution. Here he has not left us equally in the dark as to the grounds upon which his condemnation is founded. Not only does he prohibit prostitution to the Christians, but he tells them exactly why they ought not to indulge in it; and his argument upon this subject is sufficiently curious to merit a moment's examination. In the first place, then, he tells his disciples that neither fornicators, nor adulterers, nor Sodomites, nor practicers of various other vices not of a sexual nature, will inherit the kingom of God (1 Cor. vi. 9, 10; Eph. v. 5). Fornication should not even be named among the Christians (Eph. v. 3). They must mortify their members upon earth, for impure connections and sexual license bring down the wrath of God (Col. iii. 5, 6). They must exclude from their society any one who is guilty of such irregularities (1 Cor. v. 9–11). "The body is not for prostitution, but for the Lord, and the Lord for the body." The bodies of Christians are the members of Christ: "Shall I then take the members of Christ, and make them the members of a prostitute? God forbid. What! do you not know that he who is joined to a prostitute is one body? for the two [he says] shall be one flesh " (1 Cor. vi. 13–16). It was surely a very original notion of Paul's to extend to the casual connections formed by the temporary passion the solemn sanction bestowed upon the permanent union of man and wife. It is said in Genesis that a man and his wife are to be one flesh, and this is obviously an emphatic mode of expressing the closeness and binding character of the alliance into which they enter. But what may appropriately be said of married persons cannot of necessity be said of persons linked together only by the most fleeting and mercenary kind of ties. The very evil of prostitution is, that the prostitute and her companion are *not* one flesh in the allegorical sense in which husband and wife are so; and to condemn it on account of the presence of the very circumstance which is conspicuously absent, is to cut the ground from under our feet. But let us hear the apostle further. " But he that is joined to the Lord is one spirit. Flee prostitution. Every sin that a man commits is outside of the body [what can this mean?], but the fornicator sins against his own body. What! do you not know that your body is the temple of the Holy Spirit in you? which you have of God, and you are not your own " (1 Cor. vi. 17–19). Now in this singular argument it is noticeable that the ground taken up is entirely theological. Destroy the theological foundation, and the ethical superstructure is involved in its ruin. Thus, if we do not believe that our bodies are the members of Christ, nor the temples of the Holy Spirit, Paul has no moral reason to give us against the most unlimited indulgence in prostitution. While, even if we admit his premises, it is not very easy to see how his conclusion follows. For why should we not make the members of Christ those of a prostitute, unless it be previously shown that it would in any case be wrong to do so with our own members? It would not (according to Paul himself) be wrong to make the members of Christ members of a wife; why, then, should it be wrong to make them members of any other woman whatever? Clearly this question could not be answered without an attempt to prove, on independent grounds, the evil of promiscuous indulgence of the sexual passion. But no such attempt is made by Paul. He has therefore failed completely to make out a case against even the most unbridled license. Not that his conclusion need therefore be rejected. On the contrary, the danger of his arguments is not that his view of morals is fundamentally erroneous, but that he rests an important precept upon a dangerously narrow basis.

Pass we now to that which he considers as the normal relation between the sexes. The subject may be divided into three heads: that of the formation of such relations, that of their character when formed, and that of their disruption. Upon all of these the apostle has advice to give.

In the first place it appears that the Corinthians had applied to him for a solution of some question that had been raised among them as to the propriety of entering at all into the matrimonial state. In answer to their inquiries he begins by informing them that it is good for a man not to touch a woman. He would prefer it if every one were like himself unmarried. To unmarried people and widows he says that they had better remain as they are. Concerning virgins of either sex he delivers his private opinion that their condition is a good one for the present necessity. A married man indeed should not endeavor to get rid of his wife; but neither should an unmarried man endeavor to obtain a wife. The time is so short till the final judgment of the world that it makes little difference; before long both married and unmarried will be in the same position. Meantime, however, celibacy is the preferable state; and that because celibates care for the things of the Lord, how they may please the Lord; but married people care for one another, and study to please one another (1 Cor. vii. 1-34). Why Paul should suppose that married people, even while studying one another's happiness, might not also endeavor to please the Lord, it is hard to understand. He seems in this passage to lend his sanction to the very dangerous doctrine that a due discharge of the ordinary duties of life is incompatible with attention to the service of God. As if the highest type of Christian life was not precisely that in which both were combined in such a manner that neither should be sacrificed to the other. But, apart from this fundamental objection to his theory it is liable to the remark that the assumptions on which it rests are untrue. Unmarried persons, unless the whole literature of fiction, dramatic and novelistic, utterly belies them, care at least as much to become married as married persons care to promote one another's comfort. Indeed, it would be no less true to nature to say, that the unmarried in general take more pains to please some persons of the opposite sex than husbands take to please their wives, or wives their husbands. Not to dwell upon the fact that courtship involves a greater effort, mental and physical, than the mere continuance of love assured of being returned, there is the obvious consideration that the mere outward circumstances of the unmarried are far less favorable than those of the married to the enjoyment of their mutual society without considerable sacrifice of time. Hence the estimate made by Paul of the relative advantages of the two states is untrue to facts, except in the rare cases of those who have firmly resolved upon a life of celibacy, and who, in addition to this, have so perfect a control over their passions, or so little passion at all, as to be untroubled by sexual imaginations.

That these objections are well founded might be proved by reference to a picture (drawn either by Paul himself or by some one who assumed his name) of the conduct of young widows. Having to consider the question what widows may properly be supported by the charity of the Church, this writer refuses to admit any of them to the number of pensioners until they are sixty years old, apparently on the ground that they cannot be trusted to give up flirting altogether before they have reached that age. Young widows are to be rejected, for when they have begun to wax wanton against Christ, they wish to marry; a damnable tendency, but one which it is so hopeless to get rid of, that the best thing they can do is to marry, to have children, and manage their households. Otherwise they will gad about gossiping and tale-bearing from house to house; not only idle, but mischievous (1 Tim. v. 9-15). So that the ideal conception of unmarried persons caring only to please the Lord had at least no application to Christian widows.

While recommending celibacy, Paul is careful not to encourage breach of promise of marriage. If a man thinks he is behaving unhandsomely towards his betrothed, who is passing the flower of her age, he may marry her: he is not doing wrong. Nevertheless, if he feel no necessity for a sexual relation, and resolve to keep her a virgin, he does well. So then marriage is good, but celibacy is better (1 Cor. vii. 36–38).

Notwithstanding these views, Paul, or at least the Pauline Christian who wrote the first Epistle to Timothy, by no means contemplates a celibate clergy. It is specially enumerated among the qualifications of a bishop that he is to be a good manager of his household, keeping his children well in order; for (it is argued) if a man cannot rule his own house, how will he be able to take care of the Church of God? The only limitation placed upon the bishops is that they are not to be polygamists. They, as well as the deacons, are to keep to a single wife (1 Tim. iii. 1–5).

Notwithstanding his general preference for celibacy, Paul recognizes certain reasons as sufficing to excuse the establishment of a sexual relation, and it is important to note what, in the apostle's judgment, these reasons are. Now it is remarkable that he seems to perceive no consideration whatever in favor of the matrimonial condition but its ability to satisfy the sexual appetite. To avoid fornication a man is to have his own wife; if people cannot restrain themselves, they should marry, for it is better to marry than to burn. Those who marry are not guilty of sin, although they will have trouble in the flesh (1 Cor. vii. 2, 9, 28). Such a view of the functions of matrimony as this is simply degrading. It treats it as exactly equivalent to prostitution in the uses it fulfills, and as differing only in the durability of the connection. But if the whole object of the connection is merely to gratify passion, its greater durability is but a questionable advantage. For exactly as marriage is recommended "to avoid fornication," so divorce might often be recommended to avoid adultery. A union of which the main purpose is to give a convenient outlet to desire, had better be broken when it ceases to fulfill that office to the satisfaction of both the parties. It is strange that Paul should seem to have no conception whatever of the intellectual or moral advantages to be derived from the sympathetic companionship of one of the opposite sex. Perhaps his age presented him with scarcely any examples of marriages in which that companionship was carried into the higher fields of human thought or action. Yet he might still have acknowledged something more in the emotion of love than a special condition of the human body. Christianity has done much to raise the character of marriage, but not one of its achievements in that respect can be credited to the writings of its chief apostle.

Such being the grounds on which the matrimonial bond was to be contracted, it was natural that when contracted, the relation of the parties to each other should not be one of a very exalted order. Paul has, in fact, little of moment to recommend under the second head (that of the character of these relations) except the subjection of women, and on this he is certainly emphatic enough. Wives are to submit themselves to their own husbands: husbands are to love their wives (Col. iii. 18, 19.—Eph. v. 22, 25). An extraordinary reason is given in one epistle (possibly indeed not written by Paul) for requiring women to learn with subjection, and forbiding them to teach, or usurp authority over men. It is that Adam was formed first, and Eve after him, and that Adam was not deceived, but Eve was (1 Tim. ii. 11-14). Scarcely less absurd than this is the argument (and again I must note that it occurs in an epistle of doubtful authenticity) that the husband is the head of the wife, as Christ is of the Church, and that just as the Church is subject to Christ, so must wives be subject to their husbands. And as Christ loved the Church, so are husbands to love their wives, considering them as equivalent to their own bodies, which they cannot hate (Eph. v. 22-33)—although it did not appear that when man became "one body" with a prostitute he was therefore to love her. These views of the duty of submission on the part of wives are not indeed surprising in that early age, for they have continued to the present day. The writer of these epistles is only chargeable with not being in advance of his fellow-men. It required all the genius of Plato, whom not even the greatest apostle could approach, to foreshadow for women a position of equality which they are but now beginning to attain.

Besides these rules there is another laid down by Paul for the conduct of married parties which evinces his strong common sense. Husbands and wives are mutually to render one another their "due." They have not absolute power over their own bodies. They must not therefore defraud one another of conjugal rights, unless for a short time with a view to fasting and prayer, and then only with mutual consent (1 Cor. vii. 3–5). Paul therefore would. have given no sanction to that very questionable form of asceticism in which husbands deserted their wives, or wives their husbands, to pursue their own salvation, regardless of the happiness of their unfortunate consorts. All such persons he would have bidden to return to the more indisputable duties of the marriage-bed.

Such a doctrine, however, to make it properly applicable to practice, would require to be supplemented by a doctrine of divorce; otherwise there is no provision for the case of an invincible repugnance arising in one of the parties towards the other, or in both towards each other. And this brings me to the third head of the apostle's teaching; his views on the disruption of the marriage-tie. Here he has little to say except that the wife is not to quit her husband, or that, if she do, she must remain unmarried or be reconciled to her husband; and that the husband is not to put away his wife. In cases where one is a Christian and the other not, they are not absolutely under bondage: they may separate, though it does not appear that they may marry again. But the apostle strongly advises them to keep together, in the hope that the believing member of the couple may save the other (1 Cor. vii. 10–16). It is plain from this summary that the apostle, no more than his Master, faces the real difficulties of the question of divorce. For the case of unhappy unions, except in the single instance of the one party being a Christian, he has no provision whatever. It is remarkable, however, that he several times intimates in the course of this chapter that he is not speaking with the authority of Christ, but simply expressing his personal opinions, a proviso which looks as if he himself were unwilling to invest these views with full force of the sanction they would otherwise have derived from his apostolical commission.

There is another subject on which the opinions expressed by Paul are open to considerable comment — the resurrection of the dead. In a chapter which for its beauty and its eloquence is unparalleled in the New Testament, he discusses the Christian prospect of another life. Had he confined himself to rhetoric

I should have been contented simply to admire, but he has unfortunately mingled argument with poetic vision in a very unsatisfactory manner. In the first place, he attempts to deduce the resurrection of the dead from the resurrection of Christ. If, he contends, there be no resurrection of the dead, then Christ is not risen; our preaching is vain, and so also is your faith (1 Cor. xv. 12–20). He fails to perceive that the resurrection of Christ — a man whose whole life, according to him, was full of prodigies — could be no guarantee for the resurrection of any other individual whatever. Christ had already been restored to life in a manner in which no other person had ever been restored. His body had been reanimated after two days, before it had had time to suffer decomposition, and that without the intervention of any other person, competent like Christ himself, to perform a miracle. How then could so unprecedented an occurrence warrant the expectation of the reanimation of those who had been long dead, and whose bodies had suffered decomposition? Plainly there is here a palpable *non sequitur*. Christ might be raised without this fact involving a general resurrection; and a general resurrection might happen without Christ having been raised. Further on he makes a still more amazing blunder. Answering a supposed antagonist, who puts the natural question, "With what body are the dead raised?" he exclaims, "Fool! that which thou sowest is not quickened except it die;" (1 Cor. xv. 36.) implying that he conceived the change undergone by seed dropped into the ground to resemble the death of the human body. Now it is needless to point out that the organic processes constituting physical life do not cease in the grain which (as he says) grows up into wheat or some other corn; and that if they did cease, that "body that shall be," which he compares to the bodies of men in their expected resurrection, never would appear at all. The grain, in short, would not grow. An adversary, had he been on the alert, might have retorted upon Paul (borrowing his own courteous phraseology): "Idiot! that which thou sowest is not quickened *if* it die." Such a retort would have been completely crushing. Another very fatal mistake of Paul's is the contention that if the dead do not rise, we have no reason to do anything but enjoy the passing hour. "Let us eat and drink, for to-morrow

we die " (1 Cor. xv. 32).   Nothing can be more dangerous than
such language as this; for it a man bases his moral system
upon the belief in a future life, the destruction of that belief
will involve the destruction of his moral system.   It is founding
the more certain upon the less so; universal conceptions upon
special ones; that which is essential to human existence upon
the doctrines of a particular creed held only by a portion of the
human race.   The argument is a favorite one with theologians,
because it enlists in favor of the doctrine of a future state all
the strong attachment by which we cling to principles of morals.
None the less is it illegitimate, and it ought to be sternly
rejected.

Next in beauty to this eloquent description of the future
state of man may be reckoned the extremely fine chapter on
brotherly love in the same epistle.   Brotherly love, according
to Paul, never fails, though intellectual gifts, such as prophecies, tongues, and knowledge, will pass away.   Hope, faith, and
brotherly love are joined together by him as a trinity of virtues
which " now abide;" but the greatest of these is brotherly
love (1 Cor. xiii).

Scattered about in the writings of this apostle there are also
some admirable maxims of conduct, extremely similar in tone
to those of Jesus.   Thus, he tells his fellow-Christians to be
kindly affectioned one to another; to bless those that persecute them — to bless and not to curse; to return no man evil
for evil; give food to a hungry enemy and drink to a thirsty
one; and generally, not to be overcome by evil, but to overcome evil by good (Rom. xii. 10-21.—1 Thess. v. 15).   It were
much to be wished that he himself had remembered these beneficent rules of conduct in the case of Alexander the coppersmith,
who he says did him "much evil," and concerning whom he
utters the significant prayer that the Lord may reward him
according to his works (2 Tim. iv. 14).

SUBDIVISION 3.— *The Apocalypse.*

The author of the Apocalypse, or Book of Revelation, who
professes to have seen the vision he describes at Patmos, gives
himself the name of John; a circumstance which led in former

times to the belief that the work was the composition of John the disciple of Jesus. It is a rather late production, having been written subsequently to the establishment by Paul of Gentile Christian communities in various parts of Asia. It also presupposes the existence of a sect of heretics termed Nicolaitanes, who had arisen in some places, and was therefore probably not written until some time after the foundation of these churches by the great apostle.

The author endeavors to add lustre to his work by proclaiming at its outset that it was committed to writing under the direct inspiration of Jesus Christ himself, who dictated it to him, or rather showed it to him, when he was "in the Spirit on the Lord's day." Notwithstanding this exalted authorship, it is a production of very inferior merits indeed. It is conceived in that style of overloaded allegory of which the art consists in concealing the thought of the writer under images decipherable only by an initiated few. The Book of Daniel is an example of the same kind of thing. A false interest is excited by this style from the mere difficulty of comprehending the meaning. How widely it differs from that mode of allegory which possesses a real literary justification, may be shown by comparing the Apocalypse with the "Pilgrim's Progress." In Bunyan, the thought is revealed under clear and transparent images; in John, it is concealed under obscure and turbid ones. Hence there have been endless interpretations of the Apocalypse; there has been only one of the "Pilgrim's Progress." That characteristic which Holy Writ has been shown to possess of calling forth a multitude of comments and speculations upon its meaning belongs in a preëminent degree to the Revelation of John.

After writing by the instructions of Christ a letter to each of the Seven Churches, the author proceeds to describe his vision. There was a throne in heaven, upon which God himself was seated. He had the singular appearance of a jasper and a sardine stone. Beasts, elders, angels, saints, and a promiscuous company besides were around the throne, engaged in performing the ceremonies of the celestial court. Various works were executed according to orders by the attendant angels. A beast then arises out of the sea, and is worshiped by those whose names are not in Christ's book. "Babylon the Great," under the form of a harlot, is judged and put an end to. An angel comes down from heaven and binds "that old serpent, which is the Devil and Satan," for a thousand years. During this millennium Christ reigns on earth, and all who have been martyrs for his sake, or have not worshiped the beast, rise from the dead to reign with him. After the thousand years are over Satan is unfortunately released from prison, and does a great deal of mischief, but is ultimately recaptured again and cast into a lake of fire and brimstone. A second resurrection, for the unprivileged multitude, now takes place. All the dead stand before God, and are judged by reference to the records which have been carefully kept in heaven in books provided for the purpose. All who are not in the book of life are thrown into the lake of fire, to which death and hell are consigned also. The inspired seer is now shown a new heaven, a new earth, and a new Jerusalem which comes down from heaven. For a moment he rises from the extremely commonplace level upon which he usually moves to an eloquent picture of that happier world in which "God shall wipe away all tears from" the eyes of men; when "there shall be no more death, neither sorrow, nor crying, neither shall there be any more pain." The book concludes with a curse upon any one who shall in any manner tamper with it, either by way of addition or erasure, and with a promise from Jesus that he will come quickly.

SUBDIVISION 4. — *The God of Christendom.*

Although the God whom Jesus thought himself commissioned to represent, and in whom his disciples believed, is the historical continuation of the Jehovah of Hebrew Scripture, yet his character is in many important aspects widely different. No longer the arbitrary and irascible personage who continually interfered with the current of human affairs, rewarding here, punishing there; now overthrowing a monarch, now destroying a nation; he exercises a calmer and more equitable sway over the destinies of the world. As the servile occupants of the bench in former days too often combined the functions of prosecutors with those of judges, so Jehovah in the ancient times of Israel had sometimes thrown off the judicial dignity to act with all the *animus* of a party to the cause. This was natural perhaps where the subject-matter of the inquiry was the worship and honor to be paid to himself. It was natural that he should take a strong personal interest in such cases; but as all opposition (among the Jews at least) had passed away, and he remained in exclusive possession of the throne, he could afford to treat the charges with which he had now to deal—mere infractions of morality, for example—in a much more impartial spirit.

In addition to this cause of transformation, the natural growth of religious feeling had tended to replace the older deity by a modified conception, and Jesus, falling in in this respect with the course of thought already in progress, contributed to effect a still further modification in the same direction. Hence, although there is nowhere an absolute break between the old and the new conceptions, the God of the New Testament is practically a very different person from the God of the Old. We cannot conceive him doing the same things. The worst action, in the way of interference in mundane matters, of which the God of the New Testament is guilty, is, perhaps, the sudden slaughter of Ananias and Sapphira. But what is this to such enormities as the deluge, the destruction of Sodom and Gomorrah, or the commission of bears to devour little children who had ridiculed the baldness of a prophet? Horrors like these, so consistent with the general mode of proceedure of the ancient Jehovah, are wholly incompatible with the characteristics so often ascribed to the more recent God. According to the theories of the New Testament, the crime committed by the Jews in executing Jesus was at least as great as the crimes for which the antediluvians and the Sodomites had been so ruthlessly exterminated. Yet we cannot imagine Jesus as even wishing for the extermination of his contemporaries by water or by fire. The God whose love for mankind he had been teaching could not for a moment be thought of as consenting to such a course. While Elijah the Tishbite is represented as positively praying for the instant death of one hundred men who came to him with a message from his king, Jesus, on the contrary, is depicted as actually healing the only one of his enemies who had been in any way injured in effecting his arrest. Plainly when the conduct of the prophets is thus dissimilar, the deity whom they represent on earth is dissimilar also.

Another very marked alteration to be observed in passing from the character of Jehovah to that of God, is the emancipation of the object of worship from the limits of race. Jehovah was altogether a Jew. He kept the Sabbath-day; he loved fasts and festivals; he believed strongly in the virtue of circumcision; he was interested not so much in the general well-being of the human species, as in the success of the single people of whom he was the true leader in battle and the ultimate sovereign at home. What happened to all the remainder of mankind was to him a matter of trivial moment, although it might suit him occasionally to use them as instruments either for the chastisement or the restoration to favor of his beloved Israel. But God in the New Testament has largely cast off the special features of his race, and although he sometimes betrays his Judaic origin, he is in the main cosmopolite in his sympathies and impartial in his behavior. Though by no means catholic in religion, but holding exclusively to a single faith, he receives all who embrace that faith, of whatever nation, within the range of his favor. This great and deeply important change, though begun by Jesus, was in the main the work of Paul. If it was Jesus who constructed the tabernacle, it was Paul who built the temple.

While, however, there is an enormous improvement if we compare the administration of human affairs by Jehovah and by God, there is nevertheless a blot upon the character of God which suffices, if rigorously balanced against the failings of Jehovah, to outweigh them all. It is the eternity of the punishment which he inflicts in a future life. No amount of sophistry can ever justify the creation of beings whose lives are to terminate in endless suffering. But while the *reality* of condemnation to such endless suffering would be a far more gigantic crime than any of the merely terrestrial penalties inflicted by the Hebrew Jehovah, the *belief* in such endless suffering is quite consistent with a much higher general conception of the divinity than the one that coëxisted with the belief in those terrestrial penalties. The explanation of this apparent paradox is to be found in the fact that the necessary injustice of eternal punishment is not very easily perceived; that, in fact, it is not understood at all in the ruder stages of social evolution, and not by every individual even in so advanced a society as our own. Some degree of punishment for offenses is felt to be requisite; and it is not observed without considerable reflection that that punishment in order to be just must needs be finite; must needs, if imposed by absolute power, aim at the ultimate reformation of the criminal, not at his ultimate misery. And it takes a far higher degree of mental cultivation to feel this than it takes to feel the injustice of the violent outbursts attributed in the Old Testament to Jehovah. Tradition and custom alone could have prevented Jesus and his disciples from feeling shocked at these; while it was intellectual capacity which was needed to enable them to reject eternal punishment as incompatible with justice. Add to these considerations the very important fact that the conduct conducing to salvation, and avoiding condemnation in the future state, was supposed to be known to all men beforehand, being fixed by unalterable rules; while the conduct necessary to ensure the terrestrial rewards, and escape the terrestrial penalties of the Old Testament, was not known till the occasion arose; sometimes not till after it had arisen. Thus, Jesus lays down in his teaching both the rules to be observed by human beings if they would obtain the approbation of his Father, and the exact manner in which the violation of those rules will be visited upon them if they fail to repent and obtain forgiveness. But Jehovah only made his rules from time to time, and never announced beforehand what his punishments would be. Who, for instance, could tell what he would do to the Israelites for worshiping the golden calf? who could say whether he would treat gathering sticks on the Sabbath, as to which there was as yet no law, as a capital crime? still more, who could imagine that he would visit the action of a monarch in taking a census of Israel by a pestilence inflicted on the unoffending people? Plainly it was a very rude notion of deity indeed which was satisfied to suppose an arbitrary interposition in all such cases. The God of the New Testament may be more cruel, but he is also more consistent. If I may venture on a homely comparison, I should say that the Jehovah of the Israelites is like a capricious Oriental despot, whose subjects' lives are in his hand, while the God of Christendom rather resembles a judge administering a Draconian code in which there should be no gradations between capital punishment and entire acquittal. The laws may in fact demand more bloodshed than the tyrant; but their existence and administration by fixed rules would undoubtedly imply that a people had reached a higher grade of civilization. Moreover, exactly as government conducted by laws is capable of improvement by modification of the legislative enactments, while despotic government is essentially vicious, so the character of God admits of easy adaptation to the needs of a more cultivated state, while that of Jehovah can by no possibility be rendered consistent with a high ideal of divinity.

Such adaptation of the Christian God has actually taken place to a very large extent. The doctrine of Purgatory, leaving only the most incorrigible offenders to be consigned to hell, was already a considerable step in advance of the teaching of the New Testament. It got rid of the fundamental weakness in the conception of Jesus, wherein there was no proportion of punishment to offense; every sin, small or great, was either absolutely forgiven or punished to the uttermost extent. It effected the same beneficent change as Romilly effected in the English law. Precisely as our former code punished even trifling crimes with death or not all, so the God of Jesus punished sin either eternally or not at all. Precisely as the excessive severity of English law led to the entire acquittal of many criminals who should have received some degree of punishment, so the excessive severity of God led to the belief and hope that many sinners would be entirely pardoned who should in justice have received some measure of correction. Thus, in both these cases, the undue harshness of the threatened penalty tended to defeat the very object in view.

But the character of the God of Christendom admits of a much more thorough reformation than that effected by the Catholic Church. Tender spirits, offended, like Uncle Toby, at the notion that even the worst of beings should be damned to all eternity, have simply refused to accept the notion of endless torture. Thinkers, aiming at a system of abstract justice, have sought to prove that it could not be. Theologians have contrived all sorts of shifts to dispense with the necessity of believing it. Modern feeling, whether on grounds of logic or of sentiment, has gradually come to suppress it more and more as an inconvenient article in the nominal creed, to be, if not consciously rejected, at least instinctively thrust as much as possible out of sight. There has resulted an idea of the Deity in which the harsher elements are swept away, and the gentler ones, such as his fatherhood, his care, and his love, are left behind. Such writers as Theodore Parker, Francis W. Newman, and Frances Power Cobb, have carried this ideal to the highest point of perfection of which it appears to be capable. Their God is still the God of Christendom, but refined, purified and exalted. The work which the Jewish prophets began, which Jesus carried on, at which all the nations of Christendom have labored, they have most worthily completed. Whether the ideal thus attained is destined to be final, whether it really represents the ultimate possibilities of religious thought that can remain as the corner-stone of a universal faith, are questions that can be answered only when we have undertaken the complete analysis of those most general constituents of all theological systems which the foregoing examination has disclosed. On that last analysis we are about to enter.

"Ach, mein Kindchen, schon als Knabe,
Als ich sass auf Mutters Schoss,
Glaubte ich an Gott den Vater,
Der da waltet gut und gross.

"Der die schöne Erd' erschaffen,
Und die schönen Menschen d'rauf,
Der den Sonnen, Monden, Sternen,
Vorgezeichnet ihren Lauf.

"Als ich groösser wurder, Kindchen,
Noch vielmehr begriff ich schon,
Und begriff, und ward vernünftig,
Und ich glaub' auch an den Sohn;

"An den lieben Sohn, der liebend
Uns die Liebe offenbart,
Und zum Lohne, wie gebräcchlich,
Von dem Volk gekreuzight ward.

" Jetzo, da ich ausgewachsen,
Viel gelesen, viel gereist,
Schwillt mein Herz, und ganz von Herzen
Glaub, ich an den heil'gen Geist."

—HEINE.

THE

RELIGIOUS SENTIMENT ITSELF.

CHAPTER VII.

THE ULTIMATE ELEMENTS.

WE have now examined and classified the various phenomena manifested by the religious sentiment throughout the world. We have found these phenomena to have been in all ages of history, and to be now among all races of men, fundamentally alike. Diverse as the several creeds existing on the face of the earth appear to a superficial observer, yet the rites, the practices, the dogmas they contain, admit of being ranged under certain definite categories and deduced from certain invariable assumptions. The two leading ideas of consecration and of sanctity pervade them all, and while the mode of consecration, the objects consecrated, the things, places, men, or books regarded as sacred, differ in every quarter of the globe, the feelings of the religious man remain the same.

Let us take a rapid survey, before proceeding further, of the ground we have already traversed. Wherever any religion exists at all, we have found consecrated *actions:* that is, actions devoted to the service of God. Such actions, it is assumed, have some kind of validity or force, either in bringing from the deities addressed by the worshipers some species of temporal blessing, or in ensuring happiness in a future state, or in improving his moral character in this. Secondly, we no sooner rise above the very rudest forms of religion, than we find *places* set apart for worship, and entirely abstracted from all profaner uses. Thirdly, we find that it is a universal practice to dedicate certain *objects* to the special use of the divine beings received in the country; such objects being various in their nature, but very frequently consisting of gifts to the accredited ministers of the God for whom they are intended. Fourthly, we find in all the greater religions—the Confucians possibly excepted—a number of *persons* who have devoted themselves to a mode of life supposed to be especially pleasing to God, and carrying with it in their minds the notion of superior sanctity. Lastly, we have in almost every form of faith a special *class*, generally of male persons only, who are set apart, by some distinctive rite, to the performance of the consecrated actions required by the community to be done on their behalf; these actions thus acquiring a double consecration, derived primarily from their own nature, and secondarily from the character of those by whom they are performed.

Passing to the second of our main divisions, we found the conception of sanctity applied generally where that of consecration had been applied, the distinction being that while the latter was imparted by man, the former was the gift of God. Thus, in the first place, just as human beings consecrate some of their actions to the service of God, so he, in his turn, sanctifies certain *events* to the enlightenment of mankind. It is the same in the second case, that of *places;* for here the deity sometimes points out a holy spot by some special mark of his presence, sometimes (and more commonly) condescends to sanctify those which man has devoted to his worship. And, thirdly, as men set apart some of their property for him, so he imparts to some of the *objects* in their possession a holy character, which endows them with peculiar powers, either over external nature, or over the mind and conscience of those who see, touch, or otherwise use them. Fourthly, he endows the *class* who perform the ceremonies of religion with his peculiar grace; a grace commonly evinced in their power to consecrate places, things, and men, to forgive sins, to convey the apostolic succession, to administer sacraments, and so forth; but occasionally manifested in the shape of supernatural endowments. And fifthly, as there are many of both sexes who give themselves to him, so there have been a few *men* to whom he may be said to have given himself, having invested them with authority to teach infallible truth, and found religions called after their names. Sixthly, he has revealed himself in a way to which there is nothing corresponding on the human side, by means of *books* composed by authors whom he inspired with the words he desired them to write.

Viewed in the gross, as we have viewed them now, these several manifestations of religious feeling cancel one another. That feeling has indeed expressed itself in the same general manner, but with differences in detail which render all its expressions equally unimportant in the eyes of science. For, to take the simplest instance, nothing can be said by a Christian, on behalf of the inspiration of his Scriptures, which might not be said by the Buddhist, the Confucian, or the Mussulman on behalf of the inspiration of theirs. If his appear to him more beautiful, more perfect, more sublime, so do theirs to them; and even if we concede his claims, the difference is one of degree, and not of kind. So it is in reference to miracles. Christianity can point to no miracles tending to establish its truth, which may not be matched by others tending to establish the truth of rival creeds. And if we find believers of every kind in every clime, attaching the most profound importance to the exact performance of religious rites in certain exact ways, while, nevertheless, those ways differ from age to age and from place to place, we cannot but conclude that every form of worship is equally good and equally indifferent; and that the faith of the Christian who drinks the blood of Christ on the banks of the Thames, stands on the same intellectual level with that of the Brahman who quaffs the juice of the Soma on the banks of the Ganges.

But this line of argument seems to tend to nothing short of the absolute annihilation of religion. Under the touch of a comparative anatomy of creeds, all that was imposing and magnificent in the edifice of theology crumbles into dust. Systems of thought piled up with elaborate care, philosophies evolved by centuries of toilsome preparation, fall into shapeless ruins at our feet. And all this by the simple process of putting them side by side.

Can we, however, rest content in the assumption that so vast a superstructure as that of religion has no solid foundation in the mind of man? And is it destined, like the theologies it has evolved in the course of its existence to disappear entirely from a world enlightened by scientific knowledge?

Two questions must be carefully distinguished from one another in replying to the doubt thus suggested. The first is whether religion, although it may contain no objective truth, or no objective truth ascertainable by us, nevertheless possesses, from some circumstance in its own nature, or in the nature of the world we live in, a hold upon the human race, of which it cannot by any advance of knowledge be deprived. Is there, in short, if not an everlasting truth, yet an everlasting dream from which there is to be no awakening, and in which spectral shapes do duty for external realities? An affirmative reply would admit the existence of religious sentiment to be a necessary result of the constitution of the human mind, but would not concede the inference that conclusions reached by means of that sentiment had any objective validity, or any intellectual worth beyond that which they derive from the imagination of those who believe them. The second question is whether there are in the fundamental composition of religious sentiment any elements not only necessary, but true; and if so, what those elements are, and what is the proof of their credibility, if proof there be.

As a preliminary to answering either of these questions, it is needful to ascertain whether in the midst of the variety we have passed in review, there is any fundamental unity; in other words, whether the varied *forms* of religion are all we can ever know of it, or whether underlying those forms there is a permanent *structure* upon which they are superposed. For only when we know whether there is in all the creeds of the world a common element, can we proceed to inquire whether there is an element which is a necessary result of the constitution of our minds. If the phenomena evinced by the several religions to which we have referred in the previous book have no common source in human nature; if, while they differ in every article of their theology, there is nothing beyond theology in which they agree; then religion is a mere superficial product of circumstances, having no more solid guarantee than the authority of the particular teachers of each special variety. There is in fact no religion; there are only religions. There is no universal Faith; there is only particular Belief.

These, then, are the queries to which our attention must be addressed :—

1. Are there in the several religions of mankind any common elements?

2. If so, are those common elements a necessary, and therefore permanent, portion of our mental furniture?

3. If so, are those elements the correlatives of any actual truths, or not?

It may have been observed that all the phenomena we have examined in the previous Book imply one assumption, and cannot be understood without that assumption. All of them imply some kind of power or powers either behind, beyond, or external to the material world and the human beings who inhabit it, or at least involved in and manifested through that world and its inhabitants; some power whose nature is not clear to us, but whose effects are perceptible to our senses; some power to which we ourselves and the material world are equally subject. Sometimes indeed the power which religion thus assumes is broken up into several minor forces, and instead of a single deity we have several deities controlling the operations of nature. But, without dwelling now upon the fact that polytheistic creeds often look above the lesser beings whom they commonly put forward to a more mysterious and greater God, it may be observed that these minor forces are no more than forms of the one great force from which they are parted off by an imaginative subdivision. To place the ocean under one divinity, the winds under another, and the sun under a third, is practically a mental process of the same kind as to place them all under a single divinity; and the existence of some such cause of material phenomena being granted, it is a mere question of less or greater representative capacity whether we range them under numerous chiefs or comprehend them all under one. In either case we assume extra-mundane and superhuman power, and this is the essential assumption of all religion. The least assumption a religion can make is that of a single such power, and this (or more than this) it always must assume. For without this we should remain within the boundaries of science; we should examine and classify phenomena, but we could never pass beyond the phenomena themselves to their mysterious origin or their hidden cause.

But this is not the only assumption involved in every possible religion. Every religion assumes also that there is in human nature something equally hyperphysical with the power which it worships, whether we call this something soul, or mind, or spirit. And between this human essence and the divine power there is held to be a singular correspondence, their relationship finding its concrete expression in religious worship on the one side and theological dogma on the other. All the practices and all the doctrines of every positive religion are but the modes in which men have sought to give body to their idea of this relationship.

We have then, strictly speaking, three fundamental postulates involved in the religious idea: —

First, that of a hyperphysical power in the universe.

Secondly, that of a hyperphysical entity in man.

Thirdly, that of a relation between the two.

The power assumed in the first postulate we may term the objective element in religion; the entity assumed in the second postulate we may term the subjective element. In the following chapter we shall deal with the objective element in the religious idea.

CHAPTER VIII.

THE OBJECTIVE ELEMENT.

THE general result which has thus been reached by the decomposition of religion into its ultimate constituents must now be rendered somewhat more specific by illustrative examples tending to explain the character of the power the idea of whose existence forms the foundation of the religious sentiment, and such examples will tend to throw light upon the question whether the admission of such a power is or is not a necessity of thought. For the proof of necessity is twofold *a posteriori* and *a priori*. We may show by the first mode that certain assumptions are always made under certain conditions as a matter of fact; not that they are always made by every human being, but that given the appropriate grade of culture, the beliefs in question arise. And we may show by the second that no effort of ours is able to separate certain ideas which have become associated in our minds; that the association persists under every strain we can put upon it, and that the resulting belief is therefore a necessary part of the constitution of the mind. Both modes of proof must be attempted here.

Now, in the first place, it must be remarked that few, if any, of the nations of the world are wholly destitute of some religious creed; and that those which have been supposed, rightly or wrongly, to be without it, have generally been savage tribes of the lowest grade of culture. So slender is the evidence of the presence of a people without some theological conception that it may be doubted whether the travelers who have reported such facts have not been misled, either by inability to comprehend the language, or unfamiliarity with the order of thought, of those with whom they conversed.

Sometimes the absence of religion seems to be predicated of a people which does not present an example of the kind of belief which the European observer has been accustomed to consider as religious. An instance of this is afforded in Angas' account of "Savage Life in Australia." Of the Australians he states that "they appear to have no religious observances whatever. They acknowledge no Supreme Being, worship no idols, and believe only in the existence of a spirit whom they consider as the author of ill, and regard with superstitious dread." So that in the very act of denying a religion to these people he practically ascribes one to them. They, like Christians, appear to acknowledge a powerful spirit; and if they dwell upon the evil side of his works more than upon the good side, it is to be remembered that Christians too consider their deity "as the author of ill" by his action in cursing Adam with all his posterity; and that they too regard him "with superstitious dread" as a being who will send them to eternal torture if they fail to worship, to think, and to act as he enjoins them. Immediately after this, the author informs us that the Australians constantly carry firesticks at night, to repel malignant spirits, and that they place great faith in sorcerers who profess to "counteract the influence of the spirits" (S. L. A., vol. i. p. 88). So that their destitution of "religious observances" is in like manner merely comparative.

Very little, if any, belief in deity appears to exist in Kamschatka. Steller, who has described the creed of its inhabitants, states that they believe in no providence, and hold that they have nothing to do with God, nor he with them (Kamschatka, p. 269). Whether this amounts to a denial of his existence I cannot say. They have, however, another element of religion, belief in a future state, as will afterwards appear.

In primitive religions the abstract form of Deity is often filled up with the concrete figures of departed relatives. Indeed this is one of the modes in which that form acquires definiteness, becoming comprehensible to the savage mind from this limitation of its generality. Thus in Fiji, although a supreme God and various other gods exist, the ancestors appear to be the most popular objects of worship. Deceased relations of the Fijians (according to Seemann) take their place at once among the family gods (Viti, p. 389–391). Another author confirms this testimony. In Sandwich Island, in the Fijian group, he states that there are no idols. "The people worship the spirits of their ancestors " (N. Y., p. 394). In Savage Island again they pay their forefathers similar homage, and remark that they once had an image which they worshiped, but that they broke it in pieces during an epidemic which they ascribed to its influence (Ib., p. 470). Among the Kafirs the spirits of the dead are believed to possess considerable power for good and evil; "they are elevated in fact to the rank of deities, and (except where the Great-Great is worshiped concurrently with them) they are the only objects of a Kafir's adoration " (K. N., p. 161).

Similar evidence is given by Acosta in reference to Peru. In that country there existed a highly-developed and elaborated worship of the dead. The bodies of the Incas, or governors of Peru, were kept and worshiped. Regular ministers were devoted to their service. Living Incas had images of themselves constructed, termed brothers, to which, both during the lifetime of their original and after his death, as much honor was shown as to the Incas themselves. These images were carried in procession designed to obtain rain, and fair weather, and in time of war. They were also the objects of feasting and of sacrifices (H. I., b. 5, ch. vi). But the adoration of the dead was not of such exclusive importance in Peru as in some countries of inferior culture, and the most prominent positions in their system were occupied by the Sun and the soul of the world, Pachacamac, who was in fact their highest God (C. R. b. 2, ch. iii).

These last examples introduce us to the more general conception of deity which, in all religions but the very lowest, is found along with the belief in supernatural beings of an inferior class, and in some of them overshadows and expels it. The Peruvians, as just stated, assigned the first rank to him whom they conceived to have created and to animate the universe. The Fijians adored a supreme Being Degei or Tangaroa. Lastly, the "Great-Great," mentioned in the above quotation from Shooter, is a being who seems from the somewhat contradictory evidence of travelers to have been regarded as God by some of the Kafirs, but to have been wholly neglected by others. Thus, in a passage quoted from a work of Captain Gardiner's by Canon Callaway, we find a conversation of the writer's with a native, in which the latter denies all knowledge of deity whatever, and expresses a vague notion that the things in the world may "come of themselves." Of another tribe the same writer asserts that "they acknowledged, indeed, a traditionary account of a Supreme Being, whom they called Ookoolukoolu (literally the Great-Great), but knew nothing further respecting him, than that he originally issued from the reeds, created men and cattle, and taught them the use of the assagai." Canon Callaway is apparently of opinion that the word Unkulunkulu was not in use among the natives of South Africa in the sense of God until it was introduced by Captain Gardiner (R. S. A., vol. i. pp. 54, 55). Considerable suspicion is thus thrown upon any statements in which this name is employed for the Creator. If, however, we may accept a statement of Shooter's, "the Kafirs of Natal have preserved the tradition of a Being whom they call the Great-Great and the First Appearer or Exister." According to this writer "he is represented as having made all things," but this tradition "is not universally known among the people." A chief who was asked about Unkulunkulu, the Great-Great, knew nothing about him, but one of his old men, when a child, "had been told by women stooping with age that there was a great being above." There is also "a tribe in Natal which still worships the Great-Great, though its recollection of him is very dim." This tribe calls upon Unkulunkulu in the act of sacrifice and in sickness (K. N., pp. 159, 160). While this testimony leaves it doubtful whether Unkulunkulu is worshiped at all, except by this single tribe, the traditions collected by Canon Callaway in the first volume of his valuable work point to the presence of a well-marked legend of creation in which that deity figures as the originator of human life. True, he is also spoken of as the first man, and in this fact we have the probable reconciliation of the view which treats him as the Supreme Being, with that which denies that his name was used with this signification. Unkulunkulu was the primæval ancestor of mankind, but he was also the Creator. Ancestor-worship finds its culmination in him. But he has been much neglected in comparison with minor deities, and the word Unkulunkulu has been applied to the ancestor of special tribes instead of to the ancestor of all mankind.

The general result seems to be that some, though not all of the Zulus, have in their minds a more or less definite idea of a First Cause of existence, but that this First Cause is not worshiped and is but little spoken of. Thus, an old woman questioned by an emissary of Canon Callaway's related this:—

"When we spoke of the origin of corn, asking, 'Whence came this?' the old people said, 'It came from the Creator who created all things. But we do not know him.' When we asked continually, 'Where is the Creator? for our chiefs we see?' the old men denied, saying, 'And those chiefs too whom we see, they were created by the Creator.' And when we asked, 'Where is he? for he is not visible at all. Where is he then?' we heard our fathers pointing towards heaven and saying, 'The Creator of all things is in heaven. And there is a nation of people there too'" (R. S. A., vol. i. p. 52).

But while Unkulunkulu is generally considered as the Creator by the Zulus, it would appear that a neighboring people, called the Amakxosa, had heard of a "lord in heaven" even greater than him, whom they called Utikxo. According to the evidence of an old native the word Utikxo is not of foreign origin. Utikxo was appealed to when a man sneezed, and "as regards the use of Utikxo, we used to say it when it thundered, and we thus knew that there is a power which is in heaven; and at length we adopted the custom of saying, Utikxo is he who is above all. But it was not said that he was in a certain place in heaven; it was said he filled the whole heaven. No distinction of place was made" (Ib., vol. i. p. 65). In the opinion of this authority, Utikxo had been in a manner superseded by Unkulunkulu, who, because he was visible while the original power was invisible, was mistaken for the Creator and for God (Ib., vol. i. p. 67).

Testimony of a similar nature is given in regard to other regions of Africa. In Juda it is stated that the most intellectual of the great men had a confused idea of the existence and unity of a God (V. G., vol. ii. p. 160). Oldendorp states broadly that "all negro peoples believe that there is a God, whom they represent to themselves as very powerful and beneficent." He adds that among all the black nations he has known, there is none that has not this belief in God and that does not regard him as the author of the world. They call him by the same name as heaven, and it is even doubtful whether they do not take heaven for the supreme Being. "But perhaps," he adds, "they do not even think so definitely" (G. d. M., p. 318). So that the conception of the Highest God in the regions visited by this missionary is still vague and indefinite, like that we have found in Juda and in Natal.

If now we turn to another quarter of the globe we find the peculiarly degraded and ignorant Greenlanders asserting that, although they knew nothing of God before the arrival of the missionaries, yet that those of them who had reflected on the subject had perceived the necessity of creative power, and had inferred that there must be a being far superior to the cleverest man. They had, in fact, used the argument from design, and thus prepared, they had gladly believed in the God preacked by the missionaries, for they found that it was he whom they had in their hearts desired to know (H. G., p. 240). A similar conviction of the existence of a supreme God prevailed in the new world when it was discovered by Europeans. Such a God was acknowledged in Mexico and Peru, as also in the less civilized regions of the North. Speaking of the American Indians, Charlevoix observes that nothing is more certain, yet nothing more obscure, than the idea which these savages have of a primæval Being. All agree in regarding him as the first Spirit, the Ruler and the Creator of the world; but when further pressed, they have nothing to offer but grotesque fancies, ill-considered fables, and undigested systems. Nearly all the Algonquin nations (he adds) call the first Spirit the Great Hare; some term him Michabou, and others Atahocan. He was apparently supposed by some to have been a kind of quadruped, and to have created the earth from a grain of sand drawn from the bottom of .the ocean, and men from the dead bodies of animals (N. F., vol. iii. p. 343).

The great religions of the world have all of them (Buddhism alone excepted) acknowledged a God, whom they pictured to their minds in various ways according to the degree of their development and their powers of abstract thought. Dimly shadowed forth in the Confucian system under the title of Heaven, plainly acknowledged, yet mystically described by the Hindoos under many titles, whereof Brahma is one of the most usual, celebrated in plainer language by the classical heathens as Zeus or Jupiter, this great being appears in the three kindred creeds of Judaism, Islam, and Christianity, as Jehovah, as Allah, and as God. In Buddhism, however, there is no article of faith corresponding to the belief in God. The Buddha is himself the most exalted being in the universe, and he is neither almighty nor eternal. The creation of matter as also of man appears to be unaccounted for. There is no single being who can be regarded as the ruler of all things, and the highest object of Buddhist worship. But it must not be supposed that Buddhism has escaped the universal necessity of admitting spiritual powers superior to human beings. In the first place it retained the Indian deities, such as Brahma, Indra, and others, and though, subordinating all of them to Buddha, yet left them in possession of enormous capacities. In the second place, the Buddha in fact, though not in name, assumed the rank of a God. Practically, he is far more than human. He himself determines the place, time, and manner of his incarnation. He delivers infallible doctrine. He becomes an object of adoration, receiving divine honors from his followers. And although the reigning Buddha (having entered Nirvana) is non-existent, and cannot aid his disciples, the future Buddha, or Boddhisattva, can do so, and he is addressed in prayer for the same purposes for which a Christian would invoke the intercession of his Savior. Thirdly, it is to be remarked that Buddhism, free from the single idea of God, is not free from the multitudinous idea of supernatural essences. Its theology, so to speak, is quite full of celestial beings of various ranks and functions, who swarm around the terrestrial believers and perform all kinds of wonders. To these remarks it may be added that in Nepaul, one of the countries where Buddhism prevails, the non-theistic form has been superseded by a theistic form, in which there are divine Buddhas corresponding to the human Buddhas; the highest of these, Adi-Buddha, being equivalent to the highest God of other creeds. And it is at least noteworthy, that in Ceylon, where the non-theistic form prevails in all its purity, the people have a habit of invoking demons to their aid, and of employing the priests of these demons, in all the more important emergencies of their domestic lives.

It must not be imagined, however, that I wish to undervalue the importance of the exception which Buddhism presents to the general rule. Far from it. It ought, in my opinion, to be always borne in mind as a refutation of the statement that belief in a personal God is a necessary element of all religion. Europeans are apt to carry with them throughout the world their clear-cut notions of deity as a powerful being who created the world, put man into it, governs it in a certain manner, and assigns punishments and rewards to the souls of men in a future state. This belief appears to them so necessary and so natural that they expect to find it universally prevailing, and regard it as the indispensable foundation on which all religion must be built. Buddhism, however, the creed which, after Christianity, has probably exerted the greatest and most widespread influence on human affairs, knows no such article of faith; and our general ideas of the universal constituents of religion must needs be modified to embrace this fact.

Some superhuman power must, however, be recognized in every religion, and it is the manner in which this superhuman power is described, the qualities ascribed to it, its unity or plurality, its relation towards man, and similar distinctions, which serve to differentiate one form of religion from another. The degree of definiteness is one of the most important features in this differentiation. Generally speaking, the definiteness of this idea and the development of the religion vary inversely as one another. This law, however, is obscured by the continual tendency to put forward, to worship, and to speak about in ordinary cases, some inferior deity or deities, while there is lurking behind the vague idea of a higher entity who is seldom mentioned, little or never worshiped, and who possibly has no name in the language. So that the gods or idols who are worshiped by the people must not be taken as embodying the best expression of their religious thoughts. Some instances of the occurrence of this phenomenon will serve as illustrations of the foregoing statement.

On the coast of Guinea the people "have a faint idea of the

true God, and ascribe to him the attributes Almighty and
Omnipresent; they believe he created the universe, and therefore vastly prefer him before their idol-gods; but yet they do
not pray to him, or offer any sacrifices to him; for which they
give the following reasons. God, they say, is too highly exalted
above us and too great to condescend so much as to trouble
himself, or think of mankind: wherefore he commits the government of the world to their idols" (C. G., p. 348). The manner in which Utikxo, the highest God, is thrown into the shade
by the more intelligible and human Unkulunkulu (as shown in
a previous extract) is another example of the operation of this
law. And it is especially noteworthy that the Amazulu have
also a "lord of heaven," with attributes corresponding to those
of Utikxo, for whom they have no name. Anonymity, or if not
absolute anonymity, the absence of any name commonly employed in the popular language is, as we shall see, one of the
most usual features of this most exalted Being. Other travelers
give similar accounts of other regions of Africa. Winterbottom,
who was especially acquainted with Sierra Leone and its neighborhood, says that "the Africans all acknowledge a supreme
Being, the creator of the universe; but they suppose him to be
endowed with too much benevolence to do harm to mankind,
and therefore think it unnecessary to offer him any homage"
(S. L., vol. i. p. 222). Of Dahomey we learn from Winwood
Reade (a writer not likely to be partial to theism, or to discover
it where it does not exist), that the natives erect temples to
snakes, but "have also the unknown, unseen God, whose name
they seldom dare to mention" (S. A., p. 49). In another country in Africa the same writer found that the natives worshiped
numerous spirits, and believed also in an evil Genius and a
good Spirit. The former they were in the habit of propitiating
by religious service; but the latter "they do not deem it necessary to pray to in a regular way, because he will not harm
them. The word by which they express this supreme Being
answers exactly to our word God. Like the Jehovah of the
Hebrews, like that word in masonry which is only known to
masters and never pronounced but in a whisper and in full
lodge, this word they seldom dare to speak; and they display
uneasiness if it is uttered before them." The writer states that

he only heard it on two occasions; once when his men cried it out in a dangerous storm, and once when having asked a slave the name for God, the man "raised his eyes, and pointing to heaven, said in a soft voice *Njambi*" (Ib., p. 250). Again, in a lecture on the Ashantees, Mr. Reade informed his hearers that "the Oji people," although believing in a supreme Being, do not worship him: while they do worship "a number of inferior gods or demons," to whom they believe the superior God, offended with mankind, has left the management of terrestrial affairs.

Strange to say, the peculiarity thus observed in the old world is precisely repeated in the new. Of the Mexicans it is stated that "they never offered sacrifices to" Tonacatecotle who was "God, Lord, Creator, Governor of the Universe," and whom "they painted alone with a crown, as lord of all." As their explanation of this conduct "they said that he did not regard them. All the others to whom they sacrificed were men once on a time, or demons" (A. M., vol. vi. p. 107, plate 1). Concerning the Peruvians, Acosta tells us that they give their deity a name of great excellence, Pachacamac, or Pachayachacic (creator of heaven and earth), and Usapu (admirable). He remarks, however, with much surprise, that they had no proper (or perhaps general) name in their language for God. There was nothing in the language of Cuzco or Mexico answering to "Deus," and the Spaniards used their own word "Dios." Whence he concludes, somewhat hastily, that they had but a slight and superficial knowledge of God (H. I., b. 5, ch. iii).

In reference to Peru, however, we have still more trustworthy evidence from a member of the governing family, or Incas. From his statements it appears that the name applied to the Highest was pronounced only on rare occasions, and then with extremest reverence. This name was Pachacamac, a word signifying "he who animates the whole world," or the Universal Soul, as it would be termed in Indian philosophy. Like other creeds that of Peru had its secondary deity, the Sun, in whose honor sacrifices were offered and festivals held, while no temples were erected, and no sacrifices offered to Pachacamac, although the Peruvians adored him in their hearts and looked upon him as the unknown God (C. R., b. 2, ch. iii).

Ancient religion presents similar facts. In his exhaustive work on Sabaeism, Chwolsohn observes that the fundamental idea of that form of faith was not, as is often supposed, astrolatry. To Shahrastani (the Arabian scholar), and many others who followed him, Sabaeism expressed the idea "that God is too sublime and too great to occupy himself with the immediate management of this world; that he has therefore transferred the government thereof to the gods, and retained only the most important affairs for himself; that further, man is too weak to be able to apply immediately to the Highest; that he must therefore address his prayers and sacrifices to the intermediate divinities, to whom the management of the world has been intrusted by the Highest." Further on, the author asks himself whether this conception was peculiar to the Harranian Sabaeans, and replies, "Certainly not. This fundamental idea is tolerably old, and in later times found admission to some extent even among the strictly monotheistic Jews. . . . In the heathen world this view was universally shared by the cultivated classes, at least in the first centuries of the Christian era" (Ssabismus, vol. i. p. 725).

Indian theology teems with the conception of a sublime but unknowable deity far superior to the deities of popular adoration, who has no name and whose greatness cannot be adequately expressed in human language. Indian philosophy loses itself in a sea of mystic terms when it endeavors to speak of this all-pervading and preëminent Being. Take, for example, the following from the Chhandogya Upanishad, one of the treatises appended to the Sama Veda. A father is instructing his son:—

"'Dissolve this salt in water, and appear before me to-morrow morning.' He did so. Unto him said (the father), 'My child, find out the salt that you put in that water last night.' The salt, having been dissolved, could not be made out. (Unto Swetaketu said his father), 'Child, do you taste a little from the top of that water.' (The child did so. After a while the father inquired), 'How tastes it?' 'It is saltish' (said Swetaketu)." The same result followed with water taken from the middle and the bottom. "'If so (throwing it away), wash your mouth and grieve not.' Verily he did so (and said to his father), 'The salt

that I put in the water exists for ever; (though I perceive it
not by my eyes it is felt by my tongue).' (Unto him) said (his
father), 'Verily, such is the case with the Truth, my child.
Though you perceive it not, it nevertheless pervades this (body).
That particle which is the soul of all this is Truth; it is the
Universal Soul. O Swetaketu, Thou art that'" (Ch. Up., ch. vi.
sec. 13, p. 113).

Similar notions of an all-pervading and infinite Being are
found in the Bhagavat-Gita, a theological episode inserted in
the great epical poem known as the Mahabharata. There
Vishnu is not merely the ordinary god Vishnu of Indian theology; but the universe itself is expressed as an incarnation of
that deity who is seen in everything and himself is everything.
"I am the soul, O Arjuna," thus he addresses his mortal pupil,
"which exists in the heart of all beings, and I am the beginning and the middle and also the end of existing things" (Bh.
G., ch. x. p. 71).

Again, Vishnu thus describes himself in language which
translated into ordinary prose, would serve to convey the idea
embodied in Mr. Herbert Spencer's Unknowable:—

"Know that that brilliance which enters the sun and illu-
mines the whole earth, and which is in the moon, and in fire,
is of me. And I enter the ground and support all living
things by my vigor; and I nourish all herbs, becoming that
moisture of which the peculiar property is taste. And becoming fire, I enter the body of the living, and being associated
with their inspiration and expiration, cause food of the four
kinds to digest. And I enter the heart of each one, and from
me come memory, knowledge, and reason" (Ib., ch. xv. p. 100).

Nor did the writers of the Veda and the commentaries
thereupon omit to look above the concrete forms of the mythological gods who people their Pantheon to a more comprehensive and less comprehensible primordial Source. The gods were
unfitted to serve as explanations of the origin of the universe by
reason of the theory that they were not eternal, and that they
came into existence subsequently to the creation of the world.
The writer of a hymn in the tenth book of the Rig-Veda asserted
that "the One, which in the beginning breathed calmly, self-
sustained, is developed by . . . its own inherent heat, or by

rigorous and intense abstraction." But this Rishi avowed himself unable to say anything of creation, or even to know whether
there was a creator. "Even its ruler in the highest heaven
may not be in possession of the great secret." Explaining this
passage, a commentator, writing at a much later date, observes
that "the last verse of the hymn declares that the ruler of the
universe knows, or that even he does not know, from what material cause this visible world arose, and whether that material
cause exists in any definite form or not. That is to say, the
delaration that ' he knows,' is made from the stand-point of that
popular conception which distinguishes between the ruler of the
universe and the creatures over whom he rules; while the proposition that ' he does not know ' is asserted on the ground of
that highest principle which, transcending all popular conceptions, affirms the identity of all things with the supreme Soul,
which cannot see any other existence as distinct from itself "
(O. S. T., vol. v. pp. 363, 364).

In this sentence the commentator correctly points out the
distinction between the Unknown Cause of philosophic thought
and the gods of popular theology, the latter being limited, and
having the universe outside of and objective to them, the former
comprehending it within itself, and having nothing objective
whatever. And he perceives apparently that these are but different modes of conceiving the same Ultimate Essence, dependent on the varying representative capacities of those by whom
they are employed.

In India, as elsewhere, this Ultimate Essence had no proper
name. Sometimes it is spoken of as "That." Thus, in a passage quoted by Dr. Muir from the Taittirīya Brahmana we find
the following: " This [universe] was not originally anything.
There was neither heaven, nor earth, nor atmosphere. That
being non-existent (asat) resolved ' Let me be.' That became
fervent," and so forth. Hereupon the commentator states that
"the Supreme Spirit was non-existent only in respect of name
and form, but that nevertheless it was really existing (sat) " (O.
S. T., vol. v. p. 366).

Prof. Max Müller, in his essay on the Veda, has observed
that after naming the several powers of nature, and worshiping
them as gods, the ancient Hindu found that there was yet

another power within him and around him for which he had no name. This he termed in the first instance "Brahman," force, will, wish. But when Brahman too had become a person, he called the mysterious and impersonal power "âtman," originally meaning breath or spirit, subsequently Self. "Atman remained always free from myth and worship, differing in this from Brahman (neuter), who has his temples in India even now and is worshiped as Brahman (masculine), together with Vishnu and Siva and other popular gods" (Chips, vol. i. pp. 70, 71). Distinguishing these two deities, for the convenience of English readers, as Brahm, the neuter, and Brahma, the masculine God, it is to be observed that even the latter, who holds in theology the function of Creator, is but little worshiped in India, and holds no conspicuous place in the popular mind. Thus Wilson says, "It is doubtful if Brahma was ever worshiped. Indications of local adoration of him at Pushkara, near Ajmir, are found in one Purana, the Brahma Purana, but in no other part of India is there the slightest vestige of his worship" (W. W., vol. ii. p. 63). Elsewhere the same most competent authority states "it might be difficult to meet with" any Brahma-worshipers now; "exclusive adorers of this deity, and temples dedicated to him, do not now occur perhaps in any part of India; at the same time it is an error to suppose that public homage is never paid to him." Hereupon he mentions a few places where Brahma is particularly reverenced. While, however, there may be discovered some faint traces of the worship of Brahma the Creator, and first member of the Hindu Trinity, there does not appear to be any worship whatever of the more impersonal and abstract Brahm. Brahm is related to Brahma much as the Absolute or the Unknowable of philosphy is related to the God of the Hebrew and Christian Scriptures. In the conception of Brahm the idea of deity is pushed to the utmost limits of which human thought is capable, and we have a being whose very exaltation above the mythological personages who pass for gods among the people precludes him from receiving the adoration of any but philosophic minds. When therefore Professor Max Müller speaks of temples dedicated to Brahm I presume that he is speaking of the temples of Brahma, the corporeal form of this unembodied idea. For Brahm is stated to be "immaterial, invisible, unborn, uncreated, without beginning or end;" to be "inapprehensible by the understanding, at least until that is freed from the film of mortal blindness;" to be devoid of attributes, or to have only purity, and to be "susceptible of no interest in the acts of man or the administration of the affairs of the universe." Conformably to these views, adds Wilson, "no temples are erected, no prayers are even addressed to the Supreme" (W. W., vol. ii. p. 91). Thus Brahma, the God, is but little worshiped; Brahm, the infinite being, and âtman, spirit, are not worshiped at all. Now Brahma, the creative and formative power, corresponds to God the Father; while Brahm and âtman, especially the latter, bear more resemblance to the Holy Ghost; a fact to be especially noted in reference to the comparison hereafter to be made between the positions occupied by the more and the less spiritual members of the Christian Trinity.

Thus we have this singular neglect of the Supreme Divinity prevailing among ancient heathens, among modern Africans, among Hindus of all ages, and among pre-Christian Mexicans and Peruvians. Do Judaism, and its offshoot, Christianity, offer no sign of a similar relegation of the highest to an invisible background? I think they do. The evidence is not indeed quite so simple as in the other cases. But it is deserving of remark that the ordinary name for God in Hebrew, Elohim, is plural, and must at one time have signified gods; while the word which is sometimes used alone, but more commonly in combination with it, is regarded as so sacred that the Jews in reading the Scriptures never pronounce it, but substitute Adonai, my lord, in its place. Owing to this ancient custom the very sound of the word יהוה has been absolutely forgotten, and Jehovah, by which we commonly render it, has been merely constructed by supplying the vowels from Adonai. Now the existence of a most holy name, but rarely used, and then only with great reverence, is a manifestation of religious feeling exactly corresponding to that related by Reade concerning the African name Njambi. Suppose that with the progress of theological dogmas and ecclesiastical usages the use of the word Njambi should be entirely dropped, its pronunciation might then be entirely lost (if, as in Hebrew, its vowel sounds were never written). And with the adoption of a monotheistic creed some name, now belonging to an idol, might be used as synonymous with Njambi. Now something of this kind may have happened with the Hebrews. There can be little doubt that the Elohim were originally gods accepted by the Hebrews as part of a polytheistic system. Deep in the minds of Hebrew thinkers lay the more abstract notion of a single God, more powerful and more mysterious than the Elohim. They called him Jahveh, or whatever else may have been the name expressed by יהוה. But as the monotheistic view triumphed over the polytheistic, the Elohim were adopted into the framework of the new religion, and in a manner subordinated to Jahveh by a process of fusion. The name of Jahveh, which must once have been in common use, was now treated as too holy to be ever uttered by mortal lips. The ancient God who had stood at the head of the system of his party, was in a certain sense withdrawn from active life, but retained as the nominal occupant of supreme authority. Whether this account is probable or not, must be left to better judges to decide, but it tends at least to bring the history of the Jewish faith into harmony with that of other religions.

Moreover, it is interesting to observe that a process extremely similar to that here imagined as occurring in the development of Judaism, was actually passed through by its younger rival. Christianity, arising in the midst of a people who had arrived at highly abstract views of deity, proceeded at once to do what so many other creeds have done, to embody the conception of divine power in a concrete object. This concrete object was in the Christian theology a man. And as generally happens in these cases, the more abstract idea was overshadowed and to some extent driven from the field by the more concrete. Christ occupies a larger place both in authorized Christian worship and in the popular Christian imagination than does his Father. The creed no doubt treats them both with equal reverence, as persons in a single God; but to understand what is truly felt and believed by the people, we must look not to the letter of their creeds, but to their actual, and above all their unconscious practice. Doing this we find first an entire absence of any special festival in honor of the Father.* Look at the large

* The remark is not mine, but is made by Didron, a devout Roman

place occupied by the history of Jesus in ecclesiastical fast-days and feast-days. We have the Annunciation, the Nativity, the forty days of Lent, the Crucifixion, the Resurrection, the Ascension, all referring to him. But we have quite forgotten to celebrate the creation of the human species, the expulsion from Eden, the deluge. the destruction of Sodom and Gomorrah, and other mighty works due to his Father. The weekly holiday, originally a memorial of his repose on the seventh day, has indeed been retained from Judaism; yet even here its reference has been changed from the history of the first person to that of the second by its transfer from the last day of the week to the first. But this is not all. Didron remarks that in early works of art Jesus is made to take the place of his Father in creation and in similar labors, just as in heathen religions an inferior divinity does the work under a superior one. Dishonorable and even ridiculous positions were assigned to God the Father. The more ancient artists were reluctant to paint the whole of the First Person, just as Africans, Peruvians and Hebrews were reluctant to speak his name. A mere hand or an arm is held sufficient to represent him. But in the thirteenth and fourteenth centuries, God the Father begins to manifest his figure; at first his bust only, and then his whole person. In the fourteenth century we take part in the birth and development of the figure of the eternal Father. At first equal to his Son in age and station, he begins in process of time to become slightly different, until, towards 1360, the notion of paternity is attached irrevocably to him; he is thenceforth uniformly older than his Son, and assumes the first place in the Trinity. The middle age may be divided (according to Didron) into two periods. In the first, preceding the fourteenth century, we have the Father in the image and similitude of the Son. In the second, after the thirteenth century until the sixteenth, Jesus Christ loses his iconographic distinctness, and is conquered by his Father. He in his turn puts on the likeness of the Father, becoming old and wrinkled like him (Ic. Ch., p. 148–203. Basing his conclusions on these remarkable disclosures, Michelet, in his "History of France," observes with considerable reason

Catholic writer, to whom I am much indebted for this and other hints.—Ic Ch., p. 572 n.

that from the first century until the twelfth God was not worshiped by Christians. Nay, even for fifteen centuries not a temple, not an altar was erected to him. And when he did venture to appear beside his Son in Christian art, he remained neglected and solitary. Nobody made an offering to him, or caused a mass to be said in his honor (Michelet, "Histoire de France," vol. vii. p. xlix).

But while the first Person of the Trinity has now obtained, especially in Protestant countries, a degree of recognition which he did not always enjoy, there remains behind another Person, who is more abstract, more spiritual, more undefinable than either the Father or the Son. Formally included in the liturgies of the Church, having an office established in his honor, churches dedicated to his name, this member of the Trinity has nevertheless been strangely neglected by all Christian nations. Nobody practically worships the Holy Ghost; nobody pays him especial attention; nobody appears to be much concerned about his proceedings. Artists have treated him with a degree of indifference which they have never manifested towards Jesus Christ. Not only have they sometimes forgotten to include the Holy Ghost in their representations of the Godhead, but they have omitted him even from a scene where he had the best possible claim to figure, namely, the reception of the Spirit by the apostles at the feast of Pentecost. Elsewhere they have not completely left him out, but have placed him in an attitude of subordination and indignity, evincing but scant respect, as where an artist had depicted an angel as apparently restraining the impetuosity of the dove by holding its tail in both his hands. While in the Catacombs it was the Father who was suppressed, in the Trinities of the twelfth, fifteenth, and sixteenth centuries it is the Holy Ghost who is found to be missing. "Thus," observes the Roman Catholic author to whom I am indebted for these facts, "the Holy Ghost has sometimes had reason to complain of the artists" (Ic. Chr., p. 489-495).

Were this Person, in fact, disposed to be punctilious, it is not only artists, mere reflectors of the general sentiment, but the whole Christian world of whom he would have reason to complain. So little does he occupy the ordinary thoughts of Christians, that Abailard gave the greatest offense by naming a monastery after him, and this procedure of the great theologian remains, I believe, a solitary example in ecclesiastical history of such an honor being paid to the Paraclete. Yet surely he who bears the great office of the Comforter is deserving of some more express recognition than he now receives! What is the cause of this universal oblivion? I suspect it is that which leads to the neglect by the Africans of their highest god, namely, his entire innocuousness. We saw that various tribes, while omitting to worship a benevolent deity, who will never do them any kind of harm, address their prayers to a class of gods who are described by travelers as demons, or evil spirits, but whom they no doubt regard as mixtures of good qualities with bad; capable of propitiation by prayer, but resentful of irreverence. Now the Father and the Son correspond in some degree to these inferior gods. Not that they are actively malevolent, but they have certain characteristics of a terrifying order. God the Father is throughout the Bible the author of chastisements and scourges. God the Son, merciful though he be, yet intimates that he will return to judge the world, and that he will disavow those who are not truly his disciples, thus consigning them to the secular arm of God the Father, who will condemn them to eternal punishment. But God the Spirit has no share in these horrors. Whenever he appears upon the scene, he is quiet, gentle, and inoffensive; and these qualities, combined with the absence of the more definite personality possessed by his colleagues, have effectually ensured his comparative insignificance in Christian worship and in Christian thought.

While this has been the course of affairs in reference to the persons in the Trinity — who, though dogmatically one, are popularly and practically three — a simultaneous displacement of all its members by still more comprehensible objects of worship has been going on. First in rank among these stands the Virgin Mary, so universally worshiped in Catholic countries. After her come the mass of saints, some of general, some of local celebrity; but who, no doubt, receive, each from his or her particular devotees, a far larger share of devotional attention than the Father or the Son themselves. For they are requested to intercede with these more exalted potentates; and we naturally pay more regard to our intercessors, show them more assiduous respect, feel towards them more gratitude, than we do to those with whom they intercede, and who stand too far above us to be approached directly by us. Keightley, in his "History of England," expresses himself as shocked by the far larger share of the offerings of the pious received at Canterbury by the altar of Thomas-á-Becket than was received by the altars of the Virgin and of the Son. The proportion is as follows:—In one year St. Thomas received £832, 12s. 3d.; the Virgin £63, 5s. 6d.; Christ only £3, 2s. 6d. Next year the martyr had £954, 6s. 3d.; Mary £4, 1s. 8d.; and Christ nothing at all. This relation is perfectly natural. Thomas-á-Becket was the local saint. He stood nearer to the people, was more intelligible to their minds, than the Virgin Mary; and the latter, again, was more intelligible to them than Jesus Christ, whose mystic attributes she did not share. This fact does but illustrate the common tendency of mankind to neglect the worship of the highest deity recognized in their formal creed, and to offer their prayers and their sacrifices to idols of lower pretensions and more human proportions.

That which, as the upshot of these speculations, we are chiefly concerned to note, is that religion everywhere contains, as its most essential ingredient, the conception of an unknown power; which power, thus offered by religion to the adoration of mankind, becomes the object of a double tendency: a tendency on the one hand to preserve it as a dim idea, represented to the mind under highly abstract forms; a tendency on the other hand, to bring it down to common comprehension by presenting it to the senses under concrete symbols. But under all images, however material; under all embodiments, however gross; the central thought of a power hidden behind sensible phenomena, unknown and unknowable, still remains.

So far then as historical inquiry throws light upon the answer to the second question in the previous chapter, that answer will be in the affirmative. It renders it at least highly probable that the common elements of religion are, from their universal or all but universal prevalence, "a necessary and therefore permanent portion of our mental furniture." Nor is this conclusion invalidated by the hypothetical objection that there are races without a religion at all. Granting the fact, it admits of an explanation quite consistent with this view. For the races which are destitute of the religious idea may be so, not because they are superior to it, and can do without it, but because they are inferior to it, and have not yet perceived it. Thus, the savage nations who cannot count beyond their fingers, prove nothing against the necessity of numerical relations. Even though they cannot add their ten toes to their ten fingers, and thus make twenty, yet the moment we perceive that ten plus ten equals twenty, we perceive also that this relation is an absolute necessity, and it remains an unalterable fact in our intellectual treasury. No inability on the part of the savage to understand us can shake our conviction. Now the same thing may hold good of the ultimate elements of religious feeling. These also, when once the conditions are realized in thought, may prove necessary beliefs. Whether they are so or not is a question for philosophy. To the examination of that question we must now proceed.

Religion, as the foregoing analysis has shown, puts forward as its cardinal truth the conception of a power which is neither perceptible by the senses nor definable by the intellect. For sensible perception requires a material object and a material organ; and intellectual definition requires an object which can be compared with other objects that are like it, discriminated from others that are unlike it, and classified according to that likeness and that unlikeness. In either case therefore the object must be a phenomenon having its place among phenomena, whether those of the sensible or those of the intelligible sphere. But if the power accepted by religion be neither perceptible nor definable, are we obliged to believe in the existence of so abstract an entity at all, or may we reject it as a figment of the human brain?

Perhaps we shall best be able to discover whether such a belief is necessary or not by endeavoring to do without it, and to frame a consistent conception of the universe from which it is entirely excluded.

There are various ways in which such a conception might be attempted. We may regard the world from the platform of

Realism or from that of Idealism, and the nature of our Realism or of our Idealism may vary with the special school of thought to which we may belong. Realism in the first instance admits of two main subdivisions: into Common, or as Mr. Spencer calls it, Crude Realism, and into Metaphysical Realism; and these two forms of it require separate treatment.

Common Realism is the primitive opinion of uneducated and of unreflecting persons, and is in fact simply the absence of any genuine opinion at all. They, I imagine, regard the external objects by which they are surrounded as so many actual entities, not only having an independent existence of their own, but an existence like that which they possess in our consciousness. Thus, an egg they would take to be in reality a white, brittle, hard thing on the outside, having a certain shape, size, and weight, and containing inside the shell a quantity of soft whitish and yellowish substance with a given taste. These qualities, not excepting the taste, taken along with any other qualities that may be disclosed by more careful inquiry, they would conceive to constitute the whole of the egg. It is the same with other objects. What we perceive by our senses is thought by them to be a copy of the real things as they exist in nature, much as the retina of the eye, regarded from without, is seen to contain a copy in miniature of the surrounding scene. Common Realism, however, while it tacitly takes for granted an infinite number of separate entities, cannot account either for the origin of those entities or for their nature. Nor has it any account to give of the origin of life, for material things are in this system utterly destitute of life, and indeed opposed to it. They are precisely what our senses inform us of, and nothing more. Hence they furnish no answers to the questions: How did this world come into being, and how did it reach its present shape? How do men come to exist in it; for matter contains no vitality and no power of infusing vitality into itself? Therefore it is that the adherents of Common Realism are invariably driven back upon a superior being, whom they term a Creator, and who supplies the motive impulse which is wanting in their world.

Metaphysical Realism professes to be the improvement of scholars upon the unsifted notions of the vulgar. It is the system to which, in its earlier and cruder form, Berkeley a century ago gave what once appeared to be its death-blow, but what may perhaps turn out to have been a wound sufficiently severe to cause prolonged insensibility, but not absolute extinction. It is not, however, with the purpose of completing the work of destruction, but of examining whether it affords a possible escape from the necessity of the religious postulate, that I refer to it here. Metaphysical Realists perceived clearly enough that the apparent qualities of sensible objects could not be the objects themselves. Even if they did not recognize this with regard to all the apparent qualities, they did so with regard to those termed "secondary," such as taste, smell, and color. Later representatives of the school, such as Kant, extended the process by which this conclusion was reached to all apparent qualities, whatsoever. Below the apparent qualities, however, these thinkers assumed a substance, "*substantia*," in which they inhered, and by which they were bound together, so as to constitute the object. And this substance something unperceived underlying the qualities perceived — was their notion of matter. Observe now the position we have arrived at. No sooner does Realism abandon the untenable hypothesis that the qualities of the object are the object itself, than it is driven upon the assumption of an utterly unknowable and inconceivable entity; a matter which is not perceptible by any of our senses, which is below, or in addition to, phenomena concerning which we can predicate nothing, and whose relation to the qualities it is supposed to support we cannot understand. But the necessity of some such assumption is the very assertion implied in all forms of religious faith. Realism, then, does not escape the pressure of this necessity, even though the entity it assumes is not precisely of the same character.

But is the difference in its character one that tells in favor of this variety of Realism, or in favor of religion? Assuredly substance, or matter, imagined as the bond between apparent qualities, is not an easier, simpler, or more intelligible conception than that of a universal power as the origin, source, or objective side of all physical phenomena. Granting even that the latter conception cannot be represented to the mind, a representation of the former is equally impossible. But does it explain the facts better? Let us see. In the first place, we must demand an accurate definition of what this supposed matter is. Is it passive, inanimate, incapable of independent action, and unable to develop out of itself the living creatures which in some way have come to exist? If so, we plainly require another entity in addition to matter, both to account for the active forces of our universe, and to originate the phenomenon of life. For if the qualities of body need a substratum, so also do those of mind. If it be held that the power from which mind emanates be the same as that which is evinced in so-called physical forces, then we have two distinct, if not independent, substances, beings, or whatever we may prefer to call them: matter, pervading material objects in their statical condition, and force or life, pervading both consciousness and material objects in their dynamical condition. Or if the first be regarded as sufficient to account for motion as well as matter, then we have still two powers, one subsisting throughout the physical, the other throughout the mental world. How are these two substances related to one another? Is the substance of mind supreme, governing its material colleague? or is that of matter at the head of affairs, and that of mind subordinate? or are they equal and coördinate authorities, as in the Gnostic philosophy? Suppose we endeavor to elude these difficulties by the assertion that there is nothing else but the unperceivable substratum supporting material objects, and that in this all modes of existence take their rise, we are met by further and still more troublesome questions. For if, under the manifestations of this substance we include consciousness, then the distinction between matter and mind has vanished, and in calling this substance matter we are simply giving it an unmeaning name. In fact, it is a substance supporting not only the qualities of bodies, but also the chemical, electric, molar, molecular, and other forces throughout the universe, as well as sensation, thought, and emotion. Matter in short does everything which deity can be required to do; it originates motion; it produces living creatures; it feels; it thinks; it lives. Thus we have but stumbled upon God in an unexpected quarter. Suppose, however, that we take what is in this system the easier and more natural hypothesis of a substance of matter, a substance of

mind, and a still more hidden power superior to both, and from
which both are derived, then we have but abandoned the perplexing questions raised by metaphysical Realism to take refuge
in the religious position from which it seemed to offer a plausible deliverance.

Does Idealism help us? Idealism is of several forms. That
represented by Berkeley need not occupy us here, for Berkeley
not only admitted, but expressly asserted, the existence of an
all-comprehending Power, and without this his philosophy
would have appeared to himself unmeaning and incomprehensible. Nor need we stop to examine that more recent species of
Idealism, as I hold it to be, which its illustrious author, Mr. Herbert Spencer, has christened Transfigured Realism. Whatever
differences may exist between Spencer and Berkeley — and I
believe them to be more apparent than real — they are at one
in the cardinal doctrine that sensible phenomena are but the
varied manifestations of this ultimate Power. All such Idealism
as this is in harmony with religion. But there are two forms
which seem to be at variance with it, one of which I will term
Moderate, and the other Extreme Idealism.

Moderate Idealism agrees with Berkeley in dismissing to the
limbo of extinct metaphysical creatures the substance supposed
to lurk beneath the apparent qualities of bodies. It holds that
there is no such substance, and that these qualities, and therefore bodies themselves, exist only in consciousness. But it differs from Berkeley in omitting to provide any source whatever,
external to ourselves, from which these bodies can be derived.
Not only are they in their phenomenal aspect mere states of
our own consciousness, but they have no other aspect than the
phenomenal one, and are in themselves nothing but phenomena. Rather inconsistently, this school of Idealism does not
push its reasoning to its natural results, but concedes to other
human beings something more than a merely phenomenal
existence. Nothing exists but states of consciousness; but those
peculiar states of my consciousness which I term men and
women may be shown, by careful reasoning, to possess (in all
probability) an existence of their own, even apart from my seeing, hearing, or feeling them. The process by which we reach
this conclusion " is exactly parallel to that by which Newton

proved that the force which keeps the planets in their orbits is identical with that by which an apple falls to the ground."*

Those peculiar modifications of color, and that special mode of filling up empty space which I term "my friend," do indeed seem, if we push matters to an extreme, to come into existence only when he enters my room, and to cease to exist the moment he quits it. If he has any further vitality, it is only in the shape of that state of consciousness which is known as recollection. But Moderate Idealism escapes from this consequence, on the ground that modifications of body and outward actions, since they are connected with feelings in ourselves, must be connected with feelings also in the case of those other phenomena which we term human beings, and perhaps in the case of those we term animals.† But if this be so, how did so extraordinary a fact as that of consciousness arise? *Ex hypothesi*, there was nothing before it. Did it then suddenly spring into being, full-grown like Minerva, but, unlike Minerva, with no head of Jupiter to spring from? Or was it a gradual growth, and if so, from what origin? Go back as far as you will, you can find nothing but consciousness, and that the consciousness of limited beings (either men or animals); and it is no less difficult to conceive the beginning, from nothing at all, of the least atom of conscious life, than to conceive that of the profoundest philosopher. Observe, there is no world of any kind, and in this no-world (the contradiction is unavoidable) there suddenly arises, from no antecedent, a consciousness of external objects which are no-objects. Geology upon this theory is a myth; so is that branch of astronomy which treats of the formation of our planetary system from nebular matter. Stars, suns, planets, and crust of the earth only arose when they were perceived, and will cease to be when there is no living creature to perceive them any longer. Since, however, conclusions like these are in reality unthinkable, whatever efforts metaphysicians may make to think them, Moderate Idealism must of

---

* Mill's "Examination of Sir W. Hamilton's Philosophy," p. 209 (second edition).

† Mr. Mill, in treating the point, seems to have forgotten the animal world, but his argument would cover it.—Mill's "Examination of Sir W. Hamilton's Philosophy," pp. 208, 209.

necessity complete its fabric by the admission of a Power from which both consciousness and the objects of consciousness have taken their rise. Should it persist in denying anything but a mental reality to the objects of consciousness, it must still suppose an unknown source from which consciousness itself has been derived; otherwise it will entangle itself in two unthinkable propositions. First, that before men (or animals) existed there was absolute nothingness, an idea which we cannot frame; secondly, that where there was nothing at one moment there was the next moment something, a process which we *cannot* realize without supposing a time antecedent to that something, and which we *may not*, without the contradiction of introducing time in the midst of nothingness, realize by supposing a time antecedent to that something.

It was no doubt the vague feeling of these perplexities that forced John Stuart Mill, the most eminent defender of this school of thought, to denominate matter a Permanent Possibility of Sensation. This singular phrase well exemplifies the difficulties of his position. For is matter an external substance, existing independently, or not ? If it is, then what becomes of the Berkeleyan doctrine? Mill and his followers are simply metaphysical Realists. But if not, what becomes of the permanence? It is not in us, for our sensations are not permanent; it is not in the matter, for there is none. And what is there a possibility of ? Causing sensation, or having it ? Not the former, for there is nothing to cause it; not the latter, for the possibility of our having sensations is a mere fact of our nature, and cannot serve to define matter. And where is the sensation located ? The phraseology would seem to imply, that matter is in the permanent condition of possible feeling; just as the nerve may be in the permanent condition of possible excitation. But this would be placing sensation in the wrong quarter. And if sensation be in us, we have not a permanent possibility, but a permanent actuality of sensation. So that unless the words be construed to mean that there is outside of us a permanent something which excites sensation, of which the modes vary (for this is the sense of possibility), they have no assignable meaning whatever. Mill, in fact, had been compelled, without wishing it, to recognize an ultimate power in nature; and his perception of this truth conflicted strangely, in his candid mind, with his idealistic prepossessions.

A more consistent and rigorous form of Idealism is that which has been referred to as the strict consequence of Moderate Idealism. This form, which I will term Extreme Idealism, denies the existence of persons as well as things. The Extreme Idealist believes himself to be the only being in the universe. There is to him no period preceding his own existence; none succeeding it. Past and future, except in his own life, have no meaning for him. We cannot reason with him, for all we may say is only a transient mode of his own sensations. Obviously, to such a philosophy there is no reply but one: it is simply unthinkable. Were any one seriously to defend it, the very seriousness of his defense would prove that he did not believe it. For against what or whom would he be contending? Against a phantom of his own mind. And the more pains he took to prove to us that he believed us to have no existence but as a part of himself, the less credit should we attach to his assertions.

Philosophy, therefore, is under a logical compulsion to make the same fundamental assumption as Religion — that of an ultimate, unknown, and all-pervading Power Origin, or Cause. Science, in a variety of ways, does the same. It does so, first, in its belief of a past and a future in the history of the solar system far transcending the past and future of humanity, or indeed of any form of life whatever. Passing at a glance over our brief abode on the face of the earth, Geology pushes its researches back into a time preceding by innumerable ages the existence of mankind, while her elder sister Astronomy carries her vision to a still remoter age, when even the planet we now inhabit was but a fragment in one indistinguishable mass. But it is not only these two sciences that assume the continuance of nature quite independently of our presence or absence; every other science does the like. The botanist, the chemist, the physicist, all believe that the facts they assert are facts in an external nature, the relations of which as now discovered by their several sciences held good before man existed, and will hold good after he has ceased to exist. But to say this, is to say in effect that there is something more than the mere phenomena disclosed by investigation; namely, an external reality persisting through all time in which the varied series of phenomena take their rise.

More clearly still does Science assert some such reality in its great modern doctrine of the Persistence of Force. Not that this doctrine is entirely new; for regarded in its metaphysical rather than its physical aspect it is but an expression in the language of the day of a truth which has long been realized as a necessity of thought. It is the converse of the ancient axiom, "*Nihil ex nihilo fit*," for if nothing can be made from nothing, neither can something pass into nothing. The Persistence of Force is an expression of the fact that every cause must have an adequate effect; that in nature nothing can be lost, no particle of force pass into nonentity. Concentrated forces may be dissipated, and dissipated forces may be concentrated; or one variety of force may pass into another. But the ultimate fund of force remains ever unchangeable; nothing is ever created, nothing destroyed.

Observe, then, that Science, however cautiously it may keep within the range of the material world, however eagerly it may repudiate all investigation of ultimate causes as fruitless and unprofitable, cannot take one single step towards proving the propositions it advances without tacitly laying down an ontological entity as the basis of its demonstration. For to speak of its discoveries as laws of nature is simply to predicate a constant, unvarying force, which under like conditions always produces like results. And to declare the uniformity of nature, is merely to say that the methods of that force do not change -- that it is the same now as it ever was, and will be the same throughout the eternal ages.

"Thus," writes Mr. Herbert Spencer, "by the Persistence of Force, we really mean the persistence of some Power which transcends our knowledge and conception. The manifestations, as occurring in ourselves or outside of us, do not persist; but that which persists is the Unknown Cause of these manifestations. In other words, asserting the Persistence of Force, is but another mode of asserting an Unconditional Reality, without beginning or end " (Spencer's "First Principles," § 60, p. 189).

Philosophy, or Reasoned Thought, and Science, or Reasoned

Observation, have both led us to admit, as a fundamental principle, the necessary existence of an unknown, inconceivable, and omnipresent Power, whose operations are ever in progress before our eyes, but whose nature is, and can never cease to be, an impenetrable mystery. And this is the cardinal truth of all religion. From all sides then, by every mode of contemplation, we are forced upon the same irresistible conclusion. The final question still remains, Is this ultimate element of all religion "the correlative of any actual truth or not?"

But for the prevalence, in recent times, of a philosophy which denies all connection between the necessity of a belief and its truth, I should have regarded such a question as scarcely worth the answering. To say that a belief is necessary and to say that it is true, would appear to all, but adherents of the extreme experiential school, one and the same thing. But in the present day this cannot be taken for granted, and I should be the last to complain that even that which seems most obvious should be tested by adverse criticism.

Ingenious, however, as their arguments are, philosophers of this school, when driven to reason out their views, cut their own throats. They commit a logical suicide. For what is the test of truth they hold up to us in lieu of necessity? Experience. But what in the last resort does our belief in experience rest upon? Simply upon a mental necessity. Nobody can tell us *why* he believes that the laws of nature will hold good to-morrow as they do to-day. He can indeed tell us that he has always found them constant before, and therefore expects them to remain so. But this is merely to state the belief, not to justify it. Experience itself cannot be appealed to, to support our confidence in experience. True, we habitually say that we believe such and such results will follow such and such antecedents *because* we have always found them follow before. But our past experience is not the whole of the fact involved in the belief. It is our past experience, conjoined with the mental necessity of thinking that the future will resemble the past, that forms the convictions on which we act. Experience alone, without that mental necessity, could teach us nothing. If therefore our necessary beliefs need not be true, the belief in experience falls to the ground along with the rest, and experience cannot be put in place of necessity as a test of truth. In fact, every argument drawn from the past fallibility of the test of necessity might be retorted with tenfold force against the test of experience. Observation has constantly misled mankind, and thousands of alleged facts, accepted upon imagined experience, have been disproved by more accurate examination. Observation and reasoning combined (as they often are) are exposed to the double danger of false premises and false inferences from true premises; while the addition of an element of testimony (a circumstance common in scientific inquiries) exposes every conclusion to a threefold possibility of error. Human beings are no more exempt from the possibility of mistaken science than from that of hasty metaphysics. But as, in matters of physical research, we do not discredit the use of our eyes because their perceptions are sometimes inaccurate, so in matters of metaphysical inquiry we need not discredit the use of our minds because their apparent intuitions are now and then fallacious. In the one case, as in the other, the proper course is not to cast contempt upon the only instruments of discovery we have, but to apply those instruments again and again, omitting no precaution that may serve to correct an observation and to test an argument. But when we have done our utmost to attain whatever certainty the nature of the subject permits, we cannot reasonably turn round upon ourselves and say: "True, my eyes assure me of this fact, but human eyes have erred so often that I cannot accept their verdict;" or, "No doubt my mind forces this conclusion upon me as a necessity of thought, but so many assumed necessities have turned out not to be necessary at all that I must refuse to listen to my mind;" for this is not really the caution of science, but the rashness of philosophic theory. For we can have no higher conviction than that arising in a necessity of thought. Nothing can surpass the certainty of this. Grant that we may yet be wrong: we can never know it, and we can have no reason to think it. To oppose to a necessary belief such a train of reasoning as this:

Necessary beliefs (so-called) have often proved false:
This is a necessary belief (so-called):

Therefore it may prove false,

is in reality to seek to overthrow a strong conviction by a weak
one; an intuition by a syllogism; a proposition felt immediately to be true by an inference open to discussion. Arguments
like this resemble the procedure of a man who should tell us,
when we meet a friend, that we cannot possibly be sure of his
identity because on some previous occasion in our lives we mis-
took Jones for Thompson.

Exaggerated as this doctrine of the experiential school is
thus seen to be, yet it has done good service by putting thinkers
on their guard, not to accept as necessary and ultimate some
beliefs which are only contingent and dissoluble. Two conditions must be fulfilled in order to effect a presumption of necessity. The belief must always arise under certain conditions;
that is, it must be universal in the only sense in which that
term can fitly be applied. Having arisen, it must be incapable
of expulsion from the mind; its terms must adhere together so
firmly that they cannot be parted by adverse criticism, either
our own or that of others. Both these conditions are fulfilled
by the fundamental postulate of religion. Given the appropriate conditions — human beings raised even a little above the
lowest savagery — and it at once takes possession of their
minds. After this, it persists in spite of every attempt to do
without it, and the highest philosophy is compelled to give it
the place of honor in the forefront of its teaching.

Observe now, that what this philosophy accepts and incor-
porates into its system is religion and not theology. These two
must be broadly distinguished from one another. Religion might
be described as the soul of which theology is the body. Religion is an abstract, indefinable, pervading sentiment; theology a
concrete, well-defined, limited creed. The one is emotional; the
other intellectual. The one is a constant element of our nature;
the other fluctuates from generation to generation, and varies
from place to place. Theology seeks to bind down religion with
immovable forms. Against these forms there is constantly
arising both an intellectual and an emotional protest. The
intellect objects to them as untrue in the name of science (in
the largest sense); the emotions struggle against them as

cramping their freedom in the name of religion itself. Thus between the human mind and dogma, between the religious sentiment and dogma, there is going on a perpetual warfare. Religious sentiment is no sooner born than the tendency to limit and to define makes itself felt. It is confined within a set of dogmas, and forbidden under every species of pains and penalties to pass over its allotted bounds. Sooner or later, religious sentiment bursts through every restriction; seems for a moment to breathe the invigorating air of freedom, but falls again into the hands of new theologians, with another framework of dogmas; to be again broken through in its turn when its fettering influence can be no longer borne. In carrying on this continually renovated contest — which is seen in its highest activity in great religious reformations — the religious sentiment seeks the alliance of intellect, which latter supplies it with deadly weapons drawn from the armories of science, logic, and historical research. Thus the overthrow of theology is in great part an intellectual work. But it must not be forgotten that the very deepest hostility to theological systems is inspired by the very emotion to which these systems seek to give a formal and definite expression.

The historical progress of religion is thus in some degree a counterpart of the progress described by Heine (in the lines heading this Book) as that of his individual mind. First of all there arises in the mind of man, so soon as he begins to speculate on the world in which he lives, the idea of a Creator. He cannot conceive the existence of the material objects with which he is familiar without conceiving also some being more powerful than himself who has made them what they are. His notions of creation may be, no doubt often are, extremely limited. He may confine the operations of his God to that small portion of the universe with which he is most familiar. But that the idea of an invisible yet preeminent deity arises very early in the mental development of the human race, and remains brooding dimly above the popular idolatry, has been abundantly shown. This is the belief in God the Father. The second stage, so closely interwoven with the first as to be inseparable from it in actual history, is the incarnation of this idea. The supreme Creator is too lofty, too abstract, too great, to be held steadily before the mind and worshiped in his unclouded glory. The children of Israel cannot bear the immediate presence of Jehovah, nor can even Moses meet the brightness of his face. Hence the material shapes in which the objects of adoration are embodied. When divine attributes are given to idols; when a golden calf is taken instead of the invisible God; when the Father is said to assume the form of a man to live a human life, and die a human death, when apostles, saints, and virgins are addressed in prayer or celebrated in praise, an incarnation has occurred. In the language of the traditions we have quoted, the supreme God has gone away and left the government of the world to his inferiors. Practically, such incarnations belong to the earliest period of religion, and no popular creed has ever been entirely without them. No sooner is the religious idea conceived in the mind, than it begins to be clothed in flesh and bones. But in the order of thought these two stages are separable. For idols are not worshiped until the notion of some power which is not human, of which the nature is not understood, has arisen in the worshipers. Then a concrete expression is desired, and we have in poetical language the belief in God the Son.

Last of all comes the belief — more properly an emotion than a belief — in the Holy Spirit. With this step a far higher grade of religious sentiment is reached. For God is now conceived, not only as creating or as governing the world without, but as entering into the mind of man to inspire his actions and influence his heart. A relation which up to this point was merely external — like that of the Creator to the created, or of superior to inferior — is rendered internal and intimate. The Holy Spirit not only speaks *to* our souls, but it speaks in them and through them. We receive, not the arbitrary command of an almighty potentate, but the inspiring force of a being who, while raising us above ourselves, is still a part, the best part, of ourselves. This indeed, in the deep imagination of the poet, makes all men noble.

Yet not in such a creed as this, sublime as it is in comparison with those that have gone before it, is the final resting-place of religious feeling. For every word or phrase in which we endeavor to give form to that feeling tends to lower and to corrupt it by the admixture of elements which are foreign to its genuine nature. To clothe this sentiment in language is itself an incarnation. For whether we speak of a Force, a Power, or a Spirit, of an ultimate Cause, or an all-pervading Essence; of the Absolute, or of the Reality beyond phenomena, these terms are but symbols of the Supreme, not the Supreme itself.

> "Name ist Schall und Rauch
> Umnebelnd Himmelsgluth."

All that we can say is, that while we *know* nothing but that which either our senses perceive, or our minds understand, we *feel* that there is something more. Both the world without and the world within, both that which is perceived and that which perceives, require an origin beyond themselves. Both compel us to look, as their common source, to a Being alike unknown and unknowable, whose nature is shrouded in a mystery no eye can pierce, and no intellect can fathom.

This is the great truth which religion has presented to philosophy, and which philosophy, if she be truly (as her name implies) the love of wisdom, will not disdain to incorporate with the more recently discovered treasures belonging to her peculiar sphere. For it is not the part of wisdom to spurn as worthless even the childish lispings prompted by the profound idea that has inspired the faith of men, from that of the far past to that of the present hour, from that of the rudest African to that of the most enlightened European. Rather is it the part of wisdom to excavate that idea from amidst the strange incrustations under which it is hidden, to understand its significance, and to recognize its value. Thus may we assign to it a fitting place within the limits of a system which does equal honor, and accords equal rights, to the scientific faculty and to the emotional instinct.

CHAPTER IX.

WHEN speaking of the fundamental postulates involved in the religious idea, we pointed out that, besides the unknown cause of physical phenomena, "every religion assumes also that there is in human nature something equally hyperphysical with the object which it worships, whether we call this something soul, or mind, or spirit." Let us call it soul. And first let us examine what it is that religion says of the soul, after which we may be in a position to consider what degree of truth, if any, is involved in its assertions.

Now the great fact which presents itself to our notice in this inquiry is the broad line of demarcation which religion has everywhere drawn between the mental and corporeal functions of man, or in other words, between his soul and his body. Generally, it expresses this grand distinction by the assertion that the soul continues to live after the body is dissolved. This doctrine is very ancient and very wide-spread. A few illustrations of its prevalence are all that can be given here.*

The rude people of Kamschatka, who had so little notion of a providence, believed in a subterranean life after death. The soul they thought was immortal, and the body would at some time rejoin it, when the two would live on together, much as they do here but under happier conditions. Their place of abode was to be under the earth, where there was another earth resembling ours. Some of them objected to being baptized, because they would then be compelled to meet their enemies

---

* See much interesting evidence in Dulaure, "Histoire Abregee de differens Cultes," vol. i. chs. xxiv.-xxvii.; and a valuable discussion of the whole subject in Tylor's "Primitive Culture."

the Russians, instead of living among their own people under ground. Animals too were all of them to live again (Kamschatka, p. 269-273). The Tartars, when visited by Carpin, had some notion that after death they would enjoy another life where they would perform the same actions as in this (Bergeron, vol. i. art. 3, p. 32). "The most intelligent Greenlanders," writes a traveler among that people, "assert that the soul is a spiritual being quite different from the body and from all matter, that requires no material nourishment, and while the body is decaying in the ground, lives after death and needs a nourishment that is not corporeal, but which they do not know" (H. G., p. 242). The American Indians firmly believed in the immortality of the soul. They thought it would keep the same tendencies after death as the living man had evinced; hence their custom — one that is widely spread — of burying the property of the dead along with the body. The souls were obliged after death to take a long journey, at the end of which they arrived at their appropriate places of suffering and enjoyment. The Paradise of virtuous Indians consisted in the very definite pleasures of good hunting and fishing, eternal spring, abundance of everything with no work, and all the satisfactions of the senses (N. F., tome 3, p. 351 353). The Kafirs, as we have already seen, worship their ancestors, whose "Amadhlozi," or spirits, they believe to continue in existence after death. What they mean by Amadhlozi they explain with tolerable clearness by saying that they are identical with the shadow. These spirits are the true objects of a Kafir's worship, being supposed to possess great power over the affairs of their descendants and relatives for weal or woe. They are believed to reappear in the form of a certain species of harmless snakes, and should a man observe such a snake on the grave of his deceased relation, he will say, "Oh, I have seen him to-day basking on the top of the grave" (R. S. A., pt. 2, p. 142.—K. N., pp. 161, 162). Similar reverence for the dead is shown in other parts of Africa. In his lecture on the Ashantees, Mr. Reade says that, "on the death of a member of the household he is sometimes buried under the floor of the hut, in the belief that his spirit may occasionally join in the circle of the living. Food also is placed upon the grave, for they think that as the body of man con-

tains an indwelling spirit, so there exists in the corruptible
food an immaterial essence on which the ghost of the departed
will feed."

To come to races standing higher in the scale of civilization:
the Peruvians had definite notions of a future state, with an
upper world in which the good lived a quiet life, free from
trouble, and a lower world in which the bad were punished by
suffering all the miseries and troubles of this terrestrial condition without intermission (C. R., b. 2, ch. vii). In China the
utmost respect is paid to deceased progenitors, who are the
objects of a regular *cultus*. India has had from early ages its
highly-developed and subtle notions of the distinction of spirit
from body, and the former is held to prolong its existence after
its separation from the latter, both as disembodied in heavens
or hells, and embodied in animals or other men. Some schools
believed in the immortality of the soul; others asserted that its
final destination was extinction. Buddhism ranged itself with
the latter opinion, while still maintaining the doctrine of
metempsychosis, and of rewards and punishments both in this
world and in numerous others to which spirits went in the
course of their wanderings. Parsee souls hover about the
grave a few days; then proceed upon a long journey. At its
conclusion they pass over a narrow bridge, which the good
traverse in safety to enter Paradise, while the bad fall over it
and go into hell. In the Mussulman faith there are likewise
but two destinies open to man — eternal happiness and eternal
suffering. Among the Jews in the time of Christ two doctrines
prevailed. Their ancient religion, while aware of the distinction
between the spirit and the body, left the continued life of the
former an open question. Hence the Pharisees asserted, while
the Sadducees denied, a future state. Christ was in this respect
a Pharisee of the Pharisees. He, however, like Mahomet, provided only two abodes for the souls of men; one in heaven with
his Father, the other in hell, where the fire was never quenched.
It was felt, however, by the general Christian world that this
sharp separation of all mankind into black and white, goats
and sheep, was quite untenable. Hence the Catholic institution
of Purgatory, which, whatever may be said against it, is a wise
and liberal modification of the harsh doctrine of Christ, afford-

ing a resource for the vast intermediate mass who are neither wholly virtuous nor wholly wicked, and providing an agreeable exercise for that natural piety which prompts us to mingle the names of departed friends in our devotions, whether (as in Africa) to pray to them, or (as in Europe) to pray for them.

From this brief review of the opinions of various races, it will be evident that some conception of a spirit in man as distinguished from his body prevails and always has prevailed throughout the world. The special characteristic of this spiritual essence has always been held to be its immateriality. All religions conceive it as distinct from the body, most of them evincing this view by treating it as capable of independent existence. Many of them no doubt invest the spirit after death with a material form, but this is the clothing of the idea, not the idea itself. The form is received after the spirit has left its terrestrial body, and does not originally belong to it; as in the case of the serpents in South Africa, in which ancestral souls are thought to dwell. This immaterial nature is clearly expressed — so far as such an abstract idea can find clear expression from a rude people — by those Kafirs who compare the soul to a shadow. Nothing in the external world seems to have so purely subjective a character as shadows; things which cannot be felt or handled, and which appear to have no independent substance.

Immateriality then is universally asserted (or attempted to be asserted) of the soul. This is of the very essence of the idea. No race believes that any portion of the body, or the body as a whole, is the same thing as mind or spirit. But immortality is not equally involved in the idea or inseparable from it. Notably the Buddhistic creed held by a considerable fraction of mankind — teaches its votaries to look forward to utter extinction as the *summum bonum*. True, the masses of average believers may not dwell upon the hope of Nirvana, but upon that of heaven.* But the authorized dogma of the Church is, that "not enjoyment and not sorrow is our destined end" or goal, but the absolute rest, if so it may be called, of ceasing to

* See some evidence bearing on this point in a paper by the author, entitled "Recent Publications on Buddhism." "Theological Review," July, 1872, p. 313.

exist. And that this dogma was fervently accepted and thoroughly believed in as a genuine "gospel," the early literature of Buddhism amply proves. The Jews, a most religious people, had no settled hope of immortality provided by their creed, though the account of the creation of Adam shows how clearly they distinguished mind from matter. Warburton indeed infers the authenticity of the Hebrew Revelation from the very fact of the absence of the doctrine of immortality; for no author of a popular religion, except God himself, could have afforded to dispense with so important an article. The more defective Judaism was, the more clearly it was divine. Nor were the classical nations of Greece and Rome at all more certain. With them also opinions differed—some, like Plato and his followers, asserting the immortality of the soul; others, like Epicurus and his school, denying it. Cicero discusses it as an open question, though himself holding to the belief in future existence. His two possible alternatives are continued life in a condition of happiness, or utter cessation of life; either of which he accepts with equal calmness. The fear of hell did not torment him: "post mortem quidem sensus aut optandus aut nullus est" (Cato Major, xx. 74). Even if we are not to be immortal, as he hopes, nevertheless it is a happy thing for man to be extinguished at the fitting season (Ibid., xxiii. 86). Less philosophical people, however, were troubled, like Christians, with the notion of a future world of punishment; and Lucretius addresses himself with all the ardor of a man proclaiming a beneficent gospel to the dissipation of this popular delusion:—

> " Nil igitur mors est, ad nos neque pertinet hilum,
> Quandoquidem natura animi mortalis habetur." *

Like other thinkers of his time, he distinguishes between the *animus* and *anima*—spirit and soul, and this three-fold division of the nature of man subsisted for a time in the language and ideas of Christians. But the essential point is that, whatever further subdivisions may have been made, all schools, ancient and modern, pagan and Christian, agreed in the fundamental distinction between the spiritual principle and the material instruments; between mind and matter, or soul and body.

* De Rerum Nat., iii. 830.

Such, then, is the universal voice of the religious instinct. Let us test the truth of this second postulate as we did that of the first: by endeavoring to do without it. Then we have matter and motion of matter; and the problem is:—Given these elements to find the resultant, mind. Motion is merely change of matter from place to place; therefore the question is, whether in any kind of matter and any changes of matter we can discover mind. Consider the material world statically. As known to science (and we have no right to go beyond scientific observation now), it contains certain properties perceptible to the senses, such as color, sound, taste, and smell, roughness, smoothness, and other tangible qualities, with extension and resistance, discoverable by the muscular sense and touch combined. Any further properties which a deeper analysis may disclose will still belong to the domain of sensible perception, the senses being the instruments employed in their discovery. In which of these statical conditions of matter can mind be shown to be involved? Or what combination of statical conditions can produce mind as a part of the compound? Plainly any attempt to discover it in matter at rest would be an absurdity. Now consider the world dynamically. Here we have matter in motion, matter as the recipient and the transmitter of certain qualities of force. The mode of motion may be either molar (that of masses through space), or molecular (that of particles within a mass). In either case it is nothing but a change of position relatively to other objects. Now, how can change of position either be mind, or result in mind? Take the case of a planet whirling through space. Does this molar motion, considered in any conceivable light, bring us one step nearer to mental phenomena? But all molar motion is of the same kind, and however completely analyzed, can lead to nothing but matter changing its position in space. Is molecular motion in better case? When light is transmitted to the eye, the vibrations of the atmosphere, which form the objective side of this phenomenon, arriving at the optic nerve, cause corresponding vibrations in it, and these transmitted to the brain result in certain movements in its component particles. Which of all these vibrations and movements is sensation? At what point does the physical fact of changes in molecules of matter pass into the mental fact of changes in the quantity or quality of the light perceived? Evidently no such point of transition can be found. And not only can it not be found, but the bare hypothesis of its existence is negatived by the fact that every physical movement produces an exactly equivalent amount of physical movement; so that there is nothing whatever in the resultant which is not accounted for in the antecedents, and nothing in the antecedents which has not its full effect in the resultant. There is thus no room left for the passage of the objective fact of molecular motion into the subjective fact of feeling.

Although these considerations practically exhaust the question, yet another aspect of it may, for the sake of greater clearness, be briefly touched upon. If the doctrine of abiogenesis be accepted, it may be thought to afford some confirmation to the materialistic hypothesis that mind is but a function or property of matter. Do we not here see (it may be asked) life and sensation arising out of non-sentient materials? And if a single living creature can thus arise, then, by the doctrine of evolution, all mind whatever is affiliated on matter. Such a conclusion, however, would be quite unwarranted by the facts observed. In abiogenesis unorganic matter is seen to pass into organic matter, and this is the whole of the process known to science. To assume that at some period in this process the material constituents of the newly-formed creature acquire the property of sensation is, to say the least, a very unscientific proceeding. For, throughout all their permutations, the component elements can (or could with improved instruments) be exactly observed, measured, and weighed; enabling us to say that so and so much, such and such of the inorganic elements has become so and so much, such and such of the organic compound. Now the factors of this compound do not (*ex hypothesi*) contain sensation. How, then, did the compound acquire it? Where is your warrant for suddenly introducing a consequent sensation — for which you have no assignable antecedent?

Thus it is evident that between mind and matter, between spirit and body, between internal and external phenomena, there is a great gulf fixed, which no scientific or metaphysical cunning can succeed in bridging over. Matter is never sensation, and cannot be conceived as ever becoming sensation. The chain of material phenomena, with its several series of causes and effects, is never broken; no physical cause is without its adequate physical effect, nor is any physical effect without a physical cause sufficient to produce it. The body is to the mind an external, material phenomena; closely connected indeed with mental states, and always more or less present to consciousness, but no part of our true selves, no necessary element in our conception of what we actually are. Every portion of the bodily frame can be regarded by us as an outward object, wholly independent of ourselves, and logically, if not practically, separable from ourselves. Many portions, such as the limbs, are actually so separable; and all of them are separable in thought.

Still more impassable is this chasm in nature seen to be when we remark, that there are two all-pervading elements in which mind and matter have their being, and that the phenomena within each element have definite relations to other phenomena within the same element, but are incapable of being brought into a like relation with those of the other element. These two elements are Space and Time. Material particles are related to one another in space, and in space alone. They are nearer to, or more distant from, above or below, to the north, south, east, or west of, the other material particles with which we compare them. But they are not earlier or later than other particles. The existence of concrete objects may be earlier or later than that of other concrete objects; but when we talk of their existence as earlier or later, we are talking of their relation to consciousness, not of their relation to one another. It is the total framed and classified by the mind that has a relation in time to some other similar total; each total, analyzed into its ultimate atoms, has only relations in space to the other total, likewise analyzed into its ultimate atoms. Contrariwise, mental objects, or states of consciousness, are related to one another in time, and in time alone. States of consciousness can be compared as earlier or later, simultaneous or successive. They have no space-relations either to one another or to the material world. It is common indeed to consider the mind as located *in* the body, but this is incorrect. For absolutely nothing is meant by saying that anything is in a given place except that it stands in given space-relations to surrounding objects. My body is in a place because it is *upon* the ground, *in* the air, *below* the clouds, *amid* a certain environment which constitutes the country and locality of that country which it is in. But my mind has no surrounding objects of this nature at all. The thought, say, of a distant friend can by no possibility be imagined as enclosed within the grey matter of the brain, just to the right of a nerve A, and in contact with a ganglion B. This thought, and its accompanying emotion, could not be found by any vivisection (if such were possible), though its correlative physical condition might. Hence the mind is not in the body, but is an independent entity whose phenomena, successive in time, run parallel to but never intermingle with the phenomena of body, extended in space.

From the view here stated of the irremoveable distinction between mind and matter an important corollary will be seen to follow.* No physical movement (it has been shown) can be conceived as passing into a state of consciousness, for each physical movement begets further physical movement, and while it is fully spent in its physical consequent is itself fully accounted for by its physical antecedent. The converse of this doctrine must therefore be equally true. That is to say, no state of consciousness can pass into a physical movement, for, if it could, this movement would have another than a physical antecedent. In other words, the mind can in no way influence the actions of the body. It cannot stand in a casual relation to any physical fact whatever. Hence the doctrine of the will (not only of free will but of any will) falls to the ground. For the current conception of a will supposes that a chain of material events passes at some point in its course into a state of consciousness, and that this state of consciousness again originates a chain of material events. Say that I hear some one call my name, and go to the window to ascertain who it is. Then the common explanation would be, not only that the atmo-

---

* The doctrine here stated is not my own invention. It was first published (so far as I know) by Mr. Shadworth Hodgson in his "Theory of Practice," vol. i. p. 416-436, § 57; but I am indebted for my acquaintance with it to Mr. D. A. Spalding, who discovered it independently, and announced it in the *Examiner*, December 30, 1871; September 6, 1873; March 14, 1874; and in *Nature*, January 8, 1874.

spheric undulations, which are the material correlative of sound passing into the brain by the auditory nerves, produced the sensation of hearing, which is true, but that this sensation in its turn produced those exertions of the limbs which result in my arrival at the window, which is erroneous. According to the view here adopted, the atmospheric undulations stand in a direct relation of causation to the affection of the auditory nerve, and this affection, in a direct relation of causation, to the resulting movements. The states of consciousness in like manner stand in a direct relation of simple sequence to each other; the sensation of sitting in a room being followed by that of hearing my name, this by the thought that there is some one outside calling me, this by the sensation of motion through space, and this last by that of seeing the person from whom the call emanated standing in the expected' place. But at no point can the one train of events be converted into the other. And while the train of external sequences does influence the train of internal sequences, this latter has no corresponding influence upon the former. For this would imply that at some period in the succession physical movements lost themselves in consciousness; ceased to *be* physical movements, and became something of an alien nature. It would imply further that such movements originated *de novo* from something of an alien nature having no calculable·or measurable relation to them. Either of which implications would constitute an exception to the Persistence of Force.

Man is, in short, as the adherents of this opinion have called him, a "conscious automaton." He does not will his own actions, nor do external manifestations, whether those of the unconscious or the conscious orders of existence, influence his will. But along with the set of objective facts there is always present a parallel set of subjective facts, and the subjective facts stand in an invariable relation to the objective facts. So that where the material circumstances, both those of the surrounding world and those of the body, are of a given character, the non-material circumstance, the state of mind, is also of a given and precisely corresponding character. Variations in the one imply variations in the other; feelings in the one change or remain fixed with changes or fixity·in the other.

Could the friends of dogmatic religion know the things belonging to their peace, they would bestow upon this doctrine their most earnest support; for it deals the death-blow to that semi-scientific materialism which derives a certain countenance from the discoveries of the day, and which is—second to religious dogmas themselves—the most dangerous enemy of the spiritual conception of the universe and of mankind. Not that in lifting a voice against materialistic views, I mean for a moment to lend a helping hand to the vulgar and irreverent outcry which is so often raised against matter itself as something gross and degraded, and deserving only of a contemptuous tolerance at our hands. I should have thought that the endless beauty of the material universe, and the varied enjoyments to be derived from its contemplation, as also the profound instruction to be obtained by its study, would have sufficed to give it a higher place in the estimation of religious minds. With such opposition to materialism as this I can have no vestige of sympathy. The form of materialism which I contend against, not as irreligious but as unphilosophic, is that which confounds the two orders of phenomena—physical and mental—under one idea, that of matter. Matter is supposed in this philosophy to be the parent of mind. A bridge is sought to be thrown across the great gulf which is fixed between us and the world without. But the moment we seek to walk over this imaginary bridge it crashes beneath our feet, and we are hurled into the abyss below.

Between that which feels, thinks, perceives, and reasons on the one hand, and that which is felt, thought about, perceived, and reasoned on, there is no community of nature. The distinction between these two. though it need not be ultimate in the order of things, is absolutely ultimate in the order of thought. In their own undiscoverable nature these two manifestations may be one; in their relation to us they are for ever two.

CHAPTER X.

ONE final postulate has been found to be involved in all religion, namely, that between the human essence spoken of as the subjective element, and the power spoken of as the objective element, "there is held to be a singular correspondence, their relationship finding its concrete expression in religious worship on the one side and theological dogma on the other." Ritual, consecration of things and places, ordination of priests, omens, inspiration of prophets and of books, all of them imply the supposed possibility of such a relation. All of them, however, from their contradictory and variable character, prove that they are but imperfect efforts to find utterance for the emotion which underlies them all. But that this emotion is incapable of an explanation consistent with rational belief is not therefore to be taken for granted.

Consider, first, that in order to be aware of the existence of the ultimate and unknown power, we must possess some faculty in our constitution by which that power is felt. It must, so to speak, come in contact with us at some point in our nature.

Now, no sensible perception can lead us to this conception as a generalization. The whole universe, regarded merely as a series of presentations to the senses, contains not a single object which can possibly suggest it. Nor can any combination of such presentations be shown to include within them any such idea. Neither can the existence of such a power be inferred by the exercise of the reasoning faculty. There is no analogical case from which the inference can be drawn. When we reason we proceed from something known to something unknown, and conclude that the latter, resembling the former in one or more of

695

its qualities, will resemble it also in the quality yet to be established. In exploring, for instance, some deserted spot, we find traces of a building. Now, previous experience has taught us that such buildings are only found where human builders have made them. We conclude, therefore, that we have stumbled upon a work of human hands. Suppose we explore further and find the remains of the building very extensive. We now draw the further inference that it was inhabited by a wealthy man, because we know that only the wealthy can afford to live in magnificent houses. But if prolonged excavation lead to the discovery of long rows of buildings, of various sizes and having streets between them, we confidently assert that we have unearthed a ruined city; for we are aware that no single man, however rich or powerful, is likely to have built so much. Of these three inferences, the first only is, strictly speaking, infallibly true. But the others are rendered by familiar analogies so highly probable as to be practically certain. Now let the thing sought be, not some single cause of a single phenomenon, or the various causes of various phenomena, but the ultimate cause of all phenomena whatever,—where is the corresponding case on which we can proceed to argue? Plainly there is none. There is no *other* world or system to which we can appeal and say, "Those stars and those planets were made by a God, therefore our own sun and its planets must have been made by a God also." Every single argument we can frame to establish the existence of deity assumes in its major premiss the very thing to be proved. It takes for granted that phenomenal objects require a cause, and were not the idea of this necessity already in the mind it could not take one single step. For if it be contended, say, that the world could not exist without a Creator, we have but to ask, "Why not?" and our adversary can proceed no further with his argument. All he can ever do is to appeal to a sentiment in us corresponding to the sentiment of which he himself is conscious.

Thus it appears that neither direct observation, nor reasoning, which is generalized observation, supplies the material for an induction as to the existence of an Unknowable Cause. Yet this idea is so persistent in the human race as to resist every effort to do without it. In one form or another it invariably creeps in. There is but one possible explanation of such a fact: namely, that it is one of those primary constituents of our nature which are incapable of proof because they are themselves the foundations on which proof must be erected. We cannot demonstrate a single law of nature without supposing a world external to ourselves. And we cannot suppose a world external to ourselves without referring explicitly or implicitly to an unknown entity manifested in that world. The faculty by which this truth is known must be considered as a kind of internal sense. It is a direct perception. And precisely as objects of direct perception by the senses appear widely dissimilar at different distances, to different men, and to the same man at different times, so the object of the religious emotion is variously conceived in different places and ages, by different men, and by the same man at different times. Moreover, as the religious sentiment in the mind of man perceives its object, the Ultimate Being, so that Being is conceived as making itself known to the mind of man through the religious sentiment. A reciprocal relation is thus established; the Unknowable causing a peculiar intuition, the mind of man receiving it. And this is the grain of fact at the foundation of the numerous statements of religious men, that they have felt themselves inspired by God, that he speaks to them and speaks through them, that they enter into communion with him in prayer, and obey his influence during their lives. We need not discard such feelings as idle delusions. In form they are fanciful and erroneous; in substance they are genuine and true. And in a higher sense the adherent of the universal religion may himself admit their title to a place in his nature. To use the words of a great philosopher, "he, like every other man, may consider himself as one of the myriad agencies through whom works the Unknown Cause;" "he too may feel that when the Unknown Cause produces in him a certain belief, he is thereby authorized to profess and act out that belief" (Spencer's "First Principles," 2d ed., § 34, p. 123).

But we may go still deeper in our examination of the nature of the relation between the Ultimate Being and the mind of man. To do so we must briefly recur to the philosophical questions touched upon in the eighth chapter of this Book. We there discussed four possible modes of viewing the great problem presented by the existence of sensible objects: Common and Metaphysical Realism, Moderate and Complete Idealism. Let us briefly reconsider these several systems to discover whether any of them affords a satisfactory solution.

Common Realism is excluded by the consideration that it treats the qualities of external objects as existing in those objects and not in the percipient subject. It requires but little reflection to prove that such qualities are modes of consciousness, not modes of absolute being. This defect is surmounted in Metaphysical Realism, which, however, is liable to the fatal objection, that it takes for granted an abstract substance in material things, which substance is like the Unknowable, utterly inconceivable, yet is not the Unknowable, and is incapable of accounting for any of the manifestations belonging to the mental order. So that we should have a superfluous entity brought in to form the substance of matter, of which entity neither our senses, nor our reason, nor our emotions, give us any information. For matter, in the abstract, is not the matter perceived by the senses; nor is it the object of the religious sentiment; nor is its existence capable of any kind of proof save that which consists in establishing the necessity of some kind of Permanent Reality below phenomena. And this Reality is not only the substratum of material, but of all phenomena whatsoever. Moderate Idealism is in no better case. For in denying all true existence except to living creatures it fails utterly to give any rational account of that order of events which is universally and instinctively referred to external causes, nor can it find any possible origin for the living creatures in whose reality it believes. Extreme Idealism recognizes no problem to be dealt with, and can therefore offer no solution.

Each of these systems, however, while false as a whole, contains a partial truth. Extreme Idealism is the outcome of the ordinary, unreflecting Realism; for if the Common Realist be convinced that appearances do not imply existence, and if he believe in no existence but appearances, the ground is cut from under his feet, and he remains standing upon nothing. He knows only phenomena, and the phenomena are mere ideas of his own mind. The truth common to these two extremes is that so emphatically asserted by Berkeley, that the *esse* of material objects is *percipi;* that we exhaust the physical phenomenon when we describe its apparent qualities, and need not introduce besides these a material substance to which those qualities are related as its accidents. They are not the accidents, but the actual thing, in so far as it is material. Metaphysical Realism and moderate Idealism are united in the recognition of the truth that the phenomena are not the ultimate realities, and that the qualities of bodies, when analyzed, are subjective, not objective; forms of the human mind, and not independent, external existences.

Hence these various philosophies, like the various religions of which they are in some sort metaphysical parallels, must be considered as preparing the way for the admission of that all-embracing truth which is the common ground of metaphysics and religion.

Examine a simple objective phenomenon. Then you find that you can separate it into all its component qualities: its color, taste, smell, extension, and so forth; and that after all these qualities have been taken into account nothing of the object remains save the vague feeling of an unknown cause by which the whole phenomenon is produced. All the apparent qualities, without exception, are resolvable into modes of consciousness, but the whole object is not so resolvable. For the question still remains, How did we come to have those modes of consciousness? Thus the analysis of the commonest material object leads us straight to an unknowable origin of known manifestations. And each particular phenomenon brings us to the same result. But are we to assume a special Unknowable for each special object? A little consideration will show that the division and subdivision we make of the objects of sensible perception resembles their apparent qualities in being purely subjective, and indeed more than subjective, arbitrary. For I consider an object as one or many, according to the point of view from which I regard it. The glass which I hold in my hand is at this moment one; but the next moment it is shivered into a thousand atoms, and each of these atoms is of complex character, and resolvable into still simpler parts. The planet we inhabit is, for the astronomer, one object; for the geologist a number of distinct rocks; for the botanist it is composed of mineral and vegetable constituents, and of these, the latter, which alone engage his attention, are numerous and various; for the chemist it consists of an infinite multitude of elementary atoms variously combined. Hence unity and multiplicity are mere modes of subjective reflection; not ultimate modes of objective being. And the Unknowable cannot, strictly speaking, be regarded as either one or many, since each alike implies limitation and separation from something else. Rather is it all-comprehending; the Universal Foundation upon which unity and multiplicity alike are built.

Material things, then, are analyzable into modes of consciousness with an unknown cause to which these modes are due. But what is consciousness itself? Like matter, it has its subjective and its objective aspect. The subjective aspect consists of its various phenomenal conditions; the sensations which we ascribe to outward objects as their producing causes, and the emotions, passions, thoughts, and feelings which we conceive as of internal origin. The objective aspect consists of the unknown essence itself which experiences these various states; of the very self which is supposed to persist through all its changes of form; of the actual being which is the ultimate Reality of our mental lives. The existence of this ultimate Ego is known as an immediate fact of consciousness, and cannot be called in question without impugning the direct assurance which every one feels of his own being as apart from his particular and transient feelings. Nobody believes that he *is* the several sensations and emotions which he experiences in life; he believes that he *has* them. And if the existence of the Unknowable underlying material manifestations is perceived by a direct, indubitable inference, the existence of the Unknowable underlying mental manifestations is perceived without an inference at all by an intuition from which there is no appeal. For no one can even attempt to reason with me about this conviction without resting his argument upon facts, and inferences from facts, which are in themselves less certain than this primary certainty which he is seeking to overthrow.

Existence, then, is known to us immediately in our own case; mediately in every other — consequently, the only conception we can frame of existence is derived from ourselves. Hence when we say that anything exists, we can only mean one of two things: either that it exists as a mode of human consciousness, as in the case of material things; or that it exists *per se*, and is the very substance of consciousness itself. And the former of these modes of existence is altogether dependent upon a conscious subject. A material object is a congeries of material qualities, none of which can be conceived at all except in relation to some percipient subject. Take away the subject, and color, extension, solidity, sound, smell, and every other quality, vanish into nothing. The existence of these qualities, and hence the existence of matter itself in its phenomenal character, is relative and secondary. There remains therefore only the second of these two modes of existence as absolute and primary. The substance of consciousness, then, is the one reality which is known to exist; and in no other form is existence in its purity conceivable by us. For if we attempt to conceive a something as existent which is neither object nor subject, neither that which is felt nor that which feels, neither that which is thought nor that which thinks, we must inevitably fail. There is no *tertium quid* which is neither mind nor matter of which we can frame the most remote conception. We may, if we please, imagine the existence of such a *tertium quid*, but the hypothesis is altogether fanciful, and would have nothing in science, nothing in the construction of the human mind, to render it even plausible. Indeed, it would be making an illegitimate use of the word "existence" to apply it in such a sense. Existence to us *means* consciousness, and never can mean anything else. We cannot by any effort conceive a universe previous to the origin of life in which there was no consciousness; for the moment we attempt to conceive it, we import our own consciousness into it. We think of ourselves as seeing or feeling it. The effort, therefore, to frame an idea of any existing thing without including consciousness in the idea is self-defeating, and when we predicate Existence of the Unknown Cause, we predicate its kinship to that ultimate substance of the mind from which alone our conception of absolute existence is derived.

Here, then, we have a second and more intimate relationship between the objective and the subjective elements in the religious emotion. They are found to be of kindred nature; or, to speak with stricter caution, it is found that we cannot think of them but as thus akin to one another. We must ever bear in mind, however, that our thoughts upon such a subject as this can be no more than partial approximations to the truth; tentative explorations in a dark region of the mind rather than accurate measurements of the ground. Thus, in the present instance, we have spoken of the Unknowable as more or less akin to the mind of man; yet we cannot think of the Unknowable as resembling the fleeting states which are all that we know by direct observation of the constitution of the mind. It is not the passing and variable modes, but the fixed and unchangeable substratum on which those modes are conceived to be impressed, which the Unknowable must be held to resemble. And this substratum itself is an absolute mystery. We can in no way picture it to ourselves without its modes, which nevertheless we cannot regard as appertaining to its ultimate being. One further consideration will establish a yet closer relationship than that of likeness. The Unknown Reality, which is the source of all phenomena whatsoever, mental and physical, must of necessity *include* within itself that mode of existence which is manifested in consciousness; for otherwise, we must imagine yet an ther power as the originator of conscious life, and we should then have two unknown entities, still requiring a higher entity behind them both, to effect that entire harmony which actually subsists between them. The Unknowable is, therefore, the hidden source from which both the great streams of being, internal and external, take their rise. Since, then, our minds themselves originate in that Universal Source, since it comprehends every form of existence within itself, we stand to it in the relation of parts to a whole, in which and by which those parts subsist. There is thus not only likeness but identity of nature between ourselves and our unknown Origin. And it is literally true that *in* it "we live, and move, and have our being."

From the summit to which we have at length attained, we may survey the ground we have already traversed, and comprehend, now that they lie below us, a few of the intricacies which we met with on our way. The apparent puzzle of automatism, for example, may be resolved into a more comprehensive law. It was shown, at the conclusion of the preceding chapter, that a train of physical events could in no way impinge upon, or pass over into, a train of mental events, nor a state of consciousness be converted into physical movements. But it was hinted that, while the distinction between the two great series of manifestations, those of mind and those of matter, was ultimate in the order of thought, it need not be ultimate in the order of things. Of this suggested possibility we have now found the confirmation; for we have seen that material phenomena, analyzed to their lowest terms, resolve themselves into forms of consciousness, and forms of consciousness, analyzed in their turn, prove to be the varied modes of an unknown subject; and this unknown subject has its roots in the ultimate Being in which both these great divisions of the phenomenal universe find their foundation and their origin. The distinction, therefore, between the mental and the material train belongs to these trains in their character of phenomena alone. They are distinguished in the human mind, not in the order of nature. Thus, if we recur to the illustration used in explaining automatism, we pointed out that in the circumstance of hearing a call and going to the window, two series might be thus distinguished: 1. The material series, consisting of atmospheric undulations, affections of the nerves and matter of the brain, movements of the body; 2. The mental series, consisting of the sensations of sitting still, and hearing of the thought of a person, of the sensations of motion, and seeing the person.   Now, if we take the trouble to observe the terms of which the first series is composed, we shall see that they also express states of consciousness, though states of a different kind from those contained in the terms of the second series. Undulations, nervous affections, movements, and so forth, are only intelligible by us as modifications of our consciousness. To conceive in any degree the atmospheric pertubations which are the physical correlatives of sound, we must imagine them as somehow felt or perceived — for instance, as a faint breeze. To conceive the cerebral changes implied in hearing, we must imagine ourselves as dissecting and examining the interior of the brain. In other words, the external train of events to which

consciousness runs ever parallel can only be represented in
thought by translating it into terms of consciousness; and the
absolute harmony of both these trains, the fact that while
states of consciousness do not originate the movements of our
bodies, they yet bear so unvarying a relation to them as to be
mistaken for their causes, finds its solution in the reflection
that, when we look below the appearances to the reality pervading both, it is the same Universal Being which is manifested
in each alike.

Hence, too, the sense of independent power to produce physical effects in accordance with mental conceptions, which forms
the great obstacle to the general admission of the doctrine of
human automatism. Reason as we may, we still feel that we
are reservoirs of force which we give out in the shape of material movement whenever we please and as we please. And if
the doctrine of the Persistence of Force appears, by showing
that every physical consequent has a purely physical antecedent, to contradict this feeling, we naturally give the preference
to the feeling over the doctrine. But since the Persistence of
Force is itself no less firmly seated in consciousness than the
sense of independent power — since all nature would be a chaos
without the Persistence of Force — it is the part of true philosophy to give its due to each. And this may be done by admitting the particle of truth contained in the belief that the human
will influences the external world. We are indeed reservoirs of
force. But it is not our own peculiar force that is exerted
through us; it is the Universal Force, which is evinced no less
in the actions of men than in the movements of inanimate
nature. And since those actions are in constant unison with
their wishes, there is not, and cannot be, the sense of constraint
which is usually opposed to voluntary performance. Thus, to
take a simple illustration, the necessities of our physical constitution absolutely compel us to support ourselves by food; yet
no man feels that in eating his meals he is acting under external compulsion.

It would be a strange exception indeed to the universal prevalence of unvarying law, if human beings were permitted to
exert independent influence upon the order of events. Not in
so slovenly a manner has the work of nature been performed.

We are no more free to disturb the harmony and beauty of the universe than are the stars in their courses or the planets in their orbits. Our courses and orbits are no less fixed than theirs, and it is but the imperfection of our knowledge, if they have not been, and cannot yet be discovered. But it would be a lamentable blot upon a universe, where all things are fixed by a Power "in whom there is no variableness nor shadow of turning," were there permitted to exist a race of creatures who were a law unto themselves.

Again, the relation now established between the human mind and the ultimate Source both of mind and matter, serves to throw light upon that dark spot in the hypothesis of evolution — the origin of consciousness. For while in this hypothesis there is a continual progression, of which each step is the natural consequence of another, from the gaseous to the solid condition of our system, from inorganic to organic substances, from the humblest organization to the most complex, there is absolutely no traceable gradation from the absence to the presence of conscious life. No cunning contrivance of science can derive sensation from non-sentient materials, for the difference between the two is not a difference in degree of development, but in kind. There is a radical unlikeness between the two, and it is unphilosophic, as well as unscientific, to disguise the fact that a mere process of material evolution can never lead from the one to the other. "The moment of a rising of consciousness," says Mr. Shadworth Hodgson, "is the most important break in the world of phenomena or nature taken as a whole; the phenomena above and the phenomena below it can never be reduced completely into each other; there is a certain heterogeneity between them. But this is not the only instance of such a heterogeneity" (Hodgson's "Theory of Practice," vol. i. p. 340). I venture to say that it is the only instance, and that there is nothing else in nature which can properly be compared with it. The instances of similar heterogeneity which Mr. Hodgson gives appear to me less carefully considered than might have been expected from so careful a writer. That between Time and Space, which is his first case, is involved in that between mind and matter, and is only another expression of it (see *supra*, p. 447); while "curves and straight lines," and "physical and vital forces," are not truly heterogeneous at all, unless under "vital forces" we include mental effort, and so again illustrate the primary unlikeness by a case included under it. But the last example is remarkable. "Until Mr. Darwin propounded his law of natural selection, it was supposed also [that there was heterogeneity] between species of living organisms in physiology." Now it is the great triumph of the evolutional system to have rid us of this unintelligible break, and to have shown that the whole of the material universe, inorganic and organic, is the result of the unchangeable operation of laws which are no less active now than they have ever been. In other words, evolution dispenses with the necessity of supposing the existence, at some point in the history of the planet, of a special law for the production of species brought into operation *ad hoc.*

But the general principles which apply to the origin of organic products must apply also to the origin of conscious life. This also must be figured as an evolution. This also must take place without the aid of a special law brought into operation *ad hoc.* Like the evolution of material products, it can only be conceived as taking place from a preëxisting fund, containing potentially the whole of the effects which are afterwards found in actual existence.

Let us test this by trying to conceive the process in other ways. Consciousness might be supposed to arise in two ways: by special creation, and by uncaused origin, from nothing. Both possibilities are in absolute contradiction to the fundamental principles of evolution. Creation by a superior power is a hypothesis standing on a level with that of the creation of man out of the dust of the earth. To realize it in thought at all we must suppose the very thing intended to be denied, namely, the material of mind already existing in the universe, as that of body existed — in the earth. Otherwise, we should be obliged to admit the unthinkable hypothesis of the origin of something from nothing. This latter difficulty presses with its full force upon the second supposition. Mind would thereby be represented as suddenly springing into being without any imaginable antecedent. For no material antecedent can produce it without an exception to the Persistence of Force, which requires a material consequent. And it cannot arise without any antecedent but by a similar exception.

Neither creation nor destruction can in fact be represented as occurring in nature. We cannot conceive a new being arising out of nothing, or passing into nothing. As the development of the physical universe takes place by the change, composition, decomposition, and re-composition of preëxisting constituents, so it must be with the development of mind. We cannot suppose the origin of sensation, its advance to more varied and complex kinds, through emotions, passions, and reasonings to the most subtle feelings and the profoundest thoughts, without believing that all of these have their source in the Ultimate Reality of nature, which comprehends not these only, but every further perfection of which we may yet be capable in ages to come.

Here, then, is the solution of the difficulty which was shown (p. 690) to beset the theory of abiogenesis; a theory which, if ultimately accepted by science, as I believe it will be, will for the first time bring perfect unity into our conceptions of the development of the world we live in. While science will thus show that there is no impassable break between inorganic and organic forms of matter, philosophy will confirm it by showing, that there is no real distinction between the universal life which is manifested in the (so-called) inanimate forces and constituents of our system and the fragmentary life which comes to light in animated creatures. There is heterogeneity nowhere. There are no breaks in nature. There are no unimaginable leaps in her unbroken course.

From the point of view now reached we can understand also —so far as understanding is possible in such a case—the apparent riddle of our knowledge of the existence of the Unknowable. We can explain the universal sentiment of religious minds that there is some direct relation between them and the object of their worship. The sense of an intuitional perception of that object, the sense of undefinable similarity thereto, the sense of inspiration and of guidance thereby, are included under and rendered intelligible by the actual identity in their ultimate natures of the subject and the object of religious feeling. And the incomprehensibility of the latter is shown to have an obvious reason. For the part cannot comprehend the whole of which it is a part. It can but feel that there *is* a whole, in some mysterious way related to itself. But what that whole is, the conditions of its existence render it impossible that it should even guess.

Imagine the whole of the atmosphere divided into two great currents: a hot current continually ascending, and a cold current continually descending. And let the hot current represent the stream of conscious life, the cold current the stream of material things. To complete the simile, conceive that there is a sharp boundary between the two currents, so that atoms of air can never cross to and fro; while yet the conscious atoms in the hot current are aware of the existence of the unconscious atoms in the cold one. Now if the atoms or particles in the conscious current should be gifted with senses in proportion to their size, they will see and feel an infinitely minute portion both of the ascending current in which they themselves are placed, and of the descending current they are passing by. But of the whole of the atmosphere of which they are themselves fragmentary portions they will be able to form no conception whatever. Its existence they will be aware of, for it will be needed to explain their own. But of its nature they will have no idea, except that in some undefinable way it is like themselves. Nor will they be able to form any picture of the cause which is continually carrying them upwards, and forcing their homologues in the opposite current downwards. While, if we suppose these opposite movements to represent the elements of Time and Space, they will be conscious of themselves only in terms of movement upwards, and of the unconscious particles in terms of movement downwards. They will suppose these two movements to be of the very essence of hot and cold particles, and will be able to conceive them only under these terms. Suppose, lastly, that at a certain point in their progress the hot particles become cold and pass into the opposing current, losing their individual, particular life, then their fellow-particles in the hot current will lose sight of them at that point, and they will be merged in the general stream of being to emerge again in their turn into the stream of conscious being.

Imperfect as this simile is, and as all such similes must be, it serves in some faint measure to express the relation of the mind of man to its mysterious Source. And it serves also to illustrate the leading characteristics of Religion and Theology, or Faith and Belief, the function of the first having ever been to conceive the existence of that relation, and the function of the second to misconceive its character. Thus there runs through the whole course of religious history a pervading error and a general truth. In all its special manifestations these two have been mingled confusedly together, and the manifold forms of error have generally obscured from sight the single form of truth.

The relation held by Faith to Belief, by the true elements to the false, in special creeds, may be thus expressed: That the creeds have sought to individualize, and thus to limit that which is essentially general and unlimited. Thus worship, in its purest character a mere communing of the mind with its unknown Source, has been narrowed to the presentation of petitions to a personal deity. Particular places and peculiar objects have been selected as evincing, in some exceptional manner, the presence of the infinite Being which pervades all places and things alike. Certain men have been regarded as the exclusive organs of the ultimate Truth; certain books, as its authorized expressions; whereas the several races of men in their different modes of life, and in the diverse products of their art and their culture, are all in their variety, and even in their conflict, inspired workers in the hands of that Truth which is manifested completely in none, partially in all.

And as it has been with the special objects upon which Theology has fixed its gaze, so it has been with the general object which underlies them all. This, too, has been individualized, limited and defined. It has been forgotten that we are but forms of that which we are seeking to bring within the grasp of our reason, and cannot therefore see around it, above it, and below it. But this truth, which Theology is ever forgetting, Religion must ever proclaim. The proclamation of this truth is the title-deed of its acceptance by mankind. Without this, it would sink into the dishonored subject of incessant wranglings and profitless dispute. When it begins to define the Infinite, it ceases, in the purer sense of the word, to be Religion, and can only command the assent of reasonable beings in so far as its assertions comply with the rigorous methods of logical demonstration. But this condition is in fact impossible of fulfillment, for the nature of the object concerning which we reason, renders the exact terms of logical propositions misleading and inadequate. The Unknowable Reality does not admit of definition, comprehension, or description. How should we, mere fragments of that Reality, define, comprehend. or describe the Infinite Being wherein we have taken our rise, and whereto we must return ?

Thus is Religion analyzed, explained and justified. Its varied forms have been shown to be unessential and temporary; its uniform substance to be essential and permanent. Belief has melted away under the comparative method; Faith has remained behind. From two sides, however, objections may be raised to the results of this analysis. Those who admit no ultimate residuum of truth in the religious sentiment at all, may hold that I have done it too much honor in conceding so much; while those who adhere to some more positive theology than is admitted here, will think that I have left scarcely anything worth the having in conceding so little.

To the first class of objectors I may perhaps be permitted to point out the extreme improbability of the presence in human nature of a universally-felt emotion without a corresponding object. Even if they themselves do not realize in their own minds the force of that emotion they will at least not deny its historical manifestations. They will scarcely question that it has been in all ages known to history as an inspiring force, and often an overmastering passion. They will believe the evidence of those who affirm that they are conscious of that emotion now, and cannot attribute it to anything but the kind of Cause which religion postulates. The actual presence of the emotion they will not deny, though the explanation attempted of its origin they will. But those who make the rather startling assertion that a deep-seated and wide-spread emotion is absolutely without any object resembling that which it imagines to be its source, are bound to give some tenable account of the genesis of that emotion. How did it come into being at all? How having come into being, did it continue and extend? How did it come to mistake a subjective illusion for an objective reality ?

These are questions pressing for an answer from those who ask us to believe that one of our strongest feelings exists merely to deceive. But it will be found, I believe, that all explanations tending to show that this emotion is illusory in its nature assume the very unreality they seek to prove. Should it, for example, be contended that human beings, conscious of a force in their own bodies, extend the conception of this force to a superhuman being, which extension is illegitimate, it is assumed, not proved, in such an argument as this, that the force manifested in the universe at large is not in some way akin to that manifested in human beings. Again, should it be urged that man, being aware of design in his own works, fancies a like design in the works of nature, it is a mere assumption that this attribution of the ideas of his own mind to a mind greater than his is an unwarrantable process. The argument from design may be, and in my opinion is, open to other grave objections; but its mere presence cannot be used as explaining the manner in which the religious emotion has come to exist. Rather is it the religious emotion which has found expression in the argument from design. The same criticism applies to all accounts of this sentiment which aim at finding an origin for it sufficient to explain its presence without admitting its truth. They all of them assume the very point at issue.

But the real difficulty that is felt about religion lies deeper than in the mere belief that a given emotion may be deceptive. It lies in the doubt whether a mere emotion can be taken in evidence of the presence in nature of any object at all. Emotions are by their very nature vague, and this is of all perhaps the vaguest. Nor are emotions vague only; they are inexpressible in precise language, and even when we express them as clearly as we can, they remain unintelligible to those who have not felt them. Now this general and unspecific character of emotions renders it hard for those who are wanting in any given emotion to understand its intensity in others, and even fully to believe in their statements about it. Were religion a case of sensible perception they would have no such doubt. Color-blind persons do not question the faculty of distinguishing colors in others. But while the sharp definitions of these senses compel us to believe in the existence of their objects, the comparatively hazy outlines drawn by the emotions leave us at least a physical possibility of disputing the existence of theirs.

Yet the cases are in their natures identical. We see a table, and because we see it we infer the existence of a real thing external to ourselves. The presence of the sensations is conceived to be an adequate warrant for asserting the presence of their cause. Precisely in the same way, we feel the Unknowable Being, and because we feel it we infer the existence of a real object both external to ourselves and within ourselves. The presence of the emotion is conceived to be an adequate warrant for asserting the presence of its cause. Undoubtedly, the supposed object of the sensations and the supposed object of the emotion *might* be both of them illusory. This is conceivable in logic, though not in fact. But there can be no reason for maintaining the unreality of the emotional, and the reality of the sensible object. Existence is believed in both instances on the strength of an immediate, intuitional inference. The mental processes are exactly parallel. And if it be contended that sensible perception carries with it a stronger warrant for our belief in the existence of its objects than internal feeling, the reasons for this contention must be exhibited before we can be asked to accept it; otherwise, it will again turn out to be a pure assumption, constituting, not a reason for the rejection of religion by those who now accept it, but a mere explanation of the conduct of those who do not.

In fact, however, the denial of the truth of religion is no less emotional then its affirmation. It is not denied because those who disbelieve in it have anything to produce against it, but because the inner sense which results in religion is either absent in them, or too faint to produce its usual consequences. For this of course they are not to blame, and nothing can be more irrational than to charge them with moral delinquency or culpable blindness. If the Unknown Cause is not perceptible to them, that surely is not a deficiency to be laid to their charge. But when they quit the emotional stronghold wherein they are safe to speak of those to whom that Unknown Cause is perceptible as the victims of delusion, these latter may confidently meet them on the field which they themselves have chosen.

First, then, it is at least a rather startling supposition that their fellow creatures have always been, and are still, the victims of a universal delusion, from which they alone enjoy the privilege of exemption. Presumption, at all events, is against a man who asserts that everybody but himself sees wrongly. He may be the only person whose eyes have not deceived him, but we should require him to give the strongest proof of so extraordinary an assertion. And in all cases which are in the least degree similar, this condition is complied with without the smallest hesitation. There are, so far as I am aware, no instances of proved universal delusions, save those arising from the misleading suggestions of the senses. That the earth is a flat surface, that the sun moves round it, that the sun and moon are larger than the stars, that the blue sky begins at a fixed place, are inferences which the uninstructed observer cannot fail to draw from the most obvious appearances. But those who have combated these errors have not done so by merely telling the world at large that it was mistaken; they have pointed out the phenomena from which the erroneous inferences were drawn, and have shown at the same time that other phenomena, no less evident to the senses than these, were inconsistent with the explanation given. They have then substituted an explanation which accounted for all the phenomena alike, both the more obvious phenomena and the less so. Precisely similar is the method of procedure in history and philosophy, though the methods of proof in these sciences are not equally rigorous. Great historical delusions — such as the Popish plot — are put to rest by showing the misinterpreted facts out of which they have grown, exposing the misinterpretation, and substituting true interpretation. Imperfect psychological analysis, say of an emotion, is superseded by showing from what facts this analysis has been obtained, and what other facts it fails to account for.

Observe, then, that in all these cases the appeal is made from the first impressions of the mistaken person to his own impressions on further examination; not to those of another. Considerations are laid before him which it is supposed will cause him to change his mind, and in all that class of cases where strict demonstration is possible actually do so. To a man who believes the earth to be a flat extended surface we point out the fact that the top of a ship's mast is the first part of it to appear, and that this and other kindred phenomena imply sphericity. Our appeal is from the senses to the senses better informed; not from another man's senses to our own. And we justly assume that were all the world in possession of the facts we have before us, all the world would be of our opinion.

What, then, is the conclusion from these analogies? It surely is, that those who would deny the reality of the object of religious emotion must show from what appearances, misunderstood, the belief in that object has arisen, and must point out other appearances leading to other emotions which are in conflict with it. As the astronomer appeals from sensible perception to sensible perception, so they must appeal from emotion to emotion. But it must not be their own emotions to which they go as forming a standard for ours. They can demand no hearing at all until they attempt to influence the emotions of those whom they address.

Generality of belief need not, for the purposes of this argument, be taken as even a presumption of truth. We can grant our adversaries this advantage which, in the parallel cases of the illusions of the senses, was neither asked nor given. But we must ask them in return to concede to us that, if the generality of a belief entitles it to no weight in philosophic estimation, the singularity of a belief entitles it to none either. All mankind may be deluded: well and good: *a fortiori* a few individuals among mankind may be deluded too. Grant that the human faculties at large are subject to error and deception, it follows from this that the faculties of individuals lie under the same disability. No word can be said as to the general liability to false beliefs, which does not carry with it the liability to false beliefs of the very persons who are seeking to convince us.

By whom, in fact, are we asked to admit, in the interests of their peculiar theory, the prevalence of a universal deception, and a deception embracing in its grasp not only the ignorant multitude, but men of science, thinkers and philosophers of the very highest altitude of culture? By whom is it that the great mass of humankind is charged with baseless thoughts, illusory emotions, and untenable ideas? By those who, in thus denying the capacity of the whole human race to perceive the truth, nevertheless maintain their own capacity to see over the heads of their fellow men so far as to assert that they are all the victims of an error. By those who, while bidding us distrust the strongest feelings, nevertheless require us to trust them so far as to banish, at their bidding, those feelings from our hearts. Not from our reason to our more instructed reason do they appeal, only from our reason to their own. But I deny the competence of the tribunal; and I maintain that until not merely disbelief, but disproof, of the position of Religion can be offered, Religion must remain in possession of the field.

Yet there is one mistake which, as it may tend to obscure the issue, it will be desirable to clear away. It is often contended, oftener perhaps tacitly assumed, that the burden of proof must rest on those who in any case maintain the affirmative side of a belief, while the negative on its side requires no proof, but can simply claim reception until the affirmative is established. Now this principle is true, where the negative is simply a suspension of judgment; the mere non-acceptance of a fact asserted, without a counter-assertion of its opposite. To understand the true application of the rule we must distinguish between what I will term substantial affirmations or negations, and affirmations or negations in form. Thus, to assert that A. B. is six feet tall, is a substantial affirmation. Out of many possible alternatives it selects one, and postulates that one as true, while all the rest it discards as false. Since, however, there are numerous possibilities besides this one with regard to A. B.'s height—since he may be either taller or shorter by various degrees—the negative, in the absence of all knowledge on the subject, is inherently more probable, for it covers a larger ground. It is a substantial negation. That is, it affirms nothing at all, but simply questions the fact affirmed, leaving the field open to countless other substantial affirmations. So, in law, it is the prosecution which is required to prove its case; for the prosecution affirms that this man was at a given place at a given time and did the criminal action. The opposite hypothesis of this covers innumerable alternatives: not this man but another, may have been at that place, or he may have been there and not done the action charged, or some other man may have done it, or the crime may have not been committed at all, and so forth. These are cases of substantial affirmations; asserting one alone out of many conceivable possibilities, and therefore needing proof. And their opposites are substantial negations; questioning only the one fact affirmed, and even with reference to that merely maintaining that in the absence of proof there is an inherent probability in favor of the negative side.

Widely different is the case before us. Here the affirmation and negation are affirmative and negative in form alone. The assertions, "An Unknowable Being exists," and "An Unknowable Being does not exist," are not opposed to one another as the affirmative and the negative sides were opposed in the previous cases. The latter proposition does not cover a number of possible alternatives whereof the former selects and affirms a single one. Both propositions are true and substantial affirmations. Both assert a supposed actual fact. And the latter does not, as the previous negative propositions did, leave the judgment in simple suspense. It requires assent to a given doctrine. That the one cast is in a negative form is the mere accident of expression, and without in any way affecting their substance, their positions in this respect may be reversed. Thus, we may say for the first, "The universe cannot exist without an Unknowable Being;" and for the second, "The universe can exist without an Unknowable Being." There are not here a multitude of alternatives, but two only, and of these each side affirms one. Each proposition is equally the assertion of a positive belief. Thus, the reason which, in general, causes the greater antecedent probability of a denial as against a positive assertion, in no way applies to the denial of the fundamental postulate of Religion. The statement that there is nobody in a certain room is not in itself more probable than the statement that there is somebody. And the proposition: "all men are not mortal," though negative in form, is truly as affirmative as the counter-proposition: "all men are mortal."

But this argument, inasmuch as it places the denial of all truth in the religious emotion on a level with its affirmation, fails to do justice to the real strength of the case. There are not here two contending beliefs, of which the one is as probable as the other. In conceding so much to the skeptical party we have given them a far greater advantage than they are entitled to demand. Generality of belief is, in the absence of evidence or argument to the contrary, a presumption of truth; for, unless its origin from some kind of fallacy can be shown, its generality is in itself a proof that it persists in virtue of the general laws of mind which forbid the separation of its subject from its predicate. And it is not only that we have here a general belief, or, more correctly speaking, a general emotion, but we have categories in the human mind which are not filled up or capable of being filled up by the objective element in the religious idea. There is, for example, the category of Cause; Nature presents us not with Cause, but with causes; and these causes are mere antecedents, physical causation in general being nothing whatever but invariable antecedents and invariable sequence. But this analysis of the facts of nature by no means satisfies the conception of causation which is rooted in the human mind. That conception imperiously demands a cause which is not a mere antecedent, but a Power. Without that, the idea would remain as a blank form, having no reality to fill it. And how do we come to be in the firm possession of this idea if there be nothing in nature corresponding to it? From what phenomena could it be derived? Akin to our notion of Cause is our notion of Force. When the scientific man speaks of a Force, he merely means an unknown something which effects certain movements. And Science cannot possibly dispense with the metaphysical idea of Force. Yet Force is not only unknowable; but it is *the* Unknowable manifested in certain modes. Again, therefore, I ask, whence do we derive ineradicable feeling of the manifestation of Force, if that feeling be a mere illusion? Similar remarks apply to other categories which, like these, have no objects in actual existence in the conformity of the religious sentiment to truth be denied. Such is the category of Reality. Imagination cannot picture the world save as containing, though in its essence unknown to us, some real and permanent being. We know it only as a compound of phenomena, all of them fleeting, variable, and unsubstantial.

There is nothing in the phenomena which can satisfy our mental demand for absolute being. As being transient, and as being relative, the phenomena in fact are nothing. But our intellectual, our emotiónal, and our moral natures demand the τὸ ὄντως ὄν—that which really is, as the necessary completion of τὰ φαινόμεα—that which only appears. And it is precisely the unshakeable belief in an unchangeable, though unknowable Reality; an everlasting Truth amid shifting forms, a Substance among shadows, which forms the universal foundation of religious faith.

A ship that has been driven from her intended course is drifting, with a crew who have no clear knowledge of her whereabouts, upon an unexplored ocean. Suddenly her captain exclaims that he sees land in the distance. The mate, however, summoned to verify the captain's observation, fancies that the black speck on the horizon is not land, but a large vessel. The sailors and passengers take part, some with the one, some with the other; while many of them form opinions of their own not agreeing with that of either, one maintaining it to be a whale, another a dark cloud, a third something else, and so forth. Minor differences abound. Those who take it to be land are at issue as to its being a plain or a mountain, those who think it a vessel cannot agree as to the description of the craft. One solitary passenger sees nothing at all. Instead of drawing what would appear to be the most obvious conclusion, that he is either more shortsighted or less apt to discover distant objects than the rest, he infers that his vision alone is right, and that of all the others, captain, passengers, and crew, defective and misleading. Oblivious of the fact that the mere failure to perceive an object is no proof of its non-existence, he persists in asserting not only that the speck seen in the distance, being so variously described, probably does not resemble any of the ideas formed of it on board the ship, but that there is no speck at all. Even the fact that the crews of many other ships, passing in this direction, perceive the same dim outline on the horizon, does not shake his conviction that it is a mere "idol of the tribe." Such is the procedure of those who deny the reality of the object of the religious idea. Instead of drawing from the diversity of creeds the legitimate inference that the Being of whom they severally speak is of unknown nature, they conclude, from the mere absence of the idea of that Being in their individual consciousness, that its very existence is a dream.

Lastly, a few words, and a few only, must be said in reply to those who will think that the cenception of the Unknowable resulting from our analysis is too vague and shadowy to form the fitting foundation for religious feeling. They will probably object that the Being whom that feeling requires is not an inconceivable Cause or Substance of the Universe, but a Personal God; not an undefined something which we can barely imagine, but a definite Some one whom we can adore and love. There is nothing, they will say, in such a conception as this either to satisfy the affections or to impress the moral sentiments. And both purposes were fulfilled by the Christian ideal of a loving Father and a righteous Judge.

To these objections I would reply, first of all, that I have simply attempted to analyze religion as I found it, neither omitting what was of the essence of the religious idea, nor inserting what was not. If this analysis is in any respect defective, that is a matter for criticism and discussion. But if it has been correctly performed — of which I frankly admit there is abundant room for doubt — then I am not responsible for not finding in the universal elements of religion that which is not contained within them. The expression found for the ultimate truths must embrace within it, if possible, the crude notions of deity formed by the savage,.and the highly abstract ideal formed by the most eminent thinkers of modern times. Even then, if I myself held the doctrines of the personality and the fatherhood of God, I could not have required from others any admission of these views of mine as universal ingredients in religious faith. The utmost I could have done would have been to tack them on as supplementary developments of the idea of the ultimate Being. And thus it is still open to any one who wishes it to do. Difficult as it is to reconcile the ideas of Love and Justice with unlimited Power and absolute Existence, yet if there are some who find it possible to accomplish the reconciliation, it may be well for them so to do.*

---

* See an ingenious attempt to maintain the personality, along with the

Undoubtedly, however, all such efforts do appear to me mere hankerings after an incarnation of that idea which, by its very nature, does not admit of representation by incarnate forms, even though those forms be moral perfections. And I would reply, secondly, to the above objection, that, while we lose something by giving up the definite personality of God, we gain something also. If we part with the image of a loving Father, we part also with that of a stern monarch and an implacable judge. If we can no longer indulge in the contemplation of perfect virtue, embodied in an actual Person, we are free from the problem that has perplexed theologians of every age: how to reconcile the undoubted evil in the world with the omnipotence of that Person. I know that there are some who think it possible to retain the gentler features in the popular conception of deity, while dropping all that is harsh and repulsive. To them the idea of God is as free from terror as the idea of the Unknowable, and the first of these gains is therefore no gain to them. But the problem of the existence of evil presses perhaps with greater severity upon them than upon any other class of theologians. To suppose that God could not prevent the presence of wickedness, or could not prevent it without some greater calamity, is to deny his omnipotence; to suppose that he could, and did not, is to question his benevolence. But even admitting the improvement made by purging from the character of God all its severity, its vindictiveness, and its tendency to excessive punishment, the fact remains that the conception thus attained is not that of the popular creed at all, but that of a few enlightened thinkers. And it is with the former, not with the latter, that the doctrine of the Unknowable must be compared, in order fairly to estimate its advantages or disadvantages in relation to the current belief in a personal God.

Moreover, it must be borne in mind that the dim figure we have shadowed out of an inconceivable and all-embracing ultimate Existence, if widely different from the more ordinary theological embodiments of the religious idea, is altogether in harmony with many of its expressions by the most devoutly relig-

moral qualities of God, in Mr. Shadworth Hodgson's "Theory of Practice," vol. i. p. 305 ff.

ious minds. If religion has always had a tendency to run to seed in dogma, it has also always had a tendency to revert to its fundamental mysticism. The very best and highest minds have continually evinced this tendency to mysticism, and it has mixed itself up with the logical definitions of others who did not rise to so exalted a level. So that the examination of the writings of religious men will continually disclose that profound impression of the utterly incomprehensible and mysterious nature of the Supreme Being which is now, in its complete development in the form of Agnosticism, stigmatized as incompatible with genuine religious faith.

That tendency to be deeply sensible of the impossibility of conceiving the Absolute which Religion has thus evinced, it is the result of Science to strengthen and to increase. Science shows the imperfection of all the concrete expressions which have been found for the Unknowable. It proves that we cannot think of the Unknowable as entering in any peculiar sense into special objects in nature, dwelling in special places, or speaking through special channels. Miraculous phenomena, which were supposed to constitute the peculiar sphere of its manifestations, are thrown by Science completely out of the account. But all phenomena whatsoever are shown to manifest the Unknowable. Thus, while scientific inquiry tends to diminish the intensity of religious ideas, it tends to widen their extension. They do not any longer cling to partial symbols. They do not attach themselves with the same fervor to individual embodiments. But, in becoming more abstract, they become also more pervading. Religion is found everywhere and in everything. All nature is the utterance of the idea. And, as it gains in extension while losing in intensity in reference to the external world, it goes through a similar process in relation to human life. No longer a force seizing on given moments of our existence, at one moment inspiring devotional observances, at the next forgotten in the pleasures or the business of the day; at one time filling men with the zeal of martyrs or crusaders, at another leaving them to the unrestrained indulgence of gross injustice or revolting cruelty, it becomes a calm, allpervading sentiment, shown (if it be shown at all) in the general beauty and spirituality of the character, not in the state l exercises of a rigorous piety, or in the passionate outbursts of an enthusiastic fervor.

But these considerations would lead me on to a subject which I had once hoped to treat within the boundaries of the present volume, but which I am now compelled, owing to the enlargement of the scheme, to postpone to a future time. That subject is the relation of religion to ethics. It may have struck some readers as an omission that I have said nothing of religion as a force inspiring moral conduct, which is the principal aspect under which it is regarded by some competent authorities. But the omission has been altogether intentional. It would take me a long time to explain what in my judgment has been the actual influence of religion upon morals in the past, and what is likely to be its influence in the future. Meanwhile I merely note the fact that this analysis professes to be complete in its own kind; that I have endeavored to probe the religious sentiment to the bottom, and to discover all that it contains. Thus, if religion be not only an emotion, but a moral force, it must acquire this character in virtue of the relation of its emotional elements to human character, not in virtue of the presence of ethical elements actually belonging to the religious emotion, and comprehended under it by the same indefeasible title as the sense of the Unknowable itself.

At present, however, I can attempt no answer to the objection which will no doubt be urged, that so abstract and cold a faith as that expounded here can afford no satisfaction to the moral sentiments. Indeed I must to a certain extent admit the reality of the loss which the adoption of this faith entails. There is consolation no doubt in the thought of a Heavenly Father who loves us; there is strength in the idea that he sees and helps us in our continual combat against evil without and evil within; there is happiness in the hope that he will assign us in another life an infinite reward for all the endurances of this. Above all, there is comfort in the reflection that when we are parted by death we are not parted for ever; that our love for those whom we have cherished on earth is no temporary bond, to be broken ere long in bitterness and despair, but a possession never to be lost again, a union of souls interrupted for a little while by the separation of the body, only to be again renewed in far greater perfection and carried on into far higher joys than can be even imagined here. All this is beautiful and full of fascination: why should we deny it? Candor compels us to admit that in giving it up with the other illusions of our younger days we are resigning a balm for the wounded spirit for which it would be hard to find an equivalent in all the repertories in Science, and in all the treasures of philosophy. Yet it must be borne in mind that every step from a lower to a higher creed involves a precisely similar loss. How much more beautiful was nature (as Schiller has shown us in his poem on the gods of Greece) when every fountain, tree and river had its presiding genius, when the Sun was driven by a divine charioteer, when the deities of Olympus intervened in the affairs of men to prevent injustice and to maintain the right. How cold and lifeless, nay, how profoundly irreligious, would our modern conception of the earth and the solar system have appeared to the worshiper of Poseidon and Apollon. And if the loss of the Christian as compared to the Pagan is thus great, how great also is the loss of the enlightened Protestant as compared to the ignorant Catholic peasant. What comfort must be found in the immediate intervention of the Virgin in answer to prayer, what security afforded by the protection of the local saint. Or again, how great the pleasure of contributing by our piety to the release of a friend from purgatorial torment, and of knowing that our friends will do us the same kindly service.

Even without contrasting such broad and conspicuous divisions of Christianity as these, we shall find enough of the same kind of difference within the limits of Protestantism itself. What mere intellectual conviction of a future state can vie with the consoling certainty offered by the Spiritualistic belief, that those whom we have lost on earth still hover around us in our daily course; sometimes even appear to us in bodily form, and converse with us in human speech. No mere hope of meeting them again can for a moment equal the delight of seeing their well-known shapes and hearing their familiar tones. Hence the Spiritualist has undoubtedly a source of comfort in his faith which more rational creeds can offer nothing to supply. But who that does not share it can envy them so baseless a conviction, so illusory a joy?

It is, in fact, the very condition of progress that, as we advance in knowledge and in culture, we give up something on the road. But it is also a condition that we do not feel the need of that which we have lost. Not only as we become men do we put away childish things, but we can no longer realize in thought the enjoyment which those childish things brought with them. Other interests, new occupations, deeper affections take the place of the interests, the occupations, and the affections of our early years. So too should it be in religion. Men have dwelt upon the love of God because they could not satisfy the craving of nature for the love of their fellow men. They have looked forward to eternal happiness in a future life because they could not find temporary happiness in this. It is these reflections which point out the way in which the void left by the removal of the religious affections should hereafter be supplied. The effort of those who cannot turn for consolation to a friend in heaven should be to strengthen the bonds of friendship on earth, to widen the range of human sympathy and to increase its depth. We should seek that love in one another which we have hitherto been required to seek in God. Above all, we should sweep away those barriers of convention and fancied propriety which continually hinder the free expression of affection, and force us to turn from the restrictions of the world to One towards whom there need be no irksome conformity to artificial regulation, and in speaking to whom we are under no shadow of reserve.

Were we thus permitted to find in our fellow creatures that sympathy which so many mourners, so many sufferers, so many lonely hearts, have been compelled to find only in the idea of their heavenly Father, I hesitate not to say that the consolations of the new religion would far surpass in their strength and their perfection all those that were offered by the old. Towards such increasing and such deepening of the sympathies of humanity I believe that we are continually tending even now. Meantime, while we are still far from the promised land, the adherents of the universal religion are not without a happiness of their own. Their faith is at least a faith of perfect peace. Untroubled by the storms of controversy, in which so many others are tossed about, they can welcome all men as brothers in faith, for all of them, even the most hostile, contribute to supply the stones of the broad foundation upon which their philosophy is built. Those therefore who contend against them, be it even with vehemence and passion, yield them involuntary help in bringing the materials upon which their judgment is formed. No man can truly oppose their religion, for he who seems to be hostile to it is himself but one of the notes struck by the Unknowable Cause, which so plays upon the vast instrument of humanity as to bring harmony out of jangling sounds, and to produce the universal chords of truth from the individual discords of error. Scientific discoveries and philosophic inquiries, so fatal to other creeds, touch not the universal religion. .They who accept it can but desire the increase of knowledge, for even though new facts and deeper reasoning should overthrow something of what they have hitherto believed and taught, they will rejoice that their mistakes should be corrected, and their imperfections brought to light. They desire but the Truth, and the Truth has made them free. And as in their thoughts they can wish nothing so much as to know and to believe that which is true, so in their lives they will express the serenity which that desire will inevitably bring. They are not pained or troubled because other men see not as they see. They have no vain hope of a unity of thought which the very conditions of our being do not permit. They aim not at conquering the minds of men; far rather would they stimulate and help them to discover a higher Truth than they themselves have been permitted to know. And as their action will thus be inspired with hope of contributing their mite to the treasury of human knowledge, well-being, and moral good, so their death will be the expression of that peaceful faith which has sustained their lives. Even though torn away when, in their own judgment, they have still much to do, they will not repine at the necessity of leaving it undone, even though they are well aware that their names, which might have been illustrious in the annals of our race, will now be buried in oblivion. For the disappearance of a single life is but a ripple on the ocean of humanity, and humanity feels it not. Hence they will meet their end "sustained and soothed by an unfaltering trust,"

"Like one who wraps the drapery of his couch
About him, and lies down to pleasant dreams."

But the opposite fate, sometimes still more terrible, that of continuing to live when the joys of life are gone, and its purest happiness is turned into the bitterest pain, will be accepted too. Thus they will be willing, if need be, to remain in a world where their labor is not yet ended, even though that labor be wrought through suffering, despondency, and sorrow; willing also, if need be, to meet the universal lot — even though it strike them in the midst of prosperity, happiness, and hope; bowing in either case to the verdict of fate with unmurmuring resignation and fearless calm.

THE END.

INDEX.

THE ATHEIST VIEWPOINT

AN ARNO PRESS / NEW YORK TIMES COLLECTION

Amberley, [John Russell], Viscount. **An Analysis of Religious Belief.** 1877.

Atheist Magazines: A Sampling, 1927–1970. New Introduction by Madalyn Murray O'Hair. 1972.

Besant, Annie. **The Freethinker's Text-Book:** Part II—Christianity. n.d.

[Burr, William Henry.] **Revelations of Antichrist.** 1879.

Cardiff, Ira D. **What Great Men Think of Religion.** 1945.

Champion of Liberty: Charles Bradlaugh. 1934.

Cohen, Chapman. **Primitive Survivals in Modern Thought.** 1935.

Drews, Arthur. **The Witnesses to the Historicity of Jesus.** Translated by Joseph McCabe. 1912.

Ferrer [y Guardia], Francisco. **The Origins and Ideals of the Modern School.** Translated by Joseph McCabe. 1913.

Foote, G. W. and W. P. Ball, editors. **The Bible Handbook.** 1961.

Gibbon, Edward. **History of Christianity.** 1883.

Holyoake, George Jacob. **The History of the Last Trial by Jury for Atheism in England.** 1851.

Komroff, Manuel, editor. **The Apocrypha or Non-Canonical Books of the Bible:** The King James Version. 1936.

Lewis, Joseph. **Atheism and Other Addresses.** 1960.

McCarthy, William. **Bible, Church and God.** 1946.

Macdonald, George E. **Fifty Years of Freethought.** 1929, 1931. Two volumes in one.

Manhattan, Avro. **Catholic Imperialism and World Freedom.** 1952.

Meslier, Jean. **Superstition in All Ages.** Translated from the French original by Anna Knoop. 1890.

Nietzsche, Friedrich. **The Antichrist.** 1930.

O'Hair, Madalyn Murray. **What on Earth Is an Atheist!** 1969.

Robertson, J. M. **A Short History of Freethought.** 1957.

Russell, Bertrand. **Atheism: Collected Essays, 1943–1949.** 1972.

Shelley, Percy Bysshe. **Selected Essays on Atheism.** (n.d.) 1972.

Teller, Woolsey. **The Atheism of Astronomy.** 1938.

Wells, H. G. **Crux Ansata:** An Indictment of the Roman Catholic Church. 1944.